Time Out

New York

timeoutny.com

Penguin Books

Time Out New York

PENGUIN BOOKS

Published by the Penguin Group
Penguin Books Ltd, 80 Strand, London WC2R ORL, England
Penguin Books USA Inc., 375 Hudson Street, New York, New York 10014, USA
Penguin Books Australia Ltd, 250 Camberwell Road, Camberwell, Victoria 3124, Australia
Penguin Books Canada Ltd, 10 Alcorn Avenue, Toronto, Ontario, Canada M4V 3B2
Penguin Books (NZ) Ltd, cnr Rosedale and Airborne Roads, Albany, Auckland, New Zealand

Penguin Books Ltd, Registered Offices: Harmondsworth, Middlesex, England

First published 1990
Second edition 1992
Third edition 1994
Fourth edition 1996
Fifth edition 1997
Sixth edition 1998
Seventh edition 1999
Eighth edition 2000
Ninth edition 2001
Tenth edition 2002
11th edition 2003

12th edition 2004

10 9 8 7 6 5 4 3 2 1

Printed and bound by Cayfosa-Quebecor, Ctra. de Caldes, Km 3, 08 130 Sta, Perpètua de Mogoda, Barcelona, Spain

Market value Corner stores and bodegas are the heart of New York City's neighborhoods.

MINI MARK
GROCER
AWAY
DAILY NEWS
PUSH
99¢
TRADITIONAL LAGER
AMERICA'S OLDEST BREWERY.
AriZona
WaterAID
VITAMIN FORTIFIED
BIG CAN!
99¢
23.5 OZ. CANS
not too strong... not too light
Newport
Paulina
Budw

Contents

Still life Statue-esque in **Battery Park**.

Edited and designed by Time Out New York Guides
475 Tenth Avenue, 12th floor
New York, NY 10018
Tel: 646-432-3000
Fax: 646-432-3050
E-mail: guides@timeoutny.com
www.timeoutny.com

Guides Director Killian Jordan
Senior Editor Melisa Coburn **Art Director** Caroline Jackson **Project Photo Editor** Beth Ferraro
Associate Project Editors Stanley Mieses, Stephanie Rosenbaum **Guides Copy Chief** Ann Lien
Guides/Online Assistant Editor Heather Tierney **Guides/Online Editorial Coordinator** Tim McCormick
Copy Editors John House, Liz Gall **Researchers** Katie Baker, Victoria Elmacioglu, Margaret Girouard, Elizabeth King, Lisa Lavochkin
Guides Publicity and Marketing Associate Rosella Albanese

Time Out New York
E-mail: letters@timeoutny.com

President/Editorial Director Cyndi Stivers
Publisher Alison Tocci
Financial Director Daniel P. Reilly

Production Director Nestor Cervantes **Technology Director** Daniel G. Hernandez
Production Manager Audrey Calle **Associate Production Manager** Jim Schuessler
Advertising Production Manager Tom Oesau
Advertising Production Coordinator Andrea Dunn **Advertising Designers** Stephen de Francesco, Jamie Dunst, Ed Stern
Digital Imaging Specialist Chris Heins

Associate Publisher/Advertising Anne Perton **Advertising Manager** Tony Monteleone
Senior Account Managers Dan Kenefick, Ridwana Lloyd-Bey, Melissa Keller
Account Managers Julia Keefe-Chamberlain, Emily Kelton, Lauren Newman, Paula Sarapin, Angela Van Hover
Assistant to the Publisher Jahan Mantin

Associate Publisher/Marketing Marisa Guillen Fariña

Time Out Guides Ltd
Universal House
251 Tottenham Court Road
London W1T 7AB
Tel: +44 (0)20 7813 3000
Fax: +44 (0)20 7813 6001
E-mail: guides@timeout.com
www.timeout.com

Editorial/Managing Director Peter Fiennes **Series Editor** Ruth Jarvis **Art Director** Mandy Martin **Deputy Series Editor** Lesley McCave **Advertising Sales Director** Mark Phillips **Guides Production Director** Mark Lamond **Guides Coordinator** Anna Norman

Chairman Tony Elliott **Managing Director** Mike Hardwick **Group Financial Director** Richard Waterlow **Group Commercial Director** Lesley Gill **Group Marketing Director** Christine Cort **Marketing Manager** Mandy Martinez **Group General Manager** Nichola Coulthard **Group Art Director** John Oakey **Online Managing Director** David Pepper

Contributors
History Kathy Squires **Architecture** Eric P. Nash **What Lies Beneath** illustration by Takako Okuma **New York Today** Billie Cohen **Where to Stay** Heather Tierney **Sightseeing Introduction** Reed Tucker **Tour New York** Ann Lien **Downtown** Annie Bell; *Stall wonder* Heather Tierney *The Iron Age* Sam Clover **Midtown** Les Simpson **Uptown** Stanley Mieses **Brooklyn** Beth Greenfield; *Red-hot Red Hook* Anne Fifield **Queens** Karen Tina Harrison **The Bronx** Stanley Mieses **Staten Island** Peter Zaremba **Museums** Sarah Schmerler; *To each, his own art* Mark Sinclair **Restaurants** adapted from *Time Out New York Eating & Drinking 2004; Just desserts* Andrea Delbanco *Counter intelligence* Stephanie Rosenbaum **Bars** adapted from *Time Out New York Bars & Clubs 2003* **Shops & Services** Kelly McMasters, Whitney Joiner (spas); *Where to get the kinks out* Clare Lambe **Festivals & Events** Clare Lambe **Art Galleries** Sarah Schmerler **Books & Poetry** Maureen Shelly **Cabaret & Comedy** Joe Grossman (comedy), H. Scott Jolley (cabaret) **Children** Barbara Aria **Clubs** Bruce Tantum **Film & TV** Darren D'Addario **Gay & Lesbian** Beth Greenfield **Music** Mike Wolf, K. Leander Williams, Jay Ruttenberg, Leah Greenblatt (popular), Steve Smith (classical); *Scene and heard* Mike Wolf **Sports & Fitness** Reed Tucker, Whitney Joiner (yoga); *Belmont: A horse, a course* Karen Tina Harrison **Theater & Dance** David Cote (theater), Gia Kourlas (dance) **Trips Out of Town** Ann Lien; *The hills are alive!* Margaret Pouncey.

Maps J.S. Graphics (john@jsgraphics.co.uk); pages 409–412 reproduced by kind permission of the Metropolitan Transportation Authority.

Photography Stefano Giovannini *(www.stefanogiovannini.com)*, except: pages 1, 79 Patrik Rytikangis; pages 5, 52–53, 92, 163, 165, 187, 212, 224, 229, 236, 238, 243, 244, 246, 247, 247, 281, 306, 393 Lois Anshus *(www.loisanshus.com)*; pages 7, 12, 15, 25 Library of Congress, Prints and Photographs Division; page 8 courtesy of the Ellis Island Museum; page 9 Tara Giovanni; page 11, 91, 101 John Cassidy; page 14 Mollie Cohen; page 16 courtesy of Tishman Speyer Properties; page 23 Catherine Tighe; page 26 Beth Ferraro; page 30 Ramin Talaie/Corbis; page 57 Henry Chung; pages 60, 184, 241 Astrid Stawiarz; page 73, 227 Shaniqwa Jarvis; pages 75, 81, 96, 205, 209 Brian Marcus; pages 77, 141, 142, 180, 359 Noah Kalina; pages 82, 113, 195, 269, 293 Robert Granoff; pages 88, 100, 105, 117, 133, 282, 300, 331 Jeremy Balderson; page 92 David Nicolas; pages 99, 204, 222–223, 272 Caroline Jackson; page 112 Victoria Elmacioglu; page 115 Kara Flannery; page 118–119 Jesse Untracht-Oakner; pages 120, 128, 335 Cecilia Espinoza; pages 123, 154 Nick Axelrod; page 125 Jade Doskow; page 139 Mick Hales; page 148 (right) Jean-Auguste-Dominique Ingres *The Contesse d'Haussonville* (detail) and (left) Richard di Liberto courtesy the Frick Collection; page 150 Elizabeth Felicella; page 157 Val Duarte; page 159 (left) Ken Levinson and (right) Yamamoto Baiitsu *Flowers of the Four Seasons* (detail) courtesy the Japan Society; page 160 Tom Powel Imaging, Inc; pages 169, 177, 185, 189 Molly Morikawa; pages 178, 190, 196, 251, 275, 303, 317, 319 Ian Gittler; page 181 David S Allee; page 182 Brian Crumley; pages 203, 263 Jim Wall; page 226 Jordan Provost; pages 254, 279 Richard Terminel; page 259 Battman Studios; page 264 Richard Prince *Nurse Paintings* courtesy of Barbara Gladstone; page 266 Robert McKeever; page 284 D.DeMello; pages 286, 290, 291 Michael Scott Kenney; page 295 Dana Edelson, courtesy of NBC; page 297 Julie Peña; page 313 courtesy of The Social Registry; page 315 Devaunshi Mahadevia; page 322 ORF/Ali Schafler; page 324 Ken Howard; page 325 Laurie Lambrecht; page 326 Hiro Ito; page 339 Joan Marcus; page 346 Julie Lemberger; page 347 Tony Dougherty; page 349 Paul Kolnik; pages 351, 356 Bob Strovnik; page 353 Dick Lewis courtesy of Montauk Historical Society. The following images were provided by the featured establishments/artists: pages 20, 27, 35, 37, 45, 50, 55, 59, 63, 65, 71, 111, 134, 155, 219, 328, 329, 232, 235, 253, 255, 257, 273, 330, 332, 358. Photo page 89 GODLIS *(www.godlis.com)*.

Introduction

There's the hype about New York City—and then there's the reality, which you'll soon discover for yourself. Let's dispense with the hype straightaway.

Many believe the city is too crowded and the pace, overwhelming. That only applies to certain parts of town—notably, midtown Manhattan at midday. The city's center is where the congested, frenetic New York of popular imagination is most in evidence. What you'll find, though, is that Times Square at night and Fifth Avenue on a gorgeous day—with shoppers out in full force—are thrilling, and that striding along the concrete canyons of Sixth and Park Avenues during rush hour can leave you breathless (in a good way).

It's generally accepted that New York is too big to get to know in one visit (hell, even in one lifetime). Nevertheless, if you approach the city the way that natives do—by seeing New York as a series of concentrically overlapping villages—you'll find a way to focus on what's right for you, whether this is your first visit or your tenth. The fact is, Manhattan itself is tiny, relatively speaking. The sliver of an island comprises just 23 of New York's 309 square miles, and it's home to only 1.5 million of the city's 8 million, making it less populous than any borough except Staten Island. Everything is a short walk, subway or cab ride away: Chic restaurants, renowned museums, brilliantly designed parks, world-famous buildings and historic sites all await you at every turn.

Many visitors expect that they'll encounter lots of attitude here; that New York is a city of velvet-rope exclusivity. But you'll quickly find that seemingly pricey, inaccessible spots often have affordable, inviting counterparts. The funky shops in Nolita and the Lower East Side are great alternatives to the elegant boutiques of the Upper East Side and Soho; and new eateries in the Meatpacking or Flatiron Districts can compete with numerous reserve-a-month-ahead restaurants all over town. In fact, New York can be pretty democratic when it comes to cool (*see p30* **New York Today**). And increasingly, more of what's cutting-edge can be found in the outer boroughs. Williamsburg, Fort Greene and Red Hook all get their props (*see pp121–128* **Brooklyn**), as do Astoria and Long Island City (*see pp129–134* **Queens**).

Finally, there's the stereotype about New Yorkers being rude or arrogant. Visitors discover the real deal: People have always been the city's greatest resource. There's a more relaxed feeling on the street these days; time has passed since September 11, and the crime rate is at a 30-year low. You'll find New Yorkers to be hospitable—even downright friendly. But they can be impatient: Be alert and come prepared, because many New Yorkers just don't have time to say something twice.

Except the name of their town.

ABOUT THE TIME OUT CITY GUIDES

The *Time Out New York Guide* is one of an expanding series of Time Out City Guides—now numbering more than 45—produced by the people behind London and New York's successful weekly listings magazines. All the guides are written and updated by resident experts who strive to provide the most current information you'll need to explore the city, whether you're a local or a first-time visitor.

The staff of *Time Out New York* magazine worked on this 12th edition of the *Time Out New York Guide. TONY* has been "the obsessive guide to impulsive entertainment" for all inhabitants of the city (and passers-through) for eight years. Many chapters have been rewritten from scratch; all have been thoroughly revised, and offer new feature boxes.

THE LOWDOWN ON THE LISTINGS

All listings include addresses, telephone numbers (and often websites), travel directions (usually by subway), opening times, admission prices and credit-card information. We've given up-to-date details on facilities, services and events, all checked and correct at press time. However, owners and managers can—and often do—change their policies. It's always best to call and check the when, where and how much.

Throughout the book, you'll find boldfaced items (sights or restaurants, for example) with

► You can find an online version of this guide, as well as guides to more than 35 other international cities, at **www.timeout.com**.

Charge The symbol of **Wall Street**. *See p77.*

location and telephone number immediately following; alternatively, we provide the detailed listings information within that chapter or in one that is cross-referenced. For your convenience, we've included cross-reference boxes (outlined in red) throughout.

PRICES AND PAYMENT

We have noted whether establishments accept credit cards or not, and listed the major cards: American Express (AmEx), Diners Club (DC), Discover (Disc), MasterCard (MC) and Visa (V). Some businesses will also accept other cards. Most venues will accept U.S.-dollar traveler's checks issued by a major financial institution, such as American Express.

The prices listed are guidelines, not gospel. Fluctuating exchange rates and inflation can cause prices to change overnight. While every effort has been made to ensure the accuracy of this guide, the publishers cannot accept responsibility for any errors it may contain. If you find things altered beyond recognition, ask why—and please, e-mail to let us know. Our goal is to furnish the most accurate information available, so we always want to know if you've been badly treated or overcharged.

TELEPHONE NUMBERS

All telephone numbers in this guide are written as dialed within the United States, except that **you must always dial 1**, then the area code and the seven-digit phone number (from abroad, dial 00 first as well), even if the place you're calling is in the same area code as the one you're calling from. Manhattan area codes are 212 and 646; those in Brooklyn, Queens, the Bronx and Staten Island are 718 and 347; generally (but not always), 917 is reserved for cell phones and pagers. Phone numbers beginning with 800, 866, 877 and 888 are free of charge when called from anywhere in the U.S. When numbers are listed as letters for easy recall (e.g., 800-AIR-RIDE), dial the corresponding numbers on the telephone keypad.

ESSENTIAL INFORMATION

Turn to the **Directory** chapter (the blue pages at the back of this guide; *see pp359–382*) for all the practical information you might need for visiting New York, including getting into the city from the major airports nearby, visa and customs procedures, access for people with disabilities, emergency telephone numbers, a list of helpful websites and how to use the subway system.

THE LAY OF THE LAND

We've included cross streets in all of our addresses, so you can find your way more easily. And there's a series of fully indexed **color street maps**, as well as subway and bus maps, at the back of the guide, starting on page 394.

LET US KNOW WHAT YOU THINK

We hope you enjoy the *Time Out New York Guide,* and we'd like to know what you think of it. We welcome tips about places that you believe we should include in future editions, and appreciate your feedback on our choices, so please e-mail us at guides@timeoutny.com.

A note about our advertisers

We would like to stress that no establishment has been included in this guide because it has advertised in any of our publications, and no payment of any kind has influenced any review. The opinions given in this book are those of *Time Out* writers and are entirely independent.

In Context

Features

Immigrants met America at **Ellis Island**.

History

Rise, fall, bounce back, repeat: a world capital's wild ride.

New York has always been a city of superlatives. This is a town that strives to be the first, the biggest and the best. Not that it's always been easy, of course. But New York, like New Yorkers, loves to hang tough. And that has made this city the undisputed king of the comeback—as a quick look at local history amply illustrates.

TRIBES AND TOURISTS

Members of the indigenous Lenape tribe were the original native New Yorkers. They lived among the meadows, forests and farms of the land they called Lenapehoking for thousands of years, until 1524, when tourists from the Old World began to trickle in. The first European sightseer to cast his eyes upon this land was Giovanni da Verrazano, an Italian explorer commissioned by the French to find a shortcut to the Orient. Instead, he found Staten Island. Unimpressed, and recognizing that he was on the wrong track, Verrazano pulled up anchor nearly as quickly as he had dropped it, never setting foot on land.

Eighty-five years later, Englishman Henry Hudson was more favorably disposed. Sent by the Dutch, with the same goal of finding a shortcut to the Far East, Hudson hit the harbor in September 1609 and was entranced by what lay before him. He lingered long enough to explore the entire river that now bears his name, but it wasn't his fate to grow old in this place he admired as a "rich and pleasant land": On a return trip in 1611, Hudson's crew mutinied and cast him adrift. Still, his tales of the lush, river-crossed countryside captured the Dutch imagination—so much so that in 1624, the Dutch West India Company sent 110 settlers to establish a trading post here. They planted themselves at the southern end of the island called Mannahata, and christened the tip New Amsterdam. In bloody battles, they did their best to drive the local Lenape away from their little company town. But the Lenape dug in.

In 1626, a man named Peter Minuit, New Amsterdam's first governor, thought he'd solve the Lenape problem by pulling off the city's very first real-estate rip-off. Although the tribe had no concept of private land ownership, he "bought" the island of Manhattan—all 14,000 acres of it—from the Lenape for 60 guilders' worth of goods. Legend famously values the purchase price at $24, but modern historians set the amount closer to $500. (These days, that wouldn't cover a month's rent for a closet-size studio apartment.)

The Dutch quickly made New Amsterdam a center for fur trading. The population didn't grow as fast as their business, however, and the Dutch West India Company had a hard time finding recruits to move to an unknown island an ocean away. Deciding that anyone would do, the company made passage easy for servants, orphans, slaves, thieves, drunkards and prostitutes. Within ten years, the population grew to 400—about the same number that could cram into a popular Times Square restaurant today. Inevitably (given that one in every four structures was a tavern), drunkenness, crime and squalor were all too common in the community. If the colony was to thrive, it needed a strong leader. Enter Peter Stuyvesant.

THE FIRST TOUGH-GUY MAYOR

A one-legged, puritanical bully with a quick temper, Stuyvesant was less than popular. He was, however, the colony's first effective governor. He made peace with the Lenape, formed the first policing force (consisting of nine men), and cracked down on debauchery by shutting taverns and outlawing drinking on Sunday. He solidified the government and established the first school, post office, hospital, prison and poorhouse. Within a decade, the population quadrupled, and the settlement became an important trading port. Lined with canals and windmills, and dotted with gabled farmhouses, New Amsterdam began to resemble its namesake city. Newcomers came to work in the farming, fur and slave trades. Soon, a dozen and a half languages could be heard in the streets—a fact that made the bigoted Stuyvesant nervous. In 1654, he attempted to quash immigration by turning away Sephardic Jews who were fleeing the Spanish Inquisition. But, surprisingly for the time, the corporate honchos at the Dutch West India Company reprimanded him for his intolerance and overturned his decision, leading to the establishment of the earliest Jewish community in the New World. That was the first time the inflexible Stuyvesant was made to bend. The second time would put an end to the 40-year Dutch rule for good.

REVOLUTIONARY CITY

On August 27, 1664, English warships sailed into the harbor, set on taking over the now prosperous colony. Trying to avoid bloodshed and destruction, Stuyvesant immediately surrendered. Two days later, New Amsterdam was renamed New York (after the Duke of York, brother of King Charles II), and Stuyvesant quietly retired to his farmhouse, now commemorated by Stuyvesant Street in the East Village.

The English built upon Stuyvesant's foundation while continuing to battle with the Lenape. By 1695, the tribe was wiped out, and New York's population had shot up to 3,000. Over the next 35 years, Dutch-style farmhouses and windmills gave way to stately townhouses and monuments to English royals. By 1740, the slave trade had made New York the third-busiest port in the British Empire. The city, now home to more than 11,000 residents, was prosperous for a quarter-century more. But resentment of

It happened here

The **Audubon Ballroom** *(3940 Broadway at 165th St)*, will always be known as the place where Malcolm X met his untimely end: Here, on February 21, 1965, the charismatic Black Muslim spokesman was gunned down by three assailants. Exactly who and why have never been established, though the murder came shortly after a split with Nation of Islam head Elijah Muhammad. The Audubon, built in 1912, was also the site, in 1923, of the first-ever dance marathon (won by Alma Cummings, who kept going for more than 24 hours). Its illustrious facade has been preserved as a memorial to Malcolm X.

the English occupation was building, fueled by the ever-heavier burden of British taxation.

One angry young man was Alexander Hamilton, the illegitimate son of a Scottish nobleman, who arrived in New York from the West Indies in 1773. A tenacious intellectual, Hamilton enrolled in King's College (now Columbia University) and became politically active, organizing an artillery company, writing rebellious anti-British pamphlets and serving as a colonel in General Washington's army. In these and other ways, he played a key role in a movement that would change the face of the city—and the country—forever.

Upon winning the Revolutionary War, General Washington and his troops marched triumphantly down Broadway to reclaim New York City as part of the newly established United States of America.

Fearing the brewing revolution, New York's citizenry fled in droves in 1775, causing the population to plummet from 25,000 to just 5,000. The following year, 100 British warships floated into this virtual ghost town, carrying an intimidating army of 32,000—nearly four times the size of Washington's militia. Despite their presence, Washington organized a reading of the Declaration of Independence, and patriots tore the statue of King George III from its pedestal in Bowling Green. Revolution was inevitable.

The battle for New York officially began on August 26, 1776, and Washington's army sustained heavy losses. Nearly a quarter of his men were slaughtered in a single two-day period. As Washington retreated, a fire—thought to have been lit by patriots—reduced to ashes 493 buildings, including Trinity Church. The British were left with a scorched city, its populace living in makeshift tents. The city continued to suffer for seven long years. Eventually, of course, Washington's luck turned. Upon winning the Revolutionary War, he and his troops marched triumphantly down Broadway to reclaim New York City as part of the newly established United States of America. On December 4, 1783, the general bade farewell to his troops at Fraunces Tavern, which still stands on Pearl Street.

Alexander Hamilton, for his part, got busy in the rebuilding effort, laying the groundwork for major New York institutions that remain vital to this day. He started by establishing the city's first bank, the Bank of New York, in 1784. When Washington was inaugurated as the nation's first president in 1789, at Federal Hall on Wall Street, he brought Hamilton on board as the first secretary of the treasury. Thanks to Hamilton's clever new mercantile business plan, trade in stocks and bonds flourished, leading to the establishment of the New York Stock Exchange in 1792. In 1801, Hamilton founded the *Evening Post,* still circulating as the *New York Post.* By 1804, New York was a leading world financial center. That same year, political rival Aaron Burr killed Hamilton in a duel in Weehawken, New Jersey.

BOOMTOWN

New York continued to grow and prosper for the next three decades. Maritime commerce soared, and Robert Fulton's innovative steamboat made its maiden voyage on the Hudson River in 1807. Eleven years later, New York introduced regularly scheduled shipping (a novel concept at the time) between New York and Liverpool on the Black Ball Line. Reflecting the city's status as America's shipping center, the urban landscape was ringed with sprawling piers, towering masts and billowing sails. A job boom in the maritime trades lured hundreds of European laborers, and the influx left the city—still entirely crammed below Houston Street—increasingly congested. Where Dutch farms and English estates once stood, taller, more efficient structures took hold. Manhattan real estate became the most expensive in the world.

A notoriously ill-mannered fur trader named John Jacob Astor had the foresight to buy every scrap of land he could north of the city's bustling center, including most of what would become the Lower East Side, the East Village and Times Square. Like a true New York landlord, he did little to improve the property he owned; he merely held on to his parcels until the time was ripe to sell them at a staggering profit. His investments made him the city's first millionaire.

The first man to conquer the city's congestion problem was Mayor DeWitt Clinton, a brilliant politician and a protégé of Alexander Hamilton. Clinton's dream was to organize the entire island of Manhattan to cope with the eventual population creep northward. In 1807, he created a commission to map out the foreseeable sprawl. The commission presented its work four years later, and the manifest destiny of this new city was made plain: It would be a regular grid of crossing thoroughfares, 12 avenues wide and 155 streets long.

Perhaps Clinton knew that his next and most important contribution to New York would bring thousands to his city to fulfill that destiny. In

1811, he presented a plan to build a 350-mile canal linking the Hudson River with Lake Erie. Many thought this was impossible: The longest canal in the world at the time was a mere 27 miles long. But he pressed on, and, being as slick-tongued as certain modern-day Clintons, raised an unheard-of $6 million for the project. Work on the Erie Canal, begun in 1817, was completed in 1825—three years ahead of schedule. It shortened the journey between New York City and Buffalo from three weeks to one, and cut the cost of the trip from $100 to $6. Goods, people and money poured into New York, fostering a merchant elite that moved northward to escape the urban crush. More and more estates popped up above Houston Street, even as 3,000 new buildings were erected below it, each grander and more imposing than its modest Colonial cousins. Slavery was officially abolished in New York in 1827, making free blacks an essential part of the workforce. In 1831, the first public transportation system began operation, pulling passengers in horse-drawn omnibuses to the far reaches of the existing city.

BUMMERTOWN

As the population grew (swelling to 170,000 by 1830), so did New York City's problems. Tensions bubbled between immigrant newcomers and those who could trace their American lineage back a generation or two. Crime rose, and lurid tales filled the "penny press," the city's outlets for the newfangled tabloid journalism. While wealthy New Yorkers were moving as far "uptown" as Greenwich Village, the infamous Five Points neighborhood—the city's first slum—festered in the area now occupied by City Hall and the courthouses. Built on a fetid drained pond, Five Points became the ramshackle home of poor immigrants and blacks. At night, the area was patrolled by gangs with colorful names like the Forty Thieves, Plug Uglies and Dead Rabbits; and as in *Gangs of New York,* their members often met in bloody clashes. But what finally sent a mass of 100,000 people scurrying from downtown was an outbreak of cholera in 1832. In six weeks, 3,513 New Yorkers died.

Three years later, a vast swath of New York was destroyed by the largest fire the city would ever see—one that burned 20 square blocks to the ground. It began in a warehouse on Pearl Street. As fierce winds blew and icy water froze in the chilly air, some 1,900 firefighters tried desperately to snuff the flames roaring through the neighborhood's predominantly wooden structures. The next day, newspapers reported that the fire had claimed 700 buildings and caused $20- to $40 million in damages. Surprisingly, only two lives were lost, and within a year, 500 structures were rebuilt.

In 1837, a financial panic left hundreds of Wall Street businesses crumbling. Commerce stagnated at the docks, the expanding real-estate market collapsed, and all but three city banks closed down. Fifty thousand New Yorkers lost their jobs, while 200,000 teetered on the edge of poverty. The panic also sparked an era of civil unrest and violence. In 1849, a xenophobic mob of 8,000, protesting the performance of an English actor at the Astor Place Opera House, was met by a militia that resorted to gunfire, killing 22 people. But the Draft Riots of 1863, which have been called "the bloodiest riots in American history," were much worse. After a law was passed exempting men from the draft for a $300 fee, the (mostly Irish) poor rose up, forming a mob 15,000 strong that rampaged through the city. They trashed police stations, draft boards, newspaper offices, elite shops and wealthy homes before the chaos took a racial turn. Fueled by anger about the Civil

It happened here

Leave it to Marilyn Monroe to make even a subway grate sexy. It was here, on the northwest corner of **Lexington Avenue at 52nd Street**, that director Billy Wilder first filmed the blond bombshell's famous dress-blowing scene for 1955's *The Seven Year Itch*—though the version actually used in the movie was later shot in the studio. The pose Marilyn struck—mischievous and smiling as she girlishly forces the front of her white dress down with both hands—became iconic. The grate, however, lives on unheralded.

War (for which they blamed blacks), and fearful that freed slaves would take away jobs, the rioters set fire to the Colored Orphan Asylum and vandalized black homes. Blacks were beaten in the streets, and some were lynched. A federal force of 6,000 men was sent to subdue the violence. After five days and as many as 1,000 deaths, peace was restored.

PROGRESSIVE CITY

As intensely chaotic as the mid-19th century seemed, the pace of progress continued unabated. Compared with the major Southern cities, New York emerged nearly unscathed from the Civil War. The population ballooned to 2 million, and new technologies revolutionized daily life. The elevated railway, for example, helped spread the population into the Upper East and Upper West Sides, while other trains connected the city with upstate New York, New England and the Midwest. By 1871, train traffic had grown so much that rail tycoon Cornelius Vanderbilt built the original Grand Central Depot, which could accommodate a then-considerable 15,000 people at a time. (It was later replaced by the current Grand Central Terminal, which was completed in 1913.)

One ambitious project was brought to life during the harsh winter of 1867. The East River froze over, halting waterway traffic between Brooklyn and Manhattan for weeks. Brooklyn had, by then, become the nation's third most populous city, and its politicians, businessmen and community leaders quickly realized that the boroughs had to be linked. And so the New York Bridge Company was incorporated. Its goal was to build the world's longest bridge, spanning the East River between downtown Manhattan and southwestern Brooklyn. Over 16 years (four times longer than projected), 14,000 miles of steel cable were stretched across the 1,595-foot span, while the towers rose a staggering 276 feet above the river. Disasters, worker deaths and corruption dogged the project, but the Brooklyn Bridge opened with triumphant fanfare on May 23, 1883. It remains one of the city's most beloved symbols.

CORRUPT CITY

As New York recovered from the turmoil of the mid-1800s, one man—William M. Tweed, known as Boss—was pulling the strings. Using his ample charm, the six-foot, 300-pound bookkeeper, chair maker and volunteer firefighter became one of the city's most powerful politicians. He served as alderman, district leader, representative in the U.S. House, state senator, chairman of the Democratic General Committee and leader of the general committee of Tammany Hall, a political organization formed by craftsmen to keep the wealthy class's political clout in check. But even though Tweed opened orphanages, poorhouses and hospitals, his good deeds were overshadowed by his and his cohorts' gross embezzlement of city funds.

It's a stretch The **Brooklyn Bridge** was the world's longest suspension bridge in 1883.

By 1870, members of the "Tweed Ring" had pushed through a new city charter, granting themselves control of the city's treasury. Using fake leases and wildly inflated bills for city supplies and services, Tweed and his cronies may ultimately have pocketed as much as $200 million, and caused the city's debt to triple. The work of cartoonist Thomas Nast, who lampooned Tweed in the pages of *Harper's Weekly,* helped to bring the Boss's transgressions to light. Tweed was eventually sued by the city for $6 million, and charged with forgery and larceny. While being held in debtor's prison pending bail, he escaped in 1875. He was caught in Spain a year later, and died in the slammer in 1878.

As Tweed was emptying the city's coffers, poverty spread throughout New York. Starving families put their young to work, and soon, more than 100,000 children were toiling in sweatshops and factories. The bond market collapsed, the stock market took a nosedive, factories closed and railroads went bankrupt. By 1874, New York's homeless population stood at an estimated 90,000 souls. That winter, *Harper's Weekly* reported, 900 New Yorkers starved to death.

THE TWO HALVES

In September 1882, a new era dawned brightly when Thomas Alva Edison lit up half a square mile of lower Manhattan with 3,000 electric lamps. One of the newly illuminated offices belonged to J.P. Morgan, a successful financier who was essential in bringing New York's—and America's—economy back to life. By bailing out a number of failing railroads, then merging and restructuring them, Morgan jump-started commerce in New York once again. Goods, jobs and businesses returned to the city, and soon, aggressive businessmen with names like Rockefeller, Carnegie and Frick wanted a piece of the action. They made New York the headquarters for Standard Oil and U.S. Steel. Along with other rapidly growing companies such as General Electric and American Tobacco, these corporations would go on to shape America's economic future.

A shining symbol for less fortunate immigrants also made New York her home at that time. To commemorate America's freedom and to celebrate an international friendship, the French gave the Statue of Liberty to the U.S. Sculptor Frédéric-Auguste Bartholdi created the 151-foot-tall amazon using funds donated by French citizens, but their generosity could not cover the expense of building her base. Initially met with apathy by the U.S. government, Hungarian immigrant and publisher Joseph Pulitzer used his *World* newspaper to encourage Americans to pay for a pedestal. When she was finally unveiled in 1886, Lady Liberty measured 305 feet high—taller even than the towers of the Brooklyn Bridge.

Between 1892 and 1924, the Statue of Liberty welcomed 12 million immigrants into the harbor. These "huddled masses," fleeing political disruption, poverty and persecution, arrived from Europe by the boatload, weathering the treacherous journey in the steerage compartments of ocean liners. Ellis Island, a new immigration-processing center, opened in 1892, expecting to accommodate 500,000 people annually; it processed twice that number in its first year. In the 34-building complex, crowds of would-be Americans were herded through examinations, inspections and interrogations. Fewer than two percent were sent home, and others would move on; but 4 million would stay, turning New York into what British playwright Israel Zangwill would call "the great melting pot where all the races of Europe are melting and reforming."

While millionaires like the Vanderbilts were building huge French-style mansions along Fifth Avenue, immigrants on the Lower East Side were crowding into dark, squalid tenements. Jacob A. Riis, a Danish immigrant and police reporter for the *New York Tribune,* made it his business to expose this dichotomy. Using the still-new technology of photography, Riis's book *How the Other Half Lives,* published in 1890, revealed the real and desperate faces of the slums. To bring to light the bitter conditions of the city's working poor, the intrepid reporter scoured filthy alleys and overcrowded, unheated tenements, many of which lacked what we would now consider the barest minimum of light, ventilation and sanitation. Largely as a result of Riis's work, the state passed the Tenement House Act of 1901, which called for drastic housing reforms.

EXPANDING CITY

By the close of the 19th century, 40 fragmented governments had formed in and around Manhattan, creating political confusion and frustration on many levels. On January 1, 1898, the boroughs of Manhattan, Brooklyn, Queens, Staten Island and the Bronx consolidated to form New York City, America's largest city. More and more companies moved their headquarters into this new metropolis, increasing the demand for office space. With no more real estate left to develop in lower Manhattan, New York embraced the steel revolution and grew skyward. An all-out race began to build the tallest building in the world. By 1902, New York boasted 66 skyscrapers, including the 20-story Fuller Building (now known as the Flatiron Building) at

Fifth Avenue and 23rd Street, and the 25-story New York Times tower in Longacre (now Times) Square. Within four years, they would be outshone by the 47-story Singer building on lower Broadway, which enjoyed the status of tallest building in the world for only 18 months. The 700-foot Metropolitan Life Tower on Madison Square claimed the title in 1909, until the 767-foot Woolworth Building on Broadway and Park Place topped it in 1913—and held the distinction for nearly two decades.

As New York stretched up into the sky, it also burrowed underground. Not to be outdone by the subterranean networks of public transit in London, Paris, Budapest and Boston, New York began digging its own subway system in 1900. The $35 million project took nearly four and a half years to complete. Less than a decade after opening, it was carrying a billion passengers a year, making it the most heavily traveled underground transit system in the world.

CITY OF MOVEMENT

By 1909, 30,000 factories were operating in the city, churning out everything from heavy machinery to artificial flowers. Conditions were brutal, with workers toiling long hours for meager pay. The garment industry was by far the largest, and the majority of its workers were young immigrant seamstresses, working 60-plus hours for just $5 a week. Mistrusted and abused, factory workers burdened with impossible quotas had their pay docked for minor mistakes, and were often locked inside their workplaces during working hours.

On November 22, 1909, one 23-year-old garment worker decided she'd had enough. Clara Lemlich, a diminutive but tough Russian immigrant, stepped up to the podium at a large laborers' meeting at Cooper Union. Though six of her ribs had recently been broken during clashes on a picket line, Lemlich delivered (in Yiddish, which was translated throughout the room into other languages) an impassioned speech that mobilized her fellow workers to organize a mass strike. The next day, 15,000 garment workers left their machines while 5,000 other factory workers joined their cause. They staunchly sat out until February, finally defeated by owners who simply wouldn't budge. In the end, it would take a tragedy for real changes to be made.

On March 25, 1911, a fire broke out at the Triangle Shirtwaist Company. Though it was a Saturday, some 500 workers—most of them teenage girls—were toiling in the Greenwich Village factory. Flames spread rapidly through the fabric-stuffed building. But as the girls rushed to escape, they found many of the exits locked—a practice probably intended to keep workers from sneaking out with goods after finishing a shift. Roughly 350 made it out onto the adjoining rooftops before the inferno closed off all exits, but 146 young women perished. Many were engulfed by flames; others jumped to their deaths from windows on the eighth, ninth and tenth floors. Even in the face of such tragedy, justice wasn't served: The two factory owners, tried for manslaughter, were acquitted. But the disaster did spur labor and union organizations, which pushed for—and won—sweeping reforms for factory workers.

Another movement was taking hold during this time as well. Between 1910 and 1913, New York City hosted the largest women's-suffrage rallies in the country. Harriet Stanton Blatch (daughter of famed suffragette Elizabeth Cady Stanton and founder of the Equality League of Self Supporting Women) and Carrie Chapman

It happened here

Sobriety has a home on the corner of Park Avenue South and 21st Street: During the 1930s, the troubled tipplers who would eventually form Alcoholics Anonymous came to worship and seek help for their wayward souls at the **Calvary Episcopal Church** (1847). One hard drinker named Bill Wilson developed a close relationship with the rector, Samuel Shoemaker. In creating AA's influential 12-Step Program in 1935, Wilson and others incorporated many of Shoemaker's ideas about taking moral inventory and making amends, in addition to other concepts that have set the worldwide standard for sobering up.

Fountain of youth The Bethesda Terrace fountain in **Central Park** was opened in 1859.

Catt (organizer of the New York City Women's Suffrage party) arranged attention-getting demonstrations while pressuring the state to authorize a referendum on women's right to vote. The measure was defeated in 1915, but that setback only steeled the suffragettes' resolve. Finally, they gained the support of Tammany Hall. The law passed in 1919, challenging the male stranglehold on voting throughout the country. (With New York leading the nation, the 19th Amendment was ratified in 1920.)

In 1919, as New York welcomed troops home from World War I with a parade along Fifth Avenue, the city celebrated its emergence on the global stage. It had supplanted London as the investment capital of the world; it housed the most important corporate headquarters; and it was the center of publishing, thanks to two men named Pulitzer and Hearst. *The New York Times* had become the country's most prestigious newspaper; Broadway and Times Square had grown into the focal point of American theater; and Greenwich Village, once the home of an elite gentry, had evolved into a world-class bohemia. Filled with galleries, fringe theaters and coffeehouses, the Village hosted flamboyant artists, writers and political revolutionaries. John Reed, reporter on the Russian revolution and author of *Ten Days That Shook the World,* lived here, as did Edna St. Vincent Millay, famous for her poetry and her public, unfettered love life.

Social movements both personal and political found a home in New York City. A former nurse and midwife who grew up in a family of 11 children, Margaret Sanger was a fierce advocate of birth control and family planning. She opened the first birth-control clinic in Brownsville, Brooklyn, on October 16, 1916 (it was closed by police nine days later for violating state laws, and Sanger was arrested and imprisoned for 30 days). In 1921, she formed the American Birth Control League, a clinic that researched birth control and provided gynecological services. It was a forerunner of Planned Parenthood, which Sanger ardently supported until her death in 1966.

Forward-thinking women like Sanger set the tone for the Jazz Age, a time when women, now a voting political force, were growing beyond the moral conventions of the 19th century. The 18th Amendment, ratified by Congress in 1919, marked the beginning of the Jazz Age in New York. By outlawing the distribution and sale of alcoholic beverages, the so-called Prohibition amendment turned the city into the capital of bootlegging, speakeasies and organized crime. In the early 1920s, New York City boasted 32,000 illegal watering holes—twice the number of legal establishments before Prohibition.

In 1925, New Yorkers elected the charismatic James J. Walker as mayor. A charming ex-songwriter (as well as a frequenter of speakeasies and a skirt-chaser who would leave his wife for a dancer), Walker matched his city's flashy style and hunger for publicity. Fame

Well lit The first holiday tree at **Rockefeller Center** was set up by site workers in 1931.

flowed in the city's veins: Home-run hero Babe Ruth drew a million fans each season to the New York Yankees' games, and sharp-tongued Walter Winchell filled his newspaper columns and radio shows with celebrity tidbits and society scandals. Indeed, New York was fast becoming the king of all media. Vaudevillians like George Burns and Jack Benny brought entertainment to the airwaves, and Charles Scribner's Sons published *This Side of Paradise*, a promising first novel from a young author named F. Scott Fitzgerald. *The New Yorker* magazine hit the stands, and Alexander Woollcott, Dorothy Parker, Harold Ross, Robert Benchley and other writers would meet daily to trade witticisms around a table at the Algonquin Hotel on 44th Street.

The Harlem Renaissance was blooming at the same time. Such writers as Langston Hughes, Zora Neale Hurston and James Weldon Johnson transformed the African-American experience into lyrical literary works, and white society flocked to the Cotton Club to see genre-defining musicians like Eubie Blake, Bessie Smith, Cab Calloway, Louis Armstrong and Duke Ellington. (Blacks were not welcome unless they were performing.) Downtown, Broadway houses were packed, thanks to shows scored by brilliant composers and lyricists like George and Ira Gershwin, Irving Berlin, Lorenz Hart, Cole Porter, Richard Rodgers and Oscar Hammerstein II. The same year, Al Jolson wowed audiences in *The Jazz Singer,* the first talking picture.

The dizzying excitement came to an end on Tuesday, October 29, 1929, when the stock market crashed and the Depression rolled in. Corruption rocked Walker's hold on the city: Despite a tenure that saw the opening of the Holland Tunnel, the completion of the George Washington Bridge, and the construction of the Chrysler and Empire State buildings, Walker's luster faded as accusations of graft came to light. He resigned in 1932, leaving New York in the depths of the Great Depression, with a staggering 1 million inhabitants out of work.

In 1934, an unstoppable workaholic named Fiorello La Guardia took office as mayor, rolling up his sleeves to crack down on mobsters, gambling, smut and government corruption. La Guardia was the son of an Italian father and a Jewish mother—a tough-talking politician who described himself as "inconsiderate, arbitrary, authoritative, difficult, complicated, intolerant and somewhat theatrical." Violent of temper and known for nearly coming to blows with other city officials, La Guardia ushered New York into an era of unparalleled prosperity over the course of his three mayoral terms. During World War II, the city's ports and factories proved essential to the war effort, with the Brooklyn Navy Yard becoming the largest shipyard in the world. The feeling of unity pervading La Guardia's tenure was most visible on August 14, 1945, when 2 million people spontaneously gathered in Times Square to jubilantly celebrate the end of the war.

How did he do it? La Guardia streamlined city government, paid down the debt and updated the transportation, hospital, reservoir and sewer systems, making New York an efficient, modern city. Under his stewardship, Rockefeller Center opened and became home to

NBC, the Rainbow Room and the extravagant Radio City Music Hall. Highways made the city more accessible, and North Beach Airport (now La Guardia) became the city's first commercial landing field.

The metamorphosis that the city experienced during La Guardia's tenure was documented by photographer Berenice Abbott. Her *Changing New York,* published in 1939, focused on the city's growth and transformation between 1935 and 1938. Abbott's lens captured everything from sleek, towering skyscrapers to rickety fire escapes. The photos of the city's rapid modernization, juxtaposed with its antiquated remnants, showed how rapidly the old face of the city was disappearing.

Helping La Guardia to modernize the city was urban planner Robert Moses, a hard-nosed visionary who would do much to shape—and also destroy—New York's landscape. As chairman of the Council on Parks, Moses spent 44 years remaking the city with expressways, parks, playgrounds, beaches, public housing, bridges and tunnels, including such landmarks as Shea Stadium, Jones Beach, Lincoln Center, the United Nations complex and the Verrazano Bridge.

THE MODERN CITY

Despite La Guardia's belt-tightening and Moses' renovation, New York began to fall apart financially in the '50s and '60s. More crowding occurred as rural African-Americans and Puerto Ricans flocked to the metropolis seeking opportunity, only to meet with ruthless discrimination and a dearth of jobs. When WWII ended, 800,000 industrial jobs had disappeared. Factories in need of space moved to the suburbs; nearly 5 million residents also fled to the newly developing 'burbs.

Robert Moses' Slum Clearance Committee reduced many neighborhoods to rubble, forcing out residents to make room for huge, isolating housing projects that became magnets for crime. In 1963, the city also lost Pennsylvania Station, McKim, Mead & White's architectural masterpiece and once the world's largest rail terminal. Over the protests of picketers, the Pennsylvania Railroad Company demolished the site between 1961 and '63 to make way for a more modern station and Madison Square Garden. It was a giant wake-up call to New Yorkers that architectural changes in the city were hurtling out of control.

But Moses and his wrecking ball couldn't knock over one steadfast West Village woman. Jane Jacobs—a mother, architectural writer and urban-planning critic—organized local residents when the city unveiled its plan to clear a 14-block tract of her neighborhood for more high-rise public housing. With the support of an influential councilman (and fellow neighborhood resident) named Ed Koch, the group fought the plan and won, causing Mayor Robert J. Wagner to back down. As a result of the Penn Station demolition and Jacobs's efforts, in 1965 the Landmarks Preservation Commission—the first such group in the U.S—was formed to save important historical buildings.

Amid all the destruction of the era, the city still harbored its share of innovative creators. Allen Ginsberg, Jack Kerouac and their fellow Beats gathered in Village coffeehouses to create a new voice for poetry. A folk scene brewed in tiny clubs on Bleecker Street, showcasing musicians like Bob Dylan, who sang in protest of the war in Vietnam. A former shoe illustrator from Pittsburgh named Andy Warhol began turning the images of mass consumerism into deadpan, ironic art statements. Gay men and women, long a hidden part of the city's history, came out into the streets in 1969's Stonewall riots, sparked when patrons at the Stonewall Inn on Christopher Street resisted a police raid—and, in the process, gave birth to the modern gay-rights movement.

Violent of temper and known for nearly coming to blows with other city officials, La Guardia ushered New York into an era of unparalleled prosperity over the course of his three mayoral terms.

By the early 1970s, city services had dwindled, the streets were dirty, subways were dangerous, and trains and buildings were scrawled with multicolored graffiti. The quality of the public schools declined, crime skyrocketed and debt swelled to $6 billion. Thumbing its nose at the downward turn, the World Trade Center rose in 1973, its twin 110-story towers becoming the skyline's most dominant new feature. But New Yorkers didn't have much to be cocky about. As the Trade Center rose, the city became even more desperately overdrawn—so much so that Mayor Abraham Beame appealed to the federal government for a bailout in 1975. *The Daily News* summed up President Ford's response with the immortal headline FORD TO CITY: DROP DEAD.

Things didn't improve. During the mid-'70s, Times Square degenerated into a sleazy morass of sex shops and porn palaces, drug use escalated, and subway ridership hit an all-time low. In 1977, serial killer Son of Sam terrorized the city. A blackout one hot August night that same year led to widespread looting and arson. The angst of the time was reflected in the angry punk culture that rose up around clubs like CBGB. While the Ramones and other bands played fast and loud downtown, celebrities, designers and models converged on midtown to disco their troubles away at Studio 54.

The Wall Street boom of the '80s and some adept fiscal petitioning by Koch (who had become the city's mayor) brought money flooding back into New York. Gentrification glamorized neighborhoods like Soho, Hell's Kitchen and the East Village. But deeper ills persisted. In 1988, a demonstration against the city's efforts to impose a curfew and displace the homeless in Tompkins Square Park erupted into a violent clash with police. Crack use was epidemic in the ghettos, homelessness was rising, and AIDS was decimating the city's creative communities. By 1989, the end of Koch's third term, citizens were restless for change. They turned to David N. Dinkins, electing him the city's first African-American mayor. A soft-spoken, distinguished man, Dinkins held office for only a single term—one marked by a record murder rate, flaring racial tensions in Crown Heights, Flatbush and Washington Heights, and the explosion of a terrorist bomb in the World Trade Center that killed 6, injured 1,000 and foreshadowed the catastrophic attacks of a decade later.

After Dinkins, New Yorkers voted in former federal prosecutor Rudolph Giuliani. Like his predecessors Peter Stuyvesant and Fiorello La Guardia, Giuliani was an abrasive leader who used bully tactics to get things done. His "quality of life campaign" cracked down on everything from drug dealing and pornography to unsolicited windshield-washers. Even as the police were being criticized for using excessive force in several high-profile cases, crime was plummeting, tourism was soaring, and New York was

It's a date (in NYC history)

1524 Giovanni da Verrazano sails into New York Harbor.
1624 First Dutch settlers establish New Amsterdam at the foot of Manhattan Island.
1626 Peter Minuit purchases Manhattan for goods worth 60 guilders.
1635 Village of Breuckelen founded.
1639 The Broncks settle north of Manhattan.
1647 Peter Stuyvesant becomes director general.
1664 Dutch rule ends; New Amsterdam renamed New York.
1754 King's College (now Columbia University) founded.
1776 Battle for New York begins; fire ravages the city.
1783 George Washington marches triumphantly down Broadway.
1784 Alexander Hamilton founds the Bank of New York.
1785 New York becomes the nation's capital.
1789 President Washington inaugurated at Federal Hall on Wall Street.
1792 New York Stock Exchange founded.
1804 New York becomes the country's most populous city (population 80,000); New-York Historical Society founded.
1811 DeWitt Clinton's grid plan for Manhattan introduced.
1823 New York Gas Light Company installs first gas lamps on Broadway.
1825 Erie Canal completed.
1827 Slavery officially abolished in New York.
1833 The *New York Sun*'s lurid tales give birth to tabloid journalism.
1837 Financial panic nearly bankrupts the city.
1851 The *New York Daily Times* (now *The New York Times*) published.
1863 Mobs take to the streets during bloody Draft Riots.
1869 The Stuyvesant, a five-story building on 18th Street and Irving Place, houses 20 families under one roof—becoming America's first apartment house.
1870 Metropolitan Museum of Art founded.
1883 Brooklyn Bridge opens.
1886 Statue of Liberty unveiled.
1889 Barnard College opens; Stanford White designs an arch for Washington Square Park to commemorate the centennial of George Washington's inauguration.
1890 Jacob A. Riis publishes *How the Other Half Lives.*
1891 Carnegie Hall opens with a concert conducted by Tchaikovsky.
1892 Ellis Island opens.
1898 The city consolidates all five boroughs.
1902 The Fuller (Flatiron) Building becomes the world's first skyscraper.
1903 The New York Highlanders (later the New York Yankees) play their first game.

becoming cleaner and safer than it had been in decades. Times Square was transformed into a family-friendly tourist destination, and the dot-com explosion led to a generation of young wanna-be millionaires working overtime in the Flatiron District's Silicon Alley. Former President Bill Clinton moved into an office in Harlem, and a glorious restoration of Grand Central Terminal was completed. Giuliani's second term would come to a close, however, with a devastating tragedy.

On September 11, 2001, terrorists flew two hijacked passenger jets into the Twin Towers of the World Trade Center, collapsing the entire complex and killing nearly 3,000 people. A few months later, billionaire Michael Bloomberg was elected mayor, with the daunting task of repairing not only the city's skyline but also its battered economy and bruised psyche.

So far, the stock market and the businesses that survived the post-tragedy slump are slowly but surely reviving. Debate over the future of the Trade Center site sparked more than a year of conflict before architect Daniel Libeskind was awarded the redevelopment job in 2003. His plan, called "Memory Foundations," aims to reconcile rebuilding and remembrance with parks, plazas, a memorial and a sleek new tower. Bloomberg's recovering city also welcomed the $100 million Hudson River Park, which has added landscaping, bike paths and stylishly restored piers to the western edge of town.

The blackout that shut down the city (and much of the Eastern Seaboard) in August 2003 found New Yorkers sweaty but calm, with police cars prowling the streets as cafés set up candlelit tables and bodegas handed out free ice cream. New York's inhabitants remain confident in their city and like to think that, whatever surprises the future holds, they'll find a way to cope. After all, while the city may not be the capital of the U.S., it's still the capital of the world.

1904 New York's first subway line, the Interborough Rapid Transit Subway (IRT), opens.
1908 First ball dropped to celebrate the new year in Times Square.
1910 McKim, Mead & White's Pennsylvania Station opens.
1911 The Triangle Shirtwaist Fire claims nearly 150 lives, spurring labor reform.
1913 New Grand Central Terminal replaces Cornelius Vanderbilt's 1871 original.
1923 Yankee Stadium opens.
1924 First Macy's Thanksgiving parade held.
1929 The stock market crashes; Museum of Modern Art opens.
1931 Holland Tunnel and George Washington Bridge completed; the Empire State Building opens; the Whitney Museum opens.
1934 Fiorello La Guardia takes office; Tavern on the Green opens.
1939 New York holds a World's Fair.
1945 Two million gather in Times Square to celebrate the end of World War II.
1946 The New York Knickerbockers play their first game.
1950 United Nations complex completed.
1957 The New York Giants baseball team moves to San Francisco; Brooklyn Dodgers move to Los Angeles.
1962 New York Mets formed; Lincoln Center opens; first Shakespeare in the Park show.
1964 Verrazano-Narrows Bridge completed; World's Fair held in Flushing Meadows park.
1968 Columbia University students hold a sit-in.
1969 The Stonewall riots in Greenwich Village give birth to the gay-rights movement.
1970 First New York City Marathon held.
1973 World Trade Center completed; George Steinbrenner purchases the New York Yankees; CBGB opens.
1975 On the verge of bankruptcy, the city is snubbed by the federal government; *Saturday Night Live* debuts.
1977 Serial killer "Son of Sam" David Berkowitz arrested; Studio 54 opens; 4,000 arrested during citywide blackout.
1980 John Lennon murdered in front of the Dakota apartment building.
1988 Curfew protesters riot in Tompkins Square Park.
1989 David N. Dinkins elected the city's first black mayor.
1993 A terrorist bomb explodes in the World Trade Center, killing six and injuring 1,000.
2001 Two hijacked jets fly into the Twin Towers, killing nearly 2,800 and demolishing the World Trade Center.
2002 Michael Bloomberg becomes New York's 108th mayor.
2003 Smoking is banned in bars and restaurants; another blackout hits the city.

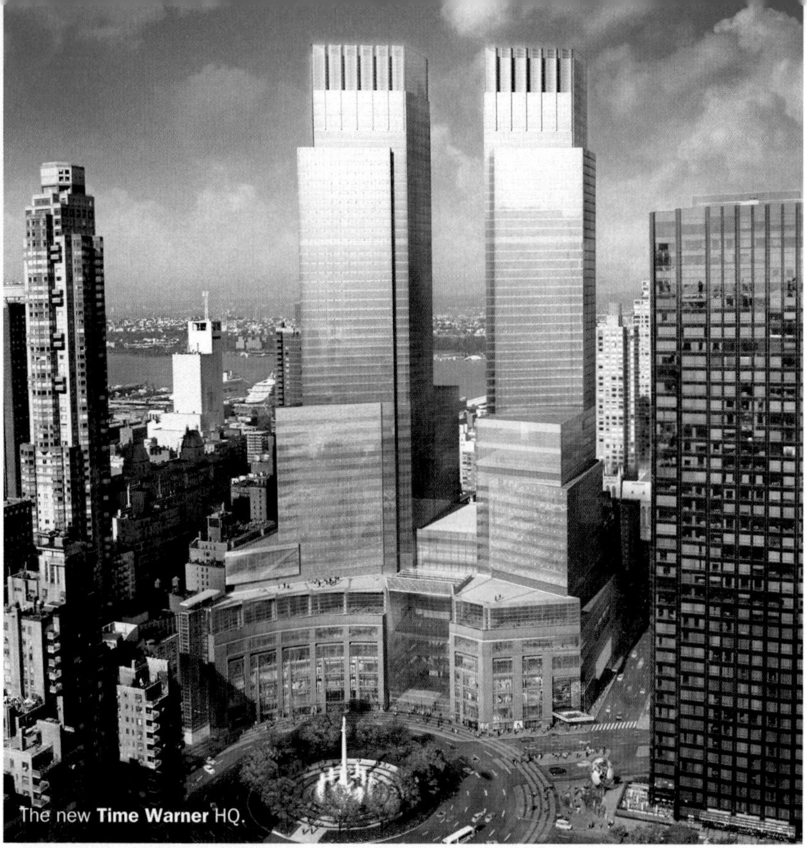

The new **Time Warner** HQ.

Architecture

A local building boom runs on "starchitect" power.

No matter what, New York rebuilds. While the events of September 11, 2001, are etched in our collective memory, the city continues to adapt and reinvent itself on a daily basis, in addition to being at the forefront of world architecture. Exciting new buildings by world-class architects—Santiago Calatrava, Daniel Libeskind, Norman Foster and Richard Meier among them—are making their New York debuts with all the fanfare of glittering first nights on Broadway.

Plans for commemorating the **World Trade Center** site continue to shift in response to the pressures of politics and commerce, but one sure bet is the spectacular **World Trade Center PATH Terminal**, to be built by the Spanish architect Calatrava, on the site of the station destroyed in the September 11 attack. Known as a "poet of movement" for his bridges and train stations, like Lisbon's soaring biomorphic Orient Station, Calatrava is creating a true downtown Grand Central Terminal, with a $2-billion project that will connect the PATH trains with 14 subway lines (it won't be ready until 2006).

The spirit of unity and cooperation in the wake of the WTC attack has been tarnished by the inevitable infighting between the powerful developer Larry A. Silverstein and the design competition winner, architect Daniel Libeskind. Silverstein unilaterally brought on board his own architect, David M. Childs, to tone down

Libeskind's original plan; already, the greatly admired crystalline shapes are being modified to accommodate more rentable office space.

Childs, a lead architect at the megafirm of Skidmore, Owings & Merrill, is the hardest-working man in showbiz these days. Even as the Twin Towers vanished, another pair of towers rose at Columbus Circle, the gateway to Central Park. Childs's **Time Warner Building** *(1 Central Park at Broadway)* is a sympathetically contextual transition between the glass-box office towers of midtown and the lower, broader residences of the Upper West Side. In addition to luxury condos, shops, restaurants, movie theaters and a Mandarin Oriental Hotel, the complex will house a new performance space for the nonprofit group Jazz at Lincoln Center.

Luckily for us, New York seems bent on having at least one building by every major world-class architect.

Besides the illuminated 777-foot-high, crinkled-glass crown of his octagonal headquarters for **Bear Stearns** *(383 Madison Ave between 46th and 47th Sts),* Childs's major mark on the Manhattan skyline will be a spectacular clamshell-shaped steel-and-glass addition to **Penn Station**, to be built behind the imposing Corinthian colonnade of McKim, Mead & White's 1913 **New York General Post Office** *(421 Eighth Ave between 31st and 33rd Sts; see p99).* The transparent, multilevel station (still in the planning stages) will revive the awesome experience of arriving by rail in the majestic original Pennsylvania Station. In its current incarnation, as the critic Vincent Scully describes it, "One scuttles in now like a rat."

The Miami-based firm of Arquitectonica, headed by the husband-and-wife team of Laurinda Spear and Bernardo Fort-Brescia, made its New York debut with the splashy **Westin** hotel *(270 W 43rd St between Seventh and Eighth Aves),* whose brightly hued glass skin, lightning-streak illumination and rollicking base in the shape of an inverted ziggurat offended some and delighted others. Some of the building's thunder was stolen by the Fox & Fowle's **Reuters Building** *(3 Times Square at 42nd St),* which by coincidence or synchronicity features the same *parti,* or overall concept, of two vertical sections split by a base-to-crown arc. Fox & Fowle's polyglot postmodern **Condé Nast Building** *(4 Times Sq at 42nd St)* and Kohn Pedersen Fox's complementing **5 Times Square** *(at 42nd St)* bracket the downtown approach to Times Square like sentinels.

Luckily for us, New York exhibits the collecting avidity of J.P. Morgan and seems bent on having at least one building by every major world-class architect. British architect Norman Foster, who created the see-through wonders of London's City Hall and the remodeled Reichstag in Berlin, is having a premiere in New York: a chrysalislike addition to the Art Deco plinth of Joseph Urban's 1928 **Hearst Magazine Building** *(959 Eighth Ave between 56th and 57th Sts).* Richard Meier's first New York effort, a pair of succinct minimalist glass apartment buildings, **173** and **176 Perry St** *(at West St),* add a sophisticated urban sheen to the westernmost West Village, especially when the floor-to-ceiling glass walls are seen illuminated from within at night.

The city quietly set another record in the new millennium for the tallest residential building in the world: Costas Kondylis's 72-story black-glass monolith, the **Trump World Tower** *(845 First Ave between 47th and 48th Sts).* Residents of Turtle Bay feared the freestanding tower would overshadow the iconic U.N. Secretariat Building to the south, but the sleek-skinned design is remarkably reticent, reflecting rather than overpowering its environs. Skyscraper buffs will be interested in comparing it with the stately 41-story Beaux Arts **Ritz Tower** *(109 E 57th St at Park Ave),* which was the world's tallest residence when it was built in 1925. You've come a long way, baby.

MORE BROWSING THAN HOUSING

Cultural institutions and stores are the other beneficiaries of New York's building boomlet. Pop artist Andy Warhol's observation that "department stores are kind of like museums" seems truer than ever, as retailers employ "starchitects" to show off their wares. The Downtown Guggenheim by Frank Gehry—which would have been moored like a shimmering vision of Bilbao in the East River—has been scrapped, but check out Gehry's free-form titanium interior for the boutique **Tribeca Issey Miyake** *(119 Hudson St between Franklin and North Moore Sts, 212-226-0100).* The **Soho Prada** store *(575 Broadway at Prince St, 212-334-8888),* by the cerebral Dutch architect Rem Koolhaas, blends high fashion and industrial tech in a chic showcase that rivals any catwalk.

▶ Other significant architectural highlights are listed in the **Sightseeing** section (*see pp69–163*).

The eccentrically angled glass facade of French architect Christian de Portzamparc's **LVMH Tower** *(19 E 57th St between Fifth and Madison Aves)* stands like a postmodernist miniglacier among more sober-sided neighboring storefronts. Equally iconoclastic is Austrian native Raimund Abraham's nearby **Austrian Cultural Institute** *(11 E 52nd St between Fifth and Madison Aves),* whose louvered facade glowers like a totemic mask.

Art museums continue to be as creative as the collections they contain. The **American Folk Art Museum** (*see p151*), by Tod Williams and Billie Tsien, is clad in panels of a delicately textured white-bronze alloy that looks like both stone and metal, and reflects the museum's mission of promoting handcrafted art. Interior walls that intersect at unexpected angles make the small-scale museum appear surprisingly spacious. The AFA's venerable neighbor, the **Museum of Modern Art** (*see p150*), has temporarily moved its masterpieces to Queens until Yoshio Taniguchi completes an addition to its midtown home base. The museum will also be restored more closely to its original 1939 design by Philip Goodwin and Edward Durell Stone. Interestingly, part of what made MoMA so revolutionary in its day was that it abandoned traditional museum trappings, like monumental stepped entrances, in favor of a simple, street-level revolving door that resembled—as Warhol noticed—a store.

If you're interested in digging some underground sounds, check out the contemporary-music scene at the Polshek Partners' spectacular new subterranean performance space, the **Arthur Zankel Hall** at Carnegie Hall (*see p321*). Another notable museum expansion is Kevin Roche, John Dinkeloo & Associates' curving granite wing of the **Museum of Jewish Heritage** (*see p160*), which shelters the permanent outdoor installation

Open sesame

We New Yorkers like to act as though we own the place. When we walk into a restaurant, it's *our* restaurant; when we sit down in a stadium, those players are working for *us;* we even get proprietary about our sidewalk space. It was only a matter of time before we started acting that way about *our* architecture. But buildings present a particular problem: access. Countless examples of the city's most creative, innovative and historical spaces are off-limits to the general public.

Enter Scott Lauer. His mission: to open dozens of sites to everyday folks—at least for a few days each year. If the first annual Open House New York was any indication, this may become the biggest native-and-tourist attraction in years. Best of all, it will be free!

While October 2003 marked the first Open House New York, the idea has been kicking around for a while, ever since Lauer was living in London as a young architect and participated in the first Open House London, in 1993. By the time he moved back to New York, London's Open House was attracting thousands of visitors each year. "It was such a great idea, I naturally assumed someone would take it on in New York," Lauer says. When four years passed and no one stepped forward, Lauer took on the job himself.

After researching some of the previously organized architectural free-for-alls—including those in Glasgow, London, Toronto and Sydney—Lauer incorporated his nonprofit organization, Open House New York, in May 2001, and became its executive director. Since then, the group's tiny staff of three (helped by more than 120 volunteers) has secured access to 60 sites, and OHNY has also joined with the New York chapter of the American Institute of Architecture's Architecture Week—which now reaches a crescendo on the weekend with the Open House New York tour. (Thus far, it's scheduled for the Saturday and Sunday of Columbus Day weekend 2004, but check the OHNY website for an up-to-date schedule).

The great charm of the initial Open House New York was that its tours combined buildings and sites of historical interest (Columbia University, City Hall and the Tweed Courthouse); the next wave of building (several architectural studio visits); newer spots of social interest (the Meatpacking District fashion boutiques as well as a brownstone—someone's private residence!); and a number of heretofore off-limits sites (Pratt Institute's 19th-century power plant in Brooklyn, a private glass-and-steel penthouse on the Lower East Side and the underground vaults beneath Green-Wood Cemetery).

The lively mix has spurred an interest in architecture among New Yorkers and visitors that's sure to, er, build for the 2004 event. In

Garden of Stones by the sculptor Andy Goldsworthy. The memorial garden comprises 18 dwarf oak saplings, each one planted in a hollowed-out boulder. In the Hebrew alphabet, 18 signifies the letter *chai,* which is also the symbol of life; the piece is therefore fitting both as a tribute to the resiliency of life after the Holocaust, and as the first major addition to downtown in the wake of September 11.

To keep track of everything new in New York architecture, visit the recently opened **American Institute of Architects (AIA) Center for Architecture** (*see p93*), a former Soho factory that has been converted into a $4 million showplace for both upcoming projects and historical conservation.

TALES OF OLD NEW YORK

Under New York's gleaming exoskeleton of steel and glass lies the heart of a 17th-century Dutch city. The city's history begins at the Battery and New York Harbor, one of the greatest naturally formed deep-water ports in the world. The former Alexander Hamilton Custom House of 1907, now the **National Museum of the American Indian** (*see p157*), was built by Cass Gilbert and is a symbol of the harbor's significance to Manhattan's growth. Before 1913, there was no income tax in the United States, and the city's chief source of revenue was from customs duties. Gilbert's domed marble edifice is suitably monumental; its carved figures of the *Four Continents* are by Daniel Chester French, the sculptor of the Lincoln Memorial in Washington, D.C.

The Dutch influence is still traceable in the downtown web of narrow, winding lanes, which resemble the centers of medieval European cities. Because the Cartesian grid that rules the city was laid down by the Commissioner's Plan in 1811, only a few samples of actual Dutch architecture remain, mostly in off-the-beaten-

addition to guided and self-guided tours of sites throughout the five boroughs, the weekend offers exhibitions, discussions and lectures (80 speakers last year).

"People understand it's a great thing on several levels," says Lauer. "It's good for New York in terms of providing a fun, free way to learn more about the city, and because it helps engage people in issues related to architecture, planning and development."

Reflecting on why OHNY seems to be an instant hit with New Yorkers, Lauer adds: "It taps into people's natural curiosity about their environment and each other, and that taps into another phenomenon—which is that, because of recent events, doors have been closing. This is an opportunity to open them up again."

OHNY's initial success in 2003 comes on the heels of more than two years of debate over the rebuilding of the World Trade Center site, which has renewed public interest in city architecture and urban planning. "People are concerned, and they want to have a say in how our city develops," Lauer says. "Our role at this stage is not so much about advocacy as it is to make people aware that these special places exist."

For more information about the 2004 event, go to www.openhousenewyork.org or call the OHNY hot line at 917-583-2398.

Industrial chic A Boerum Hill loft created by Delman or Sherman Architects.

track locales. One of these is the 1783 **Dyckman Farmhouse Museum** *(4881 Broadway at 204th St)* in north Inwood, with its double-sloped gambrel roof and decorative brickwork. The oldest house still standing in the five boroughs is the **Pieter Claesen Wyckoff House Museum** *(5902 Clarendon Rd at Ralph Ave, Flatbush, Brooklyn)*. Built around 1652, it's a typical Dutch farmhouse with shingled walls and deep eaves. The **Lefferts Homestead** *(Prospect Park, Flatbush Ave near Empire Blvd, Park Slope, Brooklyn)* of 1783 combines a gambrel roof with column-supported porches, a hybrid style popular during the Federal period.

The Dutch influence is still traceable in the downtown web of narrow, winding lanes.

In Manhattan, the only building still standing from pre-Revolutionary times is the stately columned and quoined **St. Paul's Chapel and Churchyard** (*see p78*), completed in 1766 (a spire was added in 1796). George Washington, who had been a parishioner here, was officially received in the chapel after his inauguration in 1789. The church's clear egalitarian layout was influenced by the Enlightenment ideals upon which this nation was founded. **Trinity Church** (*see p78*) of 1846 is one of the first and best Gothic Revival churches in the country, designed by Richard Upjohn, the architect of **St. Patrick's Cathedral** (*see p104*). It's difficult to imagine now that its crocketed and finialed 285-foot-tall spire held sway for decades as the tallest structure in Manhattan.

Holdouts remain from each epoch of the city's architectural history. An outstanding example of Greek Revival from the first half of the 19th century is the 1842 **Federal Hall National Memorial** (*see p78*), whose mighty marble colonnade was built to commemorate the site where George Washington took his oath of office. A larger-than-life statue of Washington by the sculptor John Quincy Adams Ward stands in front. The city's most celebrated blocks of Greek Revival townhouses (circa 1830s) are known simply as **The Row** *(1–13 Washington Sq North between Fifth Ave and Washington Sq West);* they're exemplars of the more genteel metropolis of Henry James and Edith Wharton.

Greek Revival gave way to Renaissance-inspired Beaux Arts architecture, which reflected the imperial ambitions of the wealthy young nation in the Gilded Age of the late 19th century. Like the Emperor Augustus, who boasted that he found Rome a city of brick and left it a city of marble, the firm of McKim, Mead & White built noble civic monuments and palazzi for the rich. The best-known buildings of the classicist Charles Follen McKim include the main campus of **Columbia University** (*see p115*), circa 1890s, and the austere 1917 **Morgan Library** (*see p150*). His partner, the socialite and bon vivant Stanford White (murdered in a notorious case in 1906), designed celebratory spaces, including the **Metropolitan Club** *(1–11 E 60th St at Fifth Ave),* and the extraordinarily luxe Villard Houses of 1884, now incorporated into the **New York Palace Hotel** (*see p50*). Another Beaux Arts treasure from the city's grand metropolitan era is Carrère & Hasting's sumptuous white-marble **New York Public Library** of 1911 (*see p162*), built on the site of what had once been a Revolutionary War battleground; the site later hosted a multistoried Egyptian Revival water reservoir and part of it is now the greensward of Bryant Park. The 1913 **Grand Central Terminal** (*see p104*) remains the elegant travertine-lined foyer for the city, thanks to preservationists (most prominently, Jacqueline Kennedy Onassis) who saved it from the wrecking ball.

MOVIN' ON UP

Cast-iron architecture peaked in the latter half of the 19th century, coinciding with the Civil War era and lasting until slightly after. Iron and steel components allowed architects to build higher, because they were no longer limited by the bulk, weight and cost of stone construction. Cast-iron columns could support a tremendous amount of weight and were inexpensive to mass-produce. The facades of many Soho buildings, with their intricate details of Italianate columns, were manufactured on an assembly-line basis and could be ordered in pieces from catalogs (*see p83* **The Iron Age**). This led to an aesthetic of uniform building facades, which had a direct impact on steel skyscrapers of the next generation. To enjoy one of the most telling vistas of skyscraper history, gaze uptown from the 1859 **Cooper Union** (*see p89*), the oldest existing building in America framed with steel beams.

The most visible effect of cast-iron construction was the way it opened up solid stone facades to expanses of glass. In fact, the term *window shopping* came into vogue after the Civil War. Mrs. Lincoln bought the White House china, which had been manufactured by Daniel D. Badger, at the 1857 **Haughwout Store** *(488–492 Broadway at Broome St).* The building's Palladian-style facade recalls

Heavenly A golden cross surmounts the spire of **Trinity Church** (1846). *See also p78.*

Renaissance Venice, but its regular, open fenestration was also a portent of the future. Look carefully at the front: The cast-iron ELEVATOR sign is a relic of the world's first working "safety passenger elevator," designed by Elisha Graves Otis.

Once engineers perfected steel, which is stronger and lighter than iron, and created the interlocking steel-cage construction that distributes the weight of a building over the entire frame, the sky was the limit. New York is fortunate to have one building by the great skyscraper innovator Louis Sullivan, the 1898 **Bayard-Condict Building** *(65–69 Bleecker St between Broadway and Lafayette St).* Though only 13 stories tall, Sullivan's building, covered with richly decorative terra-cotta, was one of the earliest to apply a purely vertical design, rather than imitating horizontally oriented styles of the past. As Sullivan wrote, a skyscraper "must be tall, every inch of it tall…from bottom to top, it is a unit without a single dissenting line." Chicago architect Daniel H. Burnham's 1902 **Flatiron Building** (*see p95*) is another standout example; its breathtakingly modern design, combined with traditional masonry decoration, was made possible only by steel-cage construction.

The new century saw a frenzy of skyward construction, resulting in buildings of record-shattering height, beginning with the now modest-looking 30-story, 391-foot-tall **Park Row Building** *(15 Park Row between Ann and Beekman Sts);* when it was built in 1899, it was the tallest building in the world. That record was shattered by the 700-foot-tall **Metropolitan Life Tower** *(1 Madison Ave at 24th St)* of 1909, modeled after the Campanile in Venice's Piazza San Marco; soon after, it was surpassed by Cass Gilbert's Gothic masterpiece, the 792-foot **Woolworth Building** (*see p80*). The Woolworth reigned in solitary splendor until William Van Alen's metal-spired homage to the Automobile Age, the 1930 **Chrysler Building** *(405 Lexington Ave at 42nd St),* which soared to 1,048 feet.

In a highly publicized race, the Chrysler was outstripped 13 months later, in 1931, by Shreve, Lamb & Harmon's 1,050-foot-tall **Empire State Building** (*see p103*). It has since lost its title to other buildings, beginning with the World Trade Center in 1973; the 1,454-foot Sears Tower in Chicago (1974); the 1,483-foot Petronas Towers in Kuala Lumpur, Malaysia (1996); and the current record-holder, the 1,661-foot Taipei 101 in Taiwan (2003). But the Empire State remains the iconic skyscraper, easily one of the most recognizable buildings in the world, with its broad base, narrow shaft and distinctive needled crown. (That giant ape climbing up the side might also have had something to do with it.)

The silhouette of the Empire State's setbacks, retroactively labeled Art Deco (such buildings were simply called "modern" then), was actually a response to the zoning code of 1916, which required that a building's upper stories be stepped back in order not to block sunlight and air circulation to the streets. The code engendered some of the city's most fanciful designs, like the ziggurat-crowned **Paramount Building** *(1501 Broadway between 43rd and 44th Sts)* of 1926, and the romantically slender spire of the former **Cities Service Building** *(70 Pine St at Pearl St),* illuminated from within like a rare gem.

BRAVE NEW WORLD

The post–World War II period saw the ascendance of the International Style, pioneered by such giants as Le Corbusier and Ludwig Mies van der Rohe. The style's most visible symbol was the all-glass facade, like that found on the sleek slab of the **United Nations Headquarters** (*see p106*). The International Style relied on a new set of aesthetics: minimal decoration, clear expression of construction, an honest use of materials and a near-Platonic harmony of proportions. **Lever House** *(390 Park Ave between 53rd and 54th Sts),* designed by Gordon Bunshaft of Skidmore, Owings & Merrill, was the city's first all-steel-and-glass structure when it was built in 1952 (it recently underwent an award-winning brush-up). It's nearly impossible to imagine what a radical vision of the future this glass construction represented along the all-masonry corridor of Park Avenue, because nearly every building since then has followed suit. Mies van der Rohe's celebrated bronze-skinned **Seagram Building** *(375 Park Ave between 52nd and 53rd Sts)* reigns in imperious isolation on its own plaza catercorner across the avenue, the epitome of the architect's cryptic dicta that "Less is more" and "God is in the details." The Seagram's detailing is exquisite—even the bolts securing the miniature bronze piers that run the length of the facade were custom-made, and must be hand-polished annually to keep from oxidizing and turning green. It's truly the Rolls-Royce of skyscrapers.

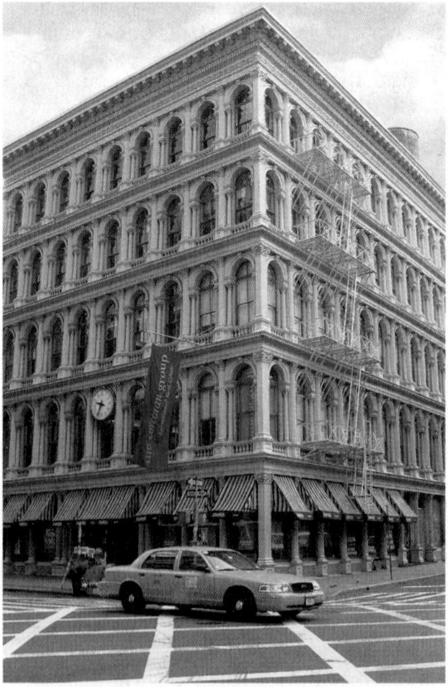

Soho's **Haughwout Building**. *See p24.*

High modernism began to show cracks in its own facade in the mid-1960s. By then, New York had built too many such structures in midtown and downtown, and besides, the public had never fully warmed to the undecorated style (though, for those provided with a little insight, the best glass boxes are fully rewarding aesthetic experiences). And the sheer arrogance of the International Style in trying to supplant the traditional city structure didn't endear it to anyone either. **The MetLife Building** *(200 Park Ave at 45th St),* originally the Pan Am Building of 1963, was the prime culprit, not so much because of its design by Walter Gropius of the Bauhaus, but because of its presumptuous location, straddling Park Avenue and looming over Grand Central. There was even a plan at the time to raze Grand Central and build a twin Pan Am. The International Style had obviously reached its end when Philip Johnson, who was instrumental in defining the movement with his book *The International Style* (co-written with Henry-Russell Hitchcock), began disparaging the style as "glass-boxitis."

POSTMODERNISM AND BEYOND

Plainly, new blood was needed. A glimmer on the horizon was Boston architect Hugh Stubbins's silvery triangle-topped **Citicorp Center** *(Lexington Ave between 53 and 54th Sts),* which utilized daring contemporary engineering (the building cantilevers almost magically on high stilts above street level), while harking back to the decorative tops of yesteryear. The sly old master Philip Johnson turned the tables on everyone with the heretical "Chippendale" crown on his **Sony Building**, originally the AT&T Building *(550 Madison Ave between 55th and 56th Sts),* a bold throwback to decoration for its own sake. Postmodernism provided a theoretical basis for a new wave of buildings that mixed past and present, often taking cues from the environs. Some notable examples include Helmut Jahn's **425 Lexington Avenue** (*between 43rd and*

Joint effort In 2007, the **Eyebeam** art and technology center will open in Chelsea.

44th Sts) of 1988; David M. Childs's retro diamond-tipped **Worldwide Plaza** *(825 Eighth Ave between 49th and 50th Sts)* of 1989; and the honky-tonk agglomeration of Skidmore, Owings & Merrill's **Bertelsmann Building** *(1540 Broadway between 45th and 46th Sts)* of 1990. But even postmodernism is becoming played out. Too many architects now rely on fussy fenestration and milquetoast "commentary" on other styles, instead of creating vital new buildings.

The vast electronic laboratory of Times Square may provide a solution. Upon seeing the myriad electric lights of Times Square in 1922, the British wit G. K. Chesterton remarked, "What a glorious garden of wonder this would be, to anyone who was lucky enough to be unable to read." This particular crossroads of the world continues to be at the cybernetic cutting edge: the 120-foot-tall, quarter-acre-in-area Nasdaq sign; the real-time stock tickers and jumbo TV screens everywhere; the news zipper on the original **New York Times** tower *(1 Times Sq between Broadway and Seventh Ave).* The public's appetite for new images seems so insatiable that a building's fixed profile no longer suffices—only an ever-shifting electronic skin will do. The iconoclastic critic Robert Venturi, who taught us how to learn from Las Vegas, calls this trend "iconography and electronics upon a generic architecture."

One firm that incorporates electronics and video in a novel way is the upstart duo of Diller & Scofidio. Known for designs that owe as much to conceptual art as to architecture, the designers are working on an eye-popping addition to staid Chelsea, the **Eyebeam** art and technology center, to be completed in 2007. The curvilinear walls of the planned museum are suggestive of film loops running through a projector. For a preview of the firm's fresh approach, check out the renovation of the windowless **Brasserie** *(100 E 53rd St between Park and Lexington Aves)* in the Seagram Building, with its space-age glass-and-steel floating staircase, gel-cushioned saddle stools at the bar, and time-delay video screens monitoring the entrance.

Computer-generated design is having as noticeable an effect on architecture as it has had on cinema. A stellar example is Kohn Pedersen Fox's stainless-steel–and–glass "vertical campus," the **Baruch College Academic Complex** *(55 Lexington Ave between 25th and 26th Sts).* The resulting phantasmic, fluid designs that curve and dart in sculptural space are so beyond the timid window-dressing of post-modernism that they really deserve a new label.

New York City may have been founded on a very deliberate grid, but it's been growing organically. And as these recent advances show, Frank Sinatra was right: "The best is yet to come."

What lies beneath

Steam, subways and sewers: underground secrets revealed.

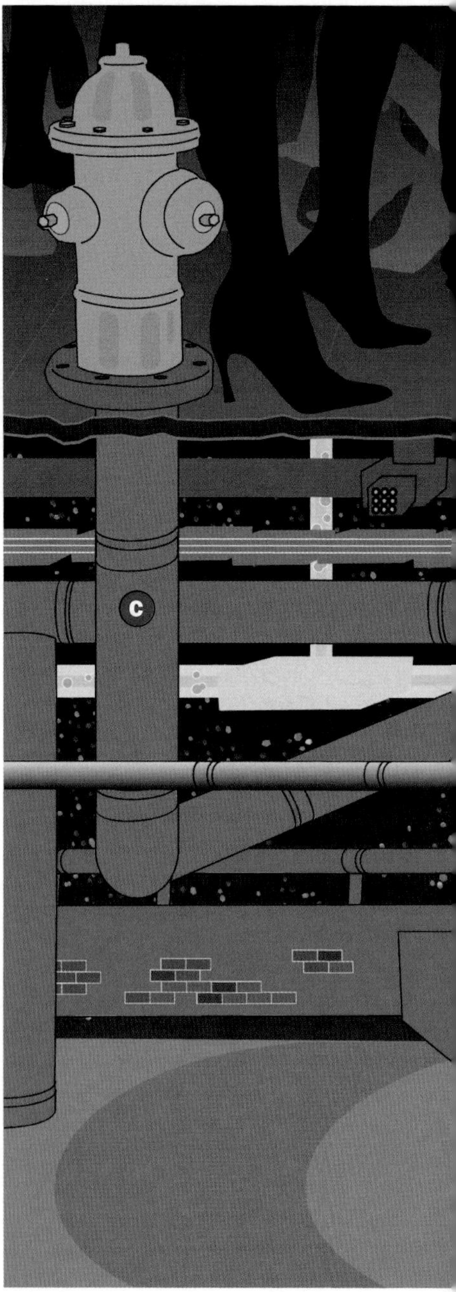

A. ELECTRICITY *(two to eight feet down)*
Juice flows over nearly 88,000 miles of copper wire (enough to encircle the globe almost four times) strung through concrete pipes.

B. TELEPHONE *(five to ten feet down)*
It takes 31 million miles of copper cable and 343,000 miles of fiber-optic cable—both housed in PVC pipe—to keep city phones ringing.

C. WATER MAINS *(four to ten feet down)*
More than 1.5 billion gallons of water flow daily through 6.6 miles of cast-iron pipe; 190,000 valves control the water's direction and pressure en route to NYC faucets.

D. STEAM *(six to eight feet down)*
Eight plants produce 13 million pounds of steam per hour, heating 2,000 buildings and more than 100,000 households.

E. GAS *(three to ten feet down)*
Piped in from Texas, Louisiana or Canada, the city's natural gas begins its long journey in 42-inch-wide cast-iron pipes. Other cities tap in along the way, so the pipes narrow as they go to keep the pressure constant. By the time the gas arrives in NYC, it's flowing through ducts just one inch wide.

F. SUBWAYS *(40 to 180 feet down)*
Along nearly 850 miles of subway tracks are more than 450 functional stations. About 4.5 million busy commuters ride the rails daily.

G. SEWERS *(40 to 54 feet down)*
Some 6,000 miles of sewer tunnels transport 1.5 billion gallons of waste and runoff each day. (Despite urban legend, the only documented alligator down there was pulled half dead out of a 123rd Street drainpipe in 1935.)

H. WATER *(250 to 800 feet down)*
Two tunnels, built in 1917 and 1938, handle the bulk of the city's water supply. A third tunnel, with a price tag of $6 billion, was begun in 1970, and should be fully operational by 2020.

N.Y.C SEWER
A
B
D
E
F
6
4
G
H

New Year's Eve in Times Square.

New York Today

In a city of constant change, the signs of the times don't last.

On the corner of 8th Street and Sixth Avenue in Greenwich Village, there's a hot-dog joint called Gray's Papaya. Not only does this fast-food eatery dish up one of the sweetest deals for meat lovers (the Recession Special is two franks and a medium drink for $2.45), it's also famous for the banners it drapes across its windows. Touting everyone from U.S. Senator Hillary Rodham Clinton to the stars of *Sex and the City,* Gray's banners are changed often, like semaphore flags that alert passersby to the shifting conditions of the city. They reflect the growing, evolving animal that is New York, for it is absolutely true that the experience of being in this city is different from what it was a few years ago, and it will be different again a few years from now.

Take the white paper banner that was recently hanging in the window of Gray's. WE ARE POLITE NEW YORKERS, it read. And we are. The old stereotype that New Yorkers have attitude is...well, to be fair, still true. But our essential niceness has really started to shine through over the past three years, like gold under gunk. After suffering a tragic loss and a crappy economy in its wake, the city is now showing a little more of its mushy inner light.

But don't go calling anyone sentimental. We'll give tourists directions when they ask, and offer opinions on the best restaurants in our neighborhoods. We might even refrain from stealing the cab you've spent 20 minutes waving down (remember, you can hail only the ones that have their top light on). Nevertheless, we're still going to be a little brusque and act a little superior. That's just part of being a New Yorker: It's a Herculean accomplishment to make it past the first month's rent, learn all the twists and turns of downtown's streets, and decode the colors, circles and squares of the subway system. And we know something about our kind. We know that when you arrive in New York for the first time, and you stand on the street with the cabs screeching by, sirens going off, lights flashing at every turn and more people than you ever imagined crammed onto one grimy sidewalk, you're going to think one of two things: "How the f*#@! does anyone live here?" or "Man, I *gotta* live here." Those who fall into the latter camp become part of a select 8 million who have either lived their entire lives in this urban jungle or decided to live the rest of their lives in this urban jungle. And making that choice makes us a little cocky. Because, after all, New York *is* the best city in the world. Period.

In New York, the average shlub can go anywhere the In Crowd can. Just act like you belong. Anyone can be fabulous.

HIP-CHECK

The good news is that it doesn't take much to fit in as a New Yorker, even when you're just visiting for a few days. The reason we can all think we're so damn great is that in NYC *anyone* can be. We have an amazingly democratic understanding of hipness, and this has always been the case. We're all members of the ruling class—we wouldn't have it any other way. In the early 1900s, immigrants who were excluded from elitist cultural circles created their own culture, giving birth to a thriving theater scene on the Lower East Side and to some of the most famous American composers, including Irving Berlin and George Gershwin. In the conservative atmosphere of the postwar '50s, a ragtag bunch led by Jack Kerouac and Allen Ginsberg turned the Village into a mixing pot of poetry and politics that lasted well into the '60s. In the '70s and '80s, social (and socialite) outcasts started to make their own scene at discos like Studio 54, where anyone could be a star—or a freak.

New York's "cool" scene has always had an inclusive aspect. The same holds true today, but even more so. If you want to be part of the in crowd, you can be—just squeeze into the bar at Lotus or at Pianos. If you want to dine with celebrities, make a reservation at Balthazar. Of course, a magazine like *Time Out New York* helps immensely with this kind of thing (nice plug, huh?), but the fact is that anyone can be trendy in this town. Hip fashions, world-class food and It bars are everywhere you look. And they're all accessible. Sometimes there's a cover fee or a long wait for a reservation, but in New York, the average shlub can go just about anywhere the In Crowd can. Just act like you belong. Anyone can be fabulous—hell, anyone can be *mayor*. Our current civic leader wasn't daunted by the fact that he's not originally from the city and never spent a day in politics before he was elected. See how it works?

Part of the reason that the New York attitude is stronger than ever, and that New Yorkers are prouder to be New Yorkers, is the time in which we're living. We're more than two years removed from September 11, 2001. Bad things happened, a lot of people died, and some people will be suffering for a long while. But those posters and T-shirts you see the vendors selling around Ground Zero are right: We do love NY more than ever. The awfulness of that tragedy brought out the best in New Yorkers, and that's the part we've hung onto. No one has forgotten exactly where he was when he first heard, saw or smelled it. But we're not dwelling on it on a daily basis. Yes, a lot of people come to see the wreckage (not that there's anything to see anymore—construction has already begun on a new building complex and transportation hub). But what happened on that day has not defined New York City. We've got too much else to boast about.

Rather than let those falling towers take the city down with them, New Yorkers have integrated the lessons of that experience into their everyday lives. Everyone's gotten a little nicer, a little more aware of their neighbors. Evidence of that change was thrown into bold relief when the largest blackout in the country's history darkened the city on August 14, 2003. It was a hot day—friggin' hot, fry-an-egg-on-the sidewalk hot. And nothing worked: Computers, traffic lights and telephones all snapped off across the Northeast. Remarkably, no one freaked out and ran amok. There wasn't looting on every corner, and there weren't any wild rage-fueled riots (as there had been in the summer of 1977, when heat and the threat of a serial killer known as Son of Sam formed ominous dark clouds over the city).

Instead, people checked on their elderly neighbors and then headed out to the bars, which were giving away beer while it was still cold, and to pizza places, which, thanks to their gas ovens, were the only restaurants that could still produce fresh food. Stiflingly hot and, as night came on, eerily dark (imagine Times Square with the neon off!), the streets became the settings for block parties, stoop-sitting and neighborly visits. The lights stayed off for 24 hours (longer in some parts of the city), but we stayed cool. We were already very familiar with major emergencies, and this was merely an inconvenience for most. A lot of people had parties that night. And a lot of people had sex. No doubt, there will be a new crop of tots hitting the city this spring—the blackout babies. More power to 'em.

SEE HER ON TOUR
WITH FRANK SINATRA
AND THE OSBOURNES.
THIS SHOULD BE THE FIRST STOP ON YOUR NEW YORK CITY TOUR. OUR AMAZINGLY LIFE-LIKE FIGURES ARE NOW INTERACTIVE. MAKE J.LO BLUSH WHEN YOU TALK TO HER. APPEAR ON TV WITH THE OSBOURNES. AND SOON, SING FOR SIMON COWELL. YOU CAN MAKE ANYTHING HAPPEN HERE.
$3.00 OFF
WHEN YOU BRING THIS AD TO MADAME TUSSAUDS NEW YORK
LOCATED AT 234 WEST 42ND STREET (BETWEEN 7TH & 8TH AVENUES). 1.800.246.8872. OPEN 365 DAYS A YEAR FROM 10:00 A.M. MONDAY THROUGH THURSDAY, LAST TICKET SOLD AT 8:00 P.M. FRIDAY THROUGH SUNDAY, LAST TICKET SOLD AT 10:00 P.M. WWW.NYCWAX.COM.
PRESENT THIS AD AT THE BOX OFFICE AND RECEIVE $3.00 OFF THE ADULT OR CHILD TICKET PRICE- VALID UP TO 4 TICKETS PER TRANSACTION. CANNOT BE COMBINED WITH ANY OTHER OFFER. RESTRICTIONS APPLY. OFFER EXPIRES 12/31/04. CELEBRITIES APPEAR IN WAX. ON OCCASION MADAME TUSSAUDS NEW YORK MAY CLOSE EARLY FOR SPECIAL EVENTS. CALL FOR UPDATES.
MADAME
TUSSAUDS
NEW YORK
C210019

WHERE IT'S AT

New York is made up of hundreds of neighborhoods, many of which we nickname so that it's easier to talk about them when they become fashionable. For instance, until recently, the area west of Times Square and south of Hell's Kitchen didn't have a moniker. It was just an anonymous, windswept wasteland waiting for something to happen. Now that the city is planning to extend the 7 subway line farther west, and is also considering the construction of a new sports stadium there, that area suddenly has a name: Hudson Yards. Cyclically, a handful of areas will emerge as the new best places to live, work, socialize or just namecheck at parties. These days, it's Harlem, Long Island City in Queens, and Brooklyn's Boerum Hill and Cobble Hill.

Although Manhattan is the borough that gets the attention (many people around the world think the island is all there is to New York City), it's often in the four other boroughs that you'll find the next up-and-coming 'hoods. In 2002, when the Museum of Modern Art moved to a temporary space in Long Island City, it directed attention to the cultural explosion happening across the East River. The formerly industrial neighborhood there is home not only to MoMA QNS but also to the P.S. 1 Contemporary Art Center, the Museum for African Art, the Isamu Noguchi Garden Museum and the Socrates Sculpture Park.

In Brooklyn, the adjacent areas of Boerum Hill, Cobble Hill and Carroll Gardens (which some people are trying to name BoCoCa) got their coolness props when Jonathan Lethem's detective novel *Motherless Brooklyn* came out in 2002. Suddenly, nearly everyone who read the book headed across the river to see the real-life places where the fictional main character worked, hung out and solved the murder of his boss. The area now boasts new restaurants, bars, stores, clubs and ever more Manhattan transplants. Smith Street is the neighborhood's restaurant row, and an influx of music venues and hangouts have made Brooklyn's Fifth Avenue, on the western edge of Park Slope, into a hipster destination.

Back in Manhattan, Harlem is experiencing yet another renaissance. This history-rich neighborhood seems to get a jolt every few years. And if someone as mainstream as former President Bill Clinton, who opened his office there in 2001, can see the change, then you know the star of Harlem has got to be shining pretty brightly. In addition to the former president, the neighborhood is attracting young professionals and, as it always has, creative types. Of course, the food ain't bad, either.

The **2003 blackout.**

On Staten Island, the most-overlooked borough of them all, St. George is the spot to keep your eye on. This area next to the ferry landing boasts amazing waterfront views from the grounds of Snug Harbor, a ton of restaurants and a great stadium for minor league baseball's Staten Island Yankees. In warm-weather months, a slew of outdoor fairs, music events and farmers' markets are all within walking distance of the ferry.

Now that you have a sense of what it's like to be in New York at this moment in time, go out and experience it. Be adventurous. Talk to locals and explore new neighborhoods. Taste, feel and see as much as you can now, because when you come back for your next trip, chances are the city will be a very different place. In the meantime, please do us a favor: Walk a little faster…and don't try to cut in front of us at the hot-dog stand.

Where to Stay

Features

Where to Stay

In the city that never sleeps, you might want to—and there are pillows aplenty.

In New York, resting your head in a place that previously housed a meat locker is hip, not horrifying. Yep, it's official: The **Meatpacking District** is the new hotel hot spot. In the past year alone, three new superstylish hostelries have opened—**Hotel Gansevoort**, the **Maritime Hotel** and **Soho House** (*see p37, p41 and p39*). Restaurateurs and nightclub promoters are quickly reaping the promised profits from the area's new inhabitants; high-design eateries like Vento and 5 Ninth, as well as sleek clubs and hangouts like PM and Pop Burger, have sprouted up along the once-grimy cobblestone streets.

On the flip side, more places are offering style on the cheap (*see p56* **High style, low budget**). New York has more small-chain and independent hotels than any other city in the country, with nearly half of its properties unaffiliated with a national or international chain. Many of these stylish smaller hotels are geared toward the discerning budget traveler, taking the minimalism made posh by boutique hoteliers like Ian Schrager and turning it into a cheap-chic design scheme.

Begin your hotel search by choosing the price range and area that interest you. The listed prices are not guaranteed, but they should give you a good idea of the hotel's average rates. And if you follow the tips below, you'll often be able to find slashed room rates, package deals and special promotions.

If you plan to travel on a weekend, be warned: Many smaller hotels adhere to a strict three-night-minimum booking policy. Beware New York's 13.25 percent room tax—it may cause sticker shock for the uninitiated. There's also a $2-per-night occupancy tax. Ask in advance about unadvertised costs—phone charges, minibars, faxes—or you might not find out about them until checkout.

HOTEL-RESERVATION AGENCIES

Booking blocks of rooms in advance allows reservation companies to offer reduced rates. Discounts cover most price ranges, including economy; some agencies claim savings of up to 65 percent, though 20 percent is more likely. If you simply want the best deal, mention the part of town you prefer and the rate you're willing to pay, and see what's available. The following agencies work with select New York hotels and are free of charge, though a few require you to pay for your rooms in advance.

> ▶ For hotel listings with direct links to booking, visit **www.timeoutny.com**.
> ▶ For more accommodations, *see p299* **Gay & Lesbian**.

Hotel Reservations Network

8140 Walnut Hill Ln, Suite 800, Dallas, TX 75231 (214-369-1264, 800-715-7666; www.hoteldiscount.com).

Quikbook

381 Park Ave South, third floor, New York, NY 10016 (212-779-7666, 800-789-9887; www.quikbook.com).

timeoutny.com

The Time Out New York website offers online reservations at more than 200 hotels. You can search by date of arrival or by name of hotel. Full disclosure: TONY receives a commission from sales made through our partner hotel-reservation sites.

BED & BREAKFAST SERVICES/ SHORT-TERM APARTMENT RENTALS

There are thousands of B&B rooms available in New York, but since there isn't a central B&B organization, some may be hard to find. Many B&Bs are unhosted, and breakfast is usually Continental (if it's served at all), but the ambience is likely to be more personal than that of a hotel. A sales tax of 8.625 percent is added on hosted rooms—though not on unhosted apartments—if you stay for more than seven days. For a longer stay, it can be cheaper and more convenient to rent a place of your own; several of the agencies listed below specialize in short-term rentals of furnished apartments. One caveat: Last-minute changes can be costly; some agencies charge a fee for cancellations less than ten days in advance. For more B&Bs, *see p299* **Gay & Lesbian**—straight guests are welcome, too.

CitySonnet

Village Station, P.O. Box 347, New York, NY 10014 (212-614-3034; www.citysonnet.com). **Rates** *$80–$165 bed-and-breakfast room; $135–$175 artist's loft; $135–$375 private apartment.* **Credit** *AmEx, Disc, MC, V.*
This friendly artist-run agency specializes in downtown locations, but has properties all over Manhattan. The B&B rooms and short-term apartment

Palace of cool Dine, drink, dance and swim on the sixth floor of the **Soho House**. *See p39.*

rentals are priced according to room size, number of guests and whether the bathroom is private or shared.

New York Habitat

307 Seventh Ave between 27th and 28th Sts, suite 306 (212-255-8018; www.nyhabitat.com). Subway 1, 9 to 28th St. **Rates** *$85–$165 unhosted studio; $135–$225 unhosted 1-bedroom apartment; $200–$375 unhosted 2-bedroom apartment.* **Credit** *AmEx, Disc, MC, V.*

A variety of services are offered, from hosted B&Bs to short-term furnished apartment rentals, which can be charged by the day, week or month.

STANDARD HOTEL SERVICES

All hotels have air-conditioning—a relief in summer—unless otherwise noted. In the accommodation categories (arranged by price) **Deluxe**, **Expensive** and **Moderate**, all hotels have the following amenities and services (unless stated otherwise): alarm clock, cable TV, concierge, conference facility, currency exchange, dry cleaning, fax (in business center or in room), hair dryer, in-room safe, laundry, minibar, modem line, radio, one or more restaurants, one or more bars, room service and voice mail. Additional services are noted at the end of each listing.

Most hotels in all categories have access for the disabled, nonsmoking rooms and an iron and ironing board in the room, or on request. Call to confirm. "Breakfast included" may mean cornflakes and tea bags, or a more generous spread of croissants, orange juice and coffee. While many hotels boast a "multilingual" staff, that term may be used loosely.

Downtown below 23rd Street

Deluxe ($350 and up)

Hotel Gansevoort

18 Ninth Ave at 13th St (212-206-6700, 877-726-7386; www.hotelgansevoort.com). Subway: A, C, E to 14th St; L to Eighth Ave. **Rates** *$395–$475 single/double; $575–$675 suite; from $2,500 duplex penthouse. 187 rooms.* **Credit** *AmEx, DC, MC, V.*

At press time, this Meatpacking District newcomer was due to swing open its doors in January 2004. Designed by architect Stephen B. Jacobs, who also designed the Library Hotel (*see p49*), this 13-floor, full-service luxury lodge will be overseen by savvy hotelier Henry Kallan (of both the Library and Hotel Giraffe. The spacious, ultracontemporary rooms come with dark wood cabinets and chocolate-colored leather headboards. Many rooms have views of the Hudson River. A lush roof garden has a glassed-in heated pool and 360-degree views of the city. Glossy, tri-level eatery Ono, owned and operated by Jeffrey Chodorow (Asia de Cuba, Rocco's), promises to have a covered terrace, private dining huts, and a specialized menu of sushi and sake (available for 24-hour room service).

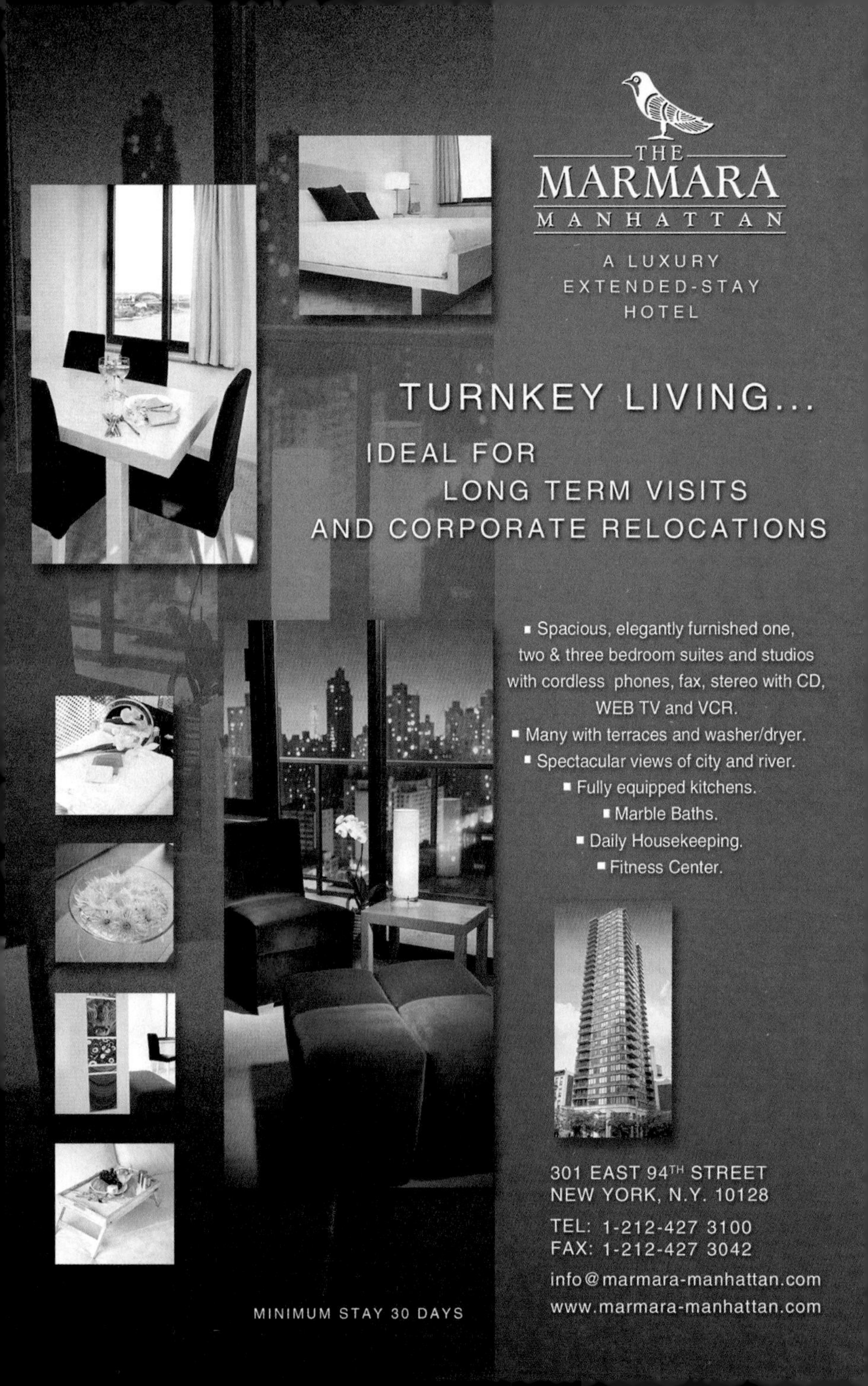
THE
MARMARA
MANHATTAN
A LUXURY
EXTENDED-STAY
HOTEL
TURNKEY LIVING...
IDEAL FOR
LONG TERM VISITS
AND CORPORATE RELOCATIONS
■ Spacious, elegantly furnished one, two & three bedroom suites and studios with cordless phones, fax, stereo with CD, WEB TV and VCR.
■ Many with terraces and washer/dryer.
■ Spectacular views of city and river.
■ Fully equipped kitchens.
■ Marble Baths.
■ Daily Housekeeping.
■ Fitness Center.
301 EAST 94TH STREET
NEW YORK, N.Y. 10128
TEL: 1-212-427 3100
FAX: 1-212-427 3042
info@marmara-manhattan.com
www.marmara-manhattan.com
MINIMUM STAY 30 DAYS

Hotel services *Fitness center. Spa. Wi-Fi.* **Room services** *CD Player. DVD player and cordless phone in some rooms. High-speed Internet. Flat-panel TVs. Room service (24hr).*

The Mercer

147 Mercer St at Prince St (212-966-6060, 888-918-6060; www.mercerhotel.com). Subway: R, W to Prince St. **Rates** *$395–$620 single/double; $1,100–$1,600 suite. 75 rooms.* **Credit** *AmEx, DC, Disc, MC, V.*
Soho's first luxury boutique hotel is in the heart of the Cast-iron District, giving it a leg up on its closest competitors, 60 Thompson and the SoHo Grand (*see below*). Rooms feature high-speed wireless Internet access, furniture by Christian Liagre and oversize bathrooms stocked with Face Stockholm products. Stay tuned for flat-panel plasma TVs in every room. The restaurant, Mercer Kitchen *(212-966-5454),* serves Jean-Georges Vongerichten's casual American cuisine.
Hotel services *Book-and-magazine library. CD and video library. Cell-phone rental. Multilingual baby-sitters. Pass to nearby gym. Ticket desk. Valet.* **Room services** *Cassette and CD players. Fireplace in some rooms. Laptop computer on request. Nintendo. PlayStation. VCR.*

The Ritz-Carlton New York, Battery Park

2 West St at Battery Pl (212-344-0800; www.ritzcarlton.com). Subway: 4, 5 to Bowling Green. **Rates** *$350–$475 single/double; $750–$4,500 suite. 298 rooms.* **Credit** *AmEx, DC, Disc, MC, V.*
For review, *see p62* **The Ritz-Carlton New York, Central Park**.

60 Thompson

60 Thompson St between Broome and Spring Sts (212-431-0400, 877-431-0400; www.60thompson.com). Subway: C, E to Spring St. **Rates** *$370–$450 single/double; $520–$630 suite; $3,500 penthouse suite. 100 rooms.* **Credit** *AmEx, DC, Disc, MC, V.*
Designed by Thomas O'Brien of Aero Studios, rooms are sleek and luxurious. Pampering elements include Frette linens, Philosophy toiletries and a pantry stocked with goodies from nearby gourmet-grocer Dean & DeLuca. Since it's the tallest building in the vicinity, the views extend to the Empire State Building and can be enjoyed from the guests-only rooftop bar, A60. Restaurant Thom *(212-219-2000)* serves creative American cuisine on a sidewalk terrace and in an indoor bamboo garden.
Hotel services *Baby-sitting. Cell-phone rental. DVD library. Laptop computer on request. Valet.* **Room services** *CD and DVD players. High-speed Internet. Microwave oven on request.*

Expensive ($200 to $350)

The Inn at Irving Place

56 Irving Pl between 17th and 18th Sts (212-533-4600, 800-685-1447; www.innatirving.com). Subway: L, N, Q, R, W, 4, 5, 6 to 14th St–Union Sq. **Rates** *$325–$415 standard/deluxe; $475–$495 junior suite. 11 rooms.* **Credit** *AmEx, DC, MC, V.*
For Victorian charm with boutique style, book a room at this 19th-century townhouse near Gramercy Park. It's one of Manhattan's smallest inns—and one of its most romantic. Some rooms are petite, but all are furnished with antiques harking back to the days of Edith Wharton. The low tables, cushy love seats and lavish tea menu of Lady Mendl's *(212-533-4466; reservations required)* make it a perfect destination for an afternoon chat. Or retreat to the downstairs lounge, Cibar *(212-460-5656),* and indulge in a meal of martinis and light bites.
Hotel services *Complimentary breakfast. Dry cleaning (24hr). Pass to New York Sports Club. Tearoom. Ticket desk. Valet.* **Room services** *CD player. Digital cable. High-speed Internet. VCR.*

SoHo Grand Hotel

310 West Broadway between Canal and Grand Sts (212-965-3000, 800-965-3000; www.sohogrand.com). Subway: A, C, E, 1, 9 to Canal St. **Rates** *$259–$429 single/double; $1,599–$1,899 suite. 366 rooms.* **Credit** *AmEx, DC, Disc, MC, V.*
Built in 1996, Soho's first high-end hotel pays homage to the neighborhood's art community and its manufacturing-district past. A dramatic stairway of bottle glass and cast iron leads up to the elegant lobby. The Bill Sofield–designed rooms are in a restrained palette of grays and beiges, and photos from local galleries hang on the walls. Sip cocktails and listen to newly released lounge albums in the Grand Bar and Lounge, or dine on haute macaroni and cheese in the Gallery. Sister location Tribeca Grand Hotel has opened Sanctum *(212-519-6677),* a classic cocktail-and-music space that exudes old Hollywood glamour.
Hotel services *Baby-sitting. Beauty salon. Cell-phone rental. Dry cleaning (24hr). Fitness center. Pets allowed. Ticket desk. Valet. Video library.* **Room services** *CD player. High-speed Internet. VCR.*
Other location *Tribeca Grand Hotel, 2 Sixth Ave between Walker and White Sts (212-519-6600).*

Soho House

29–35 Ninth Ave between 13th and 14th Sts (212-627-9800; www.sohohouse.com). Subway: A, C, E to 14th St; L to Eighth Ave. **Rates** *$250–$410 standard/deluxe; $495–$825 suite. 24 rooms.* **Credit** *AmEx, DC, Disc, MC, V.*
It's downright democratic for this supersleek club—sibling of the original Soho House in London—to give the common man access to its two dozen guest rooms. Unless you know someone who belongs (or will recommend you for a $900 annual membership), booking a room is the only way to penetrate this celeb-filled funhouse, which features a restaurant, multiple bars, a library (with more booze than books), a private screening room and the Cowshed spa. The mod-chateau rooms range from the moderate Playpen to the humongous Playground (a huge free-standing Boffi tub roosts in the corner, while the shower doubles as a steam room). All pack in a mother lode of style, thanks to Ilse Crawford's knack for mixing supermodern furniture with antiques.

Hotel services *Baby-sitting. Beauty salon. Butler. Cell-phone rental. Dry cleaning (24hr). Fitness center. Game room. Screening room. Spa. Swimming pool. Valet.* **Room services** *CD and DVD players. Flat-panel TV. Refrigerator and freezer. Room service (24hr). Wi-Fi.*

W New York–Union Square

201 Park Ave South at 17th St (212-253-9119; www.whotels.com). Subway: L, N, Q, R, W, 4, 5, 6 to 14th St–Union Sq. **Rates** *$299–$499 single/double, $599–$1,800 suite. 270 rooms.* **Credit** *AmEx, DC, Disc, MC, V.*
For review, *see p51* **W New York–Times Square**.

Moderate ($100 to $200)

Abingdon Guest House

13 Eighth Ave between Jane and W 12th Sts (212-243-5384; www.abingdonguesthouse.com). Subway: A, C, E to 14th St; L to Eighth Ave. **Rates** *$137–$187 single/double; $212–$222 suite. 9 rooms.* **Credit** *AmEx, DC, Disc, MC, V.*
This charm-saturated inn links two landmark Federal townhouses. Named for nearby Abingdon Square park, the nine-room guest house offers residential ambience for a reasonable price. Most rooms have private baths, and all have access to the leafy garden. The popular Brewbar Coffee doubles as check-in desk and café.
Hotel services *Coffeebar.* **Room services** *Free local phone service. High-speed Internet. VCR in some rooms.*

Cosmopolitan

95 West Broadway at Chambers St (212-566-1900, 888-895-9400; www.cosmohotel.com). Subway: A, C, 1, 2, 3, 9 to Chambers St. **Rates** *$119–$159 single/double. 115 rooms.* **Credit** *AmEx, DC, MC, V.*
Don't expect to be served a Cosmo at this smallish, well-maintained hotel—there isn't a bar to drink it in. Although the name suggests high style, this immaculately clean hotel is geared toward budget travelers with little need for luxuries. Open continuously since the 1850s, the hotel remains a tourist favorite for its Tribeca location and rock-bottom rates. Minilofts—multilevel rooms with sleeping lofts—start at $109.
Hotel services *Discount parking. Safe.*

Gramercy Park Hotel

2 Lexington Ave at 21st St (212-475-4320, 800-221-4083; www.gramercyparkhotel.com). Subway: 6 to 23rd St. **Rates** *$170–$185 single/double; $210–$240 suite. 455 rooms.* **Credit** *AmEx, DC, Disc, MC, V.*
Only residents of the surrounding luxury townhouses get keys to beautiful Gramercy Park. But you can gain admission by checking in to this historic hotel (now managed by Ian Schrager). JFK once lived here with his parents; Humphrey Bogart married Helen Mencken here; and a drunken Babe Ruth was escorted out of the bar more than once. The entire hotel was renovated in 2002. On balmy days, have a martini at the High Bar, a breezy rooftop annex.
Hotel services *Complimentary breakfast. Fitness center. Laundry drop-off. Valet.* **Room services** *High-speed Internet. Kitchenette. VCR.*

The Maritime Hotel

363 W 16th St between Eighth and Ninth Aves (212-242-4300; www.themaritimehotel.com). Subway: A, C, E to 14th St; L to Eighth Ave. **Rates** *$195–$260 single/double; $395–$1,100 suite. 124 rooms.* **Credit** *AmEx, Disc, DC, MC, V.*
Imagine a beautiful ship that has sailed in from Japan—by way of Palm Springs. Architects-of-cool Eric Goode and Sean MacPherson (Bowery Bar, the Park) and developers Richard Born and Ira Drukier (The Mercer and Chambers hotels) have applied

The best Inn crowd

These are the best hotels…

…for a bit of old New York
The **Pierre Hotel** (*see p61*) is the only remaining hotel with a 24/7 elevator operator.

…for couples with chemistry
The Alchemy Suite at the **Dylan Hotel** (*see p47*) is modeled after a medieval alchemist's lab.

…for never having to lift a finger
When guests check in to the **Trump International Hotel** (*see p62*), they're assigned a personal assistant and an in-room chef.

…for reliving the city's rock & roll past
Bob Dylan and Joan Baez found shelter from the storm at the **Washington Square Hotel** (*see p43*).

…for the lover of all things Italian
At the **Michelangelo** (*see p49*), Italian oil paintings hang on the walls, staff members *parlano italiano,* and breakfast is Italian pastries with espresso or cappuccino.

…for charm in the middle of Charmville
The **Abingdon Guest House** (*see left*) is a West Village delight, featuring themed rooms and a trellised garden.

their high-gloss formula to the Maritime Union's former headquarters. Opened in 2002, the hotel boasts large porthole windows and a nautical theme, with rooms designed to resemble ship cabins. The hotel's two restaurants, Matsuri (serving inventive Japanese fare) and La Bottega (an Italian trattoria which also provides round-the-clock room service), both lure a buzzing and beautiful crowd. Sip a cocktail in the outdoor garden or on the lantern-festooned patio.
Hotel services *DVD library. Fitness center. Pass to New York Sports Club.* **Room services** *CD player. Flat-panel TV. High-speed Internet. Room service (24hr). Two-line telephone.*

Surface Hotel

107 Rivington St between Essex and Ludlow Sts (212-475-2600; www.surfacehotel.com). Subway: F to Delancey St; J, M, Z to Delancey–Essex Sts. **Rates** *From $250 single/double; call or visit website for more rates. 110 rooms.* **Credit** *AmEx, Disc, MC, V.*
Owned by the hip California interior-design magazine of the same name, the hotel is slated to be completed this year. The $30 million, 20-story steel-and-glass luxury palace is guaranteed to offer spectacular views: Developer Paul Stallings used glass panels of different shapes and opacities to create what he describes as a "Mondrianesque" style. The hotel also features a private nightclub with a keyed entrance, a 5,000-square-foot bar-restaurant and a rooftop entertainment space.
Hotel services *Baby-sitting. Cell-phone rental. Complimentary breakfast. Dry cleaning (24hr). Fitness center. Gift shop. Spa. Valet. Video library.* **Room services** *CD player. High-speed Internet. VCR.*

The Wall Street Inn

9 South William St at Broad St (212-747-1500; www.thewallstreetinn.com). Subway: 2, 3 to Wall St; 4, 5 to Bowling Green. **Rates** *$169–$450 single/double. Call for corporate and weekend rates. 46 rooms.* **Credit** *AmEx, DC, Disc, MC, V.*
In recent years, this landmark district has seen new life, with patisseries, bars and restaurants sprouting along its cobblestone streets. The boutique Wall Street Inn started the trend four years ago by reincarnating an 1830s Lehman Brothers Bank building. To reach beyond the financiers, the hotel offers hefty discounts on weekends. There's no restaurant or room service, but breakfast is included.
Hotel services *Fitness center. Video library.* **Room services** *Internet. VCR.*

Washington Square Hotel

103 Waverly Pl between Fifth and Sixth Aves (212-777-9515, 800-222-0418; www.washingtonsquarehotel.com). Subway: A,C, E, B, D, F, V to W 4th St. **Rates** *$136–$165 single/double; $188 quad. 160 rooms.* **Credit** *AmEx, MC, V.*
Once you walk through its century-old doors, you'll wonder where this fabulous little gem has been all your life. Bob Dylan and Joan Baez lived in this Greenwich Village hotel, back when they sang for change in nearby Washington Square Park. The lobby was redone in 2002, and a cozy bar and lounge was added, serving afternoon tea and light fare. Rooms are small but refined, with custom-made furniture. Rates include breakfast—or splurge on the Sunday jazz brunch at North Square *(212-254-1200)*, the restaurant next door.
Hotel services *Complimentary breakfast. Fitness center.* **Room services** *High-speed Internet.*

Budget (less than $100)

Hotel 17

225 E 17th St between Second and Third Aves (212-475-2845; www.hotel17ny.com). Subway: L to Third Ave; N, Q, R, W, 4, 5, 6 to 14th St–Union Sq. **Rates** *$69–$99 single/double; $89–$120 triple. 120 rooms.* **Credit** *MC, V.*
Although still somewhat dank, the divey Hotel 17 is looking more chic than shabby after a recent renovation. The lobby was redone in 2003, and exposed pipes have been covered up. Labyrinthine hallways lead to tiny high-ceilinged rooms filled with discarded dressers and mismatched 1950s wallpaper. Ignore the permanent NO VACANCY sign, and expect to share the hallway bathroom with other guests. Madonna posed here for a magazine shoot, and Woody Allen used the place in *Manhattan Murder Mystery*. The affiliated Hotel 31 (*see p59*) has less cachet, but suffices as a midtown budget hotel.
Hotel services *Concierge. Fax. Self-serve laundry.* **Room services** *Modem. Internet.*

Larchmont Hotel

27 W 11th St between Fifth and Sixth Aves (212-989-9333; www.larchmonthotel.com). Subway: F, V to 14th St; L to Sixth Ave. **Rates** *$70–$95 single; $90–$115 double; $109–$125 queen. 60 rooms.* **Credit** *AmEx, DC, Disc, MC, V.*
Housed in a renovated 1910 Beaux Arts building, the attractive, affordable Larchmont Hotel may be the best bang for your buck in the heart of Greenwich Village. Some rooms are small, but all are clean and well maintained. Each is equipped with a washbasin, robe and pair of slippers, though all baths are shared.
Hotel services *Complimentary breakfast. Concierge. Fax. Kitchenette on some floors.* **Room services** *Alarm clock. Hair dryer. Radio. Safe. TV. Voice mail.*

Off-Soho Suites Hotel

11 Rivington St between Bowery and Chrystie St (212-979-9808, 800-633-7646; www.offsoho.com). Subway: B, D to Grand St; J, M, Z to Bowery. **Rates** *$89 2-person suite with shared bath; $149 4-person suite with private bath. 38 rooms.* **Credit** *AmEx, MC, V.*
It's all about location. These no-frill suites are a good value for the hip Lower East Side (a couple of blocks from Soho). Rooms are painfully dull yet roomy, clean and bright, with fully equipped kitchens.
Hotel services *Café. Concierge. Dry cleaning. Fax. Fitness room. Self-serve laundry.* **Room services** *Alarm clock. Hair dryer. Kitchenette. Modem line. Room service. Safe. Voice mail.*

Union Square Inn

209 E 14th St between Second and Third Aves (212-614-0500; www.unionsquareinn.com). Subway: L to Third Ave; N, Q, R, W, 4, 5, 6 to 14th St–Union Sq. **Rates** *$89–$139 single/double. 43 rooms.* **Credit** *AmEx, MC, V.*
For review, *see p59* **Murray Hill Inn**.

Hostels

Bowery's Whitehouse Hotel of New York

340 Bowery between 2nd and 3rd Sts (212-477-5623; www.whitehousehotelofny.com). Subway: B, D, F, V to Broadway–Lafayette St; 6 to Bleecker St. **Rates** *$28–$54 single/double; $71 triple. 220 rooms.* **Credit** *AmEx, DC, Disc, MC, V.*
Times are changin' on the legendarily grubby Bowery; new restaurants and flashy clubs have added some glitter to the litter. But the Bowery's Whitehouse Hotel is here to stay. Built in 1917 as housing for railroad workers, the hotel offers private rooms at unbelievably low rates. Although small, the units are clean and the mattresses are comfortable. A microwave and large-screen TV are available in the lounge at all hours. For kicks, sit down and chat with one of the resident old-timers (about 40 people live here permanently).
Hotel services *Concierge. DVD player, Internet and TV in lobby. Fax. Luggage storage. Safe-deposit boxes. Self-serve laundry.*

Midtown

Deluxe ($350 and up)

The Alex

205 E 45th St between Second and Third Aves (212-867-5100; www.thealexhotel.com). Subway: 42nd St S, 4, 5, 6, 7 to 42nd St–Grand Central. **Rates** *$375–$500 single/double; $400–$700 studio/one bedroom; $1,000–$3,000 suite. 203 rooms.* **Credit** *AmEx, Disc, MC, V.*
A-list designer David Rockwell is the man behind this bamboo-bedecked luxury hotel, along with Turkish real-estate developer Izak Senbahar and hotel mogul Simon Elias (of the Flatotel; *see p47*). Rooms feature limestone baths, Frette linens, Frédéric Fekkai bath products and gourmet goodies from Dean & DeLuca. The hotel touts a serene environment—but puts flat-panel TVs in the living room, the bedroom *and* the bathroom. Riingo, the hotel's wildly hyped Japanese restaurant, is a showcase for megastar chefs Marcus Samuelsson and Hakan Swahn of Aquavit.
Hotel services *Baby-sitting. Cell-phone rental. Fitness center. Wi-Fi.* **Room services** *DVD. Flat-screen TVs. High-speed Internet. Kitchens in some rooms. Room service (24hr).*

Four Seasons Hotel

57 E 57th St between Madison and Park Aves (212-758-5700, 800-332-3442; www.fourseasons.com). Subway: N, R, W to Lexington Ave–59th St; 4,

Chain gang

Many of the familiar global chains have locations in New York, and although they don't offer bundles of cachet, they do have reasonable rates and reliable amenities.
In the Financial District, the **Holiday Inn Wall Street** *(15 Gold St at Platt St, 212-232-7700, 800-HOLIDAY)* is actually one of the city's best business-class hotels, with automated check-in kiosks and "virtual office" rooms. See www.holidayinnwsd.com for more information. Farther up on the Lower East Side is a blessedly clean **Howard Johnson's Express Inn** *(135 E Houston St between First and Second Aves, 212-358-8844)*, serving a complimentary breakfast. Psst: The high-end rooms have two double beds and a Jacuzzi. See www.hojo.com for further details. It's hard to miss the **Westin at Times Square**'s assertive 45-floor tower *(270 W 43rd St at Eighth Ave, 888-627-7149)*. Rooms have crisp modern furnishings, fluffy duvets and flat-panel TVs. Rooms above the 15th floor have unobstructed views of Times Square. Go to www.westinny.com for more information.

The **Westin at Times Square**.

If it's romance you're after, hop over the East River to Brooklyn's **New York Marriott at the Brooklyn Bridge** *(333 Adams St between Tillary and Willoughby Sts, Brooklyn Heights; 718-246-7000)*, where, for an extra $99, starry-eyed couples can order the Elegantly White package—your room is showered with white rose petals and filled with scented candles, bubble-bath amenities and a bottle of Aria Estate Champagne. Visit www.brooklynmarriott.com for more details.

6 to 59th St. **Rates** *$455–$815 single/double; $1,350–$9,500 suite. 368 rooms.* **Credit** *AmEx, DC, Disc, MC, V.*
Everybody who's anybody—from music industry executives to political figures—has stayed at this quintessentially New York luxury hotel. Renowned architect I.M. Pei's sharp geometric design (in neutral cream and honey tones) is sleek and modern. Rooms are among the largest in the city (the three-bedroom Royal Suite measures 2,000 square feet), with bathrooms of Florentine marble, and tubs that fill in just 60 seconds. Views of Manhattan from the higher floors are superb. The hotel is known for catering to a guest's every need or craving; your 4am hot-fudge sundae is only a concierge call away.
Hotel services *Baby-sitting. Complimentary video library. Dry cleaning (24hr). Fitness center. Gift shop. Spa.* **Room services** *High-speed Internet. Flat-panel TVs. Nintendo. VCR in suites or on request.*

St. Regis

2 E 55th St at Fifth Ave (212-753-4500; www.stregis.com). Subway: E, V to Fifth Ave–53rd St; 6 to 51st St. **Rates** *$635–$760 superior/deluxe; $1,150–$11,500 suite. 315 rooms.* **Credit** *AmEx, DC, Disc, MC, V.*
The stately St. Regis is Fifth Avenue at its finest. Erected in a 1904 Beaux Arts landmark building, the glimmering hotel features Louis XVI–style furniture, crystal chandeliers, marble baths and silk wall coverings. Afternoon tea is served in the Astor Court, but if you need something stronger to make you merry, retire to the King Cole Bar (*see p207*), birthplace of the Red Snapper (a.k.a. Bloody Mary). Facials and massages are available through the Carita spa, which uses products from the exclusive Carita of Paris.
Hotel services *Baby-sitting. Beauty salon. Cell-phone rental. Fitness center. Gift shop. Spa. Ticket desk. Valet. Video library.* **Room services** *CD player. High-speed Internet. Nintendo. PlayStation. Room service (24hr). VCR.*

Expensive ($200 to $350)

The Algonquin

59 W 44th St between Fifth and Sixth Aves (212-840-6800, 800-555-8000; www.thealgonquin.net). Subway: B, D, F, V to 42nd St–Bryant Park; 7 to Fifth Ave. **Rates** *$199–$299 single/double; $299–$399 suite. 174 rooms.* **Credit** *AmEx, DC, Disc, MC, V.*
The reception area/sitting room of the venerable Algonquin lives up to its Jazz Age reputation with beautifully carved and upholstered chairs, old lamps, and a large painting of the literary greats of the 1920s and '30s, who gathered to gossip and parry at the legendary Round Table in the Oak Room (*see p274*). The rooms are on the small side but polished with a classic New York feel. The hallways are covered with *New Yorker*–cartoon wallpaper. Catch readings by local authors on some Mondays, and cabaret performances Tuesday through Saturday.

The **Alex**. *See p44.*

Hotel services *Baby-sitting. Fitness center (24hr). Ticket desk.* **Room services** *CD player and VCR in suites. High-speed Internet. PlayStation. Refrigerator in suites or on request.*

Beekman Tower Hotel

3 Mitchell Pl, 49th St at First Ave (212-355-7300, 800-ME-SUITE; www.mesuite.com). Subway: E, V to Lexington Ave–53rd St; 6 to 51st St. **Rates** *$229–$360 studio suite; $219–$400 1-bedroom; $478–$680 2-bedroom. 175 rooms.*
Credit *AmEx, DC, Disc, MC, V.*
For a tutorial in Art Deco design, book a room at this distinctive architectural landmark. Erected in 1928, the pleasant hotel belongs to Affinia, the city's largest all-suite hotel group (it has nine other properties in the city, including the Benjamin (*see below*). Rooms are large by New York standard, and all include kitchenettes. Dine on simple American cuisine at the hotel's 26th-floor restaurant, the Top of the Tower *(212-980-4796),* and enjoy a bird's-eye view of the cityscape and beyond.
Hotel services *Baby-sitting. Ballroom. Cell-phone rental. Fitness center. Valet.* **Room services** *Internet. Microwave. Kitchenette. VCR.*

The Benjamin

125 E 50th St at Lexington Ave (212-715-2500, 888-4-BENJAMIN; www.thebenjamin.com). Subway: E, V to Lexington Ave–53rd St; 6 to 51st St. **Rates** *$285–$555 single/double; $555–$1,125 suite. 209 rooms.* **Credit** *AmEx, DC, Disc, MC, V.*

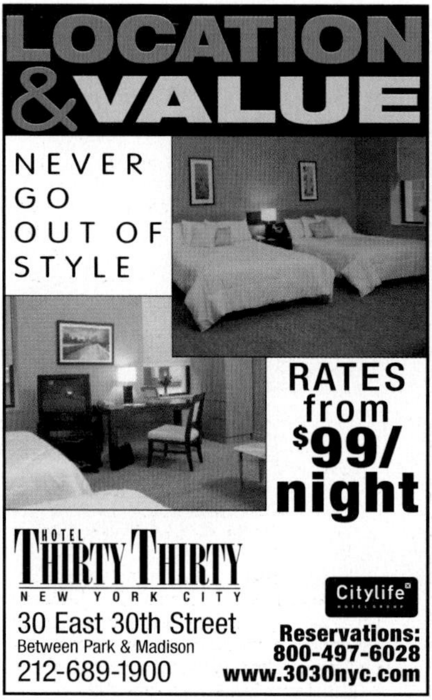
LOCATION &VALUE
NEVER GO OUT OF STYLE
RATES from $99/ night
HOTEL THIRTY THIRTY NEW YORK CITY
Citylife
30 East 30th Street
Between Park & Madison
212-689-1900
Reservations: 800-497-6028
www.3030nyc.com

New Yorks Upper West Side
HB HOTEL BEACON
BROADWAY at it's BEST
Over 240 spacious guest rooms and suites, all equipped with kitchenettes and marble bathrooms. 24-hour Restaurant.
2130 BROADWAY AT 75TH ST., NYC
212.787.1100 / 800.572.4969
www.beaconhotel.com

CHELSEA INTERNATIONAL HOSTEL
WALKING TIMES TO:
Midtown; 10 min.
So-Ho: 20 min.
Minutes to NYC's Best Clubs
Greenwich Village: 5 min.
Empire State building: 15 min.
Great Staff with vast Knowledge of NYC
Excellent location
very Clean
Extremely Safe
Parties During the week
Kitchen
Free Coffee, Tea
TV Room
Free Lockers
24-Hour Check-In
Big Backyard
$27 Per Night (inc. tax)
Travelers Checks Accepted
Free linen
Free NYC Train & Bus Maps
Laundry Room
Private Room
Internet Cafe
No Chores! No Curfews! No Hassles!
251 West 20th Street
New York, NY 10011
Tel: 212-647-0010
Fax: 212-727-7289
www.chelseahostel.com
Email: reservations@chelseahostel.com
FREE PIZZA On Wed.

Insomniacs will take heart at this sleep-obsessed executive-suite hotel—where a sleep concierge is on hand to help you choose from a customized "pillow menu" of 11 types, with fillings ranging from buckwheat hulls to water. The landmark building once housed the Hotel Beverly (which Georgia O'Keeffe used to paint from her apartment across the street). The famed Terrance Brennan's Seafood & Chop House serves choice cuts to a sophisticated, suited crowd. The green at heart will sleep well too—the Benjamin is Ecotel-certified.
Hotel services *Fitness center. Spa.* **Room services** *Cordless phone. Fax/copier. High-speed Internet. Kitchenette.*

The Bryant Park

40 W 40th St between Fifth and Sixth Aves (212-642-2200; www.bryantparkhotel.com). Subway: B, D, F, V to 42nd St–Bryant Park; 7 to Fifth Ave. **Rates** *$265–$395 single/double; $395–615 suite. 128 rooms.* **Credit** *AmEx, DC, MC, V.*
The White Stripes rock band, known for its strict red-and-white attire, would feel right at home in this modish boutique hotel, where gorgeous red-tiled walls, a sleek red desk and groovy white lamps adorn the lobby. Former Ian Schrager partner Philip Pilevsky has converted the 1924 American Radiator Building, across the street from Bryant Park, into his first New York property. Chef Rick Laakkonen prepares haute creative American cuisine at Ilo *(212-642-2255)* and at Cellar Bar (*see p207*), the hotel's vaulted lounge. Hidden beneath the lounge is a 70-seat screening room with red velour chairs and built-in desks.
Hotel services *Beauty salon. Boardroom with video conferencing. Fitness center. Screening room. Spa. Valet.* **Room services** *CD player. Digital-movies-on-demand system. High-speed Internet. Room service (24hr). VCR.*

City Club Hotel

55 W 44th St between Fifth and Sixth Aves (212-921-5500, 888-256-4100; www.cityclubhotel.com). Subway: B, D, F, V to 42nd St–Bryant Park; 7 to Fifth Ave. **Rates** *$195–$295 single/double; $225–$495 queen/king; $600 duplex suite; $695–$1,200 suite. 65 rooms.* **Credit** *AmEx, DC, MC, V.*
City Club stands out because of its excellent staff and sleek decor. The lobby is upstairs from the front desk, and the walls and rooms feature works by NYC artists. Enjoy a blend of high fashion and contemporary comfort in the stylish quarters, lavished with Jonathan Adler ceramics, Hermès bath products and windowside daybeds. DB Bistro Moderne (*see p194*) serves chef Daniel Boulud's $29 burger.
Hotel services *Baby-sitting. Beauty salon. Cell-phone rental. Complimentary access to nearby gym. Discount parking. Ticket desk. Valet. Video library.* **Room services** *CD and DVD players. Cordless phone. High-speed Internet. VCR.*

Chambers

15 W 56th St between Fifth and Sixth Aves (212-974-5656; www.chambershotel.com). Subway: F to 57th St; N, R, W to Fifth Ave–59th St. **Rates** *$315–$400 single; $350–$400 double; $475–$500 studio; $650–$1,600 suite. 77 rooms.* **Credit** *AmEx, DC, Disc, MC, V.*
Developed by Ira Drukier and Richard Born (of the Mercer and Hotel Elysée), the style-saturated Chambers features Area duvets, Bumble and bumble bath products, Mario Badescu spa services and personal shopping by Henri Bendel. David Rockwell–designed rooms contain stainless-steel fixtures and track lighting, cozied up by Tibetan rugs, taupe-and-purple bedding and plenty of textured wood. You'll find equally engaging creations—of the culinary variety—at the hotel's restaurant, Town *(212-582-4445)*.
Hotel services *Baby-sitter. CD and DVD library. Computer rental. Pass to New York Sports Club. Valet.* **Room services** *Cordless phone. High-speed Internet.*

Dylan

52 E 41st St between Madison and Park Aves (212-338-0500, 800-55-DYLAN; www.dylanhotel.com). Subway: 42nd St S, 4, 5, 6, 7 to 42nd St–Grand Central. **Rates** *$199–$399 single/double; $495–$1,200 suite. 107 rooms.* **Credit** *AmEx, DC, Disc, MC, V.*
A $30 million restoration transformed the once-crumbling 1903 landmark Chemist Club building into a breathtaking boutique hotel, with a grand marble staircase, a spacious outdoor terrace and a soaring Gothic "alchemy suite," modeled after a medieval alchemist's lab. Most rooms still have 11-foot ceilings, fluted columns, leaded floor-to-ceiling windows and beautifully ornate moldings.
Hotel services *Baby-sitting. Cell-phone rental. Fitness center. Ticket desk. Valet.* **Room services** *CD player and VCR on request. High-speed Internet.*

Flatotel

135 W 52nd St between Sixth and Seventh Aves (212-887-9400; www.flatotel.com). Subway: N, R, W to 49th St; 1, 9 to 50th St. **Rates** *$249–$349 single/double; $499–$1,800 suite. 288 rooms.* **Credit** *AmEx, DC, MC, V.*
Techno beats pump through the glossy granite lobby and backlit walnut bar. Cozy, dimly lit nooks and cowhide-and-leather couches are perfect for canoodling and cocktailing. For more private imbibing, order the in-room martini service—the staff will mix the drink right in your room and present it on a silver tray. Moda *(212-887-9880)* serves Italian-inspired fare; in temperate weather, catch a breeze while sipping your Bacardi in the restaurant's alfresco atrium.
Hotel services *Beauty salon. Business center. Cell-phone rental. Complimentary breakfast. Gift shop. Pass to nearby gym. Spa. Valet.* **Room services** *CD player. High-speed Internet. VCR.*

Hotel Elysée

60 E 54th St between Madison and Park Aves (212-753-1066; www.elyseehotel.com). Subway: E, V to Lexington Ave–53rd St; 6 to 51st St. **Rates** *$285–$345 single/double; $425–$525 suite. 101 rooms.* **Credit** *AmEx, DC, Disc, MC, V.*

Built in the '20s, the Hotel Elysée is named for one of that era's finest French restaurants. Quarters are furnished with antiques; some rooms have colored-glass conservatories and terraces. Elysée is popular with publishers and literary types, who convene over complimentary afternoon tea. Downstairs is the Steakhouse at Monkey Bar *(212-838-2600)*, where a well-coiffed clientele dines on fine cuts. For sister hotels, see Casablanca Hotel, Hotel Giraffe and the Library Hotel (*see p54 and right*).
Hotel services *Baby-sitting. Cell-phone rental. Complimentary breakfast. Dry cleaning (24hr). Pass to nearby gym. Valet. Video library.* **Room services** *CD player. High-speed Internet. VCR.*

The Iroquois

49 W 44th St between Fifth and Sixth Aves (212-840-3080, 800-332-7220; www.iroquoisny.com). Subway: B, D, F, V to 42nd St–Bryant Park; 7 to Fifth Ave. **Rates** *$249–$425 single/double; $349–$849 suite. 114 rooms.* **Credit** *AmEx, DC, Disc, MC, V.*
Once a budget hostelry, the Iroquois has morphed into a full-service luxury hotel. A polished-stone lobby, a mahogany-paneled library and marble-lined bathrooms are the result of a $13 million renovation. There's also a fitness center, a sauna and a library with computer access. Contemporary French fare is served in the hotel's two acclaimed restaurants, Triomphe and the more intimate Le Petit Triomphe *(212-453-4233)*.
Hotel services *Baby-sitting. Cell-phone rental. Dry cleaning (24hr). Fitness center. Sauna. Ticket desk. Video library.* **Room services** *CD player. High-speed Internet. Room service (24hr). VCR.*

The Kitano

66 Park Ave at 38th St (212-885-7000, 800-548-2666; www.kitano.com). Subway: 42nd St S, 4, 5, 6, 7 to 42nd St–Grand Central. **Rates** *$210–$605 single/double; $715–$2,100 suite. 149 rooms.* **Credit** *AmEx, DC, Disc, MC, V.*
This was the first Japanese-owned hotel in New York City, and it's probably the only hotel to offer heated commodes. Rooms feature silk-covered walls, smooth stone floors, Shiseido bath products and complimentary green tea. A one-of-a-kind tatami suite boasts painted shoji screens and a separate tea ceremony room. Dine with chopsticks at the hotel's two restaurants, Nadaman Hakubai *(212-885-7111)* and Garden Cafe *(212-885-7123)*.
Hotel services *Baby-sitting. Gift shop. Laundry drop-off. Ticket Desk. Valet.* **Room services** *CD player in some rooms. High-speed Internet.*

Le Parker Meridien

118 W 57th St between Sixth and Seventh Aves (212-245-5000, 800-543-4300; www.parkermeridien.com). Subway: F, N, Q, R, W to 57th St. **Rates** *$325–400 single/double; $599–$3,000 suite. 731 rooms.* **Credit** *AmEx, DC, MC, V.*
The No. 1 draw at this midtown classic is the rooftop pool. The award-winning breakfasts at Norma's *(212-708-7460)* run a close second, thanks to the "red-berry risotto oatmeal" and banana–macadamia nut flapjacks. The cute burger joint in the lobby rounds out the trifecta.
Hotel services *Cell-phone rental. Fitness center. Spa.* **Room services** *DVD player. High-speed Internet. Room service.*

The Library Hotel

299 Madison Ave at 41st St (212-983-4500). Subway: 42nd St S, 4, 5, 6, 7 to 42nd St–Grand Central; 7 to Fifth Ave. **Rates** *$255–$315 single/double; $345–$415 suite. 60 rooms.* **Credit** *AmEx, DC, MC, V.*
Literature appears even before you enter—the sidewalks of East 41st Street are inscribed with quotes from famous authors. Rooms at the mahogany-rich Library Hotel are organized according to the Dewey decimal system. Look for the autobiography of Casanova in the Love Room, appropriately curated by Dr. Ruth. Rates include breakfast and wine-and-cheese evening gatherings in the second-floor Reading Room. Hotel Giraffe, one of the Library's sister hotels, offers modern European style in the up-and-coming Rose Hill area.
Hotel services *Baby-sitting. Cell-phone rental. Complimentary breakfast. Pass to nearby gym. Ticket desk. Valet. Video library.* **Room services** *CD player. High-speed Internet. VCR.*
Other location *Hotel Giraffe, 365 Park Ave South at 26th St (212-685-7700, 877-296-0009; www.hotelgiraffe.com).*

The Mansfield

12 W 44th St between Fifth and Sixth Aves (212-944-6050, 877-847-4444; www.mansfieldhotel.com). Subway: B, D, F, V to 42nd St–Bryant Park; 7 to Fifth Ave. **Rates** *$225–$350 single/double; $325–$450 suite. 124 rooms.* **Credit** *AmEx, DC, Disc, MC, V.*
For review, *see p50* **The Roger Williams**.

The Michelangelo

152 W 51st St between Sixth and Seventh Aves (212-765-1900, 800-237-0990; www.michelangelohotel.com). Subway: N, R, W to 49th St; 1, 9 to 50th St. **Rates** *$195–$495 single/double; $395–$1,200 suite. 178 rooms.* **Credit** *AmEx, DC, Disc, MC, V.*
This lavish Old World–style hotel is appointed with Italian luxuries—peach marble, oil paintings, giant potted palms. The sizable rooms are decorated in styles ranging from French country to Art Deco; and all include two TVs, a fax machine and a giant tub. Complimentary breakfast includes Italian coffees and pastries. Fully equipped apartments are also available for extended stays ($3,500 to $9,000 per month).
Hotel services *Baby-sitting. Beauty salon. Cell-phone rental. Complimentary breakfast and limousine service to Wall Street (Mon–Fri). Dry cleaning (24hr). Fitness center (24hr). Valet.* **Room services** *CD player. Complimentary newspaper and shoe shine. Kitchenettes in suites. DVD player, laptop computer, printer and VCR on request.*

Lofty Be an artist—or just live like one—at the stylish **Chambers**. *See p47.*

The Muse

130 W 46th St between Sixth and Seventh Aves (212-485-2400; www.themusehotel.com). Subway: B, D, F, V to 47–50th Sts–Rockefeller Ctr. **Rates** *$265–$355 single/double; $450–$600 suite. 200 rooms.* **Credit** *AmEx, DC, Disc, MC, V.*

Pampering is the inspiration at the Muse. Rooms feature puffy feather beds and Philosophy toiletries. Guests can luxuriate with in-room spa treatments or indulge in Sam DeMarco's innovative American fare at District *(212-485-2999).*

Hotel services *Baby-sitting. Cell-phone rental. Fitness center. Valet. Video library.* **Room services** *CD player. High-speed Internet. VCR.*

New York Palace

455 Madison Ave between 50th and 51st Sts (212-888-7000, 800-697-2522; www.newyorkpalace.com). Subway: E, V to Fifth Ave–53rd St. **Rates** *$295–$720 single/double; $900–$7,000 suite. 896 rooms.* **Credit** *AmEx, DC, Disc, MC, V.*

The Palace is a living fairy tale, complete with red carpet, twinkling lights and fancy tea parties. Once the Villard Houses, this cluster of mansions designed by McKim, Mead & White is home to the equally high-end restaurant Le Cirque 2000 *(212-303-7788).* It's nearly impossible to make a last-minute reservation at the restaurant, but guests in the tower suites can order room service from Le Cirque's menu.

Hotel services *Complimentary limousine service to Wall Street. Complimentary shoe shine. Dry cleaning (24hr). Fitness center. Video library.* **Room services** *Complimentary breakfast, afternoon tea, evening hors d'oeuvres, desserts and newspaper in suites. Dual-line phones. Fax/copier. Room service (24hr).*

Park South Hotel

122 E 28th St between Park Ave South and Lexington Ave (212-448-0888, 800-315-4642; www.parksouthhotel.com). Subway: 6 to 28th St. **Rates** *$199–$260 single/double; $325–$345 suite. 143 rooms.* **Credit** *AmEx, DC, Disc, MC, V.*

Everything about this new boutique hotel says "I love New York." The mezzanine library is crammed with books on historic Gotham, and the walls are covered with images from the New-York Historical Society. Rooms are decorated in warm amber and brown, and some have dazzling views of the Chrysler Building. The hotel's restaurant, Black Duck *(212-204-5240),* serves live jazz with brunch.

Hotel services *Complimentary breakfast. Fitness center. Valet. Video library.* **Room services** *DVD player. Fax/copier. High-speed Internet. VCR.*

The Roger Williams

131 Madison Ave at 31st St (888-448-7788; www.rogerwilliamshotel.com). Subway: 6 to 33rd St. **Rates** *$225–$245 single/double; $405–$475 suite. 187 rooms.* **Credit** *AmEx, DC, Disc, MC, V.*

Popular with the fashion industry, the small, stylish Roger Williams offers complimentary espresso or cappuccino, and a welcome drink upon check-in—just what you'll need to warm you up amid the cool decor and even cooler clientele. The amenities (e.g., bottled water, 300-thread–count linens) make you feel as though you're in your own home—if you're lucky enough to live like this. Each room on the penthouse level has access to a shared wrap-around terrace. Other hotels in the Boutique Hotel Group include the Franklin, Hotel Wales, Mansfield and Shoreham (*see p63, p62, p49 and p56*), all located near Museum Mile.

Hotel services *Baby-sitting. CD and video library. Cell-phone rental. Complimentary breakfast. Fitness center. Meditation room. Valet. Wireless high-speed Internet.* **Room services** *VCR.*

Sofitel

45 W 44th St between Fifth and Sixth Aves (212-354-8844; fax 212-782-3002; www.sofitel.com). Subway: B, D, F, V to 42nd St–Bryant Park; 7 to Fifth Ave. **Rates** *$249–$699 single/double/suite. 398 rooms.* **Credit** *AmEx, DC, Disc, MC, V.*

Part of a French chain, Sofitel New York is a 30-story luxury business hotel with a wonderful brasserie, Gaby *(212-782-7149)*, and 52 suites with stunning views of midtown Manhattan. Rooms are contemporary and tasteful, decorated in warm, earthy colors with mahogany furniture—a perfect retreat from the hustle and bustle of Times Square.

Hotel services *Pets allowed.* **Room services** *Dataport. Internet access.*

Swissôtel The Drake New York

440 Park Ave at 56th St (212-421-0900; www.swissotel.com). Subway: E, V to Lexington Ave–53rd St; 4, 5, 6 to 59th St. **Rates** *$200–$300 single/double; $300–$1,300 suite. 495 rooms.* **Credit** *AmEx, DC, Disc, MC, V.*

The European-style Swissôtel The Drake New York is an elegant option for business travelers. Chef Rhys Rosenblum spotlights global seafood at Q56 Restaurant & Cocktails, and Park Avenue Spa & Fitness offers plenty of ways to get the office off your mind.

Hotel services *Baby-sitting. Beauty salon. Cell-phone rental. Fitness center. Gift shop. Nintendo, PlayStation and VCR rental. Parking. Spa. Valet.* **Room services** *Wireless high-speed Internet. Refrigerator. Room service (24hr).*

The Waldorf-Astoria

301 Park Ave at 50th St (212-355-3000, 800-924-3673; www.waldorf.com). Subway: E, V to Lexington Ave–53rd St; 6 to 51st St. **Rates** *$275–$450 single; $300–$450 double; $400–$900 suite. 1,425 rooms.* **Credit** *AmEx, DC, Disc, MC, V.*

The famous Waldorf salad made its debut in 1896 at the city's largest hotel—later demolished to make way for the Empire State Building. An Art Deco Waldorf opened in 1931, and now has protected status as a Historic Hotel. It still caters to New York's high society (guests have included Princess Grace, Sophia Loren and a long list of presidents).

Hotel services *Beauty salon. Cell-phone rental. Fitness center. Spa. Valet.* **Room services** *Kitchenette in some suites. VCR on request.*

The Warwick New York

65 W 54th St at Sixth Ave (212-247-2700, 800-223-4099; www.warwickhotelny.com). Subway: E, V to Fifth Ave–53rd St; F to 57th St. **Rates** *$199–$395 single/double; $425–$1,250 suite. 426 rooms.* **Credit** *AmEx, DC, MC, V.*

Built by William Randolph Hearst in 1927 and later frequented by Elvis and the Beatles, the Warwick is still polished and gleaming. Rooms are exceptionally large by midtown standards. The top-floor Suite of the Stars was once the home of Cary Grant, and comes complete with a wraparound balcony.

Hotel services *Baby-sitting. Cell-phone rental. Fitness center. Valet.* **Room services** *High-speed Internet.*

W New York–Times Square

1567 Broadway at 47th St (212-930-7400, 877-W HOTELS; www.whotels.com). Subway: N, R, W to 49th St; 1, 9 to 50th St. **Rates** *$259–$339 single/double; $499–$2,500 suite. 509 rooms.* **Credit** *AmEx, DC, Disc, MC, V.*

Starwood CEO Barry Sternlicht has founded his international W brand on four main *W*s: warm, welcoming, wired and witty. Two more *W*s come in with the hotel concierge's motto: whatever, whenever. You need a bathtub filled with chocolate? Consider it done. NYC's fifth and flashiest W location has a street-level vestibule with a waterfall, but no front desk (reception is on the seventh floor). To your right, the Living Room is a massive sprawl of white leather seating. Each room features a floating-glass desk and a sleek bathroom, but it's the bed-to-ceiling headboard mirror and sexy room-service menu that get the mind racing. Steve Hanson's Blue Fin *(212-918-1400)* serves stellar sushi and cocktails.

Hotel services *Fitness center. Gift shop. Spa. Valet. Video library.* **Room services** *CD and DVD players. VCR.*

The best Star stays

New York hotels have hosted more celebrities than Donatella Versace's Villa Il Palazzetto. Here are the places famous for putting up...

...jet-set fashion designers

The **Mercer** (*see p39*) is home to Marc Jacobs when he's in town.

...punk rock stars

Dee Dee Ramone lived in the **Chelsea Hotel** (*see p56*) for 28 years.

...women only

Grace Kelly, Liza Minnelli and Candice Bergen all stayed at the Barbizon Hotel for Women, now the **Melrose Hotel** (*see p62*).

...every celebrity under the sun

Soho House (*see p39*) is the unofficial crash pad for celebs, from Ewan McGregor to founding member David Bowie.

...ghosts of celebrities past

The Beatles frequently booked the **Warwick New York** (*see left*); Cary Grant resided there for 12 years.

Rene, owner of the **Harlem Flophouse**. *See p64.*

Alicja, housekeeper at the **Kitano**. *See p49.*

Roman, elevator operator at the **Pierre Hotel**. *See p61.*

Daniel, bellhop at **60 Thompson**. *See p39.*

Other locations *W New York, 541 Lexington Ave at 49th St (212-755-1200); W New York–The Court, 130 E 39th St between Park Ave South and Lexington Ave (212-685-1100); W New York–The Tuscany, 120 E 39th St between Park Ave South and Lexington Ave (212-686-1600); W New York–Union Square, 201 Park Ave South at 17th St (212-253-9119).*

Moderate ($100 to $200)

Casablanca Hotel

147 W 43rd St between Sixth Ave and Broadway (212-869-1212, 800-922-7225; www.casablanca hotel.com). Subway: B, D, F, V to 42nd St–Bryant Park. N, Q, R, W, 42nd St S, 1, 2, 3, 9, 7 to 42nd St–Times Sq. **Rates** *$179–$295 single/double; $265–$375 suite. 48 rooms.* **Credit** *AmEx, DC, MC, V.*

Run by the same people who own Hotel Elysée, Hotel Giraffe and the Library Hotel (*see p47 and p49*), this 48-room boutique hotel has a cheerful Moroccan theme. Rick's Café serves free wine and cheese to guests Monday through Saturday. Breakfast and a copy of *Casablanca* are complimentary.

Hotel services *Baby-sitting. Cell-phone rental. Cybercafé. Dry cleaning (24hr). Pass to nearby gym. Spa. Valet. Video library.* **Room services** *CD player. VCR. Wi-Fi.*

Hotel Edison

228 W 47th St at Broadway (212-840-5000, 800-637-7070; www.edisonhotelnyc.com). Subway: N, R, W to 49th St; 1, 9 to 50th St. **Rates** *$130 single; $170 double ($15 for each extra person, 4-person maximum); $175–$220 suite. 1,000 rooms.* **Credit** *AmEx, DC, Disc, MC, V.*

Theater lovers flock to this newly renovated Art Deco hotel for its affordable rates and convenient location. Rooms are of standard size, but are decidedly spruced-up. The coffeeshop Cafe Edison *(212-840-5000),* just off the lobby, is a longtime favorite of Broadway actors and their fans—Neil Simon was so smitten with the place that he put it in a play.

Hotel services *Fitness center. Gift shop. Tour desk. Valet.* **Room services** *High-speed Internet.*

Hotel 41

206 W 41st St between Seventh and Eighth Aves (877-847-4444; www.hotel41.com). Subway: N, Q, R, W, 42nd St S, 1, 2, 3, 9, 7 to 42nd St–Times Sq. **Rates** *$129–$149 single/double; $269–$489 suite. 47 rooms.* **Credit** *AmEx, Disc, MC, V.*

Hotel 41 looks as though it would accept payment in euros—the lobby is small and sleek, and the white-walled rooms channel that Continental combination of efficiency and charm. Although its looks are mod cool, the tiny boutique hotel feels comfy warm: Reading lamps extend from pale-wood headboards, and triple-paned windows effectively filter out the cacophony from Times Square below. Bar 41 serves breakfast, light bites and drinks.

Hotel services *Baby-sitting. CD and DVD library. Espresso bar. Valet.* **Room services** *CD and DVD players. High-speed Internet. Room service (24hr).*

Hotel Metro

45 W 35th St between Fifth and Sixth Aves (212-947-2500, 800-356-3870; www.hotelmetronyc.com). Subway: B, D, F, V, N, Q, R, W to 34th St–Herald Sq. **Rates** *$155–$325 single/double; $190–$400 suite. 179 rooms.* **Credit** *AmEx, DC, MC, V.*

It's not posh, but the Metro has good service and a convenient location. The lobby—decorated with black-and-white portraits of Hollywood legends—exudes a charmingly retro vibe. Rooms are small but neat and clean, and the rooftop bar of Metro Grill *(212-947-2500)* offers splendid views.

Hotel services *Beauty salon. Complimentary breakfast. Fitness center. Library. Ticket desk.* **Room services** *High-speed Internet. Refrigerator.*

Hotel Pennsylvania

401 Seventh Ave between 32nd and 33rd Sts (212-736-5000, 800-223-8585; www.hotelpenn.com). Subway: A, C, E, 1, 2, 3, 9 to 34th–Penn Station. **Rates** *$100–$169 single/double; $350–$1,000 suite. 1,705 rooms.* **Credit** *AmEx, DC, Disc, MC, V.*

Built in 1919 by the Pennsylvania Railroad and designed by McKim, Mead & White, Hotel Pennsylvania is one of the city's largest hotels. Its reasonable rates and good location (directly opposite Madison Square Garden and Penn Station, and one block south of Macy's) make it a popular tourist choice. Rooms are basic, with a splash of style. The hotel's Cafe Rouge Ballroom once hosted such swing-era greats as Duke Ellington and the Glenn Miller Orchestra.

Hotel services *Baby-sitting. Fitness center. Gift shop. Modem port. Ticket desk. Valet.* **Room services** *Internet.*

The Hudson

356 W 58th St between Eighth and Ninth Aves (212-554-6000; www.hudsonhotel.com). Subway: A, C, B, D, 1, 9 to 59th St–Columbus Circle. **Rates** *$175–$260 single/double; $330–$5,000 suite. 803 rooms.* **Credit** *AmEx, DC, Disc, MC, V.*

Welcome to the city's most brilliantly designed hotel. This drop-dead-gorgeous space is the fourth New York palace in Ian Schrager's hip hotel kingdom (Morgans, Paramount and Royalton). Sip one of the signature cocktails and absorb the plush surroundings: A lush courtyard is shaded with enormous potted trees, a rooftop terrace overlooks the Hudson River, and a glass-roofed lobby with imported English ivy is crawling with beautiful people. The Hudson Cafeteria and three bars lure the fabulous.

Hotel services *Cell-phone rental. Fitness center. Rooftop terrace.* **Room services** *CD player. High-speed Internet.*

Other locations *Morgans, 237 Madison Ave between 37th and 38th Sts (212-686-0300, 800-334-3408); Paramount, 235 W 46th St between Broadway and Eighth Ave (212-764-5500, 800-225-7474); Royalton, 44 W 44th St between Fifth and Sixth Aves (212-869-4400, 800-635-9013).*

Suite retreat Find peace and relative quiet above Times Square at **Hotel 41**. *See p54.*

Le Marquis

12 E 31st St between Fifth and Madison Aves (212-889-6363; www.lemarquisny.com). Subway: 6 to 33rd St. **Rates** *$179–$400 single/double; $279–$450 suite. 120 rooms.* **Credit** *AmEx, DC, Disc, MC, V.*

Rooms at this delightful hotel are style-conscious, with black-and-white photographs of New York streetscapes on the walls and Frette robes and Aveda products in the bathroom. The in-house 12:31 bar offers cocktails and light nibbles. And "good night" service at Le Marquis means a chocolate on your pillow and a next-day weather forecast.

Hotel services *DVD library. Fitness center. Valet.* **Room services** *CD and DVD players. High-speed Internet. Nintendo.*

The Marcel

201 E 24th St at Third Ave (212-696-3800; www.nycityhotels.com). Subway: 6 to 23rd St. **Rates** *$179–$220 single/double. 97 rooms.* **Credit** *AmEx, DC, Disc, MC, V.*

The sleek Marcel is frequented by fashion-industry types because of its easy access to downtown, midtown, and the Flatiron and Garment Districts. Compact rooms have nice design touches, like light blue walls with black and white photography, modern wood furniture and multicolored padded headboards. Spread *(212-683-8880),* the hotel's sexy lounge, serves pricey designer snacks, but guests looking for heartier fare will find many options on Park Avenue South, just a short walk away.

Hotel services *Cappuccino bar (24hr). Cell-phone rental. Complimentary breakfast. Ticket desk. Video library.* **Room services** *CD player. Nintendo. PlayStation. VCR on request.*

Metropolitan Hotel

569 Lexington Ave at 51st St (212-752-7000, 800-836-6471). Subway: E, V to Lexington Ave–53rd St; 6 to 51st St. **Rates** *$159–$259 single/double; $229–$699 suite. 722 rooms.* **Credit** *AmEx, DC, Disc, MC, V.*

Unveiled in 1961 as the Summit, this tropical-looking Art Deco hotel was the talk of the town. Two decades later, the look was toned down to match its new identity as the Loews New York Hotel. In 2000, architect Morris Lapidus—designer of many '50s-era hotels—returned the building to its original Coffeeshop Moderne look. The Lexington Grill and Lexy Lounge offer modern American cuisine, cocktails and late-night wine and cheese. Toiletries in the business-class rooms are just like those at home: cotton balls, Q-tips and nail files.

Hotel services *Baby-sitting. Fitness center. Gift shop. Manicurist. Ticket desk. Valet.* **Room services** *High-speed Internet. VCR rental.*

The Roger Smith

501 Lexington Ave between 47th and 48th Sts (212-755-1400, 800-445-0277; www.rogersmith.com). Subway: E, V to Lexington Ave–53rd St; 6 to 51st St. **Rates** *$195–$235 single/double; $215–$255 junior suite; $275–$400 suite. 130 rooms.* **Credit** *AmEx, DC, Disc, MC, V.*

Owned by the family of artist James Knowles, the Roger Smith is popular with touring bands. A few of Knowles's pieces decorate the lobby. Rooms are large, colorful and uniquely furnished.

Hotel services *Baby-sitting. Complimentary breakfast. Valet. Video library.* **Room services** *CD player. Coffeemaker. Free local phone calls. Kitchenette in suites. Refrigerator. VCR.*

The Roosevelt Hotel

45 E 45th St at Madison Ave (212-661-9600, 888-TEDDY-NY; www.therooseveltotel.com). Subway: 42nd St S, 4, 5, 6, 7 to 42nd St–Grand Central. **Rates** *$179–$289 single/double; $205–$2,000 suite. 1,013 rooms.* **Credit** *AmEx, DC, Disc, MC, V.*

Several films have been shot here, including *Wall Street, The French Connection* and, more recently, *Maid in Manhattan.* Built in 1924, this enormous hotel was once a haven for celebs and socialites, and the nostalgic grandeur lives on in the lobby, with its 27-foot fluted columns, acres of marble and huge sprays of flowers. The Palm Room serves snacks under a blue-sky mural, and the Madison Club Lounge *(212-885-6192)* dispenses cocktails in a clubby setting.

Hotel services *Ballroom. Fitness center. Gift shop. Ticket desk. Valet.* **Room services** *CD player and VCR in suites. High-speed Internet. Nintendo.*

The Shoreham

33 W 55th St between Fifth and Sixth Aves (212-247-6700). Subway: E, V to Fifth Ave–53rd St; F to 57th St. **Rates** *$179–$450 single/double; $450–$1,500 suite. 174 rooms.* **Credit** *AmEx, DC, Disc, MC, V.*

For review, *see p50* **The Roger Williams**.

ThirtyThirty

30 E 30th St between Madison Ave and Park Ave South (212-689-1900; www.thirtythirty-nyc.com). Subway: 6 to 28th St. **Rates** *$110–$215 single/double; $160–$305 suite. 250 rooms.* **Credit** *AmEx, DC, Disc, MC, V.*

ThirtyThirty boasts a stylish modern feel, as well as the kind of luxuries that lure budget business travelers. Ambient music sets the tone in the spare, fashionable lobby, which stretches an entire block. Standard rooms are small but sleek with clean lines and textured fabrics. Executive floor rooms are slightly larger, with nifty workspaces and slate bathrooms. The hotel's restaurant, Zanna, serves Mediterranean delicacies. ThirtyThirty's sister, On the Ave Hotel (*see p63*), offers similar style for travelers on a budget.

Hotel services *Florist. Pass to nearby gym. Ticket desk.* **Room services** *CD player. Internet.*

High style, low budget

Looking for maximum style at a minimal price? If you know where to look, you *can* find boutique hotels that offer stylish settings, superior services and modern amenities—all for about $100 a night. These six fantastic finds are scattered throughout the city, so start by choosing your neighborhood.

From Harlem to Houston Street, each 'hood has its own distinct flavor. The East Village is home to a venerable punk-rock culture, and to some of the city's coolest cheap restaurants and bars. It harbors some equally eccentric and inexpensive accommodations. Go northwest to up-and-coming Hell's Kitchen and you'll find sleek design for a steal. It's not surprising that Chelsea, with its lively gay community and many art galleries, hosts the greatest concentration of bohemian hotels. Madonna lived in this nabe in her early dancer days; in fact, a MADONNA SLEPT HERE sign could hang on the wall at several of these hotels. Farther north, the Upper West Side boasts rooms with refined elegance and modish decor, just steps away from Central Park.

To get the lowest prices listed here, be sure to book well in advance. Many hotels feature different peak and off-peak seasons, so be sure to plan ahead to secure the bottom rate. Giving up a private bathroom (for a shared one down the hall) will also help knock down your room rate. Remember to budget in the city's additional 13.25 percent hotel tax and $2-per-night occupancy tax.

Chelsea Hotel

222 W 23rd St between Seventh and Eighth Aves (212-243-3700; www.hotelchelsea.com). Subway: C, E, 1, 9 to 23rd St. **Rates** *$99–$135 single/double with shared bath; $165–$185 single/double with private bath; $225 double studio; $325 suite. 400 rooms.* **Credit** *AmEx, DC, Disc, MC, V.*

Built in 1884, this funky bohemian haunt is still one of the coolest places to stay. In 1912, *Titanic* survivors stayed here; other former residents include Dee Dee Ramone, Dylan Thomas, Mark Twain and Madonna. No evidence remains of the hotel's infamous association with the murder of Nancy Spungen by Sex Pistol Sid Vicious—Sid and Nancy's room is now an office space. The lobby doubles as an art gallery, showing work by hotel guests past and present. Rooms are generally large, with high ceilings. The basement cocktail lounge Serena *(212-255-4646)* lures a sleek crowd with nightly DJs. Cheap sleepers take note: The $99 rate applies only during the off-season (January through March); otherwise, singles start at $110.

Hotel services *Beauty salon. Concierge. Dry cleaning. Parking. Restaurant. Valet.* **Room services** *High-speed Internet. Kitchenettes or refrigerators in some rooms. Voice mail.*

The Time

224 W 49th St between Broadway and Eighth Ave (212-320-2900, 877-846-3692; www.thetimeny.com). Subway: N, R, W to 49th St. **Rates** *$189–$239 single/double; $289–$359 suite; $2,500–$6,000 penthouse suite. 193 rooms.* **Credit** *AmEx, DC, Disc, MC, V.*

This Adam Tihany–designed boutique hotel is all about color: You'll feel it, smell it, taste it and live it. Guest rooms are furnished entirely in red, blue or yellow, artfully accented with matching jelly beans, reading materials, and a chromatically inspired scent. Continental breakfast is included. Océo, a new global cuisine restaurant, is slated to open in spring 2004.

Hotel services *Cell-phone rental. Fitness center. Shopping services. Ticket desk.* **Room services** *CD player. High-speed Internet. VCR.*

Budget (less than $100)

Broadway Inn

264 W 46th St at Eighth Ave (212-997-9200, 800-826-6300; www.broadwayinn.com). Subway: A, C, E to 42nd St–Port Authority. **Rates** *$99–$185 single/double; $199–$275 suite. 41 rooms.* **Credit** *AmEx, DC, Disc, MC, V.*

Theater junkies, take note: This endearing little hotel can arrange a 35- to 40-percent discount on theater tickets; it also offers several Broadway dinner-and-show packages. The warm lobby has exposed-brick walls, ceiling fans and shelves loaded with bedtime reading material. The basic guest rooms and suites get a lot of natural light and are fairly priced. On the downside: There are no elevators, and the hotel is strict about its three-night minimum policy on weekends.

Hotel services *Complimentary breakfast. Concierge. Fax. Fitness center. Safe.* **Room services** *Alarm clock. Cable TV. Hair dryer. High-speed Internet. Kitchenette in suites. Radio. Safe.*

Carlton Arms Hotel

160 E 25th St at Third Ave (212-679-0680; www.carltonarms.com). Subway: 6 to 23rd St. **Rates** *$60–$75 single; $80–$95 double; $99–$112 triple.* **Credit** *MC, V.*

Bohemian rhapsody Artists, musicians and muses bed down at the **Chelsea Hotel**.

Chelsea Lodge

318 W 20th St between Eighth and Ninth Aves (212-243-4499; www.chelsealodge.com). Subway: C, E to 23rd St. **Rates** *$90–$105 single/double with shared bath; $135–$150 deluxe with private bath; $195–$225 suite with private bath (each additional person $15; maximum 4 guests). 26 rooms.* **Credit** *AmEx, DC, Disc, MC, V.*

In the spring of 1998, husband-and-wife team Paul and G.G. Weisenfeld turned a landmark brownstone into a boutique hotel for style-conscious budget travelers. The 22 rooms and four suites have new beds, televisions, showers and air conditioners. Although most are fairly small, the rooms are so aggressively charming that reservations fill up quickly. (*Psst!* There's no sign outside, so make sure to write down the address.)

Room services *Cable TV. Hair dryer. VCR and kitchenette in suites.*

Chelsea Star Hotel

300 W 30th St at Eighth Ave (212-244-7827, 877-827-NYNY; www.starhotelny.com). Subway: A, C, E to 34 St–Penn Station. **Rates** *$30* ▶

The Carlton Arms Art Project started in the late '80s when a small group of creative types brought new paint and fresh ideas to a run-down shelter. Today, the site is home to a cheerful, basic budget hotel with themed rooms and brightly decorated corridors, each by a different artist (check out the English-cottage room). Discounts are offered for students, overseas guests and patrons on weekly stays. Most rooms have in-room sinks but shared baths; tack on an extra $15 for a private bathroom.
Hotel services *Café. Telephone in lobby.* **Room services** *Alarm clock. Hair dryer. Internet.*

Habitat Hotel
130 E 57th St at Lexington Ave (212-753-8841; www.habitatny.com). Subway: N, R, W to Lexington Ave–59th St; 4, 5, 6 to 59th St. ***Rates*** *$75–$165 single/double; $155–$250 deluxe/suites. 450 rooms.* ***Credit*** *AmEx, DC, Disc, MC, V.*
A $20 million overhaul turned what was once a dilapidated women's residence into this reasonably priced hotel. Don't let the chic lobby fool you—rooms are as small and standard as they come. If you're searching for style, your only option is the spacious new executive floor, whose rooms come with designer bathrooms, parlors and elevated rates. The hotel also houses a Kenneth Cole store and Opia, a plush Mediterranean bistro with terrace seating and an elegant lounge. Habitat's sister hotels, On the Ave Hotel (*see p63*) and ThirtyThirty (*see p56*), are a tad pricier, but they offer better value and higher style.
Hotel services *Business center. Concierge. Fitness center. Gift shop. High-speed Internet. Parking. Restaurant.* **Room services** *Alarm clock. Cable TV. Hair dryer. Room service. Voice mail.*

The Herald Square Hotel
19 W 31st St between Fifth Ave and Broadway (212-279-4017, 800-727-1888; www.heraldsquarehotel.com). Subway: B, D, F, V, N, Q, R, W to 34th St–Herald Sq. **Rates** *$60–$120 single/double; $130 triple; $140 quad. 130 rooms.* **Credit** *AmEx, Disc, MC, V.*

▸ High style, low budget (continued)

per person in dorms; $69–$105 single–quad with shared bath; $129–$149 double with private bath; $159–$179 suite. 30 rooms. **Credit** *AmEx, MC, V.*
This whimsical hotel's claim to fame: Madonna lived here during the early '80s. Of the 16 cheaper, shared-bath theme rooms, the Shakespeare and Madame Butterfly are your best bets (unless you have a thing for floor-to-ceiling red rubber, in which case you might try begging for the Belle du Jour). A major renovation more than doubled the hotel's size; there are now 18 superior rooms and deluxe suites with custom mahogany furnishings, flat-panel TVs and stylish, private full baths. Ultracheap, hostel-style shared dorm rooms are also available.
Hotel services *Bicycle and in-line skate rental. Internet kiosk. Laundry. Safe-deposit boxes.* **Room services** *Cable TV. DVD, flat-panel TV and/or high-speed Internet in some rooms.*

East Village Bed & Coffee
110 Ave C between 7th and 8th Sts (212-533-4175; www.bedandcoffee.com). Subway: F, V to Lower East Side–Second Ave; 6 to Astor Pl. **Rates** *$65–$80 single; $75–$90 double. 8 rooms.* **Credit** *AmEx, MC, V.*
Anne Edris has transformed an unassuming East Village walk-up into a charismatic bed without the breakfast (morning caffeine is provided). The living room, bathrooms and fully equipped kitchen are all shared; the eight guest rooms come with eclectic furnishings and quirky themes. In nice weather, sip your java in the private garden.
Hotel services *Bicycle rental. Digital cable TV. Free local phone. Garden. High-speed Internet. Kitchen. Stereo. VCR. Video library.*
Other location *Second Home on Second Avenue, 221 Second Ave between 13th and 14th Sts (212-677-3161; www.secondhome.citysearch.com).*

The Gershwin Hotel
7 E 27th St between Fifth and Madison Aves (212-545-8000; www.gershwinhotel.com). Subway: R, W, 6 to 28th St. **Rates** *$33–$53 per person in 4- to 8-bed dorm; $99–$200 for one to three people in private room; $179–$289 suite. 60 beds in dorms; 133 private rooms.* **Credit** *AmEx, MC, V.*
Works by Lichtenstein and an original Warhol soup-can painting adorn the lobby of this pop-art themed hotel. Rates are extremely reasonable for a location just off Fifth Avenue. If you can afford a suite, book the Lindfors (named after the building's designer), which has screen-printed walls and a nifty sitting room. A rotating roster of entertainment (poetry readings, stand-up comedy, improv groups) livens up the evenings. In summer, the hotel's rooftop hosts Manhattan

Housed in the original Life building, the Herald Square Hotel retains its cherub-adorned entrance and corridors lined with framed *Life* illustrations. Rooms are small and basic, but tidy, and most have private bathrooms. Room discounts are offered to students with valid ID.
Hotel services *Concierge. High-speed Internet. Safe.* **Room services** *DirecTV. Modem line. Voice mail.*

Hotel 31

120 E 31st St between Park Ave South and Lexington Ave (212-685-3060; www.hotel31.com). Subway: 6 to 33rd St. **Rates** *$85–$120 single/double; $125 triple. 70 rooms.* **Credit** *MC, V.*
For review, *see p43* **Hotel 17**.

Murray Hill Inn

143 E 30th St between Lexington and Third Aves (212-683-6900, 888-996-6376; www.murrayhillinn.com). Subway: 6 to 28th St. **Rates** *$75–$95 double with shared bath; $95–$149 single/double with private bath. 50 rooms.* **Credit** *AmEx, MC, V.*
A recent renovation added carpets and new bathrooms—most of which are private—to this affordable inn. Discounted weekly and monthly rates are available. Book well in advance or try the sister locations: Amsterdam Inn, Central Park Hostel and Union Square Inn (*see p64 and p44*).
Hotel services *Alarm clock. Complimentary breakfast. Internet.* **Room services** *Cable TV. Hair dryer.*

Pickwick Arms

230 E 51st St between Second and Third Aves (212-355-0300, 800-742-5945; www.pickwickarms.com). Subway: E, V to Lexington Ave–53rd St; 6 to 51st St. **Rates** *$79–$109 single; $114–$139 double. 370 rooms.* **Credit** *AmEx, DC, MC, V.*
The decor is simple and functional, but the rooms are clean and bright, and most have private bathrooms. (Some share an adjoining facility; others share a bathroom down the hall). There are two on-site restaurants, as well as a rooftop garden.
Hotel services *Bar. Internet in lobby. Restaurants. Safe.* **Room services** *Cable TV. Voice mail.*

Head rest You'll find padded headboards and plump duvets at the **Hotel Belleclaire**.

Screenings, a series of undiscovered international feature films.
Hotel services *Concierge. Conference facility. Roof garden. Transportation desk.* **Room services** *Alarm clock. Modem line. TV in private rooms.*

Hotel Belleclaire

250 W 77th St at Broadway (212-362-7700; www.hotelbelleclaire.com). Subway: 1, 9 to 79th St. **Rates** *$99–$109 single with shared bath; $114–$189 single/double with private bath; $199–$229 suite. 185 rooms.* **Credit** *AmEx, DC, Disc, MC, V.*
Housed in a landmark building near Lincoln Center and Central Park, the Belleclaire is a steal for savvy budget travelers. Rooms feature goose-down comforters, sleek padded headboards and mod lighting fixtures. Refrigerators come in every room—perfect for chilling your protein shake while you're hitting the new state-of-the-art fitness center.
Hotel services *Business center. Cell-phone rental. Dry cleaning. Fitness center. Gift shop. Massage room. Parking.* **Room services** *Alarm clock. Cable TV. CD player. Hair dryer. Internet. Nintendo. Refrigerator. Room service. Video library. Voice mail.*

Nice package The spa at the **Mandarin Oriental** is an urban oasis. *See p61.*

Hostels

Chelsea Center

313 W 29th St between Eighth and Ninth Aves (212-643-0214; www.chelseacenterhostel.com). Subway: A, C, E to 34th St–Penn Station. **Rates** *$25–$30 per person in dorm. 20 beds.* **Credit** *Cash only.*

This small, welcoming hostel has the feel of a student dormitory, with shared rooms and a common kitchen and living room (women-only dorm rooms are available). The bathrooms are clean, and there's a patio garden out back. There's no air-conditioning or smoking in rooms, but the price includes Continental breakfast. There is a second location in the East Village; visit the website for more information.

Hotel services *Fax. Garden. Internet. Kitchen. TV.*

Above 59th Street

Deluxe ($350 and up)

The Carlyle

35 E 76th St between Madison and Park Aves (212-744-1600, 800-227-5737; www.thecarlyle.com). Subway: 6 to 77th St. **Rates** *$495–$825 single/double; $900–$3,200 suite. 180 rooms.* **Credit** *AmEx, DC, Disc, MC, V.*

An icon of New York glamour for more than 70 years, the Carlyle has attracted generations of famous guests—especially those who value privacy. The lobby (with its Matisse and Picasso artworks) and Bemelmans Bar (lined with illustrator Ludwig Bemelmans's hand-painted murals) are popular with tourists and old-money New Yorkers alike. Bathrooms are stocked with Kiehl's products. Café Carlyle (*see p273*) has been the roost of cabaret singer Bobby Short for more than three decades.

Hotel services *Baby-sitting. Cell-phone rental. Dry cleaning (24hr). Fitness center. Gift shop. Valet. Video library.* **Room services** *CD player. High-speed Internet. VCR.*

Hotel Plaza Athénée

37 E 64th St between Madison and Park Aves (212-734-9100, 800-447-8800; www.plaza-athenee.com). Subway: F to Lexington Ave–63rd St. **Rates** *$495–$615 single/double; $1,100–$3,600 suite. 150 rooms.* **Credit** *AmEx, DC, Disc, MC, V.*

On a quiet, tree-lined residential block, the Hotel Plaza Athénée impresses discerning guests right from the start with Italian-marble floors and French antique furniture—and that's just the lobby. Guest rooms are equally luxurious, with fresh-cut flowers and plush courtesy robes. European-style suites feature a terrace and a solarium. Dine on creative American cuisine at the restaurant, Arabelle *(212-606-4647)*, or retreat to the private bar to spy on media-shy celebs.

Hotel services *Fitness center. Overnight shoe shine.* **Room services** *CD player. Complimentary newspaper. Speakerphone.*

The Lowell Hotel

28 E 63rd St between Madison and Park Aves (212-838-1400, 800-221-4444). Subway: N, R, W to Lexington Ave–59th St; 4, 5, 6 to 59th St. **Rates** *$445–$575 single/double; $775–$4,575 suite. 70 rooms.* **Credit** *AmEx, DC, Disc, MC, V.*

Renovated in October 2003, this petite charmer is in a landmark Art Deco building in a posh sector of the Upper East Side. Rooms feature marble baths, Scandinavian down comforters and wood-burning fireplaces in suites. The garden suite has two private terraces and a manicured flower bed. The Post House and Pembroke Room are the hotel's two white-tablecloth dining options.
Hotel services *Baby-sitting. Cell-phone rental. Fitness center. Valet.* **Room services** *CD player. DVD player on request. Kitchenette. VCR.*

The Mandarin Oriental New York

80 Columbus Circle at 60th St (212-805-8800; www.mandarinoriental.com). Subway: A, C, B, D, 1, 9 to 59th St–Columbus Circle. **Rates** *$595–$895 single/double; $1,600–$12,000 suite. 251 rooms.* **Credit** *AmEx, DC, Disc, MC, V.*
After two years of construction, the Mandarin Oriental finally opened its polished doors in November 2003, in the massive Time Warner complex in Columbus Circle. The New York location of this luxurious chain offers serene, superplush rooms with breathtaking views of Central Park, framed by the surrounding skyline. Inside the hotel, you'll find a full-service spa and fitness center (complete with pool). Dine on refined French-Japanese cuisine at Asiate, located on the 35th floor, or stop in for a cocktail at MObar. The Lobby Lounge offers breakfast, afternoon tea and late-night desserts.
Hotel services *Baby-sitting. Cell-phone rental. Dry cleaning (24hr). DVD library. Fitness center. Gift shop. Valet.* **Room services** *CD and DVD players. High-speed Internet. Room service (24hr).*

The Mark

25 E 77th St between Fifth and Madison Aves (212-744-4300, 800-843-6275; www.themarkhotel.com). Subway: 6 to 77th St. **Rates** *$570–$600 single; $630–$660 double; $815–$2,500 suite. 176 rooms.* **Credit** *AmEx, DC, Disc, MC, V.*
Towering potted palms and arched mirrors line the entryway to this cheerful European-style hotel. The marble lobby, decorated with 18th-century Piranesi prints and Veuve Clicquot magnums, is usually swarming with mature, dressy international guests and white-gloved bellmen. Especially popular are the clubby Mark's Bar and the more elegant restaurant, Mark's *(212-879-1864).*
Hotel services *Baby-sitting. Cell-phone rental. Dry cleaning (24hr). Fitness center. Free shuttle to Wall Street and Theater District. Valet. Video library.* **Room services** *CD player. High-speed Internet. Kitchenette. Nintendo. Printer. VCR.*

The Phillips Club

155 W 66th St between Broadway and Amsterdam Ave (212-835-8800, 877-854-8800; www.phillipsclub.com). Subway: 1, 9 to 66th St–Lincoln Ctr. **Rates** *$420–$1,300 suite. 120 rooms.* **Credit** *AmEx, DC, Disc, MC, V.*
The lobby of this classy extended-stay hotel glows with lit marble and warm colors. Across from Lincoln Center, the Phillips Club is popular with patrons of the performing arts. Suites function like timeshares, available for short visits, leasing and club ownership. Each suite has a full kitchen and includes access to the luxurious Reebok Sports Club. On the ground floor, Balducci's (a gourmet grocer and the provider of the hotel's room service) ensures that all the ingredients for a fancy meal are close at hand.
Hotel services *Baby-sitting. Dry cleaning (24hr). Fitness center. Spa. Valet. Video library.* **Room services** *CD player. High-speed Internet. Kitchenette. VCR.*

The Pierre Hotel

2 E 61st St at Fifth Ave (212-838-8000, 800-PIERRE-4; www.fourseasons.com/pierre). Subway: N, R, W to Fifth Ave–59th St. **Rates** *$425–$950 single; $475–$995 double; $625–$3,800 suite. 201 rooms.* **Credit** *AmEx, DC, Disc, MC, V.*
The Pierre has been seducing guests since 1930 with old New York grandeur and accommodating service. Front rooms overlook Central Park, and wares from ritzy neighboring stores are on display in the lobby. In addition to dry cleaning, the hotel offers hand laundering for precious garments. There are three restaurants, including the opulent Cafe Pierre.

The best Services

These are the top hotels for servicing…

…your lame sex life
Soho House (*see p39*) stocks rooms with sexy thangs, from champagne and Ben & Jerry's ice cream to a copy of the *Kama Sutra.*

…your insomnia
The sleep concierge is on call at the **Benjamin** (*see p45*), ready to help you select from the 11 offerings on the hotel's "pillow menu."

…your promotion
The **Bryant Park** (*see p47*) houses everything you need for a bang-up business meeting, including a boardroom with video conferencing and a 70-seat screening room with built-in desks.

…your fashion fetish
Need a new pair of Jimmy Choos, but don't want to get out of your pj's? **Chambers** (*see p47*) offers personal shopping from Henri Bendel.

…your needs before they arise
The **Alex** (*see p44*) keeps personal profiles on regular guests. Love pistachio ice cream? Expect to find it in your fridge when you arrive.

Hotel services *Baby-sitting. Beauty salon. Cell-phone rental. Dry cleaning (24hr). Fitness center. Free shuttle to Theater District. Theater desk. Valet.* **Room services** *High-speed Internet. In-room exercise equipment. VCR on request.*

The Ritz-Carlton New York, Central Park

50 Central Park South between Fifth and Sixth Aves (212-308-9100; www.ritzcarlton.com). Subway: F to 57th St; N, R, W to Fifth Ave–59th St. **Rates** *$650–$975 single/double; $1,395–$12,500 suite. 277 rooms.* **Credit** *AmEx, DC, Disc, MC, V.*
Gilded doors swing open, a beaming doorman greets you, and bejeweled patrons drift through the high-ceilinged lobby of this renovated 1930s hotel. Frill seekers will adore the fresh flowers in the sleeping quarters. The swank on-site La Prairie at the Ritz-Carlton Spa offers treatments like a champagne-and-caviar firming facial and jet-lag therapy. The elegant dining option, Atelier *(212-521-6125)*, boasts suede walls and a chef formerly of Jean Georges. The coolest amenity: a "technology butler" is available to help you download your new MP3s or simply recover your corrupted data for tomorrow's meeting. For the Battery Park location, *see p39.*
Hotel services *Cell-phone rental. Fitness center with personal trainers. Free overnight shoe shine. Free shuttle within midtown. Laundry drop-off.* **Room services** *DVD player. High-speed Internet.*

Trump International Hotel & Tower

1 Central Park West at Columbus Circle (212-299-1000, 888-448-7867; www.trumpintl.com). Subway: A, C, B, D, 1, 9 to 59th St–Columbus Circle. **Rates** *$550–$595 single/double; $795–$1,725 suite. 167 rooms.* **Credit** *AmEx, DC, Disc, MC, V.*
After the first phase of a $10 million renovation, Donald Trump's glass-and-steel skyscraper towers are more sparkling than the window cases at Tiffany's. Remodeled suites in green, sand and cinnamon tones feature 42-inch plasma TVs and breathtaking views of Central Park. Each guest is assigned a personal assistant and in-room chef. Better yet, head downstairs to Jean Georges *(212-299-3900)*, the restaurant named for its four-star chef, Jean-Georges Vongerichten.
Hotel services. *Cell-phone rental. DVD library. Fitness center. Personal attaché service.* **Room services** *CD and DVD players. Computer. Kitchenette. Telescope.*

Expensive ($200 to $350)

The Melrose Hotel

140 E 63rd St between Lexington and Third Aves (212-838-5700; www.melrosehotel.com). Subway: N, R, W to Lexington Ave–59th St; 4, 5, 6 to 59th St. **Rates** *$199–$269 single/double; $349–$1,200 suite. 306 rooms.* **Credit** *AmEx, DC, Disc, MC, V.*
From 1927 to 1981, the former Barbizon Hotel was an exclusive women's-only hotel, host to the likes of Grace Kelly and Liza Minnelli. In 2002, the building reopened as the Melrose, spiffed up with cherrywood furniture and gilded mirrors, and with the original marble floor restored. Tower suites boast landscaped balconies with Corinthian pillars and fab views of the city lights. The Library Bar features smart cocktails and a full menu.
Hotel services *Bar. Fitness center. Spa. Ticket desk. Valet.* **Room services** *CD player. CD and video library. High-speed Internet. VCR.*

The Plaza Hotel

768 Fifth Ave at Central Park South (212-759-3000, 800-759-3000; www.fairmont.com). Subway: N, R, W to Fifth Ave–59th St. **Rates** *$269–$919 single/double; $514–$1,600 suite. 805 rooms.* **Credit** *AmEx, DC, Disc, MC, V.*
Built in 1907, and renowned for its baroque splendor, the Plaza Hotel is a neighbor to Fifth Avenue's most exclusive stores. More than half of the rooms and suites still have their original marble fireplaces. After a day of rigorous consumption, unwind at the 8,000-square-foot spa, or with wine and brasserie food at One C.P.S. *(212-583-1111)*, one of five on-site restaurants.
Hotel services *Baby-sitting. Fitness center. Salon. Spa. Ticket desk.* **Room services** *Fax. High-speed Internet. VCR on request.*

The Hotel Wales

1295 Madison Ave between 92nd and 93rd Sts (212-876-6000). Subway: 6 to 96th St. **Rates** *$209–$320 single/double; $339–$1,000 suite. 87 rooms.* **Credit** *AmEx, MC, V.*
For review, *see p50* **The Roger Williams**.

Moderate ($100 to $200)

Hotel Beacon

2130 Broadway between 74th and 75th Sts (212-787-1100, 800-572-4969; www.beaconhotel.com). Subway: 1, 2, 3, 9 to 72nd St. **Rates** *$145–$185 single/double; $185–$325 suite. 242 rooms.* **Credit** *AmEx, DC, Disc, MC, V.*
Located in a desirable residential neighborhood only a short walk from Central Park, the Beacon offers good value. Rooms are clean and spacious, with marble baths. For $5, guests can purchase passes to the Synergy gym. Quell your postworkout hunger at the 24-hour Viand Cafe, which also provides room service. You won't be needing the concierge; in-room *Time Out New York* magazines are complimentary.
Hotel services *Baby-sitting. Fitness and Internet centers.* **Room services** *Flat-panel TV. Kitchenette.*

The Bentley

500 E 62nd St at York Ave (212-644-6000, 888-66HOTEL; www.nychotels.com). Subway: N, R, W to Lexington Ave–59th St; 4, 5, 6 to 59th St. **Rates** *$135–$245 single/double; $225–$575 suite. 200 rooms.* **Credit** *AmEx, DC, Disc, MC, V.*
Once you're in one of the Bentley's sleek rooms, it's hard to notice anything other than the sweeping views from the floor-to-ceiling windows. Converted from an office building in 1998, this slender 21-story, glass-and-steel hotel is an ideal getaway for tired

Plush life All the comforts of home (and then some) in the **Mark**'s deluxe suite. *See p61.*

execs, thanks to soundproof windows and blackout shades. The mahogany-paneled library houses a complimentary cappuccino bar, and the rooftop restaurant glitters with even more views.
Hotel services *Complimentary breakfast.* **Room services** *CD and DVD players. Nintendo.*

The Empire Hotel

44 W 63rd St between Broadway and Columbus Ave (212-265-7400, 888-822-3555; www.empirehotel.com). Subway: 1, 9 to 66th St–Lincoln Ctr. **Rates** *$189–$249 single/double; $340–$1,000 suite. 381 rooms.* **Credit** *AmEx, DC, Disc, MC, V.*
The baronial Empire sits opposite Lincoln Center, its lobby decorated with wood paneling and velvet drapes. The rooms are clean and tasteful, with plenty of chintz and floral prints.
Hotel services *Cell-phone rental. Fitness center. Gift shop. Ticket desk. Video rental.* **Room services** *Cassette and CD players. High-speed Internet. Two-line phones. VCR.*

The Franklin

164 E 87th St at Lexington Ave (212-369-1000). Subway: 4, 5, 6 to 86th St. **Rates** *$179–$258 single/double. 48 rooms.* **Credit** *AmEx, DC, Disc, MC, V.*
For review, see *p50* **The Roger Williams**.

The Lucerne

201 W 79th St at Amsterdam Ave (212-875-1000, 800-492-8122; www.newyorkhotel.com). Subway: 1, 9 to 79th St. **Rates** *$150–$345 single/double; $180–$635 suite. 187 rooms.* **Credit** *AmEx, DC, Disc, MC, V.*
The landmark Lucerne has an elaborate prewar facade and ornate columns that recall the heyday of high society. A rooftop patio offers views of Central Park and the Hudson River. The rooms, though, are far from fabulous. Seek style in the breezy ground-floor French bistro, Nice Matin *(212-873-6423).*
Hotel services *Cell-phone rental. Concierge. Fitness center.* **Room services** *Internet. Nintendo.*

The Mayflower Hotel

15 Central Park West at 61st St (212-265-0060, 800-223-4164; www.mayflowerhotel.com). Subway: A, C, B, D, 1, 9 to 59th St–Columbus Circle. **Rates** *$159–$265 single/double; $225–$1,200 suite. 365 rooms.* **Credit** *AmEx, DC, Disc, MC, V.*
This musicians' haven faces Central Park, just a few blocks from Lincoln Center. Front rooms boast spectacular views of the park, and are priced accordingly. The Conservatory Café *(212-581-0896)* is a nice spot for a light breakfast.
Hotel services *Baby-sitting. Cell-phone rental. Fitness center. Valet. Video library.* **Room services** *High-speed Internet. VCR on request.*

On the Ave Hotel

2178 Broadway at 77th St (212-362-1100, 800-509-7598; www.ontheave-nyc.com). Subway: 1, 9 to 79th St. **Rates** *$159–$280 single/double; $215–$320 suite; $300–$450 penthouse. 250 rooms.* **Credit** *AmEx, DC, Disc, MC, V.*
On the Ave brings some sorely needed style to the Upper West Side's stodgy hotel scene. Winning attractions include "floating beds," industrial-style bathroom sinks and penthouse suites with fantastic balcony views of Central Park. (All guests have

access to a balcony on the 16th floor.) The hotel's Citylife Hotel Group siblings are ThirtyThirty (*see p56*) and Habitat Hotel (*see p58*).
Hotel services *Dry cleaning and laundry (24hr). Massage service. Valet. Video library.* **Room services** *High-speed Internet. VCR.*

Wyman House

36 Riverside Dr at 76th St (212-799-8281; www.wymanhouse.com). Subway: 1, 2, 3, 9 to 72th St. **Rates** *$169–$175 single/double. 6 rooms.* **Credit** *AmEx.*
Since 1986, Pamela and Ron Wyman have hosted hundreds of happy travelers at their 1888 home. Each of the six apartment-style suites has its own unique (frilly) decor. The Conservatory is the largest apartment, with sunny yellow walls, garden views and a Moroccan-themed bathroom. Note: All apartments are walk-ups, and a minimum booking of three nights is required. No children under 12.
Hotel services *Free local telephone calls.* **Room services** *Kitchenette. VCR.*

Budget ($100 or less)

Amsterdam Inn

340 Amsterdam Ave at 76th St (212-579-7500; www.amsterdaminn.com). Subway: 1, 9 to 79th St. **Rates** *$85 single/double with shared bath; $99–$129 private bath. 28 rooms.* **Credit** *AmEx, MC, V.*
For review, *see p59* **Murray Hill Inn**.

The café at **Jazz on the Park**.

The Harlem Flophouse

242 W 123rd St between Adam Clayton Powell (Seventh Ave) and Frederick Douglass Blvds (Eighth Ave) (212-662-0678; www.harlemflophouse.com). Subway: A, C, B, D to 125th St. **Rates** *$65 single; $90 double. 3 rooms.* **Credit** *MC, V.*
In 2000, new owner Rene Calvo renovated this beautiful Harlem brownstone, turning it into a B&B and art gallery. The three handsome guest rooms have Wi-Fi, hammered-tin ceilings, and antique cabinetry. A full Southern-style breakfast is available (for a fee).

Hostels

Central Park Hostel

19 W 103rd St at Central Park West (212-678-0491; www.centralparkhostel.com). Subway: B, C to 103rd St. **Rates** *$30 for a bed in shared room; $75 private room and shared bath. 250 beds.* **Credit** *Cash or traveler's checks only.*
For review, *see p59* **Murray Hill Inn**.

Hostelling International New York

891 Amsterdam Ave at 103rd St (212-932-2300; www.hinewyork.org). Subway: 1, 9 to 103rd St. **Rates** *$27–$35 dorm rooms; $120 family room; $135 private room with bath. 624 rooms.* **Credit** *AmEx, DC, MC, V.*
The city's only *real* hostel (i.e., a nonprofit accommodation that belongs to the International Youth Hostel Federation) is a gabled, Gothic-inspired brick-and-stone building the length of an entire city block. Built in 1883, it is now a protected landmark. Immaculate rooms are spare, but air-conditioned. There is a community kitchen and a large private garden.
Hotel services *Café. Conference facility. Fax. Game room. Library. Lockers. Self-serve laundry. Shuttles. Travel bureau. TV lounge.*

International House

500 Riverside Dr at 125th St (212-316-8473, in summer 212-316-8436; www.ihouse-nyc.org). Subway: 1, 9 to 125th St. **Rates** *$115–$135 single; $130–$150 double/suite. 11 rooms.* **Credit** *MC, V.*
Located on a peaceful block overlooking Grant's Tomb and the small but well-tended Sakura Park, this hostel has an inexpensive cafeteria and suites with private bathrooms and refrigerators. Summer, when foreign graduate students and visiting scholars check out, is the best time to book.
Hotel services *Bar. Cafeteria. Fax. Game room. Self-serve laundry. Parking.* **Room services** *Air conditioning. Cable TV. Voice mail.*

Jazz on the Park Hostel

36 W 106th St between Central Park West and Manhattan Ave (212-932-1600; www.jazzhostel.com). Subway: B, C to 103rd St. **Rates** *$23–$32, 4- to 12-bed dorm; $80 2-bed dorm (double occupancy); $130 private room with bath. 310 beds.* **Credit** *MC, V.*
Jazz on the Park is without a doubt the trendiest hostel in the city. The lounge, decorated like a space-age techno club, boasts a piano and pool table, while local jazz acts and karaoke swing in the

Good clean fun Scrubbing bubbles await in the **Akwaaba Mansion**'s double Jacuzzi.

basement. Weekly Block Party Mondays include special deals at nearby bars and restaurants. Linens and lockers are provided.
Hotel services *Air conditioning. ATM. Bike and in-line skate rental (summer only). Café. Complimentary breakfast. Fax. Internet. Private lockers. Self-serve laundry. TV room.*
Other location *Jazz on the Town Hostel, 130 E 57th St at Lexington Ave (212-651-3260.*

Brooklyn

Akwaaba Mansion

347 MacDonough St between Lewis and Stuyvesant Aves, Bedford-Stuyvesant, Brooklyn (718-455-5958; www.akwaaba.com). Subway: A, C to Utica Ave. **Rates** *$135–$150 weekdays; $150–$165 weekends. 4 rooms.* **Credit** *MC, V.*

This gorgeous restored 1860s mansion with a wide screened-in porch and flower gardens is worth the trek to east Brooklyn. *Akwaaba* means "welcome" in Ghanaian, which is exactly how you'll feel inside the individually themed rooms furnished with African artifacts and textiles. A hearty Southern-style breakfast is served in the dining room or on the porch. The Akwaaba restaurant *(393 Lewis Ave between Decatur and MacDonough Sts, 718-774-1444)* down the street is good for a Southern-cooking fix. Around the corner is Mirrors Coffeehouse *(401 Lewis Ave between Decatur and MacDonough Sts, 718-771-0633),* where an incredible red-velvet cake is served.

Angelique Bed & Breakfast

405 Union St between Hoyt and Smith Sts, Carroll Gardens, Brooklyn (718-852-8406). Subway: F, G to Carroll St. **Rates** *$100 single; $150 double. 6 rooms.* **Credit** *AmEx, DC, Disc, MC, V.*

Housed in an 1889 brownstone in charming Carroll Gardens, Angelique is a comfy establishment with a quasi-Victorian style. Children and pets are welcome and several rooms accommodate two adults and two children for an extra charge of $25 per child. On a warm summer day, relax in the back garden or take the F train four stops to Prospect Park. For an adventure of the culinary kind, wander along Smith Street, Brooklyn's happening restaurant row (*see p123*).

Awesome Bed & Breakfast

136 Lawrence St between Fulton and Willoughby Sts, Downtown Brooklyn (718-858-4859; www.awesome-bed-and-breakfast.com). Subway: A, C, F to Jay St–Borough Hall; M, R to Lawrence St; 2, 3, 4, 5 to Borough Hall. **Rates** *$79–$99 single/double; $120–$145 triple/quad. 7 rooms.* **Credit** *AmEx, MC, V.*

This second-floor guesthouse could be a setting for MTV's *Real World*. The themed rooms have basic furnishings but goofy details, like giant daisies and purple drapes. The snazzy bathrooms are communal. Breakfast is included, and delivered promptly to your room at 8am.

Bed & Breakfast on the Park

113 Prospect Park West between 6th and 7th Sts, Park Slope, Brooklyn (718-499-6115; www.bbnyc.com). Subway: F to Seventh Ave. **Rates** *$125–$300. 8 rooms.* **Credit** *AmEx, MC, V; checks preferred.*

Staying at this 1895 parkside brownstone is like taking up residence on the set of *Moulin Rouge*. The parlor floor is crammed with elaborately carved antique furniture, and guest rooms are outfitted with love seats, canopy beds overflowing with lacy French linens, and paintings by the proprietor's stepfather, the late William Earl Singer.

Sightseeing

Features

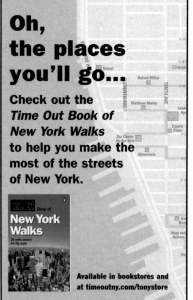

Introduction

The Bronx is up and the Battery's down. Everything in between is fabulous.

There's nothing small about New York—it's larger than life in every way. It's not a place for small ambitions either, whether you're planning to stay three days, or a lifetime. So brace yourself: The stimulation is constant, and the pace is demanding—but the energy is exciting, and the payoff for exploring the wonders of America's greatest city is huge.

However, odds are that no matter how long your visit (and no matter how determined you are to cover some serious ground), you'll leave not having done everything you wanted to do. That's just the way it is. There are people who've lived here for 20 years and who still haven't seen and done it all. The city is too vast and diverse to completely map and absorb in a lifetime, much less a vacation. Sights, attractions, museums, points of historical interest, shops and countless curiosities dot every street. And the people themselves are a whole other show.

What you need is a focus, and to that we say: Start with what you like. If you're an arty type, check out the burgeoning gallery scenes on the Lower East Side; in Williamsburg, Brooklyn; or in newly hip Long Island City, Queens (the Museum of Modern Art is there for the time being, alongside the stalwart P.S. 1). Or if architecture is more your interest, stroll through the West Village to take in its quaint historic beauty, then visit the city's impressive new AIA Center for Architecture. If you're here to shop till you drop, Nolita may become your main stomping ground. Or perhaps you'll wind up on Museum Mile, a majestic strip of Fifth Avenue (along the edge of bucolic Central Park) that's home to more famous artistic treasures than you can shake a Stickley original at. It's your call. We're here to help point you toward the best that the city has to offer.

And remember: There's always next time.

The best Sights & attractions for

...feeling alone in a crowd
The Temple of Dendur at the **Metropolitan Museum of Art** (*see p149*).

...feeling alone
The **Financial District** on a Sunday morning (*see p77*).

...feeling surrounded by a like-minded crowd
A night game at **Yankee Stadium** (*see p135*).

...a South-of-the-Border experience
Roosevelt Avenue in Jackson Heights, Queens (*see p131* **Action, Jackson**).

...a north-of-Central Park experience
Harlem's West 125th Street is the heart of the city's black cultural life (*see p116*).

...an east-of-the-East Village experience
Bedford Avenue, in Williamsburg, Brooklyn, provides an edgier alternative to Alphabet City (*see p126*).

...a west-of-the-river experience
Spectacular sunsets are best seen from **Battery Park City**'s esplanade (*see p76*).

...a taste of the Old World
Arthur Avenue in Belmont (the Bronx) is a Little Italy unto itself (*see p137*).

...a taste of the New World
The Rose Center for Earth and Space at the **Museum of Natural History** (*see p145*).

...a "what world am I in?" experience
The **Jacques Marchais Museum of Tibetan Art** on Staten Island (*see p159*).

...getting in touch with your inner child
The **Friedsam Memorial Carousel** and the **Wollman Rink** in Central Park (*see p109*).

...getting in touch with your thinner child
The **Chelsea Piers** (*see p332*) is a playground for every kind of physical endeavor.

Tour New York

On foot, on wheels, by water or air, what you see depends on how you get there.

How would you like to be introduced to New York City? Whether you want to set sail around Manhattan island, helicopter to the Statue of Liberty or discover the five boroughs on foot, there's a tour for you. Chances are, at least one of these excursions will whet your appetite for further exploration of the city that never sleeps. For more urban treks, check the Around Town section of *Time Out New York* magazine.

Sightseeing

By bicycle

For more city biking, *see p331* **Active sports**.

Bike the Big Apple

201-837-1133; www.bikethebigapple.com.
Tours *Call or visit website for schedule.*
Fees *$59–$79 (includes bicycle and helmet rental).*
Credit *AmEx, DC, Disc, MC, V.*
Licensed guides take cyclists through both historic and newly hip neighborhoods. Visit Brooklyn breweries and chocolatiers and sample their treats, or roll down the toniest Manhattan avenues. Half- and full-day rides are family-friendly and gently paced, and can be customized to your interests and riding level. Check the website for seasonal events and deals.

Central Park Bike Tours

Bite of the Apple Tours (212-541-8759; www.centralparkbiketour.com). **Tours** *Apr–Oct 10am, 1, 4pm. Nov–Mar by reservation only.*
Fees *$35, children under 15 $20 (includes bicycle rental).* **Credit** *AmEx, Disc, MC, V.*
Bite of the Apple focuses on Central Park. The main tour visits such park attractions as the John Lennon memorial at Strawberry Fields, Belvedere Castle and the Shakespeare Garden. Film buffs will enjoy the Central Park Movie Scenes Bike Tour *(Sat, Sun 10am, 1pm)*, which takes you past the film sites for movies like *When Harry Met Sally* and *Wall Street.* Most tours run a leisurely two hours; hard-core bikers might consider the three-hour Manhattan Island Bicycle Tour *($45, by appointment only).* Spanish-language tours are available, as are bike rentals if you want to ride around by yourself.

► If you plan on visiting several museums *and* taking one of the boat tours, *see p143* **Cheap tix** for reduced-fare passes.
► For more information about New York walking tours, see the Around Town section of ***Time Out New York***.

By boat

Circle Line Cruises

Pier 83, 42nd St at West Side Hwy (212-563-3200; www.circleline.com). Subway: A, C, E to 42nd St–Port Authority. **Tours** *Call or visit website for schedule.* **Fees** *$26, seniors $20, children $13.*
Credit *AmEx, DC, Disc, MC, V.*
Circle Line's famous three-hour guided circumnavigation of Manhattan is one of the best ways to take in the city's sights, from the Statue of Liberty to midtown's skyscrapers. You can also join themed tours, such as the New Year's Eve cruise, the DJ dance party or the fall foliage ride to Bear Mountain in the Hudson Valley. For a quick adventure (April to October), there's a roaringly fun 30-minute ride on a speedboat called the *Beast.*
Other location *South Street Seaport, Pier 16, South St between Burling Slip and Fulton St (212-630-8888).*

NY Waterway

Pier 78, 38th St at West Side Hwy (800-53-FERRY; www.nywaterway.com). Subway: A, C, E to 42nd St–Port Authority. **Tours** *Call or visit website for schedule.* **Fees** *two-hour Manhattan cruise $24, seniors $19, children $12.* **Credit** *AmEx, Disc, MC, V.*
The scenic two-hour ride makes a complete circuit around Manhattan's landmarks. A 60-minute tour focuses on the skyline of lower Manhattan.
Other location *South Street Seaport, Pier 17, South St at Fulton St.*

Shearwater Sailing

Hudson River between Liberty and Vesey Sts (212-619-0885, 800-544-1224; www.shearwatersailing.com). **Tours** *Apr 15–Oct 15 Mon–Thu 10am–4:30pm, 5:30–7pm; Fri, Sat 10am–4:30pm, 10–11:30pm; Sun noon–2pm.*
Fee *$40.* **Credit** *AmEx, DC, Disc, MC, V.*
Set sail on the *Shearwater,* an 82-foot luxury yacht built in 1929. Special rides, such as the champagne brunch or full-moon sail, are lovely ways to take in the skyline. The boat will celebrate its 75th anniversary in 2004 with a rechristening.

Staten Island Ferry

South St at Whitehall St (718-727-2508; www.siferry.com). Subway: 1, 9 to South Ferry; 4, 5 to Bowling Green. **Open** *24hr.* **Fee** *free.*
In a 25-minute trip on this commuter barge, you'll get stunning panoramas of lower Manhattan and the Statue of Liberty (plus smooch-worthy sunsets). Boats depart South Ferry at Battery Park. Call or visit the website for current schedules.

By bus

D3 Busline

212-533-1664, 866-D3-NITES; www.d3busline.com. **Tours** *Fri, Sat 8pm–2am.* **Fee** *$60.* **Credit** *AmEx, MC, V.*
This isn't your grandma's double-decker. A night out on the leather-seated "trans-lounge limo bus" includes an open bar and a DJ, as well as VIP entrance into select Manhattan hot spots. The new Brooklyn tour carries you to area bars for a sampling of local brews, and to hip nightclubs, where you can get your dance on. The fee includes everything but drinks at the venues.

Gray Line

777 Eighth Ave between 47th and 48th Sts (212-445-0848, 800-669-0051, ext 3; www.graylinenewyork.com). Subway: A, C, E to 42nd St–Port Authority. **Tours** *Call or visit website for schedule.* **Fees** *$35–$99.* **Credit** *AmEx, Disc, MC, V.*
This *is* your grandma's classic red double-decker (the line runs other buses too), but with something to interest everyone. Gray Line offers more than 20 bus tours, from a basic two-hour ride (with more than 40 hop-on, hop-off stops) to the guided Manhattan Comprehensive, which lasts eight-and-a-half hours and includes lunch, admission to the United Nations tour, and a ride to Ellis Island and the Statue of Liberty.

By copter, carriage or rickshaw

Liberty Helicopter Tours

VIP Heliport, West Side Hwy at 30th St (212-967-6464, 800-542-9933; www.libertyhelicopters.com). Subway: A, C, E to 34th St–Penn Station. **Tours** *Jan, Feb 9am–7pm. Mar–Dec 9am–9pm.* **Fees** *$56–$275.* **Credit** *AmEx, MC, V.*
There won't be any daredevil swooping and diving—Liberty's helicopters provide a fairly smooth flight, but the views are excitement enough. Even a five-minute ride (durations vary) is long enough to give you a thrilling look at the Empire State Building and Central Park.
Other location *Liberty Helicopter Tours, Downtown Manhattan Heliport, Pier 6, Hudson River between Broad St and Old Slip.*

Manhattan Carriage Company

200 Central Park South at Seventh Ave (212-664-1149; www.ajnfineart.com/mcc.html). Subway: N, Q, R, W to 57th St. **Tours** *Mon–Fri 10am–2am; Sat, Sun 8am–2am.* **Fees** *$40 per 20-minute ride (extended rides by reservation only). Hours and prices vary during holidays.* **Credit** *AmEx, MC, V (reserved tours only).*
The beauty of Central Park seems even more romantic from the seat of a horse-drawn carriage. Choose your carriage from those lined up on the streets on the southern end of the park, or book in advance.

The **Shearwater** sails the Hudson. *See p70.*

Manhattan Rickshaw Company

212-604-4729; www.manhattanrickshaw.com. **Tours** *Tue–Sun noon–midnight and by appointment.* **Fees** *$10–$50, depending on duration and number of passengers.* **Credit** *Cash only.*
Manhattan Rickshaw's pedicabs operate in Greenwich Village, Soho, Times Square and the Theater District in midtown. If you see one that's available, hail the driver. (Fares should be determined before you jump in.) For a prearranged pickup, make reservations 24 hours in advance.

By foot—walking tours

Adventure on a Shoestring

212-265-2663. **Tours** *Sat, Sun. Call for schedule and to make reservations.* **Fee** *$5.* **Credit** *Cash only.*
Its motto is "Exploring the world within our reach…within our means," and founder Howard Goldberg is undyingly faithful to both "real" New York and to each 90-minute tour's $5 price tag (it hasn't changed in more than 40 years). The

walks take you from one charming neighborhood to another, and topics can include Millionaire's Row and Haunted Greenwich Village. Special theme and custom tours are also available.

Big Onion Walking Tours

212-439-1090; www.bigonion.com. **Tours** *Jun–Aug Wed–Sun 1–3pm. Sept–May Fri–Sun and major holidays 1–3pm.* **Fees** *$12, seniors and students $10.* **Credit** *Cash only.*

New York was known as the Big Onion before it became the Big Apple. The tour guides will explain why, and they should know—all guides hold advanced degrees in history (or a related field), resulting in astoundingly informative tours of the city's historic districts and ethnic neighborhoods. Check the website for meeting locations. Private tours are also available.

Foods of New York Walking and Tasting Tours

212-239-1124; www.foodsofny.com. **Tours** *Tue–Sun 11am–2pm (reservations required).* **Fee** *$35 (all tastings included).* **Credit** *AmEx, Disc, MC, V.*

Eat your way through some of the best restaurants and food shops in Greenwich Village, the West Village or Chelsea. The three-hour tours provide you with a historical overview of the neighborhood, and the guides make sure you have all the info you need to return and explore on your own. Arrive hungry—there'll be ample sampling. Call or visit the website for a schedule and exact meeting locations.

Greenwich Village Literary Pub Crawl

New Ensemble Theatre Company (212-613-5796; www.geocities.com/newensemble). Tour meets at the White Horse Tavern, 567 Hudson St at 11th St. Subway: 1, 9 to Christopher St–Sheridan Sq. **Tours** *Sat 2pm (reservations requested).* **Fee** *$15 (drinks not included).* **Credit** *Cash only.*

Local actors from the New Ensemble Theatre Company take you to the former haunts of famous writers. Watering stops include Chumley's (a former speakeasy) and Cedar Tavern, where Jack Kerouac and a generation of Abstract Expressionist painters, including Jackson Pollock, clinked mugs with their peers.

Guided by voices

You may feel a little awkward at first. You may find yourself trying to be discreet, hoping to look like a neighborhood regular, like someone who normally walks into strange, dingy-looking Chinatown residences and working sweatshops. But really, you'll just be following the voice in your head—the one that starts talking when you hit the button on your CD player.

This guided stroll, called ***Soundwalk: Chinatown***, is one of three audio tours created by Manhattan-based Oversampling Inc. as a way of giving New Yorkers a fresh look at nabes they thought they knew. For the intrepid tourist, they provide immediate insight into to what life is (or was) like in Chinatown, Times Square and the Lower East Side (tours of Dumbo, the Meatpacking District and the Bronx are in the works, as are downloadable MP3 versions). Each tour is facilitated by a guiding voice—a narrator selected because of his or her strong connection to the 'hood.

On the second track of the Chinatown CD, Jami Gong, a neighborhood native, warns you that he's going to take you to places you shouldn't be in. But Soundwalk creator Stephan Crasneanscki and business developer Michel Sitruk stress that you aren't really guided anywhere you can't legally visit—just to sites you never would have considered otherwise. "We're building a scenario where you walk into a place—and you don't really know where reality stops and fiction starts," Crasneanscki says, referring to the blend of factual information provided in the tours and the anticipated reactions of the tour-takers.

The "terror upstairs at 60 Mulberry Street" turns out to be an elderly man, whose only sinister behavior is clacking his mah-jongg tiles a bit loudly. He knows that he's on the tour, but he isn't being paid to be at that location, and he isn't a prop. He's just a local character who likes to play mah-jongg. More often than not, when an earphoned tour-taker climbs to the second floor of the apartment building and follows Gong's direction to peek through the crack in the door, the man will be there, adding to the drama of Soundwalk's deftly fabricated walk-through movie.

"We grew up in the generation of visiting museums—the Vatican, the Louvre—and seeing those places through guides," says Paris-born Crasneanscki, whose ten years on the Lower East Side haven't diminished his mellifluous accent. "This is an alternative way to immerse yourself in a place and get a real sense of it."

For Crasneanscki, who selects the narrators and then works with them to lay out the tour, total immersion is the difference between

Harlem Heritage Tours

212-280-7888; www.harlemheritage.com.
Tours *Call or visit website for schedule and meeting locations.* **Fees** *$25–$100 (reservations required).* **Credit** *AmEx, MC, V.*
Now operating more than 15 bus and walking tours, Harlem Heritage shows visitors the soul of Harlem. Harlem Song, Harlem Nights takes you to landmarks such as the Apollo Theater. The Renaissance tour walks you through former speakeasies, nightclubs, and the onetime residences of artists, writers and musicians.

Municipal Art Society Tours

212-935-3960, recorded information 212-439-1049; www.mas.org. **Tours** *Call or visit website for schedule and meeting locations.* **Fees** *$12–$15 (reservations may be required for some tours).* **Credit** *Cash only.*
The society organizes bus and walking tours in New York and even New Jersey. Many, like Art Deco Midtown, have an architectural bent. There's also a free guided walk through Grand Central Terminal on Wednesdays at 12:30pm (suggested donation $10). Private tours are available by appointment.

NYC Discovery Walking Tours

212-465-3331. **Tours** *Sat, Sun. Call for schedule and meeting locations.* **Fees** *$12, food tours $17.* **Credit** *Cash only.*
These walking tours come in six varieties: American history (American Revolution to Civil War), biography (George Washington to John Lennon), culture (art to baseball), neighborhood (Brooklyn Bridge area to Central Park), indoor winter (like the Secrets of Grand Central), and tasting-and-tavern (food-and-drink landmarks). The company has 80 year-round selections; private tours are available by appointment.

Rock & Roll Walking Tour

Rock Junket NYC (212-696-6578; www.rockjunket.com). **Tours** *Sat 1pm.* **Fee** *$20.* **Credit** *Cash only.*
Rocker guides Bobby Pinn and Ginger Ail lead this East Village walk to legendary rock, punk and glam sites (famous album-cover locations; where the Ramones called home), from the 1960s to the present. Tours of Greenwich Village, or on days other than Saturday, are available by appointment.

Soundwalks and conventional tours. Recording equipment in hand, Crasneanscki becomes a fixture in each community for months at a time, interviewing anyone who'll talk to him—which is just about everyone. Then, he builds each walk like a cinematic soundtrack, layering the narrator's own tale with 360-degree recordings of site-specific street noises and clips from the nearly 100 hours of interviews.

But don't expect to be given a point-and-look rundown of historic buildings. Be prepared to put yourself entirely in your guide's hands—or, more accurately, shoes—for an hour. You'll walk with the same gait as the narrator (paced by clicking footsteps), turn right or left when instructed, and enter unmarked doors when told to do so. Soundwalk tours serve as a bridge between personal observation and real-world interaction: After hearing how longtime neighborhood denizen Mr. Wah reads his newspaper every day in the Nom Wah Tea Parlor, you walk through the door, and there he is, drinking tea and poring over a Chinese-language daily. The owners of the cafe bring out tea and cookies, unasked, for anyone that walks in with a headset—thanks to the tour, you'll feel like you're already a regular. *Soundwalk tours are available for $19.95 at www.soundwalk.com.*

Downtown

Wall Street power, Soho style, East Village edginess—and that's only half of it.

Sightseeing

Once upon a time, downtown Manhattan *was* New York. The first settlements were at the southern tip, and early immigrants flocked to the island in waves, creating communities of rich and poor, pockets of urban and rural life, all below 14th Street. Today, downtown is only a part of the borough, but it is just as rich in diversity. You can bargain for knockoff purses on Canal Street and then walk north to peruse boutiques stocked with the real (and really expensive) designer goods in **Soho**; wander along Mulberry and Grand Streets to buy fresh cannoli in one of Little Italy's pastry shops; or walk a few blocks to the **Lower East Side** for bialys and knishes. Mutability is a way of life here, too. Note the **Meatpacking District**: Until recently, butchers supplied the dominant atmosphere; now it's a chic shopping neighborhood.

Downtown New York is also where the Twin Towers once stood. Rebuilding at the **World Trade Center** site is now under way, and the area's transformation is for New Yorkers—as it is for many Americans—a symbol of hope and renewal.

Battery Park

It's most obvious that you're on an island when you explore the southern tip of Manhattan. The Atlantic Ocean breezes from the New York harbor are a vivid natural reminder of the route taken by the hope-filled millions who traveled here by ship. Trace their journey past the golden torch of the **Statue of Liberty**, through the immigration and quarantine centers of **Ellis Island** and, finally, to the statue-dotted promenade of **Battery Park**. Today, few steamships chug in; instead, the harbor is filled during summer with sailboats and Jet Ski riders who jump the wakes left by motorboats. Seagulls perch on the promenade railing, squawking at fishermen whose lines might snag a shad or a striped bass (while the Hudson River is cleaner than it's been in years, State Health Department officials advise against eating its fish more than once a month). The harbor itself is gorgeous, and one of the most peaceful experiences available in the city is sitting on a bench in Battery Park and looking toward the Statue of Liberty, Ellis Island and Staten Island.

The promenade is also a stage for applause- (and money-) hungry performers, who entertain crowds waiting to be ferried to the Statue of Liberty and Ellis Island. The park itself often plays host to events such as the **River to River Festival** (*see p255*), a celebration of downtown, featuring a variety of arty goings-on, including free outdoor music on summer evenings. **Castle Clinton**, situated inside the park, is an intimate, open-air setting for concerts. Built in 1811 to defend the city against possible attacks by the British, the castle (really a former fort) has been a theater and an aquarium; it now also serves as a visitors' center and ticket booth for the Statue of Liberty and Ellis Island tours. To the west is **Pier A** *(22 Battery Pl at West St),* Manhattan's last Victorian-era pier shed; it's currently being restored and will someday house restaurants and historic vessels.

Whether or not you join the throngs making their way to Lady Liberty, you can head east around the shore, from which several ferry terminals jut out into the harbor. The 1954 **Whitehall Ferry Terminal** is the boarding point for the famous **Staten Island Ferry** (*see p70*). The free 20-minute ride to Staten Island offers an unparalleled view of the downtown Manhattan skyline and, of course, a closer look at the iconic statue. The terminal, which was damaged by fire in 1991, remains open as it undergoes reconstruction.

In the years before the Brooklyn Bridge was built, the beautiful **Battery Maritime Building** *(11 South St between Broad and Whitehall Sts)* served as a terminal for many ferry services between Manhattan and Brooklyn. At the southeastern end of the Battery Park promenade is **American Park at the Battery** *(Battery Park, across from 17 State St at Pearl St; 212-809-5508);* the restaurant's outdoor patio overlooking the harbor is a primo spot for sipping a cocktail.

► To further explore Soho's art scene, *see pp260–269* **Art Galleries** *and pp143–163* **Museums**.

► For Soho, Nolita and Meatpacking District shops so fabulous, you won't miss the dollars spent, *see pp211–249.*

Sunset at **Battery Park**.
See p76 **A great stroll.**

Another patch of grass lies north of Battery Park: the triangle of **Bowling Green**, the city's oldest extant park. It's the front lawn of the beautiful 1907 Beaux Arts Alexander Hamilton Custom House, now home to the **National Museum of the American Indian** (*see p157*). On the north side of the triangle, sculptor Arturo DiModica's muscular bronze bull represents the massive power of this city's Financial District.

Other historical sites are close by: the rectory of the **Shrine of St. Elizabeth Ann Seton**, a 1793 Federal building dedicated to the first native-born American saint; and **New York Unearthed**, a tiny offshoot of the **South Street Seaport Museum** (*see p158*) whose collection documents 6,000 years of New York's archaeological past. The **Fraunces Tavern Museum** (*see p155*) is a restoration of the alehouse where George Washington celebrated his victory over the British. After a bite, you can examine the Revolution-era relics displayed in the tavern's period rooms.

The **Stone Street Historic District** surrounds one of Manhattan's oldest roads. The once-derelict bit of Stone Street between Coenties Alley and Hanover Square was recently spiffed up, and office workers and visitors now frequent its restaurants, bars and shops, including **Ulysses** *(95 Pearl St at Stone St, 212-482-0400),* a popular watering hole, and **Financier**, a French bakery *(62 Stone St between Mill Lane and Hanover Sq, 212-344-5600).*

Battery Park

Between State St, Battery Pl and Whitehall St. Subway: R, W to Whitehall St; 4, 5 to Bowling Green.

New York Unearthed

17 State St between Pearl and Whitehall Sts, behind Shrine of St. Elizabeth Ann Seton (212-748-8628). Subway: R, W, to Whitehall St. **Open** *Mon–Fri noon–5pm; educational programs by appointment.* **Admission** *free.*

Shrine of St. Elizabeth Ann Seton

7 State St between Pearl and Whitehall Sts (212-269-6865). Subway: R, W to Whitehall St. **Open** *Mon–Fri 6:30am–5pm; Saturdays before and after12:15pm Mass; Sundays before and after 9am and noon Masses.*

The Statue of Liberty & Ellis Island Immigration Museum

212-363-3200; www.ellisisland.org, www.nps.gov/stli. Travel: R, W to Whitehall St; 1, 9 to South Ferry, then take Statue of Liberty Ferry, departing every 45 minutes from gangway 4 or 5 in Battery Park at the southern tip of Manhattan. **Open** *Ferry runs 9:30am–5pm daily, last trip out 3:30pm, last trip back 5:15pm. Purchase tickets at Castle Clinton in Battery Park.* **Admission** *$10, seniors $8, children 4–12 $3, under 4 free.* **Credit** *Cash only.*

Frédéric-Auguste Bartholdi's *Liberty Enlightening the World,* a gift from the people of France, was unveiled in 1886. The inside of the statue (whose interior framework was designed by Gustave Eiffel) has been closed to the public for security reasons since September 11, 2001. However, tourists are still welcome to explore the exterior grounds, which provide ample room to absorb Emma Lazarus's 1883 poem, which includes the renowned lines "Give me your tired, your poor/Your huddled masses yearning to breathe free." Continue on to the Ellis Island Museum, which documents the history of the approximately 12 million immigrants who passed through Ellis Island between 1892 and 1924.

Battery Park City & Ground Zero

The streets are bustling around **Ground Zero**, well over two years after the attack on the World Trade Center. Area residential life has returned to normal, but tourists still come down to the site's memorial to pay their respects to the nearly 2,800 people who lost their lives. After a worldwide design competition, the plan created by Studio Daniel Libeskind was selected in early 2003 for the rebuilding of the WTC area. A refined version of the plan was released in fall 2003, and environmental approval could come in spring 2004—barring further political infighting. The Lower Manhattan Development Corporation (LMDC) has outlined the WTC construction process for the public, and the architectural drawings are on view at the Winter Garden.

The **World Trade Center** was Battery Park City's portal to the rest of Manhattan—residents would walk across two covered pedestrian bridges and take the subways that stopped beneath the WTC. After the events of September 11, recovery and cleanup of the area progressed at breakneck speed and were completed on May 30, 2002. The **World Financial Center**—fully recovered from September 11—is an expression of the city-within-a-city concept. Completed in 1988, architect Cesar Pelli's four glass-and-granite postmodern office towers—each crowned with a geometric form—surround an upscale retail area, a series of plazas with terraced restaurants, and a marina where private yachts and water taxis to New Jersey are docked. The glass-roofed **Winter Garden**, a popular venue for concerts and other forms of entertainment, was badly damaged in the WTC attack. But things move quickly in New York: The Winter Garden resumed its performance schedule in September 2002, and restaurants and shops such as **SouthWest NY** *(2 World Financial Center between Liberty and Vesey Sts, 212-945-0528)* and **Century 21** *(22 Cortlandt St between Broadway and Church St, 212-227-9092)* started reopening as early as February 2002.

Battery Park City was devised by Nelson Rockefeller (the governor of New York in 1966) as the site of apartment housing and schools; its public plazas, restaurants and shopping areas were designed to link with the World Financial Center. The most impressive aspects of Battery Park City are its esplanade and park (*see left* **A great stroll)**, which run north of the Financial Center along the Hudson River, and connect to Battery Park at the south. In addition to its inspiring views of the sunset behind **Colgate Center** (look for the huge COLGATE sign and clock on the Jersey side) and Jersey City across the river, the esplanade is a paradise for bikers, in-line skaters and joggers.

The northern end of the park (officially called **Nelson A. Rockefeller Park**) features the large **North Lawn**, which becomes a surrogate beach in summer. Sunbathers, kite fliers and soccer players all vie for a bit of unoccupied turf. Basketball and handball courts, concrete tables with chess and backgammon boards, and playgrounds with swings are some of the built-in recreation options. Battery Park ends at Chambers Street, but there is access to the piers that lie to the north, which are slowly being claimed for public use. In fact, some sections have already become part of the western waterfront's **Hudson River Park**, where you'll find jogging and biking trails and,

Don't miss — A great stroll

There is perhaps no better spot on Manhattan island from which to see a sunset than **Battery Park City's esplanade and park**. Beginning at Battery Park and running north to Chambers Street, the Hudson River–front esplanade is perfect for daytime bikers, in-line skaters and joggers, and its pedestrian pathway allows you to wander into the various recreation areas along the way. Strolling the promenade at night, however, is just as rewarding. The South Cove area of **Robert F. Wagner Jr. Park**, near the start of the pathway, is handsomely lit with purplish lanterns; from an observation deck, you can take in sweeping views of the New York harbor. During warmer months, you might catch an outdoor concert in front of the **Winter Garden** at the World Financial Center (*see right*). If you've gone as far as Chambers Street, you might amble up a little farther to Canal Street to watch the antics at **Trapeze School New York** (*see p335*).

From Battery Pl to Chambers St, between West St and the Hudson River (212-945-0505; www.worldfinancialcenter.com for concert info). Subway: R, W, 1, 9 to Rector St.

Left luggage Millions of arriving immigrants passed through **Ellis Island**. *See p75.*

on several of the piers, a variety of recreational possibilities—including kayaking and trapeze, just below Canal Street.

Situated between Battery Park City and Battery Park are the inventively designed **South Cove** area, the **Robert F. Wagner Jr. Park** (an observation deck offers fabulous views of the harbor and the Verrazano-Narrows Bridge) and New York City's Holocaust-remembrance archive, the **Museum of Jewish Heritage** (*see p160*). The entire park area is dotted with sculptures, such as Tom Otterness's whimsical installation *The Real World*. The park hosts outdoor cultural events during the warmer months.

Battery Park City Authority

212-417-2000; www.batteryparkcity.org.

The neighborhood's official website lists events and has a great map of the area.

Lower Manhattan Cultural Council

212-219-9401; www.lmcc.net.

An information service for artists and the public, the LMCC offers information on cultural events happening in and around lower Manhattan.

World Financial Center & Winter Garden

From Hudson River to West St, between Albany and Vesey Sts (212-945-0505; www.worldfinancialcenter.com). Subway: A, C, J, M, Z, 2, 3, 4, 5 to Fulton St; R, W to Rector St; 4, 5 to Wall St.

Call for information about free events, which range from concerts to flower shows.

Wall Street

Since the city's earliest days as a fur-trading post, wheeling and dealing have been New York's prime pastime, and commerce the backbone of its prosperity. **Wall Street** (or merely "the Street," if you want to sound like a trader) is the thoroughfare synonymous with the world's greatest den of capitalism.

Wall Street itself is actually less than a mile long; it took its name from a wooden defensive wall that the Dutch built in 1653 to mark what was then the northern limit of New Amsterdam. The southern tip of Manhattan is generally known as the **Financial District**. In the days before telecommunications, financial institutions established their headquarters in the area to be near the city's active port. Here, corporate America made its first audacious architectural statements.

Notable structures include the former **Merchants' Exchange** at 55 Wall Street with its stacked rows of Ionic and Corinthian columns, giant doors, and a remarkable interior rotunda behind the lobby that holds 3,000 people; the **Equitable Building** *(120 Broadway between Cedar and Pine Sts)*, whose greedy use of vertical space helped instigate the zoning laws now governing skyscrapers (stand across the street from the building to get the optimal view); and **40 Wall Street** (today owned by real-estate tycoon Donald Trump), which in 1929 went head-to-head with the

Chrysler Building in a battle for the title of "world's tallest building." (The Empire State Building trounced them both a year later.)

The Gothic Revival spire of the Episcopalian **Trinity Church** rises at the western end of Wall Street. It was the island's tallest structure when completed in 1846 (the original burned in 1776, and a second was demolished in 1839). Stop in and see brokers praying for a bull market, or stroll through the adjacent cemetery, where cracked and faded tombstones mark the final resting places of dozens of past city dwellers, including signers of the Declaration of Independence and the U.S. Constitution. **St. Paul's Chapel**, a satellite of Trinity Church, is an oasis of peace in the midst of frantic business activity. The chapel is New York City's only extant pre-Revolutionary building (it dates to 1766), and one of the finest Georgian structures in the country. Miraculously, both landmark churches survived the nearby World Trade Center attack; although mortar fell from their facades, the steeples remained intact.

A block east of Trinity Church, the **Federal Hall National Memorial** is a Greek Revival shrine to American inaugural history (sort of—the original building was demolished in 1812). On this spot, General Washington was sworn in as the country's first president on April 30, 1789.

The nerve center of the U.S. economy is the **New York Stock Exchange**. Unfortunately, for security reasons, the Exchange is no longer open to the public. Not to worry: People-watching on the busy street outside the NYSE is still a *great* spectator sport. It's an endless pageant, as brokers and traders and their minions march importantly up and down **Broad Street**. For a lesson on Wall Street's influence through the years, check out the **Museum of American Financial History**, on the ground floor of what was once John D. Rockefeller's Standard Oil Building.

The **Federal Reserve Bank**, a block north on Liberty Street, is an imposing structure built in the Florentine style. It holds the nation's largest store of gold—just over 9,000 tons—in a vault five stories below street level.

Federal Hall National Memorial

26 Wall St at Nassau St (212-825-6888). Subway: 2, 3, 4, 5 to Wall St. **Open** *Mon–Fri 9am–5pm.* **Admission** *free.*

Federal Reserve Bank

33 Liberty St between Nassau and William Sts (212-720-6130; www.newyorkfed.org). Subway: 2, 3, 4, 5 to Wall St. **Open** *Mon–Fri 9:30–11:30am, 1:30–2:30pm; tours every hour on the half hour.* **Admission** *free (tours must be arranged at least two weeks in advance; tickets are sent by mail).*

Museum of American Financial History

See p156 for listing.

St. Paul's Chapel

209 Broadway between Fulton and Vesey Sts (212-602-0874; www.saintpaulschapel.org). Subway: A, C to Broadway–Nassau St; J, M, Z, 2, 3, 4, 5 to Fulton St. **Open** *Mon–Sat 10am–6pm; Sun 9am–4pm.*

Trinity Church Museum

Broadway at Wall St (212-602-0872; www.trinitywallstreet.org). Subway: R, W to Rector St; 2, 3, 4, 5 to Wall St. **Open** *Mon–Fri 9am–11:45am, 1–3:45pm; Sat 10am–3:45pm; Sun 1–3:45pm; closed during concerts.* **Admission** *free.*

The Seaport

While New York's importance as a port has diminished, its initial fortune rolled in on the swells that crash around its deepwater harbor. The city was perfectly situated for trade with Europe; after 1825, goods from the Western Territories arrived via the Erie Canal and Hudson River. And because New York was the point of entry for millions of immigrants, its character was shaped by the waves of humanity that arrived at its docks.The **South Street Seaport** is the best place to see this seafaring heritage.

Redeveloped in the mid-1980s, the Seaport includes reclaimed and renovated buildings converted to shops, restaurants, bars and a museum. It's not an area that New Yorkers often visit, though it is rich in history. The Seaport's public spaces are a favorite of street performers, and the shopping area of **Pier 17** is little more than a picturesque tourist-trap-of-a-mall by day and an after-work watering hole by night (outdoor concerts in the summer do manage to attract locals). Antique vessels are docked at other piers. The **Seaport Museum** (*see p158*) details New York's maritime history and is located within the restored 19th-century buildings at **Schermerhorn Row** *(2–18 Fulton St, 91–92 South St and 189–195 Front St)*, which were constructed on landfill in 1812. At 11 Fulton Street, the **Fulton Market**, with its gourmet food stalls and seafood restaurants that open onto the cobbled streets in summer, is a great place for people-watching and oyster-slurping. Familiar national chain shops such as J. Crew and Abercrombie & Fitch line the surrounding streets.

If you enter the Seaport area from Water Street, the first thing you'll notice is the whitewashed **Titanic Memorial Lighthouse**, erected the year after the great

Flashback Following a $30 million renovation, **City Hall** looks much as it did in 1812.

ship went down (it was moved to its current location in 1976). The area offers fine views of the **Brooklyn Bridge** (*see p123*). The smell on South Street is a clear sign that the **Fulton Fish Market**, America's largest, is nearby. Opened in 1836, the market sold fish fresh from the sea until 1930, when fishing boats stopped docking here. Today, fish are trucked in and out by land. Go now (and go very early) to see the frantic predawn dance of the wholesalers and the fantastic variety of fish—the market will move to Hunts Point in the Bronx in mid-2004.

Fulton Fish Market

Pier 16, South St at Fulton St (212-406-4985). Subway: A, C to Broadway–Nassau St; J, M, Z, 2, 3, 4, 5 to Fulton St. **Open** *3:30–9am daily.*

South Street Seaport

From Water St to the East River, between John St and Peck Slip (212-732-7678; www.southstseaport.org). Subway: A, C to Broadway–Nassau St; J, M, Z, 2, 3, 4, 5 to Fulton St. **Open** *Mon–Fri 10am–9pm; Sat, Sun 10am–7pm.*

Civic Center & City Hall

The business of running New York takes place among the many grand buildings of the Civic Center, an area that formed the budding city's northern boundary in the 1700s. **City Hall Park**, where you'll find a granite time wheel that displays the park's history, was treated to an extensive renovation in 1999. The pretty landscaping and abundant benches make the park a popular lunchtime spot for area office workers. Like the steps of City Hall, the park has also been the site of press conferences and political protests for years. (Under former mayor Rudolph Giuliani, the steps were closed to such activity, though civil libertarians successfully defied the ban in April 2000.) **City Hall** itself, at the northern end of the park, houses the mayor's office and the legislative chambers of the City Council, and is therefore usually buzzing with preparations for Hizzoner's comings and goings. When City Hall was completed in 1812, its architects were so confident the city would grow no farther north that they didn't bother to put any marble on its northern side. The building, a beautiful blend of Federalist form and French Renaissance detail, is unfortunately closed to the public (except for scheduled group tours). Facing City Hall, the much larger, golden-statue–topped **Municipal Building** houses other civic offices, including the marriage bureau (note the nervous, happy brides- and grooms-to-be awaiting their ceremonies, particularly in the early morning).

Park Row, east of the park and now lined with cafés, electronics shops and the campus of Pace University, once held the offices of 19 daily papers and was known as Newspaper

Row. It was also the site of Phineas T. Barnum's sensationalist American Museum, which burned down in 1865.

Facing the park from the west is Cass Gilbert's famous **Woolworth Building** *(233 Broadway between Barclay St and Park Pl)*, a vertically elongated Gothic cathedral–style office building that has been called "the Mozart of skyscrapers" (and, alternatively, "the Cathedral of Commerce"). Its beautifully detailed lobby is open to the public during business hours.

The houses of crime and punishment are also located in the Civic Center around Foley Square—once a pond and, later, the site of the city's most notorious 19th-century slum, Five Points. These days, you'll find the State Supreme Court housed in the **New York County Courthouse** *(60 Centre St at Pearl St)*, a hexagonal Roman Revival building whose beautiful interior rotunda is decorated with a mural called *Law Through the Ages.* The **United States Courthouse** *(40 Centre St between Duane and Pearl Sts)* is crowned with a golden pyramid-topped tower above a Corinthian temple. Next to City Hall is the 1872 **New York County Courthouse**, more popularly known as the Tweed Courthouse, a symbol of the runaway corruption of mid-19th-century municipal government. Boss Tweed, leader of the political machine Tammany Hall, pocketed $10 million of the building's huge $14 million cost. The remainder was still enough to buy a beautiful edifice; the Italianate detailing is exquisite. A recent $90 million renovation has restored much of the structure's luster. (The building now houses the Board of Education.) The **Criminal Courts Building and Bernard Kerik Detention Complex** *(100 Centre St between Leonard and White Sts)* is the most intimidating in the district. Built of great granite slabs, with looming towers that guard the entrance, the architecture of this dispensary of justice suggests the Kafkaesque. The ziggurat-topped building is known familiarly as "the Tombs"—a reference not only

Stall wonder

Just steps away from the flagship Prada store on Broadway, where a pair of silver stilettos sells for $450, locals and clued-in tourists are grabbing up glittery Chinese slippers for $5. Welcome to Soho, where dozens of bohemian street stalls—selling everything from movie scripts and vintage dresses to used jazz records—vie for your attention, right outside the storefronts of such heavyweights as Chanel and DKNY. Although they are fewer in number following former mayor Rudolph Giuliani's crackdown on street-vendor permits, you'll find at least 20 to 30 of NYC's most popular vendors each weekday; on Saturdays and Sundays, expect around 70 manned stalls along West Broadway, Wooster Street, Spring Street, Houston Street and the stylin' main drag, Prince Street.

In the shadow of the historic St. Anthony's Church is **St. Anthony's Market**, which runs along Houston Street between MacDougal and Sullivan Streets. On weekends, vendors sell unique handmade rugs, Venetian glass necklaces and antique accessories. Look for a stall called **CHUU Inc.** *(800-963-CHUU; www.chuu.com)*, which sells colorful vintage kimonos for about $75—a relative bargain compared with Kimono House, a nearby shop on Thompson Street that sells the same pretty items for $150 to $450.

On **West Broadway**, Soho's central artery, the wide sidewalks allow local artists to display their work—some of which is spectacular, and some of which begs to be hung by refrigerator magnets. Check out **Isack Kousnsky**'s stall of "mixed-medium painting photography" *(www.isack-art.com)*, located on West Broadway between Prince and Spring Streets. Kousnsky creates his unusual artwork by mounting an enlarged photograph onto a painting; the vibrant colors of the painted background give the film an illusion of depth. The final product gets a chunky aluminum frame.

Wooster Street, one block east, has the only vendors who are open year-round. At the intersection of Spring and Wooster, a lovely collection of stalls has formed a small open-air market. Two noteworthy vendors are **Meehee NY** *(718-397-8165; www.meeheeny.com)* and **Sterling Stones NYC** *(917-907-4073)*. Both sell beautifully fashioned handmade jewelry, constructed of sterling silver, precious stones and freshwater pearls. A handful of vendors rotate in on weekends, selling everything from hand-knit hats and scarves to discounted shoes and studded belts.

Walk three blocks east on Spring Street and cross Broadway to reach a flock of to the architecture of its predecessor (a long-gone building inspired by a photograph of an Egyptian tomb) but also to its once deathly overcrowded prison conditions; it holds 800 prisoners today. Formerly the Manhattan House of Detention, it was renamed in honor of former Police Commissioner Bernard Kerik in 2002.

All of these courts are open to the public, weekdays from 9am to 5pm, though only some allow visitors. Your best bets for legal drama are the Criminal Courts: If you can't slip into a trial, you can at least observe hallways full of legal wheeler-dealers and the criminals they represent. Or, for a grim twist on dinner theater, you can sit and witness the pleas at **Arraignment Court**, which go on until 1am, in the same building.

A major archaeological site, the **African Burial Ground** *(Duane St between Broadway and Centre St)* is the small remnant of a five-and-a-half-acre cemetery where 20,000 African men, women and children were buried. The cemetery, which closed in 1794, was unearthed during construction of a federal office building in 1991 and designated a National Historic Landmark.

City Hall

City Hall Park between Broadway and Park Row (212-788-3000; www.nyc.gov). Subway: J, M, Z to Chambers St; 2, 3 to Park Pl; 4, 5, 6 to Brooklyn Bridge–City Hall.
For group tours, call two weeks in advance.

Tribeca & Soho

Tribeca (the Triangle Below Canal Street) today is a textbook example of the process of gentrification in lower Manhattan. It's very much as Soho was 20 years ago: A few pockets are deserted and abandoned—the cobblestones dusty and broken, and the cast-iron architecture chipped and unpainted—while the rest throbs with energy. (Developers are catching up quickly, and there's not much left in Tribeca that's not targeted for deluxe purposes.) The rich and famous weren't here first, but

street vendors perched outside of the celebrated French brasserie Balthazar. Between Broadway and Crosby Street, you'll find artists and designers selling handcrafted jewelry, modish sunglasses and stylish, soft-leather handbags. Don't miss **Chic**, which displays an array of mother-of-pearl necklaces and translucent shell earrings set in gold or silver. Similar versions can be found at nearby Banana Republic for double the price, plus tax.

Head north on Broadway to **Prince Street**—prime real estate for vendors. In midsummer, the umbrella-lined stretch of Prince Street between Broadway and Wooster could be mistaken for a small-town art fair. At Prince and Greene, ask for **Arturo**, a jolly Peruvian man who sells colorful earrings fashioned out of delicate fish scales that have been dyed rich, saturated hues. Farther down is **Cherry's Handcrafted Jewelry** *(718-693-3619)*, a wonderful stall offering a rotating selection of handmade beaded necklaces and bracelets. If you've been looking for the perfect thick-set turquoise necklace, your quest ends here. At the intersection of Wooster and Prince, clothing designer **Dawn Ebony Martin** sells her fetching reversible sundresses and skirts. For five years, Martin maintained a boutique on Thompson Street,

but taking her sales to the street allows her to retail her dresses at half the price. Keep in mind that these are only some of the neighborhood's fabulous finds. If you stray off the beaten path, you're likely to stumble upon another talented starving artist trying to make rent.

Local hero To see an old-world retail outlet in Soho, visit **Vesuvio Bakery**. *See p84.*

gentrification has turned them into "pioneers": Many big-name actors (Robert De Niro and Harvey Keitel among them) and established, successful artists such as Richard Serra live in the area. There is a host of haute restaurants, including **Bouley** and **Nobu** (*see p168*); celeb-sighting bistros, such as the long-running **Odeon** (*see p168*); and posh bars, especially in the part of Tribeca closest to Soho. Clubs and performance spaces like the **Knitting Factory** (*see p311*) contribute to the culture.

Buildings in Tribeca are generally larger than those in Soho, particularly toward the river; many are warehouses rapidly being converted into condos. There is some fine small-scale cast-iron architecture along White Street and the parallel thoroughfares, including **85 Leonard Street**—the only remaining cast-iron building attributable to James Bogardus (the developer of this building method, which prefigured the technology of the skyscraper). As in Soho, you'll find galleries, salons, furniture stores, spas and other businesses that cater to the neighborhood's stylish residents. Frank Gehry's multimillion-dollar interior for the **Tribeca Issey Miyake** boutique (*see p216*) exemplifies area developers' ambitions.

Tribeca is also the unofficial headquarters of New York's film industry. Robert De Niro's **Tribeca Film Center** *(375 Greenwich St at Franklin St)* houses screening rooms and production offices in the old Martinson Coffee Building. His **Tribeca Grill** is on the ground floor. In addition, De Niro is one of the sponsors of the **Tribeca Film Festival** (*see p252*), which draws an eager crowd to the neighborhood in May. A few blocks away, the **Screening Room** (*see p293*) shows art-house films on three screens and serves solid American cuisine in the tasteful dining room next door.

Soho, New York's glamorous downtown shopping destination, was once an industrial zone known as Hell's Hundred Acres. In the 1960s, the neighborhood was earmarked for destruction, but its signature cast-iron warehouses were saved by the many artists who inhabited them. (Urban-planning theorist Chester A. Rapkin coined the name Soho, which stands for South of Houston Street, in a 1962 study of the neighborhood.) The **King and Queen of Greene Street** *(respectively, 72–76 Greene St between Broome and Spring Sts, and 28–30 Greene St between Canal and Grand Sts)* are two prime examples of the area's landmark-designated **cast-iron architecture** (for more about cast-iron architecture, *see p83* **The Iron Age**). As loft living became fashionable and the buildings were renovated for residential use, landlords were quick to sniff the profits in gentrification. Soho morphed into a playground for the young, beautiful and rich. While it's still a pleasure to stroll around the cobbled streets, large chain stores are rapidly moving in among the elegant buildings, boutiques and bistros, causing a number of hip shops to head east. Most of the galleries that made Soho an art hot spot in the 1970s and '80s have decamped to cheaper (and now trendier) neighborhoods like West Chelsea and Brooklyn's Dumbo (*see p260*). Surprisingly, some garment-factory sweatshops remain in Soho, especially near Canal Street—though the buildings may also house businesses such as graphic-design studios, magazine publishers and record labels.

Upscale hotels, such as the **Mercer**, **SoHo Grand** and **60 Thompson** (*see p39*) keep the fashionable coming to the area, and shop names run from Banana Republic and Old Navy to Marc Jacobs and Prada. Soho is also the place to go for high-end home furnishings at design stores such as **Moss** (*see p244*). West Broadway, Soho's main shop-lined thoroughfare, is a magnet for way-out-of-towners—on the weekend, you're as likely to hear French, German and Italian as you are to catch a blast of Brooklynese. (For more on Soho street shopping, *see p80* **Stall wonder**.)

Two museums also make Soho their home: the **New Museum of Contemporary Art** (*see p150*), which has plans to begin construction on its new Bowery space in 2004; and the small, increasingly popular **New York City Fire Museum** (*see p163*), a former fire station that houses a collection of antique engines dating to the 1700s.

To the west of West Broadway, tenement- and townhouse-lined streets contain remnants of the Italian community that once inhabited this area. Elderly men and women walk along Sullivan Street to the **St. Anthony of Padua Roman Catholic Church** *(155 Sullivan St at West Houston St),* which was dedicated in 1888. You'll still find some old-school neighborhood flavor in businesses such as **Joe's Dairy** *(156 Sullivan St between Houston and Prince Sts, 212-677-8780),* **Pino's Prime Meat Market** *(149 Sullivan St between Houston and Prince Sts, 212-475-*

The Iron Age

What makes Soho so very *Soho*? Aside from perambulating supermodels and well-coiffed fashionistas, it's the cast-iron architecture that gives the neighborhood its distinctive look. In fact, Soho has the greatest concentration of buildings with cast-iron facades anywhere in the country. Balancing heft and grace, these buildings were solidly built for industrial use, but their generous interior floor space has made them ideal for residential-loft conversion in the modern era.

Soho was a manufacturing center by the mid-19th century. New factories and workrooms were needed, and in 1848, James Bogardus erected the first building with a self-supporting iron-and-glass street wall. The new cast-iron technology fit the bill in the gaslight era, as its large windows let sunlight pour into the cavernous workrooms. Bogardus also pioneered the mass production of decorative cast-iron components, making frills (like balconies) cheap and easy to add.

Stop by **565 Broadway** at Prince St (now home to a Victoria's Secret store) to admire the Italian Renaissance–style masonry. Heavier and more ornate than most buildings of this era, the structure has three rows of rigidly symmetrical windows divided by Corinthian columns and topped by an elaborate cornice. The arched lower windows are weighed down with large keystones, and the street wall is several feet thick. Compare it with the **Singer Building** next door at 561–563 Broadway. A masterwork of iron and glass, the Singer was designed by Ernest Flagg and completed in 1904. The street-level windows are divided by the thinnest of iron supports; above, wrought-iron balconies add a touch of romance.

A block south, J.P. Gaynor's **Haughwout Building** (1857) sits at 488 Broadway. Touch the surface: Painted beige, and covered with a thin layer of soot, the building looks as if it's made of stone—but, in fact, it's cast iron. Architects deliberately mimicked classical stonework, trying to capture the solidity of older buildings with the new lightweight material. On Greene Street, spot gems like **28–30 Greene Street**, with its ornate "wedding cake" facade. At the southwest corner of Greene and Prince Streets, don't miss Richard Haas's 1970s trompe l'oeil mural, painted on a brick wall. Look closely—there's a real window or two amid the trickery.

While the struggling artists who reclaimed Soho decades ago have been supplanted, their legacy lives on—not in artworks, but in the neighborhood itself. Once threatened with demolition (Robert Moses wanted to run an expressway through here in the early '60s), Soho was saved by artists who successfully petitioned the city to turn the area into a protected historic district. They succeeded in 1971, and we all reap the benefits today. Even the supermodels.

Sightseeing

8134) and **Vesuvio Bakery** *(160 Prince St between Thompson St and West Broadway, 212-925-8248),* whose old-fashioned facade has been used in dozens of commercials.

Little Italy & Nolita

Little Italy, which once ran from Canal to Houston Streets between Lafayette Street and the Bowery, hardly resembles the insular community famously portrayed in Martin Scorsese's *Mean Streets.* Italian families have fled Mott Street and gone to the suburbs, Chinatown has crept north, and rising rents have forced mom-and-pop businesses to surrender to the stylish boutiques of **Nolita**—North of Little Italy, a misnomer since it actually lies within it. Another telling change in the 'hood: **St. Patrick's Old Cathedral** *(260–264 Mulberry St between Houston and Prince Sts)* holds services in English and Spanish, not Italian. Completed in 1815 and restored after a fire in 1868, this was New York's premier Catholic church until it was demoted, upon consecration of the Fifth Avenue cathedral of the same name. But ethnic pride remains. Italian-Americans flood in from the outer boroughs to show their love for the old neighborhood during the **Feast of San Gennaro** (*see p256*) every September. Aside from the tourist-oriented Italian cafés and restaurants on Mulberry Street between Canal and Houston Streets, there remain pockets of the ethnic lifestyle. The elderly locals (and the young ones in the know) still buy olive oil and fresh pasta from venerable shops such as **DiPalo's Fine Foods** *(200 Grand St at Mott St, 212-226-1033)* and sandwiches packed with Italian meats and cheeses at **Italian Food Center** *(186 Grand St at Mulberry St, 212-925-2954).*

Of course, Little Italy is the site of several notorious Mafia landmarks. The brick-fronted **Ravenite Social Club** *(247 Mulberry St between Prince and Spring Sts)* was celebrity don John Gotti's headquarters from the mid-1980s until his arrest in 1990; it's now occupied by the accessories boutique **Amy Chan** (*see p227*). Mobster Joey Gallo was shot to death in 1972 while celebrating a birthday with his family at **Umberto's Clam House**, which has since moved around the corner *(178 Mulberry St at Broome St, 212-431-7545).* The Italian eateries in the area are mostly undistinguished, overpriced grill-and-pasta houses, but two reliable choices are **Il Cortile** *(125 Mulberry St between Canal and Hester Sts, 212-226-6060)* and **La Mela** *(167 Mulberry St between Broome and Grand Sts, 212-431-9493).* Drop in for dessert and espresso at one of the many small cafés lining the streets, such as **Caffè Roma** *(385 Broome St at Mulberry St, 212-226-8413),* which opened in 1891.

Over the past few years, chichi restaurants and boutiques seemed to open daily in Nolita. Elizabeth, Mott and Mulberry Streets, between Houston and Spring Streets in particular, are now the source of everything from perfectly cut jeans to handblown glass. Not every trendy shop lasted through the economic downturn, however, as evidenced by a number of empty storefronts. The young, the insouciant and the vaguely European still congregate outside eateries such as **Bread** and **Cafe Habana** (*see p169*). Back in 1988, long before the Nolita boom, the grand former **Police Headquarters Building** *(240 Centre St between Broome and Grand Sts)* had already been converted into luxe co-op apartments.

► For more information on downtown dining and nightlife, *see pp167–197* **Restaurants**, *pp199–209* **Bars** *and pp307–326* **Music**.

Chinatown

Take a few steps south of Broome Street and west of Broadway, and you will feel as though you've entered a completely different *country.* You won't hear much English spoken along these crowded streets, which are lined with stands stocked full of fish, fruit and vegetables. Manhattan's **Chinatown** is the largest Chinese-immigrant community outside Asia. Even though some residents eventually decamp to one of the four other Chinatowns in the city (two in Queens and two in Brooklyn), a steady flow of new arrivals keeps the original full-to-bursting. The tenements and high-rise buildings around East Canal Street house about 150,000 legal (and about 100,000 illegal) Chinese. Many work here and never leave the neighborhood. Chinatown's busy streets get even wilder during the **Chinese New Year** festivities in January or February (*see p259*), and around the Fourth of July, when the area is the city's best source of (illegal) fireworks.

Food is everywhere. The markets on Canal Street sell some of the best, most affordable seafood and fresh produce in the city—you'll see buckets of live eels and crabs, neatly stacked greens, and piles of hairy rambutans (cousins of the lychee). Street vendors sell satisfying snacks, such as pork buns and bags of sweet egg pancakes. There are also countless restaurants. Mott Street—from Worth to Kenmare Streets—is lined with Cantonese and Szechuan places,

Blow out For the **Feast of San Gennaro**, there's a parade down Mulberry Street. *See p84.*

as is East Broadway. Adding to the mix are increasing numbers of Indonesian, Malaysian, Thai and Vietnamese eateries and stores.

Canal Street is a bargain-hunter's paradise: It's infamous as a source of knockoff designer items, such as handbags and perfumes. The area's many gift shops are stocked with fun, inexpensive Chinese products, from good-luck charms to kitschy pop-culture paraphernalia.

Sites of historical interest include **65 Mott Street** *(between Bayard and Canal Sts)*, the city's first building to be erected specifically as a tenement, in 1824. The antiques shop **Chu Shing** *(12 Mott St between Chatham Sq and Mosco St, 212-227-0279)* was once the New York office of the Chinese revolutionary Dr. Sun Yat-sen, known as the father of modern China.

Wing Fat Shopping is a strange little subterranean mall with a history. Enter through its doors at Chatham Square *(to the right of the OTB parlor at No. 8)* and descend the stairs to your left; you'll find such businesses as Tin Sun Metaphysics, a well-known feng shui agency. The tunnel is rumored to have been a stop on the Underground Railroad, 25 years before the Chinese began populating this area in the 1880s. In 1906, the tunnel connected the Chinese Opera house at 5 Doyers Street with an actors' residence on the Bowery. Members of two rival tongs (Chinese organized-crime groups) staged a savage gun battle during an opera. At least four people were killed, and the gunmen escaped down the tunnels.

A statue of the Chinese philosopher marks **Confucius Plaza** at the corner of Bowery and Division Streets. In **Columbus Park**, at Bayard and Mulberry Streets, elderly men and women gather around card tables to play mah-jongg and dominoes (you can hear the clacking tiles from across the street), while younger folks practice martial arts. The **Museum of Chinese in the Americas** (*see p160*) hosts exhibitions and events that explore the Chinese immigrant experience in the Western Hemisphere. In the **Eastern States Buddhist Temple of America**, you'll be dazzled by the glitter of hundreds of Buddhas and the smell of wafting incense. Donate $1 and receive a fortune slip.

For a different perspective on Chinatown culture, visit the noisy, dingy **Chinatown Fair** *(at the southern end of Mott Street)*, an amusement arcade where some of the East Coast's best *Street Fighter* players congregate. Older kids hit Chinatown for liquid entertainment; **Good World Bar** *(3 Orchard St between Canal and Division Sts, 212-925-9975)* is a likeable locale that offers Scandinavian snacks, while the **Double Happiness** bar (*see p199*) is a popular nightspot for downtown denizens of all ethnic groups.

Chinatown

Subway: B, D to Grand St; J, M, Z, N, Q, R, W, 6 to Canal St.

Finding Nemo Dive into **Chinatown**'s fish markets for the catch of the day. *See p84.*

Eastern States Buddhist Temple of America

64 Mott St between Bayard and Canal Sts (212-966-6229). Subway: J, M, Z, N, Q, R, W, 6 to Canal St. **Open** *9am–6pm.*

Lower East Side

The **Lower East Side** tells the story of New York's immigrants, millions upon millions of whom poured into the city from the late 19th century onward. The area is densely populated with a patchwork of strong ethnic communities, and it's great for dining and exploration. Today, Lower East Side residents are largely Asian and Latino families, with an increasing number of cash-strapped hipsters sharing small apartments. The early settlers were mostly Eastern European Jews. Mass tenement housing was built to accommodate the 19th-century influx of immigrants, which included many German, Hungarian, Irish and Polish families. Their unsanitary, airless and overcrowded living conditions were documented near the end of that century by photographer and writer Jacob A. Riis in *How the Other Half Lives;* the book's publication fueled reformers, who prompted the introduction of building codes. To better understand how these immigrants lived, visit the **Lower East Side Tenement Museum** (*see p155*).

Between 1870 and 1920, hundreds of synagogues and religious schools were established. Yiddish newspapers and associations for social reform and cultural studies flourished, as did vaudeville and classic Yiddish theater. (The Marx Brothers, Jimmy Durante, Eddie Cantor, and George and Ira Gershwin were just a few of the entertainers who once lived in this district.) Today, only about 10 percent of the population is Jewish; the **Eldridge Street Synagogue** often finds it hard to round up the ten adult males required to conduct a service. Despite a shrinking congregation, the synagogue has not missed a Sabbath or holiday service in 115 years. Remarkably, in October 2001, a white-tiled *mikvah* (a small pool that collects rainwater used to cleanse Orthodox Jewish women after their menstrual cycles) was unearthed behind the synagogue; it is believed to be the oldest one of its kind in New York, dating back to 1887. **First Shearith Israel Graveyard** *(on the southern edge of Chinatown)* has gravestones that date from 1683. This is the burial ground of the oldest Jewish community in the United States—which included Spanish and Portuguese Jews who had fled the Inquisition.

Puerto Ricans and Dominicans began to move to the Lower East Side after World War II. Colorful awnings characterize the area's bodegas (groceries). Many restaurants serve Caribbean standards, such as *mofongo* and *cuchifritos*. In the summer, the streets throb with the sounds of salsa and merengue as residents hang out, savor freshly scraped ice with fruit syrup, drink beer and play dominoes.

Beginning in the 1980s, a new breed of immigrant began moving in: young artists and musicians attracted by low rents. Bars, boutiques and music venues sprang up on Ludlow Street and the surrounding area, creating an annex of the East Village. This scene is still thriving, though rents have risen sharply: The sign at **Pianos** *(158 Ludlow St at Stanton St, 212-505-3733),* a recently opened Parisian-style bi-level bar, was taken from the piano store that had been in that spot for decades. For live music, check who's playing at **Arlene Grocery** (*see p309*), the **Bowery Ballroom** (*see p309*) and **Tonic** (*see p315*). The area is also home to a burgeoning art scene. Storefront galleries such as **Rivington Arms** *(102 Rivington St between Ludlow and Essex Sts, 646-654-3213)* and **Participant Inc.** *(95 Rivington St between Ludlow and Orchard Sts, 917-488-0185)* show young artists. (For more on the LES gallery scene, *see p262* **LES is more art**.)

The Lower East Side's reputation as a haven for political radicals lives on at **ABC No Rio** (*see p272* **Our Unorganicized Reading**), which was established in 1980 after squatters took over an abandoned ground-floor space; it now houses a gallery and performance space. Meanwhile, **Surface Hotel** *(107 Rivington St between Essex and Ludlow Sts; see also p43),* a high-rise building in this low-leveled 'hood, is difficult to miss. Created by the ultrastylish magazine *Surface,* it intends to be a haven of luxury with "concept suites."

Despite the trendy shops that have cropped up along the block, Orchard Street below Stanton Street remains the heart of the **Orchard Street Bargain District**, a row of stores selling utilitarian goods. This is the place for cheap hats, luggage, sportswear and T-shirts. In the 1930s, then mayor Fiorello La Guardia forced pushcart vendors off the streets into large, indoor marketplaces. Although many of these bazaars are now a thing of the past, **Essex Street Markets** *(120 Essex St between Delancey and Rivington Sts)* is still going strong as a purveyor of all things Latino, from groceries to religious icons.

Many remnants of the neighborhood's Jewish roots remain. One of the Lower East Side's most famous eateries is the proudly shabby **Sammy's Roumanian Steak House** *(157 Chrystie St between Delancey and Rivington Sts, 212-673-0330),* where dauntingly hearty portions of Eastern European fare are served with a jug of artery-clogging *schmaltz* (chicken fat) and iced bottles of vodka. If you prefer "lighter" food, **Katz's Delicatessen** (*see p171*) sells some of the best pastrami in New York (FYI, Meg Ryan's famous faux-orgasm scene in *When Harry Met Sally* was filmed here). People come from all over for the fresh, crunchy dills at **Guss' Pickles** (*see p240*), another Lower East Side favorite and film star (it's in *Crossing Delancey*).

The Lower East Side is a nosher's paradise. Begin by paying tribute to the Eastern European origins of the neighborhood with a fresh baked bialy from **Kossar's Bialystoker Kuchen Bakery** *(367 Grand St between Essex and Norfolk Sts, 212-473-4810).* If you're in need of a sweeter hunk of dough, head a few doors over to the **Doughnut Plant** (*see below* **Cult foods**), where high-quality organic doughnuts are available in flavors such as coconut and white peach. Then

Top five Cult foods

These downtown spots may look like humble take-out joints, but to New Yorkers, they're obsessions that offer immediate gratification when a craving hits.

Cheese steaks at BB Sandwich Bar *(120 W 3rd St between MacDougal St and Sixth Ave, 212-473-7500).* This closet-size space makes just one thing, but it's beefy-cheesy heaven on a bun.

Doughnuts at the Doughnut Plant *(379 Grand St between Essex and Norfolk Sts, 212-505-3700).* Forget Krispy Kreme—New Yorkers get the jones for these handmade yeast-raised babies, in flavors like pistachio and pumpkin.

Falafel at Mamoun's Falafel *(199 MacDougal St between Bleecker and W 3rd Sts, 212-674-8685).* Loved by locals since 1971, Mamoun's fresh snacks are still only $2 apiece. Get the hot sauce.

French fries at Pommes Frites *(123 Second Ave between St. Marks Pl and E 7th St, 212-674-1234).* Soak up that beer buzz with a tall cone of freshly fried Belgian bliss, dunked in any one of two dozen zippy sauces.

Fried dumplings from Fried Dumpling *(99 Allen St between Broome and Delancey Sts, 212-941-9975).* They're so good and so cheap. A dollar's worth (five) has to be the best food bargain *ever.*

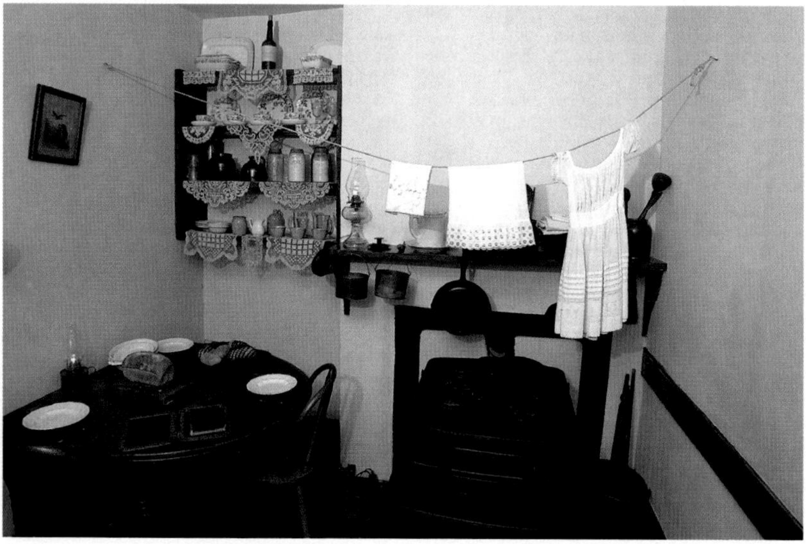

Ordinary people The **Lower East Side Tenement Museum** details immigrant life. *See p86.*

return to childhood by stocking up on nostalgic goodies like taffy and PEZ at **Economy Candy** *(108 Rivington St between Essex and Ludlow Sts, 212-254-1832).*

Eldridge Street Synagogue

12 Eldridge St between Canal and Division Sts (212-219-0888; www.eldridgestreet.org). Subway: F to East Broadway. **Open** *Tours Tue, Thu 11:30am, 2:30pm and by appointment; Sun 11am–3pm on the hour.* **Admission** *$5, seniors and students $3.*

First Shearith Israel Graveyard

55–57 St. James Pl between James and Oliver Sts. Subway: J, M, Z to Bowery.

East Village

Scruffier than its western counterpart, the **East Village** has a long history as a countercultural hotbed. Originally considered part of the Lower East Side, the neighborhood boomed in the 1960s when writers, artists and musicians moved in and turned it into the hub for the period's social revolution. (Allen Ginsberg lived at 437 East 12th Street, between First Avenue and Avenue A, until his death in 1997.) Many famous clubs and coffeehouses thrived here, including the **Fillmore East** on Second Avenue between 6th and 7th Streets (the theater has been demolished), and the **Dom** *(23 St. Marks Pl),* where the Velvet Underground often headlined; it's now being turned into condos. In the '70s, the neighborhood took a dive as drugs and crime prevailed—but that didn't stop the influx of artists and punk rockers. In the early '80s, East Village galleries were among the first to display the work of groundbreaking artists Jean-Michel Basquiat and Keith Haring. The nabe's past as an alt-scene nexus of arts and politics gets a nod with **Howl!** (*see p256*)—a new late-summer festival organized by the Federation of East Village Artists. Poetry, jazz and film events celebrate the vibrant community's development.

Today, the area east of Broadway between Houston and 14th Streets is no longer quite so edgy, though remnants of its spirited past endure. You'll find a generally amiable population of ravers, punks, yuppies, hippies, homeboys, vagrants and trustafarians (those wanna-be bohos who live off family money). This motley crew has crowded into the neighborhood's tenements—next to a few elderly residents, who tend to be holdouts from previous waves of immigration. Check out the indie record shops, bargain restaurants, grungy bars, punky clubs and funky, cheap clothing stores. At 10th Street and Second Avenue, on the eastern end of historic **Stuyvesant Street**, sits the East Village's unofficial cultural center: **St. Mark's Church in-the-Bowery** (*for listing, see p348* **Danspace Project**). St. Mark's was built in 1799 on the site of Peter Stuyvesant's farm. Stuyvesant, who was one of New York's first governors, is buried in the adjacent cemetery. The church is rented by arts groups, such as the experimental theater troupe **Ontological at St. Mark's** *(212-420-1916)*.

St. Marks Place *(8th St between Lafayette St and Ave A)* is the main drag. In earlier years, the Bolshevik Leon Trotsky once ran a printing press (1917) and poet W.H. Auden lived (1953–72) at 77 St. Marks Place—which currently houses the regional Mexican restaurant **La Palapa** (*see p179*). The street is less highbrow now. Lined with stores, bars and street vendors, St. Marks is packed until the wee hours with crowds browsing for bargain T-shirts, records and books. The more interesting places are to the east; you'll find cafés and shops on and around Avenue A between 6th and 10th Streets. Since tattooing became legal again in New York City in 1997 (it had been banned since 1961), a number of parlors have opened up, including the famous **Fun City** *(94 St. Marks Pl between First Ave and Ave A, 212-353-8282)*, whose awning advertises CAPPUCCINO & TATTOO.

Astor Place, with its 1970s revolving-cube sculpture, is always swarming with young skateboarders and other modern-day street urchins. It is also the site of Peter Cooper's recently refurbished **Cooper Union**, the city's first free private college. Opened in 1859, CU is now a design and engineering college (and still free). In the 19th century, Astor Place marked the boundary between the ghetto to the east and some of the city's most fashionable homes, such as **Colonnade Row** *(428–434 Lafayette St between Astor Pl and W 4th St)*. To the west facing these is the distinguished Astor Public building, which theater legend Joseph Papp rescued from demolition in the 1960s. Today, it's the **Public Theater**—a haven for first-run American plays, the headquarters of the **New York Shakespeare Festival** (*see p337*) and the home of trendy **Joe's Pub** (*see p311*).

East of Lafayette Street on the Bowery stand the sole vestiges of the street's notorious past: several missionary organizations that cater to the down-and-out. In recent years, a few restaurants have also set up shop. Hallowed **CBGB** (*see p310*), the birthplace of American punk, still packs in guitar bands, both new and used. Many other local bars and clubs successfully apply the formula of cheap beer and loud music, including the **Continental** and the **Mercury Lounge** (*see p310 and p313*).

East 7th Street is a Ukrainian stronghold; the focal point is the Byzantine-looking **St. George's Ukrainian Catholic Church** at No. 16–20, whose gleaming cupola was overhauled in 1977. Across the street, there's often a long line of beefy fraternity types waiting to enter **McSorley's Old Ale House** (*see p204*), which touts itself as the city's oldest pub in a single location (1854); it still serves just one kind of beer—its own brew,

Guitar heroes The Ramones' spirit lives on at **CBGB**, *the* East Village punk shrine.

Sightseeing

The **Hells Angels**' HQ.

available in light or dark versions. For those who would rather shop than sip, the eclectic boutiques of young designers and vintage-clothing dealers dot 7th, 8th and 9th Streets.

Curry Row, on 6th Street between First and Second Avenues, is one of several Little Indias in New York. Roughly two dozen Indian restaurants sit side by side (contrary to a popular joke, they do not share a single kitchen), and they remain popular with diners on an extremely tight budget. If you're wondering about the line of shiny Harleys on 3rd Street between First and Second Avenues, the New York chapter of the **Hells Angels** is headquartered here.

Alphabet City, on Avenues A through D, stretches toward the East River. The largely working-class Latino population is being overtaken by professionals willing to pay higher rents. Avenue C is known as "Loisaida" Avenue, the phonetic spelling of "Lower East Side" when pronounced with a clipped Spanish accent. The neighborhood's long, rocky romance with the drug trade is pretty much a thing of the past.

Though rough around the edges, Alphabet City has its attractions. Two churches on 4th Street are built in the Spanish-colonial style: **San Isidro y San Leandro** *(345 E 4th St between Aves C and D)* and **Iglesia Pentecostal Camino Damasco** *(289 E 4th St between Aves B and C)*. The **Nuyorican Poets Cafe** (*see p272*), a 30-year-old clubhouse for espresso-drinking beatniks, is famous for its slams, in which performance poets do lyric battle before a score-keeping audience. **Tompkins Square Park** *(from 7th to 10th Sts, between Aves A and B)* has historically been the site of demonstrations and rioting. The last uprising was about 15 years ago, when the city decided to evict squatters from the park and renovate it to suit the area's increasingly affluent residents. It was also home to the city's first drag celebration, Wigstock. These days, it's still the community park of the East Village and one of the liveliest layabout zones in the city. Latino bongo beaters, longhairs with acoustic guitars, punky squatters, mangy dogs, the neighborhood's yuppie stroller-pushers and its homeless mingle in and around the park.

North of Tompkins Square, around First Avenue and 11th Street, are remnants of earlier communities: discount fabric dealers, Italian cheese shops, Polish butchers and two great Italian coffeehouses: **De Robertis** *(176 First Ave between 10th and 11th Sts, 212-674-7137)* and **Veniero's Pasticceria and Caffe** *(342 E 11th St at First Ave, 212-674-7264)* are still wonderful for pastries and old-world ambience.

Greenwich Village

Stretching from Houston Street to 14th Street, between Broadway and Sixth Avenue, **Greenwich Village**'s leafy streets have inspired bohemian lifestyles for almost a century. It's a place for idle wandering, for people-watching from sidewalk cafés, for candlelit dining in clandestine restaurants, and for hopping between bars and cabaret venues. The Village gets mobbed in mild weather and has lost some of its quaintness, but much of what has always attracted painters and poets to New York still exists. Sip a fresh roast in honor of the Beats—Jack Kerouac, Allen Ginsberg and their buddies—as you sit in their former haunts. Kerouac's favorite was **Le Figaro Café** *(184 Bleecker St at MacDougal St, 212-677-1100).* The **Cedar Tavern** *(82 University Pl between 11th and 12th Sts, 212-929-9089),* which moved from its original location at the corner of 8th Street, is where the leading figures of Abstract Expressionism's boys' club discussed how best to apply paint: Franz Kline, Jackson Pollock and Larry Rivers drank under this banner in the 1950s.

The hippies who tuned out in **Washington Square Park**, once a potter's field, are still there in spirit, and often in person: the park hums with musicians and street artists (though the once-ubiquitous pot dealers have become victims of strict policing and hidden surveillance cameras). This is one of the best people-watching spots in the city. Chess hustlers and students from **New York University** join in, along with today's new generation of idlers: hip-hop kids who drive down to West 4th Street in their booming Jeeps, and Generation Y skateboarders who clatter around the fountain and near the base of the **Washington Arch**, a modest-size replica of the Arc de Triomphe, completed in 1895 in honor of George Washington.

The Village has been fashionable since the 1830s, when the wealthy built handsome townhouses around Washington Square. Some of these properties are still privately owned and occupied; many others have become part of the New York University campus, which seems to be ever expanding. NYU also owns the **Washington Mews**, a row of charming 19th-century buildings that were once stables; they line a tiny cobblestone cul-de-sac just north of the park between Fifth Avenue and University Place. Several literary figures, including Henry James, Herman Melville and Mark Twain, lived on or near the square. In 1871, the local creative community founded the **Salmagundi Club**, America's oldest artists' club, which is now situated north of Washington Square on Fifth Avenue (No. 47). The landmark building hosts exhibitions, lectures and art auctions.

Greenwich Village continues to change with the times, for better and worse. Eighth Street is currently a long procession of cheap-jewelry vendors, piercing parlors, punky boutiques and shoe stores; in the 1960s, it was the closest New York got to San Francisco's Haight Street. Jimi Hendrix's **Electric Lady Studios** is still at No. 52; Bob Dylan lived at and owned **94 MacDougal Street** (on a row of historic brownstones) through much of the '60s, performing in Washington Square Park and at clubs such as **Cafe Wha?** on MacDougal Street, between Bleecker and West 3rd Streets. Once the stomping ground of Beat poets and jazz musicians, **Bleecker Street** *(between La Guardia Pl and Sixth Ave)* is now a dingy stretch of poster shops, cheap restaurants and music venues for the college crowd. The famed **Village Gate** jazz club once stood at the corner of Bleecker and Thompson Streets; it's been carved up into a CVS pharmacy and a small theater, though the Gate's sign is still in evidence. The new **AIA Center for Architecture**, a comprehensive resource for building and planning in New York, is just up the road on La Guardia Place.

In the triangle formed by Sixth Avenue, Greenwich Avenue and 10th Street, you'll see the Gothic-style **Jefferson Market Library**

It happened here

The '60s radicals the Weathermen are back in the spotlight with the documentary *The Weather Underground.* The group aimed to take down the U.S. government—but they blew up their own hideout instead. The 1845 house at **18 West 11th Street** *(between Fifth and Sixth Aves),* boyhood home of poet James Merrill, served as a bomb factory for the Weather folk until March 6, 1970, when a cache of dynamite exploded, killing three group members and destroying much of the structure. (Dustin Hoffman lived next door and witnessed the explosion.) The building remained vacant for eight years before being redesigned by architect Hugh Hardy.

Sightseeing

Rack of lamb You'll find **Alexander McQueen**'s store next to active meat markets. *See p93.*

(a branch of the New York Public Library), which has served this community for 35 years. Before that, the building was a courthouse; the lovely flower-filled garden facing Greenwich Avenue once held the Art Deco Women's House of Detention (Mae West did a little time there in 1928, on obscenity charges stemming from her Broadway show *Sex*). On Sixth Avenue at 4th Street, stop by "the Cage," outdoor basketball courts where outstanding schoolyard players showcase their shake-and-bake moves.

AIA Center for Architecture

536 La Guardia Pl between Bleecker and W 3rd Sts (212-683-0023). Subway: A, C, E, B, D, F, V to W 4th St. **Open** *Mon–Fri 10am–6pm; Sat noon–4pm.* **Admission** *free.*

Jefferson Market Library

425 Sixth Ave between 9th and 10th Sts (212-243-4334). Subway: A, C, E, B, D, F, V to W 4th St. **Open** *Mon, Wed noon–8pm; Tue 10am–6pm; Thu noon–6pm; Fri 1–6pm; Sat 10am–5pm.*

Salmagundi Club

47 Fifth Ave at 12th St (212-255-7740; www.salmagundi.org). Subway: L, N, Q, R, W, 4, 5, 6 to 14th St–Union Sq. **Open** *Open for exhibitions only; phone for details.* **Admission** *free.*

Washington Square Park

From Fifth Ave to MacDougal St, between Waverly Pl and W 4th St. Subway: A, C, E, B, D, F, V to W 4th St.

West Village & Meatpacking District

While the **West Village** now harbors plenty of celebrities (Gwyneth Paltrow, Ed Koch), it has managed to retain a humble, everyone-knows-one-another feel. The area west of Sixth Avenue to the Hudson River, below 14th Street to Houston Street, still retains the features that molded the Village's character and gave it shape. Only in this neighborhood could West 10th Street cross West 4th Street, and Waverly Place cross Waverly Place. Locals fill the bistros that line Hudson Street, and patronize the shops lining Bleecker Street—you won't risk getting stuck in too many tourist traps this far west.

The northwest corner of this area is known as the **Meatpacking District**—it's been a primarily wholesale meat market since the 1930s. Until the 1990s, it was also a prime haunt for prostitutes, many of them transsexual. In recent years, the atmospheric cobblestone streets have seen the arrival of a new type of tenant: The once-lonely **Florent** *(69 Gansevoort St between Greenwich and Washington Sts, 212-989-5779)*, a 24-hour French diner that opened in 1985, is now part of a chic scene that includes swinging watering hole **APT** (*see p290*) and the restaurant **Pastis** (*see p179*).

The district also lures the fashion faithful with hot destinations like **Alexander McQueen**, **Jeffrey New York**, **Stella McCartney** and the rockin' **Dernier Cri**. As building owners raise rents, the meat dealers and artists' studios are moving out. Ten years ago, there were approximately 100 wholesale companies in the area; today, the number is down to about 30. Residents started the Save Gansevoort Market campaign to obtain landmark status for the neighborhood, and won it in September 2003.

On the corner of Bethune and Washington Streets is **Westbeth**, a block-long building formerly owned by Bell Labs (it's where the vacuum tube and the transistor were invented); the late-19th-century structure was converted to affordable lofts for artists in 1969 (Diane Arbus and Gil Evans lived and worked there; Merce Cunningham still does). The neighborhood's bohemian appeal might be diminishing, but several historic nightlife spots are alive and well: The **White Horse Tavern** *(567 Hudson St at 11th St, 212-989-3956)* is where poet Dylan Thomas went on his last drinking binge before his untimely death in 1953. Earlier in the century, John Steinbeck and John Dos Passos passed time at **Chumley's** (*see p205*), a still-unmarked Prohibition-era speakeasy at 86 Bedford Street. Writer Edna St. Vincent Millay once lived at 75½ Bedford Street, built in 1873, and later dwellers included Cary Grant and John Barrymore. At 9½ feet in width, it may be the narrowest residential building in the entire city. On and just off Seventh Avenue South are jazz and cabaret clubs, including the **Village Vanguard** (*see p318*).

The West Village is also a renowned gay neighborhood, though much of the scene has moved north to Chelsea (*see p296*). The **Stonewall** (*see p302*) on Christopher Street is next to the original Stonewall Inn, the site of the 1969 rebellion that marked the birth of the modern gay-liberation movement. Same-sex couples stroll along Christopher Street (from Sheridan Square to the Hudson River pier), and plenty of shops, bars and restaurants are out and proud.

► For a complete review of the Stonewall and other gay establishments, *see pp296–306*.
► For more on shopping in the Meatpacking District, *see p218* **From chops to shops**.

Sightseeing

Midtown

Corporate power and world-class culture rise up from the busy city streets.

Midtown Manhattan (roughly 14th Street to 59th Street, river to river) is the New York of popular imagination. The city's crowded center is where you'll find concrete canyons and glass-and-steel towers; a global mix of busy pedestrians jockeying for space on the sidewalks; fleets of yellow cabs and exhaust-belching buses charging up the avenues—and an intense energy that fuels the drive to make it in this town. Here's where many of Manhattan's most famous stars—the **Empire State Building**, the **Chrysler Building**, **Carnegie Hall**, **Rockefeller Center** and **Times Square**—find everyday work as office space for captains of industry and the arts. The biggest department stores and hotels are on display in midtown, too. And you'll see wage-earners, culture-vultures and package-laden shoppers crisscrossing the **Broadway Theater District**, **Chelsea**, **Bryant Park**, **Penn Station** and **Grand Central Terminal**—it's no exaggeration to say millions (of people *and* dollars) pass through midtown each day and night. Get set for a wild ride.

Flatiron District & Union Square

The **Flatiron District**, which runs from 14th to 29th Streets, between Fifth and Park Avenues, gives downtown a run for its money in terms of cool cachet. This chic enclave is full of retail stores that are often less expensive but just as style-conscious as those below 14th Street. The area is compact enough that tourists can hit all the sights on foot and then, after a long day of exploring, relax with a cocktail in one of the area's numerous watering holes.

There are two public squares within the district. **Madison Square** *(from 23rd to 26th Sts, between Fifth and Madison Aves)* once marked the confines of a ritzy 19th-century shopping district known as Ladies' Mile. Extending along Broadway and west to Sixth Avenue, this collection of huge retail palaces attracted the "carriage trade"—wealthy women who bought the latest fashions and household goods that had come from all over the world. By 1914, most of the department stores had moved north, leaving behind the proud cast-iron buildings that once housed them. Today, the area has reclaimed its history and is once again a prime shopping destination. Between 14th and 23rd Streets, Broadway is a tasteful home-furnishings strip: The eclectic home-design store **ABC Carpet & Home** (*see p243*) inhabits a beautiful 1882 terra-cotta–and–brick building at the corner of 19th Street. Fifth Avenue below 23rd Street is a clothing destination: Many upscale shops, including the exclusive **Paul Smith** (*see p223*), showcase the latest designs. Sixth Avenue is dotted with such chain-store behemoths as Old Navy and Bed, Bath & Beyond.

Madison Square is also rich in history. It was the site of P.T. Barnum's Hippodrome and the original Madison Square Garden—the scene of prizefights, lavish entertainment and the scandalous murder of its architect, Stanford White (later recounted in the book and film *Ragtime*). After years of neglect, the statue-filled **Madison Square Park** finally got a face-lift in 2001. For ages, the vicinity bordering the park's east side was notable only for the presence of the *Metropolis*-style **New York Life Insurance Company** building *(51 Madison Ave between 25th and 26th Sts)* and the **Appellate Division Courthouse** *(35 E 25th St at Madison Ave)*. Now several upscale dining hot spots have injected some café-society liveliness into this once-staid district, especially **Les Halles**, **Tabla** and **Craft** (*see p188 and p186*).

Just south of Madison Square is the city's famously triangular Renaissance palazzo, the **Flatiron Building** (*see also p25*). The neighborhood was christened in honor of this structure, which was the world's first steel-frame skyscraper. Today, the nabe is peppered with boutiques, bookshops, photo studios and labs (it was known as the "photo district" well into the '90s)—and wandering supermodels. In the mid-1990s, big Internet companies began colonizing the lofts on Fifth Avenue and Broadway, earning the district a new nickname: **Silicon Alley**.

► For information on multimuseum discount packages, *see p143* **Cheap tix**.
► The area's museums are detailed on *pp143–163*.

The heart of **midtown**.

Even though many dot-coms went bust and others have decamped to surrounding neighborhoods, the label remains in use.

Union Square *(from 14th to 17th Sts, between Union Sq West and Union Sq East)* is named after neither the Union of the Civil War nor the lively labor rallies that once took place there, but simply for the union of Broadway and Bowery Lane (now Fourth Avenue). From the 1920s until the early '60s, Union Square gained a reputation as the favorite location for rabble-rousing political oratory, from AFL-CIO rallies to anti–Vietnam War protests. Following September 11, 2001, the park area became the visual focal point for the city's outpouring of grief. The square itself is now best known as the site of the **Union Square Greenmarket**—an excellent farmers' market—and the buildings around the square are used for a variety of commercial purposes. They include the **W New York—Union Square** hotel (*see p41*), the giant **Zeckendorf Towers** residential complex *(1 Irving Pl between 14th and 15th Sts)*, a **Virgin Megastore** (*see p245*) and a **Barnes & Noble** bookstore. Several fine restaurants are also in close proximity, notably the **Union Square Cafe** (*see p187*). In summer, the outdoor **Luna Park** bar *(50 E 17th St between Broadway and Park Ave South)* beckons the cocktail crowd, while skateboarders commandeer the Greenmarket space on off days to practice tricks. Just off the square to the east is the **Vineyard Theater** (*see p345*), an Off Broadway venue committed to drama with a bite. It has featured the work of such well-respected resident playwrights as Craig Lucas and Paula Vogel.

Flatiron Building

175 Fifth Ave between 22nd and 23rd Sts. Subway: R, W to 23rd St.

Union Square Greenmarket

From 16th to 17th Sts, between Union Sq West and Union Sq East (212-477-3220). Subway: L, N, Q, R, W, 4, 5, 6 to 14th St–Union Sq. **Open** *Mon, Wed, Fri, Sat 8am–6pm.*

Chelsea

Not so long ago, **Chelsea** was a mostly working-class and industrial neighborhood. Now it's the epicenter of the city's gay life (*see pp296–306* **Gay & Lesbian**), but residents of all types inhabit the blocks between 14th and 29th Streets, west of Fifth Avenue. There's a generous assortment of bars and restaurants, most of them clustered on Eighth Avenue. Pioneers such as the **Dia: Chelsea** (*see p148*) have led the art crowd northward from Soho, and the whole western edge of Chelsea is now a hot gallery zone. The far-western warehouse district, currently home to fashionable lounges and nightclubs, is also seeing more residential use.

Cushman Row *(406–418 W 20th St between Ninth and Tenth Aves)*, in the **Chelsea Historic District**, is an example of how the 'hood

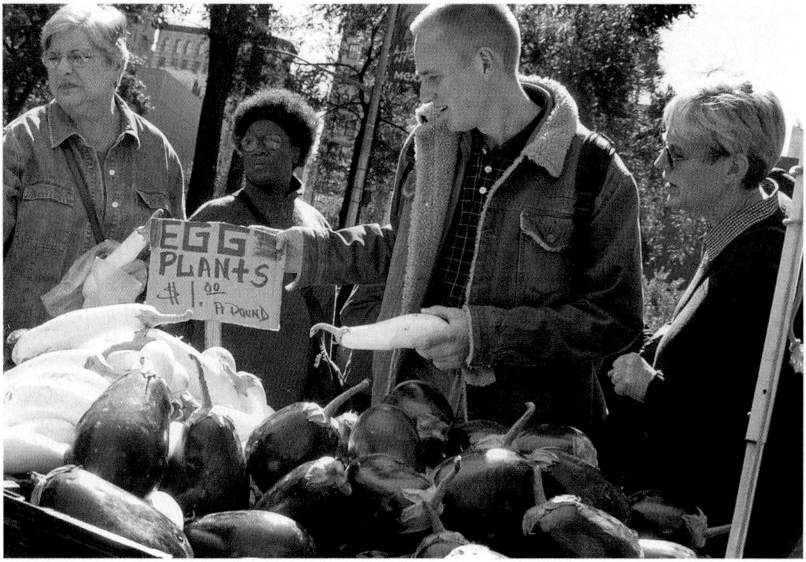

Salad days Local farm produce comes to the **Union Square Greenmarket**. *See p95.*

looked when it was developed in the mid-1800s—a grandeur that was destroyed 30 years later when noisy elevated railways were built. Just north is the block-long **General Theological Seminary of the Episcopal Church** *(175 Ninth Ave at 21st St)*, whose gardens offer a pleasant, reflective respite from active city life. The seminary's land was part of the estate known as Chelsea, which was owned by Clement Clarke Moore, best known for "'Twas the night before Christmas…"

The **Annex Antiques Fair & Flea Market** (*see p238*) operates year-round on weekends in a couple of empty parking lots, as well as in an indoor garage. An ornate wrought-iron latticework facade distinguishes the landmark **Chelsea Hotel** (*see p56* **High style, low budget**), which has been a magnet for international bohemians since the poets and painters of the '50s made it their lodging of choice. In the '60s and '70s, Andy Warhol's superstars (the "Chelsea Girls") made it infamous, and the punks made the hotel notorious in the '80s, when Nancy Spungen was stabbed to death there by boyfriend Sid Vicious. Stop by for a peek at the curious lobby artwork and the grunge-glamorous guests, and stay for a bit with a drink in the luxe basement lounge, **Serena** (in the Chelsea Hotel, *see p56*). Occupying a long city block between Ninth and Tenth Avenues is **London Terrace**, a distinctive 1920s Tudor-style apartment complex that's home to a number of celebrities, including Debbie Harry and the geographically correct Chelsea Clinton.

Chelsea has its fair share of cultural offerings. The **Joyce Theater** (*see p347*) is in a tastefully renovated Art Deco cinema house and presents some of the better-known modern dance troupes. The **Bessie Schönberg Theater** *(219 W 19th St between Seventh and Eighth Aves, 212-924-0077)* is where poets recite, participants in the **Dance Theater Workshop** perform (*see p348*), and mimes do…well, whatever mimes do. Toward the river on 19th Street is the **Kitchen** (*see p345*), a longstanding experimental-arts center.

The former Nabisco plant where the first Oreo cookie was made in 1912 has been renovated and now houses the **Chelsea Market** (the block-long factory building on Ninth Avenue is a conglomeration of 18 structures built between the 1890s and 1930s). A food arcade on the ground floor offers artisanal bread, fresh lobster, wine, hand-decorated cookies and imported Italian foods, among other things.

► Contemporary-art lovers should explore the far-western area of Chelsea. For listings *see pp261–265* **Art Galleries**.
► For more information on Chelsea's nightlife, *see pp302–305* **Gay & Lesbian**.

Chelsea's art galleries, which occupy former warehouse spaces west of Tenth Avenue in the West 20s, draw an international audience of aesthetes, especially on weekends. Many of the major galleries were priced out of Soho (in favor of retail shopping) and have found new homes here; bars and restaurants on the prowl for cheaper real estate followed the galleries—in much the same way that Soho developed. So while you're here, let's eat: The 1929 Art Deco **Empire Diner** *(210 Tenth Ave at 22nd St, 212-243-2736)* and the casual French bistro **La Lunchonette** *(130 Tenth Ave at 18th St, 212-675-0342)* have been joined by a host of newer restaurants, including the beautiful-people hot spot the **Park** (*see p206*) and the American bistro the **Red Cat** (*see p184*). **Glass** (*see p206*) is a great place to have a drink after gallery-hopping.

You can watch the sunset from one of the **Hudson River piers** in Chelsea; they were once terminals for the world's grand ocean liners. While many piers remain in a state of disrepair, the four between 17th and 23rd Streets have been transformed into a mega sports center and TV studio complex called **Chelsea Piers** (*see p332*). When you're down by the river, the stunning **Starrett-Lehigh Building** *(601 W 26th St at Eleventh Ave)* comes into view. Until 1999, the 1930s structure—acclaimed as a masterpiece of the International Style—was a neglected industrial warehouse. Today, companies such as Martha Stewart Living Omnimedia and Hugo Boss occupy the building, making a strong statement of optimism for Chelsea's far-west side.

Chelsea Historic District

From Ninth to Tenth Aves, between 20th and 22nd Sts. Subway: C, E to 23rd St.

Chelsea Market

75 Ninth Ave between 15th and 16th Sts (www.chelseamarket.com). Subway: A, C, E to 14th St; L to Eighth Ave. **Open** *Mon–Sat 8am–7pm; Sun 10am–6pm.*

General Theological Seminary

Ninth Ave between 20th and 21st Sts (212-243-5150; www.gts.edu). Subway: C, E to 23rd St. **Open** *Mon–Fri noon–3pm; Sat 11am–3pm.* **Admission** *free.*

Gramercy Park

You need a key to get inside the gates of **Gramercy Park**, a tranquil square at the bottom of Lexington Avenue *(between 20th and 21st Sts)*. Who gets a key? Only people who live in the beautiful townhouses and apartment buildings that ring the park—or those who stay at the **Gramercy Park Hotel** (*see p41*). Anyone, however, can enjoy the charm of the surrounding district, between Park Avenue South and Third Avenue. Gramercy Park was developed in the 1830s as an imitation of a London square. The **Players** *(16 Gramercy Park South at Park Ave South)*, a private club and residence, is housed in an 1845 brownstone that was owned by actor Edwin Booth; the 19th-century superstar was the brother of Abraham Lincoln's assassin, John Wilkes Booth. Edwin had it remodeled as a club for theater professionals (Winston Churchill and Mark Twain were members). No. 15 is the Gothic Revival **National Arts Club**, whose members often donate impressive works in lieu of annual dues. Its bar has what may be the only original Tiffany stained-glass ceiling left in the city.

The strip of **Irving Place**, leading south from the park to 14th Street, is named after Washington Irving. Although the author of *The Legend of Sleepy Hollow* didn't actually live on this street, it does have a literary past. O. Henry wrote "The Gift of the Magi" at **Pete's Tavern** *(129 E 18th St at Irving Pl, 212-473-7676)*, which claims to be the city's oldest bar (a title that in fact belongs to McSorley's). Near the corner of 15th Street, **Irving Plaza** (*see p311*), a medium-size live-music venue, hosts big-name acts such as Steve Earle and quirkier ones, like Rufus

Top four Views

When you need a lift, raise your spirits with a glass of spirits in an elevated place:

Top of the Tower at Beekman Tower Hotel (*see p45*)
Panoramic views from this 26th-floor restaurant include the United Nations complex and the sparkling midtown skyline.

Ava Lounge at Majestic Hotel (*see p206*)
Rise above Times Square at this seductive penthouse lounge with an open-air annex.

Metro Grill at Hotel Metro (*see p54*)
The unparalleled view of the Empire State Building makes this outdoor rooftop bar one of the city's best aeries.

The High Bar at the Gramercy Park Hotel (*see p41*)
A hip crowd takes in groovy views of the park and the nearby Flatiron Building.

Wainwright. At the corner of Park Avenue South and 17th Street stands the final headquarters of the once-omnipotent **Tammany Hall** political machine. Built in 1929, the building now contains the **New York Film Academy** and **Union Square Theater**.

A few blocks away, the **Theodore Roosevelt Birthplace**, designated as a national site, is now a small museum. The president's actual birthplace was demolished in 1916, but it has since been fully reconstructed, complete with period furniture and a trophy room. The low, fortresslike **69th Regiment Armory** *(68 Lexington Ave between 25th and 26th Sts)* is currently used by the New York National Guard, and was the site of the sensational 1913 Armory Show that introduced Americans to Cubism, Fauvism and Dadism. The tradition continues at the annual **Armory Show** (*see p259*).

Sightseeing

National Arts Club

15 Gramercy Park South between Park Ave South and Irving Pl (212-475-3424; www.nationalartsclub.org). Subway: 6 to 23rd St. **Open** *For exhibitions only.*

Theodore Roosevelt Birthplace

28 E 20th St between Broadway and Park Ave South (212-260-1616; www.nps.gov/thrb). Subway: 6 to 23rd St. **Open** *Tue–Sat 9am–5pm.* **Tours** *Tue–Sat 10am–4pm, on the hour.* **Admission** *$3, children under 18 free.* **Credit** *Cash only.*

Kips Bay & Murray Hill

Until recently, the relatively nondescript area from 23rd to 40th Streets, between Park Avenue and the East River, was dominated by large apartment buildings and hospitals. But the slightly below-market rents have attracted some stylish residents, including designer Richard Tyler. Now this newly popular neighborhood is politicking for its own acronym: Nomad (North of Madison Square Park). Maybe one day we'll all call it that. The southern, largely residential portion is known as **Kips Bay**, after Jacobus Henderson Kip, whose 17th-century farm once covered the area. Third Avenue is the main thoroughfare, and it's where you'll find ethnic eateries representing a variety of Eastern cuisines, including Afghan, Tibetan and Turkish, along with sleek nightspots such as **Spread**, a restaurant and lounge in the hotel **Marcel** (*see p55*), and the **Rodeo Bar** (*see p318*), a Texas-style roadhouse that offers food and live roots music. **Lexington Avenue** between 27th and 30th Streets is dubbed Curry Hill because of the many Indian restaurants and grocery stores here. (You can pick up one of New York's three English-language Indian newspapers in any grocery.) First Avenue, from 27th to 34th Streets, has unrivaled medical facilities: Mt. Sinai–New York University Medical Center, the city-run Bellevue Hospital Center and the Rusk Institute, a world-class rehabilitation center.

Murray Hill stretches from 30th to 40th Streets, between Third and Fifth Avenues. Townhouses of the rich and powerful were once clustered around Park and Madison Avenues. While it's still a fashionable neighborhood, only a few streets retain the elegance that once made it a tony address. **Sniffen Court** *(150–158 E 36th St between Lexington and Third Aves)* is an unspoiled row of 1864 carriage houses, located within earshot of the Queens Midtown Tunnel's ceaseless traffic. One of the area's best attractions, the **Morgan Library** (*see p150*), also on 36th Street, is closed for renovation until 2006. The charming exhibition space occupies two elegant buildings (one of which was J. Pierpont Morgan's personal library), and the library houses the manuscripts, books, prints, and silver and copper collections owned by the notorious banker.

Herald Square & the Garment District

The heart of America's billion-dollar clothing industry is New York's **Garment District** (roughly 34th to 40th Streets, from Broadway to Eighth Avenue) where every day, thousands of workers—and platoons of designers—create the clothes we'll be wearing in seasons to come. The main drag is **Seventh Avenue**, which has a stylish (if rarely used) moniker: Fashion Avenue. Although most garment manufacturing has left Manhattan, the area is still gridlocked by delivery trucks and workers pushing racks of clothes up and down the street. Trimmings, buttons and fabric shops line the sidewalks here (especially on 38th and 39th Streets), along with the last of New York's milliners. A once-thriving fur market is in retreat, now occupying only 28th to 30th Streets, between Seventh and Eighth Avenues. On Seventh Avenue at 27th Street is the **Fashion Institute of Technology** *(www.fitnyc.suny.edu)*, a state college where aspiring rivals of Calvin Klein and Jhane Barnes (both FIT graduates) dream up the modes of tomorrow. The school's gallery mounts stellar exhibitions.

Beginning on 34th Street at Broadway, and stretching all the way to Seventh Avenue, **Macy's** (*see p212*) is still the biggest—and busiest—department store in the world. Across the street is the younger, trendier chain store **H&M**, located in the Marbridge Building, which recently got a $24 million makeover.

Herald Square, named for a long-gone newspaper, is surrounded by this retail wonderland. The area's lower section is known as **Greeley Square**, after Horace Greeley, the owner of the *Herald*'s rival, the *Tribune* (which employed Karl Marx as a columnist). Once an area to be avoided, the square now offers bistro chairs and rest areas for weary pedestrians. East of Greeley Square, the many restaurants and shops of **Koreatown** line 32nd Street between Madison Avenue and Broadway.

The giant doughnut of a building on Seventh Avenue between 31st and 32nd Streets is the sports and entertainment arena **Madison Square Garden** (*see p328*). It occupies the site of the old Pennsylvania Station, a McKim, Mead & White architectural masterpiece that was razed in the 1960s—an act so outrageous that it led to the creation of the Landmarks Preservation Commission (for more on the city's architecture, *see pp20–27*). The railroad terminal's name has been shortened (as if in shame) to **Penn Station**, and it now lies beneath the Garden, where it serves approximately 600,000 people daily—more than any other station in the country. Fortunately, the aesthetic tide has turned. In 2000, the city approved a $788 million restoration-and-development project to move Penn Station to the site of the **General Post Office** *(421 Eighth Ave between 31st and 33rd Sts, 212-967-8585)*, which was designed by the original Pennsylvania Station architects in 1913 to complement the formerly majestic terminal. The project will connect the post office's two buildings with a soaring glass-and-

A la cart: Dining as a stand-up act

Midtown is busy, crowded and hectic. New York's street culture is in full throttle here, and you'll be in the thick of it. So don't waste time by breaking stride while seeing the sights; and save yourself the attitude at pricey, expense-account–supported restaurants. Grab your lunch on the go. Follow in-the-know locals to one of these top-quality sidewalk carts, then join the crowds sitting on perches along the major avenues' open plazas.

- At a mobile outpost of the popular sausage joint **Hallo Berlin** *(54th St at Fifth Ave)*, lunchtime diners line up for juicy bratwurst, smothered in the finest sauerkraut you're likely to find this side of the Rhine.
- For less than $5 each, you can get huge, wonderful crêpes at **Crêpe Cafe** *(53rd St between Fifth and Sixth Aves)*. Try one filled with broccoli, mushrooms and mozzarella, then come back for another slathered with Nutella and dusted with powdered sugar.
- Office workers cluster in droves around **Prince of Egypt** *(47th St at Sixth Ave)* for excellent falafel and solid shish kebabs.
- Any serious wiener eater will tell you that a snappy grilled frank beats a flabby boiled dog any day. And the **Hot Dog King** *(49th St at Sixth Ave)* knows how to grill 'em right.
- M.D. Rahman used to be a chef at the fabulous, dearly departed Russian Tea Room. At **Kwik Meal** *(45th St at Sixth Ave)*, he packs his pitas full of the best marinated lamb in midtown (skip the sauce). On Tuesday, Thursday and Friday, he offers spicy tiger shrimp, too.

- Why brave the crowds—and the prices—at one of those overhyped delis, when you can get a great sandwich at **Gabriel the Pastrami Guy** *(50th St between Sixth and Seventh Aves)* for less than $4? Nonmeat eaters can try the $3 veggie burger.

Light opera The neon lights of **Times Square** are positively symphonic, 24 hours a day.

nickel–trussed ticketing hall and concourse. When finally realized (no earlier than 2006), the new Penn Station will offer Amtrak service and rail links to Newark, La Guardia and JFK airports; the current Penn Station will continue as a hub for New Jersey Transit, the Long Island Rail Road and the subways.

Herald Square

Junction of Broadway and Sixth Ave at 34th St. Subway: B, D, F, V, N, Q, R, W to 34th St–Herald Sq.

Broadway & Times Square

Around 42nd Street and Broadway, which is often called "the crossroads of the world," the night is illuminated not by the moon and the stars, but by acres of blinking, glaring neon and sweeping arc lights. Even native New Yorkers are electrified—or mortified—by this larger-than-life light show. No area better represents the city's glitter and grit (though there's less of the latter now) than Times Square.

Originally called Longacre Square, **Times Square** was renamed after *The New York Times* moved to the site in the early 1900s, announcing its arrival with a spectacular New Year's Eve fireworks display. The *Times* erected the world's first "zipper" sign on its building at 1 Times Square, and the circling messages—from the stock-market crash of 1929 and JFK's assassination to the World Trade Center attack—have been known to stop midtown masses in their tracks. The Gray Lady is now located on 43rd Street between Seventh and Eighth Avenues (the paper plans to build an $84 million tower on Eighth Avenue between 40th and 41st Streets), but the sign remains at the original locale, and it marks the spot where New Year's Eve is traditionally celebrated. Times Square is really just an elongated intersection where Broadway crosses Seventh Avenue, but it's the center of the **Theater District**. More than 30 stages used for dramatic productions are situated on the streets that cross Broadway. The most notorious element of Times Square—its once-famous sex trade—is now relegated to a short stretch of Eighth Avenue, where a few peep shows and porn shops still promulgate the tawdry.

The area's transformation began in 1990, when the city condemned most of the properties along 42nd Street (a.k.a. "the Deuce") between Seventh and Eighth Avenues. A few years later, the city changed its zoning laws, making it harder for adult-entertainment establishments to operate. The result is untrue-to-their-roots places like **Show World** *(669 Eighth Ave between 42nd and 43rd Sts),* once a noted sleaze palace, which nowadays tries to get by with more PG films and live productions.

The streets west of Eighth Avenue are filled with eateries catering to theatergoers, and **Restaurant Row** *(46th St between Eighth* *and Ninth Aves)* has an unbroken string of them. Long before French bistros were commonplace downtown, midtown had places such as **Pierre au Tunnel** *(250 W 47th St between Broadway and Eighth Ave, 212-575-1220)* and **Tout Va Bien** *(311 W 51st St between Eighth and Ninth Aves, 212-265-0190),* both of which are still charming, if not gastronomically au courant.

As you'd expect, office buildings in the area are filled with entertainment companies: recording studios, theatrical management companies, record labels and screening rooms. The **Brill Building** *(1619 Broadway at 49th St)* boasts a rich history, having long been the headquarters of music publishers and producers. Such luminaries as Jerry Lieber, Mike Stoller, Phil Spector, and Carole King wrote and auditioned their hits within; it's also the building featured in the classic movie *Sweet Smell of Success.* Visiting rock royalty and aspiring musicians drool over the selection of new and vintage guitars (and countless other instruments) for sale along "Music Row" *(48th St between Sixth and Seventh Aves).* Two recent additions to the area are the colorful 863-room **Westin** hotel (*see p44* **Chain gang**) and the 110,000-square-foot **Toys "R" Us** flagship store (*see p238*), which has a 60-foot-tall indoor Ferris wheel. Nearer to the southwestern end of the square is the home base of **MTV** *(1515 Broadway at 45th St),* which often sends camera crews into the street to tape segments. During warmer months, eager teens congregate under the windows of the network's second-floor studio, hoping for a wave from guest celebrities inside. The glittering glass case that is headquarters to magazine-publishing giant **Condé Nast** *(Broadway at 43rd St)* looms at 4 Times Square. In the same building is the **Nasdaq MarketSite**. The multimedia electronic stock market dominates Times Square with its eight-story, 10,736-square-foot cylindrical video screen.

Madame Tussaud's New York, a Gothamized version of the London-based wax-museum chain, has an Opening Night Party room containing New York personalities such as Woody Allen and Barbra Streisand, along with the glamorous likes of Princess Diana and RuPaul. Matthew Broderick and Nathan Lane are also set in wax—just as their widely praised original leads in *The Producers* are set in theatrical history.

Nightlife in the square is dominated by theaters and theme restaurants. In addition to Restaurant Row, you'll find evidence of Little Brazil tucked into the Times Square side streets; try **Cabana Carioca** *(123 W 45th St between Sixth and Seventh Aves, 212-581-8088)* or the tonier **Churrascaria Plataforma** *(316 W 49th St between Eighth and Ninth Aves, 212-245-0505).*

Make a brief detour uptown on Seventh Avenue, just south of Central Park, for a glimpse of the great classical-music landmark **Carnegie Hall** (*see p321*). Across the street at the **Carnegie Deli** *(854 Seventh Ave at 55th St, 212-757-2245),* maestros of the Reuben sandwich expertly conduct its composition.

West of Times Square, past the curious steel spiral of the **Port Authority Bus Terminal** on Eighth Avenue and the **Lincoln Tunnel**'s traffic-knotted entrance, is an area historically known as **Hell's Kitchen**. During the 19th century, an impoverished gang- and crime-ridden Irish community lived here. Following the Irish were Italians, Greeks, Puerto Ricans,

It happened here

In the movie *Party Monster,* Macaulay Culkin portrays "king of the club kids" Michael Alig, who in March 1996 committed clubland's most infamous crime, at the **Riverbank West** *(560 W 43rd St between Tenth and Eleventh Aves).* Following an argument between Alig and his drug-dealing roommate Angel Melendez, the club promoter and another friend smashed Melendez on the head with a hammer, then asphyxiated him by filling his mouth with Drano. Alig dumped the body in the river, but it later washed up on Staten Island. Now it's iron bars, not velvet ropes, for Alig: He's serving 20 years for the murder.

Sightseeing

High times Views from atop the **Empire State Building** are worth a wait in line. *See p103.*

Dominicans and other ethnic groups. It remained rough-and-tumble (providing the backdrop for the hit musical *West Side Story*) through the 1970s, when, in an effort to invite gentrification, neighborhood activists renamed it Clinton, after onetime mayor and city planner DeWitt Clinton. Crime has abated, and these days, a younger, more diverse group is moving in. Ninth Avenue from 38th to 57th Streets is the area's main drag, known for its inexpensive restaurants and bars.

South of 42nd Street, the main landmark is the **Jacob K. Javits Convention Center** *(Eleventh Ave between 34th and 39th Sts)*. This black-glass palace, designed by I.M. Pei & Partners in 1986, hosts conventions and trade shows. Among the Hudson River piers is the **Circle Line** terminal (*see p70*) on 42nd Street at Pier 83. At the end of 46th Street, the aircraft carrier *Intrepid* houses the **Sea-Air-Space Museum** (*see p162*).

Madame Tussaud's New York

234 W 42nd St between Seventh and Eighth Aves (800-246-8872; www.madame-tussauds.com). Subway: N, Q, R, W, 42nd St S, 1, 2, 3, 9, 7 to 42nd St–Times Sq. **Open** *10am–8pm daily.* **Admission** *$25, seniors $22, children 4–12 $19, children under 3 free.*

Times Square

Times Square Visitors' Center, 1560 Broadway between 46th and 47th Sts, entrance on Seventh Ave (212-768-1560). Subway: N, R, W to 49th St; 1, 9 to 50th St. **Open** *8am–8pm daily.*

Fifth Avenue

Synonymous with *chic* and *sophisticated,* Fifth Avenue caters to the elite. But it is also the main route for the city's many ethnic and inclusive parades (e.g., Gay Pride). Passing in front of some of the most recognizable buildings and storefronts in town gives these public events a heightened feeling of importance.

The **Empire State Building** at 34th Street is visible from most parts of the city, and it's lit at night in various colors, according to the holiday or special event. However, it's only at the corner of Fifth Avenue and 34th Street that you can truly appreciate its height. Situated smack-dab in the center of midtown, the building's 102nd-floor observatory offers brilliant views in every direction. Go at sunset and glimpse the longest shadow you'll ever see, cast all the way across Manhattan to Queens.

Impassive stone lions guard the steps of the **New York Public Library** at 41st Street (*see p162*). This beautiful Beaux Arts building provides a quiet escape from the noise outside. The recently spiffed-up Rose Main Reading Room, on the library's top floor, is a hushed sanctuary of 23-foot-long tables and matching oak chairs, where bibliophiles can read, write and do research. Behind the library is **Bryant Park**, a well-cultivated lawn sprinkled with lunching office workers; during the summer, it hosts a dizzying schedule of free entertainment (*see p254*). The park also houses the ivy-covered American restaurant **Bryant Park Cafe and Grill** *(25 W 40th St between Fifth and Sixth Aves, 212-840-6500).* On 40th Street, the **Bryant Park** (*see p47*) is a new hotel built within the former American Radiator Building. Designed by architect Raymond Hood in the mid-1920s, the building is faced with near-black brick and trimmed in gold leaf—it seems to exemplify the term *Gotham* (if not the Bat Cave). Inside this luxurious hotel are the **Cellar Bar** lounge *(212-642-2260)* and **Ilo** *(212-642-2255),* a high-end, French-infused American restaurant. The **Algonquin** (*see p45*) is where Dorothy Parker and friends held court at Alexander Woollcott's Round Table; the lobby is still a great place to meet and have a drink.

The city's jewelry trade is located along the 47th Street strip known as **Diamond Row**. Outside the stores, in front of the glittering window displays, you'll see Orthodox Jewish traders with precious gems in their suit pockets, doing business in the street. This stretch is the most heavily surveilled block in New York City, with cameras peering out of doorways and from atop buildings.

Veer off Fifth Avenue into the 18 buildings of **Rockefeller Center** *(from 48th to 51st Sts)* and you'll understand why this masterly use of public space is so lavishly praised. As you stroll down the Channel Gardens, the stately Art Deco General Electric Building gradually appears above you. The sunken plaza in the center is the winter site of an oft-packed **ice-skating rink** (*see p333*). A giant **Christmas tree** looms above it all each holiday season (*see p258*). Gathered around the plaza's perimeter are the International Building and its companions. The center is filled with murals, sculptures, mosaics, metalwork and enamels. Of special note are José María Sert's murals in the GE Building and Sol LeWitt's primary-colored mural *Wall Drawing #896 Colors/Curves* in the lobby of Christie's auction house at 20 Rockefeller Plaza.

On weekday mornings, a crowd of (mostly) tourists gathers at the **NBC** television network's glass-walled, ground-level studio (where the *Today* show is shot), at the southwest corner of Rockefeller Plaza and 49th Street. When the show plays host to its free concert series in the plaza (featuring big-name guests like Shania Twain, Jewel and Sting), the throng swells mightily before dispersing to the chain stores above and below Rockefeller Center. **Radio City Music Hall**, on Sixth Avenue at 50th Street, was the world's largest cinema when it was built in 1932 (the backstage tour is one of the best in town). This Art Deco jewel was treated to a $70-million restoration in 1999; it's now used for music concerts, and for the traditional Christmas and Easter shows featuring the renowned Rockettes.

Across from Rockefeller Center is the beautiful Gothic Revival **St. Patrick's Cathedral**, the largest Catholic cathedral in the United States. Several museums are just a few blocks north: the newly built **American Folk Art Museum**, the **Museum of Arts and Design** and the **Museum of Television & Radio** (*see p151, p153 and p161*). The **Museum of Modern Art**'s location on West 53rd Street is closed for renovation until 2005. MoMA (*see p150*) has temporarily moved to Long Island City, Queens. **Swing Street**, on 52nd Street, is a row of former speakeasies and jazz clubs; the only remaining 1920s venue in operation is the **'21' Club** *(21 W 52nd St between Fifth and Sixth Aves, 212-582-7200).* Downstairs, the barroom buzzes at night; the upstairs restaurant is a popular power-lunch spot.

The blocks of Fifth Avenue between Rockefeller Center and Central Park boast expensive retail palaces bearing names that were famous long before the concept of branding. Along the stretch between **Saks Fifth Avenue** *(between 49th and 50th Sts; see p213)* and **Bergdorf Goodman** *(at 58th St; see p211),* the rents are among the highest in the world, and you'll find **Cartier**, **Gucci**, **Tiffany & Co.** and **Versace**. They've been joined in recent years by the first U.S. outpost of Swedish clothing giant **H&M** and by the **National Basketball Association**'s official store. Straddling the line between mass market and exclusivity is **Trump Tower** *(725 Fifth Ave at 56th St),* an ostentatious pink-marble and gilt-trim shopping mall built by "the Donald."

Fifth Avenue is crowned by **Grand Army Plaza** at 59th Street. A gilded statue of General Sherman presides over this public space; to the west is the elegant **Plaza Hotel** (*see p62*); to the east is the luxe **Pierre Hotel** (*see p61*). From here, you can enter Central Park—where a whole other world awaits you.

Empire State Building

350 Fifth Ave between 33rd and 34th Sts (212-736-3100; www.esbnyc.com). Subway: B, D, F, V, N, Q, R, W to 34th St–Herald Sq. **Open** *Observatories 9:30am–midnight daily (closed during extreme* *weather).* **Admission** *$11, seniors and children 12–17 $10, children 6–11 $6, children under 5 free; last tickets sold at 11:15pm.* **Credit** *Cash only.*

NBC

30 Rockefeller Plaza, 49th St between Fifth and Sixth Aves (212-664-3700; www.shopnbc.com). Subway: B, D, F, V to 47–50th Sts–Rockefeller Ctr. **Tours** *Mon–Sat 8:30am–5:30pm; Sun 9:30am–4:30pm; tours depart every 15–30 minutes.* **Fees** *$17.75; seniors, students and children 6–16 $15.25; children under 6 not admitted.*

Peer through the *Today* show's studio window with a horde of fellow onlookers, or pay admission for a guided tour of the interior studios. (For information on NBC show tapings, *see p295*).

New York Public Library

For listing, see p162 **Humanities and Social Services Library**.

Radio City Music Hall

See p314 for listing. **Tour fees** *$17, seniors $14, children under 12 $10.*

Rockefeller Center

From 48th to 51st Sts, between Fifth and Sixth Aves (212-632-3975; tickets 212-664-7174; www.rockefellercenter.com). Subway: B, D, F, V to 47–50th Sts–Rockefeller Ctr. **Tours** *Mon–Sat 10am–5pm; Sun 10am–4pm; tours depart every hour.* **Fees** *$10, seniors and children 6–16 $8.*

Exploring the center itself is free. For guided tours in and around the historic buildings, advance tickets are available by phone, online or at the NBC Experience Store *(30 Rockefeller Plaza, 212-664-3700).*

St. Patrick's Cathedral

Fifth Ave between 50th and 51st Sts (212-753-2261). Subway: B, D, F to 47–50th Sts–Rockefeller Ctr; E, V to Fifth Ave–53rd St. **Open** *6:30am–9:30pm daily.* **Tours** *Call for tour dates and times.* **Fees** *free.*

Midtown East

Grand Central Terminal, a 1913 Beaux Arts station, is the city's most spectacular point of arrival (unlike Penn Station, it's used only for commuter trains). The station stands at the junction of 42nd Street and Park Avenue, the latter rising on a cast-iron bridge and running around the terminal, like a roller-coaster track. Thanks to a 1998 renovation, the terminal has itself become a destination, with upscale restaurants and bars, such as the ornate cocktail lounge **Campbell Apartment** *(West Balcony, 212-953-0409);* star chef Charlie Palmer's **Métrazur** *(East Balcony, 212-687-4600);* **Michael Jordan's—The Steak House NYC** *(West Balcony, 212-655-2300);* and the grottolike **Grand Central Oyster Bar and Restaurant** (*see p191*). **Grand Central Market**, which runs along a street-level passageway, sells gourmet goodies from around the world; the Lower Concourse food court offers sophisticated, fairly priced lunch options. One notable oddity: The constellations of the winter zodiac on the ceiling of the Main Concourse were drawn in reverse (as if seen from outer space) by the original artist.

East 42nd Street holds still more architectural distinction—both in the Romanesque Revival hall of the former **Bowery Savings Bank** (at No. 110), which is now a special-events space owned by the Cipriani restaurant family, and in the Art Deco detail of the **Chanin Building** (No. 122). Completed in 1930, the gleaming chrome **Chrysler Building** *(at Lexington Ave)* pays homage to the automobile. Architect William van Alen outfitted the base of the main tower with brickwork cars, complete with chrome hubcaps and radiator-cap eagles enlarged to vast proportions and projected over the edge as "cargoyles." The building's needle-sharp stainless-steel spire was added to the original plan so that the finished building would be taller than 40 Wall Street, which was under construction at the same time. Philip Johnson's **Chrysler Trylons**—three blue-gray glass pyramids—rest between the Chrysler Building and 666 Third Avenue. These retail pavilions are Johnson's "monument to 42nd Street." The ***Daily News* Building** (No. 220), another Art Deco gem designed by Raymond Hood, was immortalized in the *Superman* films; even though the tabloid namesake no longer has offices there, the lobby still houses its giant globe.

The street ends at **Tudor City**, a pioneering 1925 residential development that's a high-rise version of Hampton Court in England. This neighborhood is dominated by the **United Nations** and its famous glass-walled Secretariat building *(U.N. Plaza, First Ave between 42nd and 48th Sts).* You won't need your passport, but you are leaving U.S. soil when you enter the U.N. complex—this is an international zone, and the vast buffet at the **Delegates Dining Room** *(fourth floor, 212-963-7626)* puts multiculturalism on the table. Optimistic sculptures dot the grounds, and the Peace Gardens along the East River bloom in season with delicate roses. Nearby, however, the serenity is disrupted (and the light nearly blotted out) by the 72-story **Trump World Tower** *(First Ave between 47th and 48th Sts),* the world's second-tallest residential building. Even a coalition of such high-powered area residents as newsman Walter Cronkite couldn't prevent Trump from erecting this behemoth.

St. Patrick's Cathedral. *See p104.*

Play on A musician serenades commuters on the move at **Grand Central Terminal**.

Rising behind Grand Central Terminal, the **MetLife Building** (*see p26*), formerly the Pan Am Building, was once the world's largest office tower. Now its most celebrated tenants are the peregrine falcons that nest on the roof and feed on pigeons snatched out of midair. Glittering **230 Park Avenue** is directly north. The building's details (by the architects of Grand Central) were later flashily gilded by the Harry and Leona Helmsley corporation.

On Park Avenue, amid the blocks of international corporate headquarters, is the **Waldorf-Astoria** (*see p51*). The famed hotel was originally located on Fifth Avenue, but was demolished in 1929 to make way for the Empire State Building; it was rebuilt on this spot in 1931. Many of the city's most famous International Style office buildings are also in the area: **Lever House** *(390 Park Ave between 53rd and 54th Sts; see also p191)* was the first (1952) and most graceful glass box on Park Avenue. The 1958 **Seagram Building** *(375 Park Ave between 52nd and 53rd Sts),* designed by Ludwig Mies van der Rohe and others, is a stunning bronze-and-glass tower that contains the landmark restaurant the **Four Seasons** *(99 E 52nd St between Park and Lexington Aves, 212-754-9494).* A postmodern Chippendale crown tops Phillip Johnson's 1980s-era **Sony Building** *(550 Madison Ave between 55th and 56th Sts).* Inside is Sony's **Wonder Technology Lab** (*see p280*), a hands-on thrill zone of innovative science-in-action.

The newest addition to this cluster of dazzling architecture is the **LVMH Tower** (*see p22*). Designed by Christian de Portzamparc (one of the youngest architects to be awarded the Pritzker Prize), this U.S. headquarters for the French conglomerate is a reworked vision of Art Deco.

Taking advantage of what was already in place, the **Bridgemarket** complex *(First Ave at 59th St)* opened in 1999 in a former farmers' market under the Queensboro Bridge. The space now contains a **Terence Conran Shop** (*see p244*) and **Guastavino Restaurant** *(409 E 59th St between First and York Aves, 212-980-2455),* named for the maker of the tiles that line its curved ceilings. The Spanish builder's legacy can also be seen in the Grand Central Oyster Bar and on **Ellis Island** (*see p75*).

Grand Central Terminal

From 42nd to 44th Sts, between Vanderbilt and Lexington Aves. Subway: 42nd St S, 4, 5, 6, 7 to 42nd St–Grand Central.
For tour information, call 212-697-1245.

United Nations Headquarters

First Ave at 46th St (212-963-7713; tours 212-963-8687; www.un.org). Subway: 42nd St S, 4, 5, 6, 7 to 42nd St–Grand Central. **Tours** *Jan, Feb Mon–Fri 9:30am–4:45pm (closed weekends). Mar–Dec Mon–Fri 9:30am–4:45pm; Sat, Sun 10am–4:30pm.* **Fees** *$10, seniors $7.50, students $6.50, children 5–14 $5; children under 5 not admitted.*

Uptown

Gorgeous greenery, great art and ethnic flavors merge up north.

Stretching from the southern edges of Central Park to the far northern tip of the city, uptown covers a lot of ground. To many, the term is synonymous with the swanky precincts of the privileged. But in truth, uptown is as much blues as blue bloods, as much jazz as opera. Columbia University students share streets with Harlem renovators, symphonygoers meet swing dancers at Lincoln Center. Upper East Side society types stand in line with Museum Mile culture hounds, and ethnic influences from Eastern Europe to the West Indies mix and mingle from block to block. And on a beautiful day, everyone goes to Central Park, the city's big backyard, where New York's democratic nature is splendidly on view.

Central Park

This 843-acre patch of the great outdoors was the first man-made, landscaped public park in the United States. In 1853, the newly formed Central Park Commission chose landscape designer Frederick Law Olmsted and architect Calvert Vaux to turn this vast tract of rocky swampland into a rambling oasis of greenery. Inspired by the great parks of London and Paris, the parks commission imagined a place that would provide the whole city with a welcome respite from the crowded streets. A noble thought, but one that required the eviction of 1,600 mostly poor and/or immigrant inhabitants who already lived there, including

Give peace a chance

There are six acres of prime parkland that most New Yorkers have never even heard of, let alone visited. That's good news for those stopping by Central Park's calm, quiet **Conservatory Garden**. Located near the northeast corner of Central Park, on Fifth Avenue at 105th Street, the garden stands behind elaborate iron gates rescued from the original mansion of Cornelius Vanderbilt II. Linked by bench-lined, blossom-filled pathways, each of the garden's three formal plots has its own distinct character. The northernmost is planted in the geometric French style, with banked rings of tulips (in spring) or chrysanthemums (in fall). This section also features a fanciful sculpture, *The Three Maidens,* that was likely rescued from Nazi thievery (it once belonged to a German-Jewish family and stood across the street from Hitler's chancellery in Berlin).

The Italianate center, bordered by crab-apple *allées,* has a long manicured lawn with a towering single-spout fountain.

The southernmost plot is the most romantic. Created in the English perennial-garden style—grasses surrounded by high hedges and a wisteria-covered pergola—this area contains one of Central Park's little treasures: a lily pond, with a sweetly sentimental sculpture and birdbath at its

head, that's dedicated to the memory of Frances Hodgson Burnett, author of the classic children's story *The Secret Garden.* What's missing from the sculpture (it was on the original plan for a larger-scale model) is this epigraph from the book: "When you have a garden, you have a future; when you have a future, you are alive." And when you're sitting there serenely, you know it's all true.

residents of Seneca Village, the city's oldest African-American settlement. But clear the area the city did, and the rest is history.

In 2003, the Park celebrated its 150th anniversary since construction began, and it has never looked better—thanks in part to the Central Park Conservancy, formed in 1990, which has been particularly instrumental in restoring and maintaining the park. A horse-drawn carriage is still the sightseeing vehicle of choice for many tourists (and even a few romantic locals, though they'll never admit it); plan on paying $40 for a 20-minute tour. (Carriages line up along Central Park South between Fifth and Sixth Avenues.)

The park is dotted with landmarks. **Strawberry Fields**, near the West 72nd Street entrance, memorializes John Lennon, who

Central Park: still evolving

Many aspects of Central Park didn't turn out as its designer, Frederick Law Olmsted, originally intended. He detested monuments. Today, the park contains 80 of them. He believed museums had no place in a city green space. Who would wish to move the **Metropolitan Museum of Art** now? Here's how a few of the other sights have evolved.

The **Pond** *(entrance on Fifth Ave at 60th St)* was intended as a bird and wildlife sanctuary when it was created in 1924. It was cut in half in 1951 to make room for the **Wollman Rink**, which was rebuilt and further enlarged in 1986, when developer Donald Trump privately took on the refurbishing job. The original carousel that was built in 1871, now called the **Friedsam Memorial Carousel** *(mid-park at 65th St)*, had real horses; the present one (built in Coney Island in 1908) contains 58 carved-wood horses, and was installed in 1951. The current **Loeb Boathouse** *(mid-park at 72nd St)* is the third to be built on the lake (it dates to 1954); the first was designed by Calvert Vaux in 1874. The authentic Venetian gondola tied up on the lake is the boathouse's second; the first, an 1862 gift, rotted away for lack of a gondolier. The **Obelisk** *(Fifth Ave at 82nd St)*, built in 1600 B.C. and known locally as Cleopatra's Needle, was presented by the khedive of Egypt in 1881. Its hieroglyphics, thousands of years old, were eroded by New York air pollution in less than a century; movie mogul Cecil B. DeMille provided plaques with translations of the vanished inscriptions. Farther north, the **Mount** *(Fifth Ave at 105th St)* was the site of a small fortress where George Washington held the British at bay in 1776; in 1846, the fort became a convent. Now there is only a bronze plaque. But not everything in the park is mutable: **Umpire Rock** *(mid-park at 62nd St, overlooking the Heckscher ball fields)* was created some 20,000 years ago by the Laurentian Glacier. And nothin's gonna change that.

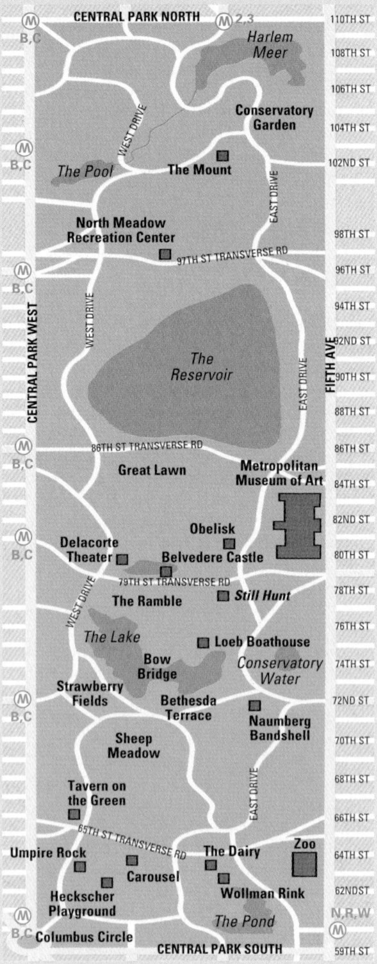

lived in the nearby **Dakota** (*see p113*). Also known as the "International Garden of Peace," this sanctuary features a mosaic of the word IMAGINE, donated by the Italian city of Naples. More than 160 species of flowers and plants from all over the world bloom here (including strawberries, of course). The statue of Balto, a heroic Siberian husky *(East Dr at 66th St),* is a favorite spot for tots. Slightly older children appreciate the statue of Alice in Wonderland, just north of the pond at the East 72nd Street park entrance.

In winter, ice skaters lace up at **Wollman Rink** *(park entrance on Central Park South at Sixth Ave, 212-439-6900; www.wollmanskatingrink.com),* where the skating comes with a postcard-perfect view of the fancy hotels surrounding the park. A short stroll to about 64th Street brings you to the **Friedsam Memorial Carousel**, still a bargain at a dollar a ride. (For more park activities for children, *see p282.*)

Come summer, kites, Frisbees and soccer balls fly every which way across the **Sheep Meadow**, the designated quiet zone that begins at 65th Street. The sheep are gone (they grazed until the 1930s), and have been replaced with sunbathers improving their tans and scoping out the throngs of thongs. The hungry (and affluent) can repair to glitzy **Tavern on the Green** *(Central Park West at 67th St, 212-873-3200),* which sets up a grand outdoor café in the summer. However, picnicking alfresco (or snacking on a hot dog from one of the park's food vendors) is the most popular option.

East of the Sheep Meadow, between 66th and 72nd Streets, is the **Mall**, where you'll find volleyball courts and plenty of in-line skaters. East of the Naumburg Bandshell is **Rumsey Playfield**—site of the annual **Central Park SummerStage** series (*see p255*), an eclectic roster of free and benefit concerts held from Memorial Day weekend to Labor Day weekend. One of the most popular meeting places in the park is the grand **Bethesda Fountain and Terrace**, near the center of the 72nd Street Transverse Road. *Angel of the Waters,* the sculpture in the middle of the fountain, was created by Emma Stebbins, the first woman to be granted a major public-art commission in New York. North of the fountain is the **Loeb Boathouse** (*see p332*), where you can rent a rowboat or gondola to take out on the lake; the lake is crossed at a narrow point by the elegant Bow Bridge. The bucolic park views that diners enjoy at the nearby **Central Park Boathouse Restaurant** *(mid-park at 75th St, 212-517-2233)* make it a lovely place for brunch or drinks. The thickly forested **Ramble**, between 73rd and 79th Streets, is a favorite spot for bird watching, offering glimpses of more than 275 species.

Farther uptown is the popular **Belvedere Castle**, a recently restored Victorian building that sits atop the park's highest peak. It offers excellent views and also houses the Henry Luce Nature Observatory. The **Delacorte Theater** hosts the **New York Shakespeare Festival** (*see p337*), a summer tradition of free performances of plays by the Bard and others. The **Great Lawn** is a sprawling stretch of grass that morphs frequently into an open-air concert spot for the New York Philharmonic, the Three Tenors, the Dave Matthews Band—just about anyone who can rally a six-figure audience. (At other times, it's the favored spot of seriously competitive soccer teams and much less competitive teams of Hacky Sackers and their dogs). Several years ago, the **Reservoir** was renamed in honor of the late Jacqueline Kennedy Onassis, who used to jog around it.

Central Park Zoo

830 Fifth Ave between 63rd and 66th Sts (212-861-6030; www.centralparkzoo.org). Subway: F to Lexington Ave–63rd St. **Open** *May–Sept Mon–Fri 10am–5pm; Sat, Sun 10am–5:30pm. Oct–Apr 10am–4:30pm.* **Admission** *$6, seniors $1.25, children $1.* **Credit** *Cash only.*

This is the only place in New York City where you can see polar bears swimming underwater. The Tisch Children's Zoo is newly spiffed up, and the George Delacorte Musical Clock delights kids every half-hour.

Charles A. Dana Discovery Center

Park entrance on Fifth Ave at 110th St (212-860-1370). Subway: 6 to 110th St. **Open** *Tue–Sun 10am–5pm.* **Admission** *free.*

Stop by for weekend family workshops, cultural exhibits and outdoor performances on the plaza next to the Harlem Meer. April through October, the center lends out fishing rods and bait.

The Dairy

Park entrance on Fifth Ave at 66th St (212-794-6564; www.centralparknyc.org). Subway: N, R, W to Fifth Ave–59th St. **Open** *Summer 11am–5pm; winter 11am–4pm.* **Admission** *free.*

Built in 1872 to show city kids where milk comes from (cows, in this case), the Dairy is now the Central Park Conservancy's information center, complete with interactive exhibits and videos explaining the park's history.

► For more information on the museums in this section, *see pp143–163.*

► For additional listings of uptown art dealers, *see p266.*

Sightseeing

Henry Luce Nature Observatory
Belvedere Castle, mid-park at 79th St (212-772-0210). Subway: B, C to 81st St–Museum of Natural History.
Open *Tue–Sun 10am–5pm.* **Admission** *free.*
Learn bird-watching techniques on ranger-led walks in the fall (every Wednesday at 8:30am). During the spring and fall hawk migrations, park rangers discuss the types of hawks found in the park and help visitors spot raptors from the castle roof. You can also sign out a bird-watching kit that includes binoculars, maps and bird-identification guides.

Upper East Side

Sightseeing

Gorgeous prewar apartments owned by society-page socialites, and soignée restaurants filled with sleek ladies who lunch: This is the picture most New Yorkers have of the **Upper East Side**. And certainly, you'll see plenty of supporting evidence along Fifth, Madison and Park Avenues. Encouraged by the opening of nearby Central Park in the late 19th century, the city's more affluent residents began building mansions along Fifth Avenue. By the beginning of the 20th century, even the superwealthy had warmed to the idea of living in apartments—provided they were close to the park. As a result, a building boom of apartment buildings and hotels began in 1881 and continued until 1932. (A few years later, working-class folks settled around Second and Third Avenues, following construction of the elevated east-side train line.) Architecturally, the overall look of the neighborhood, especially from Fifth to Park Avenues, is remarkably homogeneous. Along the strip known as the **Gold Coast**—Fifth, Madison and Park Avenues from 61st to 80th Streets—you'll see the great old mansions, many of which are now foreign consulates. The structure on **820 Fifth Avenue** (at 64th Street) was one of the earliest luxury apartment buildings on the avenue. New York's ultimate wedding cake is **45 East 66th Street** (between Madison and Park Aves). Architect Stanford White designed **998 Fifth Avenue** (at 81st Street) in the image of an Italian Renaissance palazzo. There are some wonderful old carriage houses along 63rd and 64th Streets as well.

Philanthropic gestures made by the moneyed class over the past 130 years have helped to create a cluster of art collections, museums and cultural institutions. In fact, Fifth Avenue from 82nd to 104th Streets is known as **Museum Mile** because it is lined with the **Metropolitan Museum of Art**; the Frank Lloyd Wright–designed **Guggenheim Museum**; the **Cooper-Hewitt Design Collection** (in Andrew Carnegie's former mansion); the **Jewish Museum**; the **Museum of the City of New York**; and **El Museo del Barrio** (for complete listings, *see pp143–163*).

Madison Avenue, from 57th to 86th Streets, is New York's world-class ultraluxe shopping strip. The snazzy department store **Barneys** (*see p211*) offers chic designer fashions and witty, often audacious window displays. While bars and restaurants dominate most of the north-south avenues, hungry sightseers can pick up a snack (or enough food for a picnic) at the well-stocked **Grace's Market** *(1237 Third Ave between 71st and 72nd Sts, 212-737-0600),* or at the Italian food shop **Agata & Valentina** *(1505 First Ave at 79th St, 212-452-0690).* Enjoy your meal on a park bench along the East River promenade leading to **Carl Schurz Park** (*see left* **A fine view**).

Don't miss A fine view

Lean over the railing of the elevated riverside walkway on the **Carl Schurz Park** (*see also p111*) promenade, and gaze upon the swirling waterways between Manhattan, Queens and the Bronx. Flotillas of barges and tugboats churn past on the East River below while the 59th Street Bridge sparkles above. This Upper East Side oasis, framed by classic Gracie Square to the south and Gracie Mansion to the north, is a wonderful spot to propose...that the evening not end too quickly. *86th St at East End Ave.*

Yorkville

Not much remains of the old German and Hungarian immigrant communities that filled this neighborhood with delicatessens, beer halls and restaurants. Two reminders are the 71-year-old **Elk Candy Company** *(1628 Second Ave between 84th and 85th Sts, 212-585-2303),* which is famous for its chocolates and handmade marzipan, and **Mocca Hungarian Restaurant** *(1588 Second Ave between 82nd and 83rd Sts, 212-734-6470),* where plates come heaped with goulash and chicken paprikás. Worthy newcomers in the area include **Pio Pio** *(1746 First Ave at 91st St, 212-426-5800),* a Peruvian rotisserie, and **Etats-Unis** *(242 E 81st St between Second and Third Aves, 212-517-8826),* which has good French bistro food and a comfortable neighborhood feel. (The **Bar@Etats-Unis**, a snug wine bar across the street, offers lighter fare.) For something a little more sultry, look for the long red curtains in the windows of the **Auction House** *(300 E 89th St between First*

Step right up The public is once again welcome at **Gracie Mansion**, NYC's mayoral digs.

and Second Aves, 212-427-4458), a two-story bar with velvet couches and oil paintings of lounging odalisques.

Gracie Mansion, at the eastern end of 88th Street, is the only Federal-style mansion in Manhattan, and has been New York's official mayoral residence since 1942. The yellow house with green shutters, built in 1799 by Scottish merchant Archibald Gracie, is the focal point of tranquil **Carl Schurz Park**, named in honor of the German immigrant who became a newspaper editor and U.S. senator. Gracie Mansion's living quarters are open to the public for the first time since 1942; the current mayor, billionaire Michael Bloomberg, eschews the mayor's traditional address in favor of his own Beaux Arts mansion at 17 East 79th Street (between Fifth and Madison Aves). The tour also winds through the formerly private living room, guest suite and smaller bedrooms. Reservations are a must. The **Henderson Place Historic District** *(East End Ave between 86th and 87th Sts)* is located one block from Gracie Mansion and consists of two dozen handsome Queen Anne row houses. Commissioned by furrier John C. Henderson, the cul-de-sac looks much as it did in 1882; the original turrets, double stoops and slate roofs remain intact. Although the city has approximately 400,000 Muslims, the dramatic 1990 **Islamic Cultural Center** *(1711 Third Ave at 96th St, 212-362-6800)* is New York's first major mosque.

Gracie Mansion Conservancy

Carl Schurz Park, 88th St at East End Ave (212-570-4751). Subway: 4, 5, 6 to 86th St. **Tours** *Wed 10, 11am, 1, 2pm.* **Admission** *$7, seniors $4, students and children under 12 free. Reservations required.* **Credit** *Cash only.*

Roosevelt Island

Walk along East 59th Street to the water and you'll see **Roosevelt Island**, a submarine-shaped isle located 300 yards away from Manhattan, in the East River. It is a major destination for both locals and savvy tourists on the night of July 4, as it affords prime views of the city's fireworks. The enclave, a state-planned residential community created in 1975, is home to roughly 10,000 people.

Until 1921, Roosevelt was known as Blackwell's Island, after Englishman Robert Blackwell, who bought it from the Dutch (who "bought" it from Native Americans) and moved there in 1686. The family's rebuilt clapboard farmhouse is in Blackwell Park, adjacent to Main Street (the one and only commercial strip). In the 1800s, a lunatic asylum, a smallpox hospital, prisons and workhouses were also built here.

The best way to see Roosevelt Island is to take the tram that crosses the East River from Manhattan (there's also an F subway stop). The riverfront promenades afford panoramas of the Manhattan skyline and East River. On the east side, wander down the Meditation Steps (located just north of the tram stop) for river views, or take one of the river-hugging paths down to Southpoint, a new public space at the southern tip.

Roosevelt Island Operating Corporation

591 Main St (212-832-4540; www.rioc.com). **Open** *Mon–Fri 9am–5pm. Call for details of events and free maps of the island.*

Roosevelt Island Tramway

Embark at Second Ave on 60th St in Manhattan. **Fee** *$2.*

Upper West Side

With a population that's more mature than downtown's but looser than the Upper East Side's, this four-mile-long stretch west of Central Park is culturally rich and cosmopolitan. New Yorkers were drawn here during the late 19th century after the completion of Central Park, the opening of local subway lines and Columbia University's relocation to the northern boundary of the park. In the 20th century, many Central Europeans found refuge here; in the '60s, many Puerto Ricans settled along Amsterdam and Columbus Avenues. These days, new real-estate development is reducing eye-level evidence of old immigrant life, and the neighborhood's long-standing intellectual and politically liberal spirit has waned (a bit) as apartment prices have risen. Still, parts of Riverside Drive, West End Avenue and Central Park West continue to rival the grandeur of the East Side's Fifth and Park Avenues.

The gateway to the UWS is **Columbus Circle**, where Broadway meets 59th Street, Eighth Avenue, Central Park South and Central Park West—a rare rotary in a city of right angles. The architecture around it could make anyone's head spin. A 700-ton statue of Christopher Columbus, positioned at the entrance to Central Park, goes almost unnoticed in the shadow of the new Time Warner headquarters across the street. When completed, this megacomplex will include Time Warner's corporate offices; multimillion-dollar luxury residences; an auditorium for Jazz at Lincoln Center; a Mandarin Oriental Hotel; restaurants representing top-name chefs Thomas Keller, Masa Takayama and Jean-Georges Vongerichten (*see p183* **Food court**); and shops, shops and more shops. On the south side of the circle is a windowless white-granite structure built as a modern-art gallery by Huntington Hartford in 1964. The **Museum of Arts and Design** (*see p153*) has bought the building, and after renovation, will move into its new home in 2006. The circle also bears Donald Trump's signature: He stuck his name on the former Gulf & Western Building when he converted it into the predictably glitzy **Trump International Hotel & Tower** (*see p62*).

The Upper West Side's seat of highbrow culture is **Lincoln Center** (*see p322*), a complex of concert halls and auditoriums built in 1968. The fountain in the central plaza is still a great gathering spot, especially in summer, when amateur dancers gather behind it to dance alfresco at **Midsummer Night Swing** (*see p254*). The center has begun a billion-dollar overhaul, which will include a redesign of public spaces, refurbishment of the various aging halls and construction of new buildings. The other, less formal cultural venues on the UWS include: the **Makor/Steinhardt Center** *(35 W 67th St between Central Park West and*

It happened here

Modernist painter Max Beckmann, born in 1884 in Leipzig, Germany, fled the Nazis in 1937, making stops in Amsterdam and St. Louis, Missouri, before arriving in New York City in 1949. He lived on East 19th Street until May of 1950, when he moved to West 69th Street. The artist taught painting at the Brooklyn Museum of Art, and took up bon vivantism, drinking bubbly with the swells and dining out around town—but his enjoyment was short-lived. While out for a walk, Beckmann dropped dead of a heart attack on this corner, **Central Park West at 61st Street**, on December 27, 1950.

Gold standard Gilt-y pleasures and glitz galore await in Donald's **Trump Tower**. *See p62.*

Sightseeing

Columbus Ave, 212-601-1000; www.makor.org), where you'll find lectures, films, readings and live music, often with a Middle Eastern focus; **Symphony Space** *(2537 Broadway at 95th St, 212-864-5400; www.symphonyspace.org),* where the World Music Institute books its ambitious music and dance programs; and **El Taller Latino Americano** *(2710 Broadway at 104th St, 212-665-9460; www.tallerlatino.org),* which offers a full range of Latino cultural events.

Around Sherman and Verdi Squares *(from 70th to 73rd Sts, where Broadway and Amsterdam Ave cross)* classic early-20th-century buildings stand cheek-by-jowl with newer, often mundane high-rises. The jewel is the 1904 **Ansonia Hotel** *(2109 Broadway between 73rd and 74th Sts).* Over the years, this Beaux Arts masterpiece has been home to Enrico Caruso, Babe Ruth and Igor Stravinsky. It was also the site of the Continental Baths (the gay bathhouse and cabaret where Bette Midler got her start) and Plato's Retreat (a swinging '70s sex club). On Broadway, the crowded 72nd Street subway station, which opened in 1904, is notable for its Beaux Arts entrance (a new entrance is across the street). The **Beacon Theatre** (*see p309*) was Manhattan's only rococo-style 1920s movie palace, and is now the city's premier midsize concert venue, presenting an eclectic menu of music, African-American regional theater and headliner comedy events.

Once Central Park was completed, magnificently tall apartment buildings rose up to take advantage of the views along Central Park West. The first of these great buildings was the **Dakota** (at 72nd Street). The fortresslike 1884 luxury apartment building is known as the setting for *Rosemary's Baby* and as the site of John Lennon's murder in 1980 (Yoko Ono still lives in the building). The building on **55 Central Park West** (at 66th Street) is recognizable from the film *Ghostbusters.* Built in 1930, it was the first Art Deco building on the block. Heading north on Central Park West, you'll spy the massive twin-towered **San Remo Apartments** (at 74th Street), which also date from 1930.

The **New-York Historical Society** (*see p158*) was built in 1804 and is the city's oldest museum. Across the street, the **American Museum of Natural History** (*see p145*) has been given an impressive face-lift, making even the fossils look fresh again. The museum's dinosaur skeletons, permanent rain-forest exhibit and IMAX theater (which shows Oscar-winning nature documentaries) lure adults and school groups alike. Perhaps most popular is the museum's newest wing, the **Rose Center for Earth and Space**, which includes the retooled Hayden Planetarium. The museum's overhaul has meant an astronomical leap in visitors—but it's worth suffering the crowds to marvel at this installation.

Hats off to Howard Somners, who's worked at **Zabar's** for decades because he "likes it."

Amsterdam and Columbus Avenues and Broadway are where the Upper West Side shops, drinks and eats. **H&H Bagels** *(2239 Broadway at 80th St, 212-595-8000)* is the city's largest purveyor of New York's favorite nosh. To see West Siders in their true natural habitat, get in line at the perpetually jammed smoked-fish counter at **Zabar's** *(2245 Broadway at 80th St, 212-787-2000).* This upscale gourmet shop also stocks 250 different types of cheese as well as fancy prepared foods and kitchen equipment.

On Amsterdam Avenue, the legendary **Barney Greengrass—The Sturgeon King** *(541 Amsterdam Ave between 86th and 87th Sts, 212-724-4707)* is an old-fashioned deli and restaurant that specializes in smoked fish, along with what may be the city's best chopped liver. (Don't look now—that's Philip Roth sitting next to you.) The best bang for your buck is a little farther north at **Flor de Mayo** *(484 Amsterdam Ave between 83rd and 84th Sts, 212-787-3388; 2651 Broadway between 100th and 101st Sts, 212-663-5520),* where the Peruvian *pollo a la brasa* is served to you by Chinese waiters. At **Café Con Leche** *(726 Amsterdam Ave between 95th and 96th Sts, 212-678-7000),* the coffee is strong and the accent is Dominican. At **A** *(947 Columbus Ave between 106th and 107th Sts, 212-531-1643),* the vibe and menu are more Pan-Caribbean. On Sundays, locals browse the **Greenflea** outdoor flea market and indoor farmers' market at **IHS 44** *(Columbus Ave between 76th and 77th Sts, 212-721-0900),* a New York City public high school. Before, during or after your stroll, stop by for a snack or a sandwich at the popular **Columbus Bakery** *(474 Columbus Ave between 82nd and 83rd Sts),* or head over to **Caffe La Fortuna** *(69 W 71st St between Central Park West and Columbus Ave, 212-724-5846).* A neighborhood fixture for 70 years, Fortuna features a peaceful outdoor garden and serves perfectly frothed cappuccino.

Designed by Central Park's Frederick Law Olmsted, **Riverside Park** is a sinuous stretch of riverbank that runs from 72nd to 158th Streets, between Riverside Drive and the Hudson River. You'll probably see yachts berthed at the **79th Street Boat Basin**, along with several houseboats; in the summertime, there's an open-air café in the adjacent park. Several park sites provide havens for reflection. The **Soldiers' and Sailors' Monument** *(89th St at Riverside Dr),* built in 1902 by French sculptor Paul E. M. DuBoy, honors Union soldiers who died in the Civil War, and a **1908 memorial** *(100th St at Riverside Dr)* pays tribute to fallen firemen. **Grant's Tomb**, the mausoleum of former President Ulysses S. Grant, is also located in the park. Across the street stands the towering Gothic-style **Riverside Church** *(Riverside Dr at 120th St, 212-870-6700; www.theriversidechurchny.org).* Built in 1930, it contains the world's largest carillon (74 bells, played every Sunday at 3pm) as well as peregrine falcon nests. Take an elevator ride to the top of the 21-story tower and you can see them both, along with commanding views of the city skyline and Hudson River.

General Grant National Memorial

Riverside Dr at 122nd St (212-666-1640). Subway: 1, 9 to 125th St. **Open** *9am–5pm.* **Admission** *free.*
Who's buried in Grant's Tomb? Technically, nobody—the crypts of Civil War hero and 18th president Ulysses S. Grant and his wife, Julia, are in full above-ground view.

Morningside Heights

Morningside Heights runs from West 110th Street (also called Cathedral Parkway east of Amsterdam Avenue) to West 125th Street, between Morningside Park and the Hudson River. The **Cathedral of St. John the Divine** and the campus of **Columbia University** both exert considerable influence on the surrounding neighborhood.

One of the oldest universities in the U.S., Columbia was chartered in 1754 as King's College (the name changed after the Revolutionary War). It moved to its present location in 1897. Thanks to Columbia's large student population and that of its sister school, Barnard College, the area has an academic feel, with bookshops, inexpensive restaurants and coffeehouses lining Broadway between 110th and 116th Streets. **Le Monde** *(2885 Broadway between 112th and 113th Sts, 212-531-3939),* a quiet brasserie/bar, attracts young locals with its generous selection of beers. **Mondel Chocolates** *(2913 Broadway at 114th St, 212-864-2111)* has been sating students' candy cravings since 1943, but it's perhaps best known as the late Katharine Hepburn's chocolatier of choice; her standing monthly order is still tacked on the wall behind the counter. The French restaurant **Terrace in the Sky** *(400 W 119th St between Morningside Dr and Amsterdam Ave, 212-666-9490)* offers a nicely framed view of the downtown skyline, while **Max Soha** *(1274 Amsterdam Ave at 123rd St)* serves up tasty Italian pastas.

The **Cathedral Church of St. John the Divine** is the seat of the Episcopal Diocese of New York. Known affectionately by locals as St. John the Unfinished, the enormous cathedral (already larger than Notre Dame in Paris!) will undergo hammering and chiseling well into this century. Construction began in 1892 in Romanesque style, was put on hold for a Gothic Revival redesign in 1911, then ground to a halt in 1942, when the United States entered World War II. Work resumed in earnest in 1979, but a fire in 2001 destroyed the church's gift shop and badly damaged two 17th-century Italian tapestries, further delaying completion. In addition to Sunday services, the cathedral hosts concerts and tours. In the fall, its renowned **Blessing of the Animals** (*see also p278*), during the

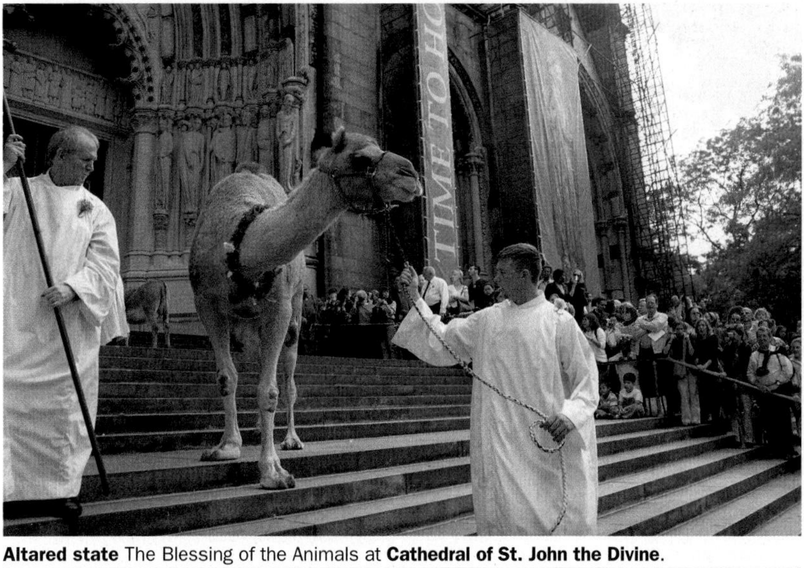

Altared state The Blessing of the Animals at **Cathedral of St. John the Divine.**

Feast of St. Francis, draws pet-lovers from all over the city. Just behind the cathedral is idyllic **Morningside Park** *(110th St at Morningside Dr).*

Cathedral of St. John the Divine

1047 Amsterdam Ave at 112th St (212-316-7540; www.stjohndivine.org). Subway: B, C, 1, 9 to 110th St–Cathedral Pkwy. **Open** *Sept–Jun Mon–Sat 7:30am–6pm; Sun 7am–7pm. Jul, Aug Mon–Sat 7:30am–6pm; Sun 7am–6pm.* **Tours** *Tue–Sat 11am; Sun 1pm.* **Fees** *$5, seniors and students $4.* **Credit** *MC, V.*

Harlem

Harlem is not just a destination on Manhattan island—it's the cultural capital of black America. More than any other New York City address, Harlem is a state of mind as well as a place in the world. Life here is lived on the street; whatever's cooking in the 'hood is right there to be seen.

Harlem today is no longer the neglected "raisin in the sun" depicted in Langston Hughes's famous poem "Harlem: A Dream Deferred," nor is it the powder keg of the '60s that Hughes's words presaged. The original Harlem Renaissance of the 1920s and '30s—a cultural explosion that gave us the likes of Hughes, Zora Neale Hurston and Duke Ellington—continues to live on in memory.

Flip your lids at **Showman's** jazz bar.

But these days, a new Harlem renaissance is burgeoning—thanks in part to real-estate investment and economic opportunity.

Harlem began as a suburb for well-to-do whites in the 19th century, after the west-side railroad was built. The area is blessed with stately brownstones in varying stages of restoration, often right next to big modern slabs of public housing. Thanks to a thriving black middle class, Harlem's cultural and religious institutions are seeing renewed interest and funding, and evidence of new commercial enterprise abounds on the streets. Still, Harlem's history remains visible. Some of the fabled locations of the original Harlem Renaissance have been restored, if not enshrined. And while many of Harlem's celebrated jazz clubs, theaters and ballrooms have had their stages replaced by pulpits, the buildings still stand.

Despite the retail explosion and influx of development money, there is still a social and psychological divide between Harlem and the rest of Manhattan that echoes an earlier time. There's an edginess that visitors might feel, due to real-estate speculation by downtowners and the infiltration of superstores. Violence and street crime are at a modern-era low, but it's not uncommon to find shops on Harlem's main avenues locked (a salesperson will buzz you in). The nabe does feel safer, and it is more welcoming to tourists than in recent memory, but street smarts and a heightened alertness to your environment always help: If you're walking in a crosstown direction (as opposed to north or south on a main avenue), walk purposefully and look for through streets that are not interrupted by blocks of housing projects.

West Harlem, from St. Nicholas to Fifth Avenues, is the Harlem of popular imagination—and 125th Street is its lifeline. Start at the crossroads: the 285,000-square-foot **Harlem USA Mall** *(300 W 125th St between Adam Clayton Powell Jr. [Seventh Ave] and Frederick Douglass [Eighth Ave] Blvds; www.harlem-usa.com).* The mall features a **Magic Johnson** multiplex movie theater *(Frederick Douglass Blvd [Eighth Ave] at 124th St, 212-665-8742)* and the **Hue-Man Bookstore** (*see p271*), the country's third-largest store specializing in African-American titles. The building also houses retail megastores such as Old Navy, Modell's, HMV, Starbucks and a Disney store. Across the street is the 87-year-old **Apollo Theater** (*see p309*), which still hosts live concerts, a syndicated television program and the classic Amateur Night on Wednesdays. A few blocks to the west is a touch of old Harlem: **Showman's Bar** *(375 W 125th St at Frederick Douglass Blvd [Eighth Ave], 212-864-8941),* a mecca for jazz lovers,

Soul kitchen This Harlem institution stirs up jazz, black culture and cool cats.

and the reconstituted **Cotton Club** *(666 W 125th St at Riverside Dr, 212-663-7980),* which hosts gospel brunches and evening jazz and blues sessions. To the east of the mall is the **Lenox Lounge** *(288 Malcolm X Blvd [Lenox Ave] between 124th and 125th Sts, 212-427-0253),* still cooking with old-school jazz. A well-regarded fine-arts center, the **Studio Museum in Harlem** (*see p151*) features work by many local artists. The offices of former President Bill Clinton are at 55 W 125th St, between Fifth Ave and Malcolm X Blvd (Lenox Ave). Harlem's rich history lives on in the archives of the **Schomburg Center for Research in Black Culture** (*see p162*). Part of the New York Public Library system, it contains more than 5 million documents, artifacts, films and prints relating to the cultures of peoples of African descent, with an emphasis on the African-American experience. The **Abyssinian Baptist Church**, where Harlem's congressman Adam Clayton Powell Jr. once preached, is celebrated for its history, political activism and rousing gospel choir. The church houses a small museum dedicated to Powell, the first black member of New York's City Council.

Harlem is also a destination for stylish plus-size fashions. Check out the **Soul Brothers Boutique** *(115 W 128th St between Adam Clayton Powell Jr. Blvd [Seventh Ave] and Malcolm X Blvd [Lenox Ave], 212-749-9005),* where you can find T-shirts celebrating the neighborhood, black political figures and '70s blaxploitation films in a very democratic size range. (You might also want to check out **Freedom Hall**, an active radical-politics lecture facility and bookstore next door.) You'll truly appreciate the generously sized clothing after sampling the smothered pork chops and collard greens with fatback at **Sylvia's**, Harlem's most renowned soul-food restaurant *(328 Malcolm X Blvd [Lenox Ave] between 126th and 127th Sts, 212-996-0660).* **Bayou**, the handsome Cajun eatery down the street *(308 Malcolm X Blvd [Lenox Ave] between 125th and 126th Sts, 212-426-3800)* is an attractive alternative. Afterward, walk off some of your meal with a stroll around **Marcus Garvey Memorial Park** *(Madison Ave between 120th and 124th Sts),* where the brownstone revival is in full swing.

Harlem's historic districts continue to gentrify. The **Mount Morris Historic District** *(from 119th to 125th Sts between Malcolm X Blvd [Lenox Ave] and Mount Morris Park West)* has charming brownstones and a collection of religious buildings in a variety of architectural styles. New boutiques, restaurants and sidewalk cafés dot the walk down Malcolm X these days. **Harlemade** *(174 Malcolm X Blvd [Lenox Ave] between 118th and 119th Sts, 212-987-2500; www.harlemade.com)* sells T-shirts with Afro- and Harlem-centric messages and images, along with postcards, books and other neighborhood-related memorabilia. **Xukuma** *(183 Malcolm X Blvd [Lenox Ave] at*

The **Graffiti Hall of Fame** in East Harlem.

119th St, 212-222-0490), a delightful home-design shop that carries its own line of body products, would seem right at home in Soho. Just a few years ago, finding bistro food or a cup of espresso was a tough task up here; now restaurant and bar **Native** (*see p194*) serves a global "all world" menu, while the **Settepani** café *(196 Malcolm X Blvd [Lenox Ave] at 120th St, 917-492-4806)* offers cappuccino, tempting pastries and Italian-style sandwiches.

Another area with a historic past is **Strivers' Row**, also known as the St. Nicholas Historic District. Running from Adam Clayton Powell Jr. Blvd (Seventh Ave) to Frederick Douglass Blvd (Eighth Ave), between 138th and 139th Sts, these three blocks of magnificent houses were developed in 1891 by David H. King Jr. and designed by three different architects, including Stanford White. In the 1920s, prominent members of the black community, like Eubie Blake and W.C. Handy, lived in this area. Now new, upwardly mobile strivers are moving in, followed by stylish boutiques like **Grandview** *(2531 Frederick Douglass Blvd [Eighth Ave] between 135th and 136th Sts, 212-694-7324).* Owner Veronica Jones sells eclectic contemporary clothing and accessories, mostly by African-American designers. The eponymous **Moshood** *(2533 Frederick Douglass Blvd [Eighth Ave] between 135th and 136th Sts, 917-507-2532; www.afrikanspirit.com)* features clothing by the Nigerian-born designer-owner, who also has a Brooklyn boutique. Along the way, there's plenty of good eating: **Londel's Supper Club** (*see p194*), owned by former police officer Londel Davis, serves some of the best blackened catfish in town; **Home Sweet Harlem Café** *(270 W 135th St at Frederick Douglass Blvd [Eighth Ave], 212-926-9616)* is the place for smoothies, soy burgers and hearty soups.

The 'hood comes alive after dark, especially at the not-to-be-missed **St. Nick's Pub** *(773 St. Nicholas Ave at 149th St, 212-283-9728),* where you can hear live jazz every night (except Tuesday) for a small cover charge. Fresh local favorites include the sophisticated **Sugar Hill Bistro** *(458 W 145th St between Amsterdam and Convent Aves, 212-491-5505)* and the new **Strivers Lounge and Café** *(2611 Frederick Douglass Blvd [Eighth Ave] at 139th St, 212-491-4422).*

Walking eastward on 116th Street, you'll pass through a dizzying smorgasbord of cultures. There's a West African flavor between Adam Clayton Powell Jr. and Frederick Douglass Blvds, especially at the Senegalese restaurant **Le Baobab** *(120 W 116th St between Malcolm X Blvd [Lenox Ave] and Adam Clayton Powell Jr. Blvd [Seventh Ave], 212-864-4700).* On the north side of the street is the Reverend Al Sharpton's favorite restaurant, **Amy Ruth's** *(113 W 116th St between Malcolm X Blvd [Lenox Ave]*

and Adam Clayton Powell Jr. Blvd [Seventh Ave], 212-280-8779), where baked ribs and chicken and waffles are de rigueur. Keep heading east past the silver-domed **Masjid Malcolm Shabazz** *(102 W 116th St at Malcolm X Blvd [Lenox Ave], 212-662-2200),* the mosque of the late Malcolm X's ministry, to the **Malcolm Shabazz Harlem Market** *(52–60 W 116th St between Fifth Ave and Malcolm X Blvd [Lenox Ave], 212-987-8131),* an outdoor bazaar where vendors hawk T-shirts, toiletries and (purportedly) African souvenirs. (Don't miss Harley the Buckle Man, custom belt-buckle maker to rap stars.)

East of Fifth Avenue is East Harlem; it's sometimes called Spanish Harlem, but is better known to its residents as El Barrio. North of 96th Street and east of Madison Avenue, El Barrio moves to a different beat. Its main east-west cross street, East 116th Street, is also the northern entrance to **La Marqueta**, an atmospheric indoor food-and-essentials bazaar that stretches down to 110th Street underneath the Metro-North railroad tracks along Park Avenue. Between Fifth and Park Avenues, East 116th Street's main attraction is actually the unusually high concentration of botanicas—shops that supply the elements (candles, charms, oils, potions, "orisha priestess" readings) of the Catholic-tinged Santeria religion. **Otto Chicas Rendon**, a.k.a. La Casa de las Velas or the House of Candles *(60 E 116th St at Madison Ave, 212-289-0378),* is particularly tourist-friendly. From 96th to 106th Streets on the east side, a little touch of East Village–style bohemia can also be detected in the appearance of such places as **Carlito's Café y Galería** *(1702 Lexington Ave between 106th and 107th Sts, 212-348-7044),* which presents music, art and poetry. Nearby is the **Graffiti Hall of Fame** *(106th St between Park and Madison Aves),* a schoolyard that celebrates great old- and new-school "writers." **El Museo del Barrio** (*see* *p158*), Spanish Harlem's community museum, is on Fifth Avenue at 104th Street.

Hamilton Heights extends from 125th Street to the Trinity Cemetery at 155th St and Riverside Drive. Named for Alexander Hamilton, who had a farm and estate here in 1802, the former factory neighborhood developed after the west-side IRT subway was built in the early 20th century. Today, it's notable for the elegant turn-of-the-century row houses in the **Hamilton Heights Historic District**, which extends along Hamilton Terrace and Convent Avenue (from 141st to 145th Streets), just beyond the Gothic Revival style campus of the City University of New York (137th Street).

The Abyssinian Baptist Church

132 W 138th St between Malcolm X Blvd (Lenox Ave) and Adam Clayton Powell Jr. Blvd (Seventh Ave) (212-862-7474; www.abyssinian.org). Subway: B, C, 2, 3 to 135th St. **Open** *Mon–Fri 9am–5pm.*

Washington Heights & Inwood

The area from West 155th Street to Dyckman (200th) Street is called **Washington Heights**; venture higher than that and you're in **Inwood**, Manhattan's northernmost neighborhood, where the Hudson River meets the Harlem River. A growing number of artists and young families are moving to these parts, attracted by Art Deco buildings, big parks, hilly streets and comparatively low rents.

Since the 1920s, waves of immigrants have settled in Washington Heights. In the post–World War II era, many German-Jewish refugees (including Henry Kissinger, Dr. Ruth Westheimer and Max Frankel, the former executive editor of the *New York Times*) moved into the neighborhood. This stretch of Broadway also housed a sizable Greek population—opera singer Maria Callas was born here. But in the last few decades, the area has become predominantly Spanish-speaking, with a large Dominican population. Today, Dyckman Street buzzes with street life and nightclubs from river to river.

Middle Aged At Manhattan's northern end, the **Cloisters** offers an oasis of calm.

A trek along Fort Washington Avenue, from 177th Street to Fort Tryon Park, puts you in the heart of what is now being called Hudson Heights—the gold coast of the neighborhood. Start at the George Washington Bridge, the city's only bridge across the Hudson River. A pedestrian walkway allows for dazzling views of Manhattan, and it's a popular route for cyclists too. Under the bridge on the New York side is a diminutive lighthouse—those who know the children's story *The Little Red Lighthouse and the Great Gray Bridge* will recognize it immediately. Stop along the way at restaurant **Bleu Evolution** *(808 W 187th St between Fort Washington and Pinehurst Aves, 212-928-6006)* for a touch of Williamsburg-like hipness, or hold out for the lovely **New Leaf Café** *(1 Margaret Corbin Dr, 212-568-5323)* within the Frederick Law Olmsted–designed **Fort Tryon Park**. At the northern edge of the park is the **Cloisters** (*see p146*), a museum built in 1938 using segments of five medieval cloisters shipped over from Europe by the Rockefeller clan. Today, it houses the Metropolitan Museum of Art's permanent collection of medieval art, including the marvelous Unicorn Tapestries, woven around 1500.

Inwood stretches from Dyckman Street up to 218th Street, the last residential block in Manhattan. The island narrows this far north, and the parks along the western shoreline culminate in the wilderness of **Inwood Hill Park**. Some believe that this is the location of the legendary 1626 transaction between Peter Minuit and the Lenape Indians for the purchase of a strip of land called "Manahatta"—a plaque at the southwest corner of the field, at approximately 214th Street, marks the purported spot. The 196-acre refuge contains the island's last swath of virgin forest and offers a view of the uncluttered part of New Jersey's Palisades. Largely owing to the efforts of Olmsted, who designed this park as well as Central and Riverside Parks, the area was not leveled in the 1800s. The massive glacier-deposited boulders (called erratics) were a factor, too. Today, with a bit of imagination, you can hike in this mossy forest and picture the beautiful land as it was before development.

Morris-Jumel Mansion

65 Jumel Terr between 160th and 162nd Sts (212-923-8008; www.morrisjumel.org). Subway: C to 163rd St–Amsterdam Ave. **Open** *Wed–Sun 10am–4pm.* **Admission** *$3, seniors and students $2, children under 12 free.*

Built in 1765, Manhattan's only surviving pre-Revolutionary manse was originally the heart of a 130-acre estate that stretched from river to river (on the grounds, a stone marker points south, with the legend NEW YORK, 11 MILES). George Washington planned the battle of Harlem Heights here in 1776, after the British colonel Roger Morris moved out. The handsome 18th-century Palladian-style villa also offers fantastic views. The villa's former driveway is now Sylvan Terrace, which boasts the largest continuous stretch of old wooden houses in Manhattan.

Brooklyn

A city unto itself, with nightlife, shopping, hipster culture—even its own accent.

More than 2.5 million residents—including a growing number of young Manhattan refugees—make Brooklyn their home, preferring tree-lined streets and a mellower pace to the crowds and nonstop hurly-burly of "the city." But Brooklyn is hardly a sleepy burg: Visiting the culture-packed borough is so wonderfully exhilarating that you could spend your entire New York vacation here and not even miss crossing the river. In the past decade, scores of fine new restaurants and boutiques have sprung up, and artists seeking affordable space have flooded the westernmost neighborhoods, bringing money and style with them. Many people now view Brooklyn as the ultimate source of New York cool.

The borough, also named Kings County, has long possessed a wealth of cultural institutions, from the Beaux Arts **Brooklyn Museum of Art**, with its renowned Egyptology collection, to the multifaceted, cutting-edge **Brooklyn Academy of Music** (BAM). The borough has first-rate shopping, too, from the antiques and furniture stores lining Atlantic Avenue to the fashion-forward clothing boutiques of Williamsburg. You'll also find endless culinary delights, thanks to thriving Caribbean, Chinese, Italian, Middle Eastern, Russian, Pakistani, Polish and Hasidic communities. Brooklyn's quaint streets, stately brownstones and vast beaches make wonderful backdrops to its ever-changing people-scape.

To become more familiar with the disparate cultures and communities, contact one of the following helpful institutions: **Brooklyn Information and Culture** *(718-855-7882; www.brooklynx.org)* or **Heart of Brooklyn: A Cultural Partnership** *(718-638-7700; www.heartofbrooklyn.org)*, which also publishes the listings-laden *BKLYN* magazine *(www.bklynmagazine.com)*.

Brooklyn Heights & Dumbo

Brooklyn Heights has been the borough's toniest neighborhood since the end of World War II. The nabe was born when entrepreneur Robert Fulton's first steam-powered ferry linked Manhattan to the quiet fishing village on western Long Island, in 1814. The streets of Brooklyn Heights—particularly Cranberry, Hicks, Pierrepont and Willow—are lined with beautifully maintained Greek Revival and Italianate row houses dating to the 1820s. In 1965, 30 blocks were designated Brooklyn's first historic district. Today, Henry and Montague Streets are the main drags, packed with shops, restaurants and bars.

Upon completion in 1881, the building that houses the **Brooklyn Historical Society** became the first structure in New York to use locally produced terra-cotta on its facade. The George B. Post creation reopened in late 2003, following an extensive restoration. Also in the area is the dignified **Plymouth Church of the Pilgrims** *(75 Hicks St between Cranberry and Orange Sts, Brooklyn Heights; 718-624-4743)*, established in 1847 under the ministry of abolitionist Henry Ward Beecher, brother of writer Harriet Beecher Stowe.

The remnants of Brooklyn's past as an independent municipality (it was incorporated into greater New York City in 1898) can be found downtown. The grand **Borough Hall** *(209 Joralemon St at Fulton St, Brooklyn Heights; www.brooklyn-usa.org)* sits in the center of this area. Completed in 1848, the Greek Revival edifice—later crowned with a Victorian cupola—was renovated in the late 1980s. The hall is linked to the **New York State Supreme Court** *(360 Adams St between Joralemon St and Tech Pl)* by **Cadman Plaza** *(from Tech Pl to Poplar St, between Cadman Plaza West and Brooklyn Bridge Blvd)*, where farmers peddle fresh produce on Tuesday, Thursday and Saturday mornings. Brooklyn's main business district is on Jay Street in **MetroTech Center** *(Tech Pl at Jay St)*. A common provides a shady place to rest, between 2 MetroTech and **Polytechnic University**, the nation's second-oldest private school of science and engineering. At the easternmost edge of the common is **Wunsch Hall** *(311 Bridge St at Johnson St)*. Long before it became part of the university campus, the 1846 Greek Revival building housed the Bridge Street African Wesleyan Methodist Episcopal Church, a stop on the Underground Railroad. (The congregation moved to Bedford-Stuyvesant in 1938.)

▶ For the **Brooklyn map**, *see p406*.

Sightseeing

Just shoot it Dumbo's **Empire State Park** has a postcard view of lower Manhattan.

Brooklyn Heights has more than history on its side; it offers spectacular vistas of Manhattan. You can get a striking view of the Financial District skyline—one you'll recognize from numerous films—on the **Brooklyn Heights Promenade**.

If the Heights is too staid for your taste, you might prefer the gruff but lovable neighborhood of Dumbo (Down Under the Manhattan Bridge Overpass). This waterside 'hood also provides impressive sight lines to Manhattan. A fine viewing perch is **Fulton Ferry Landing** (below the Brooklyn Bridge), which juts out onto the East River at Old Fulton and Water Streets, and is close to two newly refurbished green spots—**Empire State Park** and **Brooklyn Bridge Park** *(riverside between Manhattan and Brooklyn Bridges).* Also at the water's edge is the **River Café** (*see p195*); breathtaking views of the Manhattan skyline have made the adjacent garden a favorite photo spot for Chinese wedding parties. As for the famous restaurant itself, the panoramic vista (and very good food) help cushion the blow of the bill.

Artists flocked to Dumbo in the 1970s and '80s, drawn by the cobblestone streets and warehouse loft spaces, and they kept on coming through the go-go '90s. The arrival of several dolled-up boutiques, as well as the upscale chain store **ABC Carpet & Home** (*see p243*) has some people saying that the area has lost its rough-hewn charm. But the **Dumbo Arts Center** *(30 Washington St between Plymouth and Water Sts, Dumbo; 718-694-0831; www.dumboartscenter.org)* continues to promote the work of community artists through its gallery and sponsorship of the annual **Dumbo Art Under the Bridge** festival (*see p257*), in mid-October, during which dozens of artists open their studios to the public. The rest of the year, **St. Ann's Warehouse** *(38 Water St between Dock and Main Sts, Dumbo; 718-254-8779)* hosts offbeat concerts, readings and theater productions that often feature high-profile artists.

Dumbo dining also boasts its share of artistry. Pizza lovers can sample a coal-fired pie at the venerable **Grimaldi's** (*see p196*), which claims the title of America's first (and some say best) pizzeria. Ice-cream fans will find bliss at the **Brooklyn Ice Cream Factory** *(Fulton Ferry Landing between Old Fulton and Water Sts, Dumbo; 718-246-3963).* For a real sit-down meal—accompanied by a couple of good stiff drinks and the occasional live band—visit **Superfine** *(126 Front St between Jay and Pearl Sts, Dumbo; 718-243-9005),* where you'll find Mediterranean-style cuisine, plus great brunch. **Bubby's** *(1 Main St at Plymouth St, Dumbo; 718-222-0666; see also p167),* an ultrapopular eatery in Tribeca, recently opened a Dumbo outpost. And the always-packed **Jacques Torres Chocolate** shop (*see p240*) is where French confectionery artist Torres whips up his cocoa-butter masterpieces (and killer hot chocolate).

Of course, no trip to Brooklyn would be complete without a walk across the **Brooklyn Bridge**. The vision of German-born civil engineer John Augustus Roebling (who did not live to see its completion), the structure was the first to use steel cables. It connects downtown Brooklyn with Manhattan, providing glorious views of the Statue of Liberty and New York Harbor. As you walk (or bike, or blade) along its promenade, you'll find plaques detailing the story of the bridge's construction.

Brooklyn Bridge

Subway: A, C to High St; J, M, Z to Chambers St; 4, 5, 6 to Brooklyn Bridge–City Hall.

The Brooklyn Historical Society

128 Pierrepont St at Clinton St, Brooklyn Heights (718-222-4111; www.brooklynhistory.org). Subway: M, R to Court St; 2, 3, 4, 5 to Borough Hall. **Open** *Wed, Thu, Sat 10am–5pm; Fri 10am–8pm; Sun noon–5pm.* **Admission** *$6; seniors, students and children 12–18 $4; children under 12 free.* **Credit** *AmEx, MC, V.*

Boerum Hill, Carroll Gardens, Cobble Hill & Red Hook

One of Brooklyn's most striking examples of rapid gentrification can be found on **Carroll Gardens**' Smith Street, which has come to be known as the borough's Restaurant Row. Following years of decrepitude, Smith Street was targeted for urban renewal in the 1990s and given a total face-lift. Handsome new sidewalks and wrought-iron street lamps attracted trendy eateries, shops and nightspots, which transformed the strip into one of the city's hottest commercial corridors. Now a number of reliably good, affordable restaurants and cafés pack in discerning diners, some of whom are Manhattanites on a reverse bridge-and-tunnel trek. Hot eateries (serving stylish bistro fare, sandwiches, salads) along Smith Street include **Banania** *(No. 241 at Douglass St, Carroll Gardens; 718-237-9100);* **Panino'teca 275** *(No. 275 between DeGraw and Sackett Sts, Carroll Gardens; 718-237-2728);* and **Robin des Bois** *(No. 195 between Baltic and Warren Sts, Carroll Gardens; 718-596-1609).*

The most aggressively multitasking commercial enterprise on Smith Street is **Halcyon** (*see p291*), a coffeehouse, furniture store, nightspot and vinyl emporium that features some of New York's best DJs spinning after dark; by day, it's a calm, cool place to sip java—or find that Jetsons sofa you've been craving.

Many of the area's shops are run by artists and designers selling their own wares; these stand shoulder to shoulder with Latino restaurants, bodegas, junk stores and social clubs that have survived the transition. Playful, pretty women's clothing is for sale at **Frida's Closet** *(No. 296 between Sackett and Union Sts, Carroll Gardens; 718-855-0311)* and **Stacia** *(No. 267 between DeGraw and Sackett Sts, Carroll Gardens; 718-237-0078);* interior-design fanatics will appreciate **Living on Smith** *(No. 289 between Sackett and Union Sts, Carroll Gardens; 718-222-8546),* with its handmade glass, cashmere throw pillows and other homey luxuries.

Among the groovy new shops that dot nearby Atlantic Avenue are haute home furnisher **City Foundry** *(No. 365 between Bond and Hoyt Sts, Boerum Hill; 718-923-1786);* stylish women's clothier **Butter** *(No. 407 between Bond and Nevins Sts, Boerum Hill; 718-260-9033);* and **Silver Tao** *(No. 394 between Bond and Hoyt Sts, Boerum Hill; 718-422-7700),* which sells both clothing and home furnishings.

It happened here

The converted carriage houses along charming **Verandah Place** in Brooklyn's Cobble Hill neighborhood are much sought-after now. That wasn't the case in the early 1930s, when novelist Thomas Wolfe scribbled *Of Time and the River* while occupying the dank basement flat at No. 40. Back then, the narrow lane was situated in the midst of a rough blue-collar stretch—not by a park, as it is today. Wolfe later wrote: "In winter, the place sweats with clammy water; in the summer, you do all the sweating yourself." These days, though, Wolfe probably wouldn't mind going home again.

The mile-long stretch of Atlantic Avenue between Henry and Nevins, known by locals as the "Fertile Crescent," is crowded with Middle Eastern restaurants and retail food markets. The granddaddy of them all is **Sahadi Importing Company** *(No. 187 between Clinton and Court Sts, Cobble Hill; 718-624-4550)*, a 56-year-old neighborhood institution that sells olives, spices, cheeses, nuts and other gourmet treats. **Malko Karkenny Bros.** *(No. 174 between Clinton and Court Sts, Cobble Hill; 718-834-0845)* and **Hanshali International Foods** *(No. 197 between Clinton and Court Sts, Cobble Hill; 718-625-2400)* also offer Middle Eastern temptations.

Italian-food lovers may want to head to **Court Street** in Carroll Gardens, where Italian-American roots run deep. Buy a prosciutto loaf from the **Caputo Bakery** *(No. 329 between Sackett and Union Sts, Carroll Gardens; 718-875-6871)*; pick up freshly made buffalo mozzarella at **Caputo's Fine Foods** *(No. 460 between 3rd and 4th Pls, Cobble Hill; 718-855-8852)*; grab an aged *soppressata* salami from **Esposito and Sons** *(No. 357 between President and Union Sts, Carroll Gardens; 718-875-6863)*; and relax in **Carroll Park** *(Court St between Carroll and President Sts)* while watching the old-timers play bocce. Trendier eats (and a cool young crowd) can be found at the Mexican bistro **Alma** *(187 Columbia St between DeGraw and Sackett Sts, Cobble Hill; 718-643-5400)* or **Schnäck** *(122 Union St at Columbia St, Cobble Hill; 718-855-2879)*, which stuffs starving-artist types with hot dogs, tofu Reubens and cold beer.

Southwest of Carroll Gardens is rough-and-tumble **Red Hook** (*see below* **Red-hot Red Hook**), offering a mix of industrial-waterfront surrealism, local-artist studios and a still-growing crop of bars and eateries.

Park Slope & Prospect Heights

Welcome to Brooklyn's burbs. **Park Slope** has a safe, upscale feel, owing to its charming Victorian brownstones, leafy streets and proximity to Prospect Park. Although Seventh

Red-hot Red Hook

If you have completely combed the streets of Williamsburg and are dying to explore the newest pocket of Brooklyn cool, head for remote Red Hook. Surrounded by water on two sides and the Brooklyn-Queens Expressway on the third, the nabe has a laid-back vibe that mixes the rough edges of an industrial waterfront with the funky charm of a burgeoning artists' community; plus, the entire area is framed by wide-open views of the Statue of Liberty and Manhattan, just across the river.

But first, you have to get there. One of the things that has kept Red Hook funky (and affordable for residents) is its lack of a nearby subway line. For daytime venturing, catch an F train to Bergen Street, walk a couple of blocks north to Atlantic Avenue and hop aboard the B61 bus, heading west on Atlantic, then down Columbia and Van Brunt Streets. At night (or just to make it an easier, quicker trip), call for a car service (*see p364*)—and save the number for your return trip.

Life at the north end of Red Hook (closest to the BQE) centers around Columbia Street, where artisan workspaces, renovated lofts and bakeries mingle with tool shops and overgrown lots. At bar **B61** *(187 Columbia St at DeGraw St, 718-643-5400)*, grab a beer and shoot some pool. Popular Mexican eatery **Alma** (*see above*) is upstairs; its pretty terrace, festooned with colorful lights, offers killer views.

For a peek into the tough, pregentrified life of old New York, head south across the industrial corridor of Hamilton Parkway. Grand, decaying piers—once the center of a bustling commercial waterfront—make a moody backdrop for clapboard homes, empty warehouses and trucks clattering over the cobblestone streets. An episode of the HBO hit *The Sopranos* was recently filmed here; you'll often find local photographers framing the faded grandeur of the old brick factories. (Naturally, plans to convert the spaces into lofts are already afoot.)

To check out work by local artists, look for the hand-scrawled letters reading GALLERY on the doors of the **Kentler International Drawing Space** *(353 Van Brunt St between Sullivan and Wolcott Sts, 718-875-2098)*. The **Brooklyn Working Artist Coalition** (BWAC) hosts large group shows in the spring and fall; visit its website *(www.bwac.org)* or call 718-596-2507 for a calendar.

On bodega-dotted Van Brunt Street, you'll find **360** *(360 Van Brunt St at Wolcott St, 718-246-0360)*, a quirky, affordable French

Avenue is the main commercial drag, Fifth Avenue is the hot strip for great boutiques and good restaurants, including the Venetian-accented **Al Di Là** *(248 Fifth Ave at Carroll St, Park Slope; 718-783-4565; see also p196)*, eclectic, upscale **Blue Ribbon Brooklyn** *(280 Fifth Ave between Garfield and 1st Sts, Park Slope; 718-840-0404 see p194)* and the funky, affordable **Mexican Sandwich Company** *(322 Fifth Ave at 3rd St, Park Slope; 718-369-2058)*. Park Slope also has a very visible lesbian community: The **Lesbian Herstory Archives** (*see p297*) is where you can peruse books and memorabilia; **Ginger's Bar** (*see p303*) is where you can peruse the readers.

Central Park may be bigger and more famous, but **Prospect Park** has a more rustic quality than its rectangular sibling to the west, and Brooklynites adore it. This masterpiece designed by Frederick Law Olmsted and Calvert Vaux (the same architects who gave us Central Park) is a stellar spot for bird-watching, especially with a little guidance from the **Prospect Park Audubon Center at the Boathouse** *(park entrance on Ocean Ave at Lincoln Rd, Prospect Heights; 718-287-3400)*. Or pretend you've left the city altogether by boating or hiking amid the waterfalls, reflecting pools and wildlife habitats of the recently restored **Ravine** (*see p126*). Olmsted and Vaux created this 526-acre rolling green space with an equestrian's perspective in mind; you can saddle a horse at nearby **Kensington Stables** (*see p333*), or hop on a bike and pedal alongside bladers and runners. Children enjoy riding the hand-carved horses at the park's antique **Carousel** *(Flatbush Ave at Empire Blvd)* or playing with animals in the **Prospect Park Wildlife Center** *(Park entrance on Ocean Ave at Empire Blvd, Prospect Heights; 718-399-7339)*.

Another verdant expanse, **Green-Wood Cemetery**, is about a 15-minute walk from Prospect Park. A century ago, this 478-acre site vied with Niagara Falls as New York State's greatest tourist attraction. Filled with Victorian mausoleums, cherubs and gargoyles, Green-Wood is the resting place of more than a half million New Yorkers, including Jean-Michel Basquiat, Leonard Bernstein and Mae West.

bistro with an inventive menu (even in this far-flung location, it's best to reserve a table in advance). Close by, the **Hope & Anchor** *(347 Van Brunt St at Wolcott St, 718-237-0276)* offers updated diner standards, followed by drag-queen karaoke on Thursdays and Fridays.

Sunny's *(253 Conover St between Beard and Reed Sts, 718-625-8211)* is a welcoming bar where third-generation owner Sunny hosts occasional spoken-word performances and poetry readings. Or stroll over to Beard Street, where young Brooklynites hang at **Lillie's** *(46 Beard St at Dwight St, 718-858-9822)*, which has the air of an old-time saloon. Try the signature drink, a Red Hooker (rum, cranberry and pineapple juices, and brown sugar). Sunday is barbecue night, with free ribs, burgers and hot dogs (just don't forget to tip the cook).

For several years, Red Hook has been a neighborhood on the verge. Locals love it, and developers eagerly eye the undeveloped tracts of land and vacant warehouses. And better public transportation is now a possibility: **New York Water Taxi** *(www.nywatertaxi.com; 212-742-1969)* says it's considering adding a Red Hook stop in 2004. Get out there before the tide turns, and it becomes the next Soho.

Riding high Hoisting one at **Lillie's**.

The central branch of the **Brooklyn Public Library** (*Prospect Heights; 718-230-2100*) sits near Prospect Park's main entrance and the massive Civil War memorial arch at **Grand Army Plaza** *(intersection of Flatbush Ave, Eastern Pkwy and Prospect Park West).* The library's Brooklyn Collection includes thousands of artifacts, manuscripts and photos that trace the borough's history. Just around the corner is the tranquil **Brooklyn Botanic Garden** and the newly spruced-up **Brooklyn Museum of Art** (*see p145*).

Brooklyn Botanic Garden

From Eastern Pkwy to Empire Blvd, between Flatbush and Washington Aves, Prospect Heights (718-623-7200; www.bbg.org). Subway: B, Q, Franklin Ave S to Prospect Park; 2, 3 to Eastern Pkwy–Brooklyn Museum. **Open** *Apr–Sept Tue–Fri 8am–6pm; Sat, Sun 10am–6pm. Oct–Mar Tue–Fri 8am–4:30pm; Sat, Sun 10am–4:30pm.* **Admission** *$5, seniors and students $3, children free. Also free Mid-Mar–mid-Nov Tue; mid-Nov–mid-Mar Mon–Fri.*

Green-Wood Cemetery

25th St at Fifth Ave, Green-Wood Heights (718-768-7300; www.green-wood.com). Subway: M, R to 25th St. **Open** *8am–4pm.* **Admission** *free.*

Don't miss The Ravine

The **Ravine**, located between the Long Meadow and the Nethermead in Prospect Park, is defined by a steep narrow gorge, lined with the diverse foliage of Brooklyn's one and only forest. The 143-acre Ravine district has the highest elevations and the most rugged terrain in the park. As a result, not much in the way of people-pleasing activities has been built into the Ravine. However, the area did turn out to be ideally formed for a man-made watercourse, which now includes pools and a waterfall at the head of the course, and the Lake and Lullwater at the end. Since 1996, the Prospect Park Alliance's Woodlands Campaign has planted more than 250,000 trees, plants and shrubs in the Ravine and its surrounding woodlands. As of 2002, the district is fully open to the public again, and its restored lush forestry reveals Olmsted and Vaux's intention to create a little bit of the Adirondacks in the midst of Brooklyn.

Park entrances on Prospect Park West at 3rd, 9th and 15th Sts. Subway: B, Q to Seventh Ave; F to 15th St–Prospect Park; 2, 3 to Grand Army Plaza.

Prospect Park

Main entrance on Flatbush Ave at Grand Army Plaza, Prospect Heights (718-965-8999, zoo 718-399-7339; www.prospectpark.org). Subway: B, Q, Franklin Ave S to Prospect Park; F to 15th St–Prospect Park; 2, 3 to Grand Army Plaza.

Fort Greene, Greenpoint & Williamsburg

Fort Greene, with its wide Victorian brownstones and other grand buildings, has undergone a serious revival over the past decade. It has long been a center of African-American life and business—Spike Lee, Branford Marsalis, Chris Rock and Richard Wright have all called it home at some point. **Fort Greene Park** *(from DeKalb to Myrtle Aves, between St. Edwards St and Washington Park)* was conceived in 1847 at the behest of poet Walt Whitman (then the editor of the *Brooklyn Daily Eagle*); its master plan was fully realized by the omnipresent Olmsted and Vaux in 1867. At the center of the park stands the *Prison Ship Martyrs Monument,* erected in 1909 in memory of more than 11,000 American prisoners who died on British ships that were anchored nearby during the Revolutionary War.

Fort Greene's connection to history only begins there. The **Lafayette Avenue Presbyterian Church** *(85 South Oxford St at Lafayette Ave, Fort Greene; 718-625-7515)* was founded by a group of abolitionists; Abraham Lincoln's oldest son, Robert Todd Lincoln, broke ground for the church in 1860. Its subterranean tunnel once served as a stop on the Underground Railroad. The celebrated stained-glass windows created by Louis Comfort Tiffany are being restored.

A year after the church was established, the **Brooklyn Academy of Music** (*see p321*) was founded in Brooklyn Heights, later moving to its current site on Fort Greene's southern border. BAM is America's oldest operating performing-arts center. It once presented the likes of Edwin Booth and Sarah Bernhard; now it's known for ambitious cultural performances of all kinds. In recent years, it has added several venues that show cutting-edge dance, theater, music and film programs, which draw audiences from all boroughs. From October through December, BAM hosts the **Next Wave Festival** (*see p257*). Also world-famous—though perhaps to a different audience—is the cheesecake at **Junior's Restaurant** *(386 Flatbush Ave at DeKalb Ave, Fort Greene; 718-852-5257),* just three blocks away. A slew of trendy buppie-filled Fort Greene nightspots can be found nearby, including the upscale French eatery **A Table** *(171 Lafayette Ave at Adelphi St, Fort Greene;*

718-935-9121) and the always-jammin' **Frank's Cocktail Lounge** *(660 Fulton St at South Elliott Pl, Fort Greene; 718-625-9339).*

Williamsburg is further along in hipness than Fort Greene (and may even be past its peak). This is where young Manhattan transplants, most sporting way-cool haircuts and '80s fashions, slink and chain-smoke along North Sixth Street or on the neighborhood's main drag of Bedford Avenue. You'll find some of the city's trendiest nightspots here, including **Galapagos** (*see p311*), and **Pete's Candy Store** (*see p314*), plus eateries like the Thai palace **SEA** (*see p196*), and the eclectic **Chickenbone Café** (*see p195*). You'll also find the distinctly untrendy, old-time gustatory treasure **Peter Luger** (*see p196*), which grills what may be the best steak (porterhouse only) in all of the city.

The area also has dozens of art galleries, such as **Pierogi 2000** and **Roebling Hall** (*see p268*). But the core of the area's art scene is the **Williamsburg Art & Historical Center** *(135 Broadway at Bedford Ave, Williamsburg; 718-486-7372; www.wahcenter.org)*, located in a landmark 1929 bank building. The local live-music scene thrives, too; performance spaces include **Northsix** (*see p314*) and **Warsaw at the Polish National Home** (*see p316*).

Before the hipster invasion, the waterfront location made Billyburg ideal for industry, and after the Erie Canal linked the Atlantic Ocean with the Great Lakes in 1825, it became a bustling port. Companies such as Pfizer and Domino Sugar (which recently shut down its last refining operation in Williamsburg) started here. Then, in the 20th century, businesses began abandoning the enormous industrial spaces. The beloved **Brooklyn Brewery** *(79 North 11th St between Berry St and Wythe Ave, Williamsburg; 718-486-7422; www.brooklynbrewery.com)* is located in a former ironworks. Visit during happy hour on Friday evenings, or take a factory-and-tasting tour on Saturday.

Williamsburg is also one of New York's many curious multiethnic amalgams. To the south, Broadway divides a vibrant Latino neighborhood from a lively community of Hasidic Jews (known as the Satmar, a sect which has roots in Hungary), while the northern half extending into **Greenpoint** contains entrenched Polish and Italian settlements.

Bedford-Stuyvesant, Crown Heights & Flatbush

Although Harlem gets props for being the cultural capital of black America, **Bed-Stuy** is a community whose size and architectural splendor rivals that of its Manhattan counterpart. Join the annual **Brownstoners of Bedford-Stuyvesant Inc. House Tour** *(718-778-6005)*, held the third Saturday in October, rain or shine; it's a great way to see the area's historic homes. The **Concord Baptist Church of Christ** *(833 Marcy Ave between Madison St and Putnam Ave, Bedford-Stuyvesant; 718-622-1818)* offers uplifting gospel music from one of the biggest (and loudest) African-American congregations in the U.S.

There's plenty to do south of Bed-Stuy in the largely West Indian neighborhoods of **Crown Heights** and **Flatbush** (both also have sizable Jewish populations). Calypso and soca music blare from open windows, and it seems every block has a storefront selling spicy, aromatic jerk chicken or meat patties. In Flatbush, try the sublime oxtail soup at Caribbean eatery **Sybil's** *(2210 Church Ave at Flatbush Ave, Flatbush; 718-469-9049).*

Scene stealers Billyburg's **Bedford Avenue**.

Bay Ridge & Bensonhurst

Bay Ridge and **Bensonhurst** were the settings for *Saturday Night Fever,* and these mostly residential neighborhoods are always hopping. There is a host of eating options on the main drags of Third, Fourth and Fifth

Hot lips Coney Island **Sideshow** fire-eater.

Avenues, between Bay Ridge Parkway and 88th Street. For authentic Lebanese cuisine, try **Karam** *(8519 Fourth Ave between 85th and 86th Sts, Bay Ridge; 718-745-5227)*. Eighty-nine-year-old favorite **Hinsch's Confectionery** *(8518 Fifth Ave between 85th and 86th Sts, Bay Ridge; 718-748-2854)* froths a mean egg cream. Incidentally, the disco in which John Travolta strutted his stuff remains—it's now a gay club called **Spectrum** *(802 64th St at Eighth Ave, Bay Ridge; 718-238-8213)*.

You can see the **Verrazano-Narrows Bridge** from just about anywhere in Bay Ridge. Completed in 1964, it connects Brooklyn and Staten Island. **Fort Hamilton**, named after founding father Alexander Hamilton, sits at the foot of the bridge. The fort is the second-oldest continuously garrisoned federal post in the country. Originally a Dutch settlement in the 19th century, it became a summer retreat for moneyed Manhattanites. You can still find grand old homes along the quiet suburban streets—including the **Howard E. and Jessie Jones House** *(8220 Narrows Ave at 83rd St)*, an arts-and-crafts mansion known locally as the "Gingerbread House."

If you find Manhattan's Little Italy too touristy, check out **Bensonhurst**'s version on a stretch of 18th Avenue *(between 68th and 77th Sts)* known as "Cristoforo Colombo Boulevard." There are old-fashioned Italian men's social clubs, delis stocked with fresh pasta and shops selling Italian music. At **Villabate Pasticceria & Bakery** *(7117 18th Ave between 71st and 72nd Sts, Bensonhurst; 718-331-8430)*, Italian-speaking crowds shout out their orders for pastries and marzipan.

Brighton Beach & Coney Island

Brighton Beach is also known as Little Odessa because of its large Russian immigrant population. You can wander the aisles of **M&I International Foods** *(249 Brighton Beach Ave between Brighton 1st and Brighton 2nd Sts, 718-615-1011)*, a huge Russian deli and grocery, or make a reservation at one of the local nightclubs, where the dress is formal, the food and vodka are plentiful, and the dancing continues until the wee hours.

Coney Island, on the peninsula just west of Brighton Beach, is a summertime destination. After decades of decay, the weirdly wonderful community—known for its amusement park, beach and boardwalk—has made a comeback. The biggest improvement is seaside **KeySpan Park**, home to the **Brooklyn Cyclones** (*see p327*), a minor-league baseball affiliate of the New York Mets. If you're a thrill-seeker, take a spin in the Cyclone at **Astroland Amusement Park** (*see p277*); a ride on the 75-year-old wooden roller coaster lasts only two minutes, but the first drop is nearly vertical, and the cars clatter along the 2,640 feet of track at speeds of up to 60 miles per hour.

After your ride, take a stroll along the boardwalk. You'll soon hit the **New York Aquarium** (*see p284*), where you can marvel at the famous beluga whales. From July through early September, boogie to house music at the **Black Underground** dance party *(boardwalk at West 10th St; Sat 3–9pm)*. And there is always the (fairly tame) **Sideshows by the Seashore**, put on by **Coney Island USA**, an organization that keeps the torch burning for early-20th-century Coney Island. The **Mermaid Parade** (*see p254*) and **Nathan's Famous Fourth of July Hot Dog Eating Contest** (*see p255*) are two popular, appropriately quirky annual Coney Island events.

Coney Island USA

1208 Surf Ave at W 12th St, Coney Island (718-372-5159; www.coneyislandusa.com). Subway: D to Stillwell Ave–Coney Island. **Open** *Call or visit website for schedule.* **Admission** *$5, children under 12 $3.*

Queens

A fresh arts scene (including MoMA) makes this outer borough very "in."

For too long, residential Queens—"the other 718"—was regarded by lordly Manhattanites as the déclassé bridge-and-tunnel expanse where Archie Bunker and George Costanza lived, the boring borough where you went to catch a plane, a Mets game or a U.S. Open match. But all that is changing, as back-of-the-bus Queens edges into the forefront of New York happenings.

The energy behind Queens' higher profile comes from its recent cultural explosion. The Museum of Modern Art's 2002 temporary relocation to Long Island City has been the big bang of the Queens art movement. Thanks to trailblazing **MoMA QNS** (*see p150*), Manhattan culturati were finally lured across the water to the other Queens museums and galleries that had already sprouted in abandoned factories, warehouses and waterfront lots. Probably as a result of all this arty action, the borough has acquired a buzz as an affordable but not fatally uncool address. Rent refugees from Manhattan and now-hot Brooklyn have found their way to Queens' safe, Manhattan-view neighborhoods. Astoria, Long Island City and Sunnyside are now rife with postcollegiate multiroommate flats, converted lofts and 1920s co-ops that can be had for half the cost of their 212 equivalents.

Renovation-savvy professionals aren't the only ones moving to the borough. Queens has become the most ethnically diverse urban area in the world, and its street life is almost psychedelically colorful. The dazzling variety of retail outlets and restaurants can be attributed to the fact that more than a third of the borough's 2-million-plus residents are foreign-born—including Arabs, Brazilians, Chinese, Colombians, Croatians, Cubans, Greeks, Indians, Italians, Koreans, Peruvians, Thais and many others. You'll find a large mix of ethnic dishes, from *arepas* to zabaglione, that are gloriously authentic and much more reasonably priced than at places in "the city."

Your tour should commence just beyond the East River in **Long Island City**, at the 7 subway train's Vernon Blvd–Jackson Ave stop. Walk to the historic waterfront, where **Gantry Plaza State Park**, named for its towering 19th-century railroad gantries, features stunning East River views and a close-up look at a Queens landmark, the 1936 red neon **Pepsi-Cola sign**. Get a whiff of Long Island City's scrappy dockside origins in the boxing-themed bar of **Waterfront Crabhouse** *(2-03 Borden Ave at 2nd St, Long Island City; 718-729-4862)*, an old-time saloon and oyster bar in an 1880s brick edifice. Back near the subway stop are fine restaurants: **Tournesol** *(50-12 Vernon Blvd between 50th and 51st Aves, Long Island City; 718-472-4355; see p197)*, a true French bistro, and **LIC Café**, a labor of love by a passionate owner-chef *(5-48 49th Ave between Vernon Blvd and 5th St, Long Island City; 718-752-0282; see p197)*. Some of New York's best pastas and brick-oven pizzas are found at **Manetta's** *(1076 Jackson Ave at 49th Ave, Long Island City; 718-786-6171; see p197)*.

Walk a few blocks east on Jackson Avenue. You'll pass **P.S. 1 Contemporary Art Center** (*see p151*), a progressive museum that sponsors wildly popular Warm Up art parties during the summer. Stop for a look at the 1904 Beaux Arts–style **New York State Supreme Court** *(25-10 Courthouse Sq at Thompson Ave, Long Island City)*. Nearby, a well-preserved row of 1890s Italianate brownstones

Don't miss Pops's pad

Jazz legend **Louis Armstrong** (born in New Orleans in 1901) was famous and wealthy by 1943, when he and his wife Lucille purchased a modest home in Corona (*see p134*). They lived out their lives in this house—he died in 1971; she, in 1983—and it opened as a museum in the fall of 2003. The place underwent a $1.6 million restoration, but don't worry—it looks just as it did when Louis and the missus resided there. "Every chair, every couch, every tchotchke is there, as if they're frozen in time," says Michael Cogswell, director of the House & Archives. One nifty update: A sound system hidden within the walls plays excerpts from Armstrong's 600-plus home-recorded reel-to-reel tapes. Visitors hear him telling jokes, eating dinner with Lucille and playing with General, the family dog. He may have been Satchmo to the world, but to his Queens friends, he was known as Pops. You'll leave feeling like a neighbor, too.

Sightseeing

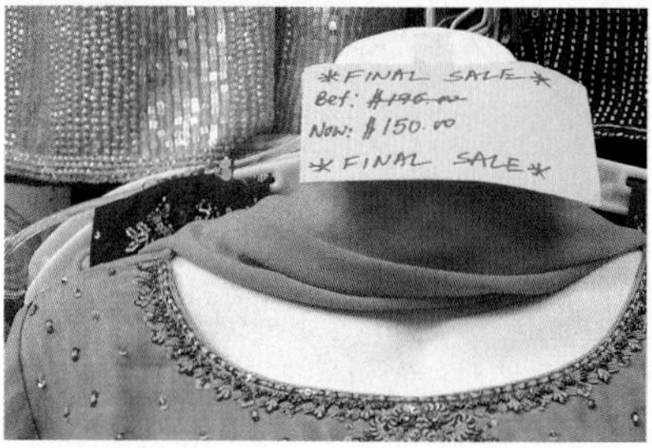

Passage to India Shops in **Jackson Heights.**

(45th Ave between 21st and 23rd Sts, Long Island City) constitutes the **Hunters Point Historic District**.

Hop back on the 7 train. When it emerges from underground, look out of the left-hand windows. You'll be treated to the marvelous graffiti-covered walls of the outdoor **Phun Phactory** and a peerless view of the Manhattan skyline. The back of the SILVERCUP sign that you see from the Queensboro Plaza platform announces **Silvercup Studios**, once a bread bakery and now a TV and film studio (*Sex and the City* and *The Sopranos* shoot interiors here). When Los Angeles was still a sleepy orange grove, western Queens was booming with filmmaking. W.C. Fields and the Marx Brothers clowned at Famous Players/Lasky Studios; now **Kaufman-Astoria Studios** (where *The Cosby Show* was shot), this 14-acre facility also houses the **American Museum of the Moving Image** (*see p161*), which holds exhibitions and screenings.

At Queensboro Plaza, transfer to an N or W train and head north into Astoria. If it's a nice day, get off at Broadway for a visit to the **Socrates Sculpture Park**, a 4.5-acre public space given to large-scale outdoor exhibits, and films and concerts during the summer. At the end of the subway line *(Astoria–Ditmars Blvd stop)*, walk west to Astoria Park, which features dramatic views of two bridges: the **Triborough Bridge**, a Robert Moses–conceived series of elevated roadways that connects Queens, the Bronx and Manhattan; and the 1916 **Hellgate**, a single-arch steel masterpiece that was the template for the Sydney Harbour Bridge in Australia and is now used only for freight trains.

Astoria, New York's Greek stronghold, bursts with Hellenic eateries specializing in impeccably grilled seafood. **Taverna Kyklades** *(33-07 Ditmars Blvd between 32nd and 33rd Sts, Astoria; 718-545-8666)* has a breezy Aegean atmosphere, while dirt-cheap **Uncle George's**, open 24/7/365, is beloved by locals *(33-19 Broadway at 34th St, Astoria; 718-626-0593)*. **Mediterranean Foods** *(30-12 34th St between 30th and 31st Aves, Astoria; 718-728-6166)*, a Greek grocery, sells low-priced, picnic-ready imported olives and cheeses. Do you fancy eating outdoors? New York's last remaining Central European beer garden, **Bohemian Hall** *(29-19 24th Ave at 29th St, Astoria; 718-274-0043)*, hosts Czech-style indoor and outdoor dining and drinking. **Steinway Street**, south of Astoria Boulevard, is a concentrated swath of the Queens mosaic. Enjoy a (legal!) hookah pipe with your coffee at one of the Egyptian cafés here.

The **Lent-Riker-Smith Homestead**, a lovingly restored historic site in the Steinway area, rates a detour. Dating from 1654, the oldest private dwelling in the five boroughs includes a stable, a gazebo and a family cemetery that has been the final resting place for generations of Rikers. This clan owned Riker's Island and a hunk of Long Island Sound waterfront once called North Beach, a former seaside amusement park now occupied by La Guardia Airport.

Find your way back to the International Express—the 7 subway line itself is a designated National Millennium Trail—and disembark at 74th St–Broadway. This is the crossroads of **Jackson Heights**, a dizzyingly multiculti neighborhood even by Queens standards—and it's a foodie's paradise (*see right* **Action, Jackson**). The large windows of **Bombay Harbour** *(72-23 Broadway between 72nd and*

Action, Jackson

Manhattan may be too pricey for new immigrants, but where there's a green card, there's a way. **Jackson Heights**, in western Queens, has become New York's most international district. In past decades, it has welcomed newcomers from South Asia, then Latinos from Argentina, Colombia and Peru. At present, Mexicans from the state of Puebla constitute the neighborhood's newest, most populous segment, and the main commercial street, **Roosevelt Avenue**, bursts with the food, fashion and festive flavor of Latin America. The 7 elevated subway train rumbling above the avenue adds to the strip's otherworldly feel.

The aroma of *pollo a la brasa* (spicy Colombian rotisserie-grilled chicken) from **Gusty Chicken** *(74-01 Roosevelt Ave at 74th St)* greets you as you step off the subway. At the restaurant **Hornado Ecuatoriano** *(76-18 Roosevelt Ave at 76th St)*, you can order in Spanish or Quechua, the language of Andean Indians. *Cuy*, a native delicacy of spit-roasted guinea pig, is available by special order only. As in every restaurant on Roosevelt Avenue, flower-selling waifs weave around tables proffering *"rosas para la señorita."* The constant lively beats you hear are emanating from **Rincon Musical** *(76-11 Roosevelt Ave at 76th St)*; the store offers a hemisphere's worth of musical styles, including Cuban *son*, Dominican merengue, Puerto Rican salsa, Brazilian samba, Argentine tango, Tex-Mex *tejano* and Colombian *cumbia*.

No. 77-02 *(between 77th and 78th Sts)* is the first of Roosevelt's many Mexican sidewalk counters that craft tacos and *tortas*—mega-sandwiches piled with ham, chorizo sausage, avocado, chipotle peppers and mild Oaxacan cheese to temper the heat. Thirsty? *Jugos naturales* are sold at a Puerto Rican–owned juice bar at **No. 79-01** *(at 79th St)*: Three bucks buys you your choice of fresh-blended Caribbean fruit flavors such as *lulo*, *curuba* and *mamey*. **Omega Tatuelas**, a New World tattoo parlor *(No. 81-09 at 81st St)*, inks Mayan designs from Chichén Itzá, Incan patterns from Peru and the Virgin of Guadelupe, Mexico's patron saint.

The 82nd Street stop on the 7 train is as abuzz with bystanders, hawkers and fluttering pigeons as any *zocalo* (Mexican town square). On nice days, it swarms with sidewalk barbers, shoeshine boys, Pentecostal orators, Chinese-Ecuadorean chair masseurs, Spanish booksellers, video pirates and flower stands. Street snacks include Mexican sugared coconut and Colombian coffee candies; double-parked trucks bag and sell freshly sliced mangoes and melons with such condiments as lemon juice and chili sauce. Flyers pressed into your palm advertise *divorcios rapidos*, bail loans, fortune-telling and by-the-minute calls to Mexico.

This section of Roosevelt teems with Latin style: **Joyeria Gemex** *(No. 83-25 between 83rd and 84th Sts)* and **Arias Jewelry** *(No. 84-01 at 84th St)* ask less than $100 for big J. Lo–style 14-karat-gold hoop earrings. **Soccer Fanatic** *(No. 84-28 between 84th and 85th Sts)* carries equipment and jerseys from South American and Mexican soccer teams, as well as the Europeans. **Zapaterio Mexicano** *(No. 88-07 at 88th St)* features well-made Tex-Mex *vaquero* (cowboy) gear. You'll find black Mexican cowboy hats, tooled leather belts and showy boots in lizard, snakeskin, ostrich and leather. Made-in-Mexico Tejas-label cowboy shirts, embroidered with stars, lariats, bulls or horses, are a steal at $40.

Cooks will appreciate **Mi Bello Mexico** *(No. 87-17 between 87th and 88th Sts)* for its assortment of dried peppers, such as ancho, *arbole*, *guajillo*, *mulatto* and *pastilla*. **Lavaza Foods** *(No. 88-13 between 87th and 88th Sts)* sells homemade corn tortillas and fresh Mexican produce like tomatillos, jalapeños and cactus leaves.

Before hopping back on the 7 at Junction Boulevard, duck into **El Rincon Criollo** *(40-09 Junction Blvd between Northern Blvd and 34th Ave)*. This '60s time capsule (dig the "fun facts about Cuba" place mats) serves first-rate Cuban eats for a tiny tab. You could be anywhere in Latin America—but you're actually two subway stops from Flushing.
Subway: E, F, V, G, R to Jackson Hts–Roosevelt Ave; 7 to 74th St–Broadway or 82nd St–Jackson Hts.

Gusty Chicken.

73rd Sts, Jackson Heights; 718-898-5500) overlook a busy intersection, and its $6 lunch buffet is exceptional. Another good option is **Ashoka** *(74-14 37th Ave between 74th and 75th Sts, Jackson Heights; 718-898-5088).* Indian sari, spice and jewelry shops line the block of 74th Street between Roosevelt and 37th Avenues. Don't miss **Patel Brothers** *(37-27 74th St between Roosevelt and 37th Aves, Jackson Heights; 718-898-3445),* an Indian supermarket and general store teeming with exotic goods.

For no-knife-required Argentine steak in a charming hacienda, try **La Fusta** *(80-32 Baxter St between Ketcham and Layton Sts, Jackson Heights; 718-429-8222).* The sprightly Peruvian ceviche at **La Pollada de Laura** would be the envy of any chichi Manhattan eatery *(102-03 Northern Blvd at 102nd St, Jackson Heights; 718-426-7818).* **Green Field** *(108-01 Northern Blvd at 108th St, Jackson Heights; 718-672-5202)* is a boisterous Brazilian *rodizio* serving an all-you-can-eat extravaganza of tropical salads and grilled meats.

Throughout Jackson Heights, look for green-and-white signs marking the **Jackson Heights Garden City Trail**. Jackson Heights has a roughly 30-square-block landmark district of notable co-op apartment buildings and private homes in Tudor and neo-Gothic styles. They were built mainly during the 1920s by visionary architects seeking to create a "garden city" with parklike interior courtyards. Outstanding examples can be found on 34th Avenue between 76th and 81st Streets.

At the end of the 7 train lies **Flushing**. It was settled as "Vlishing" by egalitarian Dutch, who were joined by pacifist Friends (a.k.a. Quakers) seeking their own freedom in the New World. These settlers authored the Flushing Remonstrance, a 1657 edict that extended freedom of worship to Jews and Muslims; it's now regarded as a precursor to the U.S. Constitution's First Amendment. Today, Flushing has churches, synagogues, mosques, and Buddhist and Hindu temples. The modest **Friends Meeting House** *(137-16 Northern Blvd between Main and Union Sts, Flushing; 718-358-9636),* built in 1694, remains.

Next door is **Kingsland Homestead**, a 1785 farmhouse that houses the **Queens Historical Society** and hosts regular exhibitions on local history. Take another step back in time at the **Voelker-Orth Museum** *(149-19 38th Ave between 149th St and 149th Pl, Flushing; 718-359-6227),* a restored 1880s Victorian gingerbread house and herb garden that sponsors tours, lectures, concerts, dances and a popular period tea party. **Flushing Town Hall**, a fanciful 1862 Romanesque Revival edifice, houses the Flushing Council on Culture and the Arts, and hosts jazz and classical concerts and multimedia exhibits. The FCCA runs free trolley tours of Queens every Sunday at noon; you can also catch the monthly **Queens Jazz Trail** *(www.queensjazztrail.com)* here. The latter is a pilgrimage to the homes of jazz greats who have resided in the borough—a Valhalla of vibe that has nurtured Louis Armstrong, Count Basie, John Coltrane, Ella Fitzgerald, Dizzy Gillespie, Billie Holiday and Charles Mingus. Armstrong's former residence, in Corona, has been dedicated as a historic-house museum (*see p129* **Pops's pad**).

If exploring Flushing has stimulated your appetite, you're in luck: The mile-and-a-half stretch of **Main Street**, south of Northern Boulevard, is one of the world's most vibrant, fastest-growing Chinatowns, welcoming newcomers—and chefs—from all over Asia.

Flushing is geared toward residents rather than tourists, so it's impossible to get an underspiced or overpriced meal here. The Pan-Asian restaurant row on Main Street includes **Sichuan Dynasty** *(135-32 40th Rd between Main and Prince Sts, Flushing; 718-961-7500),* where $16.95 buys you three, yes *three,* zesty central-Chinese entrées, like lamb with pink peppercorns, chicken with three peppers or garlicky *ma-la* shrimp. Around the corner, **Penang** *(38-04 Prince St at 38th Ave, Flushing; 718-321-2078)* cooks curry- and coconut-spiked Malaysian cuisine, a fusion of Chinese and Indonesian flavors. Twenty-four–hour Korean grills also abound in Flushing. Try **Woo Chon** *(41-19 Kissena Blvd at Barclay Ave, Flushing; 718-463-0803)* for *bulgogi* (barbecued beef) and unlimited *banchan* (side dishes).

The massive **Flushing Meadows–Corona Park** is where both the 1939 and 1964 World's Fairs were held. It contains the "Uni-five" cultural outposts, including the **Queens Zoo** (with its "natural" environments); the Philip Johnson–designed **Queens Theatre in the Park**, an indoor amphitheater; the **New York Hall of Science** (*see p163*), an acclaimed interactive museum; the **Queens Botanical Garden**, a 39-acre horizontal extravaganza; and the **Queens Museum of Art** (*see p154*), whose pièce de résistance is the 1964 *Panorama of the City of New York*—a 9,335-square-foot scale model of the five boroughs.

The park also encompasses **Shea Stadium**, the local turf for baseball's hard-luck **New York Mets** (*see p327*); the **United States**

▶ For a map of **Queens**, *see p408*.
▶ For more on **MoMA QNS**, *see p150*.

Earth to Queens The 1964 **Unisphere** is comparable in height to a 14-story building.

National Tennis Center (*see p331*), where the U.S. Open is held at the end of the summer; and the **Unisphere**, a mammoth steel globe that was the symbol of the 1964 World's Fair. Before you leave the park, try to figure out what those dual disk-topped towers are; they turned up as UFOs in *Men in Black.*

There is *still* more to Queens. Busy **Jamaica**, in the southern part of the borough, is the center of African-American commerce, hip-hop culture and—true to its name—Caribbean immigration. From the subway, walk to Jamaica Avenue, the main drag. The **Tabernacle of Prayer** is an "anointed, spirit-filled" Evangelical church set in a splendid, defunct 1940 Art Deco movie palace, the Loews Valencia. Bishop Ronny Davis's Sunday gospel service is far less overrun with tourists than are its Harlem counterparts.

Down Jamaica Avenue, within King Park, is **King Manor Museum**, the early-19th-century residence of Rufus King, a four-term senator from New York and an early opponent of slavery; his memory has been resurrected by local residents. Perhaps freethinking King would dig the soul food at **Carmichael's** *(117-08 Guy R. Brewer Blvd at Foch Blvd, Jamaica; 718-723-6908)*, a pristine '40s diner slinging all-day breakfasts of salmon croquettes and grits 'n' gravy.

At the southern tip of Queens is **Rockaway Beach** (yes, the one the Ramones sang about). A lively year-round surfing scene clusters around the sandy stretch from Beach 90th to Beach 93rd Streets; check www.newyorksurf.com and www.surfrider.com for wave conditions. Queens also boasts two alternating-season Thoroughbred tracks that sponsor world-class horse racing: **Aqueduct** (*see p330*), near JFK Airport, and **Belmont Park** (*see p330* **A horse, a course**) on Queens' eastern border. Manhattan may have the nightlife, but Queens is full of life, period.

American Museum of the Moving Image

34-12 36th St between 34th and 35th Aves, Astoria (718-784-0077; www.ammi.org). Subway: G, R, V to 36th St; N, W to 36th Ave. **Open** *Wed, Thu noon–5pm; Fri noon–8pm; Sat, Sun 11am–6pm.* **Admission** *$10, students $7.50, children 5–18 $5, children under 5 free. Free Fri 4–8pm.* **Credit** *AmEx, MC, V.*

Discover Queens

www.discoverqueens.info.
This website offers current cultural and entertainment information, as well as discount coupons.

Flushing Meadows–Corona Park

Between 111th St and Van Wyck Expwy, from Grand Central Pkwy to Flushing Bay. Subway: 7 to Willets Point–Shea Stadium.

Flushing Town Hall/Flushing Council on Culture and the Arts

137-35 Northern Blvd, Flushing (718-463-7700; www.flushingtownhall.org). Subway: 7 to Flushing–Main St. **Open** *Mon–Fri 10am–5pm; Sat, Sun noon–5pm.* **Admission** *free; Jazz Trail $26 (reservations required).* **Credit** *AmEx, MC, V.*

No waiting The 2003 Emerging Artist Fellowship Exhibition at **Socrates Sculpture Park**.

King Manor Museum
King Park, Jamaica Ave at 153rd St, Jamaica (718-206-0525). Subway: E, J, Z to Jamaica Ctr–Parsons/Archer; F to Parsons Blvd.
Open *Feb–Dec Thu, Fri noon–2pm; Sat, Sun 1–5pm.* **Admission** *$5, seniors and students $3, children 4–13 $2.* **Credit** *Cash only.*

Kingsland Homestead/ Queens Historical Society
143-35 37th Ave between Bowne St and Parsons Blvd, Flushing (718-939-0647, ext 17; www.queenshistoricalsociety.org). Subway: 7 to Flushing–Main St. **Tours** *Tue, Sat, Sun 2:30–4:30pm; and by appointment.* **Admission** *$3, seniors and students $2.* **Credit** *Cash only.*

Lent-Riker-Smith Homestead
78-03 19th Rd at 78th St, East Elmhurst (718-728-0072; www.lentrikersmithhomestead.com). Travel: N, W to Astoria–Ditmars Blvd, then Q19A bus to 78th St. Private tours available through owner Marion Smith; donation optional.

Louis Armstrong House
34-56 107th St between 34th and 37th Aves, Corona (718-478-8274; www.satchmo.net). Subway: 7 to 103rd St–Corona Plaza. **Open** *Tue–Fri 10am–5pm; Sat, Sun noon–5pm; tours on the hour till 4pm.* **Admission** *$8, seniors and children $4.* **Credit** *MC, V.*

Queens Botanical Garden
43-50 Main St between Dahlia and Elder Aves, Flushing (718-886-3800; www.queensbotanical.org). Subway: 7 to Flushing–Main St. **Open** *Apr–Oct Tue–Fri 8am–6pm; Sat, Sun 8am–7pm. Nov–Mar Tue–Fri 8am–4:30pm. Open on Monday holidays.* **Admission** *free.*

Queens Council on the Arts
718-647-3377; www.queenscouncilarts.org.
This website provides details on cultural events.

Queens Theatre in the Park
Flushing Meadows–Corona Park (718-760-0064; www.queenstheatre.org). Subway: 7 to Willets Point–Shea Stadium; take Shea Stadium exit to meet shuttle, which picks up from subway station one hour before every show. Call or visit website for show times and ticket prices.

Queens Zoo
53-51 111th St between 53rd and 54th Aves, inside park (718-271-1500; www.queenszoo.com). Subway: 7 to 111th St. **Open** *May–Sept 10am–5pm. Oct–Apr 10am–4:30pm.* **Admission** *$5, seniors $1.25, children 3–12 $1, children under 3 free.* **Credit** *Cash only.*

Socrates Sculpture Park
Broadway at Vernon Blvd, Astoria (718-956-1819; www.socratessculpturepark.org). Travel: N, W to Broadway, then Q104 bus to Vernon Blvd. **Open** *9am–sunset daily.* **Admission** *free.*

Tabernacle of Prayer
165-11 Jamaica Ave between Merrick Blvd and 165th St, Jamaica; entrance for services on Jamaica Ave (718-657-4210; www.forministry.com/11432top1). Subway: E, J, Z to Jamaica Ctr–Parsons/Archer; F to Parsons Blvd. **Tours** *Private tours available.*

The Bronx

Lions and tigers and bears—plus hikes, art and baseball.

Located north of Manhattan, the Bronx is the only New York borough attached to the U.S. mainland—but its past, present and future belong to the city in every way. While it may not top every tourist itinerary, the Bronx offers numerous attractions that are worthy of a visit, including a world-class **zoo**, the **New York Botanical Garden** and **Yankee Stadium**. It also has lively ethnic neighborhoods and serene green spaces rife with hiking trails and riverside views.

The Bronx is so named because the area once belonged to the family of Jonas Bronck, a Dutch farmer who owned a 500-acre homestead in what is now the central Morrisania section. Back in 1639, people said they were going to visit "the Broncks," and the name (along with the article) stuck. Throughout the early decades of the 20th century, the Bronx, like fellow outer boroughs Queens and Brooklyn, drew much of its population from the ever-expanding pool of Irish, German, Italian and Eastern European Jewish immigrants. These new Americans, many of whom had rarely ventured beyond their home villages before setting off to the New World, flocked to the Bronx for its cheap rents and open spaces. During the post-WWII years, as the Bronx grew more urbanized, the descendants of the old European immigrants moved farther out, to the suburbs of nearby Westchester and Long Island. Their places were taken by fresh waves of newcomers, now hailing from Central America, Puerto Rico, Albania, Russia, Haiti, the Dominican Republic and the West Indies. Jennifer Lopez grew up here, as did Secretary of State Colin Powell, Regis Philbin, former mayor Rudolph Giuliani and a host of rappers, including Slick Rick and Missy Elliott.

But the Bronx has had its share of hard knocks. Robert Moses, the city planner both revered and reviled for his remaking of the five boroughs, brought parks, playgrounds, beaches and (with less attractive results) bridges to the city's residents. Aware that traffic was fast choking New York's roadways, and prizing the automobile over public transit, Moses spanned the city with borough-linking expressways and bridges. The challenge of building such grand public works in a densely populated urban area was one that Moses met with brute force. From the late 1940s until the early '70s, thousands of Bronx residents saw their apartment buildings razed to make room for the Whitestone and Throgs Neck Bridges, the east–west Cross Bronx Expressway, and the north–south Bruckner Boulevard extension of the New England Thruway. Cut off from their surrounding communities, many neighborhoods fell into neglect, a condition exacerbated by the economic and social downturns that plagued the entire city in the '60s and '70s.

These days, the Bronx is finding its feet again. While some spots around the South, East and Central Bronx are still in transition, artists' communities have begun to sprout in **Mott Haven** and **Hunts Point**; the zoo and botanical garden are more attractive than ever; and numerous areas—the **Grand Concourse**, **Arthur Avenue**, **Riverdale**, **City Island** and **Pelham Bay Park**—are safe and welcoming to visitors.

Located at 161st Street and River Avenue, **Yankee Stadium** is one of the Bronx's best-known landmarks (*see below* **Night game**). When there are no day games, the Yankees organization gives tours of the clubhouse, the dugout and the famous center field "Monument Park." The coolest way to get to the game is by boat: **NY Waterway** (*see p70*) will ferry you to and from the stadium (from Manhattan or New Jersey) aboard the *Yankee Clipper*.

Don't miss Night game

An evening game at **Yankee Stadium** is the best reason to visit the Bronx after dark. From the platform of the elevated subway line *(B, D or 4 train to 161st Street and River Avenue)*, you're hit by the blast of bright stadium lights and the roar from a crowd of tens of thousands. Inside, the scene is as multiculti as the city: Vendors hawk Hideki Matsui bobble-head dolls and Bernie Williams CDs alongside foot-long kosher hot dogs, Italian ices, chow mein and even zinfandel (if you're in box seats). Join in—everyone else will—during the fifth inning, when the grounds crew regales fans with a spirited version of "YMCA."

Counter culture Get a taste of Italy at the **Arthur Avenue Retail Market**. *See p137.*

Baseball not on your agenda? Architecture buffs can start their Bronx tour with a stroll along the **Grand Concourse** in the west Bronx. Stretching from 138th Street to Mosholu Parkway, this four-mile boulevard was designed in 1892, six years before the Bronx would officially become one of the five boroughs of New York City. Buildings here, built mostly from the late '20s through the early '40s, are a trove of styles inspired by Art Deco and Art Moderne. Erected in 1937 at the intersection of Grand Concourse and 161st Street, **888 Grand Concourse** has a concave entrance of gilded mosaic, topped by a curvy metallic marquee. Inside, the mirrored lobby's central fountain and sunburst-patterned floor could rival those of any hotel on Miami's Ocean Drive. The grandest building on the Grand Concourse is the landmark **Andrew Freedman Home**, a 1924 French-inspired limestone palazzo between McClennan and 166th Streets. Freedman, a millionaire subway contractor, stipulated in his will that the bulk of his $7 million fortune be used to build a retirement home for wealthy people who had fallen on hard times. Today, the building still houses the elderly—but a dramatic reversal of fortune is no longer a residency requirement.

Established in 1961 and housed in a former synagogue at 1040 Grand Concourse at 165th Street, the **Bronx Museum of the Arts** is the borough's only art museum. Its high-quality exhibitions are devoted to contemporary and historical works by Bronx-based artists, including many of African-American, Asian and Latino heritage. Those interested in getting a closer look at the up-and-coming arts scene in Mott Haven and the South Bronx should hop on the **Bronx Culture Trolley**, a free shuttle that visits the hottest galleries, performance spaces and museums. Participating institutions—including the Bronx Museum, the **Hostos Art Gallery** (part of the **Center for Arts and Culture** at **Hostos Community College**), the **Pregones Theater** and the **Blue Ox Bar**—schedule screenings and performances along the trolley's route.

Farther north, at 2640 Grand Concourse (at 192nd Street), step back in time inside the **Edgar Allan Poe Cottage**, a small wooden farmhouse where the writer lived from 1846 to 1849 while he penned the poem "Annabel Lee." Moved from its original spot on Fordham Road in 1913, it's a museum with period furniture and information about Poe and his work.

Fordham Road, which runs east to west from the Harlem River to Long Island Sound, will lead you to Fordham University, the New York Botanical Garden, the Bronx Zoo, Arthur Avenue and City Island. A Jesuit institution founded in 1841, **Fordham University** *(441 E Fordham Rd between Washington and Third Aves)* has several remarkable buildings, including the grand neo-Gothic Keating Hall and the handsome Greek Revival Rose Hill Administration Building, once a manor house. Call security ahead of time *(718-817-2222);* your name will be added to a visitors' list at the gate.

Spread out over 250 acres and bisected by the Bronx River, the **New York Botanical Garden** offers a respite from cars and concrete, with 48 gardens and plant collections, including the Rockefeller Rose Garden, the Everett Children's Adventure Garden and the last 50 original acres of a forest that once covered all of New York City. In springtime, the gardens are frothy with pastel blossoms as clusters of lilac, cherry, magnolia and crab-apple trees burst into bloom, followed in fall by vivid foliage in the oak and maple groves. On a rainy day, you can stay warm and dry inside the **Enid A. Haupt Conservatory**, a striking, glass-walled greenhouse built in 1902; it offers seasonal exhibits as well as the World of Plants, a series of environmental galleries that will take you on an ecotour through tropical rain forests, deserts and palm-tree oases.

Nature lovers can continue on to the borough's most famous attraction, the **Bronx Zoo**, which opened in 1899. Spread out over 265 acres, it's the largest urban zoo in the United States. Instead of cages, there are indoor and outdoor environments that mimic the natural habitats of more than 4,000 mammals, birds, reptiles and other animals. Nearly a hundred species, including monkeys, leopards and tapirs, live inside the lush, steamy Jungle World, which re-creates an Asian rain forest inside a 37,000-square-foot building. Opened in 1999, the superpopular **Congo Gorilla Forest** has turned 6.5 acres into a dramatic Central African rain-forest habitat. A glass-enclosed tunnel winds through the forest, allowing visitors to get up-close views of the dozens of different kinds of primates in residence, including 22 majestic lowland gorillas. One of the forest's "celebrities" is native daughter Pattycake, the first gorilla born in New York City. For those who prefer cats, the newly opened **Tiger Mountain** is home to six adult Siberian tigers. If you take the **Bengali Express Monorail** (which travels through the Wild Asia Encampment), try to grab a seat up front for prime viewing of antelopes, Indian rhinos and Asian elephants.

If you're hungry after all this touring, head to nearby **Belmont**, home of the Bronx's Little Italy. You'll hear plenty of Italian spoken along lively **Arthur Avenue**, the neighborhood's main drag, which is lined with Italian delis, restaurants, markets and cafés. Stop for a hot chicken Parmesan hero sandwich at **Roma Luncheonette** *(636 E 187th St at Belmont Ave, 718-367-9189)*. If you're in the mood for a full meal, **Mario's** *(2342 Arthur Ave between 184th and 187th Sts, 718-584-1188)* and **Dominick's** *(2335 Arthur Ave between Crescent Ave and E 187th St, 718-733-2807)* are authentically old-style red-sauce joints. Browse and graze at the **Arthur Avenue Retail Market** *(Crescent Ave at 186th St)*, an indoor bazaar built in the 1940s when former mayor Fiorello La Guardia campaigned to get pushcarts off the street. (The market is closed on Sundays.) Inside is **Mike's Deli** *(2344 Arthur Ave between Crescent Ave and E 186th St, 718-295-5033)*. Try the trademark *schiacciata* sandwich of grilled vegetables, or Big Mike's Combo, a roll loaded with provolone cheese and Italian cold cuts like mortadella, prosciutto and salami. Can't see a red, white and green flag without jonesing for a slice? Stop in for a pie at the popular **Full Moon Pizzeria** *(600 E 187th St at Arthur Ave, 718-584-3451)*, where soccer fans gorge on crackling thin-crust pizza nicely balanced with sauce and cheese while watching the game on TV.

Located just west of Pelham Bay Park and surrounded by the waters of Eastchester Bay and Long Island Sound, **City Island** could pass for a sleepy New England village, except that it's accessible by crosstown city bus. Settled in 1685, it was once a prosperous shipbuilding center with a busy fishing industry, a history reflected in streets lined with Victorian captains' houses. There's plenty of nautical life still around, especially in the summer, but recreational boating is the main industry now, with seafood restaurants, marine-themed bars, six yacht clubs and a couple of sail makers crowding the docks. Join the warm-weather crowds at **Johnny's Famous Reef Restaurant** *(2 City Island Ave at Belden's St, 718-885-2086)* for steamed clams, cold beer and great views. For a romantic getaway, book a room at **Le Refuge Inn** (*see p197*), a restored 19th-century sea captain's house where you can enjoy a sophisticated French menu in elegant surroundings. Few commercial fishermen remain, but you'd hardly know it at the **Boat Livery** *(663 City Island Ave at Bridge St, 718-885-1843)*, a bait-and-tackle shop that rents motorboats by the day. The Livery also doubles as a bustling bar, known locally as the Worm Hole.

Riverdale, along the northwest coast of the Bronx, is one of the city's most beautiful neighborhoods. Situated atop a hill overlooking the Hudson River, it's filled with huge homes perched on narrow, winding streets. Theodore Roosevelt, Arturo Toscanini and Mark Twain all lived in **Wave Hill House**, an 1843 stone mansion located on a private estate that is now a cultural and environmental center. **Wave Hill**'s 28 acres of cultivated gardens and woodlands provide lovely views of the river. The art gallery shows nature-themed exhibits, and the organization presents concerts and performances year-round. If you crave a day outdoors on foot or bike, the Hudson River–hugging **Riverdale Park** *(Palisade Ave between 232nd and 254th Sts)* has quiet pathways. Enter this swath of forest preserve along Palisade Avenue. You can continue your hike or bicycle ride along Spaulding Lane (off 248th Street), which offers a gurgling stream and waterfall, or on Ladd Road (north of 255th Street), where three modernist houses sit like serene Buddhas in the woods.

Down the slope from Riverdale, you'll find **Gaelic Park**, a longtime gathering place for the area's Irish-American community. Located just west of Broadway, on the north side of 240th Street near Manhattan College, it's where Irish hurling and football teams compete regularly on weekends. The 1,100-acre **Van Cortlandt Park** *(Broadway at 249th St)* is nearby. Cricket teams, made up mostly of immigrants from the West Indies, are a common sight here; you can also hike through a 100-year-old forest, play golf on a municipal course or rent horses at stables within the park. The **Van Cortlandt House**, a fine example of pre-Revolutionary Georgian architecture, was built by Frederick Van Cortlandt in 1748; it later served as a headquarters for George Washington during the Revolutionary War. Donated to the city by the Van Cortlandt family, it remains the Bronx's oldest building.

Once you've exhausted yourself in the great outdoors, kick back at the **Riverdale Diner** *(3657 Kingsbridge Ave between Broadway and 238th St, 718-884-6050)*, which has an exhaustive classic-diner menu. Or take home a rich, velvety cheesecake from the **S&S Cheesecake Factory** *(222 W 238th St between Broadway and Review Pl, 718-549-3888)*. Local pub **An Béal Bocht** *(445 W 238th St between Greystone and Waldo Aves, 718-884-7127)* has Guinness, live Irish bands and *ceili* dancing.

Tucked in the southeastern corner of the Bronx, **Hunts Point** may look like an industrial wasteland, but over the past decade, it's become a popular live/work destination for local artists. In 1994, artists converted a 12,000-square-foot industrial building into the **Point** *(940 Garrison Ave at Manida St, 718-542-4139; www.thepoint.org)*, a performance space, gallery and business incubator. The Point holds a monthly break-dancing performance called *Breakbeats* and leads Mambo to Hip-Hop, a lively walking tour covering the history of locally born music genres. And at the nearby **Bronx Academy of Arts and Dance (BAAD!)**, creative types stage performances, while more than a dozen painters and sculptors work in the center's studios. The group annually presents "BAAD! Ass Women," a celebration of works by female artists; the springtime Boogie Down Dance Series; and Out Like That, a gay and lesbian arts festival. Hunts Point is also home to the city's largest wholesale markets for produce, meat and fish, which turn the predawn hours into a chaotic bazaar. (The markets are open to the public, but sales are in bulk only, and browsing is discouraged.)

In the northeastern corner of the borough is **Pelham Bay Park**, the city's biggest bucolic playground. You're best off with a car or bike if you want to explore the park's 2,765 acres, once home to the Siwonay Indians. Pick up a map at the Ranger Nature Center, near the entrance on Bruckner Boulevard at Wilkinson Avenue. The **Bartow-Pell Mansion Museum**, in the park's southeastern quarter, overlooks Long Island Sound. Built in the 1830s, the elegantly furnished Greek Revival building faces a reflecting pool surrounded by gardens. The park also offers 13 miles of coastline, bordering the Hutchinson River to the west and Long Island Sound and Eastchester Bay to the east. In summer, locals crowd **Orchard Beach**; created in the 1930s by Robert Moses, it's one of the few Moses projects widely welcomed in the borough. Plenty of picnic tables line the woods near the parking lot.

Bartow-Pell Mansion Museum

895 Shore Rd North at Pelham Bay Park (718-885-1461). Travel: 6 to Pelham Bay Park, then Beeline bus 45 (ask driver to stop at the Bartow-Pell Mansion; bus does not run on Sunday), or take a cab from the subway station. **Open** *Wed, Sat, Sun noon–4pm.* **Admission** *$2.50, seniors and students $1.25, children under 12 free.* **Credit** *Cash only.*

Bronx Academy of Arts and Dance (BAAD!)

841 Barretto St between Garrison and Lafayette Aves (718-842-5223; www.bronxacademyofartsanddance.org). Subway: 6 to Hunts Point Ave. **Open** *Hours and prices vary by event.*

Bronx County Historical Society

Valentine-Varian House, 3266 Bainbridge Ave between Van Cortlandt Ave and E 208th St (718-881-8900; www.bronxhistoricalsociety.org). Subway: D to Norwood–205th St. **Open** *Sat 10am–4pm; Sun 1–5pm.* **Admission** *$3; seniors, students and children $2.*

The Bronx County Historical Society offers tours that explore a variety of neighborhoods and historic periods. The society also operates the Museum of Bronx History within the Valentine-Varian House, a Federal-style fieldstone residence built in 1758.

Bronx Culture Trolley

The Bronx Council on the Arts (718-931-9500, ext 33; www.bronxarts.org). Subway: 2, 4, 5 to 149th St–Grand Concourse. **Open** *Feb–Jun Oct–Dec, first Wednesday of every month. Reception 5:30pm at Hostos Center for Arts and Culture at Hostos Community College, 450 Grand Concourse at 149th St; trolley leaves at 6pm.* **Admission** *free.*

The nonprofit Bronx Council on the Arts sponsors a once-a-month free trolley that stops at art galleries, performance spaces and museums in the South Bronx and Mott Haven.

Lush life The fertile grounds of **Wave Hill** make a vivid backdrop for concerts and art exhibits.

Bronx Museum of the Arts

1040 Grand Concourse at 165th St (718-681-6000). Subway: B, D, 4 to 161st St–Yankee Stadium. **Open** *Wed noon–9pm; Thu–Sun noon–6pm.* **Admission** *$5, seniors and students $3, children under 12 free.*

Bronx Zoo/ Wildlife Conservation Society

Bronx River Pkwy at Fordham Rd (718-367-1010; www.bronxzoo.org). Subway: 2 to Pelham Pkwy; 5 to E 180th St. **Open** *Apr–Oct Mon–Fri 10am–5pm; Sat, Sun, holidays 10am–5:30pm. Nov–Mar 10am–4:30pm.* **Admission** *$11, seniors $8, children under 12 $8. Free Wednesday. Some rides and exhibitions are $2–$3 extra.* **Credit** *Cash only.*

City Island

Travel: 6 to Pelham Bay Park, then Bx29 bus to City Island. Call or visit the website of the City Island Chamber of Commerce (718-885-9100; www.cityisland.com) for information about events and activities.

Edgar Allan Poe Cottage

Grand Concourse at Kingsbridge Rd (718-881-8900). Subway: B, D, 4 to Kingsbridge Rd. **Open** *Sat 10am–4pm; Sun 1–5pm.* **Admission** *$3, seniors and students $2.*

Grand Concourse

Between 138th and 165th Sts. Subway: 4 to 149th St–Grand Concourse or 161st St–Yankee Stadium.

Hostos Center for Arts and Culture

450 Grand Concourse at 149th St (718-518-4455; www.hostos.cuny.edu). Subway: 2, 4, 5 to 149th St–Grand Concourse. **Open** *Gallery Mon–Fri 10am–6pm.*

New York Botanical Garden

Bronx River Pkwy at Fordham Rd (718-817-8700; www.nybg.org). Travel: B, D, 4 to Bedford Park Blvd, then Bx26 bus; Metro-North (Harlem Line local) from Grand Central Terminal to New York Botanical Garden. **Open** *Apr–Oct Tue–Sun, Monday holidays 10am–6pm. Nov–Mar Tue–Sun 10am–5pm.* **Admission** *$6, seniors $3, students $2, children $1, under 2 free. Free Wednesday all day, Saturday 10am–noon.* **Credit** *Cash only.*

The basic $6 fee is for the grounds only; the $10 Garden Passport includes admission to the Adventure Garden and the Haupt Conservatory. If you're traveling from Manhattan, a $15.50 Getaway ticket (available at Grand Central Terminal) buys you round-trip travel on Metro-North's Harlem train line and a Garden Passport.

Pelham Bay Park

718-430-1890. Subway: 6 to Pelham Bay Park.

Van Cortlandt House Museum

Van Cortlandt Park, Broadway at 246th St (718-543-3344). Subway: 1, 9 to 242nd St–Van Cortlandt Park. **Open** *Tue–Fri 10am–3pm; Sat, Sun 11am–4pm.* **Admission** *$5, seniors and students $3, children under 12 free.* **Credit** *Cash only.*

Wave Hill House

249th St at Independence Ave (718-549-3200; www.wavehill.org). Travel: Metro-North (Hudson Line local) from Grand Central Terminal to Riverdale. **Open** *Apr 15–May 31, Aug 1–Oct 14 Tue, Thu–Sun 9am–5:30pm. Jun, Jul Tue, Thu–Sun 9am–5:30pm; Wed 9am–9pm.* **Admission** *$4, seniors and students $2, children under 6 free. Free Tue, Sat 9am–noon and Nov 15–Mar 14.* **Credit** *Cash only.*

Staten Island

Harborside views and historic houses are just a ferry ride away.

Wooded hills, quiet beaches and leafy suburban streets? Staten Island hardly feels as if it's a part of New York City at all. The delights of what residents like to call "New York's most beautiful borough" are largely unknown, even to dwellers in other parts of the city. Although the island has its share of typical (charm-free) suburban sprawl, it also has more wide-open green space than anywhere else in the city. Working-class neighborhood pride is strong; there's also a small but active artistic community, and a mellow selection of historic attractions. The island and its great views merit exploration, especially in fine weather.

In 1524, Giovanni da Verrazano sailed into the Narrows—the body of water separating the island from Brooklyn—and his name graces the suspension bridge that connects the two boroughs today. The island got its name from Henry Hudson, who dubbed the land "Staaten Eylandt" (Dutch for "State's Island") in 1609. Early settlement attempts were repeatedly wiped out by Native American resistance, but the Dutch finally took hold in 1661. The isle was a peaceful plot of land after that, with shipping and manufacturing developing on the north shore, and farms and small hamlets inland.

In 1898, the islanders voted to be incorporated into Greater New York City, becoming one of the city's five boroughs. Still, the predominantly rural area didn't have much of a connection to the rest of the city until the opening of the Verrazano-Narrows Bridge in 1964. That span (then the world's longest suspension bridge) opened Staten Island to modern, large-scale development.

If you'd like to escape the city for a few hours, hop the famous (and free!) **Staten Island Ferry** (*see p70*), which passes the Statue of Liberty before sliding into the St. George terminal. Near the ferry landing, soak up some history at the modest **Staten Island Institute of Arts and Science**. Baseball fans can catch a game at the **Richmond County Savings Bank Ballpark**, the harborside home of the minor-league **Staten Island Yankees**. You can also wander along the waterfront and enjoy the view of Manhattan's downtown skyline, then head south a few blocks for a burger and beer at the **Cargo Cafe** *(120 Bay St between Slosson Terr and Victory Blvd, 718-876-0539)*. A popular bar and grill, the place displays a rotating collection of paintings by local artists (there's live entertainment and a pool table, too).

If you want to explore farther in, both the buses and the single-line Staten Island Railroad depart from St. George for destinations across the island. Visitors with an interest in architecture and the arts should see the stately Greek Revival structures that form the nucleus of the 83-acre **Snug Harbor Cultural Center**. Opened in 1833 as a maritime hospital and sailor's home, the center was converted into a visual- and performing-arts complex in 1976.

The **Jacques Marchais Museum of Tibetan Art** (*see p159*), a reproduction of a small Himalayan temple with a tranquil meditation garden, is a surprisingly serene oasis. The museum showcases a collection of Tibetan and Buddhist artifacts, artworks and religious items.

Nearby, guides in period garb give tours of the 27 carefully restored buildings of **Historic Richmond Town**, the island's former county seat. Take a look at the Voorlezer's House, the nation's oldest former schoolhouse (circa 1695); there's also a general store, an on-site blacksmith and basket weaver, and a working farm.

Hungry yet? There are several options around Port Richmond. Islanders swear that the bubbling, thin-crust pie at **Denino's Tavern** *(524 Port Richmond Ave between Hooker Pl and Walker St, 718-442-9401)*, around since 1937, is the best pizza in NYC. For dessert, stroll across the street for one of **Ralph's Famous Italian Ices** *(501 Port Richmond Ave at Catherine St, 718-273-3675)*. You can also dine by candlelight at the **Parsonage** *(74 Arthur Kill Rd at Clarke Ave, 718-351-7879)*, located in a pre–Civil War home in the middle of Historic Richmond Town.

If wildlife and nature are more your scene, the **Staten Island Zoo**, located in a leafy area adjacent to Clove Lakes Park, has one of the East Coast's most important reptile collections. The compact zoo isn't as grand as its Bronx cousin, but the farm animals make it an appealing family destination.

Intrepid, outdoorsy types can take two buses from the ferry to **High Rock Park** at the heart of the island; this is the main access point for more than 30 miles of hiking trails.

Green day The 30-plus miles of trails at **High Rock Park** suit hikers of all sizes.

On a summer day, a 40-minute ride on the S78 bus will take you to the island's southeastern coast, where you can swim, picnic and even fish at relaxing **Wolfe's Pond Park** *(Cornelia Ave at Hylan Blvd, 718-984-8266).*

A little farther south, tour the **Conference House**, once the home of Capt. Christopher Billopp and now a museum of Colonial life. Just a short walk away, you can admire the passing sailboats from **Tottenville Beach**, at the very tip of the island. You'll come back to Manhattan with sand in your shoes and an insider's view of this little-known piece of the Big Apple.

Alice Austin House

2 Hylan Blvd between Bay and Edgewater Sts (718-816-4506). Travel: From the Staten Island Ferry, take the S51 bus to Hylan Blvd. **Open** *Mar–Dec Thu–Sun noon–5pm (closed major holidays).* **Admission** *suggested donation $2.* **Credit** *Cash only.*

This lovely Victorian cottage with a scenic view of the New York bay was the family home of pioneering photographer Alice Austin. It contains more than 3,000 of her glass-negative photographs, which document life in the Gilded Age. The house also hosts rotating photographic exhibits.

Conference House (Billopp House)

7455 Hylan Blvd at Craig Ave (718-984-2086; www.theconferencehouse.org). Travel: From the Staten Island Ferry, take the S78 bus to Craig Ave. **Open** *Apr 1–Dec 15 Fri–Sun 1–4pm.* **Admission** *$2, seniors and children $1.* **Credit** *Cash only.*

New York's oldest surviving manor house (circa 1680s) was already nearly 100 years old when Britain's Lord Howe parleyed with John Adams and Ben Franklin here in 1776, in an attempt to put the brakes on the American Revolution. The conference failed (obviously), but the house still commands a striking view overlooking Raritan Bay. Now fully restored, it serves as a museum of Staten Island life during Colonial times.

Garibaldi-Meucci Museum

420 Tompkins Ave at Chestnut Ave (718-442-1608; www.garibaldimeuccimuseum.org). Travel: From the Staten Island Ferry, take the S78 bus to Chestnut Ave. **Open** *Tue–Sun 1–5pm.* **Admission** *suggested donation $3.* **Credit** *Cash only.*

In 2002, Congress passed a House resolution that declared Italian-American Antonio Meucci, not Alexander Graham Bell, to be the true inventor of the telephone. The house where Meucci lived for most of his life is now a museum.

High Rock Park

200 Nevada Ave at Rockland Ave (718-667-2165; www.sigreenbelt.org). Travel: From the Staten Island Ferry, take the S62 bus to Manor Rd, then the S54 bus to Nevada Ave, and walk up Nevada Ave. **Open** *9am–dusk. Visitors' Center Mon–Fri 9am–5pm.* **Admission** *free.*

This 90-acre park is part of the Greenbelt, Staten Island's whopping 2,800 acres of parkland. Hike the mile-long Swamp Trail, climb Todt Hill, or explore trails through forests, meadows and wetlands.

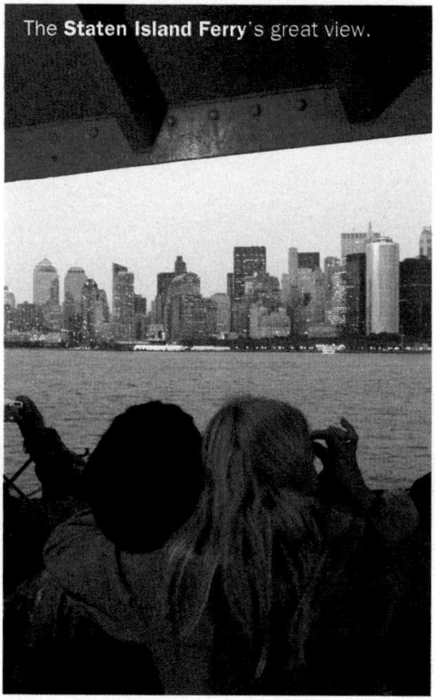

The **Staten Island Ferry**'s great view.

Historic Richmond Town

441 Clarke Ave between Richmond Rd and St. Patrick's Pl (718-351-1611; www.historicrichmondtown.org). Travel: From the Staten Island Ferry, take the S74 bus to St. Patrick's Pl. **Open** *Sept–May Wed–Sun 1–5pm; Jun–Aug Wed–Sat 10am–5pm; Sun 1–5pm.* **Admission** *$5, seniors $4, children 5–17 $3.50, children under 5 free.* **Credit** *Cash only.*

Richmond County Savings Bank Ballpark

75 Richmond Terr at Bay St (718-720-9265, tickets 718-720-9200; www.siyanks.com). Travel: From the Staten Island Ferry, walk to ballpark. **Open** *Jun–Sept.* **Admission** *reserve $8, box seats $10.* **Credit** *AmEx, Disc, MC, V.*

This stadium (known for its impressive waterside views) is the home turf of the Staten Island Yankees, a minor-league team fielded by the famed New York Yankees organization.

Staten Island Institute of Arts and Sciences

75 Stuyvesant Pl between Hamilton Ave and Wall St (718-727-1135; www.siiasmuseum.org). **Open** *Tue–Sat 9am–5pm; Sun 1–5pm.* **Admission** *suggested donation $2.50, seniors and children $1.50.* **Credit** *Cash only.*

This small museum is the island's oldest cultural organization (1881) and contains exhibits on local arts, history and nature.

Staten Island Zoo

614 Broadway between Forest Ave and Victory Blvd (718-442-3100; www.statenislandzoo.org). Travel: From the Staten Island Ferry, take the S48 bus to Broadway. **Open** *10am–4:45pm (closed major holidays).* **Admission** *$5, seniors $4, children 3–14 $3, children under 3 free. Free Wednesdays after 2pm.* **Credit** *Cash only.*

Snug Harbor Cultural Center

The colonnaded main buildings of the cultural center are stunning examples of Greek Revival architecture. An arts complex since 1976, Snug Harbor now includes the Newhouse Center for Contemporary Art and the 400-seat Music Hall, the city's second-oldest concert venue (Carnegie Hall opened one year earlier, in 1891). Also sharing the parklike grounds are the **Noble Maritime Collection**, the **Botanical Garden** and the **Children's Museum**.

Snug Harbor Cultural Center

1000 Richmond Terr between Snug Harbor Rd and Tysen St (718-448-2500, tickets 718-815-7684; www.snug-harbor.org). Travel: From the Staten Island Ferry, take the S40 bus to the north gate (tell the bus driver). **Open** *Galleries Tue–Sun 10am–5pm.* **Admission** *$2, seniors and students $1, children under 10 free.* **Credit** *AmEx, MC, V.*

The Noble Maritime Collection

Building D (718-447-6490; www.noblemaritime.org). **Open** *Thu–Sun 1–5pm.* **Admission** *$3, seniors and students $2, children under 10 free.* **Credit** *AmEx, MC, V.*

This nautically inspired collection focuses on works by noted maritime artist John A. Noble. The collection also includes his houseboat studio, created by culling parts from larger boats.

Staten Island Botanical Garden

Building H, Visitors' Center (718-273-8200; www.sibg.org). **Open** *Dawn–dusk.* **Admission** *Chinese Scholar's Garden $5; seniors, students and children $4. Grounds and other gardens free.* **Credit** *AmEx, MC, V.*

Stroll through more than 20 different themed gardens and plantings, from the White Garden (based on Vita Sackville-West's creation at Sissinghurst Castle) and the tranquil, pavilion-lined Chinese Scholar's Garden to the delightful Secret Garden, complete with a child-size castle, maze and walled "secret" garden.

Staten Island Children's Museum

Building M (718-273-2060). **Open** *Sept 2–Jul 4 Tue–Sun noon–5pm; Jul 5–Sept 1 Tue–Sun 11am–5pm.* **Admission** *$5, children under 1 free.* **Credit** *AmEx, Disc, MC, V.*

Interactive exhibits include a playground, a children's theater and family workshops.

Museums

Meteorites, mummies, Michelangelo, Monet—mercy!

What makes New York the cultural capital of the U.S.? To a large degree, the answer lies in its museums. Like the gold in Fort Knox backing up the dollar, the city's incredible holdings of artworks and cultural riches ensure New York's status as a leader in the arts. Treasures range from the most obscure artifacts on earth to meteorites from outer space; from Fabergé eggs to the most provocative of contemporary works.

Upper Fifth Avenue is known as **Museum Mile**, but cultural attractions aren't limited to Manhattan. Throughout the five boroughs, you'll find important collections and exhibitions, such as Tibetan art at the **Jacques Marchais Museum** in Staten Island, or the headline-grabbing 1999 "Sensation" show at the **Brooklyn Museum of Art**. Many sites offer activities beyond viewing paintings, sculptures and installations—there are exhibits to touch, gardens to stroll in and hands-on programs for kids (*see p279*). And you don't have to go home after dark—numerous institutions are drawing evening visitors by mixing socializing and art in a convivial atmosphere (*see p152* **Party, people**).

Attempting to cram several museum visits into a single day can be exhausting. Similarly, it's self-defeating to try to hit all the major collections during a single visit to an institution as large as the **Metropolitan Museum of Art** or the **American Museum of Natural History**. Even comparatively small venues can wear you out, so make a plan, and pace yourself: A host of excellent museum cafés and restaurants allow convenient breaks. Great places for a respite include Sarabeth's at the **Whitney**, the elegant Café Sabarsky at the **Neue Galerie**, the **Jewish Museum**'s Café Weissman and, of course, the **Metropolitan Museum**'s newly refurbished Petrie Court Cafe. While it might be tempting to save museums for a rainy day, remember that most sites offer cool air-conditioned comfort on sticky summer days and cozy warmth come winter.

Brace yourself for the fact that local admission prices can be steep. This is because most New York museums are privately funded, with little or no government subsidizing. Even so, a majority of the city's art institutions, including the **Museum of Modern Art**, the **Whitney Museum of American Art**, the **Guggenheim** and the **International Center of Photography**, offer at least one evening a week when admission fees are either waived or switched to a voluntary donation. Most museums also offer admission discounts to students and senior citizens with valid ID. And while the city's crown jewel, the Metropolitan Museum, has a suggested $12 donation for adults, you can pay what you wish at all times. That's right—you can experience one of the world's finest museums for as little as 25 cents!

Some New York venues began as private collections—among them, the **Frick Collection**, the **Morgan Library** and the **Schomburg Center for Research in Black Culture**. As a result, the collections are displayed in grand mansions that were once the residences of some of New York's wealthiest citizens.

Other major museums are housed in structures as impressive and eclectic as their holdings within. Uptown, the distinctive white spiral of the Guggenheim never fails to make passersby—tourists and jaded locals alike—stop and stare. The gray granite cube of the Whitney, with its Cyclops-eye window and concrete moat, is no less stunning. And when the sun goes down, the illuminated globe of the **Rose Center for Earth and Space** is simply breathtaking. The **Cloisters**, at the northern reaches of Manhattan in Fort Tryon

Cheap tix

If you're planning a multimuseum tour that spans several days—and you're likely to add a visit to the Empire State Building or a Circle Line tour—consider buying a **CityPass** for $38 *(children 12–17 $31)*. Similarly, the **New York Pass** covers admission to more than 40 of the city's top cultural and popular attractions, with added discounts and unlimited public transportation. The card costs $39 for the day *(children 2–12 $21)* and $119 for the week *(children $84)*. Compare benefits and purchase cards at www.citypass.com and www.newyorkpass.com.

Park, was oil magnate John D. Rockefeller's gift to New York. Its reconstructed monastery houses the Met's trove of medieval art. In summer, bring a picnic lunch and bask in the garden, which affords spectacular views of the Hudson River and the rocky cliffs of the Palisades in New Jersey.

While you may relish the freedom of exploring museums on your own, many institutions offer tours that are entertaining and educational. For example, the audio tour at the **Ellis Island Museum** and the guided tours at the **Lower East Side Tenement Museum** and the **Museum of Jewish Heritage** all provide visitors with fascinating insights into NYC's immigrant roots.

Across the Hudson, New Jersey's **Liberty Science Center** is an unexpected pleasure, with lively interactive exhibits for all ages and a rooftop overlooking Manhattan and the Statue of Liberty. You can take the **NY Waterway ferry** (*see p70*) to the museum and admire Lady Liberty along the way.

As magnificent as they are, the city's museums are constantly changing and growing. Among the most dramatic examples of this are the American Museum of Natural History's construction a few years ago of the Rose Center for Earth and Space, and the recent renovation of the Hall of Meteorites. The Brooklyn Museum of Art has undergone an incredible $63 million face-lift, adding outdoor fountains, a broad plaza and a mural by contemporary painter Alexis Rockman, which depicts a near-dystopian Brooklyn of the future. There's also the change that a number of institutions have wrought on the neighborhood of Long Island City, Queens. MoMA, the **Museum for African Art** and the **Isamu Noguchi Garden Museum**—all currently getting new or redesigned permanent homes—have put down temporary stakes here, joining Queens pioneers **P.S. 1 Contemporary Art Center** and the **American Museum of the Moving Image**. The **Dia Art Foundation** has shuttered its famed Chelsea location for renovation, but its superb satellite facility in Beacon, New York, is a Minimalist paradise (*see p146* **Hudson River school**).

Most New York museums are closed on New Year's Day, Presidents' Day, Memorial Day, Independence Day, Labor Day, Columbus Day, Thanksgiving and Christmas (*see p362* **Holidays**). However, the Metropolitan Museum has begun staying open on certain holiday Mondays, such as Columbus Day and Presidents' Day. A few places, like Dia: Beacon, change their hours seasonally; during the summer, it's wise to call before setting out.

Security has been tightened at most museums. Guards at all public institutions will ask you to open your purse or backpack for inspection; all large bags must be checked at a coatroom, along with umbrellas (there's no charge). Most museums can also provide free wheelchairs.

Major institutions

American Museum of Natural History/Rose Center for Earth and Space

Central Park West at 79th St (212-769-5000, recorded information 212-769-5100; www.amnh.org). Subway: B, C to 81st St–Museum of Natural History. **Open** *10am–5:45pm.* **Admission** *suggested donation $12, seniors and students $9, children ages 2–12 $7.* **Credit** *AmEx, MC, V.*

The thrills begin when you cross the threshold of the Theodore Roosevelt Rotunda and are confronted with a towering barosaurus, rearing high on its hind legs to protect its young from an attacking allosaurus. It's an impressive welcome to the largest museum of its kind in the world (and a reminder to visit the dinosaur halls on the fourth floor). During the museum's mid 1990s renovation, several specimens were remodeled to correspond to discoveries made during that time. The T. rex, for instance, was once believed to have walked upright, Godzilla-style; it now stalks its prey with its head lowered and its tail parallel to the ground. The rest of the site is equally dramatic. The Hall of Biodiversity examines world ecosystems and environmental preservation, while the Hall of Ocean Life features a life-size model of a blue whale, suspended from the cavernous ceiling. Reopened in the fall of 2003, the impressive Hall of Meteorites has been brushed up and reorganized. The exhibit's focal point is Anighito, an iron meteor that weights 34 tons (more than 30,000 kilos!), the largest on display anywhere in the world. The spectacular $210 million Rose Center for Earth and Space—dazzling to come upon at night—is a giant silvery globe where you can learn about the universe through 3-D shows in the Hayden Planetarium and light shows in the Big Bang Theater. An IMAX theater shows bigger-than-life nature programs, and there are always innovative temporary exhibitions, an easily accessible research library (with vast photo and print archives), several cool gift shops and a friendly, helpful staff.

Brooklyn Museum of Art

200 Eastern Pkwy at Washington Ave, Prospect Heights, Brooklyn (718-638-5000; www.brooklynart.org). Subway: 2, 3 to Eastern

► See ***Time Out New York*** for reviews and listings of current exhibitions.
► For dining options near museums, *see pp167–197.*

Pkwy–Brooklyn Museum. **Open** *Wed–Fri 10am–5pm; Sat, Sun 11am–6pm; first Saturday of each month (except September) 11am–11pm.* **Admission** *$6, seniors and students $3, children under 12 free when accompanied by an adult. Free on the first Saturday of the month (except September) 5–11pm.* **Credit** *AmEx, MC, V.*
The BMA's $63 million renovation added an impressive glass pavilion and a new public plaza along the entryway. The 560,000-square-foot space is a tranquil alternative to Manhattan's big-name spaces, and is rarely crowded. Among the museum's all-too-unsung assets is a stunning 4,000-piece Egyptian collection. Last year, more than 600 objects came out of storage and were installed in the third floor's plush new galleries. Don't miss the stunning gilded-ebony statue of Amenhotep III and, on the ceiling, a large-scale rendering of an ancient map of the cosmos. You can even find an actual mummy, preserved in its original coffin.

An impressive European painting and sculpture collection (including masterworks by Cézanne, Courbet, Degas and Monet) came out of three-year storage and is now displayed in the museum's newly renovated, skylighted Beaux Arts Court. On the fifth floor, you'll find American paintings and sculptures, such as native son Thomas Cole's *The Picnic* and Louis Rémy Mignot's *Niagara,* a stunning vista of the falls. And don't miss the impressive African and Pacific Island galleries, or the comprehensive Asian art collection.

The Cloisters

Fort Tryon Park, Fort Washington Ave at Margaret Corbin Plaza (212-923-3700; www.metmuseum.org). Travel: A to 190th St, then take the M4 bus or follow Margaret Corbin Dr north (about the length of five city blocks) to the museum. **Open** *Mar–Oct Tue–Sun 9:30am–5:15pm. Nov–Feb Tue–Sun 9:30am–4:45pm.* **Admission** *suggested donation (includes admission*

Sightseeing

Hudson River school

Take a model example of early-20th-century industrial architecture. Combine it with some of the most ambitious and uncompromising art of the past 50 years. What do you get? One of the most satisfying aesthetic experiences on the planet. Indeed, for the 24 artists whose works are on view, and for the visiting public, **Dia: Beacon**—Dia Art Foundation's magnificent new outpost in the Hudson Valley—is nothing short of a blessing.

Despite its cavernous Chelsea galleries, Dia has never had adequate space to put its massively scaled collection on permanent display. Founders Heiner Friedrich and his wife, Philippa de Menil (an heir to the Schlumberger oil fortune), acquired much of their holdings in the 1960s and '70s. They had a taste for the Minimal, the Conceptual and the monumental, and they supported artists with radical ideas about what art was, what it could do and where it should happen. Together with others of their generation, the Dia circle (Robert Smithson, Michael Heizer, Walter De Maria, Donald Judd and Dan Flavin) felt strongly that a work of art had to viewed in context, be it visual, philosophical or historical. Thanks to the institution's current director, Michael Govan, curator Lynne Cooke and board chairman Leonard Riggio (founder and chairman of Barnes & Noble Inc.), the Dia circle's vision of the proper context is now the biggest contemporary-art museum in the world.

A convenient 80-minute train ride from Grand Central, Dia: Beacon sits on a 31-acre tract overlooking the Hudson River. The nearly 300,000-square-foot complex of three brick buildings was built in 1929 as a box-printing factory for Nabisco; 34,000 square feet of north-facing skylights provide almost all the illumination within. Nowhere does that natural light serve the art more beautifully than in the immense gallery where 72 of Andy Warhol's 102 rarely exhibited *Shadows* (1978–79) canvases hang end to end, looking like solar flares on acid. It's a gorgeous presentation, and a tough act to follow, but Hanne Darboven's *Kulturgeschichte* (1980–1983) more than meets the challenge. Her labyrinthine floor-to-ceiling installation is made up of 1,590 framed sheets of newspaper articles, magazine covers and pinups, calligraphic doodles, written notations, and personal and found photographs. Flavin's white-fluorescent totems, exhibited on accordion-pleated screens, hold their own against the building's magnificent skylights and windows.

Still, all this hardly prepares you for Heizer's *North, East, South, West* (1967/2002)—four geometrically shaped, steel-lined shafts that plunge 20 vertiginous feet through the concrete floor to the basement (which is otherwise given over to a Bruce Nauman mini-retrospective), and then farther down past the building's foundation into the earth itself. Standing at the lip of one of these holes (which you can do only if accompanied by a Dia staffer and with a scheduled

to the Metropolitan Museum of Art on the same day) $12, seniors and students $7, under 12 free (must be accompanied by an adult). **Credit** *AmEx, MC, V.*
Set in a bucolic park overlooking the Hudson River, the Cloisters houses the Met's medieval art and architecture collections. A path winds through the peaceful grounds, bringing you to a castle that seems to have survived from the Middle Ages, even though it was built a mere 60 years ago. (It is constructed from the pieces of five French medieval cloisters.) Be sure to check out the famous Unicorn Tapestries, and *The Annunciation Triptych* by Robert Campin.

Cooper-Hewitt National Design Museum

2 E 91st St at Fifth Ave (212-849-8400; www.si.edu/ndm). Subway: 6 to 96th St. **Open** *Tue–Thu 10am–5pm; Fri 10am–9pm; Sat 10am–6pm; Sun noon–6pm.* **Admission** *$8, seniors and students $5, children under 12 free.* **Credit** *AmEx, Disc, MC, V.*
The Smithsonian's National Design Museum was once the home of industrialist Andrew Carnegie. Now it's the only museum in the U.S. dedicated to domestic and industrial design. Recent exhibitions have included "Solos: Smartwrap," an exploration of a revolutionary new material dubbed "the building skin of the future"; and "Creating American Lifestyle," a full-scale retrospective of furniture, dinnerware and appliances by designer Russel Wright. From April through September 2004, the museum will host the National Design Triennial, exploring new developments in architectural, interior, fashion and landscape design. Sign-language (ASL) interpretation is available upon request.

Dia: Beacon

3 Beekman St, Beacon, NY 12508 (845-440-0100; www.diacenter.org). Travel: Take Metro-North (Hudson line) to Beacon, then a seven-minute walk to gallery. **Open** *Mid-Apr–Thanksgiving Sun, Mon, Thu–Sat 11am–6pm. Late Nov–mid-Apr Sun, Mon,*

Judd's *Untitled.*

appointment), you forget where you are, which way is up, and whether you are inside or out.

What really sets the Dia: Beacon experience apart, however, is the surprising intimacy of its galleries and gardens, designed by California light-and-space artist Robert Irwin, in collaboration with the Manhattan architectural collective OpenOffice. Not only does this enormous museum feel like a private house, but the many correspondences between artworks seem to evolve into an elegant narrative of connoisseurship. Heizer's holes are the flip side of Richard Serra's *Torqued Ellipses*, which in turn make perfect antidotes to Joseph Beuys's affectless towers of felt. All three bear a relationship to Judd's 15 large plywood boxes, all of which are of equal size and volume—and yet no two are alike. Fred Sandback's architectural yarn constructions dovetail nicely with a Sol LeWitt wall drawing, making its first public appearance since 1965. Gerhard Richter's six huge cantilevered gray mirrors are similarly in a sort of dialogue with Robert Ryman's pop-from-the-wall, white-on-white paintings.

It was to be expected, perhaps, that not every project looks picture-perfect in this setting. John Chamberlain's crushed-metal sculptures seem lost in space, though the room they occupy is magnificent. And sculptor Louise Bourgeois's work remains powerful—especially the amazing, ritualistic installation entitled *The Destruction of the Father* (1974)—yet her style seems far too figurative for the rigorous abstraction that characterizes the museum's overall collection. Still, one can't get too exercised about these minor missteps. What could easily have been a parody of self-aggrandizing avant-gardism has turned out, instead, to be a triumph—an energizing symbiosis of art and architecture in an unbeatable natural setting.

Come hither The **Frick Collection**, on view in a former home, invites you to another era.

Thu–Sat 11am–4pm. **Note:** *Days and times vary with the availability of natural light. Best to call first.* **Admission** *$10, students and seniors $7.* **Credit** *AmEx, MC, V.*

Dia: Beacon (*see p146* **Hudson River school**), Dia Art Foundation's latest outpost, contains 240,000 square feet of exhibition space, lit exclusively by natural light coming through more than 34,000 square feet of skylights. Housed in a former Nabisco printing plant (redesigned by artist Robert Irwin and architectural team OpenOffice), the museum is nothing short of amazing. The gems permanently on view include Andy Warhol's multipart painting *Shadows,* sculptor Michael Heizer's plunging steel-lined columns *North, East, South, West* and three of Richard Serra's monumental steel *Torqued Ellipses.*

Dia: Chelsea

548 W 22nd St between Tenth and Eleventh Aves (212-989-5566; www.diacenter.org). **Closed until 2006.**

The Chelsea branch (usually given over to single-artist projects) of this New York stalwart is undergoing renovation and will reopen sometime in 2006 (*see p147* **Dia: Beacon**).

Frick Collection

1 E 70th St between Fifth and Madison Aves (212-288-0700; www.frick.org). Subway: N, R, W to Fifth Ave–59th St; 6 to 68th St–Hunter College. **Open** *Tue–Thu, Sat 10am–6pm; Fri 10am–9pm; Sun 1–6pm.* **Admission** *$12, seniors $8, students $5, children 10–18 $5 (must be accompanied by an adult; under 10 not admitted).* **Credit** *AmEx, Disc, MC, V.*

The opulent residence that houses this private collection of great masters (from the 14th through the 19th centuries) was originally built for industrialist Henry Clay Frick. The firm of Carrère & Hastings designed the 1914 structure in an 18th-century European style, with a beautiful interior court and reflecting pool. The permanent collections include world-class paintings, sculpture and furniture by the likes of Rembrandt, Vermeer, Renoir and French cabinetmaker Jean-Henri Riesener.

Solomon R. Guggenheim Museum

1071 Fifth Ave at 89th St (212-423-3500; www.guggenheim.org). Subway: 4, 5, 6 to 86th St. **Open** *Mon–Wed, Sat, Sun 10am–5:45pm; Fri 10am–8pm.* **Admission** *$15, seniors and students with a valid ID $10, children under 12 free (must be accompanied by an adult). Voluntary donation Fri 6–8pm.* **Credit** *AmEx, MC, V.*

Designed by Frank Lloyd Wright, the Guggenheim is itself a stunning piece of art. Even if your hectic museum-hopping schedule doesn't allow time to view the collections, you must visit this museum's dramatic white spiral of a building, if only from the outside. In addition to works by Manet, Kandinsky, Picasso and Chagall, the museum owns Peggy Guggenheim's trove of Cubist, Surrealist and Abstract Expressionist works, along with the Panza di Biumo collection of American Minimalist and Conceptual art from the 1960s and '70s. In 1992, the addition of a ten-story tower provided space for a sculpture gallery (with views of Central Park), an auditorium and a café.

Planned 2004 exhibitions Built around Umberto Boccioni's 1912 portrait of his mother, "*Materia:* A Futurist Masterpiece and the European Avant-Garde" will also show works by such Cubist masters as Duchamp and Picasso *(Feb 6–May 6)*. On loan from the Tate Modern in London, a show surveying the work of visionary modern sculptor Constantin Brancusi will include his seminal marble statue, *The Kiss (Jun 17–Sep 19)*. A major Aztec exhibit will showcase more than 600 objects dating from 1325 to 1519 *(Oct 14, 2004–Jan 16, 2005)*.

Metropolitan Museum of Art

1000 Fifth Ave at 82nd St (212-535-7710; www.metmuseum.org). Subway: 4, 5, 6 to 86th St. **Open** *Tue–Thu, Sun 9:30am–5:30pm; Fri, Sat 9:30am–9pm. No strollers on Sundays.* **Admission** *suggested donation $12, seniors and students $7, children under 12 free.* **Credit** *AmEx, MC, V.*

It could take days, even weeks, to cover the Met's 2 million square feet of exhibition space, so it's best to be selective. Besides the enthralling temporary exhibits, there are excellent collections of African, Oceanic and Islamic art, along with more than 3,000 European paintings from the medieval through the fin-de-siècle periods, including major works by Titian, Brueghel, Rembrandt, Vermeer, Goya, Manet and Degas. Egyptology fans should head straight for the glass-walled atrium housing the Temple of Dendur. The Greek and Roman halls have received a graceful face-lift, and the incomparable collection of medieval armor—a huge favorite with both adults and children—was recently enriched by new gifts of European, North American, Japanese and Islamic arms. The Met has also made significant additions to its galleries of modern art, including major works by American artist Eric Fischl and Chilean Surrealist Matta. Contemporary sculptures are displayed each year in the Iris and B. Gerald Cantor Roof Garden *(May–Oct)*, the perfect place to grab a sandwich and a cool drink while surveying the skyscrapers soaring above Central Park (*see p152* **Party, people**). The upgraded Petrie Court Cafe now offers waiter service and a better quality of food. If you're in town for a long holiday weekend, don't despair. The Met recently started their Holiday Mondays program, opening museum doors on certain holidays, including Martin Luther King Day, Presidents' Day, Memorial Day and the Monday between Christmas and New Year's.

A large, round desk in the museum's Great Hall (staffed by volunteers who speak multiple languages) is the hub of the museum's excellent Visitors' Services resources, and the best place to begin planning your visit. (Foreign-language tours are also available; call *212-570-3711.*) Once you're directed to the sort of work that interests you most—from Greek *kouroi* to colorful Kandinskys—we recommend seeking out a spot of relative privacy and calm. Surprisingly enough, the Met is dotted with plenty of them—you just have to know where to look. (*Psst!* Ask a guard for directions.) The Englehard Court, bordering on Central Park, has benches and a trickling fountain, with trees, ivy and stunning examples of Tiffany stained glass to further encourage restful contemplation. (If you'd like to grab a drink or a snack in less-than-hectic surroundings, try the recently opened American Wing Cafe.) The Astor Court on the second floor is a garden modeled on a Ming-dynasty scholar's courtyard. Wooden paths border a naturally lit atriumlike area paved with gravel and stones. (There are places to sit here, too.) The nearby East Asian Galleries (some 64,000 square feet of space) are full of superb examples of archaic bronzes, ceramics and rare wooden Buddhist images, and they seldom get a lot of foot traffic. On the western end of the museum, take a rest on the benches in the Robert Lehman Wing, then go commune with Botticelli's *Annunciation*.

Planned 2004 exhibitions "Byzantium: Face and Power (1261–1557)," a major international-loan show of Byzantine art and artifacts, is scheduled for

The best Gift shops

Want to take home something a little cooler than a green-sponge Lady Liberty crown? Museum gift shops are the best places to…

...eat like an astronaut

Freeze-dried ice cream is always a hit at the kiddie Satellite Shop in the **Rose Center for Earth and Space** (*see p145*). Star charts, mini telescopes and glow-in-the-dark "galactic goo" make great souvenirs for the young science set.

...deck the halls

Make it a modern (and monochromatic) Christmas with chic black-and-white ornaments from the **MoMA Design Store** *(44 W 53rd St between Fifth and Sixth Aves, 212-767-1050)* in midtown.

...tour the East, from Turkey to Tibet

Textiles, tea sets, jewelry, cookbooks and more from the Near to the Far East are for sale in the lavishly stocked Asia Store at **Asia Society** (*see p158*).

...settle a bet

The two gift shops in the grand **public library** building (*see p162*) are stocked with great reference books and Gotham-themed postcards and journals.

Cinematic The cavernous lobby at **MoMA QNS** doubles as a multiprojection space.

the spring *(Mar 23–Jul 4)*. A comprehensive exhibition will examine the work of Leonardo, Caravaggio and others who emerged from the northern Italian region of Lombardy during the 16th, 17th and 18th centuries *(May 27–Aug 18)*. French Deco lovers won't want to miss the Emile-Jacques Ruhlman showcase *(Jun 8–Sep 5)*. A retrospective of the paintings of American Impressionist Childe Hassam is planned for the summer *(Jun 10–Sept 12)*.

The Morgan Library

29 E 36th St between Madison and Park Aves (212-685-0008; www.morganlibrary.org). Subway: 6 to 33rd St. **Closed until early 2006.**

Undergoing a dramatic expansion, the Morgan has closed its doors until early 2006. Plans are being made to display some of the archive's rare manuscripts and books in alternative locations. Call or visit the website for details.

Museum of Modern Art, Queens

45-20 33rd St between Queens Blvd and 47th Ave, Long Island City, Queens (212-708-9400; www.moma.org). Subway: 7 (local) to 33rd St. **Open** *Mon, Thu, Sat 10am–5pm; Fri 10am–7:45pm.* **Admission** *$12, seniors and students $8.50, children under 16 free (must be accompanied by an adult). Voluntary donation Fri 4–7:45pm.* **Note**: *A ticket to MoMA QNS includes free admission (within a 30-day period) to MoMA Film at the Gramercy Theatre.* **Credit** *AmEx, MC, V.*

The Museum of Modern Art contains the world's finest and most comprehensive holdings of 20th-century art, including an unsurpassed collection of photography. The museum has moved from its West 53rd Street home to the former Swingline staple factory in Long Island City, Queens, where it will stay until 2005, when expansion of the midtown headquarters is completed. The low-slung electric-blue building, called MoMA QNS, is just a 15-minute subway ride from midtown and not far from MoMA affiliate, **P.S. 1 Contemporary Art Center** (*see p151*). Owing to space restrictions, only highlights of the permanent collection (in addition to temporary and traveling exhibitions) are on display. They include the best of Cézanne, Matisse, Picasso, Van Gogh, Giacometti, Pollock, Rothko and Warhol, among many others. Back in Manhattan, the museum's outstanding Film and Media department (it has more than 14,000 films) has taken over the Gramercy Theatre, where it will continue to host 20-plus screenings each week for the duration of MoMA's reconstruction.

Planned 2004 exhibitions German-Swiss artist Dieter Roth gets his first major U.S. museum retrospective in two decades *(Mar 12–Jun 7)*. Fashion lovers won't want to miss "Fashioning Fiction in Photography since 1990," an examination of key trends in the work of young photographers *(Apr 16–Jun 28)*. "Tall Buildings," the museum's homage to the skyscraper, focuses on the designs of the past decade *(Jul 16–Sept 27)*.

New Museum of Contemporary Art

583 Broadway between Houston and Prince Sts (212-219-1222; www.newmuseum.org). Subway: B, D, F, V to Broadway–Lafayette St; R, W to Prince St; 6 to Bleecker St. **Open** *Tue–Sun noon–6pm; Thu noon–8pm.* **Admission** *$6, children under 18 free. Thu 6–8pm $3.* **Credit** *AmEx, DC, Disc, MC, V.*

Under new management, this Soho institution has found its footing and matured into a showcase for contemporary art. Mid-career retrospectives of artists who are often under-recognized in the U.S.—South Africa's William Kentridge, Los Angeles' Paul McCarthy, New York's Carroll Dunham—attract serious crowds, though not every group show is as strong. The 24-hour street-level window displays are hard to beat; downstairs, the Zenith Media Lounge holds regular Friday-night events and is perhaps the premier spot in the city for the latest digitally based art. No admission fee is required for entrance to the museum's terrific bookstore, open seven days.

P.S. 1 Contemporary Art Center

22-25 Jackson Ave at 46th Ave, Long Island City, Queens (718-784-2084; www.ps1.org). Subway: E, V to 23rd St–Ely Ave; G to Long Island City–Court Sq; 7 to 45th Rd–Court House Sq. **Open** *Mon–Thu noon–6pm.* **Admission** *suggested donation $5, seniors and students $2.* **Credit** *Cash only.*

Cutting-edge shows and an international studio program make every visit to this freewheeling contemporary-art space a treasure hunt, with artwork turning up in every corner, from the stairwells to the basement. In a distinctive Romanesque Revival building, whose maze of exhibition rooms still bears evidence of the public school it once was, P.S. 1 mounts shows that appeal to adults and children alike. P.S. 1 became an affiliate of MoMA in 1999, but it has a wholly independent schedule of temporary exhibitions along with a decidedly global outlook.

Studio Museum in Harlem

144 W 125th St between Malcolm X Blvd (Lenox Ave) and Adam Clayton Powell Jr Blvd (Seventh Ave) (212-864-4500; www.studiomuseuminharlem.org). Subway: A, C, B, D, 2, 3 to 125th St.
Open *Wed, Thu noon–6pm; Fri noon–8pm; Sat, Sun 10am–6pm; guided tours by appointment.*
Admission *$5, seniors $3, children under 12 $1.*
Credit *Cash only.*

When Studio Museum opened in 1968, it was the first black fine-arts museum in the country, and it remains the place to go for historical insight into African-American art and the art of the African diaspora. Under the leadership of director Lowery Sims (formerly at the Met) and chief curator Thelma Golden (formerly of the Whitney), this neighborhood favorite has evolved into the city's most exciting showcase for contemporary African-American artists.

Planned 2004 exhibitions "Harlemworld: Metropolis as Metaphor" traces the area's cultural evolution *(Jan 26–Apr 14).* "Fred Wilson: Objects and Installations: 1985–2000" *(Apr 28–Jul 4)* charts one influential African-American's career.

Whitney Museum of American Art

945 Madison Ave at 75th St (212-570-3600, recorded information 212-570-3676; www.whitney.org). Subway: 6 to 77th St. **Open** *Wed, Thu, Sat, Sun 11am–6pm; Fri 1–9pm.* **Admission** *$12, seniors and students $9.50, children under 12 free. Voluntary donation Fri 6–9pm.* **Credit** *AmEx, MC, V.*

Like the Guggenheim, the Whitney is set apart by its unique architecture: a gray granite cube with an all-seeing upper-story "eye" window, designed by Marcel Breuer. When Gertrude Vanderbilt Whitney, a sculptor and art patron, opened the museum in 1931, she dedicated it to living American artists. Today, the Whitney holds about 12,000 pieces by nearly 2,000 artists, including Alexander Calder, Willem de Kooning, Edward Hopper (the museum holds his entire estate), Jasper Johns, Louise Nevelson, Georgia O'Keeffe and Claes Oldenburg. Still, the museum's reputation rests mainly on its temporary shows, particularly the exhibit everyone loves to hate: the **Whitney Biennial**. Held in even-numbered years, the biennial remains the most prestigious (and controversial) assessment of contemporary art in America. The Whitney's smaller satellite "Altria" branch (*see below*), located in an office building's atrium space across from Grand Central Terminal in midtown, mounts solo commissioned projects. At the main building, there are free guided tours daily, and live performances on Friday nights (*see p152* **Party, people**). Sarabeth's, the museum's café, is open daily till 4:30pm and offers pleasant, homey fare.

Planned 2004 exhibitions Packing all four floors of the museum with edgy fare, the 2004 Whitney Biennial may well be *the* show of the year; it's definitely the show you'll want to say you've seen *(Mar 11–May 30).* Late Cuban artist Ana Mendieta's earth-, body- and feminist-based works get the much-deserved retrospective treatment this summer *(Jun–Sept).* Seminal African-American artist Romare Bearden's watercolors, prints and collages make their NYC stop this fall after traveling through Washington, D.C. *(Oct–Jan).*
Other location *Whitney Museum of American Art at Altria, 120 Park Ave at 42nd St (917-663-2453).*

Art & design

American Folk Art Museum

45 W 53rd St between Fifth and Sixth Aves (212-265-1040; www.folkartmuseum.org). Subway: E, V to Fifth Ave–53rd St. **Open** *Tue–Thu, Sat, Sun 10am–6pm; Fri 10am–8pm.* **Admission** *$9, seniors and students $5, children under 12 free. Voluntary donation Fri 6–8pm.* **Credit** *AmEx, MC, V.*

Art is everywhere in the American Folk Art Museum (formerly the Museum of American Folk Art). Designed by architects Billie Tsien and Tod Williams, the architecturally stunning eight-floor building is four times larger than the original Lincoln Center location (now a branch of the museum) and includes a café. The range of decorative, practical and ceremonial folk art encompasses pottery, trade signs, delicately stitched log-cabin quilts and even windup toys.
Other location *2 Lincoln Sq, Columbus Ave between 65th and 66th Sts (212-595-9533).*

Dahesh Museum

580 Madison Ave between 56th and 57th Sts (212-759-0606; www.daheshmuseum.org). Subway: E, V to Lexington Ave–53rd St; 6 to 51st St. **Open** *Tue–Sun 11am–6pm; first Thursday of the month 11am–9pm.* **Admission** *$9, seniors and students $4, children free. Voluntary donation on the first Thursday of the month 6–9pm.* **Credit** *AmEx, MC, V.*

This major repository of 19th-century academic art has recently expanded its exhibition space tenfold with a new three-story Madison Avenue site (and it added an entrance fee; the museum used to be free!). Take a break here from the hubbub of nearby Niketown and other megastores to revel in the incredibly romantic fare on display in the permanent collection: dreamy exotic landscapes, lustrous marble nymphs.

Forbes Magazine Galleries

62 Fifth Ave at 12th St (212-206-5548). Subway: L, N, Q, R, W, 4, 5, 6 to 14th St–Union Sq. **Open** *Tue, Wed, Fri, Sat 10am–4pm.* **Admission** *free; children under 16 must be accompanied by an adult; no strollers or photos.*

The late magazine publisher Malcolm Forbes assembled this wonderfully personal collection, which features a dozen Imperial Easter eggs and other intricate pieces by the famous Russian jeweler and goldsmith Peter Carl Fabergé (only Queen Elizabeth has more). Gallery hours are subject to change, so call before visiting.

Isamu Noguchi Garden Museum

36-01 43rd Ave at 36th St, Long Island City, Queens (718-204-7088; www.noguchi.org). Subway: 7 (local) to 33rd St. **Open** *Mon, Thu, Fri 10am–5pm; Sat, Sun 11am–6pm.* **Admission** *suggested donation $5, seniors and students $2.50.* **Credit** *Cash only.*

In addition to his famous lamps, sculptor Isamu Noguchi designed stage sets for Martha Graham and George Balanchine, as well as furniture, sculpture parks and immense objects of great simplicity and beauty. The artist's studios in Astoria, Queens, where his work is shown in a serene garden setting, are closed for renovation until late in 2004. Meanwhile, this temporary loft space in

Party, people

In a city that never sleeps, even the museums stay open late. Whether it's sunset cocktails on the terrace or Afrobeat music in the garden, more museums are luring crowds (especially culture-minded singles) to their dramatic, party-worthy settings on weekend evenings. Held weekly or monthly, these social events usually complement later hours for the galleries themselves, and the activities are often bundled with a pay-what-you-wish admission night, making them an affordable way to start an evening on the town. All of these venues also sell cocktails and snacks; offerings can change seasonally, so always call in advance.

On the first Friday of every month, stop by **SoundCheck**, a musical-literary series organized by Whitney museum curator Debra Singer (*see p151*). It's surprisingly hip for the uptown locale, and recent performances have included the global free jazz of Sync and the bluesy roots music of the Gowanus Valley Orchestra. And since Friday from 6 to 9pm is pay what you wish, the price is right.

Also on the first Friday of each month, **Starry Nights** brings a classy, diverse crowd to the atrium of the awe-inspiring Rose Center for Earth and Space at the American Museum of Natural History (*see p145*). From 5:30 to 8pm, you can listen to live jazz, buy a drink and contemplate the solar system. Admission is included in the $12 suggested museum donation.

On the first Saturday of the month, the **Brooklyn Museum of Art** (*see p145*) stays open late, and gets down with changing programs of films, lectures and live music. If the weather's nice, expect to dance in the back garden to the sounds of worldbeat or salsa, music that's inspired by the exhibits inside. Admission is free from 5 to 11pm.

Year-round on Friday and Saturday nights, the **Great Hall Balcony Bar** in the Metropolitan Museum of Art (*see p149*) serves drinks and appetizers overlooking the museum's glamorous Beaux Arts hall from 4 to 8:30pm. Music played by small chamber groups filters in from the surrounding galleries. Admission to the area is free with your suggested $12 donation. (Drinks and food are extra.)

From May to October, on Fridays and Saturdays, a young crowd turns the **Iris and B. Gerald Cantor Roof Garden** into a sunset soiree that runs until 8:30pm (weather permitting). "I take my parents to the Great Hall," says one young art lover, "but I take my friends—or a date—to the roof garden."

From May to September, the **Arthur Ross Terrace and Garden** of the Cooper-Hewitt National Design Museum (*see p147*) comes

Long Island City features selected sculptures from the museum's permanent collection. Guided tours begin at 2:30pm.

The Museum at FIT

Seventh Ave at 27th St (212-217-5800; www.fitnyc.edu). Subway: 1, 9 to 28th St. **Open** *Tue–Fri noon–8pm; Sat 10am–5pm.* **Admission** *free.*

The Fashion Institute of Technology houses one of the world's most important collections of clothing and textiles, curated by the influential fashion historian Valerie Steele. Incorporating everything from extravagant costumes to sturdy denim work clothes, the exhibits here touch on the role fashion has played in society since the beginning of the 20th century.

The Museum of Arts and Design

40 W 53rd St between Fifth and Sixth Aves (212-956-3535; www.americancraftmuseum.org). Subway: E, V to Fifth Ave–53rd St; N, R, W to 49th St. **Open** *Mon–Wed, Fri–Sun 10am–6pm; Thu 10am–8pm.* **Admission** *$8, seniors and students $5, children under 12 free. Voluntary donation Thu 6–8pm.* **Credit** *Cash only.*

Formerly the American Crafts Museum, this is the country's leading museum for contemporary crafts in clay, cloth, glass, metal and wood. It changed its name to emphasize the correspondences among art, design and craft. This may be your last chance to visit the current location, a spacious four-floor home to works in various mediums, before the museum moves to its new home at Columbus Circle. Browse the gift shop for unexpectedly stylish jewelry and ceramics.

National Academy of Design

1083 Fifth Ave at 89th St (212-369-4880; www.nationalacademy.org). Subway: 4, 5, 6 to 86th St. **Open** *Wed, Thu noon–5pm; Fri–Sun 11am–6pm.* **Admission** *$8, seniors and students $4.50, children 6–16 free; Fri 5–8pm free.* **Credit** *Cash only.*

Housed in an elegant Fifth Avenue townhouse, the Academy's museum has more than 5,000 works of 19th- and 20th-century American art (paintings, sculptures, engravings and architectural drawings). The permanent collection includes works by Louise Bourgeois, Frank Gehry, Jasper Johns, Robert Rauschenberg and John Singer Sargent.

Light fantastic DJs rule the decks on steamy summer nights at **P.S. 1**.

alive in the evenings, with events open to the public. Expect music, refreshments and an opportunity to see the exhibitions displayed in what was originally Andrew Carnegie's enormous private mansion. Check the website for more information.

For the absolute hottest summer party, don't miss **Warm Up** nights at P.S. 1 (*see p151*). On Saturdays throughout the summer, the museum's courtyard plays host to a rotating cast of local and international DJs, spinning everything from up-front progressive house to manic breakbeat. Each spring, the museum selects an emerging architect (most recently, Tom Wiscombe, who designed the colorful work above), to transform the outdoor space into a backdrop for enthusiastic, ever-increasing crowds (which tend to be young, sweaty and shirtless, though it varies with the DJ). The action winds down around 9pm. A $6 cover includes museum admission, and beer is for sale.

Neue Galerie

1048 Fifth Ave at 86th St (212-628-6200; www.neuegalerie.org). Subway: 4, 5, 6 to 86th St. **Open** *Mon, Sat, Sun 11am–6pm; Fri 11am–9pm.* **Admission** *$10, seniors and students $7 (children 12–16 must be accompanied by an adult; children under 12 not admitted).* **Credit** *AmEx, MC, V.*

This elegant addition to the city's museum scene is devoted entirely to late-19th- and early-20th-century German and Austrian fine and decorative arts. Located in a renovated brick-and-limestone mansion that was built by the architects of the New York Public Library, this brainchild of the late art dealer Serge Sabarsky and cosmetics mogul Ronald S. Lauder has the largest concentration of works by Gustav Klimt and Egon Schiele outside Vienna. You'll also find a bookstore, a chic (and expensive) design shop and the Old-World–inspired **Café Sabarsky** (*see p193*), serving updated Austrian cuisine and ravishing Viennese pastries.

Queens Museum of Art

New York City Building, park entrance on 49th Ave at 111th St, Flushing Meadows–Corona Park, Queens (718-592-9700; www.queensmuseum.org). Subway: 7 to 111th St. **Open** *Wed–Fri 10am–5pm; Sat, Sun noon–5pm.* **Admission** *$5, seniors and students $2.50, children under 5 free.* **Credit** *Cash only.*

Located on the site of the 1939 and 1964 World's Fairs, the Queens Museum holds one of the area's most amazing sights: a 9,335-square-foot scale model of New York City that is accurate down to the square inch. It's surprisingly affecting when the ambient light turns from day to night (dusk falls every 15 minutes). The model was last updated in 1992, so some recent changes are not reflected. The World Trade Center, however, has been replaced by a miniature version of the *Towers of Light,* the city's first memorial to the lives lost on September 11, 2001. The museum is also known as a place for hometown artists to display site-specific work.

Auction houses

New York City is home to a number of the world's most esteemed auction houses, some of which preface their sales with short exhibitions of the art, furniture and decorative objects on offer. These exhibitions are designed to drum up interest among buyers, but are also open to the general public. When the museums are packed, shows at these sites can be a great alternative, especially when juicy celebrity estates are on the block.

Christie's

20 Rockefeller Plaza at 49th St between Fifth and Sixth Aves (212-636-2000, www.christies.com). Subway: B, D, F, V to 47–50th Sts–Rockefeller Ctr. **Open** *Mon–Sat 10am–5pm; Sun 1–5pm (except major holidays).* **Admission** *free.*

Dating back to 1766, Christie's joins Sotheby's (*see p155*) as one of New York's premier auction houses. Architecturally, the building alone is worth a visit, particularly its cavernous three-floor lobby featuring a mural by artist Sol LeWitt (commissioned for the space). Most auctions are open to the public, with viewing hours scheduled in the days leading up to the sale. Hours vary with each exhibition, so call or visit the website for details.

Phillips, de Pury & Luxembourg

450 W 15th St at Tenth Ave (212-940-1200; www.phillips-dpl.com). Subway: A, C, E to 14th St; L to Eighth Ave. **Open** *Mon–Sat 10am–5pm; Sun 1–5pm.* **Admission** *free.*

Held in the spring and fall, PDPL's auctions are organized into six categories: contemporary art, photography, jewelry, American art, Impressionist and modern art, and 20th- to 21st-century design. Adhering to the quality-over-quantity ethos, this

It happened here

The urinal that Marcel Duchamp submitted for a 1917 modern-art exhibit is arguably the most talked-about bathroom fixture in history. Duchamp stopped by the J.L. Mott Iron Works at **118 Fifth Avenue** and bought an ordinary porcelain basin. Dubbing it *Fountain*—and offering it for exhibit—illustrated his notion that everyday objects, or "readymades" could be art. The idea gave birth to the modern Conceptual movement, yet *Fountain* was excluded from the show after being declared "vulgar" and "nonart" by board members. The old Mott space is now occupied by a GapBody store, known for its own sort of readymades.

Iberian express The **Hispanic Society of America**'s setting is transporting. *See p159.*

auction house specializes in small sales that are meticulously curated. The art is usually on public view for one to two weeks leading up to the sale. Call first for hours and sale info.

Sotheby's

1334 York Ave at 72nd St (212-606-7000; www.sothebys.com). Subway: 6 to 68th St–Hunter College. **Open** *Mon–Sat 10am–5pm; Sun 1–5pm (weekend hours change seasonally).* **Admission** *free.*

With offices from London to Taipei, Sotheby's may be the world's most famous auction house. Its New York branch regularly holds public auctions of everything from antique furniture and jewelry to pop-culture memorabilia. Biannual sales of Impressionist, modern and contemporary art are held in spring and fall. Public exhibitions are usually short—four or five days—and held just prior to the auction. Schedules and hours vary with each show, so call or visit the website for full details.

Swann Auction Galleries

104 E 25th St between Park and Lexington Aves, sixth floor (212-254-4710). Subway: 6 to 23rd St. **Open** *Mon 10am–6pm; Tue, Wed 10pm–8pm; Sat 10am–4pm.* **Admission** *free.*

Although Swann was originally created to specialize in book sales, it has grown to include auctions in a variety of art forms. Things slow down during the summer months, but during the rest of the year, Swann holds sales every week. Works are usually exhibited beginning the Saturday before a Thursday sale, and most Saturdays also include a Gallery Walk with the Expert—a guided tour of sorts, led by the expert involved in that particular sale. Hours are subject to change, so call ahead to confirm.

Arts & culture

Historical

American Museum of Natural History

See p145 for listing.

Fraunces Tavern Museum

54 Pearl St at Broad St (212-425-1778; www.frauncestavernmuseum.org). Subway: J, M, Z to Broad St; 4, 5 to Bowling Green. **Open** *Tue, Wed, Fri 10am–5pm; Thu 10am–7pm; Sat 11am–5pm.* **Admission** *$3, seniors and children $2.* **Credit** *Cash only.*

This 18th-century tavern was George Washington's watering hole and the site of his famous farewell to the troops at the close of the Revolution. In 1887, the building became home to the fledgling nation's departments of war, foreign affairs and treasury. Re-created period rooms display artifacts, furniture and documents from the Revolutionary period and beyond. Also within the museum is a tavern and restaurant (212-968-1776) serving hearty fare at lunch and dinner Monday through Saturday.

Lower East Side Tenement Museum

90 Orchard St at Broome St (212-431-0233; www.tenement.org). Subway: F to Delancey St; J, M, Z to Delancey–Essex Sts. **Open** *Visitors' center Sun–Wed, Fri, Sat 11am–5:30pm; Thu 11am–6pm.* **Admission** *$10, seniors and students $8.* **Credit** *AmEx, MC, V.*

This 1863 tenement building is accessible only by guided tour. The tours, which regularly sell out (definitely book ahead), explain what daily life was like for typical tenement-dwelling immigrant families. The museum also has a gallery, shop and video room, and leads walking tours of the Lower East Side from April through December.

Merchant's House Museum

29 E 4th St between Bowery and Lafayette St (212-777-1089; www.merchantshouse.com). Subway: B, D, F, V to Broadway–Lafayette St; 6 to Bleecker St. **Open** *Thu–Sun 1–5pm.* **Admission** *$6, seniors and students $4, children under 12 free.* **Credit** *Cash only.*
New York City's only preserved 19th-century family home, this elegant late Federal–Greek Revival house is stocked with the same furnishings and decorations that filled its rooms when it was inhabited from 1835 to 1933 by hardware tycoon Seabury Treadwell and his descendants.

Mount Vernon Hotel Museum and Garden

421 E 61st St between First and York Aves (212-838-6878). Subway: N, R, W to Lexington Ave–59th St; 4, 5, 6 to 59th St. **Open** *Tue–Sun 11am–4pm; last tour departs at approximately 3:15pm.* **Admission** *$5, seniors and students $4, children under 12 free.* **Credit** *AmEx, Disc, MC, V.*
Formerly known as the Abigail Adams Smith Museum, this historic landmark was built in 1799 as a carriage house for Abigail Adams (daughter of John Adams, the second president of the U.S.) and her husband, Colonel William Stevens Smith. Operated as a hotel from 1826 to 1833, the museum is filled with period articles and furniture.

Museum of American Financial History

28 Broadway at Beaver St (212-908-4110; www.financialhistory.org). Subway: 1, 9 to Rector St. **Open** *Tue–Sat 10am–4pm.* **Admission** *$2.* **Credit** *AmEx, MC, V.*
The permanent collection, which traces the development of Wall Street and America's financial markets, includes ticker tape from the morning of the big crash (October 29, 1929), an 1867 stock ticker and the earliest known photograph of Wall Street.

Museum of the City of New York

1220 Fifth Ave between 103rd and 104th Sts (212-534-1672; www.mcny.org). Subway: 2, 3 to 110th St; 6 to 103rd St. **Open** *Wed–Sun 10am–5pm.* **Admission** *suggested donation $7; seniors, students and children $4; families $12.* **Credit** *AmEx, MC, V.*

To each his own art

New York City is justifiably famous for its world-class museums. But don't spend so much time in the Egyptian wing at the Met that you miss out on some of the city's lesser-known attractions. These offbeat venues celebrate diversity and eccentricity—and they'll put you face-to-face with artists, historians and obsessed connoisseurs.

Freakatorium (El Museo Loco)

57 Clinton St between Rivington and Stanton Sts (212-375-0475). Subway: F to Delancey St; J, M, Z to Delancey–Essex Sts. **Open** *Wed–Sun 1–7pm.* **Admission** *$5, children under 12 $3.*
Sword swallower and carnival enthusiast Johnny Fox is no stranger to cramming big things into small spaces. And that's just what he's done with Freakatorium, a tiny storefront on the Lower East Side that's bursting with colorful curiosities from Fox's 25 years of collecting sideshow memorabilia and cultural oddities. Frik and Frak, a real live two-headed turtle, watches over creepy photos of famous freaks, like Jo-Jo the Dog-Faced Boy and Siamese twins Cheng and Eng, along with examples of once-famous taxidermy hoaxes such as the Feejee Mermaid and the Furry Mink Fish. While the museum takes its role as cultural preservationist seriously, Fox and his staff never fail to tap into your basest desires, making you admit that, yes, you really do want to see a glass eyeball once worn by Sammy Davis Jr.

The International Salsa Museum

2127 Third Ave between 116th and 117th Sts (212-289-1368). Subway: 6 to 116th St. **Open** *Thu–Sun noon–6pm.* **Admission** *suggested donation $3.*
This crowded back room of a "Made in Puerto Rico" gift store in Spanish Harlem is stuffed with thousands of old and new salsa records (sadly, for browsing only—no listening), along with posters, magazines, guitars, drums, pianos and trumpets donated by local musicians, dancers and DJs. Capable guides like Willie Medina, a DJ and salsa-loving volunteer, will show you around, reminiscing about the glory days when Tito Puente and Machito performed at the Palladium.

Living Museum

Creedmoor Psychiatric Center, 80-45 Winchester Blvd between Seward Ave and Union Tpke, Queens Village, Queens (718-264-3490). Travel: E, F to Kew Gardens–Union Tpke, then Q46 bus to Winchester Blvd. **Open** *Mon–Thu, by appointment only.* **Admission** *free.*
For art that pushes boundaries, it's worth taking the trip out to Queens to this huge studio and exhibition space on the grounds of

Located at the northern end of Museum Mile, this institution is a treasure trove of city history, including paintings, sculptures, photographs, military and naval uniforms, theater memorabilia, manuscripts, ship models and rare books. The extensive toy collection, full of the playthings of New Yorkers dating from the Colonial era to the present, is especially well loved. Toy trains, lead soldiers and battered teddy bears share shelf space with exquisite bisque dolls (decked out in extravagant Paris fashions) and lavishly appointed dollhouses. Don't miss the amazing Stettheimer Dollhouse, created during the 1920s by Carrie Stettheimer. Passionate patrons of the avant-garde, Stettheimer and her sister Ettie had their artist friends—many of whom would later be recognized as masters of modern art—recreate their masterpieces in miniature to hang on the dollhouse's walls. Look closely and you'll even spy a tiny version of Marcel Duchamp's famous *Nude Descending a Staircase.*

Museum of Sex

233 Fifth Ave at 27th St (information 212-689-6337, tickets 866-667-3984; www.museumofsex.com). Subway: R, W, 6 to 28th St. **Open** *Sun–Fri 11am–6:30pm; Sat 11am–8pm.* **Admission** *$17; $12 before noon Mon, Tue, Thu, Fri. All visitors must be 18 or older.*

This museum opened to mixed reviews in the fall of 2002 with the inaugural exhibition "NYC Sex: How New York City Transformed Sex in America." Don't expect titillation; instead, you'll find presentations of historical documents and items—many of which were too risqué to be made public in their own time—that explore prostitution, burlesque theater, birth control, obscenity and fetishism.

National Museum of the American Indian

George Gustav Heye Center, Alexander Hamilton Custom House, 1 Bowling Green between Broadway and Whitehall St (212-514-3700, 212-514-3888; www.americanindian.si.edu). Subway: R, W to Whitehall St; 4, 5 to Bowling Green. **Open** *Sun–Wed, Fri, Sat 10am–5pm; Thu 10am–8pm.* **Admission** *free.*

This branch of the Smithsonian Institution displays its collection off the grand rotunda of the 1907 Custom House, located adjacent to Battery Park at the very bottom of Broadway (which began as a

Sightseeing

the Creedmoor Psychiatric Center. A little more than 20 years ago, this institution converted a former dining room and kitchen into an art-therapy studio for patients and an exhibition space for their work. Spread out over 40,000 square feet on two floors, much of the art is technically and conceptually sophisticated, with paintings, sculptures and drawings squeezed into every available corner—even inside an old, defunct pizza oven.

Frik and Frak at **Freakatorium.**

Micro Museum

123 Smith St between Dean and Pacific Sts, Boerum Hill, Brooklyn (718-797-3116; www.micromuseum.com). Subway: F, G to Bergen St. **Open** *Sat noon–6pm.* **Admission** *free.*

Artists William and Kathleen Laziza opened their interdisciplinary modern-art gallery way back in 1986, long before Smith Street was hopping. Now expanded to two floors, the still-tiny museum has kept its laid-back, just-for-kicks vibe. Its rotating collection of multimedia work by local artists encourages hands-on interaction.

Museum of American Illustration

128 E 63rd St between Park and Lexington Aves (212-838-2560). Subway: F to Lexington Ave–63rd St. **Open** *Tue 10am–8pm; Wed–Fri 10am–5pm; Sat noon–4pm.* **Admission** *free.*

Housed inside a beautifully appointed Upper East Side carriage house, the Society of Illustrators (a professional association for commercial artists) showcases an often-overlooked art genre. The permanent collection reads like a roll call of America's greatest illustrators: Norman Rockwell, N.C. Wyeth, Howard Pyle. Recent shows have included illustrations from *National Geographic* and cartoon artwork by Patrick McDonnell, creator of the *Mutts* comic strip.

Native American trail). A rotating series of exhibitions presents the life and culture of Native Americans—from tiny, intricately woven Pomo fiber baskets to beaded buckskin shirts and moccasins—along with contemporary Native American artworks.

New-York Historical Society

2 W 77th St at Central Park West (212-873-3400; www.nyhistory.org). Subway: B, C to 81st St–Museum of Natural History; 1, 9 to 79th St. **Open** *Tue–Sun 10am–6pm.* **Admission** *$8, seniors and students $5, children under 12 free when accompanied by an adult.* **Credit** *Cash only.*

New York's oldest museum, founded in 1804, was one of America's first cultural and educational institutions. With the opening of the vast Henry Luce III Center for the Study of American Culture, the NYHS can finally display a sizable share of its treasures. Highlights include George Washington's Valley Forge camp cot, a complete series of the extant watercolors from Audubon's *The Birds of America* and the world's largest collection of Tiffany lamps. Shows in 2004 include "Kleindeutschland: The Malleable Memory of German New York," which traces the history of German-American immigrants to NYC *(Apr–Aug)*, and "It's a Grand Old Flag," displaying both historic and contemporary examples of the Stars and Stripes from the museum's extensive collection *(Jun–Sept)*.

Sightseeing

South Street Seaport Museum

Visitors' center, 12 Fulton St at South St (212-748-8600; www.southstseaport.org). Subway: A, C to Broadway–Nassau St; J, M, Z, 2, 3, 4, 5 to Fulton St. **Open** *Apr–Sept 10am–6pm daily. Oct–Mar Sun, Mon, Wed–Sat 10am–5pm.* **Admission** *$5, students $4, children under 12 free.* **Credit** *AmEx, MC, V.*

Sprawling across 11 blocks along the East River, the museum is an amalgam of galleries, historic ships, 19th-century buildings and a visitors' center. Wander around the rebuilt streets and pop in to see an exhibition on marine life and history before climbing aboard the four-masted 1911 *Peking*. The seaport itself is generally thick with tourists, but it's still a lively place to spend an afternoon, especially for families with children, who will enjoy the atmosphere and intriguing seafaring memorabilia.

The Statue of Liberty & Ellis Island Immigration Museum

See p75 for listing.

Security concerns have closed the pedestal and crown of the Statue of Liberty to visitors—a great loss, although fund-raising efforts are in the works to effect the changes necessary to reopen the interior of the statue. The grounds of the island remain open, however, and when weather and staffing permit, park rangers offer outdoor tours. On the way back to Manhattan, the ferry will take you to the popular Immigration Museum on Ellis Island, through which more than 12 million people entered the country. The exhibitions are an evocative, moving tribute to the people from so many different countries who made the journey to America filled with dreams of a better life. The $5 audio tour, narrated by Tom Brokaw, is highly informative.

International

Asia Society and Museum

725 Park Ave at 70th St (212-288-6400; www.asiasociety.org). Subway: 6 to 68th St–Hunter College. **Open** *Tue–Thu, Sat, Sun 11am–6pm; Fri 11am–9pm.* **Admission** *$7, seniors and students $5, children under 16 free. Free Fri 6–9pm.* **Credit** *Cash only.*

The Asia Society sponsors study missions and conferences, and promotes public programs both in the U.S. and abroad. The striking, newly renovated headquarters' expanded galleries show major art exhibitions from public and private collections, including the permanent Mr. and Mrs. John D. Rockefeller III collection of Asian art. A spacious, atrium-styled café with a Pan-Asian menu and a beautifully stocked gift shop make this a one-stop destination for anyone with an interest in Asian artworks and culture, spanning dozens of countries and time periods from ancient India to medieval Persia and contemporary Japan.

China Institute

125 E 65th St between Park and Lexington Aves (212-744-8181; www.chinainstitute.org). Subway: F to Lexington Ave–63rd St; 6 to 68th St–Hunter College. **Open** *Mon, Wed, Fri, Sat 10am–5pm; Tue, Thu 10am–8pm.* **Admission** *suggested donation $3, seniors and students $2, children under 12 free.* **Credit** *AmEx, MC, V.*

Consisting of just two small gallery rooms, the China Institute is somewhat overshadowed by the nearby Asia Society. But its rotating exhibitions, ranging from works by female Chinese artists to selections from the Beijing Palace Museum, are compelling. The institute also offers lectures and courses on subjects such as calligraphy, Confucianism and cooking.

El Museo del Barrio

1230 Fifth Ave between 104th and 105th Sts (212-831-7272; www.elmuseo.org). Subway: 6 to 103rd St. **Open** *Wed–Sun 11am–5pm.* **Admission** *$5, seniors and students $3, children under 12 free when accompanied by an adult.* **Credit** *AmEx, MC, V.*

At the top of Museum Mile, not far from Spanish Harlem (the neighborhood from which it takes its name), El Museo del Barrio is dedicated to the work of Latino artists in the United States, as well as that of Latin Americans. This 8,000-piece collection ranges from pre-Columbian artifacts to contemporary installations. In 2004, the museum will present more than 100 different works by various Caribbean and Latin American artists, on loan from MoMA's permanent collection *(Mar 4–Jul 25)*. Later this year, "The One and Many Faces of Latin America" will focus on portraiture in Latin American art over the past two millennia *(Sept 15, 2004–Jan 15, 2005)*.

***Edo*-cational** The year-round garden and a silk-screen detail at the **Japan Society**.

French Institute–Alliance Française

22 E 60th St between Madison and Park Aves (212-355-6100; www.fiaf.org). Subway: N, R, W to Fifth Ave–59th St. **Open** *Mon–Thu 9am–8pm; Fri 9am–5pm; Sat 10am–1:30pm.* **Admission** *free.*

Bienvenue! Welcome to the New York home for all things Gallic: The institute (a.k.a. the Alliance Française) houses the city's most extensive all-French library, and offers numerous language classes and cultural seminars, along with screenings of French films and live performances.

Goethe-Institut New York/ German Cultural Center

1014 Fifth Ave at 82nd St (212-439-8700). Subway: 4, 5, 6 to 86th St. **Open** *Gallery Mon, Wed, Fri 10am–5pm; Tue, Thu 10am–7pm. Library Tue, Thu noon–7pm; Wed, Fri noon–5pm.* **Admission** *free.*

Goethe-Institut New York is a branch of the German multinational cultural organization founded in 1951. Located across the street from the Metropolitan Museum of Art in a landmark Fifth Avenue mansion, it mounts shows featuring German-born contemporary artists, and presents concerts, lectures and film screenings. A library offers German-language books, videos and periodicals.

Hispanic Society of America

Audubon Terrace, Broadway between 155th and 156th Sts (212-926-2234; www.hispanicsociety.org). Subway: 1 to 157th St. **Open** *Tue–Sat 10am–4:30pm; Sun 1–4pm.* **Admission** *free.*

The Hispanic Society has the largest grouping of Spanish art and manuscripts outside Spain. Look for two portraits by Goya, and for the striking bas-relief of Don Quixote in the lobby. The collection is dominated by religious artifacts, including 16th-century tombs from the monastery of San Francisco in Cuéllar, Spain. A collection of more than 176,000 black-and-white photographs document life in Spain and Latin America from the 1850s onwards.

Jacques Marchais Museum of Tibetan Art

338 Lighthouse Ave between Manor Ct and Windsor Ave (718-987-3500; www.tibetanmuseum.com). Travel: From the Staten Island Ferry, take the S74 bus to Lighthouse Ave. **Open** *Wed–Sun 1–5pm.* **Admission** *$5, seniors and students $3, children under 12 $2.* **Credit** *Cash only.*

This tiny hillside museum contains a striking Buddhist altar and the largest collection of Tibetan art in the West, including religious objects, bronzes and paintings. Every October, the museum hosts a Tibetan festival.

Japan Society

333 E 47th St between First and Second Aves (212-752-3015; www.japansociety.org). Subway: E, V to Lexington Ave–53rd St; 6 to 51st St. **Open** *Tue–Fri 11am–6pm; Sat, Sun 11am–5pm.* **Admission** *$5, seniors and students $3.* **Credit** *Cash only.*

Located in a serene space, complete with a waterfall and bamboo garden, the Japan Society presents performing arts, lectures, exchange programs and

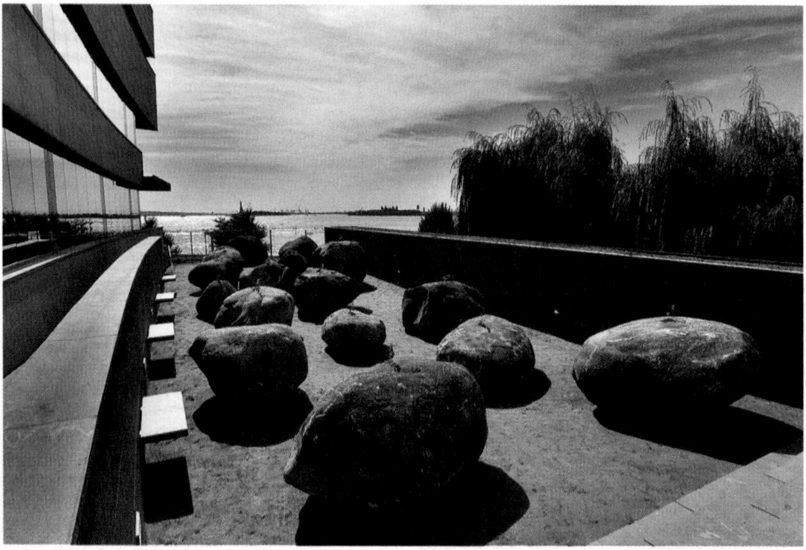

Rock solid Andy Goldsworthy's *Garden of Stones* at the **Museum of Jewish Heritage**.

special events. The gallery shows traditional Japanese art and such contemporary fare as the recent "Isamu Noguchi and Modern Japanese Ceramics." The film center is a major showcase for Japanese cinema in the U.S. There's also a language center and library (open to members and students) in the lower lobby.

Jewish Museum

1109 Fifth Ave at 92nd St (212-423-3200; www.jewishmuseum.org). Subway: 4, 5, 6 to 86th St. **Open** *Sun–Wed 11am–5:45pm; Thu 11am–8pm; Fri 11am–3pm. Closed on Jewish holidays.* **Admission** *$10, seniors and students $7.50, children under 12 free when accompanied by an adult. Voluntary donation Thu 5–8pm.* **Credit** *AmEx, MC, V.*

The Jewish Museum, housed in the 1908 Warburg Mansion, contains a fascinating collection of more than 28,000 works of art, artifacts and media installations. The two-floor permanent exhibition, "Culture and Continuity: The Jewish Journey," examines how Judaism has survived and explores the essence of Jewish identity. Temporary exhibitions in 2004 will feature works by Arnold Schoenberg, Wassily Kandinsky, Lotte Jacobi, Alfred Stieglitz and Amedeo Modigliani. The Café Weissman serves contemporary kosher fare.

Museum for African Art

36-01 43rd Ave at 36th St, Long Island City, Queens (718-784-7700; www.africanart.org). Subway: 7 to 33rd St. **Open** *Mon, Thu, Fri 10am–5pm; Sat, Sun 11am–6pm.* **Admission** *$6, seniors, students and children $3.* **Credit** *MC, V ($10 minimum).*

Adding to the recent influx of art into Queens, this attraction is now in the same building as the Isamu Noguchi Garden Museum (*see p152*), which is three short blocks from MoMA QNS. Exhibits of African art change about twice a year, and the quality of the work—often from private collections—is exceptional. There's an unusually good gift shop filled with African art objects and crafts.

Museum of Chinese in the Americas

70 Mulberry St at Bayard St, second floor (212-619-4785; www.moca-nyc.org). Subway: J, M, Z, N, Q, R, W, 6 to Canal St. **Open** *Tue–Sun noon–5pm.* **Admission** *suggested donation $3, seniors and students $1, children free.*

In the heart of downtown Manhattan's Chinatown, a century-old former schoolhouse houses a two-room museum focusing on Chinese-American history and the Chinese immigrant experience. Call for details about walking tours of Chinatown.

Museum of Jewish Heritage: A Living Memorial to the Holocaust

36 Battery Pl (212-968-1800; www.mjhnyc.org). Subway: 1, 9 to South Ferry; 4, 5 to Bowling Green. **Open** *Sun–Tue, Thu 10am–5:45pm; Wed 10am–8pm; Fri, eve of Jewish holidays 10am–3pm (until 5pm in the summer).* **Admission** *$10, seniors $7, students $5, children under 12 free.* **Credit** *AmEx, MC, V.*

Opened in 1997 and expanded in 2003, this museum offers one of the most moving cultural experiences in the city. Detailing both the horrors and the joys of Jewish existence over the past century, the collection consists of 24 documentary films, 2,000 photographs, and 800 historical and cultural artifacts, many donated by Holocaust survivors and their families. There are three main sections: Jewish Life a Century Ago; The War Against the Jews; and, lastly, Jewish Renewal. The recently opened Memorial Garden now features *Garden of Stones,* a permanent installation by English artist Andy Goldsworthy that features 18 fire-hollowed stone boulders, each planted with a dwarf oak sapling.

Scandinavia House: The Nordic Center in America

58 Park Ave between 37th and 38th Sts (212-879-9779; www.scandinaviahouse.org). Subway: 42nd Street S, 4, 5, 6, 7 to 42nd St–Grand Central. **Open** *Tue–Sat noon–6pm.* **Admission** *suggested donation $3, seniors and students $2.*

You'll find all things Nordic—from Ikea designs to the latest in Finnish film—at this modern $20 million center, the leading cultural link between the United States and the five Scandinavian countries (Denmark, Finland, Iceland, Norway and Sweden). Often incorporating works on loan from museums in those countries, the sleek glass-and-wood Scandinavia House features exhibitions, films, concerts, lectures, symposia and readings for all ages. The AQ Café is a bustling lunch spot serving updated Nordic fare.

Yeshiva University Museum

Center for Jewish History, 15 W 16th St between Fifth and Sixth Aves (212-294-8330; www.yu.edu/museum). Subway: F, V to 14th St; L to Sixth Ave. **Open** *Tue–Thu, Sun 11am–5pm.* **Admission** *$6; seniors, students and children 5–16 $4; children under 5 free.* **Credit** *Cash only.*

The museum usually hosts one major exhibition and several smaller shows each year, mainly on Jewish themes. It's located inside the Center for Jewish History, a separate organization that also offers exhibits along with numerous educational and cultural programs.

Media

American Museum of the Moving Image

35th Ave at 36th St, Astoria, Queens (718-784-0077; www.ammi.org). Subway: G, R, V to Steinway St. **Open** *Wed, Thu noon–5pm; Fri noon–8pm; Sat, Sun 11am–6pm.* **Admission** *$10, seniors and students $7.50, children 5–18 $5, children under 5 free. No strollers.* **Credit** *Cash only.*

About a 15-minute subway ride from midtown Manhattan, AMMI is one of the city's most dynamic institutions. Located within the restored complex that once housed the original Kaufman Astoria Studios (*see p130*), it offers an extensive daily program of films and videos. But that's not all; the museum also has famous movie props and costumes on display. Highlights of the permanent collection include the chariot driven by Charlton Heston in *Ben-Hur* and the Yoda puppet used in *Star Wars: Episode V—The Empire Strikes Back.*

The Museum of Television & Radio

25 W 52nd St between Fifth and Sixth Aves (212-621-6800; www.mtr.org). Subway: B, D, F to 47–50th Sts–Rockefeller Ctr; E, V to Fifth Ave–53rd St. **Open** *Tue–Sun noon–6pm; Thu noon–8pm.* **Admission** *$10, seniors and students $8, children under 14 $5.* **Credit** *Cash only.*

This nirvana for boob-tube addicts and pop-culture junkies contains an archive of more than 100,000 radio and TV programs. Head to the fourth-floor library to search the computerized system for your favorite *Star Trek* or *I Love Lucy* episode, then walk down one flight to take a seat at your assigned console. (The radio listening room operates the same way.) There are screenings of modern cartoons, as well as public seminars and special presentations.

Top five: Laugh in

Touring the town can take it out of you. One great way to relax and catch your breath (not to mention enjoy a few good belly laughs), is to plop your tired self down in a private viewing booth and watch one of these classic episodes at the Museum of Television & Radio (*see above*).

The Cosby Show, "A Shirt Story"

The only Cosbys worth watching are those with Lisa Bonet as the delightfully underachieving Denise. In this episode, she tries to copy a designer shirt for Theo.

The Bob Newhart Show, "His Busiest Season"

Christmas couldn't get worse when Bob's loser patients congregate at his apartment for a horrible holiday party.

The Mary Tyler Moore Show, "Will Mary Richards Go to Jail?"

Mary has to spend the night in jail for not revealing a source; stuck with two hookers and no toothbrush, her humiliations are endless.

Flip Wilson Show

Any episode with the genius Geraldine.

The Muppet Show, with guest host Steve Martin

Kermit auditions new talent while Martin makes balloon animals and strums the banjo; Statler and Waldorf sing "Varsity Drag." Pure heaven.

Sightseeing

Military

Intrepid Sea-Air-Space Museum

USS Intrepid, *Pier 86, 46th St at the Hudson River (212-245-0072; www.intrepidmuseum.org). Travel: A, C, E to 42nd St–Port Authority, then M42 bus to Twelfth Ave.* **Open** *Apr–Sept Mon–Fri 10am–5pm; Sat, Sun 10am–6pm. Oct–Mar Tue–Sun 10am–5pm. Last admittance one hour before closing.* **Admission** *$14; seniors, veterans and students $10; children ages 6–11 $7; children ages 2–5 $2; children under 2 and servicepeople on active duty free.* **Credit** *AmEx, MC, V.*

Climb inside a model of a wooden Revolutionary War–era submarine, try out a supersonic-flight simulator, and explore dozens of military helicopters, fighter planes and more on board this retired aircraft carrier. A barge next to the *Intrepid* displays a British Airways Concorde jet, along with exhibits on the history of supersonic flight.

Sightseeing

New York Public Library

The vast New York Public Library, founded in 1895, comprises four major research libraries and 85 local and specialty branches, making it the largest and most comprehensive library system in the world. The holdings grew from the combined collections of John Jacob Astor, James Lenox and Samuel Jones Tilden. Today, the system contains 52 million items, including more than 18 million books. Unless you're interested in a specific subject, your best bet is to visit the system's flagship, officially called the Humanities and Social Sciences Library. Information on the entire system can be found at www.nypl.org.

Donnell Library Center

20 W 53rd St between Fifth and Sixth Aves (212-621-0618). Subway: E, V to Fifth Ave–53rd St. **Open** *Mon, Wed, Fri 10am–6pm; Tue, Thu 10am–8pm; Sat 10am–5pm; Sun 1–5pm.* **Admission** *free.*

This branch of the NYPL has an extensive collection of records, films and videotapes, with appropriate screening facilities. The Donnell specializes in foreign-language books (in more than 80 languages), and there's also a children's section of more than 100,000 books, films, records and cassettes.

Humanities and Social Sciences Library

455 Fifth Ave at 42nd St (212-930-0830, recorded information on exhibits and events 212-869-8069). Subway: B, D, F, V to 42nd St–Bryant Park; 7 to Fifth Ave. **Open** *Tue, Wed 11am–7:30pm; Thu–Sat 10am–6pm.* **Admission** *free.*

This landmark Beaux Arts building is what most people mean when they say "the New York Public Library." Two massive stone lions, dubbed Patience and Fortitude by former mayor Fiorello La Guardia, guard the main portal. Free guided tours (at 11am and 2pm) include the beautifully renovated Rose Main Reading Room and the Bill Blass Public Catalog Room, which offers free Internet access. Lectures, author readings and special exhibitions are worth checking out.

Library for the Performing Arts

40 Lincoln Center Plaza at 65th St (212-870-1630). Subway: 1, 9 to 66th St–Lincoln Ctr. **Open** *Tue, Wed, Fri, Sat noon–6pm; Thu noon–8pm.* **Admission** *free.*

After a three-year, $37 million renovation, this facility is now one of the great performing-arts research centers, with a vast collection of films, letters, manuscripts, and audio- and videotapes (including half a million sound recordings). Visitors can browse through books, scores and recordings, or attend concerts and lectures.

Schomburg Center for Research in Black Culture

515 Malcolm X Blvd (Lenox Ave) at 135th St (212-491-2200). Subway: 2, 3 to 135th St. **Open** *Tue, Wed noon–8pm; Thu, Fri noon–6pm; Sat 10am–6pm.* **Admission** *free.*

This extraordinary trove of vintage literature and historical memorabilia—all relating to black culture and the African diaspora—was founded in 1926 by its first curator, bibliophile Arturo Alfonso Schomburg. The center hosts jazz concerts, films, lectures and tours.

Science, Industry and Business Library

188 Madison Ave between 34th and 35th Sts (212-592-7010). Subway: 6 to 33rd St. **Open** *Tue–Thu 10am–8pm; Fri, Sat 10am–6pm.* **Admission** *free.*

Opened in 1996, this Gwathmey Siegel–designed branch of the NYPL is dedicated to science, technology, business and economics. It has a circulating collection of 50,000 books, an open-shelf reference collection of 60,000 volumes, and it provides access (at no charge) to more than 100 electronic databases. Free 30-minute tours are given at 2pm on Tuesdays and Thursdays.

Science & technology

Liberty Science Center

251 Phillip St, Jersey City, NJ 07305 (201-200-1000; www.lsc.org). Travel: PATH to Pavonia/Newport, then NJ Transit (Hudson-Bergen Light Rail) to Liberty State Park. **Open** *Tue–Sun 9:30am–5:30pm.* **Admission** *$10, seniors and children 2–18 $8. Combined entry to center and IMAX movie $16.50, seniors and children 2–18 $14.50, children under 2 $10.* **Credit** *AmEx, Disc, MC, V.*

This science museum for kids has three floors of innovative, hands-on exhibits, including a 100-foot-long, pitch-dark "touch tunnel," a bug zoo and a scale model of the Hudson River estuary, plus daily

Tunnel vision It's never rush hour at the renovated **New York Transit Museum**.

demonstrations explaining the hows and whys of science in everyday life. The center also boasts the country's largest IMAX cinema, showing documentaries such as Volcanos of the Deep Sea and Roar: Lions of the Kalahari. From the observation tower, you get great views of Manhattan and an unusual, sideways look at the Statue of Liberty. On weekends, take the NY Waterway ferry (*see p70*).

New York Hall of Science

47-01 111th St at 46th Ave, Flushing Meadows–Corona Park, Queens (718-699-0005; www.nyhallsci.org). Subway: 7 to 111th St. **Open** *Sept–Jun Tue–Thu 9:30am–2pm; Fri 9:30am–5pm; Sat, Sun noon–5pm. Jul, Aug Mon 9:30am–2pm; Tue–Fri 9:30am–5pm; Sat, Sun 10:30am–6pm.* **Admission** *$9, seniors and students $6, children 2–4 $2.50. Free Sept–Jun Fri 2–5pm. Science playground $3 (open Mar–Dec, weather permitting).* **Credit** *AmEx, MC, V.*

Opened at the 1964 World's Fair, the New York Hall of Science demystifies its subject through fun hands-on exhibits about biology, chemistry and physics, with topics such as "The Realm of the Atom" to "Marvelous Molecules." Kids can burn off surplus energy in the 30,000-square-foot outdoor science playground. An outdoor rocket park is expected to open in July 2004.

Urban services

New York City Fire Museum

278 Spring St between Hudson and Varick Sts (212-691-1303; www.nycfiremuseum.org). Subway: C, E to Spring St; 1, 9 to Houston St. **Open** *Tue–Sat 10am–5pm; Sun 10am–4pm.* **Admission** *suggested donation $4, seniors and students $2, children under 12 $1.* **Credit** *AmEx, MC, V.*

An active firehouse from 1904 to 1954, this museum is filled with gadgetry and pageantry, from vintage fire engines to 100-year-old fire-fighting equipment. In the works is a permanent exhibit about NYC firefighters' heroic work following the World Trade Center attacks.

New York City Police Museum

100 Old Slip between South and Water Sts (212-480-3100; www.nycpolicemuseum.org). Subway: 2, 3 to Wall St; 4, 5 to Bowling Green. **Open** *Tue–Sat 10am–5pm.* **Admission** *suggested donation $5, seniors $3, children 6–18 $2.*

The NYPD's tribute to itself features exhibits on the history of the department and the tools (and transportation) of the trade. This is also the only place to get officially licensed NYPD paraphernalia.

New York Transit Museum

Corner of Boerum Pl and Schermerhorn St, Brooklyn Heights, Brooklyn (718-694-1600; www.mta.info/mta/museum). Subway: A, C, G to Hoyt–Schermerhorn. Call or visit website for details. **Open** *Tue–Fri 10am–4pm; Sat, Sun noon–5pm.* **Admission** *$5, seniors and children 3–17 $3.*

The Transit Museum, located underground in an old 1930s subway station, has reopened after a yearlong renovation. The museum also has a gallery (and great gift shop) in Grand Central Terminal.

Other location *Grand Central Terminal, 42nd St at Park Ave, adjacent to stationmaster's office off the Main Concourse (212-878-0106).*

Eat, Drink, Shop

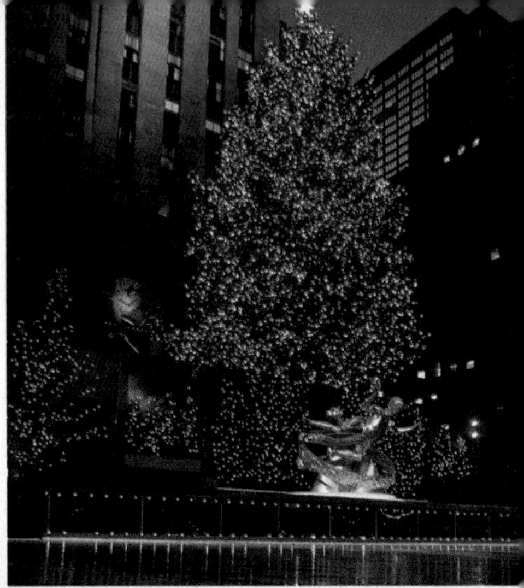

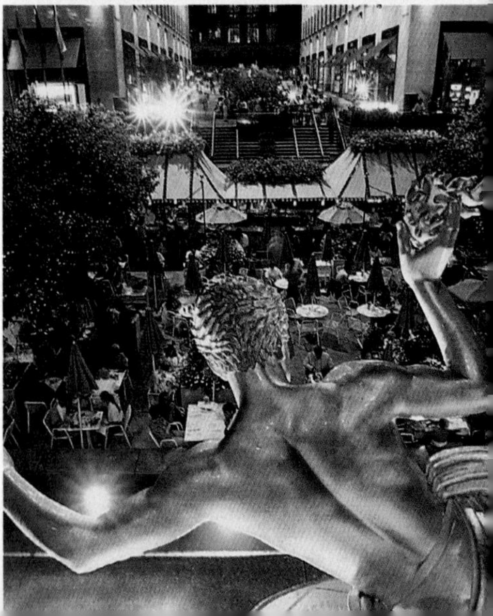

Restaurants

Endless dining options will satisfy all of your cravings.

Many people assume that New Yorkers constantly eat out because we're too busy to cook—and because our kitchens are too small to produce anything bigger than a Hot Pocket. Not true: When you're in one of the world's best food cities, you want to hit as many restaurants as possible, and New York has enough to keep us all occupied for a lifetime. Let the following list be your guide, but know that the restaurant scene changes almost daily. To keep up with openings and closings, pick up a copy of this week's *Time Out New York*. Also, be aware that some of the hottest restaurants book up months in advance; unless you're willing to eat at 5 or 11pm, you might want to belly up to the bar for a meal instead (*see p174* **Counter intelligence**). We know the restaurant options are daunting, but have fun choosing, or simply concentrate all of your energy on a luscious sweet treat (*see p186* **Just desserts**). And finally, because we're certain you won't want to stop eating for a single second, we've included great spots for brunch (*see p173*), barbecue (*see p184*), and all-night dining (*see p192*). All you have to do is figure out how to fit it all in. (If you need bigger pants, the shopping section starts on p211.)

Tribeca & South

American

Bubby's

120 Hudson St at North Moore St (212-219-0666). Subway: 1, 9 to Franklin St. **Open** *Mon–Thu 8am–11pm; Fri 8am–midnight; Sat 9am–midnight; Sun 9am–10pm.* **Average main course** *$13.* **Credit** *AmEx, DC, Disc, MC, V.*

Bubby's began with dessert and evolved backward: Founded in 1990 as a pie company, it's now an all-day source for no-nonsense food in a casual canteenlike setting. Hordes descend on weekend mornings, when a "we love kids!" attitude and no-brunch-reservations policy add up to barely controlled chaos. (Of course, if you've got energetic toddlers in tow, this can be a good thing.) For something calmer, try a weekday dinner of alphabet soup, homemade potato chips in blue-cheese sauce, mac and cheese, or slow-cooked BBQ. Mountainous servings of pie are the best dessert option.

Other location *1 Main St at Plymouth St, Dumbo, Brooklyn (718-222-0666).*

American Creative

Bridge Cafe

279 Water St at Dover St (212-227-3344). Subway: A, C to Broadway–Nassau St; J, M, Z, 2, 3, 4, 5 to Fulton St. **Open** *Sun, Mon 11:45am–10pm; Tue–Thu 11:45am–11pm; Fri 11:45am–midnight; Sat 5pm–midnight.* **Average main course** *$23.* **Credit** *AmEx, DC, Disc, MC, V.*

This cozy retreat in the shadow of the Brooklyn Bridge offers modern cooking in a historic building that dates back to 1794. The quaint tin-ceilinged dining room is the perfect romantic spot for sharing plump soft-shell crabs sautéed in lemon and scallion butter; pan-seared halibut in a sexy sake-ginger lobster broth; or good old-fashioned roasted chicken—all followed by a slice of the famous key lime mousse pie. Monday through Wednesday nights, the entire 80-bottle wine list is 30 percent off.

Chinese

66

241 Church St at Leonard St (212-925-0202). Subway: 1, 9 to Franklin St. **Open** *Sun–Thu noon–3pm, 6pm–midnight; Fri, Sat noon–3pm, 6pm–1am.* **Average main course** *$26.* **Credit** *AmEx, MC, V.*

The best Places...

...for obsessive foodies

Babbo (*see p181*), **Biltmore Room** (*see p185*), **Craft** (*see p186*), **'Cesca** (*see p193*).

...for scene-spotting

Industry (Food) (*see p177*); **Mercer Kitchen** (*see p176*), **Schiller's Liquor Bar** (*see p173*).

...for sexy sushi

Bond St. (*see p178*), **Jewel Bako** (*see p179*), **Nobu** (*see p168*), **Sui** (*see p171*).

...for the food of the future

Public (*see p176*), **WD-50** (*see p171*).

...for round-the-world cheap eats

Cafe Habana (*see p169*); **'inoteca** (*see p174*) **LIC Café** (*see p197*).

Certainly, with its elongated communal table, Eames chairs and fish-tank kitchen windows, Richard Meier's design blows away any Mott Street palace. The waitresses are even dolled up in Vivienne Tam. And as you'd expect from a restaurant run by hotshot chef Jean-Georges Vongerichten, the menu sparkles with fabulous creations: foie gras dim sum, noodles lavished with lobster, and stir-fried shrimp with a sweet-and-sour chili glaze. Getting a table takes patience, though; weekend tables are often booked a month in advance.

French

Bouley

120 West Broadway at Duane St (212-964-2525). Subway: A, C, 1, 2, 3, 9 to Chambers St. **Open** *11:30am–3pm, 5–11pm daily.* **Average main course** *$36.* **Credit** *AmEx, DC, Disc, MC, V.*
David Bouley may have an ego the size of a Sub-Zero, but there's no disputing the man's culinary legerdemain. Both of Bouley's dining spaces are lovely—the white room a bit more formal, the red room a bit more Hernando's Hideaway. Minced squab, delicately infused with lemon thyme, is swaddled with foie gras in cabbage leaves; lamb is crusted with sea salt and cardamom; lobster is coiled around mango, artichoke and *serrano* ham. Even health nuts have their day: In his mung-bean–sprout "risotto," Bouley finishes the sautéed sprouts with saffron bouillabaisse sauce. If you've got it (and you'll need plenty), spend it here.

Montrachet

239 West Broadway between Walker and White Sts (212-219-2777). Subway: A, C, E to Canal St; 1, 9 to Franklin St. **Open** *Mon–Thu 5:30–10:30pm; Fri noon–2pm, 5:30–10:30pm; Sat 5:30–11pm.* **Average main course** *$26.* **Tasting menu** *$30–$95.* **Credit** *AmEx, DC, Disc, MC, V.*
After 20 years, Montrachet is still carrying on its haute-cuisine affair with a loyal clientele. Although the wall-to-wall carpeting and '80s-style artwork may look dated, chef Chris Gesualdi prepares exquisite contemporary French food for present-day gourmands, and the polished servers know their stuff.

The Odeon

145 West Broadway between Duane and Thomas Sts (212-233-0507). Subway: A, C, 1, 2, 3, 9 to Chambers St. **Open** *Mon–Fri 11:45am–2am; Sat, Sun 11am–2am.* **Average main course** *$17.* **Credit** *AmEx, DC, Disc, MC, V.*

> ► For reviews of the newest restaurants, see the latest issue of ***Time Out New York***.
> ► The thousands of reviews in the ***Time Out Eating & Drinking*** guide are available on newsstands; they're updated weekly and searchable at **eatdrink.timeoutny.com**.

This legendary bistro, formerly a cafeteria, is still going strong. The house burger is a sirloin-chuck blend of medium-rare splendor, and other dishes, like a country frisée salad with pungent Roquefort (opt for the truffled poached egg on top) turn out nearly as well. Weekend brunch attracts a beautiful, champagne-sipping clientele.

Japanese

Nobu

105 Hudson St at Franklin St (212-219-0500). Subway: 1, 9 to Franklin St. **Open** *Mon–Fri 11:45am–2:15pm, 5:45–10:15pm; Sat, Sun 5:45–10:15pm.* **Average hot dish** *$16.* **Average sushi roll** *$8.* **Credit** *AmEx, Disc, DC, MC, V.*
Nobu turned ten last year, and it's still impossible to get a table. Celebrity sightings remain as commonplace as orders of chef Nobu Matsuhisa's signature black cod in miso. The sushi is impeccable, but the cooked dishes are downright sexy, from seared slices of fish glossed with a hint of *yuzu*, sesame and olive oils to rock-shrimp tempura with chili aioli. Even the salmon-skin roll is succulent as ever, with slices of cucumber enfolding salty salmon skin along with avocado, carrots and *shiso* leaves.
Other location *Next Door Nobu, 105 Hudson St at Franklin St (212-334-4445).*

Takahachi Tribeca

145 Duane St between Church St and West Broadway (212-571-1830). Subway: A, C, 1, 2, 3, 9 to Chambers St. **Open** *Mon–Thu noon–2:30pm, 5:30–10:30pm; Fri noon–2:30pm, 5:30–11pm; Sat 5:30–11pm; Sun 5:30–10:30pm.* **Average main course** *$20.* **Credit** *AmEx, DC, Disc, MC, V.*
An offshoot of Takahachi on Avenue A, Takahachi Tribeca is more urbane than its decent-sushi-at-decent-prices sibling. Deep-fried octopus tossed with *shiso* leaf and miso has the flavor—but not the gooeyness—of a sweet-and-sour dish. Wild-salmon sashimi is as fatty and creamy as pork belly. Cinematically inspired rolls such as the Seven Samurai—a clean combination of mackerel, cucumber and ginger, sliced into seven pieces—surmount their silly names.

Chinatown & Little Italy

American Creative

Capitale

130 Bowery at Grand St (212-334-5500). Subway: J, M, Z to Bowery; 6 to Spring St. **Open** *Mon–Sat 6pm–midnight.* **Average main course** *$25.* **Credit** *AmEx, DC, Disc, MC, V.*
Owner Seth Greenberg brings a nightclub vibe to this grandiose place, with its majestic marble columns and swags of brown velvet, but chef Fred Brightman makes sure the contemporary American menu holds its own, with options like Hudson Valley foie gras paired with lychee and pineapple, and pan-roasted venison painted with chocolate oil.

Cheap date Low prices and high-style fixins at **Schiller's Liquor Bar**. *See p173.*

Chinese

Fuleen Seafood

11 Division St between Confucius Pl and East Broadway (212-941-6888). Subway: F to East Broadway. **Open** *11:30am–3am daily.* **Average main course** *$23.* **Credit** *AmEx.*

Always inquire about the specials here: You might find yourself staring at a steaming basket of shrimp just plucked from their tank, a meltingly tender whole fish with ginger and scallions or a chili-flecked Dungeness crab. The kitchen is equally adept on dry land. Garlic-tossed baby bok choy is superb, and the deep-fried whole chicken with sticky-rice stuffing is a true showshopper. On weekdays, Fuleen doles out $5 lunch specials to long lines of food-savvy downtown professionals.

Cuban

Cafe Habana

17 Prince St at Elizabeth St (212-625-2001). Subway: R, W to Prince St; 6 to Spring St. **Open** *9am–midnight daily.* **Average main course** *$10.* **Credit** *AmEx, DC, MC, V.*

This sexy *nuevo*-Cubano café is a rare example of a place where the menu is even hotter than the trendy scene. An appetizer of taquitos *caseros* (small, deep-fried rolls stuffed with chicken) with tomatillo salsa is deliciously spicy. Chipotle chilies overwhelmed otherwise tasty pork chops in thick wild-mushroom pepper sauce. All of the elements in the empanadalike cornmeal cake—sun-dried tomatoes, goat cheese and black beans—meld together surprisingly well. For dessert, get your butt kicked by the Kahlúa-espresso flan. Dodging the downtown beau monde? Remain incognito by ordering take-out next door.

Other location *Cafe Habana to Go, 229 Elizabeth St between Houston and Prince Sts (212-625-2002).*

Italian

Bread

20 Spring St between Elizabeth and Mott Sts (212-334-1015). Subway: R, W to Prince St; 6 to Spring St. **Open** *Sun–Thu 11am–11pm; Fri, Sat 11am–midnight.* **Average sandwich** *$8.* **Credit** *AmEx, Disc, MC, V.*

This paninoteca, café and wine bar is small in size, but it has a worldly sophistication. Owner and Mercer Kitchen alum Luigi Comandatore knows his ingredients: Ciabatta, baguettes and raisin-walnut bread come from Balthazar; prosciutto di Parma, mozzarella and taleggio, from DiPalo's Fine Foods. Comandatore assembles it all, then presses each densely flavored sandwich in his panino grill. But New Yorkers cannot live by bread alone. The ravioli bolognese starter is masterful and robustly flavored, and a cutting-board spread of savory speck, salami, prosciutto, grilled zucchini and Brie is so fresh, you'll think you died and went to Parma.

Other location *Bread Tribeca, 301 Church St between Walker and White Sts (212-334-8282).*

Peasant

194 Elizabeth St between Prince and Spring Sts (212-965-9511). Subway: R, W to Prince St; 6 to Spring St. **Open** *Tue–Sat 6–11pm; Sun 6–10pm.* **Average main course** *$20.* **Credit** *AmEx, MC, V.*

Inspired by the no-frills cuisine of Apulia, chef-owner Frank DeCarlo cooks almost exclusively—and to wondrous effect—with charcoal and wood. Start with a bowl of fine ricotta, a dish of olive oil and some crusty Pugliese bread. Fresh sardines, pulled sizzling from the oven, make a juicy appetizer, while a plate of Parmigiano-Reggiano, prosciutto and pears is much more than the sum of its parts, especially when followed by the outstanding gnocchi with morels. Such purity doesn't come cheap, but simplicity this luscious is worth the price.

Va Tutto!

23 Cleveland Pl between Kenmare and Spring Sts (212-941-0286). Subway: 6 to Spring St.
Open *Noon–11pm daily.* **Average main course** *$18.* **Credit** *AmEx, MC, V.*
Visiting Europeans too cool to be called tourists sit beside Manhattanites at this modest eatery, where the dazzling food takes center stage. High-quality meats, fine cheeses and aromatic vegetables get light-handed treatment. Arugula salad is juiced up with grilled asparagus, fennel and warm *caciocavallo* cheese; ravioli are packed with supercreamy ricotta and topped with a savory mix of Swiss chard, pancetta and Parmesan.

Japanese

Sui

54 Spring St between Lafayette and Mulberry Sts (212-965-9838). Subway: B, D, F, V to Broadway–Lafayette St; 6 to Bleecker St. **Open** *Sun–Thu 5pm–midnight; Fri, Sat 5pm–1:30am.* **Average main course** *$24.* **Credit** *AmEx, DC, MC, V.*
The water theme hits you as soon as you walk into Sui—ocean-blue walls, a fish-motif bar, wave-shaped lamps, a running waterfall and several fish tanks. Not surprisingly, fresh fish is all over the menu, though it may not resemble the sushi you know. Chef and co-owner Adam Roth serves "live fish" and "live lobster" sashimi (he keeps a separate tank of live creatures behind the sushi bar), as well as ceviche and cross-cultural rolls spun with arugula, prosciutto, Boursin cheese and sun-dried tomatoes. Entrées venture into the rest of the animal kingdom: rack of lamb, miso chicken, grilled duck and a seasonal-game plate.

Pan-Asian

Lovely Day

196 Elizabeth St between Prince and Spring Sts (212-925-3310). Subway: B, D, F, V to Broadway–Lafayette St; R, W to Prince St; 6 to Spring St.
Open *Mon–Thu noon–11pm; Fri noon–midnight; Sat 11am–midnight; Sun 11am–11pm.* **Average main course** *$9.* **Credit** *AmEx.*
Lovely Day's menu gives lonely travelers some much-needed relief from Nolita's unrelenting attitude and exorbitant prices. The staff is hip and casual, but also attentive. And while owner Kazusa Jibiki serves Asian flavors, it's not a standard Asian restaurant. The flowery wallpaper and grandma's-café decor are cute without trying too hard. Two chefs cook whimsical cuisine with Japanese and Thai touches—richly flavored coconut-curry noodles, gingery fried chicken, sweet and oil-free pad thai. On weekends, Lovely Day serves brunch—eggs and bacon, coconut French toast, and bagels with smoked salmon and wasabi cream cheese.

Pizza

Lombardi's

32 Spring St between Mott and Mulberry Sts (212-941-7994). Subway: 6 to Spring St.
Open *Mon–Thu 11:30am–11pm; Fri, Sat 11:30am–midnight; Sun 11:30am–10pm.* **Large plain pizza** *$15.* **Credit** *Cash only.*
Neapolitan arrival Gennaro Lombardi opened what claims to be the city's first pizza place in 1905. It's still a contender for best pie.

Lower East Side

American

Dish

165 Allen St between Rivington and Stanton Sts (212-253-8840). Subway: F, V to Lower East Side–Second Ave. **Open** *Mon–Thu 5–11pm; Fri 5pm–midnight; Sat 10:30am–4pm, 5pm–midnight; Sun 10:30am–4pm, 5–11pm.* **Average main course** *$15.* **Credit** *AmEx, Disc, MC, V.*
How low can you go? At this charming storefront, you get a main course and two sides for $15. Caterer-turned-chef (and owner) Cheryl Perry lets diners pair punchy primary flavors—grilled pork chops, rib-eye steak, fried catfish with grilled lemon—with creative American sides like fingerling-potato salad, three-cheese macaroni and fried green tomatoes in smoked-tomato vinaigrette. Whet your appetite with small dishes like grilled shrimp with red grapefruit, smoked trout with pickled fennel, or ricotta terrine with prosciutto and poached pears.

American Creative

WD-50

50 Clinton St between Rivington and Stanton Sts (212-477-2900). Subway: F to Delancey St; J, M, Z to Delancey–Essex Sts. **Open** *Mon–Sat 6–11pm; Sun 6–10pm.* **Average main course** *$24.* **Credit** *AmEx, DC, MC, V.*
Wildly talented chef Wylie Dufresne and his partners spent months in the kitchen pushing the boundaries of ingredients and techniques before opening their new venture in 2003. Their creations are utterly new—either totally fascinating or really freaky, depending on your point of view. Food intellectuals are still discussing the merit of Dufresne shockers like pounded-flat oysters, but Dufresne has already

"Best Brewpub in New York" - New York Magazine
Only In New York!
HEARTLAND BREWERY
REAL BEER
• LUNCH • DINNER
• PRE-THEATRE
• KIDS MENU
• RATED #1 BY ZAGAT'S NIGHT LIFE GUIDE
AWARD WINNING BEER
BREWED DAILY
Plus Homemade Sodas and Great Desserts for the Kids – Award-Winning Beer for You!
TIMES SQUARE 43rd St. & B'way 646-366-0235
SEAPORT Fulton at South St. 646-572-BEER
RADIO CITY 6th Ave. at 51st 212-582-8244
UNION SQ. W at 17th 212-645-3400
www.heartlandbrewery.com
CONVENIENT TO ALL HOTELS

Thalia
AMERICAN CUISINE WITH EUROPEAN FLAVOR
Brunch
Lunch
Dinner
Late Night
Menu
DJ
828 Eighth Avenue (50th), New York City, 10019 ▪ www.restaurantthalia.com
Tel: 212-399-4444 • Fax: 212-399-3268

Brasserie
Les Halles™
www.LesHalles.net
Voted
"Best French Bistro/Brasserie"
by Time Out readers, 2003
New York
411 Park Ave. S. @ 29th St.
212-679-4111
New York Downtown
15 John Street
212-285-8585
Miami, FL
2415 Ponce de Leon
305-461-1099
Washington, DC
1201 Pennsylvania Ave. NW
202-347-6848
©
Open 7 days
Non-stop service
Noon to Midnight
AMERICAN BEEF
FRENCH STYLE

moved on to foie gras terrine topped with shiny anchovies; flaky cod with bizarre but satisfying smoked mashed potatoes; and a tender chunk of lamb topped with shavings of sharp aged goat cheese and served with hibiscus-date puree. Pastry chef Sam Mason has stuck with his popular parsnip cake and *gianduja* parfait while experimenting with lychee-cilantro sorbet and goat-cheese panna cotta.

Delis

Katz's Delicatessen

205 E Houston St at Ludlow St (212-254-2246). Subway: F, V to Lower East Side–Second Ave. **Open** *Sun–Tue 8am–10pm; Wed, Thu 8am–11pm; Fri, Sat 8am–3am.* **Average sandwich** *$11.* **Credit** *AmEx, MC, V ($20 minimum).*

This cavernous old dining hall is a repository of living history. Arrive at 11am on a Sunday morning, and the line may be out the door. Grab a ticket and approach the long counter. First, a hot dog. The wienies here are without peer—crisp-skinned, all-beef dogs that are worth the $2.50. Then shuffle down and order your legendarily shareable sandwich (half portions are now available). Roast beef goes quickly (steer clear of the evening remains). The brisket rates, but don't forget the horseradish. And the pastrami? It's simply the best. Everything tastes better with one of the 16 draft beers; if you're on the wagon, grab a bottle of Dr. Brown's Cel-Ray Tonic.

Eclectic

Schiller's Liquor Bar

131 Rivington St at Norfolk St (212-260-4555). Subway: F to Delancey St; J, M, Z to Delancey–Essex Sts. **Open** *Tue–Thu 8am–1:30am; Fri 8am–2am; Sat 10am–2am; Sun 10am–1:30am.* **Average main course** *$12.* **Credit** *AmEx, MC, V.*

Keith McNally, owner of Balthazar, Lucky Strike and Pastis, has opened yet another restaurant in a trendy neighborhood, decorated once again with old mirrors and antique subway tiles. But McNally says Schiller's Liquor Bar is "a bohemian alternative" to his style-conscious bistros; no dish except steak costs more than $15. The 95-seat restaurant serves fancy-free brunch, lunch and dinner, with a menu of Franco-Brit comfort-food staples like Welsh rarebit over toast, steak frites and lamb curry. Don't know about wine, but know what you like? Try one of the six bottles labeled simply CHEAP, DECENT or GOOD.

French

Le Père Pinard

175 Ludlow St between Houston and Stanton Sts (212-777-4917). Subway: F to Delancey St; J, M, Z to Delancey–Essex Sts. **Open** *Sun–Thu 5pm–midnight; Fri 5pm–1am; Sat 11am–1am.* **Average main course** *$15.* **Credit** *AmEx.*

Though they make it look easy in this brick-walled bistro, food doesn't get this good by accident. The steak tartare is a revelation—it's just raw beef, of course, but the taste is sublime. And maybe it helped that the capers, chopped onion, raw egg, mustard and Worcestershire sauce were mixed together at the table by a charming, bare-midriffed waitress. A Valrhona-chocolate soufflé exudes a similar Gallic confidence. A DJ spins on weekends, and the bar gets squeezed full with an international clientele.

Italian

Apizz

217 Eldridge St at Stanton St (212-253-9199). Subway: F, V to Lower East Side–Second Ave. **Open** *Mon–Sat 6–11pm.* **Average main course** *$20.* **Credit** *AmEx, Disc, MC, V.*

The best Brunches

New Yorkers take their brunch seriously, so here is a rundown of the best spots.

...for a buzzing scene

Schiller's Liquor Bar (*see left*) is McNally-magnificent (and less crowded than at dinnertime).

...for hip huevos rancheros

Even the eggs are sexy at Nolita's spicy Cuban **Cafe Habana** (*see p169*).

...for praising your pancakes

Londel's Supper Club (*see p194*) has live gospel music on Sunday from noon to 5pm.

...for waking up with the stars

At **Mercer Kitchen** (*see p176*), eggs Benedict come with a side of celebrities, like Kate Moss, Lucy Liu and Marc Jacobs.

...for big appetites

Norma's (*see p49,* **Le Parker Meridien**) serves a huge over-the-top, all-breakfast menu.

...for certified hangover relief

Prune (*see p178*) offers nine different takes on that a.m. cure, the Bloody Mary.

...for all-day eggs

At **Cafeteria** (*see p184*), you can order fluffy omelettes and golden waffles 24/7.

...for groovin' while you grub

During weekend brunch at **Café Noir** (*see p201*), DJs spin quality lounge and house.

An enormous wood-burning brick oven occupies an entire corner of the dining room at this Southern Italian restaurant, and it deserves the space: Everything on the menu is cooked in it. Owners John LaFemina and Frank DeCarlo, of the similarly rustic Peasant, fire up pizzas, whole fish and a memorable wild-boar lasagna. The 45-seat dining room, fashioned with old bricks and a cross-beamed ceiling, is simple but comfortable.

'inoteca

98 Rivington St at Ludlow St (212-614-0473). Subway: F to Delancey St; J, M, Z to Delancey–Essex Sts. **Open** *Noon–3am daily.* **Average small plate** *$8.* **Credit** *AmEx, MC, V.*

For five years, the West Village's diminutive 'ino has proved that good things come in small packages. Now 'ino has a big brother with more space and an expanded menu. The new spin-off, which offers seats in a downstairs wine cellar and a sidewalk café, is three times the size of the original. And though you can order 'ino's famed truffled egg toast, you can also choose from many more snacks, including panini, cured meats and imported cheeses—plus more than 250 mostly Italian wines, 25 of them by the glass or half-carafe.

Other location *'ino, 21 Bedford St between Sixth Ave and Downing St (212-989-5769).*

Latin American

Suba

109 Ludlow St between Delancey and Rivington Sts (212-982-5714). Subway: F to Delancey St; J, M, Z to Delancey–Essex Sts. **Open** *Mon–Thu 6–10:30pm; Fri–Sun 6–11:30pm.* **Average main course** *$20.* **Credit** *AmEx, MC, V.*

The clamor at the street-level tapas bar might be obnoxious, but down the suspended steel staircase is another scene entirely. Ethereal light plays off a moat surrounding the small dining room, and the *nuevo* Spanish/Latino fare is equally impressive. Starters are strong, particularly the *milhojas de serrano y crema cabra,* a tasty little tower of ham, goat cheese and quince paste. Among the entrées, a roasted saffron-infused duck breast is complemented with black beans, corn and guacamole, and chipotle-marinated yellowfin tuna with spinach

Counter intelligence

Sometimes it's impossible to score a reservation at the city's hottest eateries—unless you want to dine at 5 or 9:45pm. But if you show up willing to eat at the bar around 7:15, just after the 7 o'clocks are seated and before the 7:30 crew arrives, you'll often be able to wriggle into a popular place, even if the dining room is fully booked. And besides, you occasionally want to eat well without being trapped behind a formal white tablecloth for hours on end. Here are a few great places for bellying up to the bar.

From the outside, **Artisanal** (*see p191*) looks like a bustling Paris-perfect brasserie. But take a whiff as you walk inside, and you'll quickly realize that cheese is the restaurant's funky, pungent raison d'être. A long bar and a row of banquette tables means plenty of room for walk-in diners, and a simplified bar menu makes ordering less daunting. Start with a glass of wine (cheese-friendly Swiss whites are particularly well represented) and a basket of warm, puffy cheese *gougères* (trust us—you want the full order, even if you're alone). Then, move on to one of the fondues or cheese plates, or try the affordable $20 prix fixe: lively mesclun salad; nicely crisped flattened chicken, or moist skate in a sweet-tart blood-orange sauce; and sorbet or ice cream for dessert.

Down in Greenwich Village, trying to get a prime-time table at **Babbo** (*see p181*) is about as tough as getting season tickets for the Giants—tougher, actually, since you can't call a scalper in Jersey to buy an 8pm reservation. But chef-owner Mario Batali left a loophole for fans of his gratifying Italian-inspired cuisine: six walk-in tables, plus a ten-seat bar. Arrive on the early side (especially in the first half of the week) and you can grab a seat, with a forest of skinny breadsticks in front of you and a quartini (quarter-liter carafe) of Barbaresco at your elbow. You'll need fortifying, because Batali's menu will whomp you with food lust: heirloom tomatoes layered with buffalo mozzarella, fatty-delicious house-cured salami, succulent beef-cheek ravioli, toothsome *orecchiette* with sausage and broccoli rabe…the offerings are pure sexy torture. Take our advice: Make friends with your barmates so you can taste their food too.

Just a few blocks east, you can almost hear the ocean sighing inside the **Mermaid Inn** (*see p179*). The nautical theme (sailing charts on the walls, mermaids on the cocktail napkins) even extends to the bar snacks—bowls of Goldfish crackers, of course. Since no reservations are taken, most diners use the ten shiny black barstools to cool their heels while waiting for a table, but the cute (and friendly) bartenders are happy to serve a

aioli rests atop a delicate butternut-squash tortilla. The dark-chocolate almond cake with strawberry ice cream is irresistible, but a drinkable dessert, like Suba's own lime-pie cocktail, is a better match for the seductive surroundings.

Pan-Asian

Kuma Inn

113 Ludlow St between Delancey and Rivington Sts, second floor (212-353-8866). Subway: F to Delancey St; J, M, Z to Delancey–Essex Sts. **Open** *Tue–Sun 6pm–midnight.* **Average small plate** *$7.* **Credit** *Cash only.*
Don't bother trying to find the Kuma Inn without directions handy. It's on the second floor of a Lower East Side walk-up, in a former art gallery, and only a business card marks its presence at street level. Those who make their way into the snug bamboo-decorated space are rewarded with chef-owner King Phojanakong's creative Asian dishes, including grilled pork loin with *achara* (a vinegary Filipino salad of chayote, carrots, daikon and ginger) or scallops with bacon and *kalamansi,* a tropical citrus fruit. You can pair your plates with any of 20 sakes, which might make finding your way home trickier than getting here in the first place.

Soho

American

Salt

58 MacDougal St between Houston and Prince Sts (212-674-4968). Subway: C, E to Spring St; 1, 9 to Houston St. **Open** *Mon–Thu 6–11pm; Fri 6pm–midnight; Sat 11:30am–3:30pm, 6pm–midnight; Sun 11:30am–3:30pm, 6–11pm.* **Average main course** *$19.* **Credit** *AmEx, DC, MC, V.*
Melissa O'Donnell knows what it takes to create a successful neighborhood joint. This simple square room, neatly packed with a small bar and chunky white tables, is equally friendly to solo diners or cozy twosomes. Warm pancetta vinaigrette turns spinach and goat cheese into a great savory, messy salad you can really bite into. Casually prepared in a good

Pitcher perfect Arrive early to enjoy the attentive bar service at Mario Batali's **Babbo**.

whole meal at the bar. Sip a Wet Mermaid (pear gin and prosecco) or a Mermaiden (a Bloody Mary pegged with a jumbo shrimp) before diving into an icy plate of clams on the half shell, juicy fried oysters or a pair of crispy fried whole sardines, followed by a fat lobster roll with fries or a bowl of seafood-laced spaghetti, kissed with spicy tomato sauce.

Moving uptown, contemporary-French **Aix** (*see p192*) has a pleasant mix of bar seats and comfortable tables in its well-lit front lounge. If only they'd left out the huge flat-screen TV, which adds a jarring (if silent) sports-bar note to an otherwise sophisticated spot. While you watch (or ignore) the game, skip the drab café options and instead make a meal of the creative appetizers on the fusion-accented main menu. Sweet, pillowy scallops, seared with chili, ride on bright pedestals of tart cabbage and fennel slaws, while shrimp and basil brochettes arrive in a tangy saffron-mustard dressing. Or go straight to drinks and dessert. Melding Indian flavors with French techniques, pastry chef Jehangir Mehta produces surprises like coffee-nutmeg ice cream and cardamom-fig tart. As if you needed another reason to linger at the bar.

home-cooked way, entrées are built to satisfy: crisp cod on mashed potatoes; pork tenderloin wrapped in prosciutto. A popular option is the "protein + 2," a whole roasted fish or a tasty slab of duck or Newport steak, paired with a choice of two alluring vegetable sides. The short wine list is quirky but well chosen, with good offerings in the $30 range.

American Creative

Mercer Kitchen

The Mercer, 99 Prince St at Mercer St (212-966-5454). Subway: R, W to Prince St. **Open** *Mon–Thu 7am–midnight; Fri, Sat 7am–1am; Sun 7am–11pm.* **Average main course** *$27.* **Credit** *AmEx, DC, MC, V.*

Owner Jean-Georges Vongerichten believes that time-pressed New Yorkers who don't get the chance to cook at home appreciate "everyday food." Calling the dishes at upscale Jean Georges and JoJo "everyday" may be a stretch, but Mercer Kitchen, located in the achingly hip Mercer Hotel, does seem to reflect that philosophy. Chef Chris Beischer allows the flavors of organic vegetables and meats to be revealed without fuss. A tuna spring roll with soybean puree is light and satisfying. Crisp thin-crust pizzas are slicked with raw tuna and wasabi, or black truffle and fontina. Even the more straightforward entrées—roasted chicken, aged-sirloin steak with fries—are memorable. The sleek underground space draws both Soho sophisticates and savvy hotel guests.

Cafés

Palacinka

28 Grand St between Sixth Ave and Thompson St (212-625-0362). Subway: A, C, E, 1, 9 to Canal St. **Open** *10:30am–midnight daily.* **Average crêpe** *$7.* **Credit** *Cash only.*

All glinting tin tables and young Europeans, Palacinka serves good, cheap crêpes (the meaning of the eatery's Czech name) that come two to a plate, with a side of mesclun salad. Get them savory (like tarragon-herbed chicken with goat cheese and peppers) or sweet (lemon, butter and sugar, or a luscious filling of chestnut paste with crème fraîche). By night, the lights are low and seductive; by day, when it's warm, the French windows open onto the sidewalks of Soho's western frontier.

Eclectic

Public

210 Elizabeth St between Prince and Spring Sts (212-343-7011). Subway: R, W to Prince St; 6 to Spring St. **Open** *Sun–Wed 10am–midnight; Thu–Sat 10am–4am.* **Average main course** *$20.* **Credit** *AmEx, MC, V.*

Designed by Adam Farmerie and his team at AvroKo, this venture is high on concept, using machine-age glass lamps and prewar office doors to create "a utopian vision of civilized society." Farmerie's bro Brad, who worked at London's acclaimed Providores, has created the menu in tandem with Providores' chefs, New Zealanders Anna Hansen and Peter Gordon. Look for a global-Kiwi influence in dishes like grilled kangaroo on coriander falafel; scallops with plantain crisps; New Zealand venison with pomegranates and truffles; and striped bass over curried lentils.

French

Balthazar

80 Spring St between Broadway and Crosby St (212-965-1414). Subway: R, W to Prince St; 6 to Spring St. **Open** *Mon–Wed 7:30–11:30am, noon–5pm, 6pm–1am; Thu 7:30–11:30am, noon–5pm, 6pm–1:30am; Fri 7:30–11:30am, noon–5pm, 6pm–2am; Sat 10am–4pm, 6pm–2am; Sun 10am–4pm, 5:30pm–midnight.* **Average main course** *$21.* **Credit** *AmEx, MC, V.*

Is it possible that you still can't get a reservation before 10pm on a Sunday night? Well, this is Balthazar, and it's not only possible, it's likely. Even at that ungodly dinner hour (by American standards), the place will be packed with rail-thin lookers in head-to-toe Prada and equally trendy messy-haired boys in chic hoodies and too-cool sneakers. But the bread is great, the food is good, and the service is surprisingly friendly. The three-tiered Balthazar seafood platter casts the most impressive shadow of any appetizer in town. The frisée *aux lardons* is exemplary. Roasted chicken for two on mashed potatoes, *délicieux*. Skate with brown butter and capers, yum. These days, the only not-so-Gallic detail is that no one is smoking.

Italian

Fiamma Osteria

206 Spring St between Sixth Ave and Sullivan St (212-653-0100). Subway: C, E to Spring St. **Open** *Mon–Thu noon–2:30pm, 5:30–11pm; Fri noon–2:30pm, 5:30pm–midnight; Sat 5:30pm–midnight; Sun 5:30–11pm.* **Average main course** *$27.* **Credit** *AmEx, Disc, MC, V.*

Which dining room at Steve Hanson's boutique eatery is cooler, upstairs or downstairs? One group of regulars swears by the ground floor, but we overheard a bartender in the suave upstairs lounge say that the young and sexy prefer to be on top. Wherever you end up, you're in for a series of phenomenal dishes by chef Michael White, who cooks like a Tuscan, drawing on the intense flavors of a few extrafresh ingredients to punctuate every dish. The menu changes seasonally, but past options have included seared scallops with baby artichokes and porcini; creamy asparagus soup dotted with spongy, meaty morels; and tortellini stuffed with unctuous braised oxtail. Finish the feast with a cappuccino martini—it's an after-dinner drink, coffee and dessert all rolled into one.

Dos Caminos Soho.

Mexican

Dos Caminos Soho

475 West Broadway at Houston St (212-277-4300). Subway: B, D, F, V to Broadway–Lafayette St; 6 to Bleecker St. **Open** *Sun–Tue noon–11pm; Wed, Thu noon–midnight; Fri, Sat noon–12:30am.* **Average main course** *$23.* **Credit** *AmEx, DC, Disc, MC, V.*

Like the Gramercy original, the smaller Soho branch of Steve Hanson's popular Mexican restaurant knows how to throw a party. It cranks out loads of freshly mashed guacamole, gets everyone lubed up on strong margaritas, then teases appetites with warm little tortillas stuffed with spicy shredded pork. But good luck crashing the festivities. The bar is too small to accommodate all the pretty young things who yearn to crowd around it. And the highly prized patio seats (warmed by heaters during chillier months) are tough to snag during prime time. If you can't wait to join the throngs, take a shot of one of the 150 tequilas immediately upon arrival and enjoy the show.

Other location *Dos Caminos, 373 Park Ave South between 26th and 27th Sts (212-294-1000).*

East Village

American

Butter

415 Lafayette St between Astor Pl and E 4th St (212-253-2828). Subway: 6 to Astor Pl.
Open *Mon–Sat 5:30pm–midnight.* **Average main course** *$25.* **Credit** *AmEx, DC, Disc, MC, V.*

This elegant restaurant's name doesn't have anything to do with its extraordinary and imaginative cooking, but the owner does have a penchant for collecting unique butter plates, which, filled with creamy French *beurre,* adorn each tabletop. Seared scallops with foie gras are delectable, as are the roasted red snapper, pan-seared tuna and succulent pork chops. There's an extensive wine list, gorgeous (and delicious) dessert selections, and capable waiters who make recommendations enthusiastically and knowledgeably. If you're in the mood to splurge on a five-star meal, but don't want to deal with uptown traffic or attitude, this place is like Butter.

American Creative

Industry (Food)

509 E 6th St between Aves A and B (212-777-5920). Subway: F, V to Lower East Side–Second Ave. **Open** *Sun–Wed 6pm–midnight; Thu–Sat 6pm–1am.* **Average main course** *$21.*
Credit *AmEx, DC, MC, V.*

Wade past the cool kids cramming the front bar and you'll find a wood-paneled dining room where the eye candy is on the plate. Lobster bruschetta is a bon vivant's answer to the BLT: lobster, pancetta, lettuce and tomato, all piled atop buttery brioche. The bouillabaisse is an improvement on the usual fish stew—creamy saffron broth clings to tender bits of seafood bolstered with couscous. The bizarre-sounding white-chocolate margarita turns out to be a lively finish to the feast: creamy mousse topped with tangy passion-fruit gelatin and lychee sorbet. At $8, it's the cheapest thing you're going to get in a martini glass around here.

What a tomato Gabrielle Hamilton, of **Prune**; one of her nine Bloody Mary variations.

Prune

54 E 1st St between First and Second Aves (212-677-6221). Subway: F, V to Lower East Side–Second Ave. **Open** *Mon–Thu 6–11pm; Fri 6pm–midnight; Sat 10am–3:30pm, 6pm–midnight; Sun 10am–3:30pm, 5–10pm.* **Average main course** *$21.* **Credit** *AmEx, MC, V.*

There's nothing cute or safe about chef-owner Gabrielle Hamilton's food. She knows her meat: juicy roasted suckling pig complemented by a spicy salad of pickled tomatoes, black-eyed peas and aioli; rich sweetbreads topped with bacon; warm lentils with fried chicken livers. Show up at tiny Prune on weekend mornings for such delights as the popular sausages and oysters, a plate of smoked fish from nearby Russ & Daughters, or one or two of the nine Bloody Mary variations. Good luck walking a straight line out of here.

Italian

Supper

156 E 2nd St between Aves A and B (212-477-7600). Subway: F, V to Lower East Side–Second Ave. **Open** *Sun–Thu 11am–1am; Fri, Sat 11am–2am.* **Average main course** *$10.* **Credit** *Cash only.*

Remember when supper came between playing Wiffle ball and catching lightning bugs? This addition to Frank Prisinzano's team of modestly priced Italian eateries (Frank, Lil' Frankie's Pizza) brings back the charm of easy eating. Although the decor has a grown-up feel, with rustic wooden tables, antique chandeliers and a private dining room in the basement wine vault, simplicity rules the menu. Pastas—linguine with butter and mint, gnocchi with tomato sauce, spaghetti with lemon and Parmesan—allow the freshness of their ingredients to shine.

Japanese

Bond St.

6 Bond St between Broadway and Lafayette St (212-777-2500). Subway: F, V to Broadway–Lafayette St; 6 to Bleecker St. **Open** *Mon–Sat 6–11:30pm; Sun 6–10:30pm.* **Average sushi meal** *(6 pieces): $24.* **Credit** *AmEx, DC, MC, V.*

Bond St., one of the city's top fusion restaurants, attracts a lounge-cool crowd sipping design-a-tinis. Chef Linda Rodriguez mesmerizes diners with immaculate conceptions such as crisp *rouget* (red mullet) in a tomato-ginger dressing, and seared foie gras and tuna with pear chutney and basil. Succulent grilled rack of lamb, bathed in tomato confit, is dreamy. On the raw side, head sushi chef Hiroshi Nakahara's impeccable, well-chosen selection will sate by-the-book diners, but even they may be swayed by delicious heresies like sesame-crusted shrimp roll in orange-curry dressing.

Jewel Bako

239 E 5th St between Second and Third Aves (212-979-1012). Subway: F, V to Lower East Side–Second Ave; 6 to Astor Pl. **Open** *Mon–Sat 6:30–10:30pm.* **Average sushi meal** *(9 pieces, 1 roll) $29.* **Credit** *AmEx, DC, MC, V.*
This tiny 31-seat restaurant focuses on sushi and sashimi, with most fish flown in every other day from Tokyo's Tsukiji fish market. Don't leave without trying the *toro* tartare—bluefin tuna with osetra caviar and a pureed avocado sauce. If they have it, order the special of Japanese mushrooms steamed with *yuzu* zest and sake. The restaurant's stylish husband-and-wife owners, Jack and Grace Lamb, live across the street (above their latest venture, Jack's Luxury Oyster Bar) and clearly love tending to every detail of their culinary jewel box.

Mexican

La Palapa

77 St. Marks Pl between First and Second Aves (212-777-2537). Subway: 6 to Astor Pl.
Open *Mon–Fri noon–midnight; Sat, Sun 11am–midnight.* **Average main course** *$17.*
Credit *AmEx, DC, MC, V.*
Palapa means "thatched beach hut," and you'll feel like you're dining in one. Spiced catfish and cactus in a corn husk, a pre-Columbian dish, is fragrantly moist. Rich, juicy grilled duck is drizzled with a robust chocolate-accented *mole*. The good seafood selection includes a mild cod fillet that gets bite from toasted–pumpkin-seed sauce. Finish with an empanada *de arroz con leche,* a cinnamon turnover filled with sweet rice pudding.
Other location *La Palapa Rockola, 359 Sixth Ave between Washington Pl and W 4th St (212-243-6870).*

Middle Eastern

Mamlouk

211 E 4th St between Aves A and B (212-529-3477). Subway: F, V to Lower East Side–Second Ave.
Open *Tue–Sun 7–10pm.* **Prix fixe** *$30.*
Credit *AmEx, MC, V.*
There's no menu—Wissam el-Masri cooks whatever he feels like on any given day. Let the Lebanese chef take you on a six-course culinary journey that spans North Africa and the Levant. As you recline on a Moroccan settee inlaid with mother-of-pearl, a parade of dishes will be placed on the low copper-topped Egyptian table before you—a combo platter of appetizers, then soup, salad, dips, fish (perhaps on a bed of cilantro and lentils), and a main course such as braised lamb in a rich tomato sauce. (El-Masri will happily accommodate vegetarians and vegans.) The downstairs lounge is often the site of weekend birthday celebrations; weekdays, you can retire there, hookah in hand, for a sweet puff. Plan ahead, though: The restaurant seats diners only at 7 and 9pm.

Seafood

Mermaid Inn

96 Second Ave between 5th and 6th Sts (212-674-5870). Subway: F, V to Lower East Side–Second Ave; 6 to Astor Pl. **Open** *Mon–Sat 6pm–1am.* **Average main course** *$16.* **Credit** *AmEx, DC, Disc, MC, V.*
The name conjures a dive bar on the Jersey Shore, but the East Village's Mermaid Inn is about as far from Bay Head as you can get. Danny Abrams and Jimmy Bradley, the pair behind the Red Cat and the Harrison, have dressed seafood for New York palates: oysters and clams on the half shell, lobster-corn chowder, crunchy fried oysters, pan-crisped skate and fat fillets of cod (all of which taste even better in summer, when you can sit in the back garden). The menu is strictly from the sea, with a few vegetable sides. Crowds flock to its siren song, but this Mermaid accepts no reservations, so expect a wait. Dessert is limited to a small freebie from the kitchen, which keeps the tables turning.

Steakhouses

Strip House

13 E 12th St between Fifth Ave and University Pl (212-328-0000). Subway: L, N, Q, R, W, 4, 5, 6 to 14th St–Union Sq. **Open** *Mon–Thu 5–11pm; Fri, Sat 5–11:30pm; Sun 5–10pm.* **Average main course** *$32.* **Credit** *AmEx, DC, Disc, MC, V.*
Your search for an unforgettable piece of beef ends here, where a magnificently hunky New York strip for two is carved tableside into perfect four-inch squares, charred crisp and salty on the outside, red within. Unless, perhaps, you order the burly bone-in rib chop, seamed with flavorful fat. Just as impressive are chef David Walzog's sides and appetizers. Start with his creative take on a classic tomato-and-onion salad, then partner your meat with luscious creamed, truffled spinach and goose-fat–fried potatoes. As for decor, think of the Playboy Mansion, circa 1962: Strip House has a spacious cocktail lounge, red velvet walls, burgundy quilted-leather banquettes, terrazzo floors and an in-the-mood glow.

Vegetarian & Organic

Angelica Kitchen

300 E 12th St between First and Second Aves (212-228-2909). Subway: L to First Ave; N, Q, R, W, 4, 5, 6 to 14th St–Union Sq. **Open** *11:30am–10:30pm daily.* **Average main course** *$10.* **Credit** *Cash only.*
This vegetarian mecca has been around since hippie was hip, and the vibe hasn't changed much; nor has the quality of the clever dishes. A 34-term cheat sheet on the back of the menu explains what *umeboshi* and *kombu* are, and why they're good for you. The Pantry Plate is a sampler of starters like walnut-lentil pâté, pickled seasonal vegetables, or a couscous-and-vegetable salad tossed in cilantro vinaigrette. You might think you're eating a Reuben when you bite

into the fresh sourdough baguette layered with thick, marinated baked tempeh slices and homemade mushroom gravy; it's served with raw spinach, ruby kraut and mashed potatoes. With options like these, who needs meat?

West Village

American

Corner Bistro

331 W 4th St at Jane St (212-242-9502). Subway: A, C, E to 14th St; L to Eighth Ave. **Open** *11:30am–4am daily.* **Average burger** *$5.* **Credit** *Cash only.*

A Corner Bistro burger is the best in town. To get your hands on one (and you *will* need both hands), you may have to wait in line for a good hour. Fortunately, several two-dollar drafts are offered, the game is on the tube, and a jukebox covers everything from Calexico to Coltrane. The cheeseburger is just $4.75, but you might as well go for the legendary Bistro Burger, a fat patty of gloriously broiled beef, topped with cheese and several strips of supersmoky bacon, on a soft sesame-seed bun for $5.50. Grilled cheese is $2.75, and a plate of shoestring fries runs $2, but really, it's all about the beef.

Deborah

43 Carmine St between Bedford and Bleecker Sts (212-242-2606). Subway: A, C, E, B, D, F, V to W 4th St. **Open** *Tue–Sun 11am–4pm, 5–11pm.* **Average main course** *$16.* **Credit** *AmEx, DC, Disc, MC, V.*

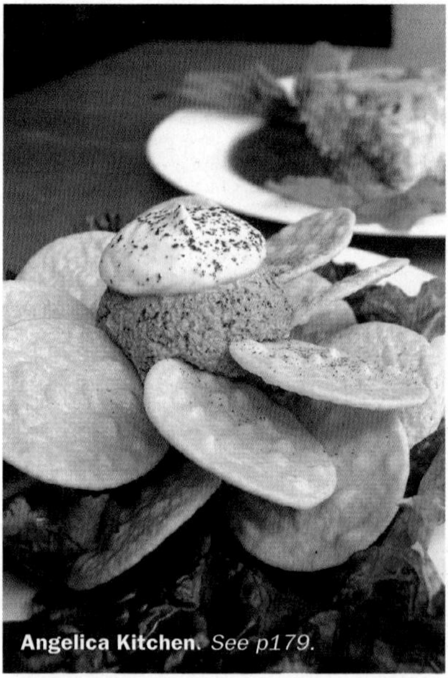

Angelica Kitchen. *See p179.*

Deborah will quickly become your new best friend. She's attractive, dressed in neat lines of red, white and black, with a spare yet comfortable style. She's familiar and grounded yet never dull, just like her moist mini meat loaf, which has an intense mushroom flavor. She's straightforward with her lightly seared tuna with carrot salad and a touch of wasabi, but a touch naughty with her smooth, rich chocolate pot de crème. Drop in for brunch in her inviting back garden or snuggle up for lunch or dinner in her tiny, square dining room.

Peanut Butter & Co.

240 Sullivan St between Bleecker and W 3rd Sts (212-677-3995). Subway: A, C, E, B, D, F, V to W 4th St. **Open** *Sun–Thu 11am–9pm; Fri, Sat 11am–10pm.* **Average sandwich** *$6.* **Credit** *AmEx, DC, Disc, MC, V.*

Tell your inner child to stop whining: Every day, the staff grinds a fresh batch of peanut butter, which is used to create gooey mood pacifiers like the popular Elvis—the King's infamous grilled favorite of peanut butter, banana and honey. The warm cinnamon-raisin–flavored peanut-butter sandwich with vanilla cream cheese and tart apple slices is good taste and texture rolled into one. And for dessert, Death by Peanut Butter is a landslide of ice cream, Peanut Butter Cap'n Crunch, peanut-butter chips and peanut-butter sauce.

American Creative

Annisa

13 Barrow St between Bleecker and W 4th Sts (212-741-6699). Subway: A, C, E, B, D, F, V to W 4th St; 1, 9 to Christopher St–Sheridan Sq. **Open** *Mon–Sat 5:30–10pm; Sun 5:30–9:30pm.* **Average main course** *$26.* **Credit** *AmEx, DC, MC, V.*

The guiding principle in this serene off-white room seems to be lightness—and it extends to the adventurous, globally inspired dishes of chef and co-owner Anita Lo. A ceviche of raw, tender sea scallops is marinated in a celery-root sauce and topped with slices of tangy green apple. A ready-to-burst soup dumpling, topped with seared foie gras, is animated by a hint of jicama. Even after one of the five- or seven-course tasting menus—which Lo often improvises according to available ingredients—you won't feel weighed down. Many great restaurants in this town leave you satisfied; Annisa is one of the few that also leaves you feeling refreshed.

Cafés

A Salt & Battery

112 Greenwich Ave between 12th and 13th Sts (212-691-2713). Subway: A, C, E to 14th St; L to Eighth Ave. **Open** *Noon–10pm daily.* **Average main course** *$10.* **Credit** *AmEx, MC, V.*

The name is one of the most painful restaurant puns ever. But A Salt & Battery is about as authentic as any non-U.K. fish-and-chips joint could be.

Eat, Drink, Shop

Flying fish The 31-seat **Jewel Bako** air-expresses seafood from Tokyo. *See p179.*

The batter is light and crisp, the cod is tender, and the chips are Brit-style soggy, even before you douse them with malt vinegar. Stick with the basic cod or try the more intensely flavored chunks of batter-fried cod roe—wrapped in a London newspaper. The chip shop now has a larger East Village location, where you can bite into savory pies or slog happily through an all-day fried breakfast.
Other location *80 Second Ave between 4th and 5th Sts (212-254-6610).*

French

Paradou

8 Little West 12th St between Ninth Ave and Washington St (212-463-8345). Subway: A, C, E to 14th St; L to Eighth Ave. **Open** *Mon–Wed 4pm–midnight; Thu 4pm–1am; Fri, Sat noon–5:30am; Sun noon–10pm.* **Average main course** *$19.* **Credit** *Disc, MC, V.*

Can't deal with the line at nearby Pastis? Duck into sweet little Paradou, and soon you'll be surrounded by hydrangea and ivy in the back garden, sharing plates like the *tartine* sampler (tiny toasts topped with delightful homemade spreads) or buckwheat crêpes filled with mushrooms, asparagus, pecorino and truffle oil. Crêpes reappear at dessert, encasing sensuous confections like chestnut cream with chopped nuts. Good news for folks who club at neighboring Cielo: Paradou now offers a scaled-down menu on Friday and Saturday after 1:30am (try the spicy merguez sandwich).
Other location *426 Seventh Ave at 14th St, Park Slope, Brooklyn (718-499-5557).*

Pastis

9 Ninth Ave at Little West 12th St (212-929-4844). Subway: A, C, E to 14th St; L to Eighth Ave. **Open** *Sun–Thu 9am–2am; Fri, Sat 9am–3am.* **Average main course** *$18.* **Credit** *AmEx, MC, V.*

Keith McNally's West Side counterpart to Soho's Balthazar is a buzzing sea of slim black-clad bodies, all crowding in for consistently pleasing bistro food. If you haven't made dining-room reservations, work your way through the crowd to stake out a small table by the bar. You'll find tomato-and-goat-cheese tart; thick, succulent steak with slender frites; meaty roasted halibut; and a piping-hot bread pudding. If you crave Pastis's food but want to avoid its clamorous scene, consider weekend brunch, when it's just marginally less packed. Lobster, steak and croque-monsieur show up alongside egg dishes dressed in their Sunday best.

Italian

Babbo

110 Waverly Pl between MacDougal St and Sixth Ave (212-777-0303). Subway: A, C, E, B, D, F, V to W 4th St. **Open** *Mon–Sat 5:30–11:30pm; Sun 5–11pm.* **Average main course** *$27.* **Credit** *AmEx, Disc, MC, V.*

Regulars know that ordering gets more frustrating with each visit. Once you taste a Babbo dish, you have to order it again. So you're either "stuck" with lamb's-tongue salad painted with the thick yolk of a poached egg, or saucy parcels of beef-cheek ravioli—or you'll have to spring for more than you could

Bliss Burgers at **Corner Bistro.** *See p180.*

possibly eat at one sitting. Who could blame you? Mario Batali's fluffy gnocchi are blanketed with tender shreds of oxtail. Two-Minute Calamari—a red soup exploding with caper berries and rings of white squid—is a bowlful of fireworks. Have it all, then throw in the *frittelle di* ricotta with caramelized bananas, gelato and chocolate sauce.

Lupa

170 Thompson St between Bleecker and Houston Sts (212-982-5089). Subway: A, C, E, B, D, F, V to W 4th St. **Open** *Mon–Fri noon–2:30pm, 5–11:30pm; Sat, Sun noon–2:15pm, 5–11:30pm.* **Average main course** *$14.* **Credit** *AmEx, MC, V.*
It may be difficult to resist the special pastas (*bigoli* with duck *ragù*—please, baby, please!), which can fetch as much as $30. But Mario Batali's Roman trattoria isn't known as the poor man's Babbo for nothing: One can eat happily and heartily here without doing serious bank-account damage. It's possible to make a meal of exquisitely earthy antipasti—say, a $12 *verdure* trio, which should definitely include the charred leeks with egg. Or stick with one of the sublime regular pastas, like ricotta gnocchi with sausage and fennel ($14). And you can pair it all with one of several worthy reds for a mere $10 a carafe. Now, that's eating well on the cheap.

Japanese

Matsuri

Maritime Hotel, 369 W 16th St at Ninth Ave (212-243-6400). Subway: A, C, E to 14th St. **Open** *Sun–Wed 6pm–midnight; Thu–Sat 6pm–1am.* **Average main course** *$18.* **Credit** *AmEx, DC, MC, V.*
This Kyoto-inspired behemoth has a 25-foot-high barrel-vaulted ceiling, blimp-size rice-paper hanging lanterns, 120 seats and two sushi bars. The food, by chef Tadashi Ono (La Caravelle, Sono) is decadent and delicious—Kobe beef with mustard-*happozu* sauce, braised sardines with salt-cured plums and succulent black cod. All of it is ripe for pairing with any of the 200 sakes.

Sumile

154 W 13th St between Sixth and Seventh Aves (212-989-7699). Subway: L to Sixth Ave. **Open** *Mon–Thu 5:30–10:30pm; Fri, Sat 5:30–11pm.* **Average main course** *$28.* **Credit** *AmEx, MC, V.*
This West Village restaurant has been suited up in cool aqua and gray tones with Japanese-inspired chairs and hanging lamps. Chef Josh DeChellis (Bouley, Union Pacific) takes his cues from Japan too, focusing his small plates ($14 each) on inventive Japanese fare, such as tea-smoked *unagi* on boiled daikon and poached *hamachi* with pickled melon and salt spiked with powdered nori.

Pizza

John's Pizza

278 Bleecker St at Jones St (212-243-1680). Subway: A, C, E, B, D, F, V to W 4th St; 1, 9 to Christopher St–Sheridan Sq. **Open** *Mon–Sat 11:30am–11:30pm; Sun noon–11:30pm.* **Large plain pizza** *$13.* **Credit** *Cash only.*
Always in the running for "best pizza," John's serves an excellent coal-oven pie (no slices). Opened in 1929, the original location dishes up pizzas with crispy-chewy crust and a sweet red sauce.
Other locations *260 W 44th St between Broadway and Eighth Ave (212-391-7560); 408 E 64th St between First and York Aves (212-935-2895).*

Seafood

Pearl Oyster Bar

18 Cornelia St between Bleecker and W 4th Sts (212-691-8211). Subway: A, C, E, B, D, F, V to W 4th St. **Open** *Mon–Fri noon–2:30pm, 6–11pm; Sat 6–11pm.* **Average main course** *$22.* **Credit** *MC, V.*

Now twice its original size (thanks to a recently added dining room), Pearl still draws crowds for chef Rebecca Charles's straightforward but superb seafood. A Maine-perfect lobster roll, made of chunky lobster salad spilling out of a toasted, butter-drenched hot-dog bun, is Charles's signature dish, but other fishy favorites include fresh steamers, clam chowder accented with smoky bacon, pan-roasted oysters and whole boiled or grilled lobster. Downhome desserts and a smart selection of well-priced wines and beers finish the winning equation.

Thai

Tangerine

228 W 10th St between Bleecker and Hudson Sts (212-463-8585). Subway: 1, 9 to Christopher St–Sheridan Sq. **Open** *Mon–Sat 5:30pm–midnight.* **Average main course** *$17.* **Credit** *AmEx, DC, Disc, MC, V.*

Leafy bamboo dots the sexy maroon lounge, and the the downstairs dining room is a streamlined box. It's an artful setting for the cuisine of chef Bangorn Changpeak, who formerly cooked in high-end restaurants in Bangkok. His famous Purple Blossoms—delicate chicken-filled dumplings shaped (and colored) like flowers—are the prettiest starter you'll ever eat. If spice is your vice, dive into one of the smoking curries, like shredded pork studded with cool Granny Smith apple slices. Got a group? Try one of the massive Tangerine Dream platters, complete with soup, seafood, rice and meat.

Vietnamese

Hue

91 Charles St at Bleecker St (212-691-4170). Subway: 1, 9 to Christopher St–Sheridan Sq. **Open** *11:30am–4pm, 6pm–midnight daily.* **Average main course** *$17.* **Credit** *AmEx, DC, Disc, MC, V.*

A waterfall, fireplace and tilted skylights make this sultry restaurant seem more Soho-sexy (and feng shui–perfect) than West Village–quaint. The chic crowd seems to have rolled straight out of the dressing rooms at nearby Marc Jacobs onto the velvet banquettes and two lounge-ready beds. On the French-Vietnamese menu: spring rolls, five-spice quail, pho (beef noodle soup) and sushi.

Food court

New York's newest, most glamorous restaurants...in a mall? Indeed. You won't find any Cinnabon stands in the snazzy new Time Warner center at Columbus Circle. The complex has a concourse food hall operated by Whole Foods Market; two dozen upscale retailers like Coach, Thomas Pink, Sephora and Face Stockholm; a splashy Williams-Sonoma operation on the ground floor and mezzanine; and, on the third and fourth floors, several high-end restaurants helmed by blockbuster chefs (another eatery, **Asiate**, is in the adjacent Mandarin Oriental Hotel). At press time, the restaurants listed below were slated to open in early to mid-2004; however, chefs, dates, concepts and names are likely to change in the interim. Two as-yet-unnamed projects are scheduled to open later in 2004: a seafood restaurant with raw bar, helmed by Chicago hotshot Charlie Trotter; and a French-accented steakhouse run by New York powerhouse Jean-Georges Vongerichten. Stay tuned.

Asiate

212-805-8800.

The French-Japanese cuisine of Noriyuki Sugie (who worked at Charlie Trotter's in Chicago) competes with fork-dropping views from the 35th floor of the Mandarin Oriental hotel.

Café Gray

212-823-9595; www.cafegray.com.

There's a lively (and eponymous) talent behind this restaurant's snooze-inducing name: Swiss-trained Gray Kunz, the genius behind the late, much-lamented Lespinasse, is planning a brasserie with an Eastern European flavor.

Masa

212-823-9800.

Sushi master Masa Takayama, whose Ginza Sushiko in Beverly Hills was a favorite among Hollywood stars and moguls, has moved east to open New York's most expensive sushi bar: At press time, dinner for one was pitched at $500. However, a small sake bar will have simpler (and less expensive) offerings.

Per Se

212-823-9335.

Perfectionist Thomas Keller, who made his name as the chef-owner of the award-winning, ultraexclusive French Laundry restaurant in California's Napa Valley, brings his exquisite culinary sensibility to the big city. If you're lucky enough to get a table, expect a pricey prix-fixe procession of 9, 12 or more small, seasonally inspired courses for lunch and dinner.

Chelsea

American

Cafeteria

119 Seventh Ave at 17th St (212-414-1717). Subway: 1, 9 to 18th St. **Open** *24hrs.* **Average main course** *$17.* **Credit** *AmEx, DC, Disc, MC, V.*
This nonstop scene has its own version of the Happy Meal: a Cosmo, some mashed potatoes and the phone number of that ripped fellow in cutoffs. Artists, designers and celebs converge on the white minimalist dining room to jadedly watch the world go by, and food is not the first thing on their minds. Still, everyone's gotta eat, and Cafeteria sates the fashionista herds with down-home favorites. The mac and cheese is nearly perfect, with a crumbly top and a gooey fontina-cheddar middle. Other classics—like gravy-heavy meat loaf served with a tomato–red-pepper relish, and a charred, juicy burger with blue cheese—are equally satisfying. If you're on a strictly liquid diet, nourish yourself in the tiny basement bar.

The Red Cat

227 Tenth Ave between 23rd and 24th Sts (212-242-1122). Subway: C, E to 23rd St. **Open** *Mon–Thu 5:30–11pm; Fri, Sat 5:30pm–midnight; Sun 5–10pm.* **Average main course** *$21.* **Credit** *AmEx, DC, MC, V.*
Art-world luminaries and locals from up the block descend on this handsome place, decorated with New England barn-wood walls and Moroccan lanterns. They come for buttery foie gras *torchon* with sautéed nectarines, hot honeyed onions and toasted pistachios; panfried mustard-crusted trout with cherry tomatoes; and a towering pistachio *semifreddo* drenched in bittersweet chocolate. The food is so self-assured, and the setting so comfortable, it's easy to overlook small touches like lustrous china and elegant table linen.

American Creative

Amuse

108 W 18th St between Sixth and Seventh Aves (212-929-9755). Subway: 1, 9 to 18th St. **Open** *Mon–Sat noon–midnight.* **Average main course** *$15.* **Credit** *AmEx, DC, MC, V.*
Under the direction of chef-owner Gerry Hayden (Aureole, Tribeca Grill) this place has become a sleek dining hall where you order by price ($5, $10, $15, $20). Portions get larger, techniques more refined and ingredients dearer with each increase. But the food doesn't need this Craft-y gimmick to

Smokin' hot

Right now, the only legal smoking going on in New York restaurants is in the barbecue pits. This all-American technique, typically associated more with Kansas City, Memphis and parts of Texas, has become hot right here. There's plenty of wrangling over who's firing up the best 'cue—these are a few of the most serious contenders:

Biscuit

367 Flatbush Ave between Seventh Ave and Sterling Pl, Park Slope, Brooklyn (718-398-2227). Subway: B, Q to Seventh Ave; 2, 3 to Grand Army Plaza. **Open** *Mon–Thu 9am–10pm; Fri, Sat 9am–11pm; Sun 9am–9pm.* **Average main course** *$7.* **Credit** *Cash only.*
Brooklyn native Josh Cohen hickory-smokes all the meats at this comfy spot.

Blue Smoke

116 E 27th St between Park and Lexington Aves (212-447-7733). Subway: 6 to 28th St. **Open** *Mon–Thu noon–1am; Fri, Sat noon–1:30am; Sun 5:30pm–1am.* **Average main course** *$20.* **Credit** *AmEx, Disc, MC, V.*
Restaurant mogul Danny Meyer (Gramercy Tavern, Union Square Cafe) draws crowds at this Flatiron District destination.

Pearson's Texas Barbecue.

Daisy May's BBQ USA

623 Eleventh Ave between 45th and 46th Sts (212-977-1500). Subway: A, C, E to 42nd St. **Open** *11am–8pm daily.* **Average main course** *$8.* **Credit** *AmEx, Disc, MC, V.*
Former Daniel chef Adam Perry Lang heats up Hell's Kitchen at this top-notch take-out joint.

Pearson's Texas Barbecue

170 E 81st St between Lexington and Third Aves (212-288-2700). Subway: 6 to 77th St. **Open** *Tue–Sun 5–10pm.* **Average main course** *$15.* **Credit** *MC, V.*
No rubs, no sauces, just pure meaty goodness, from lick-your-fingers ribs to lip-smackingly tender brisket.

hold your interest. Five-dollar fries come with an luscious eggless béarnaise, and the $10 cumin-spiced pork tortilla is like a BBQ sloppy joe with bite. On the higher end, juicy slices of peppered Long Island duck breast are bathed in a deep, dark fig reduction.

Snackbar

111 W 17th St between Sixth and Seventh Aves (212-627-3700). Subway: F, V to 14th St; L to Sixth Ave; 1, 9 to 18th St. **Open** *Mon–Sat noon–midnight; Sun 11am–midnight.* **Average main course** *$15.* **Credit** *AmEx, MC, V.*

Chef Nick Tischler and owner Krim Boughalem have taken a nontraditional approach to snacking, starting with Tischler's fancy house canapé—a frothy, offbeat blend of white chocolate, Parmesan cheese, rosemary and apricots served on a toast point. He tosses bits of glittery gold leaf into a salad of whipped goat cheese and golden beets, and places foie gras, diced watermelon and rutabaga atop lemon-thyme johnnycakes. The interior also relies on contrasting components: Rough fixtures like a concrete bar and steel screens play off luxe marble tabletops and handmade ceramic tiles.

Belgian

Markt

401 W 14th St at Ninth Ave (212-727-3314). Subway: A, C, E to 14th St; L to Eighth Ave. **Open** *Mon–Fri 11:30am–4:30pm, 5:30pm–midnight; Sat, Sun 10am–4:30pm, 5:30pm–midnight.* **Average main course** *$18.* **Credit** *AmEx, DC, MC, V.*

The brief Belgian-food craze came and went, but Markt is still going strong, offering ample seating in a gorgeous environment: a 60-foot rose-marble bar, dark-wood floors and the hanging-globe lighting of a '30s brasserie. Dozens of sidewalk tables allow for prime people-watching. Markt is best known for its jumbo-sized metal pails of fresh steamed mussels accompanied by salty frites and one of 30 types of beer. Culinary heaven this isn't, but the good-looking crowd sure doesn't care.

Mexican

Sueños

311 W 17th St at Eighth Ave (212-243-1333). Subway 1, 9 to 18th St. **Open** *Mon–Sat 6pm–midnight; Sun 11:30am–3:30pm, 6pm–midnight.* **Average main course** *$18.* **Credit** *AmEx, MC, V.*

Sue Torres (Rocking Horse Cafe, Hell's Kitchen) combines authentic food (a woman stands on a platform in the dining room mashing avocados for guacamole and cranking out handmade tortillas to order), with the fiesta factor of hot-pink and pumpkin-orange decor, glammed-up margaritas and a $50 daredevil chili-tasting menu. Lively dishes include goat-cheese empanadas in smoky jalapeño coulis, chorizo quesadillas and red snapper wrapped in a banana leaf.

People-watch at **Markt**.

Pan-Asian

Biltmore Room

290 Eighth Ave between 24th and 25th Sts (212-807-0111; www.thebiltmoreroom.com). Subway: C, E to 23rd St. **Open** *Sun–Thu 6–10:30pm; Fri, Sat 6–11:30pm.* **Average main course** *$28.* **Credit** *AmEx, DC, MC, V.*

Named after the legendary hotel, the Biltmore Room lives up to the swanky promise implicit in its name. The dining room shimmers with crystal chandeliers, mirrors, brass doors, and marble floors and columns. On the Asian-inspired menu: Goan spiced rack of lamb, giant prawns wrapped in crispy noodles, Indian spiced Alaskan salmon. The real attraction is the world's first cell-phone booth, a brass vestibule with a beige leather interior, so you can chat in comfort without broadcasting your postdessert plans to the rest of the room.

Wild Lily Tea Room

511 W 22nd St between Tenth and Eleventh Aves (212-691-2258). Subway C, E to 23rd St. **Open** *Tue–Sun 11am–10pm.* **Average main course** *$11.* **Credit** *AmEx, MC, V.*

A split-level dining area and a gurgling goldfish pool make this narrow room in Chelsea's gallery district seem spacious and tranquil. Tapa-size dishes are carefully composed. Pear salad with sugar-glazed walnuts and goat cheese is an elegant play of textures, while the Dumpling Club assortment

holds a few surprises (shrimp is pureed and buttery; shiitake is julienned for an extra burst of musky flavor). All are designed to be accompanied by sake. Dessert specials are paired with specific tea recommendations—delicately scented jade tea enhances *mochi*-wrapped ice cream. For aspiring tea connoisseurs, Wild Lily has a branch in the East Village that sells more than 50 varieties and all the tea-related items you could possibly desire.
Other location *Wild Lily Tea Market, 545 E 12th St between Aves A and B (212-598-9097).*

Gramercy & Flatiron

For Blue Smoke *see p184* **Smokin' hot**.

American Creative

Craft

43 E 19th St between Broadway and Park Ave South (212-780-0880). Subway: R, W, 6 to 23rd St. **Open** *Mon–Thu noon–2pm, 5:30–10pm; Fri noon–2pm, 5:30–11pm; Sat 5:30–11pm; Sun 5:30–10pm.* **Average main course with one side** *$36.* **Credit** *AmEx, DC, Disc, MC, V.*

Craft's chef-owner, Tom Colicchio, gives organic, seasonal cuisine a gloss of New York glamour, while the rosy lighting gives diners instant makeovers. Instead of the usual appetizers-and-entrées listings, the menu is sectioned by cooking technique. It's up to you (with some help from the well-trained waitstaff) to put your meal together from categories like raw, roasted, braised and sautéed. But you can't go wrong with glorious options like braised lobster, foie gras terrine with 100-year-old balsamic vinegar, and beef short ribs creamy enough to eat with a spoon. Don't have the big bucks? Try the elegant but less pricey Craftbar next door, or grab a panino at sandwich shop 'wichcraft down the block.
Other locations *Craftbar, 47 E 19th St between Broadway and Park Ave South (212-780-0880); 'wichcraft, 49 E 19th St between Broadway and Park Ave South (212-780-0577).*

Just desserts

Coffee and cheesecake, red wine and chocolate: New York is a great place to skip the nutritious and go straight to the delicious. Whether you're looking for a postshow wind-down or a preclub sugar bounce, a sweet spot for dessert is never far off.

Among the most refined options is **Payard Pâtisserie & Bistro**. Although this Paris-perfect spot is also a full-fledged restaurant, the patisserie up front is the main event. These gorgeous confections are as chicly turned out as the patrons. The Louvre, one of pastry chef François Payard's signature pastries, is a glossy dark-chocolate dome of hazelnut and milk-chocolate mousse over hazelnut *dacquoise,* while the haute cheesecake dubbed New York New York has a design of the city skyline wrapped around layers of lemon sponge cake and cream-cheese mousse.

For something a little less precious (but still uptown), **Blue Grotto**'s desserts are as sweet as the restaurant is stylish. The high-backed booths under the skylights, at the rear of the long, narrow restaurant, are the perfect place to indulge in the Chocolate Three Way, an orgy of flavors and textures that's wickedly delicious.

Although the polite, polished waitstaff at **Gramercy Tavern** will always allow a dessert-only diner, it's best to sit up front in the Tavern Room. Beautifully plated desserts, like smooth milk-chocolate crème brûlée and Italian-plum crisp with cinnamon ice cream, are even more engaging than the attractive crowd sipping wine at the bar.

Who needs dinner when you can have three courses of dessert? Throngs line up for a late-night seat at the chic white counter at **ChikaLicious**, the East Village's all-sweets bar. Sleek and petite (much like the clientele), the desserts here are arranged so exquisitely that it's almost a shame to eat them. Almost. The three-course prix-fixe menu costs $12 (wine pairings are available for $7 a glass) and changes daily. You'll start with an *amuse-bouche* (like basil gelée with peach sorbet), move on to a main-course dessert (like a warm chocolate tart served with pink-peppercorn ice cream and red wine sauce) and end with a selection of petit fours.

The least ceremonious (but possibly the most romantic) option is the **Magnolia Bakery**. As you wander through the picturesque West Village streets, the sweet smell of butter and sugar should lead you to a long line of cupcake-seekers winding out the door of this perpetually crowded bakery, which stays open till 11:30pm on weekdays and 12:30am on weekends. The old-timey windows are filled with trays of fluffy cupcakes topped with thick swirls of pastel-colored frosting. Mind the dozen-per-person limit and grab two (or four), find yourself a nearby stoop, and have a moment of bake-sale bliss.

Morrells Restaurant

900 Broadway at 20th St (212-253-0900). Subway: R, W to 23rd St. **Open** *Mon–Fri noon–2:30pm, 6–11pm; Sat 6–11pm.* **Average main course** *$25.* **Credit** *AmEx, Disc, MC, V.*

Morrells is a sleek Flatiron spin-off of Rockefeller Center's Morrell and Co. wine store and its adjacent Morrell Wine Bar & Café. At press time, new chef Patricia Williams was still developing her menu, but expect plenty of wine-friendly takes on contemporary American standards. The chunky wine list (more than a thousand bottles) should please oenophiles of all stripes, especially those with some cash to spend (the under-$40 section is pretty skimpy). The best value is at the bar, where great vino (150 types!) can be sampled by the glass with a reasonably priced, casual pub-food menu that includes well-chosen cheese and charcuterie plates and a solid $14 burger with zinfandel ketchup.

Other location *Morrell Wine Bar & Café, 1 Rockefeller Plaza between 48th and 49th Sts (212-262-7700).*

Union Square Cafe

21 E 16th St between Fifth Ave and Union Sq West (212-243-4020). Subway: L, N, Q, R, W, 4, 5, 6 to 14th St–Union Sq. **Open** *Sun–Thu noon–2:30pm, 6–10:15pm; Fri, Sat noon–2:30pm, 6–11:15pm.* **Average main course** *$26.* **Credit** *AmEx, DC, Disc, MC, V.*

Danny Meyer's magic formula for business-casual dining is nearly 20 years old, but it simply doesn't age. Union Square Cafe's meandering dining room is lined with high-gloss, dark-green wainscoting; servers are clad in cotton button-downs; and formalities like white tablecloths and a 13-page wine list are brought down to earth with wicker chairs and a discount wine of the night. Chef Michael Romano keeps the reliable, refined cuisine coming: creamy crab risotto with a kick of lemon, straight-off-the-grill lamb chops and buttery cod that falls apart in a sea of heartily seasoned lentils. The challenge, as every regular knows, is to finish the generous entrée and still put away a passion-fruit napoleon or an espresso-flavored panna cotta with dark-chocolate sorbet.

Blue Grotto

1576 Third Ave between 88th and 89th Sts (212-426-3200). Subway: 4, 5, 6 to 86th St. **Open** *Mon, Tue 5–10pm; Wed, Thu 5–11pm; Fri, Sat 5pm–midnight; Sun 11am–3pm, 5–10pm.* **Average dessert** *$8.* **Credit** *AmEx, DC, Disc, MC, V.*

ChikaLicious

203 E 10th St between First and Second Aves (212-995-9511). Subway: L to Third Ave; 6 to Astor Pl. **Open** *Tue–Sun 3pm–midnight.* **Average dessert** *$12.* **Credit** *MC, V.*

Gramercy Tavern

42 E 20th St between Broadway and Park Ave South (212-477-0777). Subway: R, W, 6 to 23rd St. **Open** *Sun–Thu noon–11pm; Fri, Sat noon–midnight.* **Average dessert** *$8.* **Credit** *AmEx, DC, Disc, MC, V.*

Magnolia Bakery

401 Bleecker St at 11th St (212-462-2572). Subway: 1, 9 to Christopher St–Sheridan Sq. **Open** *Sun, Mon 10am–11:30pm; Tue–Thu 9am–11:30pm; Fri 9am–12:30am; Sat 10am–12:30am.* **Average dessert** *$2.* **Credit** *AmEx, MC, V.*

Payard Pâtisserie & Bistro

1032 Lexington Ave between 73rd and 74th Sts (212-717-5252). Subway: 6 to 77th St. **Open** *Mon–Sat 7am–11pm.* **Average dessert** *$4.* **Credit** *AmEx, DC, MC, V.*

Rhymes with delicious Lick those sorbet cravings at desserts-only **ChikaLicious**.

Cafés

City Bakery

3 W 18th St between Fifth and Sixth Aves (212-366-1414). Subway: L, N, Q, R, W, 4, 5, 6 to 14th St–Union Sq. **Open** *Mon–Fri 7:30am–7pm; Sat 7:30am–6pm; Sun 9am–6pm.* **Salad bar** *$12 per pound.* **Credit** *AmEx, MC, V.*

Maury Rubin's City Bakery made its name with fabulously chic tarts and sleek, modernist cakes; though the bakery side's still going strong, most locals now come here to hit the gorgeously stocked salad bar, or to sip fresh fruit-spiked lemonade (in summer) or supercreamy, super-rich hot chocolate with housemade marshmallows (in winter). The kitchen's allegiance to fresh-from-the-Greenmarket produce is apparent in nearly every dish. Food sells by weight and adds up fast, so if you want to get off cheap, avoid heavy items (roasted beets, fruit salad) and pile on comparatively light ones (tofu-skin salad, roasted green tomatoes).

French

Les Halles

411 Park Ave South between 28th and 29th Sts (212-679-4111). Subway: 6 to 28th St. **Open** *Noon–midnight daily.* **Average main course** *$19.* **Credit** *AmEx, DC, Disc, MC, V.*

Is Anthony Bourdain in the kitchen? Fans of the hedonistic celebrity chef's books and TV shows want to know. It's certainly a packed house—loud, cramped and underlit. First clue on what to order: a meat case filled with entrecôte, *filet de boeuf* and *côte d'agneau.* Clue number two: the steak knife at every place setting. The rest of the menu includes the usual suspects: onion soup, frisée salad with *lardons,* duck confit and *boudin noir.* So, *is* Bourdain at the stove? As the French hostess told us, "'E ez not 'ere. 'E ez too famoos." No matter. The flavorful steaks still show his flair.

Other location *15 John St between Broadway and Nassau St (212-285-8585).*

Indian

Tabla

11 Madison Ave at 25th St (212-889-0667). Subway: R, W, 6 to 23rd St. **Open** *Mon–Fri noon–2pm, 5:30–10:30pm; Sat, Sun 5:30–10:30pm.* **Prix fixe** *$54–$88.* **Credit** *AmEx, DC, Disc, MC, V.*

Bombay-bred and French-trained chef Floyd Cardoz melds Indian spices with seasonal produce and a glamorous New York sensibility; imagine a hunk of flaky halibut served with bold, sweet watermelon curry. Even desserts get multiculti: Classic chocolate soufflé comes with cinnamon-clove ice cream. While the more formal Tabla on the upper floor gets all the press, the diners at the downstairs Bread Bar sometimes seem to be having more fun—sipping Tablatinis infused with lemongrass, nibbling on nan fresh from the blazing tandoor and sharing small dishes inspired by Indian street food.

Other location *Tabla Bread Bar, 11 Madison Ave at 25th St (212-889-0667).*

Vegetarian & Organic

Bonobo's Vegetarian

18 E 23rd St between Broadway and Park Ave South (212-505-1200). Subway: R, W, 6 to 23rd St. **Open** *Mon–Sat 11:30am–10pm.* **Average main course** *$12.* **Credit** *AmEx, Disc, MC, V.*

This new raw-foods (nothing is heated over 118 degrees) cafeteria is a detoxer's dream: protein-rich nut pâtes, vegetable lasagna layered with sheets of crunchy flax crackers, shredded raw squash "spaghetti" topped with vegetable puree, plus, naturally, a well-stocked salad bar. Eat up your veggies and you can splurge on dessert: loads of exotic fruit, frozen fudge and vegan ice creams and sorbets.

Midtown West

For Daisy May's BBQ USA, *see p184* **Smokin' hot**.

American

Market Cafe

496 Ninth Ave between 37th and 38th Sts (212-564-7350). Subway: A, C, E to 34th St–Penn Station. **Open** *Mon–Sat 11am–11pm.* **Average main course** *$12.* **Credit** *AmEx, DC, Disc, MC, V.*

If only every neighborhood had a place like this, where you can get straightforward food for diner prices. Stylish young things, Javits Center attendees and cops mount the '50s-era barstools at the long counter, or chat at Formica-topped tables in blue vinyl booths. A big bowl of rigatoni tossed with grilled chicken, tomato, Parmesan and basil is yours for only $9, while the steak frites is a whopping $12. Great wines by the glass add to the unhurried mood.

Mix in New York

68 W 58th St between Fifth and Sixth Aves (212-583-0300). Subway: F to 57th St; N, R, W to Fifth Ave–59th St. **Open** *Mon–Fri 11am–2:30pm, 5:30–10:15pm; Sat, Sun 5:30–10:30pm.* **Average main course** *$36.* **Credit** *AmEx, DC, MC, V.*

Trend-magnet Jeffrey Chodorow, the finance man behind Rocco's, is partnered with Alain Ducasse on this high-profile midtown restaurant. Ducasse, known for his ultra-expensive, superhaute French cuisine, has left the day-to-day cooking to the young but talented Doug Psaltis, who mixes his all-American background with Ducasse's Gallic flights of fancy. The confusing prix fixe menu can be tricky to navigate, but it's worth it for the chicken potpie, the succulent pork-greens-and-cornbread combo and at dessert time, chocolate pizza.

Mirror, mirror Located in a modernist landmark, **Lever House** reflects well on its diners. *See p191.*

Mexican

Hell's Kitchen

679 Ninth Ave between 46th and 47th Sts (212-977-1588). Subway: C, E to 50th St. **Open** *Sun, Mon 5–11pm; Tue–Fri 11:30am–3:30pm, 5pm–midnight; Sat 5pm–midnight.* **Average main course** *$18.* **Credit** *AmEx, MC, V.*

This eatery's loose but sophisticated interpretation of Mexican food starts with a complimentary crock of black beans, corn and cilantro drizzled with a creamy poblano sauce, perfect for dipping the thin triangles of sweet corn bread. Plantain empanadas filled with goat cheese or duck confit swim in pools of tomato coulis or fig *mole,* respectively. Entrées are sauced-up too: A potato pancake is piled with mushrooms and goat cheese, and it gets both sweetness and spark from a grape-chipotle sauce. Reservations are recommended.

Moroccan

Kemia Bar

630 Ninth Ave at 44th St (212-582-3200). Subway: A, C, E to 42nd St–Port Authority. **Open** *Mon–Sat 6–11pm.* **Average small plate** *$7.* **Credit** *AmEx, MC, V.*

"I love the movie *Casablanca,*" says owner Zoughbi Djamal, who set out to create a Moroccan speakeasy in the space beneath the French brasserie Marseille. Sip a lychee martini, tickle your toes on rose petals underfoot, and fall into a trance while staring at the colorful canopies overhead. Marseille chef Alex Ureña oversees the kitchen, which makes inexpensive North African meze like spicy merguez sausage and couscous-crusted shrimp, along with main dishes like chicken tagine with olives and potatoes. It's clear Djamal knows that fundamental things apply.

Steakhouses

Keens Steakhouse

72 W 36th St between Fifth and Sixth Aves (212-947-3636). Subway: B, D, F, V, N, Q, R, W to 34th St–Herald Sq. **Open** *Mon–Fri 11:45am–3pm, 5:30–10:30pm; Sat 5–10:30pm; Sun 4–8pm.* **Average main course** *$32.* **Credit** *AmEx, DC, Disc, MC, V.*

At 140-year-old Keens, once a private men's club, you get the allure of a New York that is no more. Beveled-glass doors, a working fireplace and a forest's worth of dark wood suggest the days when the legendary Diamond Jim Brady piled his table with bushels of oyster, slabs of beef and troughs of ale. Sirloin and porterhouse (for two) hold their own against any steak in the city. Lunch is a bargain in the tavern: A crisp disk of prime-rib hash topped with a fried egg is only $10.

The Buddha at **Tao.**
See p191.

Midtown East

American

Lever House

390 Park Ave between 53rd and 54th Sts (212-888-2700). Subway: E, V to Lexington Ave–53rd St; 6 to 51st St. **Open** *Mon–Thu 5:30–11pm; Fri, Sat 5:30–11:30pm; Sun 5–10pm.* **Average main course** *$27.* **Credit** *AmEx, DC, Disc, MC, V.*

When it was built in 1952, the gorgeously modernist Lever House was the talk of the town. Fifty-two years later, the trailblazing skyscraper has its first restaurant, already a power-lunching destination. Union Square Cafe veteran Dan Silverman oversees the seasonal menu. Recent dishes have included lobster tempura, salmon ceviche sparked with lime and cilantro, golden-skinned *poussin* in foie gras sauce, and Colorado lamb over fava beans. Pastry chef Deborah Snyder celebrates straightforward American flavors with treats like cranberry-pecan tart, apple beignets, even corn ice cream.

French

Artisanal

2 Park Ave at 32nd St (212-725-8585). Subway: 6 to 33rd St. **Open** *Mon–Thu noon–11pm; Fri, Sat noon–midnight; Sun 11am–3pm, 5–10pm.* **Average main course** *$23.* **Credit** *AmEx, MC, V.*

At Artisanal, 250 varieties of cheese—chèvres and cheddars, Gorgonzolas and Gruyères, Robiolas and Reblochons—are displayed as if they were prize orchids. Chef-owner Terrance Brennan nods to Alsace with his *boudin blanc,* rillettes and rabbit in riesling with shredded rutabaga "sauerkraut." Crisp skate takes to its blood-orange sauce like a party girl to a Cosmopolitan. Still, this is the place to discover just how much cheese you can really handle. An appetizer of raclette? A basket of puffy *gougères*? How about a cheese plate for dessert? About 160 wines in the cellar are available by the glass, all the better to pair with your favorite…cheese.

Kosher

Box Tree

Box Tree Inn, 250 E 49th St between Second and Third Aves (212-758-8320). Subway: E, V to Lexington Ave–53rd St; 6 to 51st St. **Open** *Mon–Thu noon–3pm, 5–11pm; Fri, Sat noon–3pm; Sun 5–10pm.* **Average main course** *$34.* **Credit** *AmEx, MC, V.*

A lovely East Side townhouse with Tiffany stained glass, gold-leaf ceilings, an Art Nouveau staircase and…a mezuzah? The contemporary kosher-French cuisine by Alexandre Petard (who worked under Christian Delouvrier at Lespinasse and Jean Georges) sets a new glatt standard with pistachio-crusted halibut and salmon-and-tuna tartare brightened by sesame, ginger and guacamole. A spectacular 22-ounce Delmonico steak, accented with soy and ginger, could easily feed four. For a more casual, less expensive option, try Branch on the main floor.

Mexican

Mamá Mexico

214 E 49th St between Second and Third Aves (212-935-1316). Subway: E, V to Lexington Ave–53rd St; 6 to 51st St. **Open** *Sun–Wed noon–midnight; Thu–Sat noon–2am.* **Average main course** *$17.* **Credit** *AmEx, MC, V.*

Around seven every night, a strolling mariachi band fills this festive cantina with song, and 100 varieties of tequila doled out by the flirtatious staff soften up the corporate masses. Color is everywhere—from wall mirrors stenciled with images of Mayan deities to seat cushions striped in eye-popping fuchsia, green and purple. Tex-Mex standards—tamales, burritos—are foolproof choices, but Mamá's fish dishes excel, especially the red snapper soup and the heaping platter of spicy seafood paella.

Other location *2672 Broadway between 101st and 102nd Sts (212-864-2323).*

Pan-Asian

Tao

42 E 58th St between Madison and Park Aves (212-888-2288). Subway: N, R, W to Fifth Ave–59th St. **Open** *Mon, Tue 11:30am–midnight; Wed–Fri 11:30am–1am; Sat 5pm–1am; Sun 5pm–midnight.* **Average main course** *$22.* **Credit** *AmEx, DC, MC, V.*

A magnificent, scenic palace, Tao is packed to the glowing Chinese lanterns with wealthy businessmen, trendy Manhattanites and intrepid suburbanites. The bar is eternally thronged, and the stunning dining room has a Hollywood-Zen feel, thanks to curly bamboo, Eastern art and a 16-foot, 4,000-pound stone Buddha. The menu—yes, there's food—offers generic small plates (dumplings, satay) and decent entrées. Tao is one of New York's first restaurants to serve Kobe beef, and it's worth ponying up for the buttery pleasure of a few ounces, which you cook at your table on a hot stone.

Seafood

Grand Central Oyster Bar & Restaurant

Grand Central Terminal, Lower Concourse, 42nd St at Park Ave (212-490-6650). Subway: 42nd St S, 4, 5, 6, 7 to 42nd St–Grand Central. **Open** *Mon–Fri 11:30am–9:30pm; Sat noon–9:30pm.* **Average main course** *$22.* **Credit** *AmEx, DC, Disc, MC, V.*

This 90-year-old landmark, nestled in the basement of Grand Central Terminal, is still Eden for oyster lovers. There are two large dining rooms, but the white-topped counter is the best place to sit. Some 30 varieties of oysters, including harder-to-find bivalves like Virginia's Chincoteagues, are served on the half shell with a kicky mignonette sauce. Creamy oyster stews, clam chowder and Dungeness-crabmeat cocktails shine, but nonoyster entrées can be lackluster. No worries, though: The Oyster Bar is also known for its gargantuan homemade desserts.

Spanish

Solera

216 E 53rd St at Third Ave (212-644-1166). Subway: E, V to Lexington Ave–53rd St. **Open** *Mon–Fri noon–11pm; Sat 4:30–11pm.* **Average main course** *$29.* **Credit** *AmEx, DC, Disc, MC, V.*
After office hours, young execs come to this brownstone tapas bar and restaurant to congregate over sangria, sherries and tasty bites like sautéed chorizo and grilled anchovies. In the lovely buttery-yellow back dining room, the chatter softens. The staff is knowledgeable about the well-prepared Iberian classics—rich garlic shrimp, sautéed matchstick-size baby eels, grilled grouper. The three-cheese plate, paired with sherry, makes a delicious, urbane finish.

Upper West Side

American Creative

Ouest

2315 Broadway between 83rd and 84th Sts (212-580-8700). Subway: 1, 9 to 86th St. **Open** *Tue–Thu 5–10:30pm; Fri, Sat 5–11:30pm; Sun 10am–2pm, 5–10:30pm.* **Average main course** *$24.* **Credit** *AmEx, DC, Disc, MC, V.*
Ouest's big round booths are filled just about every night with Upper West Side diners clamoring for braised lamb shanks and fork-tender short ribs. Chef Tom Valenti handles brawny ingredients with delicate intensity, as in a pan-roasted sturgeon served with risotto that's been cooked in a truffled wild-mushroom broth. But Sunday is still meat loaf night—high-end, dressed-down food for a dressed-up crowd.

Delis

Barney Greengrass—The Sturgeon King

541 Amsterdam Ave between 86th and 87th Sts (212-724-4707). Subway: B, C, 1, 9 to 86th St. **Open** *Tue–Fri 8:30am–4pm; Sat, Sun 8:30am–5pm.* **Average main course** *$13.* **Credit** *Cash only.*
The decor's pretty shabby, but this legendary deli and restaurant is a madhouse at weekend brunch. Egg platters with succulent sturgeon or silky Nova Scotia salmon are a relative bargain at $12, since you won't be hungry again for weeks. Ditto the sandwiches, such as satiny smoked sablefish on pumpernickel. For tasty sipping, try the cold, creamy pink borscht, served straight up in a glass.

French

Aix

2293 Broadway at 88th St (212-874-7400). Subway: 1, 9 to 86th St. **Open** *Mon–Fri 5pm–midnight; Sat 11am–4pm, 5pm–midnight; Sun 11am–4pm, 5–11pm.* **Average main course** *$22.* **Credit** *AmEx, MC, V.*

24/7

Getting up early, coming home late: No matter what time it is, you'll eat, drink and be happy at these round-the-clock establishments.

Anytime
Sandwiches, burgers and more are available for Billyburg's hungry hipsters. *93 North 6th St between Berry St and Wythe Ave, Williamsburg, Brooklyn (718-218-7272).*

Bereket
This is a Lower East Side favorite for late-night Turkish delights. *187 E Houston St at Orchard St (212-475-7700).*

Empire Diner
Glammed-up food in a slick diner setting is an all-hours must for the Chelsea art crowd. *210 Tenth Ave at 22nd St (212-243-2736).*

Florent
Drag queens mix with fashionistas at this longtime Meatpacking District fave. *69 Gansevoort St between Greenwich and Washington Sts (212-989-5779).*

Lahore
Cabbies and clubbers alike fuel up on samosas, chai and take-out Pakistani specials. *132 Crosby St between Houston and Prince Sts (212-965-1777).*

Veselka
This Ukrainian institution serves borscht, kielbasa and pierogi round the clock. *144 Second Ave at 9th St (212-228-9682).*

Won Jo
Get potent postkaraoke Korean barbecue anytime. *23 W 32nd St between Fifth Ave and Broadway (212-695-5815).*

It has to hurt a man's ego to see his namesake restaurant replaced by Britney Spears's short-lived Nyla. But Didier Virot moved on and opened Aix to great acclaim. The meandering two-story space, formerly Boulevard, has been gutted and transformed into a warm, colorful wainscoted home for Virot's creative Provençal cooking. On his inaugural menu: *pistou* with sardine tartare, *daurade* with fennel broth, and venison loin with quince-beet strudel.

Nice Matin

201 W 79th St between Amsterdam Ave and Broadway (212-873-6423). Subway: 1, 9 to 79th St. **Open** *Sun–Thu 5pm–midnight; Fri, Sat 5pm–1am.* **Average main course** *$16.* **Credit** *AmEx, DC, MC, V.*

The breezy dining room at Nice Matin, inspired by cafés of the French Riviera, is lined with busy yellow, maroon and lime-green wallpaper, and lit by giant fixtures that mimic the tops of carousels. Owner Simon Oren and chef Andy D'Amico named the place after Nice's morning paper, and they serve Niçoise flavors from start to finish: *pissaladière* (pizza with caramelized onions, olives and thyme), fennel-cured mackerel with grapefruit, and grilled leg of lamb with flageolets.

Italian

'Cesca

164 W 75th St between Columbus and Amsterdam Aves (212-787-6300). Subway: 1, 2, 3, 9 to 72nd St. **Open** *Tue–Thu, Sun 5–11pm; Fri, Sat 5–11:30pm. Wine bar Tue–Thu 5pm–midnight; Fri, Sat 5pm–1am; Sun 5–11pm.* **Average main course** *$27.* **Credit** *AmEx, DC, Disc, MC, V.*

Tom Valenti has done it again: The savvy Italian-American chef has opened another Upper West Side clubhouse for his well-heeled, pasta-loving patrons. Start with irresistible Parmesan fritters, marinated baby artichokes with creamy fresh ricotta, or wild-mushroom–studded *arancini* (fried rice balls), then move on to lusty Southern Italian–inspired pastas, followed by great *secondi* like caponata-crusted swordfish and hunky lamb shanks.

Mexican

Rosa Mexicano

61 Columbus Ave at 62nd St (212-977-7700). Subway: 1, 9 to 66th St–Lincoln Ctr. **Open** *Sun, Mon noon–3pm, 5–10:30pm; Tue–Sat noon–3pm, 5pm–midnight.* **Average main course** *$23.* **Credit** *AmEx, DC, Disc, MC, V.*

If you know Rosa's comfortably worn-in location on First Avenue, the Technicolor journey up vivid terrazzo steps into the cavernous dining room at Rosa II might make you wonder if this child is really related to its mother. But the famous guacamole is still loaded with fresh cilantro, and mahimahi ceviche teeters in a zingy tower. As the waiter unwraps a parchment package of braised lamb shank, the rich aroma of chili, cumin and cloves envelops the table. Veracruz-style red snapper is stuffed with crab in a punchy sauce of tomatoes, olives and capers. Owner Josefina Howard has retired from the kitchen, but her restaurants carry on her legacy with confidence.
Other location *1063 First Ave at 58th St (212-753-7407).*

Upper East Side

For Pearson's Texas Barbecue, *see p184* **Smokin' hot**.

American Creative

Aureole

34 E 61st St between Madison and Park Aves (212-319-1660). Subway: N, R, W to Fifth Ave–59th St. **Open** *Mon–Fri noon–2:30pm, 5:30–10pm; Sat 5–10:30pm.* **Prix fixe** *$69.* **Credit** *AmEx, DC, Disc, MC, V.*

Charlie Palmer first made his name at this glass-fronted townhouse, with its maroon leather banquettes and dramatic floral arrangements. Now Palmer's empire extends from Washington, D.C., to Vegas, which leaves Aureole in the competent hands of chef Dante Boccuzzi. Stop eating the delicious breadsticks and begin twirling a haystack of soba noodles with ruby-red tuna sashimi dressed in soy, lime and cilantro. Pan-roasting perfects a wedge of halibut, gilded with foamy asparagus sabayon. You'll be sent home with a decadent chocolate-orange tea cake—but do dip into the bowl of foil-wrapped candied citrus peels on your way out.

Argentine

Hacienda de Argentina

339 E 75th St between First and Second Aves (212-472-5300). Subway: 6 to 77th St. **Open** *Sun–Tue 5pm–midnight; Wed–Sat 5pm–3am.* **Average main course** *$18.* **Credit** *AmEx, MC, V.*

The decor here is *estancia*-chic, with high-backed cowhide chairs and candelabra from Buenos Aires. Consulting chef Patricia Douek Pirotte cooks food as authentic as the backdrop. Empanadas ring true, especially the chicken with red, yellow and green peppers. Grass-fed *bife de chorizo* (sirloin) is simply seasoned with rock salt and pepper. Indulge in an extensive Argentine wine list, and wallow in a space as wide as the pampas. Isn't it good to be *el patrón*?

Austrian

Café Sabarsky

Neue Galerie New York, 1048 Fifth Ave at 86th St (212-288-0665). Subway: 4, 5, 6 to 86th St. **Open** *Mon, Wed 9am–6pm; Thu–Sun 9am–9pm.* **Average main course** *$14.* **Credit** *AmEx, MC, V.*

Seems like Café Sabarsky gets more daytime business than the elegant museum of German and Austrian art that houses it. Superb beef goulash makes the perfect winter lunch, as does cod strudel with riesling sauerkraut. In spring, don't pass up *spargel*, the white asparagus that Austrians and Germans go crazy for. In the afternoon, a well-heeled neighborhood crowd settles in for rich *kaffee mit schlag* (coffee with whipped cream) and a spectacular spread of Viennese tortes and pastries, including marvelously flaky apple strudel and lavish chocolate-and-nut confections. On select Fridays, Sabarsky hosts a $95 prix-fixe dinner and cabaret.

French

Daniel

60 E 65th St between Madison and Park Aves (212-288-0033). Subway: F to Lexington Ave–63rd St; 6 to 68th St–Hunter College. **Open** *Mon–Sat 5:45–11pm.* **Prix fixe** *$85–$160.* **Credit** *AmEx, DC, MC, V.*

Daniel Boulud's haute French cuisine is almost upstaged by its exuberant setting; the playfully ornate ceiling, towering flower arrangements and backslapping power brokers might overwhelm food that was merely excellent. But with Boulud at the helm, that's impossible. A tower of velvety tuna is encased in radish slices, spiked with creamy wasabi and Meyer lemon dressings, and topped with sevruga caviar. Roasted lamb medallions are as tender as the tuna and jazzed up with rosemary-citrus glaze. This kind of perfection is pricey, but if you can swing it, the amazement is worth the tab. Boulud's mini-empire also includes the stylish Café Boulud and midtown's DB Bistro Moderne (home of his famous $29 truffles–and–foie-gras burger).

Other locations *Café Boulud, 20 E 76th St between Fifth and Madison Aves (212-772-2600); DB Bistro Moderne, 55 W 44th St between Fifth and Sixth Aves (212-391-2400).*

Above 116th Street

American

Kitchenette Uptown

1272 Amsterdam Ave between 122nd and 123rd Sts (212-531-7600). Subway: 1, 9 to 125th St. **Open** *8am–11pm daily.* **Average main course** *$13.* **Credit** *AmEx, DC, MC, V.*

Riding the wave of South Harlem gentrification, Kitchenette Uptown brings its Tribeca country dining to a sunlit space in Morningside Heights. At brunch, order the BLT on challah—it does cartwheels around the egg dishes. Hearty cheese grits with homemade turkey sausage and biscuits also make a great meal, followed by a down-home slice of cherry pie. The all-day breakfast and weekend brunch attract a lively group of university types, as does the BYOB dinner with chicken potpie and four-cheese macaroni.

Other location *Kitchenette, 80 West Broadway at Warren St (212-267-6740).*

American Regional

Londel's Supper Club

2620 Frederick Douglass Blvd (Eighth Ave) between 139th and 140th Sts (212-234-6114). Subway: A, C, B, D to 145th St. **Open** *Tue–Sat 11:30am–4pm, 5–11pm; Sun noon–5pm.* **Average main course** *$20.* **Credit** *AmEx, DC, Disc, MC, V.*

For a Yankee town, New York sure has a lot of soul-food options, and Londel's is one of the choicest. Tuxedoed waiters serve fried chicken that's molar-rattlingly crunchy. The secret: It's fried, then baked. Other standards prove as tasty, including the cornmeal-crusted whiting fingers, blackened catfish fillet, and mac and cheese bound by ribbons of crisped cheddar. Live music adds to the good-time feel: The third Thursday of the month is R&B; Friday and Saturday focus on jazz; and Sunday is, of course, gospel.

Caribbean

Native

101 W 118th St at Malcolm X Blvd (Lenox Ave) (212-665-2525). Subway: 2, 3 to 116th St. **Open** *Mon–Thu 11am–11pm; Fri, Sat 11am–midnight; Sun 11am–10pm.* **Average main course** *$12.* **Credit** *AmEx, MC, V.*

This loungey, brick-walled restaurant and bar draws a hip Harlem crowd. The small dining room is lined with velvet banquettes and lit with funky wall sconces. The food from chef Brian Washington-Palmer (Bleu Evolution) is just as cool, ranging from an all-in-one bowl of red rice, black beans, garlicky spinach and fried plantains to spicy blackened snapper, and a seafood cobbler of scallops and crab swimming in coconut-curry broth. And Native's take on fried chicken—a panfried cutlet over mashed potatoes and collards in cumin cream sauce—is a successful original.

Brooklyn

For Biscuit, *see p184* **Smokin' hot**.

American

Blue Ribbon Brooklyn

280 Fifth Ave between Garfield Pl and 1st St, Park Slope, Brooklyn (718-840-0404). Subway: M, R to Union St. **Open** *Tue–Thu 6pm–2am; Fri 6pm–4am; Sat noon–4pm, 6pm–4am; Sun noon–4pm, 6pm–midnight.* **Average main course** *$20.* **Credit** *AmEx, DC, MC, V.*

Park Slopers know that this moderately upscale eatery, a spin-off of Soho's Blue Ribbon, is the place to bring everyone from hamburger-chomping buddies to oyster-loving dates. While it's known for its killer raw bar and fresh seafood, the secret to its success lies in upbeat homestyle favorites: The hamburger is smothered with blue cheese; the Blue Reuben gets a little zing from chorizo. Escargots and

Say cheese Get your piece of the pie at **Grimaldi's**, a Brooklyn favorite. *See p196.*

foie gras are on the appetizer menu alongside french fries and hummus; they're all expertly prepared and presented. Everything is available until the wee hours, fueling a buzzing after-midnight scene.
Other location *Blue Ribbon, 97 Sullivan St between Prince and Spring Sts (212-274-0404).*

Diner

85 Broadway at Berry St, Williamsburg, Brooklyn (718-486-3077). Subway: J, M, Z to Marcy Ave.
Open *Sun–Thu 11am–4pm, 6pm–midnight; Fri, Sat 11am–4pm, 6pm–1am.* **Average main course** *$14.* **Credit** *MC, V.*
These days, you know that a Williamsburg restaurant called Diner won't be just a diner (the same way a Chelsea restaurant called Snackbar won't be serving just nachos and soda). Since 1999, when owners Andrew Tarlow and Mark Firth renovated an old train-car–shaped diner, Diner has proved that it's possible to be both hip and grown-up. Menu basics include sweet steamed mussels and juicy burgers, but the kitchen's real talents are revealed in the long list of specials—moist pork tenderloin, whole *branzino* with spicy Spanish rice—scribbled on the paper tablecloths.

American Creative

River Café

1 Water St at Old Fulton St, Dumbo, Brooklyn (718-522-5200). Subway: A, C to High St; F to York St. **Open** *Mon–Sat noon–3pm, 5:30–11pm; Sun 11:30am–3pm, 5:30–11pm.* **Prix fixe** *$70.*
Credit *AmEx, DC, Disc, MC, V.*
From your table aboard this genteel barge, anchored at the foot of the Brooklyn Bridge, you can gaze at the twinkling Financial District, and feel blissfully between boroughs. The menu adds global elements to make classic American dishes sparkle. Wake up your taste buds with a kicky Taylor Bay scallop ceviche. Move on to a pancetta-wrapped black sea bass with fondant potatoes and a briny vinaigrette. The wine list is pricey, but a few affordable offerings and a thoughtful selection of half bottles lessen the strain.

Eclectic

Chickenbone Café

177 South 4th St between Driggs Ave and Roebling St, Williamsburg, Brooklyn (718-302-2663). Subway: L to Bedford Ave; J, M, Z to Marcy Ave.
Open *Tue–Thu 5–11pm; Fri–Sun 5pm–2am.*
Average main course *$10.* **Credit** *MC, V.*
This former auto-repair garage has been lined with cedar planks and now resembles a brand-new mountain cabin transplanted to a scruffy Brooklyn block. The short sandwich-and-salads menu is augmented by daily specials: an addictive Cuban sandwich; braised, off-the-bone short ribs; or lacquered eel over rice. *Tartiflette* (a casserole of potato, Reblochon and bacon) is Savoyard comfort food with a bite; the luscious pressed beef-and-fontina sandwich is best balanced by a bowl of pungent North Fork greens.

Still in bloom A clubby feel, tropical drinks and fine cheap eats keep reliable **SEA** afloat.

Italian

Al Di Là

248 Fifth Ave at Carroll St, Park Slope, Brooklyn (718-783-4565). Subway: M, R to Union St.
Open *Mon, Wed, Thu 6–10:30pm; Fri, Sat 6–11pm; Sun 6–10pm.* **Average main course** *$15.* **Credit** *MC, V.*

Superb food, limited seating and a no-reservations policy means a wait no matter when you arrive. However, it's worth hanging around; husband-and-wife team Emiliano Coppa and Anna Klinger (the chef) prepare serious Northern Italian fare and serve it with uncommon grace and good nature. Entrées include diaphanous ravioli stuffed with beets and ricotta, and braised rabbit with black olives and polenta. The *gianduiotto*—a log of chocolate ice cream, chopped hazelnuts and whipped cream—is unbeatable.

Pizza

Grimaldi's

19 Old Fulton St between Front and Water Sts, Dumbo, Brooklyn (718-858-4300). Subway: A, C to High St; F to York St. **Open** *Mon–Thu 11:30am–11pm; Fri 11:30am–midnight; Sat noon–midnight; Sun noon–11pm.* **Large plain pizza** *$14.* **Credit** *Cash only.*

Long before the area was called Dumbo, Patsy Grimaldi was rotating pies in the 800-degree brick-walled coal oven. (He learned his trade from *the* Patsy, his uncle Patsy Lancieri.) The area's influx of professionals makes it hard to get a table on weekends.

Steakhouses

Peter Luger

178 Broadway at Driggs Ave, Williamsburg, Brooklyn (718-387-7400). Subway: J, M, Z to Marcy Ave.
Open *Sun–Thu 11:30am–10pm; Fri, Sat 11:30am–11pm.* **Steak for two** *$65.* **Credit** *Cash only.*

Does this Williamsburg landmark deserve its rep as one of the best steakhouses in America? You'll find few dissenters among those crowding the rustic dining rooms. Luger was established as a German beer hall in 1887, and eating here is a similarly communal, boisterous experience. The restaurant serves but one cut: a porterhouse that's charbroiled black on the outside, tender and pink on the inside. Service is slow, provided by crusty waiters who would rather give out wisecracks than water. A four-star experience this isn't, but the quality of the steak—less than one percent of all the beef slaughtered in America passes Luger's requirements—may make you forgive any shortcomings.

Thai

SEA Thai Restaurant and Bar

114 North 6th St at Berry St, Williamsburg, Brooklyn (718-384-8850). Subway: L to Bedford Ave. **Open** *Mon–Thu 11:30am–1am; Fri, Sat 11:30am–2am.* **Average main course** *$9.* **Credit** *AmEx, MC, V.*

You may mistake SEA for a nightclub, given the reverberating dance music and mod lounge furnished with a bubble-chair swing. Get a table by the central

pool, presided over by Buddha, and flip through the campy postcard menu—surprise! For a place so stylin', prices are cheap, and the food is remarkably good. Stuffed with shrimp and real crab, Jade Seafood Dumplings come with a nutty Massaman sauce, while the Queen of Siam beef with basil and red chili is best when you ask the kitchen to fire it up. Desserts are uncharacteristically hedonistic, but most diners just settle into another pomegranate mojito.
Other location *SEA, 75 Second Ave between 4th and 5th Sts (212-228-5505).*

Queens

American Creative

LIC Café

5-48 49th Ave between Vernon Blvd and 5th St, Long Island City, Queens (718-752-0282). Subway: 7 to Vernon Blvd–Jackson Ave. **Open** *Mon–Sat noon–4pm; Wed–Sat 6–10pm.* **Average main course** *$14.* **Credit** *AmEx, MC, V.*
LIC Café's owner, French-trained caterer Peter Yurasits, serves his inventive yet inexpensive cuisine to an avid audience (so far, dinner is Wednesday to Saturday only). At this comfortably modern, clubby little eatery, tablehopping, BYOB-sharing and CD requests are the norm. So are phenomenally flavorful takes on familiar dishes like pesto pasta, crab cakes and teriyaki salmon.

French

Tournesol

50-12 Vernon Blvd between 50th and 51st Aves, Long Island City, Queens (718-472-4355). Subway: 7 to Vernon Blvd–Jackson Ave. **Open** *Tue–Fri 11:30am–3pm, 5:30–11:30pm; Sat 11:30am–3:30pm, 5:30–11:30pm; Sun 11:30am–3:30pm, 5–10pm.* **Average main course** *$15.* **Credit** *Cash only.*
Someday, Long Island City sophisticates may debate what sparked the real-estate bang: MoMA QNS or this busy, terrific little restaurant. You have to leave the inner borough to score such succulent foie gras or gratifyingly garlicky escargots for under $10. Continue on with brasserie classics like tender steak frites and crisp grilled chicken, accompanied by an alluringly regional French wine list.

Italian

Manetta's Fine Foods

1076 Jackson Ave at 49th Ave, Long Island City, Queens (718-786-6171). Subway: 7 to Vernon Blvd–Jackson Ave. **Open** *Mon–Thu 11:30am–10pm; Fri 11:30am–11pm; Sat 3:30–11pm.* **Average main course** *$15.* **Credit** *AmEx, Disc, DC, MC, V.*
Owned and managed by several members of the Manetta clan, with a kitchen supervised by matriarch Filomena, this terra-cotta–tiled trattoria cossets its customers. A wood-burning brick oven produces mini marvels of crisp-crusted pizzas, topped with lusty *cacciatorini* sausage, smoked salmon or pesto. Pastas are deeply satisfying, especially the pasta *quattro formaggi,* which arrives aswim in molten cheese—it's balm for the soul.

Middle Eastern

Mombar

25-22 Steinway St between 25th and 28th Aves, Astoria, Queens (718-726-2356). Subway: G, R, V to Steinway St. **Open** *Tue–Sun 5–11pm.* **Average main course** *$18.* **Credit** *Cash only.*
Chef-owner Moustafa el Sayed designed the twinkling mosaics that adorn the walls and tables as well as the nouvelle-Egyptian menu, which is rife with creations like sesame-dipped phyllo bread, spiced sausage, crunchy garlic-kissed quail and molasses-glazed duck. Indecisive? Put yourself in the hands of the gracious, garrulous chef and simply ask for the $30 tasting menu.

Bronx

French

Le Refuge Inn

620 City Island Ave at Sutherland St, City Island, Bronx (718-885-2478). Travel: 6 to Pelham Bay Park, then Bx29 bus to Sutherland St.
Open *Tue–Sat 6–9pm; Sun noon–3pm, 6–9pm.*
Prix fixe *$45.* **Credit** *AmEx.*
A French country inn…in the Bronx? Bask in the Gallic charm of this sweet bed-and-breakfast inn and restaurant on City Island. Dine by the fireside or overlooking the harbor. As the name implies, you'll feel far, far away from the city as you choose between French classics like truffled duck-liver mousse and snails in puff pastry, followed by pan-seared striped bass or filet mignon.

Tax & tipping

Most New York restaurants don't add a service charge to the bill unless there are six or more in your party. Therefore, it's customary to add 15 to 20 percent of the total bill as a tip. The easiest way to figure out the amount is to double the 8.625 percent sales tax. Complain—preferably to a manager—if you feel service is under par, but only in the most extreme cases should you completely withhold a tip. Remember that servers are paid far below minimum wage, and rely on tips to pay the rent. Bartenders get tipped too: $1 a drink should ensure friendly pours until last call.

Bars

Here's to the high life!

Whether you're in the mood for cocktails at a posh hotel lounge, a luscious cabernet at a cozy neighborhood wine bar, or a cold brew at a dive with a rockin' juke, you've come to the right town to quench your thirst.

Downtown

Tribeca & South

Bread Tribeca

See p169 for listing.
Luigi Comandatore's ambitious sequel (to Spring Street) comes complete with a wood-burning oven and specialty cocktails to keep you toasty.

Les Halles

15 John St between Broadway and Nassau St (212-285-8585). See also p188.
A massive wooden bar welcomes Wall Streeters with 6 tap-drawn beers and 15 wines by the glass.

The Sanctum

Tribeca Grand Hotel, 2 Sixth Ave between Walker and White Sts (212-519-6800). Subway: A, C, E to Canal St; 1, 9 to Franklin St.
Open *Mon, Thu–Sat 9pm–4am.* **Average drink** *$12.* **Credit** *AmEx, DC, Disc, MC, V.*
The Tribeca Grand Hotel ups the ante on its Church Lounge with the addition of the Sanctum. Designed by Bill (Mr. Gucci Stores) Sofield and manned by a dream team of managers, music pros and bartenders, the Sanctum has a menu of ten newly minted drinks, along with ten classics, in a 50-seater with a *North by Northwest* patina of old elegance. It's white-hot—last year's New York Fashion Week found the Sanctum hosting designer Jeremy Scott's collection party, featuring DJs Trevor Jackson and Michelle Gaubert.

66

See p167 for listing.
The decor (stark white on white; Meier, Eames and Knoll) is uncommonly sleek, with drinks to match.

Chinatown & Little Italy

Bar Veloce

17 Cleveland Pl between Kenmare and Spring Sts (212-260-3200). Subway: R, W to Prince St; 6 to Spring St. **Open** *5pm–3am daily.* **Average drink** *$8.* **Credit** *AmEx, MC, V.*
That Vespa parked out front should clue you in to the crowd inside: hipsters and downtown types just ahead of the cool curve. Frederick Twomey's slim wine bar offers 30 medium-priced Italian vinos and a Mediterranean snack menu. Glowing backlit bottles and warm maple tones alternate with a rubber-and-rivets wall covering to create an aesthetic of clinical swank—even the bartenders dress in gray lab jackets and ties.
Other location *75 Second Ave between 11th and 12th Sts (212-966-7334).*

Double Happiness

173 Mott St between Broome and Grand Sts (212-941-1282). Subway: B, D to Grand St; J, M, Z to Bowery. **Open** *Sun–Wed 6pm–2am; Thu 6pm–3am; Fri, Sat 6pm–4am.* **Average drink** *$9.* **Credit** *MC, V.*
If you aren't already having an affair, you might want to start one here: This Asian-themed pub, buried underground in Chinatown, is made for trysts. Brave the steep stairs and you'll find yourself in a dark, stone-walled cave. Sources of happiness include lots of eye candy (downtowners file in Thursday through Saturday nights), clubby music (deejayed rock, funk and soul) and a cocktail list that one-ups the usual sappy choices with a soothing, potent green-tea martini.

Lower East Side

Bauhaus

196 Orchard St between Houston and Stanton Sts (212-477-1550). Subway: F, V to Lower East Side–Second Ave. **Open** *Tue–Sun 7pm–4am.* **Average drink** *$8.* **Credit** *AmEx, Disc, MC, V.*
Created by two FIT interior-design grads, Bauhaus is named after the 1920s movement that synthesized technology, craftsmanship and aesthetics. The result is a stylized, ambitious bar with an accomplished Japanese chef. DJs (including David Holland of Minimum Wage) spin high-quality electronica and house. Cocktails like the chocolate martini with a Hershey's Kiss are silly bliss.

Belly

155 Rivington St between Clinton and Suffolk Sts (212-533-1810). Subway: F to Delancey St; J, M, Z to Delancey–Essex Sts. **Open** *Sun–Wed 5pm–2am; Thu–Sat 5pm–4am.* **Average drink** *$7.* **Credit** *AmEx, MC, V.*
Navel gazing is not encouraged at this playful wine, beer and sake bar on the far eastern end of Rivington Street. Instead, Belly seeks to tickle your fancy with

► For more bar listings, *see pp285–291* **Clubs**, *pp296–306* **Gay & Lesbian** and *pp307–319* **Music**.

Major chord The bi-level **Pianos**, on Ludlow Street, plays to überfashionable LES hipsters.

its wine list, which includes fun picks like Bonny Doon French syrah and Dignas Spanish red, a rich blend of merlot, cabernet, malbec, syrah and other varietals. The snack selection is equally whimsical: Manchego cheese bathed in olive oil, wasabi shrimp chips and wedges of Toblerone chocolate.

Chibitini

63 Clinton St between Rivington and Stanton Sts (212-674-7300). Subway: F, V to Lower East Side–Second Ave. **Open** *Tue–Thu 5pm–midnight; Fri, Sat 5pm–1am.* **Average drink** *$9.* **Credit** *Cash only.*

Chibi, the pet bulldog of Marja Samson, sure gets a lot of play. First, Chibi's Bar was named after him; now there's Chibitini. Samson, who also owns the Kitchen Club, is sticking with a theme that works well for her: sake and dumplings. The orange-walled room with tangerine banquettes is a serene setting for sampling the 30-odd sakes, but if you feel that your shrimp-and-spinach dumpling goes better with a beer, no problem. On Tuesdays and Wednesdays, a free dumpling comes with your drink.

Happy Ending

302 Broome St between Eldridge and Forsyth Sts (212-334-9676). Subway: F to Delancey St; J, M, Z to Delancey–Essex Sts. **Open** *Tue, Wed 6pm–2am; Thu 6pm–3:30am; Fri, Sat 6pm–4am; Sun 9pm–4am.* **Average drink** *$7.* **Credit** *AmEx, MC, V.*

Use your imagination if you must: This buzzing two-story bar once housed an Asian massage parlor that, as the name suggests, was a full-service operation. But despite the showerheads poking out from the walls, the only lubricants passed around these days are cocktails, like the Happy Ending (Skyy Citrus vodka, lychee and lemon juices, cassis). The former sauna's underground nooks and crannies are drenched in seductive red light—still perfect for a late-night hookup.

'inoteca

See p174 for listing.

A spin-off of tiny, popular 'ino, this place is three times the size of the original, with 25 wines by the glass.

Oliva

161 E Houston St at Allen St (212-228-4143). Subway: F, V to Lower East Side–Second Ave. **Open** *Mon–Thu 5:30pm–midnight; Fri 5:30pm–1am; Sat 11am–1am; Sun 11am–midnight.* **Average drink** *$5.* **Credit** *AmEx, MC, V.*

The tight fit at this Spanish restaurant and drinking den makes it easy to jump-start a conversation with an attractive bohemian stranger. Well-made cocktails include the Spanish Prisoner, a blend of mandarin-orange vodka, raspberries and Cointreau that goes down cold and not too sweet. After 9pm, the place moves to a lively mix of Latin, funk and African music. Watch the heat rise on Wednesday and Sunday nights with live Cuban jazz.

Pianos

158 Ludlow St between Rivington and Stanton Sts (212-505-3733). Subway: F to Delancey St; J, M, Z to Delancey–Essex Sts. **Open** *5pm–4am daily.* **Average drink** *$5.* **Credit** *AmEx, DC, MC, V.*

If the subtle jungle theme at this place doesn't spark a heart-to-heart, one of the acts might: You'll find different music upstairs, downstairs and behind the back stairs. Step up to the bar or take a seat on the second floor, where a DJ sets the mood. Shows often draw insane crowds, making patrons unwitting victims of Pianos's success.

Schiller's Liquor Bar

See p173 for listing.
Keith McNally's downtown bar attracts the hip cats with decidedly unsnobbish wine-list categories ("cheap," "decent" and "good").

Smithfield

115 Essex St between Delancey and Rivington Sts (212-475-9997). Subway: F to Delancey St; J, M, Z to Delancey–Essex Sts. **Open** *2pm–4am daily.* **Average drink** *$5.* **Credit** *AmEx, MC, V.*
Named after an area in Dublin that's famous for its bustling fruit and vegetable markets, Smithfield seems right at home on a street once filled with pushcart vendors. There's plenty of group seating, and a pool table is creatively placed in the leafy garden. Choose from 12 tap beers—including one of the city's tastiest pints of Guinness—and ghetto-fabulous cocktails like the Hoodmopolitan (a Kool-Aid–infused Cosmo).

Soho

Balthazar

See p176 for listing.
Chris Goodhart, formerly of Windows on the World, is the new steward behind the French-only wine list.

Café Noir

32 Grand St at Thompson St (212-431-7910). Subway: A, C, E, 1, 9 to Canal St. **Open** *Noon–4am daily.* **Average drink** *$8.* **Credit** *AmEx.*
As with his Brooklyn enterprise *(Bar Tabac, 128 Smith St at Dean St, Boerum Hill, Brooklyn; 718-923-0918),* owner Georges Forgeois has achieved just the right look at Café Noir, making it a stylish place to top off a late night. The moody interior does justice to its French-Moroccan theme: saffron-hued stucco walls with wrought-iron accents, a honeycomb of small culs-de-sac filled with tables, and a small outdoor terrace. Make the *nuit* last with a glass of Rothbury shiraz and a selection of tapas.

Casa La Femme

150 Wooster St between Houston and Prince Sts (212-505-0005). **Open** *Sun–Tue 5pm–midnight; Wed–Sat 5pm–3am.* **Average drink** *$10.* **Credit** *AmEx, MC, V.*
In a building that once housed Mister Softee ice-cream trucks, this Egyptian bar-restaurant is sumptuously appointed with rich golden walls, billowing dining tents and more floor pillows than Bobby Trendy's showroom. The nightly belly-dancing performance, luscious Arabian Night cocktail (a chocolate martini) and meze will keep you up well past your bedtime. In the summer months, just for fun, the whole restaurant is recarpeted weekly with fresh sod.

The Ear Inn

326 Spring St between Greenwich and Washington Sts (212-226-9060). Subway: C, E to Spring St; 1, 9 to Canal St. **Open** *Noon–4am daily.* **Average drink** *$6.* **Credit** *AmEx, Disc, MC, V.*
Since it was established in 1816, the Ear Inn has been popular with those haunting the docks of the Lower West Side, from stevedores to artists. The decor is basic (dark wood, rickety tables and chairs) but its simplicity (and mellow staff) enhance the relaxed vibe. Visit Saturdays from 3 to 5pm for poetry readings; Monday, Tuesday and Wednesday nights for live music. The clientele runs the gamut from suits to old soaks. Free snacks (fried chicken, mussels or sausages) and cheap drinks are served on weekdays between 4 and 7pm.

Fanelli's Cafe

94 Prince St at Mercer St (212-226-9412). Subway: R, W to Prince St. **Open** *Mon–Thu 10am–3am; Fri, Sat 10am–3am; Sun 11am–2am.* **Average drink** *$5.* **Credit** *AmEx, MC, V.*
On a lovely cobblestone corner, this 1847 joint claims to be the second-oldest continuously operating bar and restaurant in the city. Prints of box-

The best Bars to...

...get glamorous and tipsy

File into **Beauty Bar** (*see p202*) for the $10 manicure (Wednesday to Sunday). It comes with a cocktail of your choice to complete the makeover—or start the hangover.

...take in some art with your appletini

Peruse the gallery at **Lit** (*see p204*) while the bartender knocks a few bucks off your bill ($2 Buds and $3 wells), every day but Sunday, from 5 to 9pm.

...drink like Al Capone

Find the hidden entrance to **Chumley's** (*see p205*), a former speakeasy, and you'll uncover a cozy spot with a historic past—plus sawdust on the floor and a working fireplace.

...take your breath away

Head upstairs to the **Metropolitan Museum of Art Roof Garden** (*see p208*) for spectacular views of both Central Park and the skylines on either side of it.

...get behind the eight-ball

Rack 'em up at **Smithfield** (*see above*), where the outdoor table (in warm months) makes this is one of the few spots in town where cigs and pool can coexist.

ing legends and one of the city's best burgers add to the easy feel. The banter of locals and the merry clinking of pint glasses sound just like the old days.

Fiamma Osteria

See p176 for listing.
Full of twinkling tea lights and fresh flowers, this boutique resto and lounge packs in the lovelies.

Mercer Kitchen

See p176 for listing.
In the bright street-level bar area of this popular spot, the "almost famous" crowd is sleek and seductive.

Ñ

33 Crosby St between Broome and Grand Sts (212-219-8856). Subway: 6 to Spring St. **Open** *Sun–Thu 5pm–2am; Fri, Sat 5pm–4am.* **Average drink** *$7.* **Credit** *Cash only.*
Those lucky enough (and Lara Flynn Boyle–thin enough) to squeeze their way into tiny, sexy Ñ can broaden their drink repertoire. Bartenders at this crowded haunt will help you navigate the list of Spanish sherries, both dry and sweet. Or keep it simple and order a tasty tapa, like the *gambas ajillo* (garlicky sautéed shrimp) with a glass of mellow *tempranillo* or sangria.

Thom Bar

60 Thompson Hotel, 60 Thompson St between Broome and Spring Sts (212-219-2000). Subway: C, E to Spring St. **Open** *5pm–2am daily.* **Average drink** *$11.* **Credit** *AmEx, DC, MC, V.*
This palace of cool comprises a James Bond–meets–Bond Street lobby, a shimmering seated lounge and a members-only rooftop annex. Cocktails are masterful: The Thom, an assimilationist cousin of the mojito, blends citrus vodka, fresh lime and mint. A different DJ every night keeps the beat bumping.

East Village

Beauty Bar

231 E 14th St between Second and Third Aves (212-539-1389). Subway: L to Third Ave; N, Q, R, W, 4, 5, 6 to 14th St–Union Sq. **Open** *Mon–Fri 5pm–4am; Sat, Sun 7pm–4am.* **Average drink** *$6.* **Credit** *MC, V.*
Outside, it looks like Grandma's hair salon. Inside, Beauty Bar is a shrine to glamour days gone by, saluting everything from AquaNet to stand-alone hair dryers, without feeling the least bit forced. Nightly DJs provide a soundtrack that ranges from punk to funk—all very loud.

Lovely 'rita, neatly made

We crave margaritas—in the dead of winter or when the summer sun is blazing. Luckily, the cold concoction, in its many flavors and various lethal preparations, can be found all over NYC these days. Whether you're a lime-on-the-rocks lover or a top-shelf tequila tippler, there's a margarita in this city with your name on it.

THE BEST MARGARITA...

...based on presentation: Salón Mexico

Discover a new way to use and abuse limes in a cocktail. In each of its margaritas, Salón Mexico floats a hollowed inside-out lime half, filled with a shot of tequila (in the Salón Margarita, $10) or 100-year-old Grand Marnier (in the Salón Especial, $20). Down the contents like a shot, or capsize the lime to give your drink an extra kick. *134–136 E 26th St between Lexington and Third Aves (212-685-9400).*

...to kill the pain: Zarela

Two of these 16-ounce behemoths ($8 to $10 each)—available frozen in guava, white peach, passion fruit, strawberry or lime—will leave you unable to spell the word *pain,* let alone feel it. *953 Second Ave between 50th and 51st Sts (212-644-6740).*

...in cool flavors: El Rey del Sol

El Rey offers on-the-rocks options of lime, orange, grapefruit, cantaloupe, watermelon and apple ($8 to $10), each topped with a sweet splash of juice—honey-hued apple or crisp, pink grapefruit. Yum! *232 W 14th St between Seventh and Eighth Aves (212-229-0733).*

...made with alternative citrus: Zócalo

At trendy margarita joints, blood orange is the new lime. And this stylish Mexican nook puts it to use in one of the best 'ritas ($7) in town. The secret? A blood-orange puree brought in from France. *Grand Central Terminal, Lower Concourse, 42nd St at Park Ave (212-687-5666); 174 E 82nd St between Lexington and Third Aves (212-717-7772).*

...for people who love tequila: Mi Cocina

Head to this restaurant's lounge to enjoy the Doña margarita ($8), a potent blend of Cuervo Gold, Grand Marnier, triple sec, and fresh lemon and lime juices. The traditional ingredients create a strong drink that allows the agave flavor to shine. *57 Jane St at Hudson St (212-627-8273).*

Black & White

86 E 10th St between Third and Fourth Aves (212-253-0246). Subway: L to Third Ave; 6 to Astor Pl. **Open** *Sun–Tue 6pm–2am; Wed–Sat 6pm–4am.* **Average drink** *$6.* **Credit** *AmEx, DC, Disc, MC, V.*
One of the best rock & roll bars in Manhattan is actually a restaurant on the tamer side of the East Village. There are booths for daters and a lively bar scene for singles. The liberal tip of the bartender's wrist makes Black & White a final destination.

Bond St.

See p178 for listing.
The lower-level bar-lounge hosts a crowd of under-30 gabbers sipping cocktails like the Sweet Saketini.

Butter

See p177 for listing.
Count on up-to-the-minute music and spare lighting that makes everyone look good.

First

87 First Ave between 5th and 6th Sts (212-674-3823). Subway: F, V to Lower East Side–Second Ave; 6 to Astor Pl. **Open** *Mon–Thu 6pm–2am; Fri, Sat 6pm–3am; Sun 11am–1am.* **Average drink** *$7.* **Credit** *AmEx, MC, V.*
The bar that brought the East Village drinking landscape a shot of chichi eight years ago shows no sign of slowing down. Take a seat at the dark-wood, candlelit bar and sample a basket of warm soft pretzels with a dunking vat of whole-grain mustard. The Tiny 'Tinis that made First popular still fuel a vibrant late-night scene. The cocktails range from savory (the Salt & Pepper combines Absolut Peppar and *peperoncino* juice) to sweet (the Key Lime Pie 'Tini is made with Smirnoff vanilla vodka, Sprite and a graham-cracker–dusted rim).
Other location *Merge, 142 W 10th St between Greenwich Ave and Waverly Pl (212-691-7757).*

Industry (Food)

See p177 for listing.
By 10pm, sexpots and scene-seekers jam in for ginger Cosmos and other dressy drinks.

Le Souk/Harem

47 Ave B between 3rd and 4th Sts (212-777-5454). Subway: F, V to Lower East Side–Second Ave; 6 to Astor Pl. **Open** *6pm–4am daily.* **Average drink** *$10.* **Credit** *AmEx, DC, MC, V.*
Harems don't traditionally allow men in—but such a policy wouldn't fly at an East Village hangout. So

...with guac and chips: Rosa Mexicano

Prepared tableside, this buttery mash of avocado, cilantro and onion is served with salt-dashed tortilla chips and tastes so good you'll want to hug the guy behind the guac cart. The only item here that *may* make you happier is the smooth-tasting frozen pomegranate margarita ($9). *See also p193 for listing. 1063 First Ave at 58th St (212-753-7407); 61 Columbus Ave at 62nd St (212-977-7700).*

...to go with dinner: Mexicana Mama

A spectacular drink will enhance the flavors of your meal—like the house margarita ($7) at this always-packed eatery. Made from freshly squeezed limes and Montezuma Blue tequila, it has a crisp tanginess that readies the palate for each new bite of Mama's cooking. *525 Hudson St between Charles and W 10th Sts (212-924-4119).*

...to sip outside: Dos Caminos Soho

This Mexican chainlet (only Soho has the patio) has received a lot of buzz—and has given plenty too. It offers more than 150

El Rey del Sol.

tequila selections. Instead of calling your usual brand for a rocks version, order one of Dos Caminos's signature frozen prickly-pear margaritas ($9) and enjoy gazing at the sharp-looking ladies and gents who pack the outdoor patio bar. *See also p177 for listing. 475 West Broadway at Houston St (212-277-4300); 373 Park Ave South between 26th and 27th Sts (212-294-1000).*

Egyptian brothers Marcus and Sam Jacob, who own the restaurant Le Souk, went coed with Harem, their seductive lounge next door. Under the aqua-blue ceiling of the bi-level space, girls and boys can nibble on meze such as spicy merguez and Tunisian *briks* (phyllo stuffed with tuna, potatoes, capers and egg). Much of Harem's menu is finger food, the better to munch while moving to live bands and DJs playing mostly Mediterranean. Less coordinated patrons can watch the dancing bellies, sip rose-water martinis and stay put on the *sariar*, a comfy ottoman the size of a queen bed.

Lit

93 Second Ave between 5th and 6th Sts (212-777-7987). Subway: F, V to Lower East Side–Second Ave; 6 to Astor Pl. **Open** *Mon–Sat 5pm–4am; Sun 9pm–4am.* **Average drink** *$5.* **Credit** *AmEx, Disc, MC, V ($20 minimum).*

Fledgling Lit breaks the East Village–lounge mold with its weekly basement parties. Thursday's Tilt soiree features glammed-up punk and dubby electropop; Fridays, Justine D (of the roving party Motherfucker, *see p291*) hosts DJs spinning trash rock, '80s pop and other goodies. In the rear is the Fuse Gallery, which is supported by the bar's proceeds and has featured the work of Mick Rock, Paul Booth and H.R. Giger, among others.

Mannahatta

316 Bowery at Bleecker St (212-253-8644). Subway: 6 to Bleecker St. **Open** *Mon–Sat 6pm–4am.* **Average drink** *$8.* **Credit** *AmEx, MC, V.*

The new owners of this formerly lifeless corner drink spot have brought some big changes to the Bowery: They've gutted the sprawling space and swapped dining tables for lounge furniture, converting a former bar area into a private dining room, and adding a menu with midnight munchies like jerk chicken wings. A DJ lounge downstairs attracts all kinds of night owls.

McSorley's Old Ale House

15 E 7th St between Second and Third Aves (212-473-9148). Subway: F, V to Lower East Side–Second Ave; R, W to 8th St–NYU. **Open** *Mon–Sat 11am–1am; Sun 1pm–1am.* **Average drink** *$2.* **Credit** *Cash only.*

It would take days to read the appreciative newspaper clips on the walls of this drinking landmark, established in 1854. Order one of the house beers—Dark Ale (sweet and smooth) or Light Ale (smooth with a bite)—and the veteran Irish waiters will bring you double mugs of suds. The sawdusted floor and never-dusted chandelier add to the old-time feel. Look up bartender-poet Geoffrey Bartholomew's book, *The McSorley Poems.*

Plant Bar

217 E 3rd St between Aves B and C (212-375-9066). Subway: F, V to Lower East Side–Second Ave. **Open** *7pm–4am daily.* **Average drink** *$5.* **Credit** *AmEx, MC, V.*

The brainchild of trendsetting DJs Marcus and Dominique, Plant is not only one of the hipper places to drink in the East Village, it's also one of the most pleasant. For quiet conversation, swoop down on one of the low, plush couches in the back. The good-looking locals don't get motivated until around midnight, so the place is all yours in the early evening.

West Village

APT

See p290 for listing.

By shifting its focus from door attitude to DJs, APT lives up to the polish of India Mahdavi's sleek design.

Ara

24 Ninth Ave between 13th and 14th Sts (212-242-8642). Subway: L to Eighth Ave; 1, 9 to 14th St. **Open** *Mon–Thu 6pm–1am; Fri, Sat 6pm–2am; Sun 4–10pm.* **Average glass of wine** *$8.* **Credit** *AmEx, Disc, MC, V.*

It happened here

There are competing theories about the origin of the term *eighty-sixed*—meaning to be unceremoniously tossed out—but the likeliest involves **Chumley's**, the long-standing West Village pub (*see p205*). In its speakeasy days, it had multiple exits, good for getaways when the fuzz showed up. Patrons would yell "Eighty-six it!" and head for 86 Bedford—then the side door. The bar has also been the hangout of the International Workers of the World (the Wobblies), as well as writers ranging from Hemingway to Kerouac. Today, you'll probably get eighty-sixed only if you light up a smoke.

Eat, Drink, Shop

Midnight at the oasis The Meatpacking District's **PM** gives you a rum for your money.

If you're in need of some personal attention, drop by Ara—only 25 people can fit into this 600-square-foot space, luxuriously decorated with Indian pillows, jade-colored marble tabletops and vintage mirrors. The owners are serious about wine; Joshua Wesson (founder of Best Cellars wine stores) oversees the 15 to 20 bottles available by the glass.

Chumley's

86 Bedford St between Barrow and Grove Sts (212-675-4449). Subway: 1, 9 to Christopher St–Sheridan Sq. **Open** *Mon–Thu 4pm–midnight; Fri 4pm–2am; Sat, Sun noon–2am.* **Average drink** *$6.* **Credit** *Cash only.*

The two unmarked entrances to Chumley's reflect its speakeasy roots. Since opening in 1922, the place has poured pints for its share of famous authors; the walls display countless book covers. A working fireplace, free-roaming Labradors and sawdusted floors maintain the scruffy-genteel sensibility.

Cielo

See p286 for listing.

Dig the soulful house music and sip from a $9 flute of champagne at this cool, attitude-free Village spot.

Paradou

See p181 for listing.

Paradou is the Provençal word for "paradise"—a fitting name for such a fetching wine bar.

Pastis

See p181 for listing.

Work through the sea of slim black-clad bodies to the bar, where you can enjoy any of 25 wines by the glass or a cocktail made with its namesake aniseed liqueur.

PM

50 Gansevoort St between Greenwich and Washington Sts (212-255-6676). Subway: A, C, E to 14th St; L to Eighth Ave. **Open** *Tue–Sat 8pm–4am.* **Average drink** *$10.* **Credit** *AmEx, DC, Disc, MC, V.*

This voodoo-themed lounge in the trendy Meatpacking District is meant to evoke a long-forgotten gentlemen's club in the tropics. Haitian owners Kyky Conille and Unik Ernest have combined luxury (leather banquettes, dramatic skylights) with offbeat touches like ornamental cement blocks, photos of Haitian crowds and antique voodoo bottles. Creole-style tapas cost a hefty $10 to $15 a pop, but that's the price of good people-watching.

Midtown

Chelsea

Amuse

See p184 for listing.

Modern in design and concept (you select menu items by price), Amuse also has a 40-foot mahogany bar.

Bungalow 8

515 W 27th St between Tenth and Eleventh Aves (212-629-3333). Subway: C, E to 23rd St. **Open** *10pm–4am daily.* **Average drink** *$12.* **Credit** *AmEx, DC, MC, V.*

The Fantasy Island of bars. Beyond the $12 champagne cocktails and a menu of gourmet snacks (like a $20 lobster club), there is a concierge service that will help fill your prescription—or book you a last-minute helicopter ride to Atlantic City.

Once perceived as a private club, it's now said to welcome all well-dressed, well-behaved patrons. Call ahead for details and be prepared to spend.

Cafeteria
See p184 for listing.
It's 3am and you're not ready to stop, so cruise to Cafeteria, where the night is just beginning.

Coral Room
See p286 for listing.
The Beauty Bar folks bring you this aquatic-themed nightclub, complete with a 10,000-gallon aquarium.

Glass
287 Tenth Ave between 26th and 27th Sts (212-904-1580). Subway: 1, 9 to 28th St. **Open** *Tue–Fri 6pm–4am; Sat 8pm–4am.* **Average drink** *$9.* **Credit** *AmEx, DC, Disc, MC, V.*
The owners of Bottino hired German-born architect Thomas Seeser to design Glass, a visually stunning bar, with Jacobsen egg chairs and custom-made cocktail tables. The washroom's one-way mirror allows pedestrians to witness plenty of nose powdering. In the all-season bamboo garden (open for smokers), artful young things while away the night stargazing. A mix of Latin and house music plays, and bar nibbles (panini and bruschetta) soak up the cheap wine from nearby art openings.

Markt
See p185 for listing.
Spacious, Belgian-themed Markt endures and endears, thanks to its 50-foot-long rose-marble bar, dark-wood floors and plentiful seats.

The Park
118 Tenth Ave between 17th and 18th Sts (212-352-3313). Subway: A, C, E to 14th St; L to Eighth Ave. **Open** *Sun–Thu 11:30am–2am; Fri, Sat 11:30am–4am.* **Average drink** *$10.* **Credit** *AmEx, DC, Disc, MC, V.*
A flash-with-cash clientele favors this former taxi garage's pastiche elegance. Equal parts ski chalet, Southeast Asian cliché and '50s Palm Springs, the decor includes Indonesian shell lamps and stuffed songbirds. Depending on the weather, you can lounge before a roaring glazed-brick fireplace or hot-tub it on the upstairs deck.

Passerby
436 W 15th St between Ninth and Tenth Aves (212-206-7321). Subway: A, C, E to 14th St; L to Eighth Ave. **Open** *Mon–Sat 6pm–2am.* **Average drink** *$8.* **Credit** *AmEx, MC, V.*
The unmarked Passerby is a sort of clubhouse for arty types (and their imitators) represented by the art gallery Gavin Brown's Enterprise. Flashing colored floor panels, created by artist Piotr Uklansky, almost synchronize with the DJ's beats and lend an ambient glow. Early evening, this is a civilized place for a drink; later, things get deliciously raucous.

Rub a dub dub Sip and soak at the **Park.**

Midtown West

Artisanal
See p191 for listing.
Don't feel overwhelmed by the 200 cheeses or 160 wines by the glass. Relish your many options or just try a wine flight paired with cheese selections.

Ava Lounge
Majestic Hotel, 210 W 55th St between Seventh Ave and Broadway (212-956-7020). Subway: N, Q, R, W to 57th St. **Open** *Mon–Wed 5pm–2am; Thu, Fri 5pm–4am; Sat 6pm–4am; Sun 6pm–1am.* **Average drink** *$9.* **Credit** *AmEx, Disc, MC, V.*
Attractive blonds in black serve key lime martinis and raspberry-vodka-champagne Flirtinis while undistinguished rock blares (via DJs on the weekends). You're afforded views west, into a residential area, and south, toward Times Square. Ava's main attraction, however, is its rooftop, open for drinks when weather permits.

Hudson Bar
The Hudson, 356 W 58th St between Eighth and Ninth Aves (212-554-6343). Subway: A, C, B, D, 1, 9 to 59th St–Columbus Circle. **Open** *Mon–Wed 4pm–2am; Thu–Sat 4pm–3am; Sun 4pm–1am. Library Sun–Wed noon–1am; Thu–Sat noon–2am. Private Park Mon–Fri 4pm–midnight; Sat, Sun noon–1am (weather permitting).* **Average drink** *$10.* **Credit** *AmEx, DC, Disc, MC, V.*

Bamboozled The rooftop bar of **Ava Lounge** is a great midtown getaway. *See p206.*

Like a lime-green stairway to heaven, an escalator leads to the lobby of Ian Schrager's Hudson hotel, where you'll find three separate bars. Most dazzling is the postmodern Hudson Bar, with a backlit glass floor and a ceiling fresco by Francesco Clemente. Try a sip of Paradise: vanilla-infused vodka, *crème de fraise,* strawberries and coconut cream. The Library bar marries class (leather sofas) and kitsch (photos of cows wearing pillbox hats). If that's too cute, get some air in the Private Park, the leafy, cigarette-friendly outdoor bar, lit by candle chandeliers.

Kemia Bar

See p189 for listing.
A subterranean lounge where guests may sip wine, enjoy tapas and groove to world beats.

Oak Bar

The Plaza Hotel, 768 Fifth Ave at Central Park South (212-759-3000). Subway: N, R, W to Fifth Ave–59th St. **Open** *Mon–Sat 11:30am–1:30am; Sun 11:30am–midnight.* **Average drink** *$10.* **Credit** *AmEx, DC, Disc, MC, V.*
Small wonder Gloria Steinem once refused to vacate this stunning classic (formerly open to men only), even after the manager removed her table. Study the Ashcan School murals by Everett Shinn while sipping a single malt ($13 to $24 per glass), and bend an elbow in the famous room where Diamond Jim Brady and George M. Cohan once tippled.

Rosa Mexicano

See p193 for listing.
The frozen pomegranate margarita packs a punch, as do the 38 tequilas and freshly made guacamole.

Midtown East

Cellar Bar

The Bryant Park, 40 W 40th St between Fifth and Sixth Aves (212-642-2260). Subway: B, D, F, V to 42nd St–Bryant Park; 7 to Fifth Ave. **Open** *Mon 5pm–midnight; Tue–Sat 5pm–2am.* **Average drink** *$13.* **Credit** *AmEx, DC, MC, V.*
At the Bryant Park hotel's pretty Mediterranean-style bar, recline beneath vaulted ceilings and snack on creations (crispy fried oysters, California rolls or smoked salmon) by chef Rick Laakkonen, who runs the hotel's renowned restaurant, Ilo. The hotel is named for the graceful park across the street, which is tented twice yearly for Fashion Week. It's only fitting that the house cocktail be au courant: The Razmopolitan (Absolut Citron, Cointreau, raspberry syrup and homemade sour mix) is a welcome break from the tired Cosmo.

King Cole Bar

St. Regis Hotel, 2 E 55th St between Fifth and Madison Aves (212-339-6721). Subway: E, V to Fifth Ave–53rd St. **Open** *Mon–Thu 11:30am–1am; Fri, Sat 11:30am–2am; Sun noon–midnight.* **Average drink** *$13.* **Credit** *AmEx, DC, Disc, MC, V.*
As you'd expect at a grand-hotel bar, there are mahogany walls and leather club chairs—along with a jacket requirement and a male-to-female ratio of four to one. The Bloody Mary was reputedly born here and is referred to by its original name, the Red Snapper. Payback for the hefty bar tab and crowded lounge: the famous Maxfield Parrish mural and free wasabi peas.

Tao

See p191 for listing.

This sceney palace is forever packed up to the Chinese lanterns; a stone Buddha towers over the dining room.

Uptown

Upper West Side

Soha

988 Amsterdam Ave between 108th and 109th Sts (212-678-0098). Subway: 1, 9 to 110th St–Cathedral Pkwy. **Open** *4pm–4am daily.* **Average drink** *$5.* **Credit** *AmEx, MC, V.*

Soha's style is as diverse as its clientele, a mix of Harlemites, Columbia kids and Upper West Siders. Walls are made of brick and faux-wood siding; on a recent visit, they were decorated with artist Brian Potter's work. There's an open-mike night on Sunday; live bands, DJs and the jukebox fill the airtime the rest of the week.

Upper East Side

Barbalùc Wine Bar

135 E 65th St between Park and Lexington Aves (212-774-1999). Subway: F to Lexington Ave–63rd St; 6 to 68th St–Hunter College. **Open** *Sun, Mon 5:30–10pm; Tue–Sat 5:30–11pm.* **Average drink** *$9.* **Credit** *AmEx, DC, Disc, MC, V.*

Named after "the [Italian] spirit of wine who warms your heart," Barbalùc has a ground-floor bar with groovy wood paneling, itty-bitty two-top tables and colored-glass place mats. The bar focuses on the Friuli region of Italy; its signature is a white variety called Tocai Zamo & Zamo. The clientele (largely 30 and over) can choose from nearly two dozen vinos by the glass from the 175-bottle list. Just don't be too surprised if you see an elf after you've had a few—that would be Barbalùc.

Bemelmans Bar

The Carlyle, 35 E 76th St between Madison and Park Aves (212-744-1600). Subway: 6 to 77th St. **Open** *Mon–Wed noon–1am; Thu–Sat noon–2am; Sun noon–midnight.* **Cover** *varies.* **Average drink** *$14.* **Credit** *AmEx, DC, Disc, MC, V.*

Ludwig Bemelmans's whimsical murals at this bar exude the same magic as his *Madeline* books. Sip one of the spiffy cocktails introduced by mixologist Dale DeGroff: The Old Cuban blends champagne with aged rum, bitters and fresh mint. Waiters in white jackets and piano music (Tuesday through Saturday) make Bemelmans timeless.

▶ For a comprehensive guide to notable New York bars, pick up a copy of the ***Time Out New York Nightlife*** guide, or subscribe to the online version at **eatdrink.timeoutny.com**.

Metropolitan Museum of Art Balcony Bar and Roof Garden

1000 Fifth Ave at 82nd St (212-535-7710). Subway: 4, 5, 6 to 86th St. **Open** *Balcony Bar Fri, Sat 4–8pm. Roof Garden May–Oct Tue–Thu, Sun 9:30am–5:15pm; Fri, Sat 9:30am–8pm.* **Average drink** *$7.* **Credit** *AmEx, DC, Disc, MC, V.*

Among the Met's countless treasures is the Balcony Bar, which springs to life on weekends. Thirty café tables, a few makeshift bars and a string quartet are set up under the watch of Canova's *Perseus.* If you'd rather survey the magnificent skyscrapers rising above Central Park, visit the Iris and B. Gerald Cantor Roof Garden for piña coladas and breathtaking views.

Above 116th Street

Lenox Lounge

288 Malcolm X Blvd (Lenox Ave) between 124th and 125th Sts (212-427-0253). Subway: 2, 3 to 125th St. **Open** *11am–4am daily.* **Cover** *varies.* **Average drink** *$5.* **Credit** *AmEx, DC, MC, V.*

This is where a street hustler named Malcolm worked before he got religion and added *X* to his name. Now the famous Harlem bar, lounge and jazz club welcomes a mix of old-school cats and unobtrusive booze hounds. Settle into the refurbished Art Deco area in front or take a table in the zebra-papered back room, and tune in to the haunting presence of Billie Holiday and Miles Davis.

Paris Blues

2021 Adam Clayton Powell Jr. Blvd (Seventh Ave) between 121st and 122nd Sts (212-864-9110). Subway: A, C, B, D, 2, 3 to 125th St. **Open** *11am–2am daily.* **Average drink** *$4.* **Credit** *Cash only.*

Named for the 1961 Sidney Poitier movie, this locals' dive has more soul than all the new bars in the neighborhood combined. Knock on the small window in the door; a woman on a stool might let you in if she likes the looks of you. The decor is proudly unchic—family photos and booths festooned with Christmas lights. The jukebox is the real attraction; everyone from Nat King Cole to En Vogue gets a turn.

Brooklyn

Boogaloo

168 Marcy Ave between Broadway and South 5th St, Williamsburg (718-599-8900). Subway: J, M, Z to Marcy Ave. **Open** *Tue–Fri 5pm–4am; Sat 7pm–4am.* **Average drink** *$6.* **Credit** *AmEx, Disc, MC, V.*

Chance Johnston knew that the glory days of the Internet-design company Razorfish were waning, so he decided to take his skills offline. The result is Boogaloo, a sleek, futuristic club. Johnston designed the furniture, including a series of sectionals that form a giant red bed. The cocktails are named for Williamsburg's celebrated old theaters, such as the Commodore (a guava margarita), and DJs spin a blend of funk, Afro-Cuban and soul.

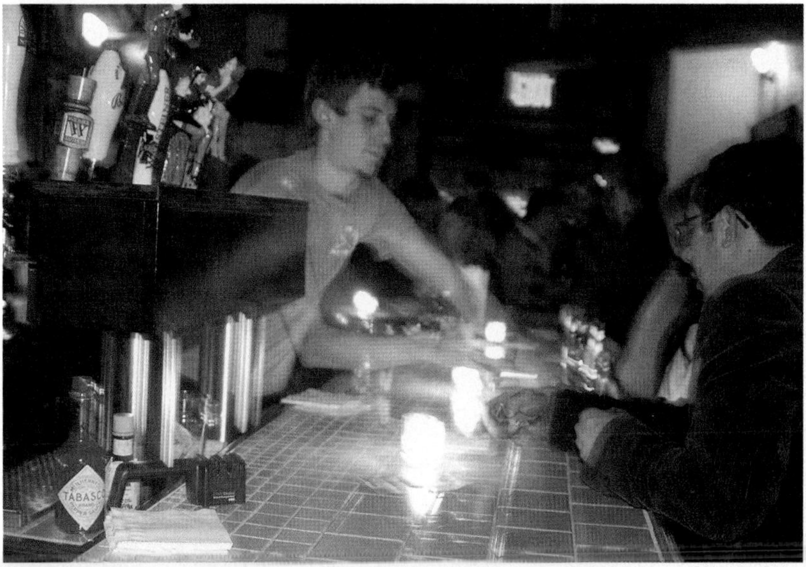

Fit for a king Head to **Royal Oak** in Williamsburg, Brooklyn, for a toast with the locals.

Galapagos

See p311 for listing.

A perennial Williamsburg fave, and another one that doubles as a performance space for all kinds of art.

Halcyon

See p291 for listing.

A varied program of live music, DJs, video artists, screenings and literary events attracts devotees.

Martinez Gallery

37 Greenpoint Ave at West St, Greenpoint (718-706-0606). Subway: G to Greenpoint Ave. **Open** *Thu–Sun 7pm–4am.* **Average drink** *$5.* **Credit** *Cash only.*

Together with dad Hugo, sibling gallerists Blanca and Erik Martinez abandoned the congested Chelsea art scene for the post-industrial desolation of waterfront Greenpoint, opening this triplex showcase in 2002. By day, contemporary art is shown. After dark, DJs like Bobbito and Citizen Kane spin breakdance beats, classic boogaloo and other Latin-infused sounds. You won't mind paying a few bucks more than at other neighborhood dives—once you're handed a tumbler-size cocktail of premium stuff.

Moto

394 Broadway at Hooper St, Williamsburg (718-599-6895). Subway: J, M to Hewes St. **Open** *Sun–Thu 5:30pm–2am; Fri, Sat 5:30pm–3am.* **Average drink** *$6.* **Credit** *Cash only.*

Owners Billy Phelps and John McCormick have somehow created a café-bar, evocative of a 1930s Parisian café, out of a former check-cashing store beneath the J-M-Z subway tracks. The menu (panini and more elaborate dishes) is as foolproof as the hand-picked list of wines and beers, which includes the popular Belgian ale Corsendonk. (A hard-liquor license is in the works.) On some nights you might have to step in through a live band—it's just that kind of friendly little place.

Robin des Bois

195 Smith St between Baltic and Warren Sts, Carroll Gardens (718-596-1609). Subway: F, G to Bergen St. **Open** *Mon–Fri 4pm–midnight; Sat, Sun 11am–1am.* **Average drink** *$7.* **Credit** *Cash only.*

Robin des Bois quadruples as a beer-and-wine bar, café, gallery and antiques shop. On sunny weekend mornings, the garden is the most pleasant brunch spot around. After night falls, it's a great place to make like Friar Tuck and partake heartily of ale and food. Come winter, seat yourself near the fireplace and warm up with hot spiced red wine.

Royal Oak

594 Union Ave at Richardson St, Williamsburg (718-388-3884). Subway: L to Bedford Ave. **Open** *5:30pm–4am daily.* **Average drink** *$6.* **Credit** *Cash only.*

Just follow your nose: This new lounge sits directly across the street from a chocolate factory. Benjamin Shih, owner of nearby Sweet Ups, has converted this space into a meandering bar, with a music venue called Feelings in the back. Shih serves the drinks our grandparents loved: sidecars, Tom Collinses, gimlets. Show up between 5:30 and 8:30pm, and it's buy a round, get a round free.

Shops & Services

Finding the useful, the one-of-a-kind and the best for the least is what we live for.

From dirt-cheap thrift shops in the outer boroughs to pricey, posh department stores on Fifth Avenue, New York is a shopaholic's paradise. But the best bargains don't just fall into your lap—you have to hunt them down. This chapter will help clue you in to sweetheart spots and favorite local destinations, so you can shop like a true New Yorker.

SHOP AROUND

Shopping events such as Barneys' ever-popular semiannual warehouse sale and the frequent designers' sample sales are excellent sources for low-priced clothing by fashion's biggest names. To find out who's selling where during any given week, consult the Check Out section of *Time Out New York*. The ***S&B Report*** *($15; 877-579-0222; www.lazarshopping.com)* and the **SSS Sample Sales hot line** *(212-947-8748)* are also great discount resources. Sales are usually held in the designers' shops or in rented loft spaces. Typically, you'll find the loft sales are not equipped with changing rooms, so bring a courageous spirit (and plenty of cold hard cash!), and remember to wear appropriate undergarments.

The cutting edge of fashion has spread beyond the Lower East Side and Nolita. In the past few years, trendy designers have gone farther afield: Harlem, the Meatpacking District, and Brooklyn's Williamsburg are now on the fashion-forward radar map. To find out who's making waves in New York's fashion scene, visit the *TONY* website at www.timeoutny.com, click on Check Out and scan the archives.

Pressed for time? Head to one of New York's shopping malls…yes, we said shopping mall. You won't get the best deals, or the uniqueness of smaller New York shops, but the **Manhattan Mall** *(Sixth Ave at 33rd St)*, **Trump Tower** *(Fifth Ave at 56th St)* and South Street Seaport's cobblestoned **Pier 17** *(Fulton St at the East River)* are good for one-stop shopping.

Most downtown shops stay open an hour or two later than those uptown. Thursday is the universal—though unofficial—shop-after-work night; most stores remain open then until at least 7pm. Certain stores have multiple locations. If a shop has more than two branches, check the business pages in the phone book for additional addresses.

Fashion

Department stores

Barneys New York

660 Madison Ave at 61st St (212-826-8900; www.barneys.com). Subway: N, R, W to Fifth Ave–59th St; 4, 5, 6 to 59th St. **Open** *Mon–Fri 10am–8pm; Sat 10am–7pm; Sun 11am–6pm.* **Credit** *AmEx, MC, V.*

All the top designers are represented at this bastion of New York style. At Christmastime, Barneys has the most provocative windows in town. Its Co-op branches carry young designers, as well as secondary lines from the heavies, like Marc Jacobs and Theory. Every February and August, the Chelsea Co-op hosts the Barneys Warehouse Sale, where prices are reduced 50 to 80 percent.

Other locations *Barneys Co-op, 116 Wooster St between Prince and Spring Sts (212-965-9964); Barneys Co-op, 236 W 18th St between Seventh and Eighth Aves (212-716-8816).*

Bergdorf Goodman

754 Fifth Ave at 57th St (212-753-7300; www.bergdorfgoodman.com). Subway: E, V to Fifth Ave–53rd St; N, R, W to Fifth Ave–59th St. **Open** *Mon–Wed, Fri, Sat 10am–7pm; Thu 10am–8pm; Sun noon–6pm.* **Credit** *AmEx, DC, MC, V.*

While Barneys aims for a young, trendy crowd, Bergdorf's is dedicated to an elegant, understated one with a suitably disposable income. As department stores go, it's one of the best for clothing and accessories. The famed men's store is across the street *(745 Fifth Ave).*

Bloomingdale's

1000 Third Ave at 59th St (212-705-2000; www.bloomingdales.com). Subway: N, R, W to Lexington Ave–59th St; 4, 5, 6 to 59th St. **Open** *Mon–Fri 10am–8:30pm; Sat 10am–7pm; Sun 11am–7pm.* **Credit** *AmEx, MC, V.*

Bloomie's is a gigantic, glitzy department store, offering everything from handbags and cosmetics to furniture and designer duds. Brace yourself for crowds—it ranks among the city's most popular tourist attractions, right up there with the Empire State Building. Look for the downtown Soho branch *(Broadway between Prince and Spring Sts)* in early 2004.

Century 21

22 Cortlandt St between Broadway and Church St (212-227-9092; www.c21stores.com). Subway: R, W to Cortlandt St. **Open** *Mon–Wed*

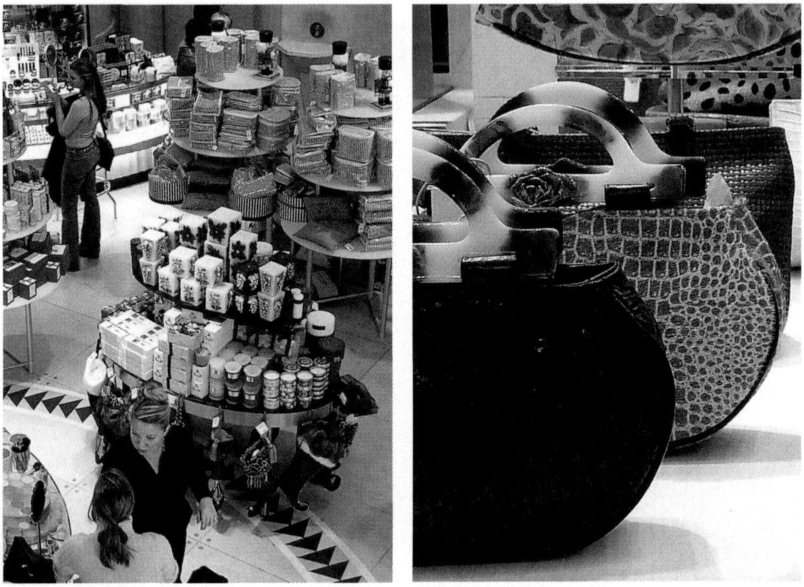

Bare necessities Busy cosmetic counters and the handbag department at **Henri Bendel**.

7:45am–8pm; Thu, Fri 7:45am–8:30pm; Sat 10am–8pm; Sun 11am–7pm. **Credit** *AmEx, MC, V.*
A white Gucci men's suit for $300? A Marc Jacobs cashmere sweater for less than $200? Roberto Cavalli sunglasses for a scant $30? You're not dreaming—you're shopping at Century 21. The score is rare but intoxicating; savings are usually between 25 and 75 percent off regular retail. Located directly across the street from Ground Zero.

Henri Bendel

712 Fifth Ave at 56th St (212-247-1100; www.henribendel.com). Subway: E, V to Fifth Ave–53rd St. **Open** *Mon–Wed, Fri, Sat 10am–7pm; Thu 10am–8pm; Sun noon–6pm.* **Credit** *AmEx, DC, Disc, MC, V.*
Bendel's lavish quarters resemble an opulently appointed townhouse. There are elevators, but it's nicer to saunter up the elegant, winding staircase. Prices are comparable to those of other upscale stores, but the merchandise seems more desirable here—must be those darling brown-striped shopping bags.

Jeffrey New York

449 W 14th St between Ninth and Tenth Aves (212-206-1272). Subway: A, C, E to 14th St; L to Eighth Ave. **Open** *Mon–Wed, Fri 10am–8pm; Thu 10am–9pm; Sat 10am–7pm; Sun 12:30–6pm.* **Credit** *AmEx, MC, V.*
Jeffrey Kalinsky, a former Barneys shoe buyer, was a pioneer in the Meatpacking District with his namesake shop, a branch of the Atlanta original. Designer clothing abounds—Helmut Lang, Versace and Yves Saint Laurent. But the centerpiece is the shoe salon, which features Manolo Blahnik, Prada and Robert Clergerie. Take advantage of this store's Bigelow outpost (*see p232*) for your makeup needs.

Lord & Taylor

424 Fifth Ave between 38th and 39th Sts (212-391-3344). Subway: B, D, F, V to 42nd St–Bryant Park; 7 to Fifth Ave. **Open** *Mon, Wed–Fri 10am–8:30pm; Tue 9am–8:30pm; Sat 10am–7pm; Sun 11am–7pm.* **Credit** *AmEx, Disc, MC, V.*
Classic goes far at Lord & Taylor, in both clothing and presentation; this is where the tradition of dramatic Christmas window displays began. Check out the recent additions of the restaurant An American Place and the Signature Café, both run by celebrity chef Larry Forgione.

Macy's

151 W 34th St between Broadway and Seventh Ave (212-695-4400; www.macys.com). Subway: B, D, F, V, N, Q, R, W to 34th St–Herald Sq; 1, 2, 3, 9 to 34th St–Penn Station. **Open** *Mon–Sat 10am–8:30pm; Sun 11am–7pm.* **Credit** *AmEx, MC, V.*
Behold the real miracle on 34th Street. Macy's has everything: designer labels and lower-priced knock-offs, a pet-supply shop, a restaurant in the cellar, a Metropolitan Museum of Art gift shop and—gulp—a McDonald's on the kids' floor. The store also offers Macy's by Appointment, a free service that allows shoppers to order goods or clothing over the phone and have those purchases shipped anywhere in the world *(800-343-0121).*

Saks Fifth Avenue
611 Fifth Ave at 50th St (212-753-4000). Subway: E, V to Fifth Ave–53rd St. **Open** *Mon–Wed, Fri, Sat 10am–7pm; Thu 10am–8pm; Sun noon–6pm.* **Credit** *AmEx, DC, Disc, MC, V.*
Saks is the classic upscale American department store. It features all the big names in women's fashion (and some of the better lesser-known ones), one of the city's best shoe departments, an excellent menswear department, fine household linens and attentive customer service.

Takashimaya
693 Fifth Ave between 54th and 55th Sts (212-350-0100). Subway: E, V to Fifth Ave–53rd St. **Open** *Mon–Sat 10am–7pm; Sun noon–5pm.* **Credit** *AmEx, DC, MC, V.*
Step out of the Fifth Avenue hustle and bustle into Takashimaya and behold the Zen rock garden of the retail world. Explore floor by floor, indulging your senses as you pass by beauty essentials, the men's and women's signature clothing collection, and furniture. A spot of brewed jasmine tea and a plate of chocolate-covered pear, apricot and ginger slivers in the basement Tea Box makes the perfect end to a trip to consumer nirvana.

National chains

Many New Yorkers regard chain stores as unimaginative places to shop, but that doesn't mean you won't have to stand behind a long line of locals while making your way to the register. Stores such as **Anthropologie**, **Banana Republic**, **Express**, **H&M**, **Old Navy** and **Urban Outfitters** abound. To find the nearest location of your favorite, refer to the phone book.

Fashion's A-list

These big-name designers have clothes horses champing at the bit for their new designs and seasonal collections.

Alexander McQueen
417 W 14th St between Ninth and Tenth Aves (212-645-1797). Subway: A, C, E to 14th St; L to Eighth Ave. **Open** *Mon–Sat 11am–7pm; Sun 12:30–6pm.* **Credit** *AmEx, DC, Disc, MC, V.*
The rebellious Brit's new Meatpacking District boutique feels like a religious retreat, with its barrel-vaulted ceilings and quiet white lighting. But the clothing—topstitched denim skirts, brown-leather jeans—is far from monastic.

Burberry
9 E 57th St between Fifth and Madison Aves (212-407-7100). Subway: N, R, W to Fifth Ave–53rd St. **Open** *Mon–Fri 9:30am–7pm; Sat 9:30am–6pm; Sun noon–6pm.* **Credit** *AmEx, DC, Disc, MC, V.*
Now that Burberry has ballooned to 24,000 square feet in this six-story glass, bronze and stone tower, it can peddle more of its trademarked tartan-plaid wares, as well as its new baby and home-accessories lines. Check out the recently launched custom-trenchcoat service, Art of the Trench.
Other location *131 Spring St between Greene and Wooster Sts (212-925-9300).*

Catherine Malandrino
468 Broome St at Greene St (212-925-6765). Subway: C, E to Spring St; R, W to Prince St. **Open** *Mon–Sat 11am–7pm; Sun noon–6pm.* **Credit** *AmEx, MC, V.*
Take refuge from Soho's chain-store madness at this colorful boutique, which showcases the breathtaking fashions and accessories of its owner-designer.

Chanel
15 E 57th St between Fifth and Madison Aves (212-355-5050). Subway: N, R, W to Fifth Ave–53rd St. **Open** *Mon–Wed, Fri 10am–6:30pm; Thu 10am–7pm; Sat 10am–6pm; Sun noon–5pm.* **Credit** *AmEx, DC, MC, V.*
The spirit of Mme. Chanel lives on in this opulent flagship store, particularly in the Chanel Suite—a Baroque salon modeled after the divine Coco's apartment on the Rue Cambon in Paris. (The suite is open only for private events.)

The best Shops...

...for avant-garde labels
Opening Ceremony (*see p218*)

...for designer-label bargains
Century 21 (*see p211*)

...for baubles, bangles and beads
Agatha (*see p228*)

...for coed shopping
Steven Alan (*see p219*)

...for that impossible-to-find book
Strand Book Store (*see p236*)

...for turntable tuneage
Fat Beats (*see p246*)

...for lox, chicken stock and barrels of coffee
Zabar's (*see p241*)

...for outfits that will make your pet lick you
Spot (*see p248*)

...for outfits that will make your lover happy
Agent Provocateur (*see p220*)

...for a bag to carry your finds
Destination (*see p227*)

Other locations *139 Spring St at Wooster St (212-334-0055); 737 Madison Ave at 64th St (212-535-5505).*

Diane von Furstenberg, the Shop

385 W 12th St between Washington St and West Side Hwy (646-486-4800; www.dvf.com). Subway: A, C, E to 14th St; L to Eighth Ave. **Open** *Mon–Wed, Fri 11am–7pm; Thu 11am–8pm; Sat 11am–6pm; Sun noon–5pm.* **Credit** *AmEx, Disc, MC, V.*

Although she's known for her classic wrap dress, Diane von Furstenberg has installed much more at this soigné space, intended to look like the inside of a glittery jewel box. Whether you go for ultra-feminine dresses or sporty knits, you'll emerge from the changing room feeling like a princess.

Dolce & Gabbana

825 Madison Ave between 68th and 69th Sts (212-249-4100). Subway: N, R, W to Fifth Ave–53rd St. **Open** *Mon–Wed, Fri, Sat 10am–6pm; Thu 10am–7pm; Sun noon–5pm.* **Credit** *AmEx, DC, MC, V.*

The Italian design team of Domenico Dolce and Stefano Gabbana gives love to uptowners and downtowners alike. Shop the 5,000-square-foot West Broadway store for the D&G line, or visit the tonier Madison Avenue flagship (and see for yourself how close the Canal Street knockoffs get to the real thing).

Other location *D&G, 434 West Broadway between Prince and Spring Sts (212-965-8000).*

Donna Karan New York

819 Madison Ave between 68th and 69th Sts (212-861-1001). Subway: 6 to 68th St–Hunter College. **Open** *Mon–Wed, Fri, Sat 10am–6pm; Thu 10am–7pm; Sun noon–5pm.* **Credit** *AmEx, DC, MC, V.*

Donna Karan's flagship for her upscale namesake line caters to men, women and the home, and is designed around a central garden with a bamboo forest. Check out the organic café at the nearby DKNY store, as well as Donna-approved reads, clothing, shoes and vintage furniture.

Other location *DKNY, 655 Madison Ave at 60th St (212-223-3569).*

Gucci

685 Fifth Ave at 54th St (212-826-2600). Subway: E, V to Fifth Ave–53rd St. **Open** *Mon–Wed, Fri 10am–6:30pm; Thu, Sat 10am–7pm; Sun noon–6pm.* **Credit** *AmEx, DC, Disc, MC, V.*

When Tom Ford revitalized Gucci a few years back (at press time, he was slated to leave the label), he made this old-lady label hip again. No fashionista is without at least one pair of shoes from his wildly popular line. Ford also designed the Abstract Decadent look inside this New York flagship store.

Helmut Lang

80 Greene St between Broome and Spring Sts (212-925-7214). Subway: R, W to Prince St; 6 to Spring St. **Open** *Mon–Sat 11am–7pm; Sun noon–6pm.* **Credit** *AmEx, MC, V.*

This 3,000-square-foot store houses the Austrian designer's cool suits and dresses, along with his accessories collection. The casual Helmut Lang Jeans line, which features denim pants, sweaters and killer jean jackets, is also available.

Jill Stuart

100 Greene St between Prince and Spring Sts (212-343-2300). Subway: R, W to Prince St; 6 to Spring St. **Open** *Mon–Sat 11am–7pm; Sun noon–6pm.* **Credit** *AmEx, MC, V.*

This cavernous boutique features Stuart's young, modern women's wear (including shoes, handbags and casual clothes). Be sure to check out the shop's boudoirlike enclave downstairs, complete with an antique four-poster bed, antique armoire and Victorian-era garment rack, devoted to handpicked vintage clothes.

Louis Vuitton

703 Fifth Ave at 55th St (212-758-8877). Subway: N, R, W to Fifth Ave–53rd St. **Open** *Mon–Wed, Fri, Sat 10am–7pm; Thu 10am–8pm; Sun noon–6pm.* **Credit** *AmEx, DC, Disc, MC, V.*

When French luxury-goods company Louis Vuitton hired American Marc Jacobs as artistic director, everyone knew Vuitton's staid lines of monogrammed luggage and accessories were sure to get a fresh spin. At the Soho outpost, a full range of men's and women's ready-to-wear collections is also on display. For its 150th anniversary in mid-2004, the store will be relocating to Fifth Avenue at 57th Street. Call 866-VUITTON for information.

Other location *116 Greene St between Prince and Spring Sts (212-274-9090).*

Marc Jacobs

163 Mercer St between Houston and Prince Sts (212-343-1490). Subway: B, D, F, V to Broadway–Lafayette St; R, W to Prince St; 6 to Bleecker St. **Open** *Mon–Sat 11am–7pm; Sun noon–6pm.* **Credit** *AmEx, DC, Disc, MC, V.*

The Soho boutique exclusively sells women's ready-to-wear, accessories and shoes collections, while the Bleecker Street shop offers impeccable men's clothes, shoes and accessories in an airy space with dark oak flooring, floor-to-ceiling windows and large khaki leather sofas.

Other location *Marc by Marc Jacobs, 403 Bleecker St at 11th St (212-924-0026).*

Prada

575 Broadway at Prince St (212-334-8888). Subway: R, W to Prince St. **Open** *Mon–Sat 11am–7pm; Sun noon–6pm.* **Credit** *AmEx, Disc, MC, V.*

Prada remains the label of choice for New York's fashion fleet (yes, you still have to put your name on a waiting list to buy the latest shoe styles). If you're interested only in the accessories, skip the crowds at the two larger stores and stop by the small 57th Street location. If you're downtown, the new space-age branch is a must-see.

Other locations *724 Fifth Ave at 57th St (212-664-0010); 841 Madison Ave at 70th St (212-327-4200).*

Cantaloup owner Heleyne Mishan-Tamir. See p217.

Ralph Lauren

867 Madison Ave at 72nd St (212-606-2100). Subway: 6 to 68th St–Hunter College. **Open** *Mon–Wed, Fri, Sat 10am–6pm; Thu 10am–7pm; Sun noon–5pm.* **Credit** *AmEx, DC, Disc, MC, V.*

Ralph Lauren spent $14 million turning the old Rhinelander mansion into an Ivy League dream of a superstore, filled with oriental rugs, English paintings, riding whips, leather club chairs, old mahogany and fresh flowers. The young homeboys, skaters and bladers who've adopted Ralphie's togs head straight to Polo Sport across the street. His small but well-stocked West Village boutique caters to women only.

Other location *Ralph Lauren Boutique, 380 Bleecker St between Charles and Perry Sts (212-645-5513).*

Stella McCartney

429 W 14th St between Ninth and Tenth Aves (212-255-1556). Subway: A, C, E to 14th St; L to Eighth Ave. **Open** *Mon–Sat 11am–7pm; Sun 12:30–6pm.* **Credit** *AmEx, DC, Disc, MC, V.*

Celeb designer McCartney, who won acclaim for her rock-star collections for Chloé, now showcases her pricey line of glam-sprite womenswear, shoes and accessories at her first-ever store.

Tribeca Issey Miyake

119 Hudson St at North Moore St (212-226-0100). Subway: 1, 9 to Franklin St. **Open** *Mon–Sat 11am–7pm; Sun noon–6pm.* **Credit** *AmEx, MC, V.*

The collaboration between mega-architect Frank Gehry and forward-thinking fashion designer Issey Miyake is an eyeful. This flagship store is jam-packed with the Japanese designer's head-turning pieces.

Boutiques

Bird

430 Seventh Ave between 14th and 15th Sts, Park Slope, Brooklyn (718-768-4940). Subway: F to 15th St–Prospect Park. **Open** *Mon–Fri noon–8pm; Sat, Sun noon–6pm.* **Credit** *AmEx, MC, V.*

Park Slope's Bird is an impeccable boutique for "real girls with real bodies." Clothing from Built by Wendy, Diane von Furstenberg and Bird's own label is up front; lingerie and shoes are in the back. The windows are wonders unto themselves.

Bond 07

7 Bond St between Broadway and Lafayette St (212-677-8487). Subway: B, D, F, V to Broadway–Lafayette St; 6 to Bleecker St. **Open** *Mon–Sat 11am–7pm; Sun noon–7pm.* **Credit** *AmEx, MC, V.*

Selima Salaun, of the famed Le Corset (*see p220*) and Selima Optique (*see p226*), has branched out from undies and eyewear, this time offering an eclectic mix of clothing (Alice Roi, Colette Dinnigan), accessories and French furniture—though vintage eyewear and bags are also available here.

Calypso on Broome

424 Broome St between Crosby and Lafayette Sts (212-274-0449). Subway: 6 to Spring St. **Open** *Mon–Sat 11am–7pm; Sun noon–6pm.* **Credit** *AmEx, DC, MC, V.*

While customers can still shop at the original Calypso on Mott Street *(between Houston and Prince Sts)*, this location—which is four times larger—features more upscale merchandise and different vendors. Stop by either shop for gorgeous slip dresses, suits, sweaters and scarves, many from little-known French designers.

Cantaloup

1036 Lexington Ave at 74th St (212-249-3566). Subway: 6 to 77th St. **Open** *Mon–Sat 11am–7pm; Sun noon–6pm.* **Credit** *AmEx, MC, V.*
This boutique gives UES girls a reason to skip the trip down to Nolita. Cantaloup is chock-full of emerging labels, such as James Coviello and Chanpaul, and less picked-over than the below-Houston boutiques.

Castor & Pollux

67½ Sixth Ave between Bergen St and Flatbush Ave, Park Slope, Brooklyn (718-398-4141). Subway: 2, 3 to Bergen St. **Open** *Tue–Sat noon–7pm; Sun 1–6pm.* **Credit** *AmEx, MC, V.*
The stock is eclectic, from old-school floral bedding to leather-trimmed fedoras, La Cosa tees and Rozae Nicols dresses.

Diesel

1 Union Sq West at 14th St (646-336-8552). Subway: L, N, Q, R, W, 4, 5, 6 to 14th St–Union Sq. **Open** *Mon–Sat 11am–9pm; Sun 11am–8pm.* **Credit** *AmEx, DC, Disc, MC, V.*
This 14,000-square-foot emporium will satisfy any denim craving you have. The 55 DSL line is carried exclusively at the Union Square store.
Other locations *throughout the city.*

Earl Jeans

160 Mercer St between Houston and Prince Sts (212-226-8709). Subway: B, D, F, V to Broadway–Lafayette St; R, W to Prince St; 6 to Bleecker St. **Open** *Mon–Sat 11am–7pm; Sun noon–6pm.* **Credit** *AmEx, DC, Disc, MC, V.*
Industrial design meets country comfort at this Soho shop. Earl's form-fitting jeans bring it all together—whether you like yours dark, light, stretchy or tight, you've got a good shot at scoring a new favorite pair.

Find Outlet

229 Mott St between Prince and Spring Sts (212-226-5167). Subway: B, D, F, V to Broadway–Lafayette St; 6 to Bleecker St. **Open** *Noon–7pm daily.* **Credit** *MC, V.*
Skip the sample sales and head to Find Outlet instead. Deeply slashed prices (50 percent on average) on high-fashion samples and overstock let you dress like a fashion editor on an editorial assistant's budget.
Other location *261 W 17th St between Eighth and Ninth Aves (212-243-3177).*

Hotel Venus by Patricia Field

382 West Broadway between Broome and Spring Sts (212-966-4066). Subway: C, E to Spring St. **Open** *11am–8pm.* **Credit** *AmEx, Disc, MC, V.*
Patricia Field is a virtuoso at blending club and street fashions (she assembled the costumes for *Sex and the City*). Her idiosyncratic mix of jewelry, makeup and clubwear proves it.

Intermix

125 Fifth Ave between 19th and 20th Sts (212-533-9720). Subway: R, W, 6 to 23rd St. **Open** *Mon–Sat 11am–8pm; Sun noon–7pm.* **Credit** *AmEx, DC, Disc, MC, V.*
The buyers know what they're doing at Intermix, selecting pieces from Catherine Malandrino, Paul & Joe, Trosman Churba, Urchin and Vanessa Bruno.

ISA

88 North 6th St between Berry St and Wythe Ave, Williamsburg, Brooklyn (718-387-3363). Subway: L to Bedford Ave. **Open** *Mon–Fri 1–9pm; Sat noon–10pm; Sun 1–7pm.* **Credit** *AmEx, MC, V.*
A sleek glass-and-concrete motif sets this warehouse-style shop apart from the rest of the street's grunge. The aluminum roller racks—full of A.P.C., Marc Jacobs and Pleasure Principle, along with a prime sneaker selection—make you feel like you're in Manhattan, but the young sales clerk/DJ reminds you you're in B-burg.

Kirna Zabête

96 Greene St between Prince and Spring Sts (212-941-9656). Subway: C, E to Spring St; R, W to Prince St. **Open** *Mon–Sat 11am–7pm; Sun noon–6pm.* **Credit** *AmEx, MC, V.*
The Nick Dine–designed, futuristic-feeling store carries more than 50 designers from around the globe, including Balenciaga, Hussein Chalayan and Jean Paul Gaultier.

Lacoste

608 Fifth Ave at 49th St (212-459-2300). Subway: B, D, F, V to 47th–50th Sts–Rockefeller Ctr. **Open** *Mon–Sat 10am–7:30pm; Sun 11am–6pm.* **Credit** *AmEx, MC, V.*
The country-club crowd had better get used to sharing: This superpreppy 70-year-old label has been embraced by hipsters and trendsetters as well.

Language

238 Mulberry St between Prince and Spring Sts (212-431-5566). Subway: R, W to Prince St; 6 to Spring St. **Open** *Mon–Wed, Fri, Sat 11am–7pm; Thu 11am–8pm; Sun noon–6pm.* **Credit** *AmEx, DC, Disc, MC, V.*
Language is an upscale clothing boutique, furniture store, art gallery and bookstore—a can't-miss for folks who buy into the lifestyle-shopping aesthetic. You'll find Chloé, Stella and Marc here, along with Language's own label.

Lucy Barnes

117 Perry St between Greenwich and Hudson Sts (212-647-0149). Subway: A, C, E to 14th St; L to Eighth Ave; 1, 9 to Christopher St–Sheridan Sq. **Open** *Mon–Sat 11:30am–7:30pm; Sun noon–6pm.* **Credit** *AmEx, MC, V.*
This homey shop, lit by crystal-trimmed hanging lightbulbs, looks primed for a tea party. Scottish designer Barnes's prim-with-a-twist threads include tulle blouses, patchwork skirts and frilly camisoles bedecked with organza flowers, with a sprinkling of vintage pieces throughout the store.

Martin

206 E 6th St between Second and Third Aves (212-358-0011). Subway: L to First Ave; 6 to Astor Pl. **Open** *Tue–Sun 1–7pm.* **Credit** *AmEx, Disc, MC, V.*

Welcome to the androgynous zone. Anne Johnston Albert's spartan boutique may be girls-only (though it is named for her husband), but it's *not* girly. Low-slung denims and corduroys, drapey tops and fitted army-style jackets are Johnston's signatures.

Miss Sixty

246 Mulberry St between Prince and Spring Sts (212-431-6040). Subway: R, W to Prince St; 6 to Spring St. **Open** *Mon–Wed noon–7:30pm; Thu–Sat 11am–8pm; Sun 11am–7pm.* **Credit** *AmEx, MC, V.*

The trendy Italian label's first American outpost looks like a '50s-era vision of the future: A white, cube-shaped portal leading up to the second level could be the entrance to a spaceship. Denim, cut far south of the belly button, stars in curve-clinging jeans and microscopic minis. The new flagship store on West Broadway carries a line of luxury denim.

Other location *386 West Broadway between Broome and Spring Sts (212-334-9772).*

Opening Ceremony

35 Howard St between Broadway and Lafayette St (212-219-2688). Subway: J, M, Z, N, Q, R, W, 6 to Canal St. **Open** *Mon–Sat 11am–8pm; Sun noon–7pm.* **Credit** *AmEx, MC, V.*

Proprietors Carol Lim and Humberto Leon (who also designs the store's namesake label) offer a stylish trip around the world in a warehouse-size space, done up with grape-colored walls and crystal chandeliers. The duo presents the fashions of one country per year (2004 kicked off with Brazil), culling from established couture labels, independent designers, mass-market brands and open-air markets. Rising stateside labels Benjamin Cho and Mary Ping have permanent citizenship.

Scoop

873 Washington St between 13th and 14th Sts (212-929-1244). Subway: A, C, E to 14th St; L to Eighth Ave. **Open** *Mon–Fri 11am–8pm; Sat 11am–7pm; Sun noon–6pm.* **Credit** *AmEx, DC, Disc, MC, V.*

Scoop is the ultimate fashion editor's closet. Clothing from Juicy Couture, Diane von Furstenberg, Philosophy and others are arranged by hue, not label. Hit the Soho shop for women only; uptown for a more classic look for guys and gals; or the newest outpost in the Meatpacking District for fab finds for both genders.

Other locations *532 Broadway between Prince and Spring Sts (212-925-2886); 1275 Third Ave between 73rd and 74th Sts (212-535-5577).*

From chops to shops

The Meatpacking District has been braising in its own fabulousness for several years, thanks to a thriving restaurant-and-nightlife scene. But it's finally catching fire as the city's Next Big Shopping Hub.

In 1999, the hyperstylish **Jeffrey New York** (*see p212*) opened on the far-west reaches of 14th Street. Parodied on *Saturday Night Live*, the mini department store—à la Barneys, except smaller and snobbier—has been drawing a steady stream of label-fastidious men and women since its debut (on opening day, it did more than $100,000 in sales). Soon, two interior-design stores that would delight aficionados of *Wallpaper** followed suit: **Auto** (*see p242*) and **Move Lab** (*see p242*).

The nabe didn't remain under wraps for long after that. Since spring 2001, sophisticated boutiques have set up camp amid still-operating meat lockers and an ever-expanding parade of eateries. The first pioneers included women's clothier **Shelly Steffee** *(34 Gansevoort St between Hudson and Little West 12th Sts, 917-408-0408)*, up-market Euro accessories store **Destination** *(see p227)*, urbane custom clothier **Jussara Lee** *(11 Little W 12th St between Ninth Ave and Washington St, 212-242-4128)* and wrap-dress maven **Diane von Furstenberg** (*see p215*). When Stacia Valle opened **Dernier Cri** *(869 Washington St between 13th and 14th Sts, 212-242-6061)* in July of 2002, stocking it with labels like Preen, the store became a stylists' haunt.

Hot on Valle's heels, **Alexander McQueen** (*see p213*) opened a glimmering 3,600-square-foot architectural marvel that's as drop-dead good-looking as Prada's Soho flagship: Modular, mirrored units showcase McQueen's signature Victorian punk-rock getups, as well as his shoes and accessories for women. McQueen (with H. Huntsman and Sons, a 150-year-old Savile Row tailor) also offers a custom-tailoring service for men. Fellow Brit **Stella McCartney** (*see p216*) swung open her gleaming door in the fall of 2002. (Both McQueen and McCartney chose this area over London for their debut boutiques.) The Chloé alum's serene, glossy environment—which includes a shimmering built-in pool—befits her ethereal clothes.

Across from these glitterdomes—and facing Western Beef—is Sonja Rubin and Kip Chapelle's **Rubin Chapelle** *(410 W 14th St between Ninth Ave and Washington St, 212-647-9388)*, a stylish co-ed shop whose former incarnations include meat locker and sex club. Flanking Rubin Chapelle are the

Selvedge

250 Mulberry St between Prince and Spring Sts (212-219-0994). Subway: R, W to Prince St; 6 to Spring St. **Open** *Mon–Sat 11am–7pm; Sun noon–6pm.* **Credit** *AmEx, DC, Disc, MC, V.*

Did you know that in 1944, because of wartime rationing, the seams on Levi's 501 bluejeans were screen-painted on, instead of actually being sewn in? At Selvedge, a boutique fittingly named after a stitched-fabric edge, you can score a pair of these old denims, plus other replicas of archival styles that were once crafted on looms.

Steven Alan

103 Franklin St between Church St and West Broadway (212-343-0692). Subway: 1, 9 to Franklin St. **Open** *Mon–Wed, Fri–Sun noon–7pm; Thu noon–8pm.* **Credit** *AmEx, MC, V.*

Decorated like an old-school general store, this roomy shop tends to lean slightly in favor of the ladies—the front section is earmarked for hot-chick labels such as Bruce, United Bamboo and Vanessa Bruno. The back area does right by the gents, though, with Rogan jeans and items from Filson, an outdoorsmen's line.

Other location *See p225.*

Sude

829 Ninth Ave between 54th and 55th Sts (212-397-2347). Subway: A, C, B, D, 1, 9 to Columbus Circle–59th St. **Open** *Mon, Wed–Sun noon–8pm.* **Credit** *AmEx, MC, V.*

A small but brilliantly edited collection in fashion-starved Hell's Kitchen. Shop for jeans by Seven, tops by Juicy Couture and pieces from new designers such as Escape Velocity, MarieMarie and Leona Edmiston.

TG-170

170 Ludlow St between Houston and Stanton Sts (212-995-8660). Subway: F, V to Lower East Side–Second Ave. **Open** *Noon–8pm daily.* **Credit** *AmEx, MC, V.*

Terri Gillis has an eye for emerging designers: She was the first to carry Built by Wendy and Pixie Yates. Nowadays, you'll find Jared Gold and Liz Collins pieces hanging in her newly expanded store.

Leather goods

Barbara Shaum

60 E 4th St between Bowery and Second Ave (212-254-4250). Subway: F, V to Lower East Side–Second Ave. **Open** *Wed–Sat 1–6pm.* **Credit** *AmEx.*

nascent stores of **Yigal Azrouël** *(408 W 14th St between Ninth Ave and Washington St, 212-929-7525)* and **Carlos Miele** *(408 W 14th St between Ninth Ave and Washington St, 646-336-6642).* Israeli designer Azrouël's stark 2,500-square-foot, high-ceilinged boutique, opened in 2003, features his refined look-at-me clothes, characterized by skirts with asymmetrical hemlines, tailored high-collar coats, and skinny trousers (Azrouël has crafted getups for Lenny Kravitz). The curtain went up on Miele's digs (the first outside his native Brazil) in February 2003, and the ultramodern white space does double duty as a performance-art venue. Miele's curve-hugging styles, in suede and Lycra, are aces in the hole for modish local nightlifers. And if there is a harbinger of trendiness, it's the appearance of youthful-fashion franchise **Scoop** (*see p218*). Co-owners Stefani Greenfield and Uzi Ben-Abraham snagged this prime location for their fifth mecca of boys' and girls' goods from Marc by Marc Jacobs, Paul Smith, 7 for All Mankind and the like.

If all of this shopping leaves you exhausted, fret not: The third outpost of Ji Baek's celeb-drawing downtown spa **Rescue Beauty Lounge** (*see p235*) has touched down on Gansevoort Street with 13 manicure and pedicure stations, four treatment rooms and fancy pampering options, such as Crème de la Mer facials. And the new **Hotel Gansevoort** (*see p37*), a 187-room boutique hotel from the folks who brought us the **Library** (*see p49*) and **Hotel Giraffe** (*see p49*), has arrived on the very same strip.

Hang time Dressing the filly *mignonne.*

Tag, you're it Undies at **Agent Provocateur**.

The couture cobblers at Barbara Shaum's shop will make your ten toes love you. Shaum has been handcrafting leather sandals for city slickers since 1954, and her chic, meticulously made creations have long lives, too. Unless you'd prefer your hippie cousin's Birkenstocks?

Carla Dawn Behrle

646-825-9065. **Open** *By appointment only; call for details.* **Credit** *AmEx, MC, V.*
CDB features leather pants and skirts, brightly colored stretch-leather tees, and tanks that can be best described as chic duds for the next Bond girl (or boy). Just ask devotees Bono and Alicia Keys.

Jutta Neumann

158 Allen St between Rivington and Stanton Sts (212-982-7048). Subway: F, V to Lower East Side–Second Ave. **Open** *Mon–Sat noon–8pm.* **Credit** *AmEx, MC, V.*
Jutta Neumann handcrafts leather sandals and bags, as well as belts and jewelry. Always wanted that one-of-a-kind Cinderella moccasin? This is the place to get your dream pair.

Lingerie

Victoria's Secret shops are all around, but these spots are special places to go for underthings that are decidedly not your grandmother's (and not your next-door-neighbor's either).

Agent Provocateur

133 Mercer St between Prince and Spring Sts (212-965-0229). Subway: F, V to Broadway–Lafayette St; R, W to Prince St. **Open** *Mon–Sat 11am–7pm; Sun noon–6pm.* **Credit** *AmEx, MC, V.*
If you're looking for something to rev up his heartbeat, check out this patron saint of provocative panties. British husband-and-wife team Joe Corre and Serena Rees have dolled up their perky salesgirls in pink '50s-style beautician dresses, designed by Corre's mom—*ahem,* Vivienne Westwood—worn unbuttoned for ample indecent exposure.

Azaleas

223 E 10th St between First and Second Aves (212-253-5484). Subway: 6 to Astor Pl. **Open** *Tue–Sat noon–8pm; Sun noon–7pm.* **Credit** *AmEx, MC, V.*
Nothing should come between a girl and this year-old hotbed of undergarments. Its lust-inspiring booty includes baby-soft briefs by Saint Grace and Deborah Marquit's glow-in-the-dark (!) neon-lace bras and thongs. In the dressing rooms, walls are plastered with Polaroids of eligible bachelors.

La Petite Coquette

51 University Pl between 9th and 10th Sts (212-473-2478). Subway: R, W to 8th St–NYU. **Open** *Mon–Wed, Fri, Sat 11am–7pm; Thu 11am–8pm; Sun noon–6pm.* **Credit** *AmEx, MC, V.*
Liv, Uma and Sarah Jessica join the throngs who flip through the panels of pinned-up bras and panties at La Petite Coquette. If your selection isn't in stock, owner Rebecca Apsan will order it for you.

Le Corset by Selima

80 Thompson St between Broome and Spring Sts (212-334-4936). Subway: C, E to Spring St. **Open** *Mon–Wed, Fri 11am–7pm; Thu noon–8pm; Sat 11am–8pm.* **Credit** *AmEx, DC, Disc, MC, V.*
In addition to Selima Salaun's slinky designs, this spacious boutique stocks antique camisoles, comely lingerie and Renaissance-inspired girdles.

Mixona

262 Mott St between Houston and Prince Sts (646-613-0100). Subway: B, D, F, V to Broadway–Lafayette St; R, W to Prince St; 6 to Bleecker St. **Open** *11:30am–7:30pm.* **Credit** *AmEx, MC, V.*
This boutique sells luxurious underthings by 30 different designers, including Christina Stott's leather-trimmed mesh bras and Passion Bait's lace knickers.

Only Hearts

386 Columbus Ave between 78th and 79th Sts (212-724-5608). Subway: B, C to 81st St–Museum of Natural History; 1, 9 to 79th St. **Open** *Mon–Sat 11am–8pm; Sun noon–6pm.* **Credit** *AmEx, Disc, MC, V.*
The dainty delicates at Only Hearts are the work of a hopeless romantic—designer Helena Stuart. The downtown store also carries her new ready-to-wear line, plus jewelry and shoes.
Other location *230 Mott St between Prince and Spring Sts (212-431-3694).*

Religious Sex

7 St. Marks Pl between Second and Third Aves (212-477-9037). Subway: 6 to Astor Pl. **Open** *Mon–Wed noon–8pm; Thu–Sat noon–9pm; Sun 1–8pm.* **Credit** *AmEx, Disc, MC, V.*

Religious Sex is a playpen for your inner fetishist. You'll find mesh tops with FUCK printed all over them, panties the size of eye patches and rubber corsets that all but guarantee a dangerous liaison—or a rash.

Swimwear

Most department stores have comprehensive swimwear sections, but check these specialty stores for all your bathing-beauty needs.

Eres

621 Madison Ave between 58th and 59th Sts (212-223-3550). Subway: N, R, W to Fifth Ave–59th St. **Open** *Mon–Sat 10am–6pm.* **Credit** *AmEx, DC, Disc, MC, V.*

Paris's reigning queen of sophisticated bathing togs fits in just swimmingly on New York's toniest avenue. The boutique's sunny white walls and serene blond-wood floors and counters give the merchandise the pedestal treatment: Precious intimates and colorful bathing suits are displayed on custom-made hangers, fabric busts and mannequins.

Other location *98 Wooster St between Prince and Spring Sts (212-431-7300).*

Malia Mills

199 Mulberry St between Kenmare and Spring Sts (212-625-2311). Subway: 6 to Spring St. **Open** *Noon–7pm daily.* **Credit** *AmEx, MC, V.*

Ever since one of her designs made the cover of *Sports Illustrated*'s swimsuit issue a few years ago, Malia Mills's swimwear has become a staple for folks who spend New Year's Eve on St. Bart's. This downtown location is open seven days a week, April through August.

Other location *960 Madison Ave between 75th and 76th Sts, second floor (212-517-7485).*

OMO Norma Kamali

11 W 56th St between Fifth and Sixth Aves (212-957-9797). Subway: F to 57th St; N, R, W to Fifth Ave–59th St. **Open** *Mon–Sat 10am–6pm.* **Credit** *AmEx, MC, V.*

The bathing-suit section is located in the atmospheric lower level of Kamali's flagship store, where you'll also find new and vintage womenswear, menswear and accessories, plus bathing-suit separates.

Vilebrequin

1070 Madison Ave at 81st St (212-650-0353). Subway: 6 to 77th St. **Open** *Mon–Sat 10am–6pm; Sun 11am–5pm.* **Credit** *AmEx, DC, MC, V.*

This St. Tropez–based company has boxer-style swimshorts (men's suits only) that come in five adult styles, and one for boys. Styles and patterns include seahorses and demure blue-and-white stripes.

Other location *436 West Broadway at Prince St (212-431-0673).*

Streetwear

Mr. Joe

500 Eighth Ave between 35th and 36th Sts (212-279-1090). Subway: A, C, E to 34th St–Penn Station. **Open** *Mon–Sat 9:30am–7:30pm; Sun 11am–6pm.* **Credit** *AmEx, DC, Disc, MC, V.*

What started in 1975 as a spot to buy Converse sneakers and Jordache jeans has evolved into an essential destination for hip-hop shoes and clothing. DJ Clue and Mark Wahlberg are patrons.

Phat Farm

129 Prince St between West Broadway and Wooster St (212-533-7428). Subway: R, W to Prince St. **Open** *Mon–Wed 11am–7pm; Thu–Sat 11am–8pm; Sun noon–7pm.* **Credit** *AmEx, Disc, MC, V.*

This store showcases Def Jam impresario Russell Simmons's classy, conservative take on hip-hop couture: phunky-phresh baggy clothing, and for gals, the curvy Baby Phat line.

Recon

237 Eldridge St between Houston and Stanton Sts (212-614-8502). Subway: F, V to Lower East Side–Second Ave. **Open** *Noon–7pm daily.* **Credit** *AmEx, MC, V.*

The joint venture of one-time graffiti artists Stash and Futura, Recon offers graf junkies a chance to wear the work, on clothing and accessories.

Stüssy

140 Wooster St between Houston and Prince Sts (212-274-8855). Subway: R, W to Prince St. **Open** *Mon–Thu noon–7pm; Fri, Sat 11am–7pm; Sun noon–6pm. Credit AmEx, MC, V.*

Tricky isn't the only one who wants to be dressed up in Stüssy. Come here for all the skate and surf wear that made Sean Stüssy famous.

Critics' picks Top 'hoods

Lower East Side

Doyle & Doyle *(see p228)*
Foley & Corinna *(see p226)*
TG-170 *(see p219)*
VICE *(see p222)*

Nolita (North of Little Italy)

Geraldine *(see p229)*
Language *(see p217)*
Selvedge *(see p219)*
Triple Five Soul *(see p222)*

Upper East Side

Cantaloup *(see p217)*
Christian Louboutin *(see p228)*
Donna Karan New York *(see p215)*
Tiny Doll House *(see p248)*

Triple Five Soul

290 Lafayette St between Houston and Prince Sts (212-431-2404). Subway: B, D, F, V to Broadway–Lafayette St; R, W to Prince St; 6 to Bleecker St.
Open *Sun–Thu 11am–7pm; Fri, Sat 11am–7:30pm.*
Credit *AmEx, Disc, MC, V.*
It's no longer a label exclusive to New York, but the city does still boast the brand's only store. Find the very necessary hooded sweatshirts and tees stamped with the Triple Five logo at this Soho streetwear store.

Union

172 Spring St between Thompson St and West Broadway (212-226-8493). Subway: C, E to Spring St. **Open** *Mon–Thu 11am–7pm; Fri, Sat 11am–7:30pm; Sun noon–6pm.* **Credit** *AmEx, MC, V.*
This closet-size shop is the exclusive New York purveyor of the Duffer of St. George, the famed streetwear sold at British shops of the same name. You'll also find Maharishi and Union labels.

VICE

252 Lafayette St between Prince and Spring Sts (212-219-7788). Subway: R, W to Prince St; 6 to Spring St. **Open** *Mon–Sat 11:30am–8pm; Sun noon–6pm.* **Credit** *AmEx, MC, V.*
Both a magazine and clothier extraordinaire, VICE is poised to take over the world. Peruse the racks full of Brooklyn Industries, Ben Sherman, Crypto, Religion and (of course) VICE, among other style superstars.

Menswear

agnès b. homme

79 Greene St between Broome and Spring Sts (212-431-4339). Subway: C, E to Spring St; R, W to Prince St. **Open** *11am–7pm daily.* **Credit** *AmEx, MC, V.*
French New Wave cinema from the 1960s is clearly an inspiration for agnès b.'s designs. Men's basics include her classic snap-button cardigan sweater and striped, long-sleeved T-shirts.

Bobby 2000

104 E 7th St between First Ave and Ave A (212-674-7649). Subway: 6 to Astor Pl.
Open *1–8pm daily.* **Credit** *AmEx, MC, V.*
A neighborhood staple, Bobby 2000 rescues boys from female-skewed vintage boutiques. The subterranean trove stocks almost all guy gear: worn corduroys and jeans, Lacoste and Izod polos, kitschy Hawaiian shirts and 1970s Martha's Vineyard tees.

Get your kicks

Pity the footwear purveyors who haven't figured out that the most coveted sneakers *aren't* the ones you can find at Foot Locker. In the hunt for the ultimate pair of rare kicks, skaters, hip-hop heads and collector-whores chat on sneaker sites or prowl the selection on eBay. When they're not surfing for shoes, sneaker freaks troll the shelves and shell out hundreds of dollars at the following stores.

Adidas Originals

136 Wooster St between Houston and Prince Sts (212-777-2001). Subway: B, D, F, V to Broadway–Lafayette St; R, W to Prince St; 6 to Bleecker St.
This market-style boutique (the first U.S. Adidas store) specializes in sneakers emblazoned with the classic trefoil—so stop slogging through those Salvation Army piles. *Adidas "Brougham," $75.*

Alife Rivington Club

158 Rivington St between Clinton and Suffolk Sts (212-375-8128). Subway: F to Delancey St; J, M, Z to Delancey–Essex Sts.
Sneakers equal religion in this tiny out-of-the-way shop, which is arguably the city's main hub for hard-to-get shoes. Check out the rotating selection of 60 or so pairs. (Ring the bell for entry.) *Alife "Kennedy," $110.*

Autumn

150 E 2nd St between Aves A and B (212-677-6220). Subway: F, V to Lower East Side–Second Ave.
Proprietor and amateur skateboarder David Mims and his wife, Kristen Yaccarino, stock DVS, Emerica, Etnies, iPath, Lakai and Vans for your half-piping pleasure. *Etnies "SLB," $60.*

D/L Cerney

13 E 7th St between Second and Third Aves (212-673-7033). Subway: 6 to Astor Pl.
Open *Noon–7pm daily.* **Credit** *AmEx, MC, V.*
Specializing in timeless original designs for the stylish fellow, the store also carries vintage menswear from the 1940s to the '60s. An adjacent shop carries D/L Cerney's new women's line.

Duncan Quinn

8 Spring St between Bowery and Elizabeth St (212-226-7030). Subway: R, W to Prince St; 6 to Spring St. **Open** *Tue–Sun noon–8pm.*
Credit *AmEx, DC, Disc, MC, V.*
Young Brit Duncan Quinn aims to clean up scruffy boys with old-fashioned tailored suits and shirts in eye-popping colors and prints. His namesake shop stocks slim-fitting button-downs in windowpane checks and candy-colored stripes, along with narrow-cut suits and flamboyant silk ties.

INA Men

For listing, see p226 **INA**.

Jack Spade

For listing, see p227 **Kate Spade**.

Paul Smith

108 Fifth Ave between 15th and 16th Sts (212-627-9770). Subway: L, N, Q, R, W, 4, 5, 6 to 14th St–Union Sq. **Open** *Mon–Wed, Fri, Sat 11am–7pm; Thu 11am–8pm; Sun noon–6pm.* **Credit** *AmEx, Disc, MC, V.*
Paul Smith devotees love this store's raffish English-gentleman look, with designs and accessories that combine elegance, quality and wit (and some serious price tags).

Scoop Men

For listing, see p218 **Scoop**.

Sean

132 Thompson St between Houston and Prince Sts (212-598-5980). Subway: C, E to Spring St.
Open *Mon–Sat 11am–8pm; Sun noon–7pm.*
Credit *AmEx, MC, V.*
Gents who wish to make a thrilling style statement on a Gap-size budget should stock up at this cool Soho shop. Owner Sean Cassidy stocks his store with French designer Pierre Emile Lafaurie's suits, corduroy jackets and poplin shirts (in 23 colors!).
Other location *224 Columbus Ave between 70th and 71st Sts (212-769-1489).*

Nort 235

235 Eldridge St between Houston and Stanton Sts (212-777-6102). Subway: F, V to Lower East Side–Second Ave.
Nort 235's proprietor, Stash, is a former graffiti artist and the co-owner of **Recon** (*see p221*). Stash assembles sought-after vintage editions and hard-to-find new releases, such as reissue Dunks, Terminators and a remake of the original 1984 Air Jordans.

Nike "Air Force 1 Laser Edition" (limited), $275.

Puma

521 Broadway between Broome and Spring Sts (212-334-7861). Subway: 6 to Spring St.
Head to the basement floor of this futuristic sportswear space to check out Pumas for both men and women, in all colors and styles. *Puma "Klim," $80.*

Premium Goods

694 Fulton St between South Oxford St and South Portland Ave, Fort Greene, Brooklyn (718-403-9348). Subway: C to Lafayette Ave; G to Fulton St; 2, 3, 4, 5 to Nevins St.
More than just a retail outlet for rare and limited-edition kicks, this shop also serves as an underground art gallery, which hosts graffiti shows and the work of local artists.

Bathing Ape "Bape Sta," $275.

Supreme

274 Lafayette St between Houston and Prince Sts (212-966-7799). Subway: 6 to Bleecker St.
The city's top-dog skate shop can generate lines half a block long when small-production and widely coveted sneakers get shipped in.

Nike "Supreme Dunk High SB" (limited), $178.

Welcome to the fold Vintage cords and tees await trendy boys at **Bobby 2000**. *See p222.*

Seize sur Vingt

243 Elizabeth St between Houston and Prince Sts (212-343-0476). Subway: B, D, F, V to Broadway–Lafayette St; R, W to Prince St; 6 to Bleecker St. **Open** *Mon–Wed, Fri, Sat 11am–7pm; Thu 11am–8pm; Sun noon–6pm.* **Credit** *AmEx, Disc, MC, V.*

Ready-to-wear men's shirts are available, but the real draws for the highly discriminating man are the custom-cut button-downs. Shirts come in Wall Street pinstripes and preppy gingham, with mother-of-pearl buttons and short square collars. The women's line is also popular.

Steven Alan

See p219 for listing.

Ted Baker London

107 Grand St at Mercer St (212-343-8989). Subway: J, M, Z, N, Q, R, W, 6 to Canal St. **Open** *Mon–Sat 11:30am–7pm; Sun noon–6pm.* **Credit** *AmEx, DC, MC, V.*

The Ted Baker label has been popular in London for more than a decade. This recently expanded shop now features the entire Ted Baker line, whose focus is short- and long-sleeved shirts in bright colors, plus crease-resistant Endurance suits. (The brand's new women's line is available in this store as well.)

Thomas Pink

520 Madison Ave at 53rd St (212-838-1928). Subway: E, V to Fifth Ave–53rd St. **Open** *Mon–Wed, Fri 10am–7pm; Thu 10am–8pm; Sat 10am–6pm; Sun noon–6pm.* **Credit** *AmEx, DC, MC, V.*

Thomas Pink's shirts are made in bold, dynamic colors that animate conservative suits. But the shop is no longer strictly for men: The women's department includes accessories, jewelry and—of course—shirts.
Other location *1155 Sixth Ave at 44th St (212-840-9663).*

Children's clothes

For Children's toys, *see p238.*

Babybird

428 Seventh Ave between 14th and 15th Sts, Park Slope, Brooklyn (718-788-4506). Subway: F to Seventh Ave. **Open** *Mon–Fri 10:30am–6:30pm; Sat, Sun noon–6pm.* **Credit** *AmEx, MC, V.*

An offshoot of the neighboring Bird (an ultracool store for grown-up girls), Babybird is filled with comfy basics in stylish colors. Lilliputians will love the tropical-fish tank built into the register counter.

Bonpoint

1269 Madison Ave at 91st St (212-722-7720). Subway: 6 to 96th St. **Open** *Mon–Sat 10am–6pm.* **Credit** *AmEx, MC, V.*

Perfect for toddlers with expense accounts, this Upper East Side institution carries frilly white party dresses and starched sailor suits.
Other location *811 Madison Ave at 68th St (212-879-0900).*

Calypso Enfants

426 Broome St between Crosby and Lafayette Sts (212-966-3234). Subway: 6 to Spring St. **Open** *Mon–Sat 11am–7pm; Sun noon–7pm.* **Credit** *AmEx, MC, V.*

Fans of Calypso adore this Francophile children's boutique: The tiny wool coats look as if they were lifted from the pages of the *Madeline* books.
Other location *See p216* **Calypso on Broome**.

City Cricket

215 W 10th St between Bleecker and W 4th Sts (212-242-2258). Subway: A, C, E, B, D, F, V to W 4th St; 1, 9 to Christopher St–Sheridan Sq. **Open** *Mon–Sat 11am–7pm; Sun noon–5pm.* **Credit** *AmEx, MC, V.*
Owner Ann Marie Romanczyk designs bibs, blankets and one-of-a-kind quilts in such retro prints as wide-eyed paper dolls and tin-can robots. Heirloom-caliber goodies—wee antique and custom-made baby chairs—make this a perfect gift-giving stop.

Sam & Seb

208 Bedford Ave between North 5th and North 6th Sts, Williamsburg, Brooklyn (718-486-8300). **Open** *Mon–Fri noon–8pm; Sat, Sun 11am–8pm.* **Credit** *AmEx, DC, Disc, MC, V.*
For style-conscious procreators who won't settle for generic baby clothes, Sam & Seb delivers groovy '60s- and '70s-inspired playclothes and funky consignment pieces by local designers, along with silk-screened Jimi Hendrix and Bob Marley tees.

Steven Alan

60 Wooster St between Broome and Spring Sts (212-334-6354). Subway: C, E, 6 to Spring St. **Open** *Noon–7pm daily.* **Credit** *AmEx, MC, V.*
After unveiling his Tribeca emporium last year, Steven Alan revamped his Soho space, this time focusing on the little guys. Labels such as Charlotte Corday and Golden Goose are carried here.

Maternity wear

Liz Lange Maternity

958 Madison Ave between 75th and 76th Sts (212-879-2191). Subway: 6 to 77th St. **Open** *Mon–Fri 10am–7pm; Sat 10am–6pm; Sun noon–5pm.* **Credit** *AmEx, MC, V.*
Former *Vogue* editor Liz Lange is the mother of hip maternity wear, and high-profile moms like Catherine Zeta-Jones and Iman are among her many customers.

Pumpkin Maternity

407 Broome St at Lafayette St (212-334-1809). Subway: 6 to Spring St. **Open** *Mon–Sat noon–7pm; Sun noon–5pm.* **Credit** *AmEx, DC, Disc, MC, V.*
At former rocker Pumpkin Wentzel's store, you'll find casual, tailored, machine-washable essentials for the expectant mother, particularly in denim.

Veronique

1321 Madison Ave at 93rd St (212-831-7800). Subway: 6 to 96th St. **Open** *Mon–Thu 10am–7pm; Fri, Sat 10am–6pm; Sun noon–5pm.* **Credit** *AmEx, MC, V.*
Veronique is dedicated to providing clothes just as cool as your regular duds. The collection in this spunky store will deliver you from muumuus and Peter Pan collars. Try the sexy Seven low-cut jeans (perfect for preggers) and styles by Nicol Caramel, Amy Zoller and Cadeau.

Vintage & thrift boutiques

Goodwill and the Salvation Army are great for vintage finds, but it can take hours of digging to pull out a single gem. Enter thrift boutiques, where the digging's been done for you; a number of them have been popping up lately in the East Village and Williamsburg. We've listed a wide range here, from the more extravagant (which cherry-pick vintage YSL and Fiorucci at not-so-vintage prices) to your general worn-in T-shirt havens, as well as a few that fall in between.

Alice Underground

481 Broadway at Broome St (212-431-9067). Subway: R, W to Prince St; 6 to Spring St. **Open** *11am–7:30pm daily.* **Credit** *AmEx, MC, V.*
This vintage mainstay houses gear from the 1940s to the present day, in varied condition. Prices are high, but it's always worth rooting through the bins at the front and back for a bargain.

Beacon's Closet

88 North 11th St between Berry St and Wythe Ave, Williamsburg, Brooklyn (718-486-0816). Subway: L to Bedford Ave. **Open** *Mon–Fri noon–9pm; Sat, Sun 11am–8pm.* **Credit** *AmEx, Disc, MC, V.*
The prices are great and so is the selection of clothing at this Brooklyn fave.
Other location *220 Fifth Ave between President and Union Sts, Park Slope, Brooklyn (718-230-1630).*

Cherry

19 Eighth Ave between Jane and W 12th Sts (212-924-1410). Subway: A, C, E to 14th St; L to Eighth Ave. **Open** *Mon–Sat noon–9pm; Sun noon–7pm.* **Credit** *AmEx, MC, V.*
This is New York's headquarters for Joseph La Rose shoes, which will make even the least shoe-fetishy girl go gaga. Cherry also stocks an irresistible collection of premier designer coats, evening wear, accessories and separates, for both men and women.

Edith & Daha

104 Rivington St between Essex and Ludlow Sts (212-979-9992). Subway: F to Delancey St; J, M, Z to Delancey–Essex Sts. **Open** *Mon–Fri 1–8pm; Sat, Sun noon–8pm.* **Credit** *AmEx, MC, V.*
This slightly below-street-level shop stocks one of the best collections of (mostly) fine-leather handbags (plus armies of shoes). You'll find no trash here—only the cream of the vintage crop. Check the front rack for Edith & Daha's own line of clothing.

Filth Mart

531 E 13th St between Aves A and B (212-387-0650). Subway: L to First Ave; N, Q, R, W, 4, 5, 6 to 14th St–Union Sq. **Open** *Sun–Tue 1–7pm; Wed–Sat noon–8pm.* **Credit** *AmEx, Disc, MC, V.*

Cool, baby B-burg's **Sam & Seb**. *See p225.*

This East Village store (co-owned by *Sopranos* star Drea De Matteo) specializes in white-trash and rock memorabilia from the 1960s through the early '80s: lots of leather, denim and T-shirts.

Foley & Corinna

108 Stanton St between Essex and Ludlow Sts (212-529-2338). Subway: F to Delancey St; J, M, Z to Delancey–Essex Sts. **Open** *Mon–Fri 1–8pm; Sat, Sun noon–8pm.* **Credit** *AmEx, MC, V.*
Vintage-clothing fiends like Liv Tyler and Donna Karan know they can have it both ways here: Shoppers freely mix old (Anna Corinna's vintage finds) with new (Dana Foley's original creations, including lace tops, leather-belted pants and sheer wool knits) to compose a truly one-of-a-kind look.

INA

101 Thompson St between Prince and Spring Sts (212-941-4757). Subway: C, E to Spring St. **Open** *Noon–7pm daily.* **Credit** *AmEx, MC, V.*
For the past ten years, INA on Thompson Street has reigned supreme over the downtown consignment scene. The Soho location features drastically reduced couture pieces, while the Nolita shop on Prince Street carries trendier clothing. Be sure to visit the men's store on Mott Street.
Other locations *21 Prince St between Elizabeth and Mott Sts (212-334-9048); 208 E 73rd St between Second and Third Aves (212-249-0014); INA Men, 262 Mott St between Houston and Prince Sts (212-334-2210).*

Lint

318 Bedford Ave between South 1st and South 2nd Sts, Williamsburg, Brooklyn (718-387-9508). Subway: L to Bedford Ave. **Open** *Wed–Fri 3–8pm; Sat, Sun 1–8pm.* **Credit** *AmEx, MC, V.*
Tiny vintage emporium Lint has a coolness uncharacteristic of the thrift-shop lot. Alongside the used clothes on display here ('70s rockabilly shirts and '80s microminis), local Williamsburg creative types showcase their jewelry and deconstructed duds here.

Marmalade

172 Ludlow St between Houston and Stanton Sts (212-473-8070). Subway: F, V to Lower East Side–Second Ave. **Open** *12:30–8:30pm daily.* **Credit** *AmEx, MC, V.*
One of the cutest vintage-clothing stores on the Lower East Side, Marmalade also has some of the hottest '70s and '80s threads to be found below Houston Street. That slinky cocktail dress or ruffled blouse can be found amid a selection of well-priced, well-cared-for items. Accessories, vintage shoes and a small selection of men's clothing are also available.

Resurrection

217 Mott St between Prince and Spring Sts (212-625-1374). Subway: R, W to Prince St; 6 to Spring St. **Open** *Mon–Sat 11am–7pm; Sun noon–7pm.* **Credit** *AmEx, MC, V.*
This vintage boutique (located in a former funeral home) is a Pucci wonderland, where Anna Sui and Kate Moss come for 1960s and '70s clothing.

Accessories

Eyewear

Fabulous Fanny's

335 E 9th St between First and Second Aves (212-533-0637). Subway: 6 to Astor Pl. **Open** *Noon–8pm daily.* **Credit** *AmEx, MC, V.*
The city's premier source of period eyeglasses for more than 17 years (and originally a fixture at the 26th Street flea market), Fabulous Fanny's has taken up permanent residence in the East Village. You'll find more than 10,000 pairs of old-time spectacles, an extraordinary collection that includes everything from WWII aviator goggles to pink-rhinestone–encrusted Versace shades from the '70s, all amid the granny's-attic–inspired decor.

Selima Optique

59 Wooster St at Broome St (212-343-9490). Subway: C, E to Spring St. **Open** *Mon–Sat 11am–8pm; Sun noon–7pm.* **Credit** *AmEx, MC, V.*
Selima Salaun's wear-if-you-dare frames are popular with such famous four-eyes as Lenny Kravitz and Sean Lennon (both of whom have frames named for them). Salaun also stocks Face à Face, Gucci, Matsuda and more.
Other locations *throughout the city.*

Sol Moscot Opticians
118 Orchard St at Delancey St (212-477-3796). Subway: F to Delancey St; J, M, Z to Delancey–Essex Sts. **Open** *Mon–Fri 9am–6pm; Sat 10am–6pm; Sun 9am–5pm.* **Credit** *AmEx, DC, Disc, MC, V.*
This 84-year-old family-run emporium offers the same big-name frames you'll find uptown, for about 20 percent less. Sol Moscot also carries vintage glasses (starting at $49), wrap-shield sunglasses by Chanel and Gucci, and bifocal contacts.
Other locations *69 W 14th St at Sixth Ave (212-647-1550); 107-20 Continental Ave between Austin St and Queens Blvd, Forest Hills, Queens (718-544-2200).*

Handbags

See also p219.

Amy Chan
247 Mulberry St between Prince and Spring Sts (212-966-3417). Subway: B, D, F, V to Broadway–Lafayette St; R, W to Prince St; 6 to Spring St. **Open** *Mon–Sat 11:30am–7:30pm; Sun noon–7pm.* **Credit** *AmEx, DC, MC, V.*
Designer Chan made her mark a few years back when she launched a collection of handbags made from brilliantly pattered Chinese silk, glittering sari fabric and feathers; they're now the centerpiece of her Nolita store.

Blue Bag
266 Elizabeth St between Houston and Prince Sts (212-966-8566). Subway: B, D, F, V to Broadway–Lafayette St; 6 to Bleecker St.
Open *11am–7pm daily.* **Credit** *AmEx, Disc, MC, V.*
Blue Bag is the walk-in handbag closet of your dreams. Its delicious bags (no, they're not all blue) are popular with the likes of Cameron Diaz and Courtney Love.

Destination
32–36 Little West 12th St between Ninth Ave and Washington St (212-727-2031). Subway: A, C, E to 14th St; L to Eighth Ave. **Open** *Mon–Sat 11am–8pm; Sun noon–7pm.* **Credit** *AmEx, MC, V.*
Manhattan's largest accessories boutique is right here in the Meatpacking District. The bags, shoes, hats and jewelry, created by more than 30 designers, include Vegas-worthy baubles and handbags crafted of film stock (from Vietnamese movies).

Kate Spade
454 Broome St at Mercer St (212-274-1991). Subway: R, W to Prince St; 6 to Spring St.
Open *Mon–Sat 11am–7pm; Sun noon–6pm.*
Credit *AmEx, Disc, MC, V.*
Popular handbag designer Kate Spade sells her classic boxy tote as well as other smart numbers in this sleek store. Spade also stocks shoes, pajamas and rain slickers. Accessories for men are sold at Jack Spade.
Other location *Jack Spade, 56 Greene St between Broome and Spring Sts (212-625-1820).*

Ro
267 E 10th St between First Ave and Ave A (212-477-1595). Subway: F, V to Lower East Side–Second Ave. **Open** *Sat, Sun noon–7pm; call on other days.*
Credit *AmEx, Disc, MC, V.*
Chic carryall designer Ro operated a showroom out of a tiny space for four years, before turning part of it into a shop. Hanging on pegs in the foyer-size storefront are company founders Gene Miao and Yvonne Roe's signature travel accoutrements, such as sleek chocolate-brown wallets shaped like suitcases.

Hats

Arnold Hatters
535 Eighth Ave between 36th and 37th Sts (212-768-3781). Subway: A, C, E to 34th St–Penn Station. **Open** *Mon–Sat 9am–7:15pm; Sun 10am–5pm.* **Credit** *AmEx, DC, Disc, MC, V.*
At 76-year-old family-owned Arnold Hatters (the old sign outside says Knox Hats), the selection includes Kangols (widest array in the U.S.), Stetsons, fedoras and caps. Call before you visit: The shop may be moving to a nearby location.

Cha-Cha's House of Ill Repute
154½ Suffolk St between Houston and Stanton Sts (212-420-7450). Subway: F, V to Lower East Side–Second Ave. **Open** *Mon–Fri noon–7pm; Sat, Sun by appointment only.* **Credit** *MC, V.*
Milliner Dina Pisani fashions almost all the ready-to-wear toppers here, and will custom-make virtually any chapeau you can dream up. Her own styles

Selima Optique. *See p226.*

blend the glamour of past eras with vamped-up twists—witness a Victorian-inspired black-velvet top hat with red-satin corset laces up the front.

Eugenia Kim

203 E 4th St between Aves A and B (212-673-9787). Subway: F, V to Lower East Side–Second Ave. **Open** *Mon–Fri 11am–8pm; Sat noon–8pm; Sun 1–7pm.* **Credit** *AmEx, MC, V.*
Eugenia Kim's creations for men and women run the gamut—from funky cowboy hats and newsboy caps to cloches and more, all fully customizable to fit your swelled head perfectly.

Hats. By Bunn

2283 Adam Clayton Powell Jr. Blvd (Seventh Ave) between 134th and 135th Sts (212-694-3590). Subway: B, C, 2, 3 to 135th St. **Open** *Mon–Sat 11:30am–7pm.* **Credit** *AmEx, Disc, DC, MC, V.*
Bunn (that's right, just Bunn) has been making exquisite hats by hand for 20 years. At his Harlem store and studio, he fashions and sells classic fedoras from Czechoslovakian wool felt and coaxes whimsical shapes from grosgrain ribbon. Best of all, his custom headgear costs a fraction of what you'd pay in Nolita.

Jewelry

Agatha

611 Madison Ave at 58th St (212-758-4301). Subway: N, R, W to Fifth Ave–59th St; 4, 5, 6 to 59th St. **Open** *Mon–Sat 10am–7pm; Sun noon–6pm.* **Credit** *AmEx, Disc, MC, V.*
The queen of the costume-jewelry joints, Agatha stocks low-priced baubles that look like a million bucks. Jumbo pearls, chunky rings and graphic, modern designs abound.
Other location *159A Columbus Ave between 67th and 68th Sts (212-362-0959).*

Borealis

229 Elizabeth St between Houston and Prince Sts (917-237-0152). Subway: B, D, F, V to Broadway–Lafayette St; 6 to Bleecker St. **Open** *Mon–Sat noon–7pm; Sun 1–6pm.* **Credit** *AmEx, MC, V.*
Borealis showcases the work of more than 38 different designers, including shop co-owner and designer Aurora Lopez, who hand-stamps her popular silver and gold charm necklaces, bracelets and pendants with such messages as MUCH WAS DECIDED BEFORE YOU WERE BORN.

Doyle & Doyle

189 Orchard St between Houston and Stanton Sts (212-677-9991). Subway: F, V to Lower East Side–Second Ave. **Open** *Tue, Wed, Fri–Sun 1–7pm; Thu 1–8pm.* **Credit** *AmEx, Disc, MC, V.*
Specialists in estate and antique jewelry. Whether your taste runs to Art Deco or Nouveau, to Victorian or Edwardian, gemologist sisters Pam and Elizabeth Doyle will have that intimate one-of-a-kind piece you're looking for (yes, they carry engagement rings and eternity bands).

Fragments

116 Prince St between Greene and Wooster Sts (212-334-9588). Subway: C, E to Spring St; R, W to Prince St. **Open** *Mon–Sat 11am–7pm; Sun noon–6pm.* **Credit** *AmEx, DC, Disc, MC, V.*
Over the years, Fragments owner Janet Goldman has assembled an exclusive stable of more than 100 artists. The jewelers first offer their designs at this Soho store before Goldman sells them to department stores such as Barneys.

Me & Ro

241 Elizabeth St between Houston and Prince Sts (917-237-9215). Subway: B, D, F, V to Broadway–Lafayette St; 6 to Bleecker St. **Open** *Mon–Sat 11am–7pm; Sun noon–6pm.* **Credit** *AmEx, MC, V.*
Michele Quan and Robin Renzi, the dynamic duo behind Me & Ro jewelry, are inspired by ancient Chinese, Tibetan and Indian traditions (like tying bells around the wrist as a form of protection).

Push

240 Mulberry St between Prince and Spring Sts (212-965-9699). Subway: 6 to Spring St. **Open** *Tue–Sat noon–7pm; Sun 1–6pm.* **Credit** *AmEx, MC, V.*
Jewelry maker Karen Karch's Nolita store, a small, fairyland-feeling spot, is almost as beautiful as her rings, bracelets, necklaces and tiaras.

Tiffany & Co.

721 Fifth Ave at 57th St (212-755-8000). Subway: N, R, W to Fifth Ave–59th St. **Open** *Mon–Fri 10am–7pm; Sat 10am–6pm; Sun noon–5pm.* **Credit** *AmEx, DC, Disc, MC, V.*
Tiffany's heyday was around the turn of the last century, when Louis Comfort Tiffany, son of store founder Charles Lewis Tiffany, took the reins and began designing his famous lamps and sensational Art Nouveau jewelry. Today, the big stars are Paloma Picasso and Elsa Peretti. Three floors are stacked with precious jewels, silver accessories, chic watches, stationery and porcelain, as well as the classic Tiffany engagement rings. FYI: They don't serve breakfast.

Shoes

Camper

125 Prince St at Wooster St (212-358-1842). Subway: R, W to Prince St; 6 to Spring St. **Open** *Mon–Sat 11am–8pm; Sun noon–6pm.* **Credit** *AmEx, DC, MC, V.*
This large corner store stocks dozens of styles from its line of Spanish-made casual shoes.

Christian Louboutin

941 Madison Ave between 74th and 75th Sts (212-396-1884). Subway: 6 to 77th St. **Open** *Mon–Sat 10am–6pm.* **Credit** *AmEx, MC, V.*
Serious shoehounds should plan to drop several C-notes on Christian Louboutin's irresistibly sexy shoes, distinguished by vertiginous heels and the signature scarlet sole. The racy footwear could easily convince you that you could walk on water (or

Booty-licious Serious shoe hounds hoof it to **Otto Tootsi Plohound** for the latest styles.

glide over slush puddles, at the very least). Don't try it—and don't try walking great distances in these fierce kicks, either.

Chuckies

1073 Third Ave between 63rd and 64th Sts (212-593-9898). Subway: F to Lexington Ave–63rd St. **Open** *Mon–Fri 10:45am–7:45pm; Sat 10:45am–7pm; Sun 12:30–7pm.* **Credit** *AmEx, DC, Disc, MC, V.*

An alternative to department stores, Chuckies carries high-profile labels for men and women. Its stock ranges from old-school Calvin and Jimmy Choo to up-and-coming Ernesto Esposito.

Geraldine

246 Mott St between Houston and Prince Sts (212-219-1620). Subway: B, D, F, V to Broadway–Lafayette St; R, W to Prince St. **Open** *Mon–Sat 11:30am–7:30pm; Sun noon–6pm.* **Credit** *AmEx, MC, V.*

Owner Bethany Mayer stocks cool creations from noted designers, such as Olivia Morris, Chloé, Narcisco Rodriguez and Michel Perry.

Jimmy Choo

645 Fifth Ave at 51st St (212-593-0800). Subway: E, V to Fifth Ave–53rd St. **Open** *Mon–Wed, Fri, Sat 10am–6pm; Thu 10am–6pm; Sun noon–5pm.* **Credit** *AmEx, MC, V.*

Jimmy Choo, famed for conceiving Princess Diana's custom shoe collection, is conquering America with his six-year-old emporium, which features chic boots, sexy stilettos, curvaceous pumps and kittenish flats, with prices starting at $450.

Manolo Blahnik

31 W 54th St between Fifth and Sixth Aves (212-582-3007). Subway: E, V to Fifth Ave–53rd St. **Open** *Mon–Fri 10:30am–6pm; Sat 10:30am–5:30pm.* **Credit** *AmEx, MC, V.*

The high priest of timeless glamorous shoes will put high style in your step—and a deep, deep dent in your wallet.

Otto Tootsi Plohound

137 Fifth Ave between 20th and 21st Sts (212-460-8650). Subway: R, W to 23rd St. **Open** *Mon–Fri 11:30am–7:30pm; Sat 11am–8pm; Sun noon–7pm.* **Credit** *AmEx, DC, Disc, MC, V.*

One of the best places for the latest shoe styles, Tootsi has a big selection of trendy (and slightly overpriced) imports for women and men.

Other locations *throughout the city.*

Sigerson Morrison

28 Prince St between Elizabeth and Mott Sts (212-219-3893). Subway: B, D, F, V to Broadway–Lafayette St; R, W to Prince St; 6 to Bleecker St. **Open** *Mon–Sat 11am–7pm; Sun noon–6pm.* **Credit** *AmEx, MC, V.*

Stop by this cultish women's shoe store for cleanly designed styles in the prettiest colors: baby blue, ruby red and shiny pearl.

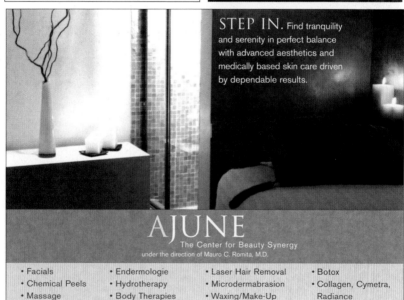

Health & Beauty

Bath, body & beauty booty

Alcone

235 W 19th St between Seventh and Eighth Aves (212-633-0551). Subway: 1, 9 to 18th St.
Open *Mon–Sat 11am–6pm.* **Credit** *AmEx, MC, V.*
Frequented by makeup artists on the prowl for the German brand Kryolan and for kits of fake blood and bruises, this shop also attracts mere mortals looking to score some of the shop's own line of sponges or its premade palettes—trays of a dozen or more eye, lip and cheek colors.

Aveda

233 Spring St between Sixth Ave and Varick St (212-807-1492). Subway: C, E to Spring St; 1, 9 to Houston St. **Open** *Mon–Fri 9am–9pm; Sat 9am–7pm; Sun 10am–6pm.* **Credit** *AmEx, Disc, MC, V.*
Aveda's exclusive line of makeup and products for hair and skin is available in this spacious, tranquil store. Create your own personal perfume by blending selections from its stock scents.
Other locations *throughout the city.*

Face Stockholm

110 Prince St at Greene St (212-966-9110). Subway: R, W to Prince St. **Open** *Mon–Wed, Fri, Sat 11am–7pm; Thu 11am–8pm; Sun noon–6pm.* **Credit** *AmEx, MC, V.*
Along with a full line of eye shadows, lipsticks, blushes and tools, Face offers makeup application and lessons to help improve your own techniques.
Other locations *226 Columbus Ave between 70th and 71st Sts (212-769-1420); 1263 Madison Ave between 90th and 91st Sts (212-987-1411).*

Fresh

57 Spring St between Lafayette and Mulberry Sts (212-925-0099). Subway: R, W to Prince St; 6 to Bleecker St. **Open** *Mon–Sat 10am–8pm; Sun noon–6pm.* **Credit** *AmEx, MC, V.*
Fresh is a Boston company that bases its soaps, lotions, candles and other products on natural ingredients such as honey, milk, soy and sugar. Stores are sleekly modern; goodies such as the Brown Sugar Body Polish smell divine.
Other location *388 Bleecker St at Perry St (917-408-1850).*

Kiehl's

109 Third Ave between 13th and 14th Sts (212-677-3171). Subway: L to Third Ave; N, Q, R, W, 4, 5, 6 to 14th St–Union Sq. **Open** *Mon–Sat 10am–7pm; Sun noon–6pm.* **Credit** *AmEx, MC, V.*
It's now 153 years old, but this venerable New York institution is often a mob scene. Check out the Motorcycle Room, full of vintage Harley-Davidsons (the owner's obsession). One dab of Kiehl's moisturizer, lip balm or body lotion from the plentiful free samples, and you'll be hooked.

M.A.C

14 Christopher St at Gay St (212-243-4150). Subway: A, C, E, B, D, F, V to W 4th St.
Open *Mon–Sat 11am–7pm; Sun noon–6pm.*
Credit *AmEx, Disc, MC, V.*
Makeup Art Cosmetics is famous for lipsticks and eye shadows that come in exotic colors.
Other locations *113 Spring St between Greene and Mercer Sts (212-334-4641); 202 W 125th St between Adam Clayton Powell Jr. Blvd (Seventh Ave) and Frederick Douglass Blvd (Eighth Ave) (212-665-0676).*

Make Up Forever

409 West Broadway between Prince and Spring Sts (212-941-9337). Subway: C, E to Spring St; R, W to Prince St. **Open** *Mon–Sat 11am–7pm; Sun noon–6pm.* **Credit** *AmEx, MC, V.*
Make Up Forever's line of French cosmetics is popular with glam women and drag queens alike. Colors range from bold purples and fuchsias to muted browns and soft pinks. The mascara is a must-have.

Make Up Mania

154 Orchard St between Rivington and Stanton Sts (212-533-5900). Subway: F, V to Lower East Side–Second Ave; J, M, Z to Bowery. **Open** *Wed, Thu 2–7pm; Fri–Sun noon–7pm; or by appointment.*
Credit *AmEx, Disc, MC, V.*
Owner and professional makeup artist Eva Marie Denst offers tricks-of-the-trade brands such as Cinema Secrets and Joe Blasco, and makeup classes ranging from Injury Simulation to Retro Hollywood.

Ricky's

718 Broadway at Washington Pl (212-979-5232). Subway: R, W to 8th St–NYU. **Open** *10am–8pm daily.* **Credit** *AmEx, Disc, MC, V.*
Stock up on tweezers, cheap travel containers and makeup cases that look like souped-up tackle boxes. Ricky's in-house makeup line, Mattése, includes fake lashes and glitter nail polish.
Other locations *throughout the city.*

Santa Maria Novella

285 Lafayette St between Houston and Prince Sts (212-925-0001). Subway: B, D, F, V to Broadway–Lafayette St. **Open** *Tue–Wed, Fri, Sat 11am–7pm; Thu 11am–8pm; Sun noon–6pm.* **Credit** *AmEx, MC, V.*
This store is a retail outlet for the hard-to-find Florentine toiletries line of the same name. The legendary skin creams and fragrances—470 concoctions in all—are still produced at the Italian monastery where they were conceived in 1210.

Sephora

555 Broadway between Prince and Spring Sts (212-625-1309). Subway: R, W to Prince St.
Open *Mon–Thu 10am–8pm; Fri, Sat 10am–8:30pm; Sun 11am–7pm.* **Credit** *AmEx, Disc, MC, V.*
A French beauty chain is devouring America. The downtown location looks like the first floor of a department store, but staffers hang back until you seek them out.
Other locations *throughout the city.*

Test drive Try the luscious free samples (not the bikes) at the **Kiehl's** flagship. *See p231.*

Shu Uemura
121 Greene St between Houston and Prince Sts (212-979-5500). Subway: B, D, F, V to Broadway–Lafayette St; R, W to Prince St; 6 to Bleecker St. **Open** *Mon–Sat 11am–7pm; Sun noon–6pm.* **Credit** *AmEx, MC, V.*
The entire line of Shu Uemura Japanese cosmetics is available at this stark, well-lit Soho boutique. For a truly eye-opening experience, check out the best-selling eyelash curler.

Perfumeries

Creed
9 Bond St between Broadway and Lafayette St (212-228-1940). Subway: B, D, F, V to Broadway–Lafayette St; 6 to Bleecker St. **Open** *Mon–Sat 11am–8pm; Sun noon–6pm.* **Credit** *AmEx, MC, V.*
Oliver Creed is a sixth-generation master perfumer and fragrance supplier to the British royals. His shop sells more than 200 scents—even to commoners. **Other locations** *Creed on Mad, 897 Madison Ave at 73rd St (212-794-4480); Creed on Mad II, 680 Madison Ave at 61st St (212-838-2790).*

Jo Malone
949 Broadway at 22nd St (212-673-2220). Subway: R, W, 6 to 23rd St. **Open** *Mon–Sat 10am–8pm; Sun noon–6pm.* **Credit** *AmEx, DC, Disc, MC, V.*
British perfumer Jo Malone champions the "layering" of scents as a way of creating a personalized aroma. Along with perfumes and colognes, her Flatiron District boutique offers candles, skin-care products and superpampering facials.

Pharmacists

For 24-hour pharmacies, *see p369.*

C.O. Bigelow Chemists
414 Sixth Ave between 8th and 9th Sts (212-533-2700). Subway: A, C, E, B, D, F, V to W 4th St. **Open** *Mon–Fri 7:30am–9pm; Sat 8:30am–7pm; Sun 8:30am–5:30pm.* **Credit** *AmEx, Disc, MC, V.*
A Greenwich Village institution, Bigelow is the complete apothecary—you name it, they have it.

Zitomer
969 Madison Ave between 75th and 76th Sts (212-737-4480). Subway: 6 to 77th St. **Open** *Mon–Fri 9am–8pm; Sat 9am–7pm; Sun 10am–6pm.* **Credit** *AmEx, DC, Disc, MC, V.*
On its ground floor, Zitomer stocks seemingly every beauty and health product under the sun.

Salons & spas

Salons

New York is the city of fresh starts; what better way to begin anew than with your hair? Whether you want a full-out makeover, a rock & roll 'do or just a trim, we have the salon for you. The stylin' superstars at **Frédéric Fekkai Beauté de Provence** *(212-753-9500)* and **Louis Licari** *(212-758-2090)* are top-notch, but they charge hair-raising prices. The following salons offer specialized services—budget, rocker, ethno-friendly—and unique settings for your special NYC cut.

Astor Place Hair Stylists

2 Astor Pl at Broadway (212-475-9854). Subway: R, W to 8th St–NYU; 6 to Astor Pl. **Open** *Mon–Sat 8am–8pm; Sun 9am–6pm.* **Credit** *Cash only.*
This is the classic New York hair experience. An army of barbers does everything from neat trims to shaved designs, all to pounding music (usually hip-hop). You can't make an appointment; just take a number and wait outside with the crowd. Sunday mornings are quiet. Cuts start at $12; blow-drys, at $20; dreads, at $75.

DopDop

170 Mercer St between Houston and Prince Sts (212-965-9540). Subway: R, W to Prince St. **Open** *Sun, Mon noon–6pm; Tue, Thu–Sat 10:30am–7:30pm; Wed 10:30am–5pm.* **Credit** *AmEx, MC, V.*
Jo Blackwell, one of the country's top colorists, is co-owner of this sleek Soho salon, which caters to a neighborhood clientele—fashion designers, painters, photographers, actors and makeup artists. Slip into one of DopDop's handmade silk robes and enjoy the surprisingly relaxed atmosphere. Cuts start at $65; highlights, at $90 (face-frame).

Ebony 2000

831 Third Ave between 50th and 51st Sts, third floor (212-750-8950). Subway: E, V to Lexington–53rd St; 6 to 51st St. **Open** *Tue–Fri 10am–6pm; Sat 8am–3pm.* **Credit** *AmEx, MC, V.*
Specializing in African-American hair, Ebony 2000 will color, press-and-curl, relax or weave the way to a new you. Coloring starts at $75.

Laicale

129 Grand St between Broadway and Crosby St (212-219-2424). Subway: J, M, Z, N, Q, R, W, 6 to Canal St. **Open** *Tue, Wed, Fri 11am–8pm; Thu 11am–10pm; Sat 9am–6pm.* **Credit** *AmEx, MC, V (gratuities accepted in cash only).*
Get your locks chopped at this industrial chrome-and-glass hair mecca while the shop's own DJ spins tunes. Most of the stylists here also work for magazines and runway shows. Cuts start at $75; highlights, at $125 (half-head).

Miwa/Alex Salon

24 E 22nd St between Broadway and Park Ave (212-228-4422). Subway: R, W, 6 to 23rd St. **Open** *Mon 8:30am–5:30pm; Tue–Sat 8:30am–7pm.* **Credit** *MC, V.*
Tucked inside a posh, friendly space in the Flatiron District, Miwa/Alex delivers the sort of cut you expect in New York: smart, unique and perfectly coordinated with color. Consultations are complimentary, and postappointment touch-ups are free.

Mudhoney

148 Sullivan St between Houston and Prince Sts (212-533-1160). Subway: C, E to Spring St. **Open** *Tue–Fri noon–8pm; Sat, Sun noon–6pm.* **Credit** *Cash only.*
This is the premier rock & roll salon in the city. Don't be surprised if your stylist colors your hair without removing his orange-tinted sunglasses (perhaps hiding bloodshot eyes?). The decor alone—featuring a torture chair and lascivious stained-glass eye candy—will make your time under the dryer fly by in this tiny, attitude-packed salon.
Other locations *7 Bond St between Broadway and Lafayette St (212-228-8128); 888 Broadway at 19th St (212-473-7407).*

Ouidad

846 Seventh Ave between 54th and 55th Sts, fifth floor (212-333-7577). Subway: B, D, E to Seventh Ave. **Open** *Tue, Wed, Fri 9:30am–6:30pm; Thu 10am–7pm; Sat 9am–5pm.* **Credit** *MC, V.*
Lebanese-born Ouidad founded the first curl-centric salon and product line 20 years ago. She is still the gold standard, and even maintains a private room for veiled clients.

Spas

Acqua Beauty Bar

7 E 14th St between Fifth Ave and Union Sq West (212-620-4329; www.acquabeautybar.com). Subway: L, N, Q, R, W, 4, 5, 6 to 14th St–Union Sq. **Open** *Mon, Thu 10am–9pm; Tue, Wed, Fri 10am–8pm; Sat, Sun 10am–7pm.* **Credit** *AmEx, MC, V.*
Besides the standard manicure and pedicure, this spa offers a dizzying array of Asian-themed facials, massages, body wraps and scrubs. Wild ginseng and freshwater pearls are used in the Chinese-inspired Wu-Hang Facial; the Balinese Retreat is an aromatherapeutic fruit-acid peel. Go all out with the Indonesian Ritual of Beauty, which includes a massage, scrub and mask inspired by the beauty regimens of Southeast Asia.

Amore Pacific

114 Spring St between Greene and Mercer Sts (212-966-0400). Subway: A, C, E to Spring St; B, D, F, V to Broadway–Lafayette St; R, W to Prince St; 6 to Spring St. **Open** *Tue–Sat 11am–7pm; Sun noon–6pm.* **Credit** *AmEx, DC, Disc, MC, V.*
Amore Pacific's Soho location is the first place in the U.S. where clients have been able to experience this established Korean company's superswanky product line. Amore has devised its own skin-care system, in which botanicals (red ginseng, bamboo sap) are used in conjunction with a high-tech process to create treatments that quickly penetrate and revitalize the skin. Reflexology and massages are available as well.

Be Mini Spa

173 Ludlow St between Houston and Stanton Sts (212-253-5665). Subway: F, V to Lower East Side–Second Ave. **Open** *Tue–Fri 12:30–8pm; Sat, Sun 11am–8pm.* **Credit** *AmEx, Disc, MC, V.*
It's located in the heart of hipster central, but Be Mini has a refreshingly unpretentious atmosphere. (You can sit and gossip long after your treatment is over.) The reasonably priced manicures and pedicures take place upstairs; facials, waxing and eyebrow-shaping are done downstairs.

Bliss 57

19 E 57th St between Fifth and Madison Aves, third floor (212-219-8970; www.blissworld.com). Subway: N, R, W to Fifth Ave–59th St.
Open *Mon, Tue, Thu, Fri 9:30am–8:30pm; Wed 12:30–8:30pm; Sat 9:30am–6:30pm.*
Credit *AmEx, DC, Disc, MC, V.*
A New York institution, Bliss is famous for its high-quality treatments and signature line of body products. Besides its immensely popular (and pricey) facials and massages, Bliss offers a host of new facial treatments, including a wrinkle- and pore-reducing "sleeping peel" and a deep-tissue treatment that promises to instantly relax your facial muscles.
Other location *568 Broadway between Houston and Prince Sts, second floor (212-219-8970).*

Eden Day Spa

388 Broadway between Walker and White Sts (212-226-0515; www.edenspany.com). Subway; N, Q, R, W, 6, to Canal St. **Open** *Mon–Sat 10am–9pm; Sun 10am–7pm.* **Credit** *AmEx, DC, Disc, MC, V.*
Eden's modest storefront doesn't hint at the glamorous spa behind the tall wooden screens: lots of low beige couches, candles and flowering plants give it a luxurious Asian vibe. Eden offers massages, facials and body treatments for both men and women; try its luscious-sounding Cocoa Wrap (a milk bath and deep-conditioning vanilla hair treatment, followed by a skin-softening warm chocolate–and–cocoa-butter body wrap) or its Deep Sea Dive, a mineral-rich mud-and-seaweed wrap.

Exhale

980 Madison Ave between 76th and 77th Sts (212-249-3000; www.exhalespa.com). Subway: 6 to 77th St. **Open** *Mon–Fri 6am–10pm; Sat, Sun 7am–9pm.*
Credit *AmEx, MC, V.*
This spot boasts an endless selection of treatments: laser therapy and microdermabrasion, in addition to plain old massages and facials. Acupuncture and yoga—including Exhale's own popular "core fusion" style that's designed to create long, lean muscles—are also offered. The reception area includes a meditation lounge, gift shop and organic café.
Other location *150 Central Park South between Sixth and Seventh Aves (opening January 2004).*

Mezzanine Medical Day Spa

62 Crosby St between Broome and Spring Sts (212-431-1600). Subway: R, W to Prince St; 6 to Spring St. **Open** *Tue, Wed noon–8pm; Thu, Fri 9am–8pm; Sat, Sun 10am–6pm.* **Credit** *AmEx, MC, V.*
Located above the Soho Integrative Health facility, Mezzanine's treatments mix East and West. Besides its detoxifying facials, you can opt for a banana-leaf wrap or a brown-sugar body polish.

Nickel

77 Eighth Ave at 14th St (212-242-3203; www.nickelformen.com). Subway: A, C, E to 14th St; L to Eighth Ave. **Open** *Sun, Mon 1–9pm; Tue–Fri 11am–9pm; Sat 10am–9pm.* **Credit** *AmEx, Disc, MC, V.*
This temple of male grooming offers facials, waxing, massages, manicures and pedicures. Nickel's own product line includes the butchly named

Spas that leave you lunch money

Feeling good in New York often comes at a price—pampering yourself can cost more than a pretty penny. But there are smaller, low-key alternatives to the bigger, well-known spas. Here are several places we recommend.

Artista Salon & Day Spa

Frills: herbal tea, mineral water
The lowdown: Artista's huge treatment rooms, laden with objets d'art and plush furniture, are warm and inviting. Heated blankets enhance the $95 aromatherapy massage experience. Pedicures ($44) are done in a room with Turkish bath–style foot sinks that are filled with smooth pebbles to massage aching feet; in the deluxe version ($54), fresh kiwi, orange and banana puree are used to soften and scent the skin. *138 Fifth Ave at 19th St (212-242-7979; www.artistasalon.com).*

Le Petit Spa

Frills: herbal tea, robe, mineral water infused with fresh strawberries, a 100-title CD library
The lowdown: Tucked behind a busy perfumery, this place is a favorite with locals in the know. Most of all, they savor the $100 Super Special treatment, which includes a deep-cleansing facial, paraffin hand treatment, digital-pressure back massage and a foot rub with chocolate and raspberry oil. In the summer, you can have your session in the spa's lovely jewel-box garden. *140 E 34th St between Lexington and Third Aves (212-685-0773; www.lepetitspanyc.com).*

Opal Center

Frills: cookies, a 157-title CD library
The lowdown: Opal's draw is Swedish-based massage in a casual, soothing environment; the emphasis is on blending top-quality technique with holistic, therapeutic benefits. Treatment rooms are spacious, furnished with beautiful rugs, flowers, candles and a sturdy massage table. After a brief consultation, your Swedish Institute–trained therapist will customize your rubdown (aromatherapy, hot stones and heated clay packs are among the

Washing Machine shower gel and Fire Insurance aftershave—as well as Self-Absorbed suntan oil, for the Narcissus in all of us.

StoneSpa

125 Fourth Ave between 12th and 13th Sts (212-254-3045; www.stonespa.com). Subway: L, N, Q, R, W, 4, 5, 6 to 14th St–Union Sq. **Open** *Mon–Sat 10am–9pm; Sun 9am–6pm.* **Credit** *AmEx, MC, V.*
As the name suggests, this place is famous for its signature Stone Massage, which uses heated river rocks to help melt away tension. After relaxing in the Moroccan-inspired tea lounge, try a hydrotherapy bath with the spa's own line of yummy-smelling salts and botanicals, or slather on a variety of skin-soothing muds and head for the lavender-scented steam room (the Maya treatment). StoneSpa also offers selected treatments for couples; the outdoor, candlelit partner massages are especially romantic.

Nails

Rescue Beauty Lounge

34 Gansevoort St between Greenwich and Hudson Sts, second floor (212-206-6409; www.rescuebeauty.com). Subway: A, C, E, 1, 2, 3, 9 to 14th St; L to Eighth Ave. **Open** *Tue–Fri 11am–8pm; Sat, Sun 10am–6pm.* **Credit** *AmEx, MC, V.*
Rescue might look nondescript, but it doesn't skimp on luxury or cost, with manicures starting at $23 and pedicures at $43. This stylishly minimalist salon is also well stocked with high-end beauty products—tony moisturizers from the La Mer line, Go Smile tooth whitener, and Dr. Hauschka lotions and oils. **Other location** *8 Centre Market Pl at Grand St (212-431-0449).*

Sweet Lily

222 West Broadway between Franklin and North Moore Sts (212-925-5441; www.sweetlilyspa.com). Subway: A, C, E to Canal St; 1, 9 to Franklin St. **Open** *Mon–Fri 11am–8pm; Sat 10am–6pm.* **Credit** *AmEx, MC, V (gratuities accepted in cash only).*
Although it's in the middle of trendy Tribeca, Sweet Lily has the feel of a country cottage, with a comforting shabby-chic decor. Sink into the giant overstuffed floral armchairs (instead of generic pedicure chairs) and treat yourself to a seasonal pedicure—such as grapefruit and mint in the summer; apple, brown sugar and cinnamon in the fall.

Objects of desire

Bookstores

Chain stores

Throughout the city, **Barnes & Noble** has opened a number of conveniently located megastores, a few of which feature readings

options). Sessions cost $80 for 70 minutes. *158 Fifth Ave between Lincoln and St. Johns Pls, Park Slope, Brooklyn (718-857-6183; www.opalcenter.com).*

Shangri-La Day Spa

Frills: mineral water
The lowdown: This intimate day spa has a nurturing, earthy atmosphere. For the signature Tibetan Herbal Body Wrap ($90), your skin is first gently exfoliated; next, your body is wrapped in towels steeped in medicinal herbs, oils and minerals; then, you're covered in warm blankets for 45 relaxing minutes, after which you shed the wrap, and specially blended oils are massaged all over your skin. You emerge deeply calmed, with skin that's smooth, supersoft and detoxified. An aromatherapy antistress facial will also leave you feeling blissful. *247 W 72nd St between Amsterdam and West End Aves, suite 1RE (212-579-0615; www.shangri-ladayspa.com).*

Foot fetish The pedicure station at **Artista.**

Eat, Drink, Shop

Comix relief Inventory at **Forbidden Planet** includes TV tie-ins and graphic novels. *See p237.*

by visiting authors. To a somewhat lesser extent, **Borders** (the other major bookstore chain) provides similar under-one-roof browsing. Check the phone book for the store nearest you, and pick up *Time Out New York* for weekly listings of readings at bookstores and other venues.

General interest

Coliseum Books

11 W 42nd St between Fifth and Sixth Aves (212-803-5890; www.coliseumbooks.com). Subway: B, D, F, V to 42nd St–Bryant Park; 7 to Fifth Ave. **Open** *Mon–Fri 8am–10pm; Sat 11am–10pm; Sun noon–7pm.* **Credit** *AmEx, DC, Disc, MC, V.*

Coliseum is something of a miracle: In 2002, this beloved haunt of bibliophiles was forced out of its 57th Street location by a rent hike. A year later, it magically reopened 15 blocks south, with many of the same staffers and fixtures.

Housing Works Used Book Cafe

126 Crosby St between Houston and Prince Sts (212-334-3324; www.housingworks.org/usedbookcafe). Subway: B, D, F, V to Broadway–Lafayette St; R, W to Prince St; 6 to Bleecker St. **Open** *Mon–Fri 10am–9pm; Sat noon–9pm; Sun noon–7pm.* **Credit** *AmEx, MC, V.*

We try not to play favorites, but the Housing Works bookstore is something special. The two-level Soho loft space—which stocks a variety of literary fiction, nonfiction and collectibles—is a peaceful spot for solo relaxation or for meeting friends over coffee or wine. All proceeds go to support services for homeless people living with HIV and AIDS.

St. Mark's Bookshop

31 Third Ave between 8th and 9th Sts (212-260-7853; www.stmarksbookshop.com). Subway: R, W to 8th St–NYU; 6 to Astor Pl. **Open** *Mon–Sat 10am–midnight; Sun 11am–midnight.* **Credit** *AmEx, Disc, MC, V.*

Students, academics and arts professionals gravitate to this East Village bookseller, which maintains strong inventories on cultural theory, graphic design, poetry and film studies, along with avant-garde journals and zines.

Strand Book Store

828 Broadway at 12th St (212-473-1452; www.strandbooks.com). Subway: L, N, Q, R, W, 4, 5, 6 to 14th St–Union Sq. **Open** *Mon–Sat 9:30am–10:30pm; Sun 11am–10:30pm.* **Credit** *AmEx, DC, Disc, MC, V.*

Owned by the Bass family since 1927, the legendary Strand—with its famous "16 miles of books"—offers incredible deals on new releases, loads of used books and the city's largest rare-book collection. If King Kong had been a reader, he'd have climbed the Strand.

Other locations *Hacker/Strand Art Books, 45 W 57th St between Fifth and Sixth Aves, fifth floor (212-688-7600); Strand Annex, 95 Fulton St between Gold and William Sts (212-732-6070); Strand Kiosk, Central Park, Fifth Ave at 60th St (646-284-5506).*

Specialty stores

East West

78 Fifth Ave between 13th and 14th Sts (212-243-5994). Subway: L, N, Q, R, W, 4, 5, 6 to 14th St–Union Sq. **Open** *Mon–Sat 10am–7:30pm; Sun 11am–6:30pm.* **Credit** *AmEx, Disc, MC, V.*
Equal space is given to Eastern and Western traditions at this spiritual titleholder, which has been helping harried urbanites follow their bliss for 27 years. An excellent source for books on philosophy, alternative health, meditation and yoga.

Forbidden Planet

840 Broadway at 13th St (212-475-6161). Subway: L, N, Q, R, W, 4, 5, 6 to 14th St–Union Sq.
Open *Mon–Sat 10am–10pm; Sun 11am–8pm.*
Credit *AmEx, Disc, MC, V.*
Embracing both the pop-culture mainstream and the cult underground, the Planet takes comics seriously. You'll find graphic novels (*Sandman, Blankets*), serials (*Asterix, Batman*) and film/TV tie-ins (*The Simpsons, Star Wars, The X-Files*).

Kitchen Arts and Letters

1435 Lexington Ave between 93rd and 94th Sts (212-876-5550). Subway: 6 to 96th St.
Open *Mon 1–6pm; Tue–Fri 10am–6:30pm; Sat 11am–6pm.* **Credit** *MC, V.*
Who knew that just reading about food could be so delicious? Lining the walls of this diminutive storefront are countless cookbooks, culinary histories and other food- and wine-related titles, including hard-to-get older editions.

The Mysterious Bookshop

129 W 56th St between Sixth and Seventh Aves (212-765-0900; www.mysteriousbookshop.com). Subway: F, N, Q, R, W to 57th St. **Open** *Mon–Sat 11am–7pm.* **Credit** *AmEx, DC, Disc, MC, V.*
If you're a devotee of the mystery, crime, suspense, spy or detective genres, you're probably familiar with owner Otto Penzler, both as an editor and from his book recommendations on Amazon.com. His brownstone shop's ground floor displays a wealth of paperbacks; climb the spiral staircase for hardcovers (including many autographed first editions).

Spoonbill & Sugartown

218 Bedford Ave between North 4th and North 5th Sts, Williamsburg, Brooklyn (718-387-7322; www.spoonbillbooks.com). Subway: L to Bedford Ave. **Open** *11am–9pm.* **Credit** *AmEx, MC, V.*
This hipster haven, located in Williamsburg's minimall, specializes in new and used books on contemporary art, art history, architecture and design. It also carries an eclectic array of fiction and nonfiction.

Cameras & electronics

When buying expensive electronic gear, check newspaper ads for price guidelines (start with the inserts in Sunday's *New York Times*). It pays to go to a well-known store to get reliable advice about a device's compatibility with systems in the country where you plan to use it. What's more, store return policies are friendlier than those of street hustlers you might see hawking the same goods. For specialized photo processing, we recommend **Duggal** (*see p374*).

B&H

420 Ninth Ave at 34th St (212-444-5040). Subway: A, C, E to 34th St–Penn Station.
Open *Mon–Thu 9am–7pm; Fri 9am–1pm; Sun 10am–5pm.* **Credit** *AmEx, Disc, MC, V.*
B&H is the ultimate one-stop shop for all your photographic, video and audio needs (including pro audio and discounted Bang & Olufsen products). Note that B&H is closed Friday afternoon, all day Saturday and on Jewish holidays.

Harvey

2 W 45th St between Fifth and Sixth Aves (212-575-5000). Subway: B, D, F, V to 42nd St–Bryant Park; 7 to Fifth Ave. **Open** *Mon–Wed, Fri 10am–7pm; Thu 10am–8pm; Sat 10am–6pm; Sun noon–5pm.* **Credit** *AmEx, MC, V.*
Though Harvey is known mainly for its huge selection of high-end products, it stocks plenty of realistically priced items and stereo furniture, too.
Other location *ABC Carpet & Home, 888 Broadway at 19th St (212-228-3354).*

J&R Music and Computer World

23 Park Row between Ann and Beekman Sts (212-238-9000, 800-221-8180). Subway: A, C to Broadway–Nassau St; J, M, Z, 4, 5 to Fulton St; 2, 3 to Park Pl. **Open** *Mon–Sat 9am–7:30pm; Sun 10:30am–6:30pm.* **Credit** *AmEx, Disc, MC, V.*
This block-long row of shops carries every electronic device you could possibly need (from PCs and TVs to CDs…and battery-powered nose-hair trimmers).

Gadget repairs

Computer Solutions Provider

See p365 for listing.

Photo-Tech Repair Service

110 E 13th St between Third and Fourth Aves (212-673-8400). Subway: L, N, Q, R, W, 4, 5, 6 to 14th St–Union Sq. **Open** *Mon, Tue, Thu, Fri 8am–4:45pm; Wed 8am–6pm; Sat 10am–3pm.*
Credit *AmEx, Disc, MC, V.*
This shop, open since 1959, has 18 on-site technicians, and guarantees that it can right your camera wrongs, regardless of the brand. Rush service is available.

Tekserve

119 W 23rd St between Sixth and Seventh Aves (212-929-3645). Subway: C, E to 23rd St.
Open *Mon–Fri 9am–7pm; Sat 10am–5pm; Sun noon–5pm.* **Credit** *AmEx, DC, MC, V.*
Tekserve is the city's resident Apple specialist. Lines are long, but take a ticket and check out the new products, or sit in the movie-theater/waiting-room section until your number is called.

Bear with me Soho's **Enchanted Forest**.

Children's toys

Sadly, at press time, famed toy emporium FAO Schwarz was set to close its doors due to financial woes. Check www.fao.com to see if the chain managed to get a reprieve.

Enchanted Forest

85 Mercer St between Broome and Spring Sts (212-925-6677). Subway: R, W to Prince St; 6 to Spring St. **Open** *Mon–Sat 11am–7pm; Sun noon–6pm.* **Credit** *AmEx, DC, Disc, MC, V.*
The forest may be enchanted, but it's hardly make-believe: Those are real trees growing inside the two-story shop. Go upstairs to sit in the treehouse, or just browse through the gallery of beasts, books and handmade toys in a magical jungle setting.

Kidding Around

60 W 15th St between Fifth and Sixth Aves (212-645-6337). Subway: F, V to 14th St; L to Sixth Ave. **Open** *Mon–Wed 10am–7pm; Thu, Fri 10am–9pm; Sun 11am–6pm.* **Credit** *AmEx, Disc, MC, V.*
Loyal customers frequent this quaint shop for learning toys and clothing for the brainy baby. The play area in the back will keep your little one occupied while you shop.

The Scholastic Store

557 Broadway between Prince and Spring Sts (212-343-6166). Subway: B, D, F, V to Broadway–Lafayette St; R, W to Prince St. **Open** *Mon–Sat 10am–7pm; Sun noon–6pm.* **Credit** *AmEx, Disc, MC, V.*
After checking out the huge selection of Scholastic books, move along to the toy section. This is the city's Harry Potter headquarters.

Toys "R" Us Times Square

1514 Broadway between 44th and 45th Sts (800-869-7787). Subway: N, Q, R, W, 42nd St S, 1, 2, 3, 9, 7 to 42nd St–Times Sq. **Open** *Mon–Sat 9am–10pm; Sun 11am–6pm.* **Credit** *AmEx, Disc, MC, V.*
The chain's flagship location is the world's largest toy store—big enough to hold an animatronic T. rex greeter and a 60-foot-high Ferris wheel inside. The store also has a two-story Barbie Dollhouse, a café and its very own sweetshop, Candy Land (designed to look just like the board game).
Other locations *throughout the city.*

Flea markets

Among bargain-hungry New Yorkers, flea-market rummaging is pursued with religious devotion. What better way to walk off that overstuffed omelette–and–Bloody Mary brunch than to explore aisles of vintage vinyl records, eight-track tapes, clothes, books and furniture?

Annex Antiques Fair & Flea Market

Sixth Ave between 24th and 26th Sts (212-243-5343). Subway: F, V to 23rd St. **Open** *Sat, Sun sunrise–sunset.* **Credit** *Cash only.*
Designers and the occasional dolled-down celebrity hunt regularly—and early—at the well-known-about-town Annex. Divided into scattered sections (one of which charges a $1 admission fee), the market has heaps of secondhand and antique clothing, old bicycles, birdcages, household items and various accessories (vintage eyewear, funky hats, scarves and handbags, platform shoes and much more). The nearby Garage indoor market, heavenly on a cold day, is a treasure trove of unusual items.
Other location *The Garage, 112 W 25th St between Sixth and Seventh Aves (212-243-5343).*

Greenflea

Intermediate School 44, Columbus Ave at 76th St (212-721-0900). Subway: B, C to 72nd St; 1, 9 to 79th St. **Open** *Sun 10am–5:30pm.* **Credit** *Cash only.*
Greenflea is an expansive market that offers everything from rare books, African art and handmade jewelry to vegetables and spiced cider (hot or cold, depending on the season). Visit both the mazelike interior and the schoolyard.
Other location *Greenwich Ave at Charles St (212-721-0900).* **Open** *Sat 10am–5:30pm.*

The Market NYC

286 Mulberry St between Houston and Prince Sts (212-580-8995). Subway: 6 to Spring St. **Open** *Sat 11am–7pm.* **Credit** *Cash only.*
Yes, it's housed in the gymnasium of a church youth center, but this market is no small shakes. Every Saturday, contemporary fashion and accessory designers hawk their wares at this Nolita address.

Florists

Although every corner deli sells flowers—especially hum-drum carnations—they usually last just a few days at best. For striking arrangements that stick around a while and aren't filled with baby's breath, try some of Manhattan's finer florists.

Banchet

809 Washington St between Gansevoort and Horatio Sts (212-989-1088). Subway: A, C, E to 14th St; L to Eighth Ave. **Open** *Mon–Fri 9am–7pm; Sat 10am–6pm.* **Credit** *AmEx, MC, V.*

Owner Bianca Jaigler, a flower-business veteran from Thailand, makes frequent jaunts to Holland to hunt down unique and obscure flora. Her bouquets (which start at $100) are jaw-droppingly dramatic constructions, bound with dogwood stems or natural twine.

Hudson River Flowers

541 Hudson St between Charles and Perry Sts (212-929-1202). Subway: A, C, E, B, D, F, V to W 4th St; 1, 9 to Christopher St–Sheridan Sq. **Open** *Mon–Sat, some Sundays 10am–7:30pm.* **Credit** *AmEx, MC, V.*

Minimalism is not a word you'll find in the lexicon of owners Mike Davis and Neno Pessoa. Their fragrant arrangements teem with discordant shapes such as hypericums, blackberries and spiky miniature proteas. Posies begin at $45.

Polux Fleuriste

248 Mott St between Houston and Prince Sts (212-219-9646). Subway: B, D, F, V to Broadway–Lafayette St; R, W to Prince St. **Open** *Mon–Sat 10am–7pm.* **Credit** *AmEx, MC, V.*

Paris-born co-owner Anouchka Levy assembles bouquets that are sweetly old-fashioned and exquisitely detailed. The shop itself is a charming sanctuary that looks as if it were uprooted from a cobblestone *rue* in Paris. Prices start at $25.

Food & drink

There is no shortage of farm-fresh, high-quality produce, meats, cheeses and grains in New York: It's expected—no, demanded, by city dwellers. Listed below are a few locally loved city markets and sweet spots.

Chocolate Bar

48 Eighth Ave between Horatio and Jane Sts (212-366-1541). Subway: A, C, E to 14th St; L to Eighth Ave. **Open** *Mon–Fri 8:30am–10pm; Sat 9am–10pm; Sun 10am–8pm.* **Credit** *AmEx, MC, V.*

Chocoholics, beware: This store gives new meaning to the word *barfly.* Owners Matt Lewis and Alison Nelson are dedicated to updating classics; 1950s-inspired chocolate clusters are redone in flavors like strawberry shortcake and cherry-coconut jubilee. Start the day with a *pain au chocolat* and a steaming cup of Chocolate Bar Chai.

Confection oven The **Jacques Torres** shop in Dumbo will cook your goose. *See p240.*

Dean & DeLuca

560 Broadway at Prince St (212-431-1691). Subway: R, W to Prince St. **Open** *Mon–Sat 10am–8pm; Sun 10am–7pm.* **Credit** *AmEx, Disc, MC, V.*

Dean & DeLuca's flagship store (one of only two that offer more than just a fancy coffeebar) provides the most sophisticated selection of specialty food items in the city. Neither residents nor visitors seem to mind the sky-high prices.

Dylan's Candy Bar

1011 Third Ave at 60th St (646-735-0078). Subway: N, R, W to Lexington Ave–59th St. **Open** *Mon–Fri 10am–9pm; Sat 10am–11pm; Sun 10am–8pm.* **Credit** *AmEx, Disc, MC, V.*

Dylan Lauren, the daughter of Ralph Lauren, runs this refined sugar-snack emporium, which has thousands of different items and a well-stocked soda fountain. The Candy Land decor is sweet!

Guss' Pickles

85–87 Orchard St between Broome and Grand Sts (917-805-4702). Subway: F to Delancey St; J, M, Z to Delancey–Essex Sts. **Open** *Mon–Thu 9:30am–6:30pm; Fri 9:30am–4pm; Sun 10am–6pm.* **Credit** *AmEx, MC, V.*

Its wandering days are over. After moving twice in recent times, the Pickle King has settled down, and his complete line of sours and half-sours, pickled peppers, watermelon rind and sauerkraut is once again available in this new location.

Jacques Torres Chocolate

66 Water St between Dock and Main Sts, Dumbo, Brooklyn (718-875-9772). Subway: A, C to High St; F to York St. **Open** *Mon–Sat 9am–7pm.* **Credit** *AmEx, MC, V.*

This small treasure trove is run by the man known to Food Network fans as "Mr. Chocolate." Sip a cup of deliciously thick hot chocolate, and watch through the large plate-glass windows as Torres's helpers work their magic in the chocolate factory next door.

McNulty's Tea and Coffee

109 Christopher St between Bleecker and Hudson Sts (212-242-5351). Subway: 1, 9 to Christopher St–Sheridan Sq. **Open** *Mon–Sat 10am–9pm; Sun 1–7pm.* **Credit** *AmEx, DC, Disc, MC, V.*

The original McNulty began selling tea in 1895; in 1980, the shop was taken over by the Wong family. There's coffee for sale here, of course, but the real draw is the tea—from the rarest White Flower Pekoe

Get the kinks out

We turned up the collar of our best raincoat and went in search of the city's seamier delights—all for you. Do a little browsing and buying of naughty nifties, then hit the town (or your hotel room). Be forewarned: Events below are subject to change, so call ahead to check that what gets you off is definitely going on.

Where to get your goodies

Eve's Garden

119 W 57th St between Sixth and Seventh Aves, suite 1201 (212-757-8651; www.evesgarden.com). Subway: N, Q, R, W to 57th St.

Bright, serene and discreet, this well-hidden store (located on the 12th floor of an office building) stocks vibrators, dildos and women-friendly erotic literature and videos. The no-hassle atmosphere is supported by an eager-to-please staff that wants you to leave with exactly the right pair of vibrating panties.

Leather Man

111 Christopher St between Bleecker and Hudson Sts (212-243-5339; www.theleatherman.com). Subway: 1, 9 to Christopher St.

Hello! Cock rings, padlocks and sturdy handcuffs greet you from wall-mounted cabinets on the first floor, while the basement (of course) is where serious bondage apparel is hung. There are also fake penises of every imaginable (and unimaginable) description. The store is oriented toward gay men, so it might intimidate all but the ballsiest of chicks.

Purple Passion

211 W 20th St between Seventh and Eighth Aves (212-807-0486; www.purplepassion.com). Subway: C, E to 23rd St; 1, 9 to 18th St.

The walls are lined with harnesses, corsets, whips and cuffs; cabinets overflow with butt plugs, ball gags and other mind-and-body–boggling devices. You get the picture.

Toys in Babeland

94 Rivington St between Ludlow and Orchard Sts (212-375-1701; www.babeland.com). Subway: F, V to Lower East Side–Second Ave.

At this friendly sex-toy boutique—run by women, for women—engrossed browsers are encouraged to handle all manner of buzzing, wriggling and bendable playthings. Attitude-free guys are welcome, and seem equally at home perusing the toys, books, videos and accessories that pack the shelves. The (harvested once a year in China and priced at $25 per quarter pound) and peach-flavored green tea (at $6 per quarter pound) to basic Darjeeling.

M2M

55 Third Ave at 11th St (212-353-2698). Subway: L to Third Ave; 6 to Astor Pl. **Open** *Sun–Thu 9am–midnight; Fri, Sat 9am–2am.* **Credit** *AmEx, MC, V.*
The Asian convenience store M2M (its name stands for "morning to midnight") is like a Japanese 7-Eleven. You won't find Slim Jims, but the selection of squid jerky is robust. The store specializes in edibles of all kinds from the Pacific Rim.

Myers of Keswick

634 Hudson St between Horatio and Jane Sts (212-691-4194). Subway: A, C, E to 14th St; L to Eighth Ave. **Open** *Mon–Fri 10am–7pm; Sat 10am–6pm; Sun noon–5pm.* **Credit** *AmEx, MC, V.*
This charming English market is a frequent stop for Brits and local Anglophiles. While some come looking for a hint of home or a jolly good meet-and-greet, others flock to the store for Cornish pasties, homemade sausages, baked beans, steak-and-kidney pies and assorted British candies and tea biscuits.

Russ & Daughters

179 E Houston St between Allen and Orchard Sts (212-475-4880). Subway: F, V to Lower East Side–Second Ave. **Open** *Mon–Sat 9am–7pm; Sun 8am–5:30pm.* **Credit** *AmEx, Disc, MC, V.*
You'll feel like a circus seal when the jovial men behind the counter of this legendary shop start tossing you bits of lox, but who's complaining? Russ & Daughters, open since 1914, sells eight other kinds of smoked salmon and many Jewish-inflected Eastern European delectables, along with Russian and Iranian caviar.

Zabar's

2245 Broadway at 80th St (212-787-2000). Subway: 1, 9 to 79th St. **Open** *Mon–Fri 8am–7:30pm; Sat 8am–8pm; Sun 9am–6pm.* **Credit** *AmEx, MC, V.*
Zabar's is more than just a market—it's a New York City landmark. You might leave the place feeling a little light in the wallet, but you can't do better than their topflight prepared food. Besides the famous smoked fish and rafts of Jewish-style delicacies, Zabar's has a fabulous selection of bread, cheese and coffee—and an entire floor of decently priced gadgets and housewares.

broads at Babeland also host frank sex-ed classes (open to all genders and sexualities), covering multiple subjects.
Other location *43 Mercer St between Broome and Grand Sts (212-966-2120).*

Where to party

Fetish Retinue

212-529-5964; www.baroness.com.
Roll up in your latex, leather or fetish outfit—the dress code is strictly enforced—and pay court to the Baroness, whose monthly downtown fetish parties have made her a brand name.

One Leg Up

www.onelegupnyc.com.
At these exclusive fleshfest soirees, there's a rigorous vetting process: You must submit a saucy photo and write an erotic essay in advance before you're given a secret password that allows you to wriggle and writhe with other hot straight couples.

Paddles

250 W 26th St between Seventh and Eighth Aves (212-629-1854; www.paddlesnyc.com).
If the sight of slave auctions is your idea of a spanking good time, then check out this

Attention! Vibrators at **Toys in Babeland**.

Chelsea institution, home to DomSubFriends and a raft of other naughty nighttime types. You'll find the floor shows so intoxicating, you won't notice the no-booze policy.

SPAM

718-789-4053.
Gay men and lesbians frolic in their undies at this monthly play party. Onlookers get an eyeful of all-gender cross-pollination (picture femme guys going down on strap-on wearing butch dykes) at this feverish gathering of sadists, punks and masochists (SPAM).

Farmers' markets

There are more than 20 open-air markets sponsored by city authorities in various locations and on different days. The largest and best-known is at **Union Square** (*see p95*), where small producers of cheese, flowers, herbs, honey, and fruits and vegetables sell their wares. Arrive early, before the good stuff sells out. For information about other venues, call or visit the website of the **Council on the Environment of New York City** *(212-477-3220; www.cenyc.org)*.

Liquor stores

Most supermarkets and corner delis sell beer. To buy wine or spirits, you need to go to a liquor store (most of them don't sell suds, however, and all are closed on Sundays).

Astor Wines & Spirits

12 Astor Pl at Lafayette St (212-674-7500). Subway: R, W to 8th St–NYU; 6 to Astor Pl. **Open** *Mon–Sat 9am–9pm.* **Credit** *AmEx, Disc, MC, V.*

This modern wine supermarket could serve as the perfect blueprint for a chain, were it not for legal obstacles that prevent liquor stores from branching out.

Sherry-Lehmann

679 Madison Ave at 61st St (212-838-7500). Subway: F to Lexington Ave–63rd St; N, R, W to Fifth Ave–59th St. **Open** *Mon–Sat 9am–7pm.* **Credit** *AmEx, MC, V.*

Perhaps the most famous of New York's numerous upscale liquor stores, Sherry-Lehmann has a vast selection of liquors, as well as a superb assortment of American, French and Italian wines.

Vintage New York

482 Broome St at Wooster St (212-226-9463). Subway: C, E to Spring St; 1, 9 to Canal St. **Open** *Mon–Sat 11am–9pm; Sun noon–9pm.* **Credit** *AmEx, Disc, MC, V.*

Technically, Vintage is an outpost of an upstate winery, which means it's open for business on Sundays. One catch: It only sells wines from New York vineyards, but you can sample any wine before buying. **Other location** *2492 Broadway at 93rd St (212-721-9999).*

Gift shops

Auto

805 Washington St between Gansevoort and Horatio Sts (212-229-2292). Subway: A, C, E to 14th St; L to Eighth Ave. **Open** *Tue–Sat noon–7pm; Sun noon–6pm.* **Credit** *AmEx, MC, V.*

This cool, white-walled store-cum-gallery is also warm and welcoming. The owners select gifted artisans who dabble in everything from handblown glass pieces and personalized ceramic shrinky-dink necklaces to paintings and bedding.

Breukelen

369 Atlantic Ave between Bond and Hoyt Sts, Boerum Hill, Brooklyn (718-246-0024). Subway: A, C, G to Hoyt–Schermerhorn. **Open** *Tue–Sat noon–7pm; Sun noon–6pm.* **Credit** *AmEx, MC, V.*

Incongruously situated in the middle of Atlantic Avenue's three-block stretch of antiques shops, this contemporary-design store features clean, pared-down household objects, including pet dishes, table lamps, salad bowls, flatware, sleek glass carafes and tumblers. The Manhattan branch specializes in larger items—attractive but spare, mod furniture—and goods come with slightly larger price tags, too. **Other location** *68 Gansevoort St between Greenwich and Washington Sts (212-645-2216).*

Love Saves the Day

119 Second Ave at 7th St (212-228-3802). ubway: 6 to Astor Pl. **Open** *Noon–9pm daily.* **Credit** *AmEx, MC, V.*

Kitsch reigns here: Yoda dolls, Elvis lamps, ant farms, lurid machine-made tapestries of Madonna, glow-in-the-dark crucifixes, collectible toys and Mexican Day of the Dead statues. Vintage clothing is peppered throughout the store.

Metropolitan Opera Shop

136 W 65th St at Broadway (212-580-4090). Subway: 1, 9 to 66th St–Lincoln Ctr. **Open** *Mon–Sat 10am–10pm; Sun noon–6pm.* **Credit** *AmEx, Disc, MC, V.*

In the Metropolitan Opera House at Lincoln Center, this shop sells CDs and cassettes of—yep—operas. You'll also find a wealth of opera books, memorabilia and DVDs. Kids aren't forgotten, either: The children's department stocks plenty of educational CDs.

Move Lab

803 Washington St between Gansevoort and Horatio Sts (212-741-5520). Subway: A, C, E to 14th St; L to Eighth Ave. **Open** *Tue–Sat noon–7pm; Sun noon–6pm.* **Credit** *AmEx, MC, V.*

The store is packed with quirky, modern-looking objects that bear visible marks of craftsmanship and a sense of history. Move Lab's blend of furniture, jewelry (including Braille-inscribed rings) and other objects is anything but monotonous.

Mxyplyzyk

125 Greenwich Ave at 13th St (212-989-4300). Subway: A, C, E to 14th St; L to Eighth Ave. **Open** *Mon–Sat 11am–7pm; Sun noon–5pm.* **Credit** *AmEx, MC, V.*

The moniker doesn't mean anything, though it's reminiscent of a character in the Superman comics. Mxyplyzyk offers cool gifts, lighting, furniture, housewares, stationery, toys, pet gear and lots of novelty books—on important topics such as paranoid taxi-driver wisdom.

Pearl River Mart

477 Broadway between Broome and Grand Sts (212-431-4770). Subway: J, M, Z, N, Q, R, W to Canal St; 6 to Spring St. **Open** *10am–7:20pm.* **Credit** *AmEx, Disc, MC, V.*

It's in the cards Mother-of-pearl bowls at **Saigoniste** get a saucy price tag.

This downtown emporium is crammed with all things Chinese: bedroom slippers, clothing, gongs, groceries, medicinal herbs, stationery, teapots, woks and all sorts of little gift items. Fun for browsing, the loft-size shop is an ideal spot to pick up trinkets to take home.
Other location *200 Grand St between Mott and Mulberry Sts (212-966-1010).*

Saigoniste

239 Mulberry St between Prince and Spring Sts (212-925-4610). Subway: R, W to Prince St; 6 to Spring St. **Open** *Mon–Fri 11am–7pm; Sat, Sun 11am–6pm.* **Credit** *AmEx, MC, V.*
The colors of this store's Vietnamese-made lacquerware, fashions and home accessories change every season, so there's always something new. Load up your shopping basket with pillows, bamboo and lacquer bowls, and traditional tea sets.

Home & design

ABC Carpet & Home

888 Broadway at 19th St (212-473-3000). Subway: R, W to 23rd St. **Open** *Mon–Thu 10am–8pm; Fri, Sat 10am–6:30pm; Sun noon–6pm.* **Credit** *AmEx, Disc, MC, V.*
At this shopping landmark, the selection of accessories, linens, rugs, reproduction and antique (Western and Asian) furniture is unbelievable; so are the mostly steep prices. For bargains, head to ABC's warehouse outlets in the Bronx or Brooklyn.
Other location *20 Jay St at Plymouth St, Dumbo, Brooklyn (718-643-7400); ABC Carpet & Home Warehouse, 1055 Bronx River Ave between Westchester Ave and Bruckner Blvd, Bronx (718-842-8772).*

The Apartment

101 Crosby St between Prince and Spring Sts (212-219-3066). Subway: R, W to Prince St; 6 to Spring St. **Open** *Mon, Tue by appointment only; Wed–Sat noon–7pm; Sun noon–6pm.* **Credit** *AmEx, MC, V.*
Owners Gina Alvarez and Stefan Boublil have designed this lifestyle shop to look like a Tribeca loft occupied by some pretty young thing and her perfect boyfriend. You, the shopper, are meant to lounge on the minimalist Dutch furniture as if *chez vous*. All that you see is for sale: the Moderno Lifestyle Emmanuele bed, ogle the Duravit bathroom fixtures by Philippe Starck—everything.

Area I.D. Moderne

262 Elizabeth St between Houston and Prince Sts (212-219-9903). Subway: B, D, F, V to Broadway–Lafayette St; 6 to Bleecker St. **Open** *Mon–Fri noon–7pm; Sat, Sun noon–6pm.* **Credit** *AmEx, MC, V.*
Home accessories and furniture from the 1950s, '60s and '70s, both vintage and reproduction, are this shop's métier—*except* that all of its furniture has been reupholstered in luxurious fabrics. The store also carries a wide selection of fur throws and rugs.

Arredo

23–25 Greene St between Canal and Grand Sts (212-334-2363). Subway: A, C, E to Canal St; R, W to Prince St. **Open** *Tue–Fri 10am–6pm; Sat noon–6pm.* **Credit** *Cash only.*

Letter perfect The selection at **ABC** is dazzling. The prices are dazing. *See p243.*

Arredo specializes in sleek goods from Vivendum, a consortium of seven Italian interior companies. Buttery leather Matteograssi couches and luxe wooden walk-in closets by Lema are laid out around the showroom in the style of a posh Manhattan loft.

Bodum Café and Home Store

413–415 W 14th St between Ninth and Tenth Aves (212-367-9125). Subway: A, C, E to 14th St; L to Eighth Ave. **Open** *Mon–Sat 10am–7pm; Sun noon–6pm.* **Credit** *AmEx, MC, V.*

Bodum isn't just about coffee presses: Its smartly designed Meatpacking District store also has kitchen, office, dining room and bathroom supplies. If the sheer number of items overwhelms you, take a break at the coffeebar and regain your strength.

Chelsea Garden Center

435 Hudson St at Morton St (212-727-7100). Subway: 1, 9 to Houston St. **Open** *Mon–Fri 11am–7pm; Sat 10am–7pm.* **Credit** *AmEx, MC, V.*

Chelsea Garden Center's 6,000-square-foot, sun-filled garden, home and lifestyle store has plenty of how-to and coffee-table books, furniture, plants, seeds, pottery and tools that are sure to brighten your host's pad (or your own). The uptown location focuses on outdoor plants.

Other location *455 W 16th St between Ninth and Tenth Aves (212-929-2477).*

Design Within Reach

142 Wooster St between Houston and Prince Sts (212-475-0001). Subway: B, D, F, V to Broadway–Lafayette St; R, W to Prince St. **Open** *Mon–Sat 11am–7pm; Sun noon–6pm.* **Credit** *AmEx, MC, V.*

This is a 3-D version of the California-based company's catalogs—which are themselves the aesthete's equivalent of the King James Bible. All the greats are here: George Nelson, Philippe Starck, and Charles and Ray Eames, among others.

Other location *408 W 14th St between Ninth and Tenth Aves (212-242-9449).*

MoMA Design Store

44 W 53rd St between Fifth and Sixth Aves (212-767-1050). Subway: E, V to Fifth Ave–53rd St. **Open** *Sun–Thu, Sat 10am–6:30pm; Fri 10am–8pm.* **Credit** *AmEx, MC, V.*

The store is as eclectic as the museum itself. On display: state-of-the-art home items, from casseroles to coffee tables, as well as an assortment of high-design chairs, lighting, office workstations, kids' furniture, jewelry and calendars.

Other location *81 Spring St at Crosby St (646-613-1367).*

Moss

146 Greene St between Houston and Prince Sts (212-204-7100). Subway: B, D, F, V to Broadway–Lafayette St. **Open** *Mon–Sat 11am–7pm; Sun noon–6pm.* **Credit** *AmEx, Disc, MC, V.*

Many of the streamlined clocks, curvy sofas and funky saltshakers are kept under glass in this museumlike temple of contemporary home design.

The Terence Conran Shop

407 E 59th St between First and York Aves (212-755-9079). Subway: N, R, W to Lexington Ave–59th St; 4, 5, 6 to 59th St. **Open** *Mon–Fri 11am–8pm; Sat 10am–7pm; Sun noon–6pm.* **Credit** *AmEx, DC, MC, V.*

Sir Terence Conran's shop, nestled beneath the Queensboro Bridge, stocks a vast selection of trendy products—new and vintage—for every room of the house: cabinets, dishes, lighting, rugs, sofas, draperies, beds, linens and much more.

Urban Archaeology

143 Franklin St between Hudson and Varick Sts, second floor (212-431-4646). Subway: A, C, E to Canal St; 1, 9 to Franklin St. **Open** *Mon–Fri 8am–6pm; Sat noon–6pm.* **Credit** *AmEx, Disc, MC, V.*

Old building parts are salvaged, refurbished and sold here as architectural artifacts, from Corinthian columns and lobby-size chandeliers to bathtubs and doorknobs, as well as reproductions of favorites.

Other location *239 E 58th St between Second and Third Aves (212-371-4646).*

West Elm

75 Front St at Main St, Dumbo, Brooklyn (718-875-7757). Subway: A, C to High St; F to York St. **Open** *Mon–Sat 10am–9pm; Sun 11am–7pm.* **Credit** *AmEx, Disc, MC, V.*

The younger, hipper sibling of Pottery Barn has finally gone from catalog to a bricks-and-mortar outpost in the arty 'hood of Dumbo. This 5,000-square-foot flagship store showcases affordable minimalist furniture and accessories in a starkly modern, skylighted space. Look for couches, futons, beds, sturdy tables and more, all displayed in a showroom-like setting.

Music

Superstores

HMV

308 W 125th St between Frederick Douglass Blvd (Eighth Ave) and St. Nicholas Ave (212 932-9619). Subway: A, C, B, D to 125th St. **Open** *Mon–Thu 9am–9pm; Fri, Sat 9am–10pm; Sun 11am–8pm.* **Credit** *AmEx, Disc, MC, V.*

HMV has a colossal multigenre selection of cassettes, CDs, videos and vinyl.

Other location *565 Fifth Ave at 46th St (212-681-6700).*

J&R Music & Computer World

See p237 for listing.

Tower Records

692 Broadway at 4th St (212-505-1500, 800-648-4844). Subway: R, W to 8th St–NYU. **Open** *9am–midnight daily.* **Credit** *AmEx, Disc, MC, V.*

Tower has all the current sounds on CD and tape. Visit the clearance store down the block *(22 E 4th St at Lafayette St, 212-228-5100)* for markdowns in all formats, including vinyl (especially classical).

Other locations *throughout the city.*

Virgin Megastore

52 E 14th St at Broadway (212-598-4666). Subway: L, N, Q, R, W, 4, 5, 6 to 14th St–Union Sq. **Open** *Mon–Sat 9am–1am; Sun 10am–midnight.* **Credit** *AmEx, Disc, MC, V.*

Besides a huge selection of music in all genres, Virgin Megastore has in-store performances and a great selection of CDs from the U.K. Books and videos are also available.

Other location *1540 Broadway between 45th and 46th Sts (212-921-1020).*

Multigenre

Bleecker Bob's

118 W 3rd St between MacDougal St and Sixth Ave (212-475-9677). Subway: A, C, E, B, D, F, V to W 4th St. **Open** *Sun–Thu 11am–1am; Fri, Sat 11am–3am.* **Credit** *AmEx, MC, V.*

Come for hard-to-find new and used music, especially on vinyl.

Etherea

66 Ave A between 4th and 5th Sts (212-358-1126). Subway: F, V to Lower East Side–Second Ave. **Open** *Sun–Thu noon–10pm; Fri, Sat noon–11pm.* **Credit** *AmEx, Disc, MC, V.*

Etherea stocks mostly electronic, experimental, house, indie and rock CDs.

Mondo Kim's

6 St. Marks Pl between Second and Third Aves (212-598-9985). Subway: 6 to Astor Pl. **Open** *9am–midnight daily.* **Credit** *AmEx, MC, V.*

This minichain of movie-and-music stores offers a great selection for collector geeks: electronic, indie, kraut, prog, reggae, soul, soundtracks and used CDs.

Other locations *throughout the city.*

Other Music

15 E 4th St between Broadway and Lafayette St (212-477-8150). Subway: R, W to 8th St–NYU; 6 to Astor Pl. **Open** *Mon–Fri noon–9pm; Sat noon–8pm; Sun noon–7pm.* **Credit** *AmEx, MC, V.*

This wee audio temple is dedicated to small-label, often-imported new and used CDs and LPs. It organizes music by arcane categories (for instance, "La Decadanse" includes lounge, Moog and soft-core soundtracks); and it sends out a free weekly e-mail with staffers' reviews of their favorite new releases.

St. Marks Sounds

16 St. Marks Pl (212-677-2727) and 20 St. Marks Pl (212-677-3444) between Second and Third Aves. Subway: 6 to Astor Pl. **Open** *Sun–Thu noon–8pm; Fri, Sat noon–9pm.* **Credit** *Cash only.*

Consisting of two neighboring stores, Sounds is the best bargain for new and used music on the block. The eastern branch specializes in jazz and international recordings.

Subterranean Records

5 Cornelia St between Bleecker St and W 4th St (212-463-8900). Subway: A, C, E, B, D, F, V to W 4th St. **Open** *Mon–Wed noon–8pm; Thu–Sat noon–10pm; Sun noon–7pm.* **Credit** *MC, V.*

This just-off-Bleecker shop carries new, used and live recordings, as well as a large selection of imports. Vinyl LPs and 45s fill the basement.

Tracking it down Vinyl rules at **Fat Beats**, the tip-top one-stop hip-hop record shop.

Classical

Gryphon Record Shop

233 W 72nd St between Broadway and West End Ave (212-874-1588). Subway: 1, 2, 3, 9 to 72nd St. **Open** *Mon–Fri 9:30am–8pm; Sat 11am–8:30pm; Sun noon–6pm.* **Credit** *MC, V.*
This solidly classical store has traditionally stocked vinyl only, but the nascent 21st century has swept in a wave of CDs. Gryphon also carries a sprinkling of jazz, as well as drama and film books.

Electronica

Dance Tracks

91 E 3rd St at First Ave (212-260-8729). Subway: F, V to Lower East Side–Second Ave. **Open** *Mon–Fri noon–9pm; Sat noon–8pm; Sun noon–7pm.* **Credit** *AmEx, Disc, MC, V.*
European imports hot off the plane (and nearly as cheap here) are what make this store a must. But it also has racks of domestic house, enticing bins of Loft/Paradise Garage classics and private decks on which to listen.

Hip-hop & R&B

Beat Street Records

494 Fulton St between Bond St and Elm Pl, Downtown Brooklyn (718-624-6400). Subway: A, C, G to Hoyt–Schermerhorn; 2, 3, 4, 5 to Nevins St. **Open** *Mon–Wed 10am–7pm; Thu–Sat 10am–7:30pm; Sun 10am–6pm.* **Credit** *AmEx, Disc, MC, V.*
A block-long basement with two DJ booths, Beat Street has the latest vinyl to go with that phat new sound system. CDs run from dancehall to gospel, but the reggae boom shots, 12-inch singles and new hip-hop albums make this the first stop for local DJs seeking killer breakbeats and samples.

Fat Beats

406 Sixth Ave between 8th and 9th Sts, second floor (212-673-3883). Subway: A, C, E, B, D, F, V to W 4th St. **Open** *Mon–Sat noon–9pm; Sun noon–6pm.* **Credit** *MC, V.*
This tiny West Village shrine to vinyl is the epicenter of local hip-hop. Everyone—Beck, DJ Evil Dee, DJ Premier, Mike D, Q-Tip—shops here regularly for treasured hip-hop, jazz, funk and reggae releases, as well as for underground magazines (*Wax Poetics*) and cult flicks (*Wild Style*).

Jazz

Jazz Record Center

236 W 26th St between Seventh and Eighth Aves, room 804 (212-675-4480). Subway: C, E to 23rd St; 1, 9 to 28th St. **Open** *Mon–Sat 10am–6pm.* **Credit** *Disc, MC, V.*
The best jazz store in the city stocks current and out-of-print records, books, videos and other jazz-related merchandise. Worldwide shipping is available.

World music

World Music Institute

49 W 27th St between Broadway and Sixth Ave, suite 930 (212-545-7536). Subway: R, W to 28th St. **Open** *Mon–Fri 10am–6pm.* **Credit** *AmEx, MC, V.*
The store is small, but if you can't find what you're looking for, WMI's expert, helpful employees can order sounds from the remotest corners of the planet and have them shipped right to you, usually within two to four weeks.

Specialty stores

Arthur Brown & Brothers

2 W 46th St between Fifth and Sixth Aves (212-575-5555). Subway: B, D, F, V to 47–50th Sts–Rockefeller Ctr; 7 to Fifth Ave. **Open** *Mon–Fri 9am–6:30pm; Sat 10am–6pm.* **Credit** *AmEx, DC, Disc, MC, V.*
A staggering selection of pens includes Cartier, Dupont, Montblanc, Porsche and Schaeffer.

Big City Kites

1210 Lexington Ave at 82nd St (212-472-2623). Subway: 4, 5, 6 to 86th St. **Open** *Mon–Wed, Fri 11am–6:30pm; Thu 11am–7:30pm; Sat 10am–6pm. Call for summer hours.* **Credit** *AmEx, Disc, MC, V.*
Act like a kid again and go fly a kite. There are more than 150 to choose from.

Carrandi Gallery

138 W 18th St between Sixth and Seventh Aves (212-206-0499, 212-242-0710). Subway: 1, 9 to 18th St. **Open** *Tue–Sat noon–6pm.* **Credit** *AmEx, Disc, MC, V.*
Carrandi stocks original advertising posters from both sides of the Atlantic, dating as far back as 1880.

Evolution

120 Spring St between Greene and Mercer Sts (212-343-1114). Subway: C, E to Spring St. **Open** *11am–7pm daily.* **Credit** *AmEx, Disc, MC, V.*
If natural history is your obsession, look no further. Fossils, giraffe skulls, wild-boar tusks, dinosaur eggs and insects mounted behind glass are among the quirky items for sale inside this relatively politically correct store. Fret not: All of the animals died of natural causes or were "culled." (*See also p280* **Shopping is child's play**.)

F.M. Allen

962 Madison Ave between 75th and 76th Sts (212-737-4374). Subway: 6 to 77th St. **Open** *Mon–Sat 10am–6pm; Sun noon–5pm.* **Credit** *AmEx, DC, Disc, MC, V.*
Colonialism may be dead, but its distinctive aesthetic lives on at this luxury safari boutique. British campaign furniture from the 19th and early-20th centuries is showcased alongside new, utilitarian-chic bags. A canvas tent serves as a dressing room, and sturdy totes are built to survive the bush, as is the nouveau-safari clothing line.

Game Show

1240 Lexington Ave between 83rd and 84th Sts (212-472-8011). Subway: 4, 5, 6 to 86th St. **Open** *Mon–Wed, Fri, Sat 11am–6pm; Thu 11am–7pm; Sun noon–5pm.* **Credit** *AmEx, MC, V.*
Head to Game Show to let your inner-child run wild. Scads of board games are sold here, many of them guaranteed to leave you intrigued or possibly even embarrassed (a few of the games are nicely off-color).
Other location *474 Sixth Ave between 11th and 12th Sts (212-633-6328).*

Jerry Ohlinger's Movie Material Store

242 W 14th St between Seventh and Eighth Aves (212-989-0869). Subway: A, C, E, 1, 2, 3, 9 to 14th St; L to Eighth Ave. **Open** *1–7:45pm daily.* **Credit** *AmEx, Disc, MC, V.*
On premises: the most extensive stock of "paper material" from movies past and present, including photos, posters, programs and fascinating celebrity curios.

Kate's Paperie

561 Broadway between Prince and Spring Sts (212-941-9816). Subway: R, W to Prince St; 6 to Spring St. **Open** *10am–7:30pm daily.* **Credit** *AmEx, Disc, MC, V.*
Kate's is the ultimate paper mill—you can choose from more than 5,000 different kinds of paper, and also mine the rich vein of stationery, custom printing, journals, photo albums and creative, amazingly beautiful gift-wrapping paper.
Other locations *throughout the city.*

Handpressed at **Kate's Paperie**.

Nat Sherman

500 Fifth Ave at 42nd St (212-764-5000). Subway: B, D, F, V to 42nd St–Bryant Park; 7 to Fifth Ave. **Open** *Mon–Fri 10am–8pm; Sat 10am–7pm; Sun 11am–5pm.* **Credit** *AmEx, DC, MC, V.*

Located across the street from the New York Public Library, Nat Sherman has its own brand of slow-burning cigarettes, as well as cigars and related accoutrements (such as cigar humidors and smoking chairs). Flick your Bic in the famous smoking room upstairs.

Pearl Paint

308 Canal St between Broadway and Church St (212-431-7932). Subway: J, M, Z, N, Q, R, W, 6 to Canal St. **Open** *Mon–Fri 9am–7pm; Sat 10am–6:30pm; Sun 10am–6pm.* **Credit** *AmEx, Disc, MC, V.*

This art- and drafting-supply commissary is bigger than a supermarket, and sells everything you could possibly need to create your masterpiece.

Other location *207 E 23rd St between Second and Third Aves (212-592-2179).*

Quark International

537 Third Ave between 35th and 36th Sts (212-889-1808). Subway: 6 to 33rd St. **Open** *Mon–Fri 10am–6:30pm; Sat noon–5pm.* **Credit** *AmEx, DC, Disc, MC, V.*

Spy wanna-bes and budding paranoids can buy body armor or high-powered bugs here. The store will also custom-bulletproof your favorite jacket.

Sam Ash Music

160 W 48th St between Sixth and Seventh Aves (212-719-2299). Subway: B, D, F, V to 47–50th Sts–Rockefeller Ctr; N, R, W to 49th St. **Open** *Mon–Sat 10am–8pm; Sun noon–6pm.* **Credit** *AmEx, MC, V.*

This 80-year-old musical-instrument emporium dominates its midtown block with four neighboring shops. New, vintage and custom guitars are available, along with amps, DJ equipment, drums, keyboards, recording equipment, turntables and a wide array of sheet music.

Other locations *throughout the city.*

Spot

78 Seventh Ave between 15th and 16th Sts (212-604-0331). Subway: F, V, 1, 2, 3, 9 to 14th St. **Open** *Mon–Sat 11am–8pm; Sun noon–6pm.* **Credit** *AmEx, Disc, MC, V.*

Perfect for the shopper who pantingly parts with cash in order to better outfit his or her pug. This compact lime-green space is stocked with clothes (hoodie sweatshirts that have BITCH or STUD stitched across the back), beds, toys and tons of treats for your favorite four-legged friend. Merchandise is seasonal, so your pooch or pussycat will never be out of fashion.

Stack's Coin Company

123 W 57th St between Sixth and Seventh Aves (212-582-2580). Subway: F, N, Q, R, W to 57th St. **Open** *Mon–Fri 10am–5pm.* **Credit** *Cash only.*

The oldest, largest coin dealer in the U.S. trades in rare coins from all over the world.

Tiny Doll House

1179 Lexington Ave between 80th and 81st Sts (212-744-3719). Subway: 6 to 77th St. **Open** *Mon–Fri 11am–5:30pm; Sat 11am–5pm.* **Credit** *AmEx, MC, V.*

Everything here is itty-bitty: miniature furniture and wares for dollhouses include beds, chests, cutlery, kitchen fittings—even tiny potted palms with accompanying bags of Miracle-Gro. Kids of all ages will fall for this place in a big way.

West Marine

12 W 37th St between Fifth and Sixth Aves (212-594-6065). Subway: B, D, F, V, N, Q, R, W to 34th St–Herald Sq. **Open** *Mon–Fri 10am–6pm; Sat, Sun 10am–3pm.* **Credit** *AmEx, Disc, MC, V.*

Basic seafaring supplies, deck shoes and fishing gear is for sale. Or perhaps you need a $2,000 global positioning system unit?

Sports

Blades, Board and Skate

659 Broadway between Bleecker and Bond Sts (212-477-7350). Subway: B, D, F, V to Broadway–Lafayette St; 6 to Bleecker St. **Open** *Mon–Sat 10am–9pm; Sun 11am–7pm.* **Credit** *MC, V.*

This is *the* place for in-line skates, skateboards, snowboards, and the requisite clothing and gear.

Other locations *throughout the city.*

Gerry Cosby & Co.

3 Pennsylvania Plaza, Madison Square Garden, Seventh Ave at 32nd St (212-563-6464, 877-563-6464). Subway: A, C, E, 1, 2, 3, 9 to 34th St–Penn Station. **Open** *9:30am–7:30pm.* **Credit** *AmEx, Disc, MC, V.*

Cosby has a huge selection of official team wear and other sporting necessities. The store remains open during—and until 30 minutes after—evening Knicks and Rangers games, just in case you're feeling celebratory.

Niketown

6 E 57th St between Fifth and Madison Aves (212-891-6453, 800-671-6453). Subway: N, R, W to Fifth Ave–59th St. **Open** *Mon–Sat 10am–8pm; Sun 11am–7pm.* **Credit** *AmEx, Disc, MC, V.*

Don't despair if you have difficulty choosing from among the 1,200 models of footwear. A huge screen drops down every 23 minutes and plays a Nike ad to focus your desires. Look also for sports attire to outfit men, women and kids for all kinds of play.

Paragon Sporting Goods

867 Broadway at 18th St (212-255-8036). Subway: L, N, Q, R, W, 4, 5, 6 to 14th St–Union Sq. **Open** *Mon–Sat 10am–8pm; Sun 11:30am–7pm.* **Credit** *AmEx, DC, Disc, MC, V.*

Three floors of equipment and clothing for almost every activity (at every level of expertise) make this the New York sports gear mecca.

Sit, stay, shop Find the perfect canine accessory at **Spot**, in Chelsea. *See p248.*

Tattoos & piercing

Tattooing was made legal in New York in 1998; piercing, however, remains relatively unregulated, so mind your nipples.

New York Adorned

47 Second Ave between 2nd and 3rd Sts (212-473-0007). Subway: F, V to Lower East Side–Second Ave. **Open** *Sun–Thu 1–9pm; Fri, Sat 1–10pm.* **Credit** *AmEx, MC, V (cash only for tattoos).*
Proprietor Lori Leven recruits world-class tattoo artists to wield the needles at her seven-year-old gothic-elegant establishment. For those with a low pain threshold, there are gentler body decorations—in the form of henna tattoos—and jewelry, such as ethereal white-gold cluster earrings crafted by Leven herself, as well as pieces by a group of emerging body jewelry designers.

Venus Modern Body Arts

199 E 4th St between Aves A and B (212-473-1954). Subway: F, V to Lower East Side–Second Ave. **Open** *Sun–Thu 1–9pm; Fri, Sat 1–10pm.* **Credit** *AmEx, Disc, MC, V.*
Venus has been tattooing and piercing New Yorkers since 1992—before body art became *de rigueur*. It also offers an enormous selection of jewelry, so you can put diamonds in your navel and platinum in your tongue.

Travel & luggage

Bag House

797 Broadway between 10th and 11th Sts (212-260-0940). Subway: L, N, Q, R, W, 4, 5, 6 to 14th St–Union Sq. **Open** *Mon–Sat 11am–7pm; Sun 1–6pm.* **Credit** *AmEx, MC, V.*
Find all sorts of bags, from the tiniest tote to something that could hold every towel in the Plaza Hotel.

Coach

595 Madison Ave at 57th St (212-754-0041). Subway: N, R, W to Lexington Ave–59th St; 4, 5, 6 to 59th St. **Open** *Mon–Sat 10am–8pm; Sun 11am–6pm.* **Credit** *AmEx, DC, Disc, MC, V.*
Coach's butter-soft leather briefcases, wallets and handbags have always been exceptional, but the Manhattan Coach stores now also stock the label's luxurious outerwear collection.
Other locations *throughout the city.*

Flight 001

96 Greenwich Ave between Jane and W 12th Sts (212-691-1001). Subway: A, C, E to 14th St; L to Eighth Ave. **Open** *Mon–Fri 11am–8:30pm; Sat 11am–8pm; Sun noon–6pm.* **Credit** *AmEx, DC, Disc, MC, V.*
This one-stop West Village shop carries guidebooks and chic luggage, along with fun travel products such as pocket-size aromatherapy kits. Forget something? Flight 001's "essentials" wall features packets of Woolite, mini-dominoes and everything in between.

Arts & Entertainment

Features

Festivals & Events

There's always something to celebrate.

As the weather changes by the season, so too does New York's constant buzz of activity. Spring brings parades and early outdoor events, while hot, sticky summer revelers celebrate with alfresco concerts, waterfront carnivals and Independence Day fireworks. Street fairs, Halloween parties and the famous Macy's Thanksgiving parade draw autumn crowds, followed by winter's sparkling multicultural holiday festivities.

We've listed some of the city's popular annual happenings (look in this **Arts & Entertainment** section for additional seasonal music, film and performance festivals). But before you set out or book a trip around an event, call to make sure the fling is still set to swing.

Spring

Whitney Biennial

See p151 for listing. **Dates** *Mar–May.*
This provocative show of important contemporary works by both established and emerging artists happens every two years. The next show will be held in spring 2004.

St. Patrick's Day Parade

Fifth Ave from 44th to 86th Sts (718-793-1600; www.saintpatricksdayparade.com). **Date** *Mar 17.*
Join the green-clad crowds a-cheering as wave upon wave of pipe bands and marchers roll by. Celebrations continue late into the night as the city's Irish bars teem with suds-swigging revelers.

Ringling Bros. and Barnum & Bailey Circus Animal Parade

34th St from the Queens Midtown Tunnel to Madison Square Garden, Seventh Ave between 31st and 33rd Sts (212-307-7171; www.ringling.com). **Dates** *Mar 16, midnight; Apr 11, midnight.*
The sight of elephants, horses, camels and zebras walking the city streets is an unmissable spectacle—so stay up late and witness this free midnight parade of animals, which opens (and closes) the circus's run in Manhattan.

> ▶ **NYC & Company** *(www.nycvisit.com),* the convention and visitors' bureau, has additional info on year-round events.
> ▶ See Around Town in ***Time Out New York*** for more seasonal events.
> ▶ Go to **www.timeoutny.com** and click on This Week's Picks for *TONY* critics' picks for each day of the week.
> ▶ For film festivals, *see p294.*
> ▶ For sports seasons, *see pp327–335.*

New York International Auto Show

Jacob K. Javits Convention Center, Eleventh Ave between 34th and 39th Sts, entrance at 35th St (800-282-3336; www.autoshowny.com). Subway: A, C, E to 34th St–Penn Station. **Dates** *Apr 9–18.*
More than a thousand autos—plus some futuristic concept cars—are on display at this huge motorfest.

Easter Parade

Fifth Ave from 49th to 57th Sts (212-484-1222; www.nycvisit.com). Subway: E, V to Fifth Ave–53rd St. **Date** *Easter Sunday, Apr 11.*
Starting at 11am on Easter Sunday, Fifth Avenue becomes a car-free promenade of gussied-up crowds sporting extravagant bonnets. Arrive early to secure a prime viewing spot near St. Patrick's Cathedral at 50th St.

New York Antiquarian Book Fair

Park Ave between 66th and 67th Sts (212-777-5218; www.sanfordsmith.com). Subway: 6 to 68th St–Hunter College. **Dates** *Apr 15–18.*
More than 200 international book dealers showcase first editions, illuminated manuscripts, and all manner of rare and antique tomes.

You Gotta Have Park

Parks throughout the city (212-360-3456).
Dates *May.*
Created to launch the summer season of outdoor events, this celebration of public greenery includes music concerts, markets, kids' events and cleanup days in NYC's major parks.

Cherry Blossom Festival

For listing, see p126 **Brooklyn Botanic Garden**.
Dates *May 1, 2.*
See nature's glorious springtime bouquet adorn the garden's 200-plus cherry trees at this annual festival. Performances, demonstrations and workshops celebrate and explain *sakura matsuri,* the traditional Japanese cherry-blossom rituals.

Tribeca Film Festival

Throughout Tribeca (212-941-2400; www.tribecafilmfestival.org). Subway: A, C, 1, 2, 3, 9 to Chambers St.
Dates *May 1–9.*
Organized by Tribeca champion Robert De Niro, this festival is packed with hundreds of screenings attended by more than 300,000 film fans.

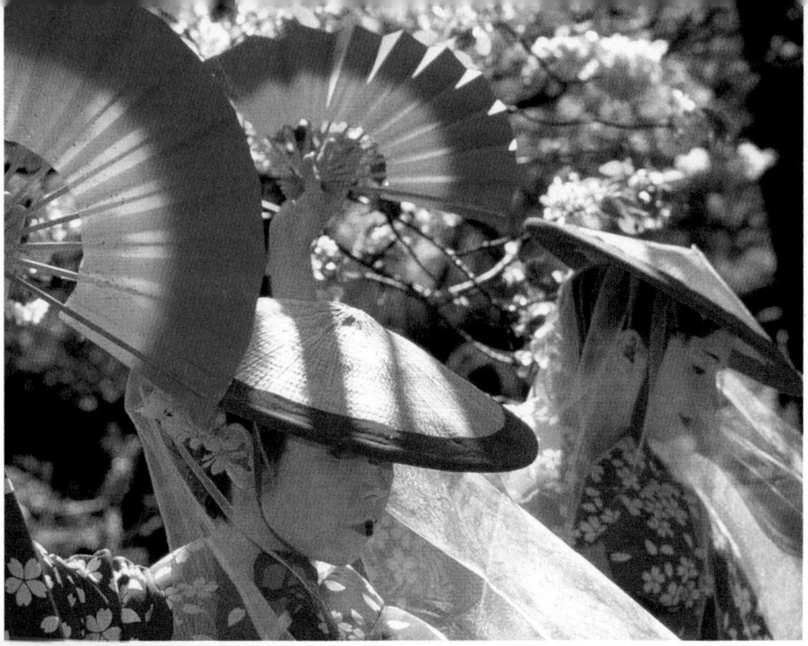

Spring role Fans wave at Brooklyn's **Cherry Blossom Festival**. *See p252.*

Bike New York: The Great Five Boro Bike Tour

Battery Park to Staten Island (212-932-2453; www.bikenewyork.org). Subway: 4, 5 to Bowling Green. **Date** *May 2.*

Thousands of cyclists kick cars to the curb and take over the city for a 42-mile (68-kilometer) Tour de New York. Advance registration required.

Red Hook Waterfront Arts Festival

Various locations, Red Hook, Brooklyn (718-287-2224; www.dancetheatreetcetera.org). Subway: F, G to Carroll St or Smith–9th Sts. **Date** *May 15.*

Red Hook's annual open-air festival celebrates the neighborhood's renaissance with the Brooklyn Working Artists' Pier Show, an Earth and Surf Parade, and music and dance performances.

Ninth Avenue International Food Festival

Ninth Ave between 37th and 57th Sts (212-581-7029). Subway: A, C, E to 42nd St–Port Authority. **Dates** *May 15, 16.*

This kaleidoscope of international cuisine attracts huge crowds of chowhounds, who come to sample round-the-world wares from the festival's hundreds of food stalls.

Fleet Week

For listing, see p162 **Intrepid** ***Sea-Air-Space Museum.*** **Dates** *Last week in May.*

New York's streets swell with sailors—and all varieties of military personnel—during this weeklong event honoring the armed forces. Naval maneuvers and air displays occur throughout the week.

Lower East Side Festival of the Arts

Theater for the New City, 155 First Ave at 10th St (212-254-1109; www.theaterforthenewcity.net). Subway: L to First Ave; 6 to Astor Pl. **Dates** *Last weekend in May.*

This celebration of artistic diversity on the Lower East Side features performances by more than 20 theatrical troupes, as well as appearances by local celebrities.

Washington Square Outdoor Art Exhibit

Various streets surrounding Washington Square Park (212-982-6255). Subway: A, C, E, B, D, F, V to W 4th St; R, W to 8th St–NYU. **Dates** *May 29–31; Jun 5–6.*

Since 1931, this outdoor exhibit has filled the area around Washington Square with photography, sculpture, paintings and one-of-a-kind crafts.

Summer

Met in the Parks

Various locations (212-362-6000; www.metopera.org). **Dates** *June.*

The Metropolitan Opera stages free open-air opera performances in Central Park and other NYC parks. Grab a blanket, pack a picnic (no alcohol or glass bottles) and show up in the afternoon to nab a good spot.

JVC Jazz Festival

Various locations (212-501-1390; www.festivalproductions.net). **Dates** *Mid-June.*

A direct descendant of the original Newport Jazz Festival, this jazz bash is an NYC institution. The festival not only fills Carnegie and Avery Fisher halls with big draws, but also sponsors gigs in Harlem and at downtown clubs.

Mermaid Parade

Coney Island, Brooklyn (718-372-5159; www.coneyisland.com). Subway: D to Coney Island–Stillwell Ave. **Date** *Jun 26.*

Come rain or shine, scantily clad mermaids and mermen of all shapes and sizes share the parade with elaborate floats at a sublimely kitschy seaside party. Check the website for details, as the parade location varies from year to year.

Summer Restaurant Week

Various locations (www.restaurantweek.com). **Dates** *Late Jun–early Jul.*

Twice a year, for two weeks at a stretch, some of the city's finest restaurants dish up three-course prix-fixe lunches for $20.04 (the bargain price reflects the year), and some offer dinner for $30.04. For the full list of participating restaurants, visit the website. You'll need to make reservations well in advance.

Gay and Lesbian Pride March

From Fifth Ave at 52nd St to Christopher St (212-807-7433; www.nycpride.org). **Date** *Last Sunday in June.*

Greenwich Village and Chelsea become a sea of rainbow flags as gays and lesbians from New York and beyond parade in commemoration of the 1969 Stonewall riots. Thousands of visitors come for the fest, which includes dozens of club events and a flamboyant dance party on the West Side piers.

Midsummer Night Swing

Lincoln Center Plaza, Columbus Ave between 64th and 65th Sts (212-875-5766; www.lincolncenter.org). Subway: 1, 9 to 66th St–Lincoln Ctr. **Dates** *Late Jun–mid-Jul.*

Lincoln Center's plaza is transformed into a giant outdoor dance floor as hot dance bands play salsa, Cajun, swing and other music. Each night is devoted to a different style of dance, and performances are preceded by free dance lessons.

Celebrate Brooklyn! Performing Arts Festival

Prospect Park Bandshell, Prospect Park West at 9th St, Park Slope, Brooklyn (718-855-7882; www.celebratebrooklyn.org). Subway: F to Seventh Ave. **Dates** *Late Jun–late Aug Thu–Sat.*

This diverse festival of outdoor events features music, dance, film and spoken-word performances. Huge crowds flock to the park's bandshell to hear major artists like Erykah Badu and Joan Armatrading. A $3 donation is requested, and admission is charged for a few benefit shows.

Bryant Park Free Summer Season

Bryant Park, Sixth Ave at 42nd St (212-768-4242; www.bryantpark.org). Subway: B, D, F, V to 42nd St–Bryant Park; 7 to Fifth Ave. **Dates** *Jun–Aug.*

The highlight of the park's free-entertainment season is the ever-popular Monday-night alfresco movie series. But during the daytime, things are equally busy as urban inmates escape sizzling streets and bask in this verdant oasis, taking in lunchtime excerpts from Broadway shows and breakfast concerts from the likes of Ringo Starr.

Midsummer Night Swing at Lincoln Center.

Central Park SummerStage

Rumsey Playfield, Central Park entrance on Fifth Ave at 72nd St (212-360-2777; www.summerstage.org). Subway: 6 to 77th St. **Dates** *Jun–Aug.*

The free concerts just keep getting better (both Ben Folds and the White Stripes played here in 2003), and there are occasional spoken-word and dance performances. Admission is charged for a few benefit shows.

New York Shakespeare Festival

See p337 for listing. **Dates** *Jun–Aug.*

This free festival is one of Manhattan's best summertime events, with big-name stars pulling on their tights for a whack at the Bard.

River to River Festival

Various venues along the west side and southern waterfronts of Manhattan (www.rivertorivernyc.org). **Dates** *Jun–Sept.*

Lower Manhattan organizations present more than 500 free summer shows, with performers ranging from James Brown to Ryan Adams. The Hudson River Festival *(212-528-2733; www.hudsonriverfestival.com)* is part of this production and offers visual-arts shows, theater, dance and family events.

Lincoln Center Festival

See p323 for listing. **Dates** *July.*

Dance, music, theater, opera and more are all part of this ambitious festival of classic and contemporary works.

Nathan's Famous Fourth of July Hot Dog Eating Contest

Nathan's Famous, 1310 Surf Ave at Stillwell Ave, Coney Island, Brooklyn (718-946-2202; www.nathansfamous.com). Subway: D to Coney Island–Stillwell Ave. **Date** *Jul 4, noon.*

How many wieners can you stuff down your gullet in 12 minutes? Diminutive Takeru Kobayashi (personal best: 51½ dogs) has won this Coney Island showdown three years in a row.

Macy's Fireworks Display

Location to be announced (212-494-4495). **Date** *Jul 4, 9:30pm.*

This spectacular fireworks display is the star attraction on Independence Day. Millions of New Yorkers watch as the city shimmers beneath the multicolored explosions of 30,000 shells and more than $1 million worth of pyrotechnics. The best viewpoints are along lower FDR Drive or on rooftops overlooking the East River.

Rock Steady Crew Anniversary

Various locations (www.rocksteadycrew.com). **Dates** *Mid- to late July.*

New York's premier practitioners of breakdancing (the crew formed in 1977) celebrate their birthday and the evolution of hip-hop with a celebrity basketball game, a film festival, a fashion show, MC and B-boy battles, and concerts.

Hello, gorgeous A **BARC** beauty. *See p256.*

New York Philharmonic Concerts

Various locations (212-875-5709; www.newyorkphilharmonic.org). **Dates** *Jul–Aug.*

The New York Philharmonic presents a varied program of classical music in many of New York's larger parks.

Seaside Summer and Martin Luther King Jr. Concert Series

Various locations (718-469-1912; www.brooklynconcerts.com). **Dates** *Jul–Aug.*

Grab a lawn chair and listen to free funk, soul and gospel at these outdoor concerts in Brooklyn.

Mostly Mozart

Lincoln Center, Columbus Ave between 64th and 65th Sts (212-875-5766; www.lincolncenter.org). Subway: 1, 9 to 66th St–Lincoln Ctr. **Dates** *Late Jul–Aug.*

For more than 35 years, the Mostly Mozart festival has been mounting a packed four-week performance schedule of works by Mozart and his contemporaries.

New York International Fringe Festival

Various downtown locations (212-279-4488; www.fringenyc.org). **Dates** *August.*

Wacky, weird and sometimes great, downtown's Fringe Festival shoehorns hundreds of performances into 12 theater-crammed days.

Central Park Zoo Chill Out Weekend

Park entrance on Fifth Ave at 66th St (212-861-6030). Subway: N, R, W to Fifth Ave–59th St.
Dates *Early August.*
This weekend freezefest features penguin and polar bear talent shows, games, zookeeper challenges and other frosty fun at the Central Park Zoo's annual two-day party dedicated to keeping it cool.

Harlem Week

Throughout Harlem (212-862-8477; www.harlemdiscover.com). Subway: B, C, 2, 3 to 135th St. **Dates** *Third week in August.*
Get in the groove at this massive street fair on 135th Street, which serves up live music, arts and food. Concerts, film, dance, fashion and sports events are on tap throughout the week.

Howl!

Throughout East Village (212-505-2225; www.howlfestival.com). **Dates** *Third week in August.*
An action-packed celebration of East Village counterculture with art events, films, performance art, readings and much more.

U.S. Open

See p331 for listing. **Dates** *Aug 30–Sept 12.*
This Grand Slam event is one of the most entertaining tournaments on the international tennis circuit. Tickets are hard to come by for the later rounds.

West Indian–American Day Carnival

Eastern Pkwy from Utica Ave to Grand Army Plaza, Prospect Park, Brooklyn (718-625-1515; www.wiadca.com). Subway: 3, 4 to Crown Hts–Utica Ave. **Dates** *Labor Day weekend.*
The streets come alive with the jubilant clangor of steel-drum bands and the steady throb of calypso and soca music. Thousands of participants dance on sidewalks packed with vendors selling Caribbean crafts, clothing, souvenirs and food.

Fall

Broadway on Broadway

43rd St at Broadway (212-768-1560). Subway: N, Q, R, W, 42nd St S, 1, 2, 3, 9, 7 to 42nd St–Times Sq.
Dates *Early September.*
In the middle of Times Square, Broadway's biggest stars convene to belt out show-stopping numbers. The season's new shows put on sneak previews, and it's all free!

Atlantic Antic

Atlantic Ave from Fourth Ave to Hicks St, Brooklyn Heights, Brooklyn (718-875-8993; www.atlanticave.org). Subway: B, Q, 2, 3, 4, 5 to Atlantic Ave. **Dates** *Mid- to late September.*
Entertainment, ethnic foods, kids' activities and the World Cheesecake-Eating Contest fill the streets at this monumental Brooklyn block party.

BARC's Annual Dog Parade, Show and Fair

Wythe Ave at North 1st St to McCarren Park, Williamsburg, Brooklyn (718-486-7489; www.barcshelter.org). Subway: L to Bedford Ave.
Date *Sept 19, noon.*
Doggy marchers in adorable costumes make this a lovable mutt of a parade. The Brooklyn Animal Resource Coalition hosts this poochfest, which includes a dog show where pups vie for awards such as Best Butt and Best Kisser. The show's 2004 theme will be Wild, Wild West.

Feast of San Gennaro

Mulberry St from Canal to Houston Sts (212-768-9320; www.sangennaro.org). Subway: J, M, Z, N, Q, R, W, 6 to Canal St. **Dates** *Mid-September.*
Religious processions, parades, game booths, rides and tons of Italian food (including a cannoli-eating contest) fill the center of Little Italy in honor of San Gennaro, the patron saint of Naples. The festival is most fun after dark, when sparkling lights arch over Mulberry Street and the smells of frying *zeppole* and sausages hang in the sultry air.

New York Is Book Country

Various locations (www.nyisbookcountry.com).
Dates *Late September.*
This five-day literary festival culminates in a massive street fair *(Fifth Ave from 48th to 57th Sts)* where more than 200 literary booths line the sidewalks, and author signings, antiquarian books and children's events all vie for your attention.

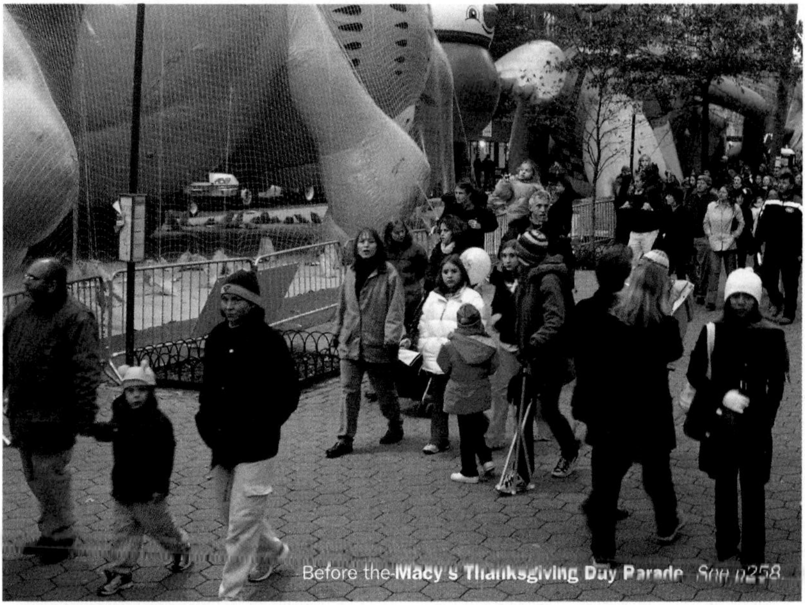
Before the Macy's Thanksgiving Day Parade. See p258.

***New Yorker* Literary Festival**

Various locations (www.festivalnewyorker.com).
Dates *Late September.*
Get up close and personal with some big names in the highbrow lit world at a three-day literary festival, organized by the *New Yorker* magazine. Expect readings, interviews, performances, lectures and walking tours. Both the website and a hot line will become active around June.

New York Film Festival

Alice Tully Hall at Lincoln Center, Broadway at 65th St (212-875-5050; www.filmlinc.com). Subway: 1, 9 to 66th St–Lincoln Ctr.
Dates *Late Sept–early Oct.*
Founded in 1965, this prestigious cinematic showcase presents premiers, features and short flicks from around the globe—and a stellar list of celebrities for the red-carpet events.

Next Wave Festival

For listing, see p321 **Brooklyn Academy of Music.**
Dates *Late Sept–Dec.*
This lengthy festival has become a premier showcase for avant-garde music, dance, theater and opera.

Open House New York

Various locations (917-583-2398; www.openhousenewyork.org). **Dates** *Early to mid-October.*
More than 60 sites of architectural interest—normally off-limits to visitors—throw open their doors and welcome the curious during this weekend of urban revelation. Past spaces available for perusal include City Hall and the Tweed Courthouse, the Jefferson Market Library Tower, and the interior of Washington Square Arch.

Dumbo Art Under the Bridge

Various locations in Dumbo, Brooklyn (718-694-0831; www.dumboartscenter.org). Subway: A, C to High St; F to York St.
Dates *Mid-October.*
Open studios, concerts, forums, a short-film festival, parties—and arty happenings aplenty—take place in Brooklyn's Dumbo (Down Under the Manhattan Bridge Overpass) neighborhood during this weekend of art appreciation.

CMJ Music Marathon, MusicFest and FilmFest

Various venues (917-606-1908; www.cmj.com).
Dates *Late October.*
Hosted by trade publisher *College Music Journal,* this industry schmoozefest is attended by thousands of music aficionados. Check out exhibits and panel discussions, and listen to live bands play rock, indie rock, hip-hop or electronica.

***Time Out New York* Literary Festival**

Various locations (www.timeoutny.com/litfest2004).
Dates *Late Oct–early Nov.*
Novelists, poets, playwrights and critics hold forth at this sprawling, multicultural literary celebration, organized around an annual theme.

Big Apple Circus

See p278 for listing. **Dates** *Late Oct–early Jan.*

Village Halloween Parade

Sixth Ave from Spring to 22nd Sts (www.halloween-nyc.com). **Date** *Oct 31, 7pm.*

Dress up in ghoulish duds and join the effervescent parade. March side by side with enormous puppets and all manner of costumed craziness at this friendliest of Village traditions (parade lineup starts at 6pm on Sixth Avenue at Spring Street).

New York City Marathon

Staten Island side of the Verrazano-Narrows Bridge to Tavern on the Green in Central Park (212-423-2249; www.nycmarathon.org). **Date** *Nov 7, 10:50am.*

A sweaty crowd of 30,000 marathoners hotfoot it through all five boroughs over a 26.2-mile (42-kilometer) course.

Macy's Thanksgiving Day Parade

Central Park West at 77th St to Macy's, Broadway at 34th St (212-695-4400). **Date** *Thanksgiving Day, Nov 25, 9am.*

The stars of this nationally televised parade are the gigantic, inflated cartoon-character balloons, elaborate floats, and good ol' Santa Claus. Watch the rubbery colossi take shape at the inflation area on the night before Thanksgiving *(from 77th to 81st Sts, between Central Park West and Columbus Ave).*

The best Places to...

...pick up a sailor

Fleet Week (*see p253*) fills the city with men (and women) in uniform.

...see an elephant in midtown

Either you've had three saketinis too many, or it's time for the **Ringling Bros. and Barnum & Bailey Circus Animal Parade** (*see p252*).

...think pink

Trees bloom in Brooklyn during the spring **Cherry Blossom Festival** (*see p252*).

...sniff out the "best butts"

Lovable mutts compete for canine accolades at **BARC's Annual Dog Parade, Show and Fair** (*see p256*).

...read poetry with Patti Smith

Start the new year with the hip crew at the **New Year's Day Marathon Poetry Reading** (*see p259*).

...samba under the stars

Get your groove on at Lincoln Center's **Midsummer Night Swing** (*see p254*).

Winter

The Nutcracker

New York State Theater, Lincoln Center, Columbus Ave at 63rd St (212-870-5570; www.nycb.org). Subway: 1, 9 to 66th St–Lincoln Ctr. **Dates** *Day after Thanksgiving–first week of January.*

As performed by the New York City Ballet, Tchaikovsky's fantasy world of fairies, princes and toy soldiers is a much-loved Christmas tradition.

Radio City Christmas Spectacular

Radio City Music Hall, 1260 Sixth Ave at 50th St (212-247-4777). Subway: B, D, F, V to 47–50th Sts–Rockefeller Ctr. **Dates** *Nov–early Jan.*

Unbeatable Christmas cheer, starring the high-kicking Rockettes.

Christmas Tree Lighting Ceremony

Rockefeller Center, Fifth Ave between 49th and 50th Sts (212-332-7654). Subway: B, D, F, V to 47–50th Sts–Rockefeller Ctr. **Date** *In first week of December.*

Big-name talents perform while expectant crowds wait to see 30,000 lights twinkle to life on the giant evergreen in Rockefeller Center. The tree, towering over twirling ice skaters, is the centerpiece of the city's most enchanting Christmas locale.

Messiah Sing-In

Avery Fisher Hall, Lincoln Center, Columbus Ave at 65th St (212-333-5333). Subway: 1, 9 to 66th St–Lincoln Ctr. **Dates** *Mid-December.*

Hallelujah! Chase those holiday blues by joining hundreds of amateur singers in a rehearsal and performance of Handel's *Messiah.* No experience is necessary, and you can buy the score on site.

New Year's Eve Ball Drop

Times Square (212-768-1560; www.timessquarebid.org). Subway: N, Q, R, W, 42nd St S, 1, 2, 3, 9, 7 to 42nd St–Times Sq. **Date** *Dec 31.*

Meet up with a half-million of your closest friends and watch the giant illuminated ball descend into the new year, amid a blizzard of confetti and cheering. Expect freezing temperatures, densely packed crowds—and very tight security.

New Year's Eve Fireworks

Naumberg Bandshell, middle of Central Park at 72nd St (212-423-2284; www.nyrrc.org). Subway: B, C to 72nd St; 6 to 68th St–Hunter College. **Date** *Dec 31.*

The fireworks explode at midnight, but there are plenty of evening festivities (*see below*), including dancing and a costume contest. The best viewing points are Tavern on the Green (at 67th Street), Central Park West at 72nd Street and Fifth Avenue at 90th Street.

New Year's Eve Midnight Run

Naumberg Bandshell, middle of Central Park at 72nd St (212-423-2284; www.nyrrc.org). Subway: B, C to 72nd St; 6 to 68th St–Hunter College. **Date** *Dec 31.*

Dragon breath The Chinese New Year is celebrated with a parade through Chinatown.

Start the new year with a four-mile jog through the park. There's also a masquerade parade, fireworks (*see p258*), prizes and a booze-free sparkling toast at the run's halfway mark.

New Year's Day Marathon Poetry Reading

For listing, see p272 **The Poetry Project**. **Date** *Jan 1.*
Big-name bohemians (Patti Smith, Richard Hell, Jim Carroll) step up to the mike during this free all-day spoken-word spectacle.

Winter Antiques Show

Seventh Regiment Armory, Park Ave at 67th St (718-292-7392; www.winterantiquesshow.com). Subway: 6 to 68th St–Hunter College. **Dates** *Jan 15–24, 2005.*
The city's most prestigious antiques fair includes expert lectures and a loan exhibition of the "best of the best" from MoMA's American Wing.

Chinese New Year

Around Mott St, Chinatown (212-226-6280; www.nycvisit.com). Subway: J, M, Z, N, Q, R, W, 6 to Canal St. **Dates** *Late January.*
Chinatown bustles with energy during the two weeks of the Lunar New Year. Winter festivities include a staged fireworks display (personal fireworks are now forbidden), a dragon parade, lion-dancing exhibitions, various performances and delicious food.

Outsider Art Fair

The Puck Building, 295 Lafayette St at Houston St (212-777-5218; www.sanfordsmith.com). Subway: B, D, F, V to Broadway–Lafayette St; 6 to Bleecker St. **Dates** *Late January.*
This three-day, world-class showcase for self-taught, intuitive and visionary artists draws browsers and buyers from all over the world.

Winter Restaurant Week

See p254 **Summer Restaurant Week**.
Dates *Late Jan, early Feb.*

The Art Show

Seventh Regiment Armory, Park Ave at 67th St (212-940-8590; www.artdealers.org). Subway: 6 to 68th St–Hunter College.
Dates *Mid-February.*
Many of America's most prominent dealers offer paintings, prints and sculptures (dating from the 17th century to the present) at this vast art fair.

International Artexpo

Jacob K. Javits Convention Center, Eleventh Ave between 34th and 39th Sts, entrance at 35th St (888-322-5226; www.artexpos.com). Subway: A, C, E to 34th St–Penn Station.
Dates *Late February.*
Artexpo, the world's largest art exhibition and sale, features original artwork, fine-art prints, limited-edition lithographs and more.

The Armory Show

Piers 88 and 90, Twelfth Ave between 48th and 50th Sts (212-645-6440; www.thearmoryshow.com). Subway: C, E to 50th St. **Dates** *Mid-March.*
It's now a huge contemporary-art fair, but this was the show that heralded the arrival of modern art into America in 1913.

Art Galleries

What's the next hot neighborhood? A vibrant art scene points the way.

Art connoisseurs in New York will rarely feel shortchanged. For those who want visual comfort food, uptown emporiums are filled with works by the old masters: Drop by any of 57th Street's big-name galleries for a host of haute options. Chelsea is the white-hot center of the contemporary scene, where you'll find everything from the blue-chip to the trendy. And Williamsburg, now home to some 40 galleries, has made Brooklyn a must-visit to see the latest work.

Spurred by a museum migration to Long Island City, galleries are popping up in Queens—a number of them in the shadow of **P.S. 1** (*see p151*). In Manhattan, quite a few call the former hinterland of the Meatpacking District home, and savvy dealer Gavin Brown just moved his business to the West Village. You can also find new venues in Harlem and the Lower East Side, and even along the banks of the Brooklyn waterfront in Dumbo. Basically, if an area feels revitalized, fresh and fun, chances are it's because pioneering artists (and real-estate–canny gallerists) are calling it home.

The most reliable gallery listings and reviews can be found in *Time Out New York* and in the Friday and Sunday editions of *The New York Times*. Always consult them before heading out. For unopinionated (but extensive) listings, pick up a monthly *Art Now Gallery Guide (www.galleryguide.org)*. It's usually available for free in galleries, or for around $3 at newsstands and bookstores.

Hours listed are for September through May or June. Summer visitors should note that from late June to early September, most galleries are open only on weekdays, and some close for the entire month of August. Summer hours are listed for some galleries that have set their calendar, but it's always best to call before visiting.

Lower East Side

The edgy Lower East Side is experiencing something of a renaissance (*see p262* **LES is more art**). For an overview of its ever-changing scene (which includes artist-run spaces too numerous to mention), your best bet is to take the **ELS-LES** self-guided walking tour.

Subway: F, V to Lower East Side–Second Ave; J, M, Z to Delancey–Essex Sts.

ELS-LES (Every Last Sunday on the Lower East Side) Open Studios

Various studios and galleries (646-602-2338; www.elsles.org). Subway: F to Delancey St; J, M, Z to Delancey–Essex Sts. **Open** *Noon–6pm.* **Admission** *free.*

On the last Sunday of every month, a number of artist- and artisan-run studios on the Lower East Side throw open their doors to the public. Participants vary; ABC No Rio, Altared Objects, Metalstone Gallery and Zito Studio Gallery are likely to be among them. For participating venues, you can download a map from the website.

Maccarone Inc.

45 Canal St between Ludlow and Orchard Sts (212-431-4977). Subway: F to East Broadway; J, M, Z, N, Q, R, W, 6 to Canal St. **Open** *Sept–May Wed–Sun noon–6pm. Jun, Jul Tue–Fri noon–6pm.*

Run by former Luhring Augustine director Michele Maccarone, the gallery has a roster of museum-quality installations and emerging European and local talents.

Participant Inc.

95 Rivington St between Ludlow and Orchard Sts (917-488-0185). Subway: F to Delancey St; J, M, Z to Delancey–Essex Sts. **Open** *Wed–Sun noon–7pm.*

This glass-fronted gallery is a Lower East Side hot spot. Expect freewheeling yet thoughtful exhibitions crossbreeding visual and performing arts with literature and new media.

Rivington Arms

102 Rivington St between Essex and Ludlow Sts (646-654-3213). Subway: F, V to Lower East Side–Second Ave. **Open** *Tue–Fri 11am–6pm.*

This modest storefront space, run by Sarah Lawrence grads Melissa Bent and Mirabelle Marden, has attracted a trendy crowd of followers.

Soho

The main concentration of Manhattan galleries may have shifted to the western blocks of Chelsea, but notable galleries still call Soho home, and a number of the city's most important nonprofit venues (*see p268*) continue to make the area a vital stop on the art map.

Subway: A, C, E, J, M, Z, N, Q, 1, 9 to Canal St; B, D, F, V to Broadway–Lafayette St; R, W to Prince St; 6 to Spring St.

Watch your step A Yoko Ono exhibit at Soho's **Deitch Projects** tips the scale.

Deitch Projects

18 Wooster St between Canal and Grand Sts (212-941-9475). **Open** *Tue–Sat noon–6pm. Call for summer hours.*

Jeffrey Deitch is an art-world impresario whose gallery features live spectacles almost as often as it presents large-scale—and sometimes overly ambitious—efforts by artists who work in virtually all media. (By comparison, Deitch's original Grand Street site seems small and sedate, but it's the one we most confidently recommend.) Solo shows here, by the likes of Chris Johansen and Yoko Ono, aim to be both complex and accessible.

Other location *76 Grand St between Greene and Wooster Sts (212-343-7300).*

Ronald Feldman

31 Mercer St between Canal and Grand Sts (212-226-3232; www.feldmangallery.com). **Open** *Sept–Jun Tue–Sat 10am–6pm. Jul, Aug Mon–Thu 10am–6pm; Fri 10am–3pm.*

This Soho pioneer has brought us landmark shows of such legendary avant-gardists as Eleanor Antin, Leon Golub and Hannah Wilke. Feldman also regularly takes chances on new talents like Williamsburg's Bruce Pearson—all to good effect.

Leo Koenig Inc.

249 Centre St between Broome and Grand Sts (212-334-9255). **Open** *Tue–Sat 10am–6pm.*

Leo Koenig's dad is Kasper Koenig, the internationally known curator and museum director, but the 26-year-old son has been making a name for himself by showcasing cutting-edge American and German talents—Tony Matelli, Torben Giehler and Nicole Eisenman among them.

Satellite (a division of Roebling Hall)

94 Prince St at Mercer St, second floor (718-599-5352). **Open** *Wed–Sat noon–6pm.*

This new Soho enterprise by dealers Christian Viveros-Fauné and Joel Beck of Williamsburg's Roebling Hall (*see p268*) shows the likes of Sebastiaan Bremer, Bjørn Melhus and Guy Richard Smit.

The Work Space

96 Spring St between Broadway and Mercer St, eighth floor (212-219-2790). **Open** *Mon–Fri 10am–5pm; Sat 1–5pm.*

Housed in the offices of a Soho law firm, this insider's gem, run by curator Lesley Heller, offers solid themed group shows by emerging and mid-career artists.

Chelsea

Chelsea has the city's greatest concentration of galleries; just be advised that it can be hard to see even half the neighborhood in one day. The subway takes you only as far as Eighth Avenue, so you'll have to walk at least one long block westward to get to the galleries. You can also take the M23 crosstown bus.

Subway: A to 14th St; C, E to 23rd St; L to Eighth Ave.

Alexander and Bonin

132 Tenth Ave between 18th and 19th Sts (212-367-7474; www.alexanderandbonin.com). **Open** *Tue–Sat 10am–6pm. August by appointment only.*

This long, cool drink of an exhibition space features contemporary painting, sculpture and photography by artists such as Willie Doherty, Mona Hatoum, Rita McBride, Doris Salcedo and Paul Thek.

Galeria Ramis Barquet

532 W 24th St between Tenth and Eleventh Aves (212-675-3421; www.ramisbarquet.com). **Open** *Tue–Sat 10am–6pm. Call for summer hours.* For review, *see p265.*

Mary Boone Gallery

541 W 24th St between Tenth and Eleventh Aves (212-752-2929; www.maryboonegallery.com). **Open** *Tue–Fri 9am–6pm; Sat 10am–5pm.*

Mary Boone made her name repping Julian Schnabel, Jean-Michel Basquiat and Francesco Clemente at her Soho gallery in the '80s. She later moved to midtown (*see p265*) and, in 2000, added this sweeping space in Chelsea, showing established artists like Ross Bleckner, Barbara Kruger and Damian Loeb.

Paula Cooper

534 W 21st St between Tenth and Eleventh Aves (212-255-1105). **Open** *Sept–May Tue–Sat 10am–6pm. Jun–Aug Mon–Fri 9:30am–5pm.*

First in Soho and early to Chelsea, Cooper has built an impressive art temple. (She has also opened a second space, across the street.) The gallery is known for Minimalist and Conceptual work, including photographers Zoe Leonard and Andres Serrano, and sculptors Carl Andre, Donald Judd, Sherrie Levine and Tony Smith.

Other location *521 W 21st St between Tenth and Eleventh Aves (212-255-5247).*

LES is more art

On a chilly night in January 2002, young downtown art fans—Sean Lennon and Bijou Phillips among them—packed into a tiny gallery for its first-ever opening. As the teeming crowd spilled onto the street, police ordered the swarm into a single-file line on the sidewalk. When nobody responded, one canny officer marched to his car, picked up a megaphone and announced the name of the bar where the after-party would be held. The mob soon dispersed, streaming over to Pioneer on the Bowery.

The gallery, **Rivington Arms**, certainly made a splashy entrée into New York's art scene that winter evening. Even more remarkable was its location: not in established Chelsea, but the emerging, oh-so-cool Lower East Side. The arrival of this and other spaces proves that the LES is distinguishing itself as New York's independent, upstart art scene. By our estimate, some 20 artists' and artisan-run studios, alternative exhibition venues and serious dealer-run galleries now reside here.

The 'hood is no stranger to brushes and canvases. In the '70s and '80s, East Village artists attempted to create another Soho, but galleries never quite took root amid the bodegas. Then, beginning in the '90s and into the new millennium, the neighborhood began to gentrify and became too expensive for career bohemians; they headed south to set up their studios.

Michele Maccarone laid the foundation when she opened **Maccarone Inc.**, a showcase for emerging international talent and museum-quality installations, in November 2001. Rivington Arms soon followed, along with **Participant Inc.**, run by Lia Gangitano, who once curated the now-defunct Thread Waxing Space. If this burgeoning art scene signals anything, it's that the pattern of Manhattan gentrification doesn't always follow the arc of studios and galleries to boutiques and expensive chain stores. On the Lower East Side, trendy boutiques have already flourished. "We never thought about opening a gallery anywhere else," says Melissa Bent, 26, who owns the Rivington Arms storefront with Mirabelle Marden, 25. "This is our neighborhood."

Bent and Marden (daughter of painter Brice Marden) started their Rivington Street space after graduating from Sarah Lawrence. Because they're self-funded, Bent says, "We can try anything we want. There are no rules." For the last couple of years, they've been focusing on shows of young artists like Britain's Daisy de Villeneuve, who draws diaristic marker portraits on notebook paper; and Marc Hundley, who specializes in hostile spray-paintings of lyrics by folk duo the McGarrigle Sisters.

As the former director of Chelsea mainstay Luhring Augustine, Michele Maccarone has a firm grip on the gallery business. "I didn't open this thing out of the blue," she says of her gallery, which shows a mix of up-and-coming American and prominent European artists.

Located at 45 Canal Street, the gallery occupies all four floors of a building that once

Gagosian

555 W 24th St between Tenth and Eleventh Aves (212-741-1111; www.gagosian.com).
Open *Tue–Sat 10am–6pm. Call for summer hours.*
Larry Gagosian's mammoth (20,000-square-foot) contribution to 24th Street's top-level galleries was launched in 1999 with a thrilling Richard Serra show. Follow-up exhibitions have featured works by Ellen Gallagher, Damien Hirst, Anselm Kiefer, Ed Ruscha, Julian Schnabel and Andy Warhol.

Barbara Gladstone

515 W 24th St between Tenth and Eleventh Aves (212-206-9300). **Open** *Sept–mid-Jun Tue–Sat 10am–6pm. Mid-Jun–Labor Day weekend Mon–Fri 10am–6pm.*
Gladstone is strictly blue-chip, with a heavy emphasis on the Conceptual, the philosophical and the daring. Matthew Barney, Richard Prince, Anish Kapoor and Rosemary Trockel show here.

Gorney Bravin + Lee

534 W 26th St between Tenth and Eleventh Aves (212-352-8372; www.gblgallery.com).
Open *Sept–Jun Tue–Sat 10am–6pm. Jul Tue–Fri 10am–6pm. August by appointment only.*
This refreshingly friendly gallery is especially strong in photography and sculpture. It has an attention-getting stable of contemporary artists, including Sarah Charlesworth, Justine Kurland, Catherine Opie and James Siena.

Greene Naftali Gallery

526 W 26th St between Tenth and Eleventh Aves, eighth floor (212-463-7770). **Open** *Sept–Jun Tue–Sat 10am–6pm. Jul Mon–Fri 10am–6pm.*
This gallery is worth a visit just for its wonderful light and spectacular bird's-eye city view. Greene Naftali has a reputation in the neighborhood for hosting potent rock 'em–sock 'em Conceptualist group shows.

belonged to an electrical-appliance store called (as Maccarone enjoys pointing out) Kunst, which happens to be German for "art." It burst onto the scene with a knockout exhibition by the Swiss artist Christoph Büchel, which pushed the concept of installation to the extreme by forcing visitors to navigate through a series of tight, filthy environments. "Our program is very site-specific in nature," says Maccarone. "Actually, I like to think of this as more of a house filled with art than a gallery."

Maccarone hopes her space will become the next art-world destination, akin to what Gavin Brown's Passerby was to Chelsea (Brown, incidentally, has relocated his exhibition space to the West Village). In January 2002, she went so far as to allow emerging artist Mike Bouchet to transform her basement-level exhibition space into a social club—of sorts. "The idea was more for artists to have an intimate space where they can discuss things, bounce ideas around," she says.

Gangitano's Participant Inc. is located on Rivington Street, a block west of Bent and Marden's space, in a building as unconventional as the work it exhibits: massive multimedia pieces, as well as more animated projects, including literary readings, lectures and film screenings. From the street, passersby are able to view both the first-floor exhibition space and the basement offices through an all-glass facade. "I was attracted to a building where you could see two levels at once," Gangitano says.

Gallery grrrls Art-gallery owners (from left) Mirabelle Marden, Melissa Bent, Lia Gangitano and Michele Maccarone.

After looking into more "art-gallery central" locations, Gangitano settled here. "The kind of audience I want is much broader than a Chelsea audience," she says. "The art world is confined to a certain geography. But the Lower East Side resists categorization—it's too diverse."

For specific info on Maccarone Inc., Participant Inc. and Rivington Arms—as well as details about a monthly tour of other galleries and artists' studios in the area—see p260.

This won't hurt a bit Richard Prince portraits at the **Barbara Gladstone** gallery. *See p263.*

Anton Kern Gallery
532 W 20th St between Tenth and Eleventh Aves (212-367-9663; www.antonkerngallery.com). **Open** *Sept–Jul Tue–Sat 10am–6pm.*
The son of artist Georg Baselitz, Kern presents young American and European artists. The futuristic, sometimes melancholy installations have provided the New York art scene with some of its most visionary shows. The likes of Kai Althoff, Sarah Jones, Michael Joo, Jim Lambie and scary Monica Bonvicini show here.

Andrew Kreps Gallery
516A W 20th St between Tenth and Eleventh Aves (212-741-8849). **Open** *Sept–Jul Tue–Sat 10am–6pm.*
The radicals in Kreps's adventurous stable include Ricci Albenda, Roe Ethridge, Robert Melee and Ruth Root.

Lehmann Maupin
540 W 26th St between Tenth and Eleventh Aves (212-255-2923; www.lehmannmaupin.com). **Open** *Sept–Jun Tue–Sat 10am–6pm. Jul 4–30 Tue–Fri 10am–6pm. August by appointment only.*
This gallery left its Rem Koolhaas–designed loft in Soho for new Koolhaas-designed digs in an old garage. Epic exhibitions feature hip Americans and Europeans, including Teresita Fernandez, Do-Ho Suh, Kutlug Ataman and Tracy Emin.

Luhring Augustine
531 W 24th St between Tenth and Eleventh Aves (212-206-9100; www.luhringaugustine.com). **Open** *Sept–May Tue–Sat 10am–6pm. Jun–Aug Mon–Fri 10am–5pm.*
Designed by the area's architect of choice, Richard Gluckman, this cool gallery features work from an impressive index of artists that includes Briton Rachel Whiteread; Swiss video star Pipilotti Rist; Japanese photo artist Yasumasa Morimura; and Americans Janine Antoni, Larry Clark, Jenny Gage, Paul McCarthy and Christopher Wool.

Matthew Marks
523 W 24th St between Tenth and Eleventh Aves (212-243-0200; www.matthewmarks.com). **Open** *Sept–Jun Tue–Sat 10am–6pm. Jul, Aug Mon–Fri 10am–6pm.*
The Matthew Marks gallery was a driving force behind Chelsea's transformation into an art destination, and it remains one of the neighborhood's biggest draws; its 9,000-square-foot, two-story locale has a second-floor public gallery. Marks showcases Lucian Freud, Nan Goldin, Andreas Gursky, Ellsworth Kelly, Willem de Kooning, Brice Marden and Ugo Rondinone.

Robert Miller Gallery
524 W 26th St between Tenth and Eleventh Aves (212-366-4774; www.robertmillergallery.com). **Open** *Sept–Jun Tue–Sat 10am–6pm. Call for summer hours.*
This former 57th Street stalwart often shows work you might expect to see at a museum: Al Held, Lee Krasner, Joan Mitchell, Alice Neel and Philip Pearlstein, as well as photographers Bruce Weber and Diane Arbus.

Paul Morris
465 W 23rd St between Ninth and Tenth Aves (212-727-2752). **Open** *Sept–Jun Tue–Sat 10am–6pm. Jul, Aug Mon–Fri 10am–6pm.*

Paul Morris may have one of Chelsea's rare shoe-box galleries, but the talents on display are huge, especially photographers Esko Männikkö, Tracey Moffatt and Arnold Odermatt, and superior draftsmen Robert Crumb and Ewan Gibbs.

PaceWildenstein Gallery

534 W 25th St between Tenth and Eleventh Aves (212-929-7000; www.pacewildenstein.com).
Open *Sept–May Tue–Sat 10am–6pm. Jun–Aug Mon–Thu 10am–6pm; Fri 10am–4pm.*
In a space designed by artist Robert Irwin, this welcoming branch of the famous 57th Street gallery (*see p266*) houses grand-scale shows by big-time contemporaries, including Georg Baselitz, Chuck Close, Alex Katz, Sol LeWitt, Elizabeth Murray and Kiki Smith.

Postmasters

459 W 19th St between Ninth and Tenth Aves (212-727-3323; www.postmastersart.com).
Open *Sept–Jul Tue–Sat 11am–6pm.*
Postmasters is an intriguing international gallery run by Magdalena Sawon, who presents decidedly techno-savvy art (most of which has Conceptualist leanings) in the form of sculpture, painting, new media and installations. Some of Sawon's brighter stars include Diana Cooper, Christian Schumann, Wolfgang Staehle and Claude Wampler.

Andrea Rosen

525 W 24th St between Tenth and Eleventh Aves (212-627-6000; www.andrearosengallery.com).
Open *Sept–Jun Tue–Sat 10am–6pm. Jul, Aug Mon–Fri 10am–6pm.*
This venue shines a light on Wolfgang Tillmans's uneasy fashion photos and Andrea Zittel's compact model homes. Before his high-profile exit in 2003, John Currin hung his unsettling romantics here.

Sonnabend

536 W 22nd St between Tenth and Eleventh Aves (212-627-1018). **Open** *Sept–Jul Tue–Sat 10am–6pm. August by appointment only.*
A well-established standby in a museumlike space shows new work by Ashley Bickerton, Gilbert & George, Candida Höfer, Jeff Koons, Haim Steinbach and Matthew Weinstein.

303 Gallery

525 W 22nd St between Tenth and Eleventh Aves (212-255-1121; www.303gallery.com).
Open *Tue–Sat 10am–6pm. Call for summer hours.*
Expect to see critically acclaimed artists who work in a variety of media—among them, sculptor Daniel Oates, photographers Thomas Demand and Collier Schorr, and painters Inka Essenhigh, Karen Kilimnik and Sue Williams.

David Zwirner

525 W 19th St between Tenth and Eleventh Aves (212-727-2070; www.davidzwirner.com).
Open *Sept–Jun Tue–Sat 10am–6pm. Jul, Aug Mon–Fri 10am–6pm.*
This maverick German expatriate has moved his shop to spiffy new white-box quarters, taking along its head-turning roster of international contemporary artists, including Stan Douglas, Marcel Dzama, Toba Khedoori, Neo Rauch and Diana Thater. (*See also p266* **Zwirner & Wirth**).

57th Street

The home of Carnegie Hall, Tiffany & Co., Bergdorf Goodman and a number of art galleries, the area around 57th Street is a beehive of cultural and commercial activity—expensive, lively and chic.
Subway: E, V to Fifth Ave–53rd St; F, V to 57th St; N, R, W to Fifth Ave–59th St.

Artemis Greenberg Van Doren

730 Fifth Ave at 57th St, seventh floor (212-445-0444; www.agvdgallery.com). **Open** *Sept–May Tue–Sat 10am–6pm. Jun–Aug Mon–Fri 10am–5:30pm.*
It may sound like a law firm, but this gallery shows established artists like Jennifer Bartlett and Richard Diebenkorn, as well as younger talent, like painters Benjamin Edwards and Lane Twitchell. Look out for new photographers like Jessica Craig-Martin, Katy Grannan and Malerie Marder.

Galeria Ramis Barquet

41 E 57th St between Madison and Park Aves (212-644-9090; www.ramisbarquet.com). **Open** *Mon–Fri 10am–6pm; Saturday by appointment.*
On a prime stretch of midtown real estate, Ramis Barquet shows prominent Latin American artists, including Marco Arce, Marta Maria Pérez Bravo, Ernesto Pujol and Betsabeé Romero. The gallery has also opened a space in Chelsea (*see p262*).

Mary Boone

745 Fifth Ave between 57th and 58th Sts, fourth floor (212-752-2929; www.maryboonegallery.com).
Open *Tue–Sat 10am–6pm.*
Onetime Soho celeb Boone continues to produce hit shows, featuring young artists, on 57th Street. But her prized possession is her newer gallery in Chelsea (*see p262*), where the star attractions include established players Ross Bleckner, Peter Halley, Barbara Kruger and hip British provocateur Damian Loeb.

Marian Goodman Gallery

24 W 57th St between Fifth and Sixth Aves, fourth floor (212-977-7160; www.mariangoodman.com).
Open *Sept–Jun Mon–Sat 10am–6pm. Jul, Aug Mon–Fri 10am–6pm.*
This well-known space in the heart of midtown offers a host of world-renowned names. Look for artists such as John Baldessari, Christian Boltanski, Maurizio Cattelan, Gabriel Orozco, Gerhard Richter, Thomas Struth and Jeff Wall.

► For weekly reviews and listings, pick up a copy of ***Time Out New York***.

PaceWildenstein Gallery

32 E 57th St between Madison and Park Aves (212-421-3292; www.pacewildenstein.com).
Open *Sept–May Tue–Sat 9:30am–5:30pm. Jun–Aug Mon–Fri 9:30am–5:30pm.*
For some of the 20th century's most significant art stalwarts, head to this institution; you'll find pieces by Chuck Close, Agnes Martin, Pablo Picasso, Ad Reinhardt, Mark Rothko and Lucas Samaras, along with Elizabeth Murray and Kiki Smith. Pace Prints and Primitives, at this same location, publishes works on paper—by everyone from old masters to big-name contemporaries—and keeps a fine collection of African art (*see also p265*).

Upper East Side

Many galleries on the Upper East Side sell masterpieces to millionaires. Still, anyone can look for free, and some pieces are treasures that could vanish from public view for years.
Subway: 6 to 68th St–Hunter College or 77th St.

C&M Arts

45 E 78th St at Madison Ave (212-861-0020; www.c-m-arts.com). **Open** *Tue–Sat 10am–5:30pm. Summer Mon–Fri 10am–5:30pm.*
If you'd like to view or study the works of historic figures like Joseph Cornell, Franz Kline, Mark Rothko, Cy Twombly and Andy Warhol, check out this major player in the secondary art market.

Gagosian

980 Madison Ave at 76th St (212-744-2313; www.gagosian.com). **Open** *Tue–Sat 10am–6pm. Summer Mon–Fri 10am–6pm.*
During the 1980s, Larry Gagosian was a force to be reckoned with in the world of contemporary art. Today, he's just as important to the scene. Regularly featured artists include Francesco Clemente, Damien Hirst and Richard Serra, as well as newer Brit Pack stars Cecily Brown and Jenny Saville. Gagosian has also succeeded in the resale market and maintains a premier exhibition space in Chelsea (*see p263*).

M Knoedler & Co.

19 E 70th St between Fifth and Madison Aves (212-794-0550). **Open** *Sept–May Tue–Sat 9:30am–5:30pm. Jun–Aug Mon–Sat 9:30am–5pm.*
The oldest gallery in New York (and in the country, having opened in 1846) represents museum-quality postwar and contemporary art, including works by Lee Bontecou, Helen Frankenthaler, Nancy Graves and John Walker.

Mitchell-Innes & Nash

1018 Madison Ave between 78th and 79th Sts, fifth floor (212-744-7400; www.miandn.com).
Open *Sept–Jun Tue–Sat 10am–5pm. Jul Mon–Fri 10am–5pm. Call for August hours.*
This seven-year-old gallery is run by two former Sotheby's specialists with an ambitious program of Impressionist, modern and contemporary works.

Zwirner & Wirth

32 E 69th St between Madison and Park Aves (212-517-8677; www.zwirnerandwirth.com).
Open *Tue–Sat 10am–6pm.*
This recently renovated townhouse space exhibits modern and contemporary masters like Dan Flavin, Martin Kippenberger and Bruce Nauman. (*See also p265* **David Zwirner**.)

Harlem

Triple Candie

461 W 126th St between Morningside and Amsterdam Aves (212-865-0783; www.triplecandie.org). Subway: A, C, B, D, 1, 9 to 125th St.
Open *Thu–Sun noon–6pm.*
This multiculturally minded contemporary-arts center brings exhibitions and educational programs to the west side of Harlem.

Brooklyn

There are about 60 galleries in Brooklyn, and that number is growing. Most are open on Sundays and Mondays, when the majority of Manhattan galleries are closed. Artists living and working in Brooklyn have created a thriving gallery scene, and Williamsburg is its uncontested hub. (For a printable map, visit www.williamsburggalleryassociation.com.) You can also head to the next-up neighborhood of Dumbo, where artist studios and new galleries roost amid the massive moorings of the Manhattan Bridge.
Subway: L to Bedford Ave; J, M, Z to Marcy Ave.

Bellwether

335 Grand St between Havemeyer St and Marcy Ave, Williamsburg (718-387-3701; www.bellwethergallery.com). Subway: J, M, Z to Marcy Ave. **Open** *Sept–Jul Sun, Mon, Thu–Sat noon–6pm.*
Setting trends since 1999, Bellwether represents such up-and-coming talents as Ellen Altfest, Sarah Bedford, Adam Cvijanovic and Matt Ducklo.

Kontiki LLC

653 Metropolitan Ave between Leonard St and Manhattan Ave, Williamsburg (212-334-9255). Subway: L to Graham Ave. **Open** *Sept–Jul Thu–Sun noon–6pm.*
This small-project space in Williamsburg features curated mixed-media exhibitions of "very, very young work," including such artists as Frank Benson and Los Angeles' Matt Johnson.

Jessica Murray Projects

210 North 6th St between Driggs Ave and Roebling St, Williamsburg (718-384-9606). Subway: L to Bedford Ave. **Open** *Sun, Mon, Thu–Sat noon–6pm.*
Dealer Murray comes to Billyburg by way of a curatorial background, and shows emerging artists who work in all media—among them, Brady Dollarhide, Jackie Gendel and Mark Dean Vecca.

Cy Twombly's *A Gathering of Time* at **Gagosian** uptown. *See p266.*

Pierogi 2000

177 North 9th St between Bedford and Driggs Aves, Williamsburg (718-599-2144; www.pierogi2000.com). Subway: L to Bedford Ave. **Open** *Sept–Jul Mon–Fri noon–6pm, and by appointment.*

One of Williamsburg's more established galleries, Pierogi presents the *Flat Files,* a series of drawers containing works on paper by some 700 artists. Don't pass up the chance to don white gloves and handle the filed artworks yourself.

Plus Ultra Gallery

235 South 1st St at Roebling St, Williamsburg (718-387-3844; www.plusultragallery.com). Subway: J, M, Z to Marcy Ave; L to Bedford Ave. **Open** *Sun, Mon, Fri, Sat noon–6pm.*

Run by artist Joshua Stern and art entrepreneur Ed Winkleman, the newly expanded Plus Ultra Gallery has a serious-fun feel, mounting shows by such artists as Leslie Brack, Joe Fig and Andy Yoder.

Roebling Hall

390 Wythe Ave at South 4th St, Williamsburg (718-599-5352; www.brooklynart.com). Subway: J, M, Z to Marcy Ave; L to Bedford Ave. **Open** *Sun, Mon, Fri, Sat noon–6pm.*

Directors Joel Beck and Christian Viveros-Fauné cook up provocative shows, featuring emerging local and international talents.

Nonprofit spaces

Apexart

291 Church St between Walker and White Sts (212-431-5270; www.apexart.org). Subway: 1, 9 to Franklin St. **Open** *Sept–Jul Tue–Sat 11am–6pm.*

At this unconventional space, the inspiration comes from the independent critics, curators and artists selected for Apexart's curatorial program. The work rarely follows prevailing fashions; more often than not, it anticipates them.

Art in General

79 Walker St between Broadway and Lafayette St (212-219-0473; www.artingeneral.org). Subway: J, M, Z, N, Q, R, W, 6 to Canal St. **Open** *Sept–Jun Tue–Sat noon–6pm.*

Now celebrating its 23rd year, this Chinatown oddball has a vigorous artist-residency program, introducing newcomers—from New York, Europe, Cuba and elsewhere in Latin America—in a homey, almost familial atmosphere.

The Drawing Center

35 Wooster St between Broome and Grand Sts (212-219-2166; www.drawingcenter.org). Subway: A, C, E, J, M, Z, N, Q, R, W, 6 to Canal St. **Open** *Sept–Jul Tue–Fri 10am–6pm; Sat 11am–6pm.*

This 26-year-old stronghold of works on paper has assembled critically acclaimed programs of emerging art stars, as well as major museum-caliber shows with such artists as James Ensor, Ellsworth Kelly—and even Rembrandt. A Soho standout.

Grey Art Gallery at New York University

100 Washington Sq East between Washington and Waverly Pls (212-998-6780; www.nyu.edu/greyart). Subway: A, C, E, B, D, F, V to W 4th St; R, W to 8th St–NYU. **Open** *Mid-Sept–mid-Jul Tue, Thu, Fri 11am–6pm; Wed 11am–8pm; Sat 11am–5pm.* **Admission** *Suggested donation $3.*

Founded in 1958, NYU's museum/laboratory has a multimedia collection of nearly 6,000 works covering the entire range of visual art. The museum's emphasis is on the late 19th and 20th centuries.

Momenta

72 Berry St between North 9th and North 10th Sts, Williamsburg, Brooklyn (718-218-8058; www.momentaart.org). Subway: L to Bedford Ave. **Open** *Sept–Jun Mon–Fri noon–6pm.*

Momenta is housed in a tiny Brooklyn space, yet it manages to convey the importance of a serious Soho white-box gallery. You'll find solo and group exhibitions from a mix of emerging artists—most of them with an intellectual Conceptual bent.

Sculpture Center

44-19 Purves St at Jackson Ave, Long Island City, Queens (718-361-1750; www.sculpture-center.org). Subway: E, V to 23rd St–Ely Ave; G to Long Island City–Court Sq; 7 to 45th Rd–Court House Sq. **Open** *Sun, Mon, Thu–Sat 11am–6pm.*

One of the best places to see work by emerging and mid-career artists, this gallery is known for its very wide-ranging definition of sculpture. The impressive steel-and-brick digs, designed by architect Maya Lin, opened in December 2002.

Smack Mellon

56 Water St between Dock and Main Sts, Dumbo, Brooklyn (718-422-0989; www.smackmellon.org). Subway: A, C to High St; F to York St. **Open** *Wed–Sun noon–6pm.*

Avant-garde group shows fill this multidisciplinary nonprofit gallery's drafty but accommodating quarters. Originally a foundry, the 6,000-square-foot structure dates back to before the Civil War.

Photography

New York is photo country, no doubt about it. For a comprehensive overview of local photo shows, look for the bimonthly directory *Photograph* ($5).

Howard Greenberg Gallery

Fuller Building, 41 E 57th between Madison and Park Aves, 14th floor (212-334-0010; www.howardgreenberg.com). Subway: N, R, W to Fifth Ave–59th St. **Open** *Tue–Sat 11am–6pm.*

Photographic masters like Henri Cartier-Bresson, Gordon Parks and Edward Weston are mainstays of this established midtown gallerist, who also represents the estates of Imogen Cunningham and Edward Steichen, among others.

Now look here Exhibits at **ICP** emphasize the centrality of photography in cultural life.

Edwynn Houk Gallery

745 Fifth Ave between 57th and 58th Sts, fourth floor (212-750-7070; www.houkgallery.com). Subway: N, R, W to Fifth Ave–59th St.
Open *Sept–Jul Tue–Sat 11am–6pm. Call for summer hours.*
This respected specialist in vintage and contemporary photography shows such artists as Brassaï, Lynn Davis, Elliott Erwitt, Dorothea Lange, Annie Leibovitz, Man Ray and Alfred Stieglitz, each commanding top dollar.

International Center of Photography

1133 Sixth Ave at 43rd St (212-857-0000; www.icp.org). Subway: B, D, F, V to 42nd St–Bryant Park; 7 to Fifth Ave. **Open** *Tue–Thu 10am–5pm; Fri 10am–8pm; Sat, Sun 10am–6pm.*
Admission *$10, seniors and students $7, children under 12 free. Voluntary donation Fri 5–8pm.*
ICP's galleries, once split between locations in midtown and uptown, were consolidated in this redesigned building in 2001. There are also a school and library—a major photographic resource—that includes back issues of photography magazines and thousands of biographical and photographic files. Begun in the 1960s as the International Fund for Concerned Photography, ICP houses work by photojournalists Werner Bischof, Robert Capa, David Seymour and Dan Weiner, all of whom were killed on assignment. News and documentary photography remains an important part of the center's program, which also includes contemporary photos and video (last year, the first-ever ICP Photo Triennial further solidified ICP's presence on the contemporary photo scene). Two floors of exhibition space often showcase retrospectives devoted to single artists; recent shows have focused on the work of Sebastião Salgado, Weegee and Garry Winogrand.

Klotz/Sirmon Gallery

511 W 25th St between Tenth and Eleventh Aves, suite 701 (212-741-4764; www.klotzsirmon.com). Subway: C, E to 23rd St. **Open** *Sept–Jun Wed–Sat 11am–6pm; Tuesday by appointment.*
In addition to its stock of vintage and high-quality contemporary works, this gallery also operates as the New York agent for the photo archives of *The New York Times*, which comprises some 5 million prints. If you're in New York in December, don't miss the annual Holiday Sale. Curators and collectors rub elbows with just plain folks—and they're all looking for bargains.

Pace/MacGill Gallery

32 E 57th St between Madison and Park Aves, ninth floor (212-759-7999). Subway: N, R, W to Lexington Ave–59th St; 4, 5, 6 to 59th St.
Open *Sept–late Jun Tue–Fri 9:30am–5:30pm; Sat 10am–6pm. Late Jun–Aug Mon–Thu 9:30am–5:30pm; Fri 9am–4pm.*
This established gallery frequently shows work by such well-known names as Walker Evans, Robert Frank, Irving Penn and Alfred Stieglitz, in addition to groundbreaking contemporaries like Guy Bourdin, Chuck Close, Philip-Lorca DiCorcia and Kiki Smith.

Books & Poetry

To get a read on the local literary scene, drop by one of these bookish events.

On any given night, dozens of authors are greeting rapt audiences around the boroughs—reading from their work, answering questions, accepting the odd manuscript. New York is a writers' town, for both best-selling authors and weblog diarists. Established writers—such as Salman Rushdie (Greenwich Village), Amy Tan (Soho), even Thomas Pynchon (sorry, our lips are sealed)—tend to stake out digs in Manhattan, while younger writers like Jhumpa Lahiri, Jonathan Lethem and Colson Whitehead favor slightly more down-to-earth (and affordable) Brooklyn.

All that literary ambition in the air must be contagious. Many New Yorkers cure their itch for recognition with regular appearances at local spoken-word series, where they can practice their verse or storytelling skills before a roomful of peers. Gut-wrenching? Sure. Exhilarating? If you're lucky. And if you're *very* lucky, you may end up meeting your future agent/editor/mentor in the process.

For a current schedule of who's reading where, and when, call or visit each venue's website, or pick up a copy of *Time Out New York.*

Author appearances

Asian-American Writers Workshop

16 W 32nd St between Fifth Ave and Broadway, tenth floor (212-494-0061; www.aaww.org). Subway: B, D, F, V, N, Q, R, W to 34th St–Herald Sq. Weeknights. **Admission** *suggested donation $5.*

Renowned writers of Asian heritage—including Maxine Hong Kingston and Jessica Hagedorn—and up-and-comers lecture on the publishing biz or share their work at this respected organization.

Barbès

376 9th St at Sixth Ave, Park Slope, Brooklyn (718-965-9177; www.barbesbrooklyn.com). Subway: F to Seventh Ave; M, R to Fourth Ave–9th St. Evenings. **Admission** *free–$2.*

Too many cafés host a few readings and suddenly declare themselves "community centers." Barbès, a bar and performance space owned by two French musicians, is one of the few places that really earns the appellation. At press time, alternate Sunday evenings were devoted to such local authors as Katy Lederer and Hal Sirowitz, while Thursdays belonged to writers from the lit journal *McSweeney's.*

> ► Check the Around Town and Books sections of ***Time Out New York*** for weekly listings and reviews.
> ► For more bookstores, *see p296* **Gay & Lesbian** and *pp235–237* **Shops & Services.**

Barnes & Noble

33 E 17th St between Broadway and Park Ave South (212-253-0810; www.barnesandnoble.com). Subway: L, N, Q, R, W, 4, 5, 6 to 14th St–Union Sq. Evenings and weekend afternoons. **Admission** *free.*

Nearly every author tour touches down at a Barnes & Noble. (This Union Square location offers an especially varied schedule.) Keep your eyes open for moonlighting celebs from other industries—like chef Daniel Boulud or *SNL*'s Jimmy Fallon.

Bluestockings

172 Allen St between Rivington and Stanton Sts (212-777-6028; www.bluestockings.com). Subway: F to Delancey St; J, M, Z to Delancey–Essex Sts. Evenings and weekend afternoons. **Admission** *suggestion donation free–$10.*

This self-proclaimed "progressive" bookstore and café hosts frequent readings and discussions, often on feminist and lesbian themes.

Books of Wonder

16th W 18th St between Fifth and Sixth Aves (212-989-3270; www.booksofwonder.net). Subway: 1, 9 to 18th St. Evenings and weekend afternoons. **Admission** *free.*

Given the many successful authors turning their hand to children's books, you're as likely to see Michael Chabon reading at this kiddie shop as you are to hear Maurice Sendak.

Coliseum

See p236 for listing. Evenings. **Admission** *free.*

The new and improved Coliseum draws the big guns: Recent readings have included Susan Sontag, Art Spiegelman and Linda Fairstein.

Galapagos Art and Performance Space

See p311 for listing. Evenings. **Admission** *free–$5.*

Irony-soaked, self-referential *McSweeney's* contributors favor this quirky Brooklyn bar, which hosts regular readings and literary variety shows.

The Half King

505 W 23rd St between Tenth and Eleventh Aves (212-462-4300; www.thehalfking.com). Subway: C, E to 23rd St. Mon 7pm. **Admission** *free.*

Co-owned by *Perfect Storm* author Sebastian Junger, this Chelsea pub features mostly literary novelists and journalists.

All lit up Young literary luminaries and a downtown crowd gather at bastion of cool, **KGB**

Housing Works Used Book Cafe

See p236 for listing. Evenings. **Admission** *free–$15.*
The emerging and the illustrious mingle at the mike and in the audience at this Soho bookstore and café. Profits go to provide shelter and support services to homeless people living with HIV and AIDS.

Hue-Man Bookstore

2319 Frederick Douglass Blvd (Eighth Ave) at 125th St (212-665-7400; www.hueman bookstore.com). Subway: A, C, B, D to 125th St. Evenings and weekend afternoons. **Admission** *free.*
This spacious Harlem bookstore features frequent readings and signings, with an emphasis on African-American writers and topics.

Humanities and Social Sciences Library

See p162 for listing. Evenings. **Admission** *$10.*
The Celeste Bartos Forum at the main research library presents excellent live interviews with influential authors, such as J.M. Coetzee and Walter Mosley, as well as literary lectures and readings.

KGB

85 E 4th St between Second and Third Aves, second floor (212-505-3360; www.kgbbar.com). Subway: F, V to Lower East Side–Second Ave; 6 to Astor Pl. 7–9pm. **Admission** *free.*
This East Village hangout runs themed series that feature NYC writers, poets, fantasy authors and so on. Recent guests have included Melissa Bank, Heidi Julavits and Chuck Klosterman.

National Arts Club

15 Gramercy Park South between Park Ave South and Irving Pl (212-475-3424; www.nationalartsclub.org). Subway: 6 to 23rd St. Evenings. **Admission** *free, except for benefits.*
A posh Gramercy Park address and splendidly grand Victorian interiors make this a suitably dramatic setting for gazing upon your literary idol. Lectures and readings are open to the public as space permits; check the website for upcoming events. And leave that hoodie and trucker cap at home—business attire is required.

New School University

66 W 12th St between Fifth and Sixth Aves (212-229-5353, tickets 212-229-5488; www.newschool.edu). Subway: F, V to 14th St; L to Sixth Ave. Evenings. **Admission** *free–$10; students free.*
Mark Doty, Rita Dove and Jonathan Franzen are a few of the notable writers to participate in the university's wide-ranging readings and literary forums. Look also for political discussions and poetry nights.

92nd Street Y

1395 Lexington Ave at 92nd St (212-415-5500; www.92y.org). Subway: 6 to 96th St. Evenings. **Admission** *$16–$25.*
Canonical novelists, journalists and poets preside over grand intellectual feasts. A recent schedule offered a tribute to poet Anthony Hecht; a double bill of Margaret Atwood and William Gibson; and a discussion on "Writing New York" by Brooklyn darling Jonathan Lethem, Colson Whitehead and Edgardo Vega Yunqué.

Soft Skull Shortwave

71 Bond St at State St, Boerum Hill, Brooklyn (718-643-1599; www.softskull.com/shortwave.php). Subway: F, G to Bergen St. Evenings. **Admission** *free.*
Discover gritty, experimental poets and edgy new fiction writers at this avant-garde Brooklyn bookstore in up-and-coming Boerum Hill.

Sunny's Bar

253 Conover St between Beard and Reed Sts, Red Hook, Brooklyn (718-625-8211). Travel: F, G to Smith–9th Sts, then B77 bus to Conover St. Evenings. **Admission** *free.*
If you're feeling adventurous, make the trip out to this old waterfront joint to hear an eclectic lineup of on-the-verge locals such as Blake Nelson and Susan Choi. Scheduling varies, so be sure to call ahead.

Spoken word

Most spoken-word events begin with a featured poet or two before moving on to an open mike. If you'd like to participate, show up a little early and ask for the sign-up sheet. Remember to adhere to poetry slam etiquette: Feel free to express your approval out loud, but keep criticism to yourself (silence speaks louder than words). For an up-to-date schedule of events throughout the city, check out the **Ultimate NYC Poetry Calendar** *(www.poetz.com).*

Event-full Slams, jams and hip-hop poetry.

Bowery Poetry Club

308 Bowery between Bleecker and Houston Sts (212-614-0505; www.bowerypoetry.com). Subway: B, D, F, V to Broadway–Lafayette St; 6 to Bleecker St. Evenings and weekend afternoons. **Admission** *free–$15.*
Celebrating the grand oral traditions and cyberific future of poetry, the funky BPC features high-energy spoken-word events every night, with readings and performance workshops in the afternoon. The Urbana National Slam team leads an open mike on Thursdays.

Cornelia Street Café

29 Cornelia St between Bleecker and W 4th Sts (212-989-9319; www.corneliastreetcafe.com). Subway: A, C, E, B, D, F, V to W 4th St. Evenings. **Admission** *free–$5 (one-drink minimum).*
This charming West Village restaurant is the home of several long-running series. At press time, the café's basement performance space was devoting various nights to Arab-American, Greek-American and Italian-American writers. The popular open-mike Pink Pony series continues on Fridays.

The Moth StorySLAM

www.themoth.org.
Better at talking than at writing? The Moth, known for its big-name monthly storytelling shows, also sponsors open slams in various venues. Ten raconteurs get five minutes each to tell a favorite story (no notes allowed!) to a panel of judges.

Nuyorican Poets Cafe

236 E 3rd St between Aves B and C (212-505-8183; www.nuyorican.org). Subway: F, V to Lower East Side–Second Ave. Evenings. **Admission** *$5–$15.*
This 30-year-old community arts center, deep in the heart of the East Village, is known for its long history of raucous poetry slams, jam sessions and anything-goes open mikes.

Our Unorganicized Reading

ABC No Rio, 156 Rivington St between Clinton and Suffolk Sts (212-254-3697; www.abcnorio.org). Subway: F to Delancey St; J, M, Z to Delancey–Essex Sts. Sun 3pm. **Admission** *$2.*
Down on the Lower East Side, ABC No Rio's long-running Sunday-afternoon open mike promises a welcoming vibe, no time limits and, best of all, "no b.s." Just remember, brevity is still the soul of wit.

The Poetry Project

St. Mark's Church in-the-Bowery, 131 E 10th St at Second Ave (212-674-0910; www.poetryproject.com). Subway: L to First Ave; 6 to Astor Pl. Evenings. **Admission** *$8, seniors and students $7.*
Housed in a beautiful old church, the Project has hosted an amazing roster of poets since its inception in 1966, including Allen Ginsberg, Michael Ondaatje and Adrienne Rich. It also offers workshops, lectures, book parties and an open poetry reading on the first Monday of each month.

Cabaret & Comedy

Know where I can get a drink around here? No, but if you hum a few bars…

Cabaret

New York is the cabaret capital of the U.S. and, quite possibly, of the world. In what other city can you find a dozen different shows on any given night?

The term *cabaret* covers both the venue and the art form. It encompasses the club where songs are sung, generally by one person, but sometimes by an ensemble; it is also the vocal interpretation of songs, usually drawn from what's known as the Great American Songbook, a vast repertoire of tunes that are derived from the American musical theater, supplemented with occasional new numbers by contemporary composers. More than anything else, however, cabaret is an act of intimacy: The best singers are able to draw in the audience until each member feels as if he or she is being personally serenaded.

The Golden Age of cabaret in New York spanned the 1950s and early '60s. With the advent of rock & roll, the velvet-edged lure of cabaret waned, but plenty of singers and fans still keep the classic sound alive. Mid-October marks the Cabaret Convention at **Town Hall** (*see p315*), which attracts top performers for a weeklong showcase of the best in the genre.

Today's venues fall into two groups: expensive boîtes tucked into hotels (**Cafe Carlyle**, **Feinstein's at the Regency**) and less formal, less pricey neighborhood clubs (**Don't Tell Mama**, the **Duplex**). After a spate of closings a few years back, new venues for cabaret are now popping up all over town.

Bobby Short at the **Cafe Carlyle**.

Classic nightspots

Cafe Carlyle

The Carlyle Hotel, 35 E 76th St at Madison Ave (212-744-1600, 800-227-5737; www.thecarlyle.com). Subway: 6 to 77th St. **Shows** *Mon–Thu 8:45pm; Fri, Sat 8:45, 10:45pm.* **Cover** *$50–$75.* **Credit** *AmEx, DC, MC, V.*

This is the epitome of chic New York, especially when Bobby Short performs. Woody Allen sometimes sits in as clarinetist with Eddie Davis and his New Orleans Jazz Band for Monday-night shows (call ahead to confirm). Don't dress casually—embrace the high life. To drink in some atmosphere without spending so much, try Bemelmans Bar across the hall, which always features an excellent pianist *(Tue–Sat 9:40pm–12:30am; $20 cover).* The murals of Ludwig Bemelmans, creator of the lovable *Madeline* books, adorn the walls.

The Duplex

61 Christopher St at Seventh Ave South (212-255-5438; www.theduplex.com). Subway: 1, 9 to Christopher St–Sheridan Sq. **Shows** *Times vary. Piano bar 9pm–4am.* **Cover** *$5–$25, two-drink minimum.* **Credit** *Cash only.*

The Duplex may not have classic glamour, but it's the city's oldest cabaret. Going strong for 50-plus years, the place is known for campy, good-natured fun. But such top acts as chanteuse Barbara Fasano have recently appeared here, earning the Duplex a *Time Out New York* award for Best Cabaret.

Feinstein's at the Regency

Regency Hotel, 540 Park Ave at 61st St (212-339-4095; www.feinsteinsattheregency.com). Subway: N, R, W to Lexington Ave–59th St; 4, 5, 6 to 59th St. **Shows** *Tue–Thu 8:30pm; Fri, Sat 8:30, 11pm.* **Cover** *$60–$70, $30 food-and-drink minimum.* **Credit** *AmEx, DC, Disc, MC, V.*

Cabaret's crown prince, Michael Feinstein, draws A-list talent to this swank room in the Regency Hotel. Past performers have included singer-guitarist John Pizzarelli and his wife, the phenomenal singer Jessica Molaskey, as well as Broadway star Betty Buckley and the swellegant Ann Hampton Callaway.

The Oak Room

Algonquin Hotel, 59 W 44th St between Fifth and Sixth Aves (212-840-6800). Subway: B, D, F, V to 42nd St–Bryant Park; 7 to Fifth Ave. **Shows** *Tue–Thu 9pm; Fri, Sat 9, 11:30pm.* **Cover** *$50–$60, $20 drink minimum; dinner compulsory at first Friday and Saturday shows.* **Credit** *AmEx, DC, Disc, MC, V.*

This resonant, banquette-lined room is the place to enjoy such cabaret luminaries as Karen Akers and Andrea Marcovicci, plus rising stars Stacey Kent and Jane Monheit. And yes, all you Dorothy Parker fans, it's *that* Algonquin (*see p45*).

Standards

Danny's Skylight Room

Grand Sea Palace, 346 W 46th St between Eighth and Ninth Aves (212-265-8130, 212-265-8133; www.dannysgsp.com). Subway: A, C, E to 42nd St–Port Authority. **Shows** *Times vary. Piano bar 8–11pm.* **Cover** *free–$25, $10 food-and-drink minimum; no cover for piano bar.* **Credit** *AmEx, DC, Disc, MC, V.*

A pastel-hued nook within the Grand Sea Palace restaurant, "where Bangkok meets Broadway" on touristy Restaurant Row, Danny's usually features the smooth sounds of standards and pop. In addition to up-and-comers, a few mature cabaret and jazz standbys, such as Blossom Dearie, perform here.

Don't Tell Mama

343 W 46th St between Eighth and Ninth Aves (212-757-0788; www.donttellmama.com). Subway: A, C, E to 42nd St–Port Authority. **Shows** *4pm–4am, 4–8 shows per night.* **Cover** *free–$20, two-drink minimum; no cover for piano bar, two-drink minimum.* **Credit** *Cash only.*

Showbiz pros and piano-bar buffs adore this Theater District stalwart, where acts range from strictly amateur to potential stars of tomorrow. The nightly lineup may include pop, jazz or Broadway singers, as well as female impersonators, magicians, comedians or musical revues.

Triad

158 W 72nd St between Columbus Ave and Broadway (212-799-4599). Subway: B, C, 1, 2, 3, 9 to 72nd St. **Shows** *Times vary.* **Cover** *$5–$20, two-drink minimum.* **Credit** *AmEx, Disc, MC, V ($20 minimum).*

This spot has been the launching pad for many revues over the years; some (like *Forbidden Broadway* and *Forever Plaid*) later moved on to larger Off Broadway venues. Dinner is also available.

Alternative venues

Dillon's

245 W 54th St between Broadway and Eighth Ave (212-307-9797). Subway: B, D, E to Seventh Ave. **Shows** *Times vary.* **Cover** *$10–$30, $10 food-and-drink minimum.* **Credit** *AmEx, MC, V.*

Musical-theater veterans (award-winning Margaret Wright) and Broadway stars of tomorrow (the swinging Judy Barnett) take the stage at this new venue just north of Times Square.

Joe's Pub

See p311 for listing.

This plush club and restaurant in the Public Theater is both hip and elegant. Frequent performers include the bebopping Lea DeLaria, the angular German diva Ute Lemper and the luminescent Audra McDonald, as well as singing sensations as diverse as Aimee Mann and Mo' Guajiro. Show times and cover prices vary.

King Kong Room

Supper Club, 240 W 47th St between Broadway and Eighth Ave (212-921-1904; www.kingkongroom.com). Subway: C, E, 1, 9 to 50th St. **Shows** *Mon 8:30pm.* **Cover** *$15–$25, $15 drink minimum.* **Credit** *AmEx, Disc, MC, V ($10 minimum).*

This upstairs boîte at the Supper Club hosts some of cabaret's brightest lights: Recent performers have included the bubbly KT Sullivan and cheeky singer-songwriter Amanda Green. Don't miss Jim Caruso's Cast Party every Monday at 10pm, where such stars as Alan Cumming, Lauren Bacall and Matthew Broderick have mingled with a crowd fueled by martinis and an anything-goes attitude.

Mama Rose's

219 Second Ave between 13th and 14th Sts (212-533-0558; www.mamaroses.net). Subway: L, N, Q, R, W, 4, 5, 6 to 14th St–Union Sq. **Shows** *Times vary.* **Cover** *prices vary; two-drink minimum.* **Credit** *AmEx, MC, V.*

Sing out, Louise! This new club, named after *Gypsy*'s stage-mother–from–hell, is designed specifically for cabaret performances (indeed, everyone from the lighting designer to the sound technician has had years of cabaret experience). The recent shows with Martha Lorin and the outrageous Mark Nadler proved to be an auspicious beginning; it looks as though Mama's is here to stay.

Comedy

It's the great paradox of NYC's comedy scene: The best shows are often found not at the established clubs, but rather at quirky little out-of-the-way places. Sure, we've spent many fine evenings at **Carolines on Broadway**, **Gotham Comedy Club** and other well-known venues. But sometimes, you're not in the mood for typical stand-up—and in New York, you have other options. Want some music and variety with your jokes? Check out ***Automatic Vaudeville***. Looking for an improvised talk-show parody? Drop by the **Upright Citizens Brigade Theatre**.

Of course, many of the best acts work both sides of the fence. Colin Quinn is a regular at **Comedy Cellar**, but he also pops up at obscure East Village lounges. The magnificently dry Todd Barry performs at every major club in town, but you might also catch him doing an extended set at a Williamsburg bar. And no comic can claim to have made it in NYC until they've been invited back to the stalwart ***Eating It***. If you're looking for less edgy comedy, you'd be wise to check out the more mainstream places. Here's a sampling of the best of both worlds.

Automatic Vaudeville

Ars Nova Theater, 511 W 54th St between Tenth and Eleventh Aves (info 212-489-9800, SmartTix 212-868-4444; www.arsnovanyc.com). Subway: A, B, D, 1, 9 to 59th St–Columbus Circle; C, E to 50th St. **Shows** *Thu 10pm.* **Cover** *$5.* **Credit** *AmEx, Disc, MC, V.*
Local favorites Dannah Feinglass and Paul Scheer host this cozy theater's weekly variety show. Every venue claims to spotlight NYC's best local comics; this one delivers the goods. The schedule can be erratic, though, so call before you head out.

Boston Comedy Club

82 W 3rd St between Sullivan and Thompson Sts (212-477-1000; www.bostoncomedyclub.com). Subway: A, C, E, B, D, F, V to W 4th St. **Shows** *Mon 8, 9:30pm; Tue 5, 9:30pm; Wed 9:30pm; Thu 7:45, 9:30pm; Fri, Sat 7:45, 10pm, 12:15am; Sun 9:30pm.* **Cover** *$7–$12 (Mon–Thu one-drink minimum; Fri, Sat two-drink minimum).* **Credit** *AmEx, MC, V.*
This isn't the classiest joint in town, but it's in a great Village location, and the club gets its share of high-quality acts and rising stars.

Carolines on Broadway

1626 Broadway between 49th and 50th Sts (212-757-4100; www.carolines.com). Subway: N, R, W to 49th St; 1, 9 to 50th St. **Shows** *Mon–Wed 7, 9:30pm, Thu, Sun 8, 10pm; Fri, Sat 8, 10:30pm, 12:30am.* **Cover** *$15–$35, two-drink minimum.* **Credit** *AmEx, DC, MC, V.*

Seeing red Saturn Returns performs at Ars Nova's ***Automatic Vaudeville*** variety show.

If you're nostalgic for the 1980s comedy boom, you can occasionally find guys like Gilbert Gottfried and Emo Philips doing their schtick here, mixed in with newer stars such as Dave Attell, Dave Chappelle and Janeane Garofalo.

Comedy Cellar

117 MacDougal St between Bleecker and W 3rd Sts (212-254-3480; www.comedycellar.com). Subway: A, C, E, B, D, F, V to W 4th St. **Shows** *Sun–Thu 9, 11pm; Fri 9, 10:45pm, 12:30am; Sat 7:30, 9:15, 11pm, 12:45am.* **Cover** *$10–$15, two-drink minimum.* **Credit** *AmEx, MC, V.*

For a sense of the talent that stalks the stage at this Village club, tune in to Comedy Central's *Tough Crowd.* Host Colin Quinn practically lives at Comedy Cellar, and most of his TV show's panelists (including Patrice O'Neal, Greg Giraldo, Jim Norton and Nick DiPaolo) are also regulars onstage.

Comic Strip Live

1568 Second Ave between 81st and 82nd Sts (212-861-9386; www.comicstriplive.com). Subway: 4, 5, 6 to 86th St. **Shows** *Mon–Thu 8:30pm; Fri 8:30, 10:30pm, 12:30am; Sat 6, 8, 10:15pm, 12:30am; Sun 8pm.* **Cover** *$12–$17, two-drink minimum.* **Credit** *AmEx, Disc, MC, V.*

Chris Rock, Adam Sandler and Jerry Seinfeld have all performed here, albeit years before you'd ever heard of them. Always on the lookout for future stars, the Strip continues to showcase some of New York's most promising young acts.

Dangerfield's

1118 First Ave between 61st and 62nd Sts (212-593-1650; www.dangerfields.com). Subway: N, R, W to Lexington Ave–59th St; 4, 5, 6 to 59th St. **Shows** *Sun–Thu 8:45pm; Fri 8:30, 10:30pm; Sat 8, 10:30pm, 12:30am.* **Cover** *$15–$20.* **Credit** *AmEx, DC, MC, V.*

Opened by Rodney Dangerfield in 1969, this old-school lounge predates not only its competitors but also many of its performers. The club offers food, no drink minimum, and $4 parking, which alone is worth the cover charge.

Eating It

Luna Lounge, 171 Ludlow St between Houston and Stanton Sts (212-260-2323; www.eatingit.net). Subway: F to Delancey St; J, M, Z to Delancey–Essex Sts. **Shows** *Mon 8pm.* **Cover** *$8, includes one drink ticket.* **Credit** *Cash only.*

This haven for experimental comedy places as much emphasis on the experimental as on the comedy. Not every act will make you fall out of your chair laughing, but there are good reasons why *Eating It* has become a must-see show for audiences and industry people alike. Expect to see performers who have been (or will soon be) on *Conan, Letterman* and *SNL.*

Gotham City Improv

158 W 23rd St between Sixth and Seventh Aves (212-367-8222; www.gothamcityimprov.com). Subway: F, V, 1, 9 to 23rd St. **Shows** *Times vary.* **Cover** *$5–$10.* **Credit** *Cash only.*

GCI presents improv, both short-form (the kind seen on *Whose Line Is It Anyway?*) and long-form (the more experimental, theatrical style). The group also trains students in both styles.

Gotham Comedy Club

34 W 22nd St between Fifth and Sixth Aves (212-367-9000; www.gothamcomedyclub.com). Subway: F, V, R, W to 23rd St. **Shows** *Sun–Thu 8:30pm; Fri 8:30, 10:30pm; Sat 8:30, 10:30pm, 12:30am.* **Cover** *$10–$16, two-drink minimum.* **Credit** *AmEx, DC, MC, V.*

You may not know their names, but if you follow stand-up, you'll recognize many of the faces that show up at this relatively upscale club in Chelsea. Regulars have included Jim Gaffigan, Judy Gold, Ted Alexandro and Jim David.

New York Comedy Club

241 E 24th St between Second and Third Aves (212-696-5233). Subway: 6 to 23rd St. **Shows** *Weeknight show times vary. Fri 8, 9, 10, 11:30pm; Sat 8, 9, 10, 11:30pm, midnight.* **Cover** *$8–$10, two-drink minimum.* **Credit** *AmEx, MC, V.*

This gritty Gramercy club has two separate rooms, each with a bargain cover price and a packed line-up. Particularly popular are the weekend shows dedicated to NYC's best acts by black *(Fri, Sat 11:30pm)* and Latino *(Fri 8pm; Sat 9pm)* acts.

The People's Improv Theater

154 W 29th St between Sixth and Seventh Aves (212-563-7488). Subway: 1, 9 to 28th St. **Shows** *Sun–Thu 8, 9:30pm; Fri, Sat 8, 10pm.* **Cover** *$6–$10.* **Credit** *Cash only.*

Founded by expats from the Upright Citizens Brigade (*see below*), the upstart PIT specializes in the same kind of innovative improv and sketch comedy that its predecessor, Improv Olympic, imported from Chicago in the late '90s.

Stand-Up New York

236 W 78th St at Broadway (212-595-0850; www.standupny.com). Subway: 1, 9 to 79th St. **Shows** *Mon 8:30pm; Tue, Wed 6, 9pm; Thu 6, 9, 11:15pm; Fri, Sat 8, 10pm, 12:15am; Sun 7, 9pm.* **Cover** *$5–$15, two-drink minimum.* **Credit** *AmEx, Disc, MC, V.*

The Upper West Side's only club features a mix of circuit regulars (Paul Mecurio, Jim Gaffigan and Dave Attell), along with fresh new talents.

Upright Citizens Brigade Theatre

307 W 26th St between Eighth and Ninth Aves (212-366-9176; www.ucbtheater.com). Subway: C, E to 23rd St. **Shows** *Times vary.* **Cover** *$5–$7.* **Credit** *Cash only.*

The UCBT presents some of the most adventurous comedy in NYC. You can catch sketches and long-form improv at a budget price every night, and you might even see performers from *Conan, Saturday Night Live* and *The Daily Show,* in the audience or honing their chops onstage. (Sunday is the typical night for celebrity drop-ins.)

Children

These are a few of our favorite things.

New York City's children have raised the bar on what is cool—and visiting kids will be grateful for it. Young seen-it-alls know that the best thing this town has to offer is its mix of well-kept secrets and tried-and-true traditional fare.

We've listed destinations that grab the imagination of New York kids, but don't ignore the simple thrills of street life: Times Square at night is a sight to behold, and no child will fail to gaze wide-eyed at live crabs threatening to tumble out of barrels and onto crowded Chinatown sidewalks. If you're looking for free activities to fill an hour or two between longer outings, pick up a copy of *Events for Children* from any branch of the New York Public Library (*see p162*); listings cover storytelling, puppet shows, films and workshops. For more in-depth exploration, Alfred Gingold and Helen Rogan's savvy *The Cool Parents' Guide to All of New York* (Universe, $15) is indispensable.

Classic kids' New York

Astroland Amusement Park

1000 Surf Ave at West 10th St, Coney Island, Brooklyn (718-372-0275; www.astroland.com). Subway: D to Stillwell Ave–Coney Island.
Open *Mid-Apr–mid-Jun Sat, Sun noon–6pm, weather permitting. Mid-Jun–Labor Day noon–midnight.* **Admission** *$2–$5 per ride; $17.99–$21.99 per six-hour session.*
Credit *MC, V.*
This well-aged Coney Island amusement park has an appealing grunginess that makes it a welcome alternative to certain slick, mouse-themed parks.

Kid-friendly restaurants

Lots of eateries welcome young'uns with kiddie-friendly menus, crayons on the table, or just the promise of huge, supergooey desserts. Here are some places that keep tots—*and* parents—happily fed.

America

9 E 18th St at Broadway (212-505-2110). Subway: L, N, Q, R, W, 4, 5, 6 to 14th St–Union Sq.
This popular spot offers mac and cheese, miniburgers and a cute Statue of Liberty theme. There are grown-up salads and regional specialties for the over-12 set.

Brooklyn Diner USA

212 W 57th St between Seventh Ave and Broadway (212-977-1957). Subway: N, Q, R, W to 57th St.
On your way to *The Lion King*? Stop here for big portions of updated diner fare, with a side of nostalgia for both old Brooklyn and the former Brooklyn Dodgers.

Bubby's

See p167 for listing.
Expect big slabs of pie at both branches of this loud, kid-loving bakery-turned-restaurant. Brunch can be a zoo at the Tribeca location, but yummy soups and all-American basics make Bubby's a crowd-pleaser anytime.

Cowgirl Hall of Fame

519 Hudson St at 10th St (212-633-1133). Subway: 1, 9 to Christopher St–Sheridan Sq.
Western kitsch, mile-high nachos and Frito pie are a few of the reasons to visit this West Village favorite. And for Mom and Dad: killer margaritas.

Genki Sushi

9 E 46th St between Fifth and Madison Aves (212-983-5018). Subway: B, D, F, V to 42nd St–Bryant Park; 7 to Fifth Ave.
Precocious youngsters can pick out their own California rolls from the plates of sushi zooming by on a conveyor belt.

Serendipity3

225 60th St between Second and Third Aves (212-838-3531). Subway: N, R, W to Lexington Ave–59th St; 4, 5, 6 to 59th St.
Huge goblets of "frozen hot chocolate" (a brain-freezing chocolate slushie) keep generations coming back to this longtime kids' hangout.

Older kids can ride the world-famous Cyclone roller coaster ($5); the young ones will prefer the Tilt-a-Whirl, the Pirate Ship or one of the three carousels.

Blessing of the Animals

For listing, see p116 **Cathedral of St. John the Divine**. **Open** *First Sunday in October 11am.* **Admission** *free.*

One of the sweetest ceremonies a child can witness is the procession of animals to this cathedral's grand altar, on the day of the Feast of St. Francis. Free tickets are distributed at 9am; the line forms earlier (count on a sellout). An outdoor fair starts at 1pm.

Dinosaurs at the Museum of Natural History

For listing, see p145 **American Museum of Natural History**.

Children of all ages request repeat visits to this old-fashioned exhibit-based museum—especially to see the dinosaurs, the enormous blue whale and, in the colder months, the free-flying butterflies. During the holiday season, look for the Christmas tree decorated with masterfully folded origami ornaments (they include dinosaur shapes). Paper-folders are on hand to help visitors make their own.

The Nutcracker at City Ballet

For listing, see p323 **New York State Theater**.

Generations of New York kids have counted on the New York City Ballet to provide this Balanchine holiday treat. The pretty production features an onstage snowstorm, a one-ton Christmas tree and tutu-wearing child dancers.

Storytelling at the Hans Christian Andersen Statue

Central Park, entrance on Fifth Ave at 72nd St (www.hcastorycenter.org). Subway: 6 to 77th St. **Open** *Jun–Sept Sat 11am–noon.* **Admission** *free.*

Children five and older have gathered for decades at the foot of this statue to hear master storytellers from all over America tell folk and fairy tales—a New York tradition that's not to be missed.

Temple of Dendur at the Met

For listing, see p149 **Metropolitan Museum of Art**.

The Met can be overwhelming—unless you make a beeline for one or two galleries. The impressive Temple of Dendur, a real multiroomed temple with carvings and reliefs, was brought here from Egypt, stone by stone, and it's a perennial hit. Also check out the mummies in the Egyptian room.

Winnie the Pooh and Friends

For listing, see p162 **Donnell Library Center**. **Open** *Mon, Wed, Fri noon–6pm; Tue 10am–6pm; Thu noon–8pm; Sat noon–5pm; Sun 1–5pm.* **Admission** *free.*

The original toys that belonged to Christopher Robin Milne are famously ensconced in a glass case in this library's Central Children's Room.

Arts festivals

Some of the city's annual arts festivals incorporate interesting kids' programming. Of particular note is the **Lincoln Center Out of Doors** festival (August), which offers pared-down performances for children. For details, go to www.lincolncenter.org. The **New York International Fringe Festival** (*see p255*) also offers theater and dance programs for kids.

Circuses

Each spring, **Ringling Bros. and Barnum & Bailey**'s three-ring circus *(see p252)* comes to Madison Square Garden—along with animal-rights picketers. You can't beat it for spectacle, but the smaller alternatives are more fun.

Big Apple Circus

Damrosch Park, Lincoln Center, 62nd St between Columbus and Amsterdam Aves (212-268-2500; www.bigapplecircus.org). Subway: 1, 9 to 66th St–Lincoln Ctr. **Open** *Oct–Jan. Call or visit website for schedule and prices.* **Credit** *AmEx, MC, V.*

New York's traveling circus was founded 27 years ago as an intimate one-act-at-a-time answer to the Ringling Bros.' extravaganza. The clowns in this nonprofit show are among the most creative in the country.

UniverSoul Big Top Circus

800-316-7439; www.universoulcircus.com. **Open** *Call or visit website for venue, schedule and prices.* **Credit** *AmEx, DC, Disc, MC, V.*

This one-ring African-American circus has the requisite clowns and animal acts with a twist: Instead of familiar circus music, you get hip-hop, R&B and salsa—and a great ringmaster, Casual Cal Dupree. The group usually appears in Brooklyn's Prospect Park in the spring.

Dance

Family Matters

Dance Theater Workshop, 219 W 19th St between Seventh and Eighth Aves (212-924-0077; www.dtw.org). Subway: C, E to 23rd St; 1, 9 to 18th St. **Open** *Call or visit website for schedule.* **Admission** *$20, children $10.* **Credit** *AmEx, MC, V.*

Curated by a pair of choreographer-parents for children ages six and up, Family Matters is a quirky variety show that blends art, dance, music and theater.

New York Theatre Ballet

Florence Gould Hall, 55 E 59th St between Madison and Park Aves (212-355-6160; www.nytb.org). Subway: N, R, W to Lexington Ave–59th St; 4, 5, 6 to 59th St. **Open** *Call or visit the website for schedule.* **Admission** *$25, children under 12 $20.* **Credit** *AmEx, MC, V (through Ticketmaster).*

Hop to it The *Carnival of the Animals* at **New York Theatre Ballet**. *See p278.*

NYTB stages one-hour adaptations of classic ballets and literary works for young children, such as the holiday favorite *The Nutcracker.* The interactive *Carnival of the Animals* teaches the audience basic dance moves, and *Alice in Wonderland* is a lively, kooky vaudevillian romp.

Film

New York International Children's Film Festival

Various venues (212-349-0330; www.gkids.com). **Open** *February or March. Call or visit website for schedule and prices.* **Credit** *AmEx, MC, V.*
This three-week fest is a hot ticket. An exciting mix of shorts and full-length features is presented to everyone from tots through teens. Many of the films are by indie filmmakers from around the world—and not necessarily those who make kids' flicks. Children determine the festival's winners, which are then screened at an awards ceremony. It's a great party for all ages, with door prizes and a celebrity host.

Tribeca Film Festival

Various Tribeca venues (866-941-FEST; www.tribecafilmfestival.org). **Open** *May. Call or visit the website for schedule and prices.*
Robert de Niro's newcomer schedules two weekends of screenings for kids, including commercial premieres and shorts programs, plus an outdoor street festival.

Museums & exhibitions

Both children's museums and those not devoted to kids offer weekend and school-break workshops as well as interactive exhibitions. Youngsters love exploring the **American Museum of Natural History** (*see p145*). The museum's **Rose Center for Earth and Space** (*see p145*) features exhibits and a multimedia space show within the largest suspended-glass cube in the U.S. Children of all ages will be fascinated by the amazing *Panorama of New York City* scale model at the **Queens Museum of Art** (*see p154*). Hands-on fun can be had inside the pitch-black Touch Tunnel at the **Liberty Science Center** (*see p162*). At the **American Museum of the Moving Image** (*see p161*), *Behind the Screen* lets kids mess with *Jurassic Park* sound effects and play with moving-image technology. The ***Intrepid*** **Sea-Air-Space Museum** (*see p162*)

► For more great ideas on where to take the kids, see ***Time Out New York Kids*** (the obsessive guide for impulsive parents), on newsstands now, or visit www.timeoutnykids.com.
► Need a baby-sitter? *See p365.*

houses interactive battle-related exhibits on an aircraft carrier. Many art museums offer family tours and workshops that include sketching in the galleries. To find out what's available, visit the websites of the **Brooklyn Museum of Art**, the **Met**, the **Whitney** and **MoMA QNS** (*see pp145–151*).

Brooklyn Children's Museum

145 Brooklyn Ave at St. Marks Ave, Crown Heights, Brooklyn (718-735-4400; www.bchildmus.org). Travel: 3 to Kingston Ave, then the B43 bus to St. Marks Ave. **Open** *Sept–Jun Wed–Fri 1–6pm; Sat, Sun 11am–6pm. Jul, Aug Tue–Fri 1–6pm; Sat, Sun 11am–6pm. Call or visit website for holiday hours.* **Admission** *$4.* **Credit** *AmEx, Disc, MC, V.*

Founded in 1899, BCM was the world's first museum designed for kids. It has more than 27,000 artifacts in its Collection Central gallery, including prehistoric fossils and present-day toys from around the world. Hands-on exhibits (and live small animals) are in the Animal Outpost, and the People Tube, a huge sewer pipe, connects four exhibit floors. Weekends, a free shuttle bus makes a circuit from the Grand Army Plaza subway station to the Brooklyn Museum of Art and this museum.

Children's Museum of the Arts

182 Lafayette St between Broome and Grand Sts (212-274-0986; www.cmany.org). Subway: 6 to Spring St. **Open** *Wed, Fri–Sun noon–5pm; Thu noon–6pm.* **Admission** *$6. Voluntary donation Thu 4–6pm.* **Credit** *AmEx, MC, V.*

Kids under seven love this low-key museum, with its floor-to-ceiling chalkboards, art computers and vast store of art supplies.

Children's Museum of Manhattan

212 W 83rd St between Amsterdam Ave and Broadway (212-721-1234; www.cmom.org). Subway: 1, 9 to 86th St. **Open** *Wed–Sun 10am–5pm. Call for summer and holiday hours.* **Admission** *$6.* **Credit** *AmEx, MC, V.*

This children's museum promotes several types of literacy through its playful interactive exhibitions. In the Inventor Center, computer-savvy kids can take any idea they dream up—a flying bike, a talking robot—and design it on-screen using digital imaging.

Sony Wonder Technology Lab

Sony Plaza, 56th St between Fifth and Madison Aves (212-833-8100; www.sonywondertechlab.com). Subway: E, V to Fifth Ave–53rd St; 6 to 51st St. **Open**

Shopping is child's play

Sure, all kids love a toy store. Big fun palaces like Toys "R" Us lure tots in with grand displays and let them play, no questions asked. But they can also be crowded, and challenging for parents—unless you *like* saying no. Below, we have listed alternative browsing spots that local parents use as substitutes for museumlike experiences; shops where you can kill an hour without salespeople hovering, and where kids can pick up a trinket or two to bring home. Or, grab a book at any branch of Barnes & Noble, sit in the cafe, and read a story over hot chocolate. At the **American Girl Place** *(609 Fifth Ave at 49th St, 877-247-5223)*, girly girls can admire the collection of cuddle-ready (but pricey) dolls in historical costumes that are thrillingly accessorized. They can even tuck their own dolls into tiny high chairs in the café while they eat. Boisterous boys and their sporty sisters can let off steam at the nearby **NBA Store** *(666 Fifth Ave at 52nd St, 212-515-6221)*, where there's a half-court on the lower level.

Abracadabra

19 W 21st St between Fifth and Sixth Aves (212-627-5194). Subway: F, V, R, W to 23rd St. **Open** *Mon–Sat 11am–7pm.* **Credit** *AmEx, DC, Disc, MC, V.*

More than 20,000 toys fill this cavernous store: costumes, tricks, severed arms, a fart machine (with remote), a fake corpse—you get the picture. Professional magicians buy their supplies here, which gives the place extra cachet; they also perform free magic shows on weekends *(Sat 2, 5pm; Sun 1, 3pm)*.

Enchanted Forest

See p238 for listing.

A collection of exotic stuffed animals, marionettes, handmade toys and baskets of tiny, mysterious 50-cent objects occupies this fairy-tale–like store, which resembles a two-floor tree house, complete with forest critters hanging from the ceiling and a wooden bridge. Most magical of all is the fact that, however packed the place gets, it always sounds rather hushed, making this a good place to recover from a Soho shopping blitz.

Evolution and Maxilla & Mandible

For listing, see p247 **Evolution**. *Maxilla & Mandible, 451 Columbus Ave between 81st and 82nd Sts (212-724-6173). Subway: B, C to 81st St–American Museum of Natural History.* **Open** *Mon–Sat 11am–7pm.* **Credit** *AmEx, Disc, MC, V.*

Arts & Entertainment

Tue, Wed, Fri, Sat 10am–6pm; Thu 10am–8pm; Sun noon–6pm. **Admission** *free; reservations required.*
Recently refurbished, this digital wonderland lets visitors (or "media trainees") use state-of-the-art communication technology to play at designing video games, assisting in surgery, editing a TV show and operating robots. Kids eight and older get the most out of this place.

Music

Carnegie Hall Family Concerts

See p321 for listing. **Admission** *$5.*
Even kids who profess to hate classical music are impressed by a visit to Carnegie Hall. The Family Concert series, which includes world-music and jazz programs, is held at Carnegie's more intimate Zankel Hall. The series features first-rate performers; concerts are held fall through spring for ages seven and up. Preconcert activities include workshops and storytelling.

Jazz for Young People

For listing, see p323 **Alice Tully Hall. Admission** *$20, children under 18 $15.* **Credit** *AmEx, Disc, MC, V.*
These participatory concerts are led by trumpeter and jazz great Wynton Marsalis, and are modeled on the New York Philharmonic Young People's Concerts. Check www.jazzforyoungpeople.com for schedule.

Little Orchestra Society

www.littleorchestra.org.
The group, founded in 1947, was the first orchestra to present professional classical concerts for kids. The most popular productions include an interactive *Peter and the Wolf* for preschoolers and December's spectacular *Amahl and the Night Visitors,* complete with live sheep.

Outdoor places

For zoos, *see p284.*

Nelson A. Rockefeller Park

Battery Park City, Hudson River at Chambers St (212-267-9700; www.bpcparks.org). Subway: A, C, 1, 2, 3, 9 to Chambers St. **Open** *6am–1am.* **Admission** *free.*
Besides watching the boats along the Hudson, kids can enjoy one of New York's best playgrounds, which has balls, board games and other toys for the

Imagine small natural-history museums where you can not only see but also handle and buy weird specimens. A resource for serious collectors, Evolution has likewise become a favorite spot for kids in the nine-and-up range, who gravitate to the rows of luminescent butterflies and fascinating seashells, or to sections devoted to bones, skulls and fossil dinosaur eggs. The smaller Maxilla & Mandible offers a similar selection—plus lollipop eyeballs.

Tah-Poozie

50 Greenwich St between Sixth and Seventh Aves (212-647-0668). Subway: 1, 9 to Christopher St–Sheridan Sq. **Open** *Mon–Fri noon–8pm; Sat noon–10pm; Sun noon–7pm.* **Credit** *AmEx, DC, Disc, MC, V.*
West Village schoolkids fill this cluttered store on weekday afternoons and—after killing quite a bit of time inspecting the merchandise—they nearly always find something fun to buy that costs not much more than a candy bar. This is *the* place for knickknacks and the latest tween fads: rubber-duck key rings, magic bubbles (they don't pop), secret-message capsules, glow-in-the-dark statues of the "Patron Saint of TV" and stickers, stickers, stickers. A smaller branch is in Chelsea *(78A Seventh Ave between 14th and 15th Sts, 646-638-0750).*

Evolution.

Shear genius *Munchy* welcomes kids to the **New York Botanical Garden**. *See p139.*

borrowing. Events for children—like chess, drawing and drumming lessons—are held May through October (visit the website for a schedule).

Piers 25 and 26

Hudson River Park, Hudson River at North Moore St (212-791-2530). Subway: 1, 9 to Franklin St.

Pier 25 has the ramshackle feel of a kid-friendly seaside town, with a mini-golf course ($2), a snack shack with a barbecue grill, a water-and-sand play area, easels for making art and a volleyball court. On Pier 26, volunteers at Downtown Boathouse *(646-613-0740; www.downtownboathouse.org)* let you take out one- to three-person kayaks for a free, half-hour paddle between piers (summer weekends and holidays, 9am to 6pm).

Riverbank State Park

Hudson River at 145th St (212-694-3600). **Open** *6am–11pm (ice skating Nov–Jan).* **Admission** *free.*

The main reason to trek uptown to this unusual 28-acre park (it's built on top of a water-treatment facility) is for the Totally Kid Carousel (open June through August).

Science Playground

For listing, see p163 **New York Hall of Science**.

The 30,000-square-foot outdoor playground (March through December) is the biggest of its kind in the Western hemisphere. Children can engage in whole-body science exploration, discovering principles of balance, gravity, energy and so on while they play on a giant seesaw, or turn a huge Archimedes' screw to push water uphill.

Central Park

New Yorkers don't have yards—they have parks. The most popular one is Central Park, which has places and programs designed just for kids. (Visit www.centralparknyc.org for a calendar.) Don't miss the beautiful antique carousel ($1 a ride) and the Heckscher Playground (one of 20), which has handball courts, softball diamonds and a puppet theater.

Central Park Zoo

See p109 for listing.

The stars of this refurbished wildlife center are the polar bears and penguins, which live in glass-sided habitats so you can watch their underwater antics. They're celebrated each July during the Chill Out festival (*see p256*).

Conservatory Water

Central Park, entrance on Fifth Ave at 72nd St. Subway: 6 to 77th St. **Open** *Jul, Aug Sun–Fri 11am–7pm; Sat 2–7pm, weather permitting.* **Admission** *free.*

Stuart Little Pond, named after E.B. White's storybook mouse, is the city's mecca for model-yacht racers. When the boat master is around, rent a remote-controlled vessel ($10 per hour). Nearby, a large bronze Alice in Wonderland statue makes for great climbing.

Henry Luce Nature Observatory

See p110 for listing.

Inside the Gothic-style Belvedere Castle, you'll find telescopes, microscopes and hands-on exhibits that teach kids about the plants and animals living (or hiding) in the park. With proper ID, you can borrow the Discovery Kit—a backpack containing binoculars, a bird-watching guide and cool tools.

North Meadow Recreation Center

Central Park, mid-park at 97th St (212-348-4867; www.centralpark2000.com/database/nm_rec_center.html). Subway: B, C, 6 to 96th St. **Open** *Check website for seasonal hours.* **Admission** *free.*

This park facility allows families to check out (with a parent's photo ID) the Field Day Kit, which includes a Frisbee, hula hoop, jump rope, kickball, and Wiffle ball and bat.

Gardens

Brooklyn Botanic Garden

See p126 for listing.

In the 13,000-square-foot Discovery Garden, children can play botanist, make toys out of natural materials, weave a wall and generally get their hands dirty.

New York Botanical Garden

See p139 for listing.

The Everett Children's Adventure Garden is a whimsical museum of the natural world, with interactive "galleries," both indoors and out. In the Family Garden (early spring through late October), kids can run under a giant caterpillar topiary, poke around in a touch tank, and plant or harvest vegetables.

Play spaces

Creatability

500 E 88th St between York and East End Aves (212-535-4033; www.creatability.us). Subway: 4, 5, 6 to 86th St. **Open** *Call or visit website for schedule and prices.* **Fee** *$21.70.* **Credit** *AmEx, MC, V.*

During midday, evening and weekend hours, this tiny Yorkville storefront is open to walk-ins who want to spend an hour or two making a puppet, a comic strip, a floatable boat—just about anything. **Other location** *201 E 31st St between Second and Third Aves (212-725-1418).*

Sydney's Playground

66 White St between Broadway and Church St (212-431-9125; www.sydneysplayground.com). Subway: 1, 9 to Franklin St. **Open** *Mon, Wed, Fri 8:30am–6pm; Tue, Thu, Sat, Sun 10am–6pm.* **Admission** *$8.50.* **Credit** *AmEx, Disc, MC, V.*

This huge, architecturally striking play space has been designed to resemble a streetscape, complete with a multilevel "climbing city," a "roadway" for ride-on toys and a high-end café.

Sports

For kayaking, *see p334* **Piers 25 and 26.** For bicycling, horseback riding and ice-skating, *see p331 and p333.*

Chelsea Piers

See p332 for listing.

A roller rink, gymnasium, toddler gym and an extreme-skating park all help kids burn energy. You'll also find ice-skating rinks, batting cages and two rock-climbing walls in this vast complex. Day passes are available. The Flip 'n Flick program (6:30 to 10:30pm) allows parents to get a night off while the kids enjoy athletic activities and a movie.

Trapeze School New York

See p335 for listing.

Kids over the age of six can fly through the air with the greatest of ease—and so can their parents. (You can also just stop along the esplanade and watch.)

Theater

The Adventures of Maya the Bee

45 Bleecker Theater, 45 Bleecker St at Lafayette St (212-253-9983; www.45bleecker.com/maya.html). Subway: B, D, F, V to Broadway–Lafayette St; 6 to Bleecker St. **Shows** *Oct–Jun Sat 11am.* **Admission** *$12.* **Credit** *AmEx, MC, V.*

The star of the Culture Project's long-running jazz puppet play may be the sweetest little bee that kids are likely to meet. But some of the creatures the bee encounters are not so nice—this is the insect world, after all. The music's great. Recommended for children ages five to nine.

Kids 'n Comedy

Gotham Comedy Club, 34 W 22nd St between Fifth and Sixth Aves (212-877-6115; www.kidsncomedy.com). Subway: R, W to 23rd St. **Shows** *Call or visit website for schedule.* **Admission** *$15, one-drink minimum.* **Credit** *AmEx, MC, V.*

Kids 'n Comedy has developed a stable of funny kids, ages 9 to 15, who deliver their own stand-up material (much of it in the homework-sucks vein).

The New Victory Theater

See p343 for listing.

As New York's only full-scale young people's theater, the New Victory presents the most accomplished work in theater and dance at junior prices. Shows often sell out well in advance, so reserve seats early.

Swedish Cottage Marionette Theater

Central Park West at 81st St (212-988-9093). Subway: B, C to 81st St–Museum of Natural History. **Shows** *Nov–Jun Mon–Fri 10:30am, noon; Sat 1pm. Jul, Aug Mon–Fri 10:30am, noon.* **Admission** *$6, children $5.* **Credit** *Cash only.*

Mommies dearest The **Bronx Zoo**'s ambitious breeding program bears fruit.

Reservations are essential at this intimate theater in an old Swedish schoolhouse, which is run by the City Parks Foundation.

Urban Word

www.urbanword.org.

A DJ hosts poetry slams and open mikes for "the next generation." Teens bring their own (uncensored) poems and freestyle rhymes, or give props to the kids performing theirs. The group's 11-day slam fest is in March.

Tours

ARTime

718-797-1573. **Open** *Oct–Jun first Saturday of the month 11am–12:30pm.* **Admission** *$25 per parent-child pair, additional child $5.* **Credit** *Cash only.*

Since 1994, art historians with education backgrounds have led contemporary-art tours of Soho galleries for kids ages five to ten.

Lower East Side Tenement Museum

See p155 for listing. **Open** *Sat, Sun, holidays noon, 1, 2, 3pm.* **Admission** *$9, children $6.* **Credit** *AmEx, MC, V.*

This museum features a weekly interactive tour (ages 7 to 14) that teaches kids about immigrant life in early-20th-century New York through game playing, trying on period costumes and handling knickknacks from that time.

Wildman Ecology Walks

Various city parks (914-835-2153; www.wildmansteve brill.com). **Open** *Weekends, some holidays 11:45am–3:45pm; reservations required 24hrs in advance.* **Admission** *suggested donation $10, children $5.* **Credit** *Cash only.*

Wildman Steve Brill, an urban forager and wild-food expert, gives kids a chance to dig, gather and taste all kinds of wild foods growing right in the center of Manhattan.

Zoos

Bronx Zoo

See p139 for listing.

Inside the Bronx Zoo is the Bronx Children's Zoo, with lots of domesticated animals to pet, plus exhibits that show the world from an animal's point of view. Camel rides are available from April through October. Don't miss the sea lion feeding *(11am, 3pm).*

New York Aquarium

Surf Ave at West 8th St, Coney Island, Brooklyn (718-265-3474; www.nyaquarium.com). Subway: D to Coney Island–Stillwell Ave. **Open** *Visit website for hours.* **Admission** *$11, seniors and children 2–12 $7.* **Credit** *AmEx, Disc, MC, V.*

Like Coney Island itself, this aquarium is a little shabby, but kids enjoy seeing the famous Beluga whale family and the scary sharks. They can also take in a sea lion show and glimpse the kinds of fish brave enough to call the East River home.

Clubs

You love the nightlife; you've got to boogie. Here's where to find your groove.

New York was once the world's undisputed clubbing capital. Fabled venues such as Studio 54, Danceteria, Twilo and Limelight ruled the after-dark scene and often the tabloid columns the following day. Clubs became the setting for the new democratic demimonde. Club freaks mingled with society dames, drag queens gamboled with truck drivers, and boldface names hobnobbed with the hoi polloi. Add to that the birth of the beat: This is the city that spawned disco, hip-hop and electroclash—and played a leading role in the development of house music. For decades, the dedicated party person had an amazing array of choices.

These days, to be honest, New York is no longer the ecstatic epicenter of club culture (it's been eclipsed in recent years by Berlin and Barcelona). Largely to blame is a string of city administrations zealously enforcing the antiquated cabaret-license laws, which limit dancing to all but a few venues. The current mayor added to the squeeze with his stringent antismoking ordinances. And the timeless greedy–club-owner factor cannot be overlooked.

Despite all the forces aligned against it, however, the nightlife scene here is thriving. The notorious Limelight has recently reopened as the **Avalon** superclub, and a branch of the famed **Crobar** chain is plying its trade across the street from the old Twilo—which itself is slated to reopen as **Spirit**. The city has an energetic underground scene as well (*see p288* **How low can you go?**). And at long last, there is movement in City Hall to revise the cabaret laws. There's plenty of life left in NYC's clubs. You just have to know when to look (often, not before midnight)—and where.

This chapter includes both dance clubs and lounges (where dancing is typically verboten), in addition to live-music venues that feature dancing (*see also pp307–319*). And since clubland exists in a state of flux, it's wise to call the venue or consult a current issue of *Time Out New York* before heading out.

Clubs

Arc

6 Hubert St at Hudson St (212-226-9212; www.arcspace.net). Subway: A, C, E, 1, 9 to Canal St. **Open** *Fri midnight–10am; Sat 11pm–10am.* **Cover** *$15–$25.* **Average drink** *(nonalcoholic) $5.*

The boxy two-room space is one of the great survivors of NYC's club scene—it was known as Area in the mid '80s, Shelter in the early '90s and Vinyl in the late '90s. It's been without a liquor license for years—something to do with a shooting in one of its former incarnations—but it turns out that people come more for the music than for the boozin' and cruisin'. On Fridays, the great Danny Tenaglia throws his long-running Be Yourself party, and Saturdays feature big-name techno and progressive-house DJs from around the world.

Avalon

660 Sixth Ave at 20th St (212-807-7780). Subway: F, V, R, W to 23rd St. **Open** *Wed, Thu 10pm–4am; Fri–Sun 10pm–7am.* **Cover** *$15–$25.* **Average drink** *$8.*

Limelight got a new lease on life when the folks behind Boston superclub Avalon took over the space and reopened the landmark-church–cum–dance hall last fall. (Some NYC clubbers thought it

The best Clubs

These are the coolest nightspots to...

...have a religious experience
Avalon (*see above*), formerly Limelight, is located in a pretty church; its house beats are heavenly as well.

...dance without going deaf
Cielo (*see p286*) features such crystal-clear sounds that cranking the volume to 11 is unnecessary for sonic bliss.

...dance till dawn and beyond
Club Shelter (*see p286*) revs up at 11pm and keeps going until noon the next day.

...feel close to your neighbors
Sapphire (*see p289*) has the city's tiniest dance floor, yet still manages to pack 'em in.

...listen to the world's top DJ
Arc (*see left*) is the place to hear the great Danny Tenaglia's prog-tech beats.

...avoid the trendies
Filter 14 (*see p287*) is perhaps the city's friendliest and least pretentious nightspot.

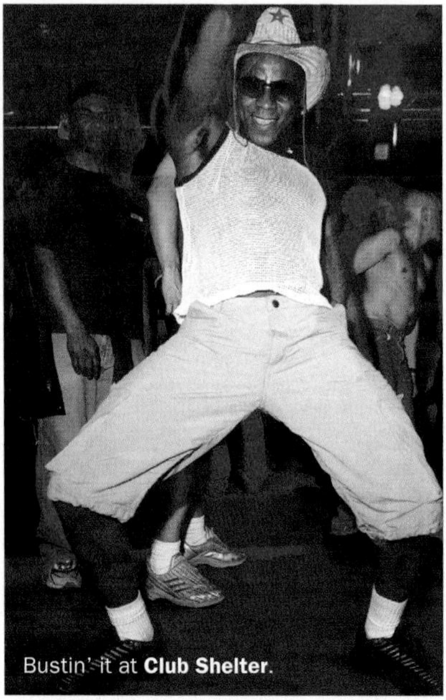
Bustin' it at **Club Shelter**.

pathetic that the local scene had sunk to the point where Bostonites were determining the direction of the town's nightlife.) Avalon may not pack the punch of its predecessor, but there's still something about partying in a church (even a deconsecrated one) that can make you feel slightly wicked.

Centro-Fly

45 W 21st St between Fifth and Sixth Aves (212-627-7770; www.centro-fly.com). Subway: F, V, R, W to 23rd St. **Open** *Thu–Sat 10pm–5:30am.* **Cover** *$15–$25.* **Average drink** *$8.*

Named and modeled after a late-1960s Italian disco, Centro-Fly relies on decor—op art, futuristic furniture and a round sunken bar—to set the mood. It looks fabulous, and for a time, its music policy was equally great, with innovative house and techno DJs like Felix da Housecat and Slam manning the decks. Lately, though, the club's bookers have gone a little conservative and are showcasing a more mainstream brand of party beat. Nonetheless, it's one of the city's best spaces and is well worth a visit.

► Get a close-up look at queer nightlife on *pp296–306*.
► For a listing of nightly club events, pick up a copy of ***Time Out New York***.
► For a comprehensive guide to notable New York clubs, pick up a copy of the ***Time Out New York Nightlife*** guide.

Cielo

18 Little West 12th St between Ninth Ave and Washington St (212-645-5700; www.cieloclub.com). Subway: A, C, E to 14th St; L to Eighth Ave. **Open** *10pm–4am daily.* **Cover** *free, except for special events.* **Average drink** *$10.*

You'd never guess from the red carpet and the Eurodude manning the door that the attitude inside this boîte is zero, at least on weeknights.It's a wonderful little joint—the urban ski-lodge decor looks great, the sunken dance floor is a nice touch, and the place boasts one of the city's clearest sound systems. Cielo features top-shelf house from world-class DJs (including the fabled Frankie Knuckles); on Mondays, the club is treated to DJ deity François K.'s dub-heavy Deep Space sessions. Though the music is still great on weekends, if you're not dressed to the nines or if your party is particularly testosterone-heavy, you'll have to talk a good game to gain entry. And if you *do* get in, be prepared to part with some cash to secure one of the booths—they're reserved for bottle-service patrons only.

Club Shelter

20 W 39th St between Fifth and Sixth Aves (212-719-4479; www.clubshelter.com). Subway: B, D, F, V to 42nd St–Bryant Park; 7 to Fifth Ave. **Open** *Sat 11pm–noon.* **Cover** *$15–$20.* **Average drink** *$6.*

There's really only one thing you need to know about Club Shelter: It's the home of the world-famous Shelter shindig. DJ Timmy "the Maestro" Regisford is the ringmaster of this long-running Saturday-night affair, spinning soulful house and classics to an enthusiastic (and sexually and racially mixed) crowd that doesn't leave until long after the sun rises on Sunday. It's a throwback to a style of clubbing that's all too rare in NYC nowadays. Club Shelter also hosts the occasional Dance Ritual bash *(www.danceritualnyc.com)*, with Master at Work Louis Vega on the wheels of steel.

Copacabana

560 W 34th St at Eleventh Ave (212-239-2672). Subway: A, C, E to 34th St–Penn Station. **Open** *Tue 6pm–3am; Fri, Sat 10pm–5am.* **Cover** *$10–$25.* **Average drink** *$9.*

Miami meets Las Vegas in the Copa's pink-palm-tree–lined lobby. Women throw curves in skintight pants and peekaboo blouses; gentlemen take it up a notch with suits and ties. Some 3,000 Latinos—and those who love them—pack the Copa's 48,000 square feet to dance through the night. Upstairs, live bands play salsa and merengue while synchronized showgirls shake the large dance floor; house music plays downstairs. Be forewarned: The $11 Cosmopolitans tasted not unlike a sizable helping of cough syrup.

Coral Room

512 W 29th St between Eleventh and Twelfth Aves (212-244-1965; www.coralroomnyc.com). Subway: A, C, E to 34th St–Penn Station; 1, 9 to 28th St. **Open** *10pm–4am daily.* **Cover** *varies.* **Average drink** *$8.*

After a promising start in early 2003, the club has devolved into just another NYC meat market, attracting a crowd that looks upscale but acts lowbrow. Still, the Coral Room does have one of the best gimmicks going: a kitschy live mermaid gallivanting for patrons in the midst of a giant fish-filled aquarium.

The Duplexx

46 Washington Ave between Flushing and Park Aves, Fort Greene, Brooklyn (718-643-6400; www.theduplexx.com). Subway: G to Clinton–Washington Aves. **Open** *Thu–Sun 10pm–4am.* **Cover** *$5–$10.* **Average drink** *$6.*

Serious dancers trek to this outpost by the Brooklyn Navy Yard to get a dose of funky R&B, house and reggae. The setup hasn't changed much since the place was called Caviar: You'll still find a mirrored dance floor and stiff drinks upstairs, while head-wrapped bohemians lounge on the lower level. The best thing about it? E-man's soulful-house hootenanny Bang the Party *(www.bangtheparty.com),* which rules the club on Friday nights.

Filter 14

432 W 14th St at Washington St (212-366-5680). Subway: A, C, E to 14th St; L to Eighth Ave. **Open** *10pm–4am daily.* **Cover** *$5–$12.* **Average drink** *$7.*

Though tucked in amid the snooty boîtes in the Meatpacking District, the midsize Filter 14 is an attitude-free oasis. A mellow door policy, no-frills decor, and relatively cheap cocktails are a welcome contrast to the I'm-on-the-list vibe of the area's other nightspots. The music policy is also much cooler than that of many local competitors: Sounds range from glitchy minimalist techno and deep house to ghetto-tech and hip-hop, and the club has one of the most bass-thumping, bottom-heaviest sound systems in the city.

Lotus

409 W 14th St between Ninth Ave and Washington St (212-243-4420; www.lotusnewyork.com). Subway: A, C, E to 14th St; L to Eighth Ave. **Open** *10pm–4am daily.* **Cover** *$10–$20.* **Average drink** *$7.*

Lotus was one of the first upscale clubs to invade the once-scuzzy Meatpacking District, and it immediately attracted legions of celebs, models and gawkers. Happily, the venue's patina of trendiness has faded, and now Lotus can be appreciated as a well-furnished restaurant–lounge–dance club, whose DJs spin a mainstream mix of sounds to an upscale bridge-and-tunnel crowd. Getting past the doorman is still a task, so dress to impress.

Marquee

289 Tenth Ave between 26th and 27th Sts (646-473-0202). Subway: C, E to 23rd St. **Open** *Tue–Sat 10pm–4am.* **Cover** *$20.* **Average drink** *$10.*

Located in a former garage, the centerpiece is a spectacular double-sided staircase that leads to a mezzanine level, where a glass wall overlooks the action below. Up to 600 people can fit inside, but this spot is so hot, you'll probably still have trouble getting past the velvet rope.

Club rules

Clubbing in NYC can be a little intimidating. Keep this simple advice in mind to avoid the most common pitfalls.

Avoid run-ins with the law

Know that you may be searched—so leave any weapons at home (duh). Also, the city's nightlife crackdown has made clubs *very* paranoid about drug use. Be smart.

Dress the part

If you're going to a trendy spot, look sharp—those dirty Cons and XXL-size tees ain't gonna cut it. But if you're heading to a grunge pit, leave the Armani at home.

Guys, don't travel in packs

Straight-oriented venues often refuse entry to large groups of men in order to maintain a gender balance. But if you're heading to a gay-leaning spot, the more the merrier!

Make nice at the door

Screaming "I'm on the list!" (even if you are) won't get you anywhere with seen-it-all doormen. However, a smile and a bit of patience may. And don't forget ID!

Phone ahead

Parties can change lineup or location at a moment's notice. Before you leave, call the club, hit its website or check out a current issue of *Time Out New York.*

Pick your night wisely

If you have a choice, hit the clubs any night except Friday and Saturday; going out on weekdays insures you'll be hanging with the cool kids.

Play it safe

The subways are a lot safer than they used to be, but if you're out late, we still recommend that you take a cab or car service home (*see p364*).

Nells

246 W 14th St between Seventh and Eighth Aves (212-675-1567; www.nells.com). Subway: A, C, E, 1, 2, 3, 9 to 14th St; L to Eighth Ave. **Open** *Sun–Thu 9pm–3am; Fri 6pm–4am; Sat 9pm–4am.* **Cover** *$10–$15.* **Average drink** *$8.*

Nells spent its youth as a hot spot for champagne-swilling hipsters, young bankers and literary wild children. Nearly two decades on, the club has gracefully evolved into an institution. Upstairs, groove to jazz and soul, often with live bands. DJs spin hip-hop, funk, R&B, reggae and classics downstairs. The Wednesday-night Cubansoul party is a great place to dance to *charanga* and salsa. The crowd is straight, multiracial, dressed up and ready to spend.

Pyramid

101 Ave A between 6th and 7th Sts (212-228-4888). Subway: F, V to Lower East Side–Second Ave; 6 to Astor Pl. **Open** *10pm–4am daily.* **Cover** *$5–$15.* **Average drink** *$7.*

Back in the '80s and early '90s, this little dive was one of downtown's performance-art and drag-scene epicenters. Since then, the joint has been lying fallow; Monday night's Konkrete Jungle drum 'n' bass bash is the only real shindig of note. But longtime promoter Chip Duckett has recently taken over, and fun parties such as Saturday night's Bang Bang Burlesque have recently made the Pyramid their home, so the Avenue A hot spot may once again heat up.

Rare

416 W 14th St between Ninth Ave and Washington St (212-675-2220). Subway: A, C, E to 14th St; L to Eighth Ave. **Open** *10pm–4am daily.* **Cover** *varies.* **Average drink** *$7.*

The former Cooler—and onetime abattoir—is among the least la-di-da hangouts in the ultratrendy Meatpacking District. All sorts of wingdings go down in this low-ceilinged space—from glitchy electronica to

How low can you go?

By its very nature, the underground clubbing scene in NYC thrives in the shadows. Its clandestine existence has always been its allure. And for those willing to do a little digging, clubland's hypogeal side can yield a rich vein of nightlife. Whether you want to plunge into a genre's deepest reaches or simply skim the surface, the following chart will help you start your trip down the mine shaft of after-dark delights. Find the party that's down there for you.

	CLASSICS, SOULFUL HOUSE	DEEP HOUSE, TECH-HOUSE, TECHNO	DRUM 'N' BASS
CRUST	**Paradizo** *Fridays at Cielo* Cielo residents Nicolas Mater and Willie Graff serve up sweet beats at this jewel box of a boîte.	**Mix Fridays** *Fridays at Avalon* The former church (and former Limelight) snags some of the scene's biggest names to bang out the beats.	**Acupuncture** *Fridays at Halcyon* Breakbeat Science hosts a night of "mature" drum 'n' bass at this cool little Brooklyn spot with a big-time sound system.
MANTLE	**Deep See** *Tuesdays at Sapphire* Lola and E-man's mellow shindig is for lovers of the prototypically NYC mix of R&B-derived dance music.	**Mondaze** *Mondays at Sapphire* This tiny, unpretentious Lower East Side venue scores the area's best spinners for its long-running Monday-night wingding.	**Direct Drive** *Saturdays at Rare* DJ Seoul's no-frills affair supplies straight-ahead, heavy-hitting rhythms for its crowd of young junglists.
CORE	**Shelter** *Saturdays at Club Shelter* DJ Timmy Regisford isn't called "the Maestro" for nothin'; his fans treat him like a latter-day Toscanini.	**Be Yourself** *Fridays at Arc* All bow down before the king of prog-tech, Mr. Danny Tenaglia. Note: This club doesn't serve alcohol.	**Konkrete Jungle** *Mondays at Pyramid* Even if this place has seen better days, a jackhammer-hard noise attack still draws crowds of beat-crazy kids.

mainstream hip-hop affairs—but our favorite night is the drum 'n' bass–heavy Direct Drive blast, which coaxes major stars of the scene (Doc Scott and Bryan Gee, for example) to rinse it out on the decks.

Roxy

515 W 18th St between Tenth and Eleventh Aves (212-645-5156; www.roxynyc.com). Subway: A, C, E to 14th St; L to Eighth Ave. **Open** *Wed 8pm–2am (roller skating only); Fri 10pm–4am; Sat 11pm–5am.* **Cover** *$12–$30.* **Average drink** *$8.*

Roxy began life as a humongous roller-skating rink (the immense main room can squeeze 3,000 revelers onto its dance floor), but in the early '80s, it became a great cross-cultural hangout, with B-boys poppin' and lockin' as downtown arty types looked on. Nowadays, it's known for Saturday night's massive boy bash, with thousands of hedonists (including a smattering of women and straight men) dancing to house beats all night long. Fridays showcase mixed sounds, ranging from hip-hop hoedowns to nights featuring superstar DJs like Paul Van Dyke. On Wednesdays, Roxy stays true to its roots with a roller-skating jam.

Sapphire

249 Eldridge St between Houston and Stanton Sts (212-777-5153; www.sapphirenyc.com). Subway: F, V to Lower East Side–Second Ave. **Open** *7pm–4am daily.* **Cover** *$5.* **Average drink** *$5.*

The lilliputian Sapphire was one of the first Lower East Side bars to feature DJs, and its management had the foresight to secure a cabaret license before the city clamped down. Sunday through Wednesday, the music falls somewhere along the techno-house-disco continuum, with local heroes E-man and Adam Goldstone being joined by the occasional slumming-it big name. Thursday through Saturday, hip-hop and funk rule, with the beloved veteran DJ Nice often running things. Warning: Weekends can be brutally crowded, so dress to sweat.

GLITCH-TECH, ILLBIENT, LAPTOP	NU-DUB, NU-JAZZ, NU-LATIN	HIP-HOP, R&B, SOUL
Share *Sundays at Openair* This sleek East Village club provides an open forum for the laptop-geek set, with video artists adding to the general spaciness.	**Turntables on the Hudson** *Various venues* Nickodemus, Mariano and guests pump out sublimely funky, dubbed-out worldbeat.	**Webster Hall** There's always some MTV-style hip-hop to be had at this megaclubbing mainstay.
Undercity *Sundays at Halcyon* Electronic experimentalists work their magic over Halcyon's hallowed speakers. Sheer sonic bliss.	**Rude Movements** *Second Tuesday of the month at APT* DJs Tyler Askew, Karl Injex, Gamall and top guests spin "interplanetary soul–based sounds."	**Variety** *Fridays at Sapphire* For years, nightlife hero DJ Jazzy Nice has been heating up this tiny sweatbox with his funkified fuel.
Phonomena *Thursdays at Subtonic Lounge* Illbient doesn't get much iller than at this night of laptop mangling and turntable abuse.	**Deep Space** *Mondays at Cielo* Dance-music deity Francois K. focuses on dub in all of its glorious echo-drenched forms. Great sound system.	**Little Ricky's Rib Shack** *Wednesdays at APT* This chic hangout gets treated to mouthwateringly down-and-dirty tuneage, courtesy of DJ Rich Medina.

DJ Spinoza at **Subtonic Lounge**.

Subtonic Lounge at Tonic

107 Norfolk St between Delancey and Rivington Sts (212-358-7501). Subway: F to Delancey St; J, M, Z to Delancey–Essex Sts. **Open** *Sun–Wed 7:30pm–midnight; Thu–Sat 7:30pm–2am.* **Cover** *free–$12.* **Average drink** *$6.*

Subtonic Lounge, the unadorned basement of the avant-bohemian Tonic performance space (*see p315*) on the Lower East Side, features DJs spinning underground sounds that range from soothing chill-out ambient to full-tilt techno. The sound system might not be all that, but the space's party-throwers and patrons (who seat themselves on banquettes inside giant, ancient wine casks) make up for it with sheer exuberance.

Webster Hall

125 E 11th St between Third and Fourth Aves (212-353-1600; www.webster-hall.com). Subway: L, N, Q, R, W, 4, 5, 6 to 14th St–Union Sq. **Open** *Thu–Sat 10pm–5am.* **Cover** *free–$30.* **Average drink** *$8.*

If you crave the sight of acid-washed jeans, big hair, muscle shirts and gold chains, Webster Hall offers all that too and…well, not much more. The grand space inside the 1800s landmark East Village building is nice enough, if you ignore the crowd. Choose among four floors of blasting disco, hip-hop, soul, Latin, progressive house or the latest pop hits. The DJs are actually good, but it's hard to forget you're sharing the dance floor with bridge-and-tunnel bottom-feeders.

Lounges & DJ bars

APT

419 W 13th St between Ninth and Tenth Aves (212-414-4245; www.aptwebsite.com). Subway: A, C, E to 14th St; L to Eighth Ave. **Open** *6pm–4am daily.* **Cover** *varies.* **Average drink** *$9.*

Labeled snootissimo when it opened, this bi-level boîte is now thought of as the city's prime place for hearing cool underground beats. Everyone from techno deity Carl Craig to Zulu Nation founder Afrika Bambaataa has played the platters in either the sleek basement bar or the cozy, well-appointed street-level room. The lounge's resident spinners are themselves no slouches: loungey-kitsch slinger Ursula 1000; the electrofunky Negroclash crew; the nouveau-disco Metro Area duo; and the red-hot punk-funkers from the DFA label. It gets sardine-packed on weekends, but at least you're squeezed in with one of the city's best-looking crowds.

Church Lounge

Tribeca Grand Hotel, 2 Sixth Ave between Walker and White Sts (212-519-6677; www.tribecagrand.com). Subway: A, C, E to Canal St; 1, 9 to Franklin St. **Open** *Mon–Thu 7am–2am; Fri 7am–3am; Sat 7am–4am; Sun 7am–midnight.* **Average drink** *$12.*

When the Tribeca Grand first started featuring DJs and live music in its posh pub, it unexpectedly became one of the city's top spots for underground beats. That happened largely because of its taste in tuneage—totally-of-the-moment electroclash and nu-rock. Things have calmed down a bit, but the place still rocks when a big-name act takes over the joint. Even on a regular night, the top-notch array of spinners can include the Turntables on the Hudson crew (*see below*).

Halcyon

227 Smith St between Butler and Douglass Sts, Carroll Gardens, Brooklyn (718-260-9299; www.halcyonline.com). Subway: F, G to Bergen St. **Open** *Noon–2am daily.* **Average drink** *$5.*

Pretty much the only thing that isn't mellow about Halcyon—wine bar, cafe, record shop, furniture store *and* music venue—is the decor, which is chockablock with mid-century furnishings and knickknacks. (They're all for sale.) It has one of the finest sound systems in NYC—a cut above most other lounges in the city, and better than most clubs. That, plus its array of top DJs (spinning everything from tech-house to hip-hop), make it a great spot to have a sip and absorb some fine tunes.

Openair

121 St. Marks Pl between First Ave and Ave A (212-979-1459; www.openairbar.com). Subway: L to First Ave; 6 to Astor Pl. **Open** *Sun–Thu 5pm–4am; Fri, Sat 8pm–4am.* **Average drink** *$6.*

Nearly invisible from the street, this semisecret lounge is one of the coolest high-tech venues in the city. House, hip-hop, techno, drum 'n' bass and ambient pump through an ace sound system.

The Park

See p206 for listing.

A flash-with-cash crowd mingles in a remodeled garage complete with garden and penthouse lounge.

Roving parties

New York has a number of peripatetic soirees. Nights, locations and prices vary, so telephone, e-mail or hit the websites for the latest updates.

Motherfucker

www.motherfuckernyc.com.

The Motherfucker gang celebrates messy omnisexual rock & roll hanky-panky, long a favored form of entertainment in the Big Apple. Michael T. and Justine D. play power pop, glam, new wave and disco, usually on those drunken nights before a big national holiday. Many of the city's nightlife veterans consider this the best party going in town right now, and they ought to know.

Turntables on the Hudson

212-560-5593; www.turntablesonthehudson.com.

This ultrafunky affair pops up all over the place. DJs Nickodemus, Mariano and guests do the dub-funky, worldbeaty thing, with live percussionists adding to the flavor. If you like to shake it, this is as good as it gets—wherever the party happens, the dance floor is packed all night long.

Cool customers at **APT**. *See p290.*

Film & TV

New York is a born scene-stealer, in any medium.

On-screen and off, this city is a dream come true for film and television buffs. You can trip along in the footsteps of Carrie Bradshaw and Holly Golightly (or Tony Soprano); sink into the jazz-soaked nostalgia of *New York, New York* or *Manhattan;* or walk straight into the "Lights! Camera! Action!" of a sidewalk film crew shooting a hot new movie. You can even be part of the action, by nabbing seats for a live taping of *Saturday Night Live, The Daily Show* and other popular TV programs.

Film

On any given day, there are hundreds of different films playing around town. Splashy multiplexes, many built during the cash-rich '90s, carry all the latest Hollywood releases. But New York's real cinematic riches lie in the dozens of revival, art and foreign-film houses that offer everything from Brazilian documentaries to Hong Kong action flicks. Films may unspool at boutique art houses, elegant historic theaters or intimate museum screening rooms. And film festivals, director retrospectives, theme nights and cult-classic revivals are yours for the price of a ticket.

For current listings, check the daily newspapers or pick up a copy of *Time Out New York*.

Art & revival houses

Angelika Film Center

18 W Houston St at Mercer St (212-995-2000; www.angelikafilmcenter.com). Subway: B, D, F, V to Broadway–Lafayette St; R, W to Prince St; 6 to Bleecker St. **Admission** *$10, seniors and children under 12 $6.50.* **Credit** *AmEx, MC, V.*

The six-screen Angelika emphasizes new American independent and foreign films. The complex is a zoo on weekends, so come extra early or visit the website to buy tickets in advance.

> ▶ For movie reviews and show times, check out **www.timeoutny.com**, or pick up a copy of ***Time Out New York***.
> ▶ Purchase tickets in advance through **www.moviefone.com**, or by calling 212-777-FILM or 800-535-TELL.
> ▶ Museums other than those listed here often host special film series and experimental films. *See pp143–163.*

BAM Rose Cinemas

For listing, see p321 **Brooklyn Academy of Music. Admission** *$10, seniors and children under 12 $6, students $7 (Mon–Thu).* **Credit** *AmEx, MC, V.*

Brooklyn's premier art-house theater pulls double duty as a repertory house and a first-run multiplex for independent films.

Cinema Village

22 E 12th St between Fifth Ave and University Pl (212-924-3363; www.cinemavillage.com). Subway: L, N, Q, R, W, 4, 5, 6 to 14th St–Union Sq. **Admission** *$9, seniors and children under 13 $5.50, students $7.* **Credit** *MC, V.*

Three-screen Cinema Village specializes in American indies and foreign films. Check out the subway turnstile that admits ticket-holders in the lobby.

Film Forum

209 W Houston St between Sixth Ave and Varick St (212-727-8110; www.filmforum.com). Subway: 1, 9 to Houston St. **Admission** *$10, seniors and children under 12 $5 (senior discount is honored Mon–Fri at shows before 5pm).* **Credit** *Cash only at box office; AmEx, MC, V on website.*

Even though the seats and sight lines leave something to be desired, this art-house theater offers great new films and documentaries, as well as a revival series.

Landmark's Sunshine Cinema

143 E Houston St between First and Second Aves (212-330-8182; 212-777-FILM). Subway: F, V to Lower East Side–Second Ave. **Admission** *$10, seniors over 63 $6.50.* **Credit** *AmEx, MC, V.*

This beautifully restored 1898 Yiddish theater is now one of New York's best art houses, presenting some of the finest new independent cinema.

Leonard Nimoy Thalia

At Symphony Space, 2537 Broadway at 95th St, entrance on 95th St (212-864-5400). Subway: 1, 2, 3, 9 to 96th St. **Admission** *$10, seniors $8.* **Credit** *AmEx, MC, V ($15 minimum).*

The famed Thalia art house—featured in *Annie Hall*—was recently rebuilt. It's much more comfortable now, and it offers both contemporary world cinema and retrospectives of classics.

Lincoln Plaza Cinemas

30 Lincoln Plaza, entrance on Broadway between 62nd and 63rd Sts (212-757-0359, tickets 212-757-2280; www.lincolnplazacinema.com).

Four-star popcorn at the **Film Forum**. *See p292.*

Subway: A, C, B, D, 1, 9 to 59th St–Columbus Circle. **Admission** *$10, seniors over 64 and children under 11 $6.50.* **Credit** *Cash only at box office; AmEx, V over the phone or on website.*
Commercially successful American and European independent films can be seen at this movie house near Lincoln Center. All six theaters are equipped with assisted-listening devices for the hearing-impaired, and are wheelchair-accessible.

Paris Theatre
4 W 58th St between Fifth and Sixth Aves (212-688-3800; 212-777-FILM). Subway: F to 57th St; N, R, W to Fifth Ave–59th St. **Admission** *$10, seniors and children $6.* **Credit** *Cash only at box office; AmEx, MC, V on website.*
Located near the Plaza Hotel, this posh theater is de rigueur for cinéastes who love foreign-language films.

Quad Cinema
34 W 13th St between Fifth and Sixth Aves (212-255-8800; www.quadcinema.com). Subway: F, V to 14th St; L to Sixth Ave. **Admission** *$9.50, seniors and children 5–12 $6.50.* **Credit** *Cash only at box office; AmEx, MC, V on website.*
Four small screens show a broad selection of foreign and American independent films, as well as documentaries; many deal with political, sexual and gay-themed issues. Children under five are not admitted.

Screening Room
54 Varick St at Canal St (212-334-2100). Subway: A,C, E, 1, 9 to Canal St. **Admission** *$9.50, seniors and children $6.50.* **Credit** *AmEx, MC, V.*
This Tribeca theater is your one-stop date destination: It has a cocktail lounge, a swank bistro and a snug movie theater with love seats for two. It shows first-run films, and screens *Breakfast at Tiffany's* every Sunday afternoon at 1:30pm.

Two Boots Pioneer Theater
155 E 3rd St between Aves A and B (212-254-3300). Subway: F, V to Lower East Side–Second Ave. **Admission** *$9; seniors, students and children $6.50.* **Credit** *Cash only.*
Phil Hartman, founder of the Two Boots pizza chain, also runs the East Village's only first-run alternative film center, showing a mix of new indies, revivals and themed festivals.

Museums & societies

American Museum of the Moving Image
See p161 for listing.
AMMI, the first American museum devoted solely to moving pictures, shows an impressive selection of more than 700 films a year.

Anthology Film Archives
32 Second Ave at 2nd St (212-505-5181). Subway: F, V to Lower East Side–Second Ave; 6 to Bleecker St. **Admission** *$8, seniors and students $5.* **Credit** *Cash only.*
Housed in a crumbling landmark building, Anthology is a fiercely independent cinema showcasing foreign and experimental film and video.

Brooklyn Museum of Art
See p145 for listing.
The eclectic roster at Brooklyn's stately palace of fine arts concentrates on offbeat foreign films and smart documentaries.

Film Society of Lincoln Center
Walter Reade Theater, Lincoln Center, 165 W 65th St between Broadway and Amsterdam Ave, plaza level (212-875-5601, tickets 212-496-

3809; www.filmlinc.com). Subway: 1, 9 to 66th St–Lincoln Ctr. **Admission** *$9.50, seniors $4.50 (Mon–Fri before 6pm), students $7.* **Credit** *Cash only at box office; MC, V on website.*
The FSLC was founded in 1969 to support filmmakers and to promote contemporary film and video. It operates the Walter Reade Theater, a state-of-the-art venue in Lincoln Center with the city's most comfortable theater seats and best sight lines. Programs are usually thematic, and they often have an international perspective. Each autumn, the society hosts the New York Film Festival (*see p257*) at Alice Tully Hall.

Guggenheim Museum

For listing, see p148 **Solomon R. Guggenheim**.
The Guggenheim often presents long-running programs focusing on provocative themes.

IMAX Theater

For listing, see p145 **American Museum of Natural History**.
The IMAX screen is an eye-popping four stories high; the kid-friendly films explore the myriad wonders of the natural world.

Metropolitan Museum of Art

See p149 for listing.
The Met offers a program of documentary films on art—many relating to current museum exhibitions—in the Uris Center Auditorium (near the 81st Street entrance).

Museum of Modern Art

Gramercy Theatre, 127 E 23rd St between Park and Lexington Aves (212-777-4900; www.ticketweb.com). Subway: R, W, 6 to 23rd St. **Admission** *$6; children under 16 free, when accompanied by an adult. Pay what you wish Fridays after 4pm.* **Credit** *Cash only.*
During the restoration of MoMA's main building, the museum has relocated its film program to the Gramercy Theatre, where it screens roughly 25 films each week, typically highlighting the work of a particular director. Entry is free with MoMA QNS admission, within a 30-day period.

The Museum of Television & Radio

See p161 for listing.
The museum's collection includes thousands of TV programs that can be viewed at private consoles.

Foreign-language films

Many of the institutions listed above screen films in languages other than English, but the following organizations show exclusively foreign-language films.

Asia Society and Museum

See p158 for listing.
See works from China, India and other Asian countries, as well as Asian-American productions.

French Institute–Alliance Française

See p159 for listing.
The institute shows French movies as well those made in Francophone countries.

Goethe-Institut New York

See p159 for listing.
The Goethe-Institut shows German films in various locations around the city, as well as in its own opulent auditorium.

Japan Society

See p159 for listing.
The Japan Society Film Center organizes a full schedule of Japanese movies.

Film festivals

Each spring, MoMA (*see left*) and the FSLC (*see p293*) sponsor the highly regarded **New Directors/New Films** series, presenting works by on-the-cusp filmmakers from around the world. The FSLC, together with *Film Comment* magazine, also presents the popular ***Film Comment* Selects** series, which allows the magazine's editors to list their favorite movies that have yet to be distributed in the U.S. Every September and October since 1963, the FSLC has also hosted the prestigious **New York Film Festival**. (For more information on any of these three festivals, visit www.filmlinc.com.) The **New York Independent Film and Video Festival** *(212-777-7100; www.nyfilmvideo.com)* lures cinéastes three times a year—in April, September and December. In May, Robert De Niro rolls out the new but influential **Tribeca Film Festival** *(www.tribecafilmfestival.org).* The popular **New York Lesbian & Gay Film Festival** screens in early June *(212-571-2170; www.newfestival.org).* January brings the annual **New York Jewish Film Festival** *(212-875-5600),* playing at Lincoln Center's Walter Reade Theater.

Television

Studio tapings

Tickets are available to several popular TV shows taped in New York City. Many shows book up far in advance, so if you can't plan ahead, try for standby or cancellation tickets.

The Daily Show with Jon Stewart

513 W 54th St between Tenth and Eleventh Aves (212-586-2477; www.comedycentral.com/dailyshow). Subway: A, C, B, D, 1, 9 to 59th St–Columbus Circle. **Tapings** *Mon–Thu 5:30pm.*

Reserve tickets at least three months ahead by phone, or call at 11:30am on the Friday before you'd like to attend, to see if you can take advantage of someone else's last-minute cancellation. You must be at least 18 and have a photo ID.

Last Call with Carson Daly

888-4LC-TIXX; www.1iota.com. Subway: B, D, F, V to 47–50th Sts–Rockefeller Ctr. **Tapings** *Call or visit website for schedule.*

A couple of weeks in advance, make a reservation online or by phone. For standby tickets, get in line at NBC's 49th Street entrance (between Fifth and Sixth Avenues) no later than 11am on weekdays. After that, leftover tickets might be available in the lobby's NBC Experience store. *Total Request Live* fans, take note: You must be at least 16 to attend *Last Call*.

Late Night with Conan O'Brien

212-664-3056; www.nbc.com/conan. Subway: B, D, F, V to 47–50th Sts–Rockefeller Ctr. **Tapings** *Tue–Fri 5:30pm.*

Call at least three months in advance for tickets (four tickets max). A limited number of same-day standby tickets are distributed at 9am *(30 Rockefeller Plaza at Sixth Ave, 49th St entrance)*; one ticket per person. You must be at least 16 and have a photo ID.

Late Show with David Letterman

212-975-1003; www.cbs.com/lateshow. Subway: B, D, E to Seventh Ave. **Tapings** *Mon–Wed 5:30pm; Thu 5:30, 8pm.*

You can try to request tickets for a specific date by filling out a form on the show's website. You may also be able to get a standby ticket by calling 212-247-6497 at 11am on the day of taping. You must be at least 18 and have a photo ID.

Saturday Night Live

212-664-3056; www.nbc.com/snl. Subway: B, D, F, V to 47–50th Sts–Rockefeller Ctr. **Tapings** *Dress rehearsal at 8pm; live show at 11:30pm.*

This show is notoriously difficult to get into, so don't get your hopes up. Tickets for the season are assigned by lottery every fall. To be eligible, send an e-mail to snltickets@nbc.com, anytime during August, or try the standby-ticket lottery on the day of the show. Line up by 8:15am under the NBC Studio marquee *(50th St between Fifth and Sixth Aves)*. You must be at least 16.

Tours

These tours sell out, so reserve in advance.

Kramer's Reality Tour

The Producers Club, 358 W 44th St between Eighth and Ninth Aves (800-KRAMERS; www.kennykramer.com). Subway: A, C, E to 42nd St–Port Authority. **Tours** *Sat, Sun 11:45am.* **Fee** *$39.50.* **Credit** *AmEx, Disc, MC, V.*

Night air Ten years on, **Conan** stands tall.

Kenny Kramer (yes, the real guy that Michael Richards's *Seinfeld* character was based on) takes you to many of the show's locations via tour bus.

Sex and the City Tour

Pulitzer Fountain near Plaza Hotel, Fifth Ave between 58th and 59th Sts (212-209-3370; www.sceneontv.com). **Tours** *Mon, Fri, Sat 3pm; Sun 10:30am. Subway: N, R, W to Fifth Ave–59th St.* **Fee** *$33.* **Credit** *AmEx, Disc, MC, V.*

Visit more than 40 sites where Carrie & Co. ate, drank, looked for men, worked out, gossiped and shopped.

The Sopranos Tour

At the giant button sculpture, 39th St at Seventh Ave (212-209-3370; www.sceneontv.com). Subway: N, Q, R, W, 42nd St S, 1, 2, 3, 9, 7 to 42nd St–Times Sq. **Tours** *Sat, Sun 2pm.* **Fee** *$35.* **Credit** *AmEx, Disc, MC, V.*

This bus tour takes you to Jersey to check out Tony's haunts, from the Bada-Bing to Pizzaland.

Gay & Lesbian

Out, loud and proud: Here's where the boys and girls are.

New York is a city that may be accurately described as—okay, we use the term grudgingly—metrosexual: Same-sex couples canoodle openly all over town, straight men now resemble well-coiffed gay boys and the annual **Gay Pride March** (*see p254*) attracts a whopping half-million spectators, including everyone from suburban grandmothers to rainbow-clad eight-year-olds.

There's a multitude of possible reasons why New Yorkers have moved to acceptance and beyond: NYC's rich gay history (it was the site of the 1969 Stonewall riots and the wellspring of the American gay-rights movement); the preponderance of queer role models (openly gay politicians, artists, performers, writers and teachers); the profusion of gay-centric shops, bars and eateries, from the East Village to Harlem; the influence of New York City's progressive laws, which criminalize antigay violence, forbid discrimination in the workplace and afford same-sex couples comprehensive domestic-partnership rights. Whatever the reason, this town is an absolute homo heaven.

A helpful first stop for any queer visitor to New York is the **Lesbian, Gay, Bisexual & Transgender Community Center** (*see p297*), a downtown nexus of essential information on culture, politics, health and entertainment. And don't miss *Time Out New York*'s lively Gay & Lesbian listings for the latest happenings.

Although the gay and lesbian population of New York is quite diverse, the club and bar scenes don't always reflect that; most places are gender-segregated and tend to attract the single 35-and-under crowd. However, the social alternatives are varied and plentiful—queer coffeebars, bookstores, restaurants and cafes, as well as a full roster of film, theater and music performances can be found all over the city (*see pp273–276, pp292–295 and pp337–349*).

Books & media

Because of the mainstreaming of gay culture (and the rise of the Internet), gay bookstores haven't fared well in recent years. But don't despair: The three establishments below are great places to browse or catch a reading.

Bluestockings

172 Allen St between Rivington and Stanton Sts (212-777-6028; www.bluestockings.com). Subway: F, V to Lower East Side–Second Ave. **Open** *1–10pm.* **Credit** *MC, V.*

Founded in 1999, this bookshop formerly known as feminist now bills itself more broadly as a radical bookstore, fair-trade café and activist resource center. Still, it continues to stock plenty of LGBT writings and erotica, and it hosts regular events (the Dyke Knitting Circle meets here).

Creative Visions

548 Hudson St between Charles and Perry Sts (212-645-7573; www.creativevisionsbooks.com). Subway: 1, 9 to Christopher St–Sheridan Sq. **Open** *Sun–Thu noon–10pm; Fri, Sat noon–11pm.* **Credit** *AmEx, Disc, MC, V.*

Housed in the original location of A Different Light's now-defunct New York outpost, this gay emporium offers an impressive collection of new and vintage gay books and magazines, including rare and out-of-print erotica.

Oscar Wilde Bookshop

15 Christopher St between Sixth and Seventh Aves (212-255-8097; www.oscarwildebooks.com). Subway: 1, 9 to Christopher St–Sheridan Sq. **Open** *11am–7pm.* **Credit** *AmEx, Disc, MC, V.*

The world's first gay bookstore (it opened in 1967) is small, but loaded with atmosphere. Come for the history, the picturesque neighborhood, and the store's collection of new and used books, including some first-edition classics.

Publications

Both of New York's weekly gay entertainment magazines—*HX* and *Next*—include extensive boy-centric information on bars, clubs, restaurants, events and group meetings. *HX*'s Getting Off section lists loads of private sex parties. The monthly *Go NYC,* "a cultural road map for the city girl," gives the lowdown on the local lesbian scene. The newspaper *Gay City News* provides feisty political coverage with an activist slant; its arch-rival, the *New York Blade,* focuses on queer politics and news. All five are free and widely available in street boxes or at gay and lesbian bars and bookstores. *MetroSource* ($4.95) is a bimonthly glossy with a guppie slant and tons of listings. Daniel Hurewitz's *Stepping Out* (Owlet, $16), which details nine walking tours of gay and lesbian NYC, is another fine resource.

Trigger happy The **Gay Pride Parade** draws fags, dykes, trannies—even grannies. *See p296.*

Television & Radio

New York has a hodgepodge of gay-related broadcasting, though much of it appears only on public-access cable channels. Programming varies by cable company, so you may not be able to watch these shows on a hotel TV. *HX* and *Next* provide the most current TV listings. On the radio, NYC's community-activist station, WBAI 99.5-FM, features the progressive gay talk show *Out-FM* on Mondays at 11am.

Centers & phone lines

Gay & Lesbian Switchboard of New York Project

212-989-0999; www.glnh.org. **Open** *Mon–Fri 4pm–midnight; Sat noon–5pm.*

This phone service offers excellent peer counseling, legal referrals, details on gay and lesbian organizations, and information on bars, hotels and restaurants. Outside New York (but within the U.S.), callers can use the toll-free Gay & Lesbian National Hotline *(888-THE-GLNH).*

Gay Men's Health Crisis

119 W 24th St between Sixth and Seventh Aves (212-367-1000, AIDS advice hot line 212-807-6655; www.gmhc.org). Subway: F, V, 1, 9 to 23rd St. **Open** *Hot line Mon–Fri 10am–9pm; Sat noon–3pm; recorded information in English and Spanish at other times; office Mon–Fri 11am–8pm.*

GMHC was the world's first organization dedicated to helping people with AIDS. It has a threefold mission: to push for better public policies; to educate the public to prevent the further spread of HIV; and to assist the sick by providing services and counseling to them and their families. Support groups usually meet in the evening.

Lesbian, Gay, Bisexual & Transgender Community Center

208 W 13th St between Seventh and Eighth Aves (212-620-7310; www.gaycenter.org). Subway: F, V, 1, 2, 3, 9 to 14th St; L to Eighth Ave. **Open** *9am–11pm daily.*

This is where ACT UP and GLAAD got started. After a major renovation, the center is up and running again, providing political, cultural, spiritual and emotional support to the 300-odd groups that meet here. The center houses both the National Museum and Archive of Lesbian and Gay History and the Pat Parker/Vito Russo Library; it also offers info to gay tourists (*see p298* **Sexual orientation**).

Lesbian Herstory Archives

484 14th St between Eighth Ave and Prospect Park West, Park Slope, Brooklyn (718-768-3953; www.datalounge.net/lha). Subway: F to 15th St–Prospect Park. **Open** *By appointment only.*

Located in Brooklyn's Park Slope area, the Herstory Archive contains more than 10,000 books (cultural theory, fiction, poetry, plays), 1,600 periodicals and assorted memorabilia. The cozy space also hosts occasional film screenings, readings and social gatherings.

► For more on the **Pride March**, *see p254.*

Arts & Entertainment

Michael Callen–Audre Lorde Community Health Center

356 W 18th St between Eighth and Ninth Aves (212-271-7200; www.callen-lorde.org). Subway: A, C, E to 14th St; L to Eighth Ave. **Open** *Mon 12:30–8pm; Tue, Thu, Fri 9am–4:30pm; Wed 2:30–8pm.*

This is the country's largest health center primarily serving the gay, lesbian, bisexual and transgender community. It offers comprehensive primary care, HIV treatment, STD screening and treatment, mental-health services, peer counseling and free adolescent services (including the youth hot line HOTT, 212-271-7212).

NYC Gay & Lesbian Anti-Violence Project

240 W 35th St between Seventh and Eighth Aves, suite 200 (212-714-1184, 24-hour hot line 212-714-1141; www.avp.org). Subway: A, C, E, 1, 2, 3, 9 to 34th St–Penn Station. **Open** *Mon–Thu 10am–8pm; Fri 10am–6pm.*

The project provides support to victims of antigay and antilesbian crimes. Working with the police department, volunteers offer advice on seeking police help. Long- and short-term counseling is available.

Queer perspective

Which neighborhood is the gayest these days? The most *visibly* queer area is bustling **Chelsea**, where hot, upwardly mobile men cruise one another along the "runway"—Eighth Avenue between 16th and 23rd Streets.The strip is bulging with boutiques hawking club clothing and sleek home designs, as well as lounges and eateries offering froufy cocktails and a range of gastronomic goodies. And while the 'hood's reputation as a magnet for supermen is only slightly exaggerated, it does draw queers of all types, mainly because so many of Manhattan's happening dance clubs are either in Chelsea or just a hop, skip or jump away from it (*see p303*).

There are other queer nabes, though—and they're far more ethnically and stylistically diverse. Christopher Street in the **West Village** (NYC's internationally renowned gay ghetto) draws crowds of young African-American and Latino men and women, especially along the recently remodeled Christopher Street Pier. Dykes of all types gather at the popular lesbian bars here. The Village is also home to historical gay sites such as the **Stonewall** (*see p302*), as well as friendly show-tune piano cabarets and stores full of rainbow knickknacks and slogan T-shirts.

A more eclectic crowd thrives in the **East Village**'s network of small, divey bars. There's a heavy bohemian contingent here—

Sexual orientation

As a gay visitor to NYC, you'll find it pretty hard to miss the slew of queer offerings, no matter which part of town you're in. But if you'd like official guidance that's both warm and personal, head directly to the **Lesbian, Gay, Bisexual & Transgender Community Center**, which celebrated its 20th anniversary last year.

"We give tourists a big gay welcome," says Richard Burns, the Center's executive director. To receive your hearty greeting—along with a stack of event listings, informative pamphlets and periodicals—just stop by the information desk any day of the week.

Since gay life is practically mainstream in NYC, you might wonder why more than 6,000 people per week continue to come through the Center's doors.

"People are still coming out of the closet and struggling to come to terms with their sexuality," says Burns. "And we're still in a health crisis with HIV and AIDS. This center is also a way for us to take care of the next generation—by providing programs, role models and a safe space for queer youth."

Attendance has been steadily rising since the space's renovation in 2001 (and the addition of bisexual and transgender to its name). About 300 groups gather in the 25 meeting rooms, including the Lesbian Sex Mafia, the New York Bears, Orthodykes and Veg Out. The Center hosts 60 12-step meetings a week; sponsors film festivals, lecture series, art shows and family programs; and claims a 50,000-household mailing list. Run by a staff of more than 70 employees and 300 volunteers, the Center provides a friendly, energetic environment, and of the 137 LGBT Centers in the country, the New York branch is second only to that of Los Angeles in size and scope. Ector Simpson, director of cultural programs, makes it his mission to ensure that the Center's offerings are diverse, running the gamut from special-interest-group meetings to yoga classes.

"The Center has to be a crossroads for the whole community," Burns says, adding that the definition of "the community" (and its needs) has changed over the 20 years of the artists, drag queens, punk-rock baby dykes—but you'll also find the yuppies and college students who've given the neighborhood a more gentrified feel.

Outside Manhattan, the tree-lined **Park Slope** neighborhood of Brooklyn is a major lesbian enclave; a fair share of mellow gay men also seek refuge here from mad Manhattan. During the first weekend in June, the Slope hosts the annual Brooklyn Pride March, a much more intimate version of the citywide celebration and parade. The Brooklyn neighborhoods of **Williamsburg** and **Boerum Hill** are always jam-packed with hipster queers.

Men of all ages, shapes and sizes frequent fetish bars and clubs, like the **Eagle** (*see p302*) in Chelsea. For open-air cruising, try the **Ramble** in Central Park, between the 79th Street transverse and the Lake (but beware of police entrapment for drugs). And despite the city's efforts to clean up Times Square and turn it into a neon-flashing, family-oriented Disney World, you can still find nude male burlesque at the **Gaiety Theatre** *(201 W 46th St between Broadway and Eighth Ave, 212-221-8868)*. The **West Side Club** bathhouse *(27 W 20th St between Fifth and Sixth Aves, 212-691-2700)* in Chelsea and its brother establishment, the **East Side Club** *(227 E 56th St at Second Ave, 212-888-1884)* provide old-school, towel-clad shenanigans. Libidinous lesbians should head to one of the friendly dyke-owned **Toys in Babeland** sex-toy shops (*see p240* **Get the kinks out**), or to the wild women's sex party **Submit** *(718-789-4053),* where a den of slings, shower rooms, rubber mats—and plates of cookies—awaits you monthly.

Accommodations

Chelsea Mews Guest House

344 W 15th St between Eighth and Ninth Aves (212-255-9174). Subway: A, C, E to 14th St; L to Eighth Ave. **Rates** *$100–$200 single/double.* **Credit** *Cash only.*

Built in 1840, this guest house caters to gay men. Rooms are comfortable and well furnished, and in most cases, have semiprivate bathrooms. Laundry service and bicycles are complimentary.

Chelsea Pines Inn

317 W 14th St between Eighth and Ninth Aves (212-929-1023, 888-546-2700; www.chelseapinesinn.com). Subway: A, C, E to 14th St; L to Eighth Ave. **Rates** *$99–$139 double/triple (slightly higher rates during June's Pride Week and holidays).* **Credit** *AmEx, DC, Disc, MC, V.*

B-fabulous Sybill Bruncheon calls the shots during Bingo nights at the **Center**.

Center's existence: "For example, our Family Project has grown and changed, and there are now 2,500 families involved. We have programs for everyone—teenage children of gay parents, pregnant lesbians and wanna-be gay daddies."

Robert Woodworth, director of institutional services, has been with the Center since its inception and has witnessed a slew of changes, though there are a few constants. "Some people are here because they're desperate; others come because they just want to have fun. That hasn't changed," he observes. "The world isn't entirely welcoming to LGBT people—that hasn't changed, either."

You can always count on this institution to greet you with open arms; a stop here should be one of your first in the city.

LGBT Community Center

208 W 13th St between Seventh and Eighth Aves (212-620-7310; www.gaycenter.org). 9am–11pm daily. See also p297.

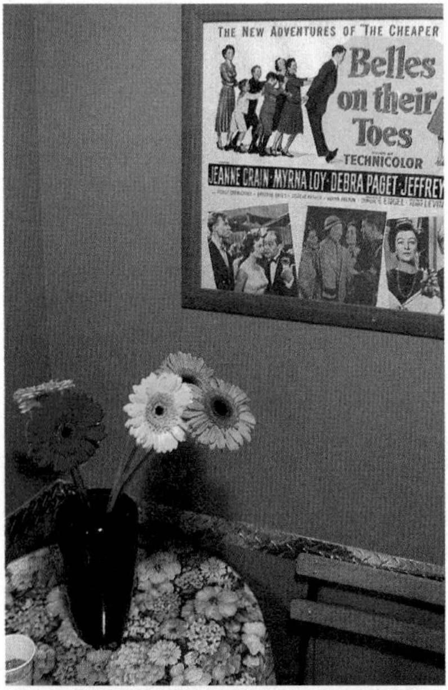

Pretty and witty and gay You'll feel right at home at the **Chelsea Pines Inn**. *See p299.*

On the border of Chelsea and the West Village, this inn welcomes gay guests, both male and female. The 25 rooms are clean and comfortable; the majority have private bathrooms; and all include a radio and TV, plus a refrigerator. Continental breakfast is included.

Colonial House Inn

318 W 22nd St between Eighth and Ninth Aves (212-243-9669, 800-689-3779; www.colonialhouseinn.com). Subway: C, E to 23rd St. **Rates** *$80–$125 single/double, shared bath; $125–$140 single/double, private bath (higher rate on weekends).* **Credit** *MC, V.*
This beautifully renovated 1880s townhouse sits on a quiet street in the heart of Chelsea. Run by and primarily for gay men, Colonial House is a great place to stay, even if some of the less expensive rooms are a bit snug. Bonuses: free Continental breakfast, a fireplace in three of the deluxe rooms, and a rooftop deck for all (nude sunbathing allowed!).

East Village B&B

244 E 7th St between Aves C and D (212-260-1865). Subway: F, V to Lower East Side–Second Ave. **Rates** *$75 single; $100 double; $275 entire apartment; breakfast included. Cash only.*
Tucked into a turn-of-the-century apartment building on a quiet East Village block, this lesbian-owned gem is quite a find. The recently remodeled space has gleaming wood floors and exposed brick, plus an explosion of eclectic artwork that the owners have collected from around the country. The bedrooms are done up in bold colors, one of the bathrooms has a tub (though it's small), and the living room has a TV and CD player. The ever-popular Meow Mix is just a few blocks away.

Incentra Village House

32 Eighth Ave between Jane and W 12th Sts (212-206-0007). Subway: A, C, E to 14th St; L to Eighth Ave. **Rates** *$119–$169 single/double; $149–$199 suites.* **Credit** *AmEx, MC, V.*
Two cute 1841 townhouses, perfectly situated in the West Village, make up this guest house run by gay men. The rooms are spacious and come with private bathrooms and kitchenettes; some have working fireplaces. There's also a 1939 Steinway baby-grand piano in the parlor for show-tune enthusiasts.

Ivy Terrace

230 E 58th St between Second and Third Aves (516-662-6862; www.ivyterrace.com). Subway: N, R, W to Lexington Ave–59th St; 4, 5, 6 to 59th St. **Rates** *$175–$200; $1,100–$1,300 weekly; breakfast included.* **Credit** *AmEx, MC, V.*
This lovely lesbian-owned B&B sits on the same block as boy-haunts O.W. Bar and the Townhouse. The three cozy rooms feature wood floors and lacy bedspreads on old-fashioned sleigh beds. Owner Vinessa Milando (who runs the inn with partner and lesbian-party promoter Sue Martino) delivers breakfast to your room each morning. You're also free to create your own meals: Each room is equipped with a gas stove and full-size fridge.

Bars

Most bars in New York offer theme nights, drink specials and happy hours, and the gay establishments are no exception. Don't be shy, remember to tip the scantily-clad bartender and carry plenty of business cards. (*See also* *pp199–209 and pp273–276.*)

Lower East Side & East Village

The Cock

188 Ave A at 12th St (212-946-1871). Subway: L to First Ave; N, Q, R, W, 4, 5, 6 to 14th St–Union Sq. **Open** *Mon 9pm–4am; Tue–Sun 10pm–4am.* **Average drink** *$6.* **Credit** *Cash only.*

The Cock is location No. 1 for the hip, randy crowd, many of whom don't roll in until after 2am. Depending on the night, the music includes campy '80s standards or good old rock & roll.

Meow Mix

269 E Houston St at Suffolk St (212-254-0688). Subway: F, V to Lower East Side–Second Ave. **Open** *5pm–4am daily.* **Average drink** *$5.* **Credit** *Cash only.*

This lesbian lair hosts local acts, mainly of the glam and garage varieties. DJs typically favor funk, disco, new wave, hip-hop, reggae and R&B. Thursday night is boisterous Gloss, which the promoters call the "glammest girly night around."

Phoenix Bar

447 E 13th St between First Ave and Ave A (212-477-9979). Subway: L to First Ave. **Open** *4pm–4am daily.* **Average drink** *$5.* **Credit** *Cash only.*

A friendly, spacious watering hole, this spot attracts an attitude-free crowd—and even a few gals!—all jamming in for strong drinks, eclectic sounds and some pool-table action.

The Slide

356 Bowery between Great Jones and E 4th Sts (212-420-8885). Subway: B, D, F, V to Broadway–Lafayette St; 6 to Bleecker St. **Open** *5pm–4am daily.* **Average drink** *$6.* **Credit** *Cash only.*

Located in the same space that housed one of Manhattan's first openly gay bars in the 1800s, the Slide is one of the newest—and liveliest—gay bars in the neighborhood. Theme nights abound, from '80s music soirees to variety shows. Saturday is the bawdiest eve, when drag queen Sweetie presents wacky acts and dirty go-go boys.

Starlight Bar and Lounge

167 Ave A between 10th and 11th Sts (212-475-2172). Subway: L to First Ave; N, Q, R, W, 4, 5, 6 to 14th St–Union Sq. **Open** *Sat, Sun 7pm–3am; Sun–Thu 7pm–4am.* **Average drink** *$6.* **Credit** *AmEx, Disc, MC, V.*

On weekends, this bar is almost too popular for its own good. During the week, the scene is more manageable, and a nice bonus is that top-notch local entertainers often perform free shows in the comfy back lounge (usually around 10pm). By 10pm on Sundays, the popular lesbian party Starlette is in full swing. It has a mix of glamour gals, tomboys and college students, but a sexy East Village style prevails. DJ Mickey Dulanto spins lush house.

Urge

33 Second Ave at 2nd St (212-533-5757). Subway: F, V to Lower East Side–Second Ave. **Open** *8pm–4am daily.* **Average drink** *$6.* **Credit** *Cash only.*

This den of iniquity features a small stage that's dominated by gyrating go-go boys—who provide the dimly lit joint with a naughty, sexually charged atmosphere. Video screens often feature hard-core porn, and DJs provide pounding beats. The faint of heart should stick to the front of the establishment, which serves strong coffee and sweet snacks during the innocent daylight hours.

West Village

Bar d'O

29 Bedford St at Downing St (212-627-1580). Subway: A, C, E, B, D, F, V to W 4th St; 1, 9 to Houston St. **Open** *Mon–Fri 6pm–3am; Sat, Sun 7pm–4am.* **Average drink** *$7.* **Credit** *AmEx, Disc, MC, V.*

On Saturdays and Sundays, this inviting, candlelit haunt features intimate performances by the city's most talented drag queens. Catch Cashetta, Raven O or Sade Pendavis—all of whom really sing, not lip-synch. On Mondays, Bar d'O transforms into Pleasure, the long-running lesbian lounge night. The music (provided by DJ Darrel) is a mellow hip-hop groove, and the place is always full of rap and hip-hop enthusiasts who truly believe in "ladies first."

Don't miss **Places to...**

...gain some perspective
Lesbian Herstory Archives (*see p297*).

...cruise wet 'n' wild Chelsea guys
SBNY (*see p304*).

...rest your head after a long night at Meow Mix
East Village B&B (*see p300*).

...find a Fill-in-the-blank Anonymous meeting
Lesbian, Gay, Bisexual & Transgender Community Center (*see p297*).

...find real-life, old-school dandies
The **Townhouse** (*see p306*).

Cubbyhole

281 W 12th St at 4th St (212-243-9041). Subway: A, C, E to 14th St; L to Eighth Ave. **Open** *Mon–Fri 4pm–4am; Sat, Sun 2pm–4am.* **Average drink** *$6.* **Credit** *Cash only.*

The legendary lesbian spot is always chock-full of girls tying one on, with the standard set of Melissa Etheridge or k.d. lang blaring in the background. Chinese paper lanterns, tissue-paper fish and old holiday decorations add to the homemade charm.

The Eagle

554 W 28th St between Tenth and Eleventh Aves (646-473-1866; www.eaglenyc.com). Subway: C, E to 23rd St. **Open** *Mon–Sat 10pm–4am; Sun 5pm–4am.* **Average drink** *$5.* **Credit** *Cash only.*

The Meatpacking District—recently overtaken by French bistros and designer boutiques—was once home to NYC's outpost of kink, the Lure. Now all the action has moved to this Levi's-and-leather classic fetish bar. It features beer blasts on Sundays, foot-worship fetes on Tuesdays and Pork, a raunchy party for the young ones, on Wednesdays.

Henrietta Hudson

438 Hudson St at Morton St (212-924-3347). Subway: 1, 9 to Christopher St–Sheridan Sq. **Open** *Mon–Fri 4pm–4am; Sat, Sun 1pm–4am.* **Average drink** *$6.* **Credit** *Cash only.*

This casual lesbian watering hole is a magnet for young hottie girls from all over the New York area, especially the New Jersey and Long Island 'burbs. You'll see everything from long-nailed J. Lo types and cute baby butches to old-school gym teachers and their wives. Various DJs mix it up on weekends, and the pool table provides endless entertainment.

The Monster

80 Grove St at Sheridan Sq (212-924-3558). Subway: 1, 9 to Christopher St–Sheridan Sq. **Open** *Mon–Fri 4pm–4am; Sat, Sun 2pm–4am.* **Average drink** *$6.* **Credit** *Cash only.*

This bi-level landmark offers an old-school piano lounge upstairs, where locals gather to sing show tunes. (And honey, you haven't lived till you've witnessed a bunch of tipsy queers belting out the best of Broadway.) The downstairs disco caters to a young outer-borough crowd just itchin' for fun.

Rubyfruit Bar & Grill

See p306 for listing.

The Stonewall

53 Christopher St between Seventh Ave and Waverly Pl (212-463-0950). Subway: 1, 9 to Christopher St–Sheridan Sq. **Open** *3pm–4am daily.* **Average drink** *$6.* **Credit** *Cash only.*

This is *the* gay landmark, next door to the actual location of the 1969 gay rebellion against police harassment. For years, the joint was a snore, but lately it's had an infusion of sexy shenanigans, including go-go boys, guest appearances by various porn stars and strip contests. Wednesday is the packed-to-the-rafters Latin night called Uncut. Don't worry, circumcised guys are welcome, too.

► For more nightlife, *see pp199–209* **Bars** *and pp285–291* **Clubs**.

Chelsea

Barracuda

275 W 22nd St between Seventh and Eighth Aves (212-645-8613). Subway: C, E to 23rd St. **Open** *4pm–4am daily.* **Average drink** *$6.* **Credit** *Cash only.*

This bar continues to draw hordes of boys, maybe because it's friendlier and more comfortable than its neighborhood competition. The space is split in two, with a traditional bar up front and a frequently redecorated lounge in back. Drag-queen celebrities perform throughout the week, and there's never a cover.

G

225 W 19th St between Seventh and Eighth Aves (212-929-1085). Subway: 1, 9 to 18th St. **Open** *4pm–4am daily.* **Average drink** *$6.* **Credit** *Cash only.*

This lounge is one of the area's most popular destinations, especially for the well-scrubbed, fresh-faced set—there's even a juice bar in the back to comfort those too health-obsessed for liquor. Late in the evening, the space is often filled to capacity, so go early to stake your place.

xl Chelsea

357 W 16th St between Eighth and Ninth Aves (212-995-1400). Subway: A, C, E to 14th St; L to Eighth Ave. **Open** *4pm–4am daily.* **Average drink** *$6.* **Credit** *Cash only.*

This sleek tri-level bar is a study in style: witness the 30-foot aquarium in the unisex bathroom. Fashion divas, muscle men, fag hags and a few trannies run amok under one roof. On Monday nights, there are free shows starring top-notch Broadway and cabaret performers.

Midtown

O.W. Bar

221 E 58th St at Second Ave (212-355-3395). Subway: N, R, W to Lexington Ave–59th St; 4, 5, 6 to 59th St. **Open** *Mon–Sat 4pm–4am; Sun 2pm–4am.* **Average drink** *$6.* **Credit** *AmEx, MC, V.*

This East Side watering hole (whose initials stand for "Oscar Wilde") features a slick lounge area, a jam-packed digital jukebox and a lovely patio, where you can partake in a free barbecue on summer Sunday afternoons.

Stella's

266 W 47th St between Broadway and Eighth Ave (212-575-1680). Subway: N, Q, R, W, 42nd St S, 1, 2, 3, 9, 7 to 42nd St–Times Sq. **Open** *Noon–4am daily.* **Cover** *$5 (Thu–Sun after 8pm).* **Average drink** *$6.* **Credit** *Cash only.*

Cat scratch fever Claw your way into the Lower East Side girl bar, **Meow Mix**. See p301.

One of the last gay vestiges of pre-Disneyfied Times Square, Stella's offers go-go–boy floor shows starting around 11pm. Connoisseurs of Latin and African-American homeboys will be especially enthralled.

The Townhouse

See p306 for listing.

Uptown

Saints

992 Amsterdam Ave at 109th St (212-961-0599). Subway: 1, 9 to Cathedral Pkwy–110th St. **Open** *4pm–4am daily.* **Average drink** *$6.* **Credit** *AmEx, DC, MC, V.*

Both wispy Columbia students and uptown homeboys converge at this wonderfully divey hangout, which features blue velvet, exposed brick, shabby couches, quirky theme nights and an absurdly welcoming staff. The soundtrack is a fun mix of R&B, funk and throbbing electrodance favorites.

Brooklyn

Excelsior

390 Fifth Ave between 6th and 7th Sts, Park Slope, Brooklyn (718-832-1599). Subway: M, R to Union St. **Open** *6pm–4am daily.* **Average drink** *$6.* **Credit** *Cash only.*

Refined Excelsior, bathed in red, black and chrome, has a spacious back deck, a beautiful garden, an eclectic jukebox and an excellent selection of beers on tap. And the boys are mighty fine.

Ginger's Bar

363 Fifth Ave between 5th and 6th Sts, Park Slope, Brooklyn (718-788-0924). Subway: M, R to Union St. **Open** *Mon–Fri 5pm–4am; Sat, Sun 2pm–4am.* **Average drink** *$6.* **Credit** *Cash only.*

The front room, with its dark-wood bar, looks out onto a bustling street scene. The back, with an always-busy pool table, has a rec-room feel. Come summertime, the outdoor patio feels like a pal's yard. This friendly local hang (and Excelsior neighbor) is full of all sorts of dykes, many with their dogs—or favorite gay boys—in tow.

Clubs

A number of New York clubs have gay nights; many of the following are one-nighters rather than permanent venues. For more clubs, plus additional information about some of those listed below, *see pp285–291.*

Dance clubs & parties

Avalon Sunday

660 Sixth Ave between 20th and 21st Sts (212-807-7780). Subway: F, V, R, W to 23rd St. **Open** *Sun 10pm.* **Cover** *$15–$20.* **Average drink** *$8.* **Credit** *MC, V.*

John Blair, the legendary gay-party promoter, is throwing his latest massive boy bash at the recently reopened Limelight. Expect throngs of young studs writhing to the pounding big-room beats of rotating big-name DJs.

Cheeky A go-go dancer's perspective on the wild weekend scene at the **Roxy**.

Club Heaven

579 Sixth Ave at 16th St (212-539-3982, www.juliesnewyork.com). Subway: F, V to 14th St; L to Sixth Ave. **Open** *Wed, Sun 7pm; Fri 10pm.* **Cover** *free–$12.* **Average drink** *$7.* **Credit** *Cash only.*

This Chelsea club has recently become the headquarters for a slew of lesbian bashes offered by Girl Club Events and Julie's NYC. Wednesday is Noche Latina, with merengue and salsa beats. Kaleidoscope Friday offers such treats as thong contests and sexy go-go dancers. Fantasy Sundays have DJ Tanco spinning everything from reggae to hip-hop.

Lovergirl

Club Shelter, 20 W 39th St between Fifth and Sixth Aves (212-252-3397). Subway: B, D, F, V to 42nd St–Bryant Park; 7 to Fifth Ave. **Open** *Sat 10pm–5am.* **Cover** *$10–$12.* **Average drink** *$6.* **Credit** *Cash only.*

Lovergirl, the popular women's party, takes advantage of Club Shelter's dynamite sound system and state-of-the-art lighting. The multiracial crowd enthusiastically shakes its groove thang to hip-hop, R&B, funk, reggae and Latin music, while ultrasexy go-go gals sport the latest in fashionable G-strings.

Motherfucker

www.motherfuckernyc.com. *See also p291.*

If rock & roll is your style, you'll want to check out Motherfucker, the wildly popular polysexual dance party that takes place about seven times a year, and which almost always changes its location.

Roxy

515 W 18th St between Tenth and Eleventh Aves (212-645-5156). Subway: A, C, E to 14th St; L to Eighth Ave. **Open** *Sat 11pm.* **Cover** *$25.* **Average drink** *$8.* **Credit** *MC, V.*

Promoter John Blair still packs this megaclub with a tasty range of muscle-bound boys who shake it to house and techno, spun by some of the biggest names on the DJ circuit. There's a classic-rock lounge upstairs for old-school boys who prefer beers over bumps.

Saint at Large

212-674-8541; www.saintatlarge.com.

The now-mythical Saint was one of the first venues where New York's gay men could enjoy dance-floor freedom. The club closed, but the clientele keeps its memory alive with four huge parties each year (the S&M Black Party, the White Party, Halloween and New Year's Eve), which attract image-conscious men from around the U.S.

SBNY

50 W 17th St between Fifth and Sixth Aves (212-691-0073; www.splashbar.com). Subway: F, V to 14th St; L to Sixth Ave. **Open** *Sun–Thu 4pm–4am; Fri, Sat 4pm–5am.* **Cover** *$5–$15.* **Average drink** *$6.* **Credit** *Cash only.*

This Chelsea institution offers a large dance floor as well as the famous onstage showers, where hunky go-go boys get wet and wild. And can it be that the supermuscular bartenders are bigger than ever? Nationally known DJs rock the house, local drag celebs give good face, and in-house VJs flash eclectic snippets of classic musicals and videos.

Shescape

212-686-5665; www.shescape.com.
For about 20 years, Shescape has been offering lesbian get-togethers at nightclubs all over town. The crowd tends to be on the guppie side, though the new promoter is doing a good job at recruiting younger, hipper partyers. The most popular events are a mammoth Thanksgiving-eve bash and various dances during Gay Pride Month.

Restaurants & cafés

Few New York restaurants would bat an eye at a same-sex couple enjoying an intimate dinner. The neighborhoods mentioned above have hundreds of venues that are de facto gay restaurants, but here are a few of the most obvious gay places in town.

Big Cup

228 Eighth Ave between 21st and 22nd Sts (212-206-0059). Subway: C, E to 23rd St.
Open *Mon–Fri 7am–12:30am; Sat, Sun 8am–1am.* **Average sandwich** *$5.75.* **Credit** *Cash only.*
Big Cup is as unmistakably Chelsea Boy as a pair of shiny polyester bikini briefs. The coffee is fine, as are the snacks—brownies and Rice Krispies Treats, plus sandwiches and soups. But no one pays much attention to those, because Big Cup is one of New York's classic gay meet markets. After all, you don't hang a disco ball in a Chelsea coffeebar and expect the patrons to lose themselves in Kafka and Kierkegaard.

Cowgirl Hall of Fame

519 Hudson St at 10th St (212-633-1133). Subway: 1, 9 to Christopher St–Sheridan Sq. **Open** *Mon–Thu 10am–11pm; Fri, Sat 11am–midnight; Sun 11am–11pm.* **Average main course** *$13.* **Credit** *AmEx, MC, V.*
Cheerful waitresses welcome girls and boys to this retro ranch-hand lounge, which has a sapphic-tinged Patsy Cline charm that's especially popular with kid-toting gay moms and dads. Specialties include trailer-park originals like Fritos Chili Pie. Chase it with a margarita served in a mason jar.

Eighteenth & Eighth

159 Eighth Ave at 18th St (212-242-5000). Subway: A, C, E to 14th St; L to Eighth Ave; 1, 9 to 18th St. **Open** *Sun–Thu 9am–midnight; Fri, Sat 9am–12:30am.* **Average main course** *$15.* **Credit** *AmEx, MC, V.*
On summer evenings, the sidewalk tables in front of Eighteenth & Eighth are rife with clinking wineglasses, laughter and the bare legs of well-sculpted men. The weekend brunch is one of the best in Chelsea.

Elmo

156 Seventh Ave between 19th and 20th Sts (212-337-8000). Subway: 1, 9 to 18th St. **Open** *Mon–Thu 11am–1am; Fri, Sat 11am–2am, Sun 10am–1am.* **Average main course** *$14.* **Credit** *AmEx, Disc, MC, V.*
This spacious, brightly decorated eatery has good, reasonably priced food and a bar that offers a view of the dining room, which is jammed with guys in clingy tank tops—regardless of the weather.

Love thy neighbor Boys (and girls!) make friends at **Therapy** in Hell's Kitchen. See p306.

Bar & girl Ladies make a love connection.

Foodbar

149 Eighth Ave between 17th and 18th Sts (212-243-2020). Subway: 1, 9 to 18th St. **Open** *11am–4pm, 5pm–midnight.* **Average main course** *$17.* **Credit** *AmEx, MC, V.*

Foodbar's globally influenced American menu will get your mouth watering—if the customers haven't already. Balsamic-glazed roasted chicken, Moroccan salad and steak au poivre are entirely satisfying. Servers are efficient and flirty.

44 & X Hell's Kitchen

622 Tenth Ave at 44th St (212-977-1170). Subway: A, C, E to 42nd St–Port Authority. **Open** *Mon–Wed 5:30pm–midnight; Thu, Fri 5:30pm–12:30am; Sat, Sun 11am–12:30am.* **Average main course** *$15.* **Credit** *AmEx, MC, V.*

Fabulous queens pack into the sleek dining space of this one bright spot on a bleak strip of Tenth Avenue. It's situated alongside the Theater District and the Manhattan Plaza high-rises, home to thousands of actors and other dramatic types. Oh, and the grub's great too—high-end comfort food like creamy mac and cheese, turkey meat loaf, buttermilk–fried chicken, and portobello-and-polenta stew. It's the perfect posttheater or preclub pit stop.

Lips

2 Bank St at Greenwich Ave (212-675-7710). Subway: 1, 2, 3, 9 to 14th St. **Open** *Mon–Thu 5:30pm–midnight; Fri, Sat 5:30pm–1am; Sun 11:30am–4pm, 5:30–11pm.* **Average main course** *$17.* **Credit** *AmEx, DC, MC, V.*

This festive restaurant certainly does provide a jovial atmosphere: The drag-queen waitstaff serves tasty meals *and* performs for very enthusiastic patrons. Weekdays, like Wednesday's Bitchy Bingo, tend to be a lot gayer than the weekends, when scores of shrieking straight chicks come to celebrate bridal showers.

Rubyfruit Bar & Grill

531 Hudson St between Charles and Washington Sts (212-929-3343). Subway: 1, 9 to Christopher St–Sheridan Sq. **Open** *Mon–Thu 2pm–4am; Fri, Sat 3pm–4am; Sun 11:30am–2am.* **Average main course** *$20.* **Average drink** *$6.* **Credit** *AmEx, DC, Disc, MC, V.*

The only dedicated lesbian restaurant and bar in town. Although the food is good, it's not the main selling point. Cabaret, an eclectic mix of music and congenial customers make this a great place for fun-loving, old-school dykes.

Therapy

348 W 52nd St between Eighth and Ninth Aves (212-397-1700). Subway: C, E to 50th St. **Open** *Sun–Wed 5pm–2am; Thu–Sat 5pm–4am.* **Average main course** *$10.* **Credit** *AmEx, MC, V.*

One of the newest gay lounges catering to a cocktail-swilling, professional midtown crowd, this one has the added attraction of decent grub. To go with that vodka tonic, try grilled chicken skewers with mango salsa, a grilled veggie sandwich on *ciabatta* or the Atkins-happy Therapy burger dripping with Roquefort cheese and bacon.

The Townhouse

206 E 58th St at Third Ave (212-826-6241). Subway: N, R, W to Lexington Ave–59th St; 4, 5, 6 to 59th St. **Open** *Mon–Thu noon–3:30pm, 5–11pm; Fri, Sat noon–3:30pm, 5pm–midnight; Sun noon–4pm, 5–11pm.* **Average main course** *$20.* **Credit** *AmEx, DC, MC, V.*

If you're a reasonably attractive man under 40, you're likely to be greeted—or at least ogled—by one of the soused middle-aged regulars at this "gentlemen's" restaurant. In the dining room beyond the bar, you'll spot couples in various stages of courtship; the flirty service makes this a good place for solo diners as well.

Music

From rock to Rachmaninoff, here's music for your ears.

Popular Music

The sonic boom of the "New York sound," which got international press for bands like the Strokes and the Yeah Yeah Yeahs, is a little quieter these days. Of those much-hyped groups, only the Strokes—who took two years to roll out a suitable sophomore album, *Room on Fire*—look likely to retain a global profile. The Yeah Yeah Yeahs' debut sputtered, and the buzz generated by the Rapture's dance hit "House of Jealous Lovers" fizzled as the band played the major-label bidding game, finally dropping the decent but unspectacular *Echoes* last year. The Walkmen are up next, with a major-label debut slated for winter 2004. Other local pop bands have remained in thrall to retromania, but the '70s influences are almost over, and even the synth-and-skinny-ties '80s are nearly played out.

Still, there's a lot going on here beyond the glitzy rock scene. Every night, a mind-blowing, world-spanning blend of sounds pumps through the city's bars and clubs. Jazz, hip-hop, soul, folk and pretty much every international flavor and fusion you can think of are mixing it up in Brooklyn, the Bronx and all stops in between. All you need to get in the groove is a subway map, a night's worth of concert listings and the joie de vivre that brought you to the city in the first place.

To help you guide your own sonic world cruise, we've organized the city's major venues by genre. Keep in mind that these categories are loose. Many clubs can throb with a techno beat one night and rock out the next, or skip from hip-hop to Brazilian music in one evening. A relaxed attitude helps, as does a willingness to hang around: If a listing says your favorite band is going on at 11pm, be prepared to wait till midnight or beyond.

A valid photo-ID (passports and driver's licenses are best) proving that you're 21 or over is essential, not just to drink but, often, just to get in. NYC bouncers are notoriously impervious to creative excuses, mainly because there are plenty of other paying customers lining up behind you.

Tickets are usually available from clubs in advance and at the door. A few small and medium-size venues also sell advance tickets through local record stores. For larger events, it's wise to buy through **Ticketmaster** (*see p378*) on the web, over the phone or at one of the outlets located throughout the city. Tickets for some events are available through **Ticket Web** *(www.ticketweb.com)*. You can also purchase online from websites of specific venues (web addresses are included in venue listings where available). For more ticket details, *see p378*. And remember to call first for info and show times, which may change without notice.

Arenas

Continental Airlines Arena

East Rutherford, NJ (201-935-3900; www.meadowlands.com). Travel: NJ Transit Meadowlands Sports Complex bus from Port Authority Bus Terminal (212-564-8484), Eighth Ave at 42nd St; $3.25 each way. **Tickets** *From $25.* **Credit** *Cash only at box office.*

North Jersey's answer to Madison Square Garden recently played host to Shania Twain, Justin Timberlake and Christina Aguilera. Big radio-sponsored pop and hip-hop extravaganzas also happen here.

Madison Square Garden

Seventh Ave between 31st and 33rd Sts (box office 212-465-6741; www.thegarden.com). Subway: A, C, E, 1, 2, 3, 9 to 34th St–Penn Station. **Box office** *Mon–Sat noon–6pm.* **Tickets** *$25–$350.* **Credit** *AmEx, DC, Disc, MC, V.*

Bob Dylan, Bruce Springsteen, Madonna and the Dixie Chicks are but a few who've sold out this venue, which doubles as a sports arena. Be forewarned: The cost of a good seat is high—tickets for special occasions can sell for more than $1,000; regular shows can easily top $100.

Nassau Veterans Memorial Coliseum

1255 Hempstead Tpke, Uniondale, Long Island (516-794-9303; www.nassaucoliseum.com). Travel: From Penn Station, Seventh Ave at 32nd St, take

► For a calendar of annual happenings, *see pp252–259* **Festivals & Events**.
► For more live-music venues, *see pp273–276* **Cabaret & Comedy**, *pp285–291* **Clubs** *and pp296–306* **Gay & Lesbian**.
► Pick up a copy of ***Time Out New York***, which lists specific shows and previews upcoming concerts.

Arts & Entertainment

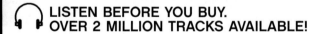

LIRR (www.lirr.org) to Hempstead, then N70, N71 or N72 bus to the coliseum. **Tickets** *From $25.* **Credit** *AmEx, Disc, MC, V.*
Long Island's arena tends to host mostly mainstream performers such as Phish and Fleetwood Mac, and back-together-again tours of aging rockers. Styx and Journey, party on!

Rock, pop & soul

Apollo Theater

253 W 125th St between Adam Clayton Powell Jr. Blvd (Seventh Ave) and Frederick Douglass Blvd (Eighth Ave) (212-531-5301, 212-531-5305; www.apollotheater.com). Subway: A, C, B, D, 1, 9 to 125th St. **Box office** *Mon, Tue, Thu, Fri 10am–6pm; Wed 10am–8:30pm; Sat noon–6pm.* **Tickets** *$16–$39.* **Credit** *AmEx, DC, Disc, MC, V.*
New York's hub for R&B music, Harlem's venerable Apollo helped launch the careers of Ella Fitzgerald, Michael Jackson and D'Angelo, just to name a few. The theater continues to host the revamped Showtime at the Apollo TV program. And the stars of tomorrow continue to line up for Wednesday's Amateur Night.

Arlene Grocery

95 Stanton St between Ludlow and Orchard Sts (212-358-1633; www.arlenegrocery.com). Subway: F to Delancey St; J, M, Z to Delancey–Essex Sts. **Cover** *free–$10; doors open at 6pm.* **Credit** *Cash only.*
Named for the Lower East Side bodega that it replaced, Arlene Grocery runs as many as seven groups a night through its top-notch sound system. Channel your inner Alice Cooper at heavy-metal karaoke on Monday night.

BAMcafé at Brooklyn Academy of Music

For listing, see p321 **Brooklyn Academy of Music**.
Like Brooklyn itself, the Brooklyn Academy of Music offers a winning mix of genres. On weekend nights, the BAMcafé above the lobby features everything from folk and spoken word to hip-hop and world music. BAM's NextNext series emphasizes performers under the age of 30: Carl Hancock Rux, Duncan Sheik, Chocolate Genius and Antibalas.

B.B. King Blues Club & Grill

237 W 42nd St between Seventh and Eighth Aves (212-997-4144; www.bbkingblues.com). Subway: A, C, E to 42nd St–Port Authority; N, Q, R, W, 42nd St S, 1, 2, 3, 9, 7 to 42nd St–Times Sq. **Box office** *10am–midnight daily.* **Tickets** *$12–$150.* **Credit** *AmEx, DC, Disc, MC, V.*
B.B.'s joint in Times Square is a squeaky-clean showcase for a wide variety of music: Cover bands and soul tributes fill the gaps between big-name bookings such as Ray Charles, Jeff Beck and George Clinton. The supper-club concept means the best seats are at the dinner tables up front, but menu prices are steep. The Harlem Gospel Choir buffet brunch on Sundays raises the roof, while live classic rock, jazz and blues play for free most nights at Lucille's, the cozy restaurant named for King's cherished guitar.

Beacon Theatre

2124 Broadway at 74th St (212-496-7070, 212-307-7171). Subway: 1, 2, 3, 9 to 72nd St. **Box office** *Mon–Fri 11am–7pm; Sat noon–6pm.* **Tickets** *$15–$175.* **Credit** *Cash only at box office.*
The classic alt-country of Lucinda Williams, the cosmopolitan pop of Norah Jones and the English soul of Simply Red all find a home in the gilded interior of the Beacon. The gigantic statues guarding either end of the stage provide extra character.

Bowery Ballroom

6 Delancey St between Bowery and Chrystie St (212-533-2111; www.boweryballroom.com). Subway: J, M, Z to Bowery; 6 to Spring St. **Box office** *At Mercury Lounge (see p313).* **Tickets** *$13–$40.* **Credit** *AmEx, MC, V (bar only).*

The best Scenes

Come here to hang with

...two-steppers and two-fisters

Rodeo (*see p318*) is one of the few spots in town for those who are a little bit country and a little bit rock 'n' roll—and there's never a cover.

...the most persnickety jazz purists

Over the past 70 years, the **Village Vanguard** (*see p318*) has hosted such one-name-only jazz legends as Dizzy, Miles and Coltrane (make sure your cell phone is off!).

...dyed-in-the-wool indie kids

Bowery Ballroom (*see above*) features the best alternative bands, like the Shins, the New Pornographers, Le Tigre and Broadcast.

...the musicians

At cozy **Joe's Pub** (*see p311*), you'll feel like you're in a spacious living room rather than a club, and the musicians—from hip-hoppers to world-music stars—are *right there.*

...the next guy's elbow

Pete's Candy Store (*see p314*) is so tiny that folks cram together to hear the cool, rootsy singer-songwriters that play here (and the shows are always free).

Karaoke at **Arlene Grocery**. *See p309.*

This is a great place to catch indie-rock stars like Broadcast and the New Pornographers. The stage, sound and sight lines are solid, and there's plenty of space, including a downstairs bar where you can escape an opening band that should never have left the garage.

Bowery Poetry Club

308 Bowery at Bleecker St (212-614-0505; www.bowerypoetry.com). Subway: B, D, F, V to Broadway–Lafayette St; 6 to Bleecker St. **Cover** *$3–$10; check website for schedule.* **Credit** *AmEx, MC, V (Internet reservations only).*

As you'd guess from its name, this colorful joint has its roots in the poetry-slam scene, but it's friendly to all sorts of jazz, folk, hip-hop and interdisciplinary artists, connecting the dots between Saul Williams and Tuli Kupferberg.

CBGB

315 Bowery at Bleecker St (212-982-4052; www.cbgb.com). Subway: B, D, F, V to Broadway–Lafayette St; 6 to Bleecker St. **Cover** *$3–$12, two-drink minimum; check website for schedule.* **Credit** *Cash only.*

The progressive spirit and crazy diversity that helped launch Blondie, the Ramones and Talking Heads is all but gone; rote metal and punk bands now rule the stage at CBGB. There are exceptions, including a set in which classical cellist Matt Haimovitz served up Bach and Hendrix. But no matter who's playing, you owe it to yourself to visit this legendary New York club (most shows begin between 6:30 and 7pm)—just avoid its equally notorious bathrooms.

CB's 313 Gallery + CBGB's Downstairs Lounge

313 Bowery at Bleecker St (212-677-0455; www.cbgb.com). Subway: B, D, F, V to Broadway–Lafayette St; 6 to Bleecker St. **Cover** *$5–$10; shows start around 7pm.* **Credit** *AmEx, MC, V ($20 minimum).*

Located right next door, these two small venues are CBGB's more cultivated cousins (the Lounge is downstairs from the Gallery), with acoustic fare and local singer-songwriters dominating the schedules. On Sunday, the lounge hosts the weekly Freestyle Avant Jazz and Other Musics, a hot event on the local jazz scene.

Continental

25 Third Ave at St. Marks Pl (212-529-6924; www.continentalnyc.com). Subway: R, W to 8th St–NYU; 6 to Astor Pl. **Cover** *free–$6; doors open at 4pm.* **Credit** *Cash only.*

As with CBGB, the Continental's best days are long gone; tribute bands and often-tuneless hardcore, metal and street-punk acts fill the rectangular room these days. Still, it remains a favorite haunt for some truly great bands, like Boston's Real Kids.

Don Hill's

511 Greenwich St at Spring St (212-219-2850; www.donhills.com). Subway: C, E to Spring St; 1, 9 to Canal St. **Cover** *free–$10; doors open at 7:30pm.* **Credit** *AmEx, DC, Disc, MC, V.*

This divey little West Village bunker recently celebrated its tenth anniversary. It's known for its weekly events: Saturday night's groovy, Britpoppy Tiswas party; Thursday's long-running '80s-dance party BeavHer; and Wednesday's rotation of glam-punk bonanza Röck Cändy and metal-karaoke party Bitch.

Fez

Inside Time Cafe, 380 Lafayette St at Great Jones St (212-533-2680). Subway: B, D, F, V to Broadway–Lafayette St; 6 to Bleecker St. **Cover** *$8–$20, two-drink minimum; doors open one hour before show.* **Credit** *AmEx, MC, V (food and drinks only).*

Fez is one of the city's finest venues for burgeoning pop, rock and lounge acts. On Thursdays, the Mingus Big Band plays the sanctified jazz of the late Charles Mingus. Fez also has a sweet tooth for kooky drag, from Karen Finley channeling Liza Minnelli to gender-bending entertainment by Jackie Beat and Kiki & Herb. The dinner theater–style seating leaves little standing room, so make reservations, arrive early and prepare for a strictly enforced two-drink minimum.

Galapagos

70 North 6th St between Kent and Wythe Aves, Williamsburg, Brooklyn (718-782-5188; www.galapagosartspace.com). Subway: L to Bedford Ave. **Cover** *free–$7; shows start around 8pm.* **Credit** *Cash only.*

As much a gallery as it is a music club, this spacious Williamsburg venue has suffered a bit since the (presumably temporary) closing of its back room. However, shows continue seven nights a week in the front room. Burlesque and vaudeville nights are weekly staples.

Hammerstein Ballroom

Manhattan Center, 311 W 34th St between Eighth and Ninth Aves (212-279-7740, 212-564-4882). Subway: A, C, E to 34th St–Penn Station. **Box office** *Mon–Sat noon–5pm.* **Tickets** *$10–$50.* **Credit** *AmEx, MC, V.*

This midsize venue may not be the best place to see a show—the security staff is a pain, the sound is crummy and if you get stuck upstairs, the stage can seem miles away. But the management books top acts: Foo Fighters, Pet Shop Boys, Blur and the Chemical Brothers have tackled the mighty Ballroom, as have local bands on the rise, such as Interpol and the Strokes.

Irving Plaza

17 Irving Pl at 15th St (212-777-6800; www.irvingplaza.com). Subway: L, N, Q, R, W, 4, 5, 6 to 14th St–Union Sq. **Box office** *Mon–Fri noon–6:30pm; Sat 1–4pm.* **Tickets** *$15–$45.* **Credit** *AmEx.*

Irving Plaza, the city's original midsize venue, pulls in an excellent roster of artists from around the globe. The room routinely features indie bands that have "made it," such as Mogwai and Fountains of Wayne, as well as moonlighters like Bruce Willis and Billy Bob Thornton. Generous elbow room keeps even a full house comfortable, but those stiff bar prices can be a drag.

Joe's Pub

425 Lafayette St between Astor Pl and E 4th St (212-539-8770; www.joespub.com). Subway: R, W to 8th St–NYU; 6 to Astor Pl. **Box office** *1–7:30pm daily.* **Tickets** *$12–$30.* **Credit** *AmEx, MC, V.*

When it comes to eclectic, adult-oriented fare, the tiny, tony Joe's Pub is one of the most satisfying places in town. Recent performers have included Malian guitarist Djelimady Tounkara, Indian-Australian singer Susheela Raman and latter-day jazz crooner Boz Scaggs. Joe's is also a major hip-hop hangout, due to its regular late-night parties and select live-music events. It helps to look sharp for some of these later events: The door policy can be selectively enforced.

Knitting Factory

74 Leonard St between Broadway and Church St (212-219-3006; www.knittingfactory.com). Subway: A, C, E to Canal St; 1, 9 to Franklin St. **Box office** *Noon–11pm daily.* **Tickets** *$5–$20.* **Credit** *AmEx, MC, V ($15 minimum).*

Once it was the city's home for avant-garde jazz, but the new owners have now instituted a broader (read: more rock-oriented) booking policy. Still, you can traverse entire galaxies of music just by moving from room to room (the Factory has three). The main performance space hosts legends (Jonathan Richman, the Fall), indie stalwarts (the Clean, Ted Leo) and genre jumpers (Arto Lindsay, Sun City Girls). Poetry and potent jazz happen in the Tap Bar and the Old Office.

Lakeside Lounge

162 Ave B between 10th and 11th Sts (212-529-8463; www.lakesidelounge.com). Subway: L to First Ave; N, Q, R, W, 4, 5, 6 to 14th St–Union Sq. **Cover** *free; shows start at 9:30 or 10pm.* **Credit** *AmEx, MC, V.*

The Lakeside remains one of the city's scruffier, more endearing little clubs. There's no stage, but that doesn't keep class acts like Kevin Salem and onetime MC5 manager John Sinclair from dropping in to play. Co-owner Roscoe Ambel has been a producer for the Bottle Rockets, Cowslingers and Mojo Nixon, so bands in the roots-rock scene frequent the joint.

The Living Room

154 Ludlow St between Rivington and Stanton Sts (212-533-7235; www.livingroomny.com). Subway: F to Delancey St; J, M, Z to Delancey–Essex Sts. **Open** *Mon–Sat 6pm–4am; Sun 6pm–2am.* **Cover** *free, one-drink minimum.* **Credit** *Cash only.*

Befitting its name, the Living Room is an intimate, low-key lounge that lets singer-songwriters play right-up-close and personal to the audience. The club boasts a piano donated by Norah Jones—no surprise, as she played some of her earliest gigs here. Equal talents (like Chris Lee) enjoy doing weekly shows.

Luna Lounge

171 Ludlow St between Houston and Stanton Sts (212-260-2323; www.lunalounge.com). Subway: F, V to Lower East Side–Second Ave. **Cover** *free; shows start around 8pm.* **Credit** *Cash only.*

An unassuming Lower East Side hangout with the best kind of cover: none. Free shows by a number of promising (and less promising) pop bands make it a favorite neighborhood destination, as the audience flows back and forth between the sofa-filled barroom in front and the boxy performance space in back.

Scene and heard

Like little individual solar systems fueled by talent, fashion, buzz and drink tickets, music scenes can coalesce around anything from a fresh sound to a hip neighborhood. Lately, the coolest shows and must-go parties are being sponsored by some of the city's small and feisty independent record labels. Run mostly by energetic, creative and terminally broke twentysomethings, these labels promote their on-the-edge bands with gigs and club events all around town. To find out who's playing where while you're here, check out the latest issue of *Time Out New York* or look for party and band info on the labels' websites.

One of the busiest labels in the area is actually based in Jersey. **Troubleman Unlimited** *(www.troublemanunlimited.com),* seems to have a hand in every cool underground-rock event happening in the city. With the Troubleman stamp of approval, even the label's non-NYC artists (Erase Errata, Glass Candy and Wolf Eyes) get enough local support to seem like hot-ticket hometown bands when they play here. The label's catalog (including Milky Wimpshake, Subtonix and Zs) primarily revolves around the newest wave of new wave and punk, but dips into everything from folk to noise. Two of NYC's finest bands, Dan Melchior's Broke Revue and the Rogers Sisters, are also two of Troubleman's top acts. A show by either of these exciting bands is a bona fide NYC-flavored event (and bound to be packed).

The Brooklyn-based **Arena Rock** *(www.arenarockrecordingco.com)* has a diverse roster of local groups: the Stones-ish Grand Mal; pop maniac Mink Lungs; indie-rock traditionalist Pilot to Gunner, whose smart lyrics and sturdy riffs conjure visions of Fugazi and Superchunk; Calla, whose noirish, desert-kissed pop has made the trio one of the city's hottest bands; and Onairlibrary!, which has been trying to update the dreamy sound of the 4AD label, with mixed results. Arena Rock also presaged the current Brooklyn music scene with its 40-artist double CD, *This Is Next Year,* put out in 2001, just as musicians were leaving Manhattan in droves to find cheaper living—and soon, a scene of their own—in Williamsburg and beyond.

Also from Brooklyn is the **Social Registry** *(www.thesocialregistry.org),* probably the most promising of the new indie labels. So far, the Registry's listings include the Pavement-inspired Icewater Scandal, electro outfit Ghost Exits and experimental rockers, ElectroPutas, along with new signees Blood on the Wall and Artanker Convoy (featuring members of Stratotanker, a popular NYC band from the '90s). The Social Registry also

Makor

35 W 67th St between Central Park West and Columbus Ave (212-601-1000; www.makor.org). Subway: 1, 9 to 66th St–Lincoln Ctr. **Box office** *Mon–Thu 9am–9pm; Fri 9am–5pm; Sat (only open when events are scheduled); Sun 10am–8pm.* **Tickets** *$9–$15.* **Credit** *AmEx, MC, V.*

Makor, an Upper West Side Jewish cultural center affiliated with the 92nd St Y, presents music shows in the basement. The programming includes a diverse mix of folk, blues, roots, world music and local singer-songwriters.

Maxwell's

1039 Washington St at 11th St, Hoboken, NJ (201-798-0406; www.maxwellsnj.com). Travel: PATH train to Hoboken, then cab, Red Apple bus or NJ Transit #126 bus to Washington St. **Box office** *Visit website.* **Tickets** *$6–$20.* **Credit** *AmEx, Disc, MC, V.*

Maxwell's has been the most consistently forward-looking rock club in the metropolitan area for more than 20 years. Yes, it's in Jersey, but the round-the-clock PATH train makes the trip a breeze. The music ranges from punk and garage (Jersey's own Swinging Neckbreakers, Holly Golightly) to indie and roots. Hometown trio Yo La Tengo's annual run of Hanukkah shows is always a blast.

Meow Mix

See p301 for listing.

Known for its girl power, the Mix has hosted legends Sleater-Kinney, Luscious Jackson and Kiki & Herb.

Mercury Lounge

217 Houston St at Ave A (212-260-4700; www.mercuryloungenyc.com). Subway: F, V to Lower East Side–Second Ave. **Box office** *Mon–Sat noon–7pm.* **Cover** *$8–$15; some shows require advance tickets.* **Credit** *Cash only.*

There's a recognizable name, from either the local scene or elsewhere, playing here pretty much every night of the week. The crowded bar is usually a tight squeeze, but beyond it lies the slightly more roomy brick-walled live-music space. The sound is great, you can see from just about anywhere (as long as you're not too short), and the staff is friendly. The Mercury specializes in indie and roots rock. From Dead Meadow and the Lilys to Tift Merritt and Steve Wynn, the sounds are always varied and usually top-notch.

sponsors Mutiny, a new, eclectic monthly event where balls-out rock shows might alternate with psychedelic-tinged folk singers.

A few labels are developing middle-of-the-road indie rock: **StarTime International** *(718-636-9755; www.startimerecords.com)* helped get the Walkmen's career rolling (the quintet recently signed with Warner Bros.). The label is also home to French Kicks, the white female hip-hop trio Northern State and the prep-school rock trio Natural History. **Ace-Fu** *(212-352-8052; www.acefu.com)* mines more jagged postpunk terrain, having worked with the Ex-Models and Secret Machines (both of which have moved to bigger labels). Its current lineup includes indie-pop revivalists the Eaves, as well as Soundtrak and Aqui. At **Self-Starter Foundation** *(www.selfstarterfoundation.com),* recent signee Sea Ray is a local rising star for its lush pop updates. Palomar and Les Savy Fav also remain strong draws.

NYC's best-known label has to be **DFA** *(www.dfarecords.com),* whose reputation probably outstrips its actual accomplishments. But through a handful of singles by the Rapture, Juan Maclean and LCD Soundsystem, these producers and their imprint have juiced the local rock scene back to the early '80s, when punk and disco made peace, as well as some of the best music in NYC's history. While most of DFA's following is in the club scene, the label's best group, the Black Dice, has partisans among trend-conscious DFA fans, and among local artists and filmmakers (who've found the perfect soundtrack material in Black Dice's abstract noise).

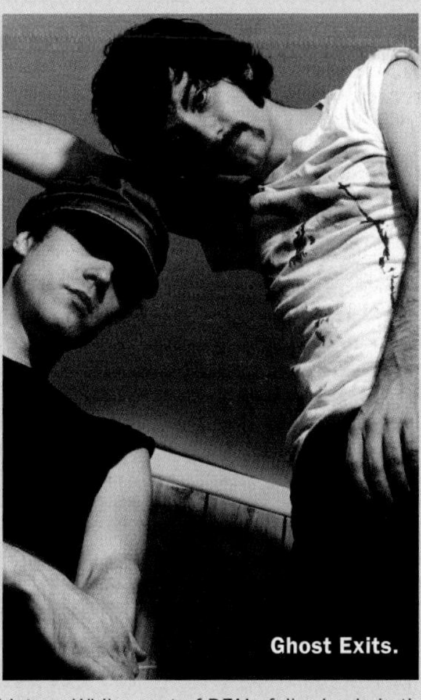

Ghost Exits.

Din and tonic Get up close and personal with the music makers at **Tonic**. *See p315.*

New Jersey Performing Arts Center

1 Center St at the waterfront, Newark, NJ (888-466-5722; www.njpac.org). Travel: PATH train to Newark, then Loop shuttle bus to NJPAC. **Box office** *Visit website.* **Tickets** *$12–$100.* **Credit** *AmEx, Disc, MC, V.*

You might think it'd be a schlep to get here, but Newark's gorgeous performing-arts center is only 15 or 20 minutes from midtown. Both the 2,750-seat Prudential Hall and the cozier 510-seat Victoria Theater feature top-rank stars, including Johnny Mathis, Paula West and Hilton Ruiz.

92nd Street Y

See p271 for listing.

The Y's popular music schedule extends to gospel, mainstream jazz and indigenous folk. Jazz in July lures swingers young and old to the comfy surroundings. Summer's Lyrics & Lyricists series celebrates the tunesmiths who wrote the classics of the American songbook.

Northsix

66 North 6th St between Kent and Wythe Aves, Williamsburg, Brooklyn (718-599-5103; www.northsix.com). Subway: L to Bedford Ave. **Box office** *Advance purchase online recommended.* **Tickets** *$5–$15.* **Credit** *AmEx, Disc, MC, V (advance purchases only).*

Music fans come to Northsix for the bargain happy hour, the great jukebox and a consistent roster of well-honed local and touring bands, from NYC old-timer Luna to Northwest favorite Quasi.

Pete's Candy Store

709 Lorimer St between Frost and Richardson Sts, Williamsburg, Brooklyn (718-302-3770; www.petescandystore.com). Subway: G to Metropolitan Ave; L to Lorimer St. **Open** *Sun–Wed 5pm–2am; Thu–Sat 5pm–4am.* **Cover** *free.* **Credit** *AmEx, Disc, MC, V.*

Shaped like an old railroad car, the performance space at Pete's is as snug as a Manhattan living room. In such environs, performances usually take on the intimacy of a basement show, but when singer-songwriters such as Cass McCombs and Burd Early play, the vibe is just right.

Radio City Music Hall

1260 Sixth Ave at 50th St (212-247-4777; www.radiocity.com). Subway: B, D, F, V to 47–50th Sts–Rockefeller Ctr. **Box office** *Mon–Sat 10am–8pm; Sun 11am–8pm.* **Tickets** *$25–$125.* **Credit** *AmEx, DC, Disc, MC, V.*

Walking through this awe-inspiring Art Deco hall is almost as exciting as watching the superstars who perform: Björk, Mariah Carey and Aretha Franklin are just three divas who have graced its stage in recent years.

Roseland

239 W 52nd St between Broadway and Eighth Ave (212-245-5761, concert hot line 212-249-8870; www.roselandballroom.com). Subway: C, E, 1, 9 to 50th St. **Box office** *At Irving Plaza (see p311).* **Tickets** *$17–$75.* **Credit** *Cash only.*

Although Portishead recorded a great live album at this 1930s-era ballroom, the sound system can leave something to be desired. Still, it's spacious (thanks to the addition of a balcony) and it's a great place to catch a mix of established acts like Marilyn Manson, Steely Dan and Dashboard Confessional, as well as such rising stars as Interpol and the Mars Volta.

Sidewalk

94 Ave A at 6th St (212-473-7373). Subway: F, V to Lower East Side–Second Ave; 6 to Astor Pl. **Cover** *free, two-drink minimum; shows start around 7:30pm.* **Credit** *AmEx, MC, V.*
The latest act to break out of Sidewalk, the unofficial headquarters of the antifolk scene, is singer-songwriter Nellie McKay; before her, it was the Moldy Peaches. Open mikes and jam sessions occur frequently.

Sin-é

150 Attorney St between Houston and Stanton Sts (212-388-0077; www.sin-e.org). Subway: F to Delancey St; J, M, Z to Delancey–Essex Sts. **Open** *7:30pm–1am daily.* **Cover** *$7–$15.* **Credit** *Cash only.*
Recently reopened in a larger space on the Lower East Side, this club has jumped right back to hosting some of the best local and touring talent, including Dan Melchior's Broke Revue, White Magic and James Chance and the Contortions—reconstituted, just like this venue.

S.O.B.'s

204 Varick St at Houston St (212-243-4940; www.sobs.com). Subway: 1, 9 to Houston St. **Box office** *Mon–Sat 11am–6pm.* **Tickets** *$10–$25.* **Credit** *AmEx, DC, Disc, MC, V (food and drinks only).*
Brazilian and Caribbean sounds (samba, reggae and salsa) continue to heat up S.O.B's, but the club has also turned into one of the city's prime venues for neosoul, urban rock and hip-hop acts: Within the past year, Clipse, Cee-Lo, Dead Presidents and Talib Kweli have all rocked its stage.

Southpaw

125 Fifth Ave between Sterling and St. Johns Pls, Park Slope, Brooklyn (718-230-0236; www.spsounds.com). Subway: B, Q, 2, 3, 4, 5 to Atlantic Ave; D, M, N, R to Pacific St. **Box office** *Visit website or www.ticketweb.com.* **Tickets** *$7–$20.* **Credit** *Cash only.*
One of Brooklyn's finest rock venues is in residential Park Slope, not hipster-haven Williamsburg. A spacious stage, an ace sound system and excellent sight lines make this a great place to see a band. The club presents a good mix of indie acts, both local (Essex Green, Jean Grae, Out Hud) and touring (the Legendary Shack Shakers, Vic Chesnutt).

The Theater at Madison Square Garden

Seventh Ave between 31st and 33rd Sts (212-465-6741, 212-307-7171; www.thegarden.com). Subway: A, C, E, 1, 2, 3, 9 to 34th St–Penn Station. **Box office** *Mon–Sat noon–6pm.* **Tickets** *vary.* **Credit** *AmEx, DC, Disc, MC, V.*
This smaller, classier extension of Madison Square Garden has better sound than the arena. The theater has hosted world-music celebrations, mainstream hip-hop shows, R&B extravaganzas, and medium-size rock shows with the Strokes, James Taylor and Bonnie Raitt.

Tonic

107 Norfolk St between Delancey and Rivington Sts (212-358-7503; www.tonic107.com). Subway: F to Delancey St; J, M, Z to Delancey–Essex Sts. **Cover** *$5–$40; doors open at 7:30pm.* **Credit** *Cash only.*
Tonic, a former kosher winery on the Lower East Side, has become one of the world's leading venues for avant-garde, creative and experimental music. Rock, pop and electronic sounds routinely mix it up with jazz and improvised music. Downtown icon John Zorn treats Tonic as his home away from home, and recently performed here every night for a month, to mark his 50th birthday. In Subtonic, the basement DJ lounge, guests can loll around inside giant (but alas, empty) wine casks.

Town Hall

123 W 43rd St between Sixth and Seventh Aves (212-997-1003; www.the-townhall-nyc.org). Subway: B, D, F, V to 42nd St–Bryant Park; N, Q, R, W, 42nd St S, 1, 2, 3, 9, 7 to 42nd

It happened here

If Jimi Hendrix came back to life, he probably wouldn't recognize his own studio: The distinctive curved-brick facade of the **Electric Lady Studios** *(52 W 8th St between Fifth and Sixth Aves)* was demolished in 1997. Originally a big-band dance hall, the building was converted to a studio in 1970. Hendrix recorded most of his final album there, but died within a month of the official opening on August 26. Some of the original interior—along with the Hendrix-commissioned wall murals—remains.

St–Times Sq. **Box office** *Mon–Sat noon–6pm.* **Tickets** *$15–$85.* **Credit** *AmEx, DC, MC, V ($2 surcharge for credit-card orders).*
An 82-year-old theater with superb acoustics, Town Hall was conceived as the "people's auditorium." Its democratic bookings keep that spirit alive. The summer is slow, but the fall season brings cabaret, folk and traditional-music artists from around the world (including many Persian and Indian talents), as well as a mix of pop artists ranging from Elvis Costello to the Folksmen.

Warsaw at the Polish National Home

261 Driggs Ave at Eckford St, Greenpoint, Brooklyn. (718-387-0505; www.warsawconcerts.com). Subway: G to Nassau Ave. **Box office** *Tue–Sun 5pm–midnight; advance purchase online recommended.* **Tickets** *$10–$25.* **Credit** *Cash only at the box office; MC, V accepted online.*
The Polish National Home is a spacious, old-fashioned ballroom with a bar in front that serves affordable Polish beers and pierogi. The cavernous main room offers a schedule of quality rock bands, both old (Love, the Residents) and new (Polyphonic Spree, Mogwai). The sound has been a problem here, but a recent upgrade to the system should help.

Jazz & experimental

Birdland

315 W 44th St between Eighth and Ninth Aves (212-581-3080; www.birdlandjazz.com). Subway: A, C, E to 42nd St–Port Authority. **Box office** *Reservations required; call club.* **Tickets** *$20–$50, $10 food-and-drink minimum.* **Credit** *AmEx, DC, Disc, MC, V.*
The flagship venue for midtown's recent jazz resurgence, Birdland takes its place among the neon lights of Times Square seriously. That means it's a haven for great jazz musicians (Joe Lovano, Kurt Elling) as well as performers like John Pizzarelli and Aaron Neville. The club is also notable for its roster of bands in residence. Sundays belong to the Chico O'Farrill Afro-Cuban Jazz Orchestra. Swing tubaist David Ostwald pilots the Gully Low Jazz Band every Tuesday.

Blue Note

131 W 3rd St between MacDougal St and Sixth Ave (212-475-8592; www.bluenote.net). Subway: A, C, E, B, D, F, V to W 4th St. **Box office** *Call or visit website.* **Tickets** *$10–$65, $5 food-and-drink minimum.* **Credit** *AmEx, DC, MC, V.*
"The jazz capital of the world" is how this famous club describes itself, and the big names who play are often greeted like visiting heads of state. Major players such as Pharoah Sanders, Eddie Palmieri and Abbey Lincoln have all had recent runs here. The glamour comes at a price, though: Dinner will cost you at least $25 a head.

Carnegie Hall

See p321 for listing.
Playing venerable Carnegie Hall remains synonymous with hitting the big time. While the acoustics of the main hall, the Isaac Stern Auditorium, were designed for classical music, the space has proved increasingly amenable to performers like Keith Jarrett, João Gilberto and Emmylou Harris. The newly opened Zankel Hall, a subterranean state-of-the-art, 644-seat theater, has significantly expanded the amount of pop, jazz and world music presented at Carnegie Hall.

Cornelia Street Cafe

29 Cornelia St between Bleecker and W 4th Sts (212-989-9318; corneliastreetcafe.com). Subway: A, C, E, B, D, F, V to W 4th St. **Cover** *$5–$15, $6 drink minimum; doors open at 6 and 9pm.* **Credit** *AmEx, DC, MC, V.*
Something about walking down the stairs of this Greenwich Village eatery mellows out even the scene's most adventurous jazz and world-music players, including Romanian singer Sanda Weigl and pianist Arturo O'Farrill. The result is dinner music with a contemporary edge.

55 Bar

55 Christopher St between Seventh Ave South and Waverly Pl (212-929-9883; www.55bar.com). Subway: 1, 9 to Christopher St–Sheridan Sq. **Open** *Doors open Fri, Sat 5:30pm; Sun 9:30pm.* **Cover** *free–$15.* **Credit** *Cash only.*
This Prohibition-era Greenwich Village dive has upped the quality of its jazz and blues bookings of late; you can catch Kurt Rosenwinkel, Tony Malaby and Lonnie Plaxico at reasonable prices and in a loose, friendly atmosphere.

Iridium

1650 Broadway at 50th St (212-582-2121; www.iridiumjazzclub.com). Subway: 1, 9 to 66th St–Lincoln Ctr. **Box office** *11am–11pm.* **Tickets** *$25–$35, $10 food-and-drink minimum; reservations recommended.* **Credit** *AmEx, DC, Disc, MC, V.*
Iridium lures upscale crowds with a lineup that's split between household names and those known only to the jazz-savvy. The sight lines and sound system are truly worthy of celebration. Recent guests have included Steve Lacy, Ravi Coltrane and Jimmy Scott. Monday nights belong to guitar hero Les Paul, while the Sunday brunch crowd is entertained by *Schoolhouse Rock* composer Bob Dorough.

Jazz Gallery

290 Hudson St between Dominick and Spring Sts (212-242-1063; www.jazzgallery.org). Subway: C, E to Spring St. **Box office** *Reservations strongly recommended; call club.* **Tickets** *$12–$15.* **Credit** *Cash only.*
It's a tad snug, but the acoustics at this jazz haunt make it a prime place to get intimate with the music. No wonder top-shelf musician Roy Hargrove appears

weekly. Jazz Gallery's weekend showcases have also become a draw for folks like Orrin Evans, Jason Lindner and Vijay Iyer.

Jazz Standard

116 E 27th St between Park and Lexington Aves (212-576-2232; www.jazzstandard.com). Subway: R, W, 6 to 28th St. **Box office** *Visit website.* **Tickets** *$15–$30.* **Credit** *AmEx, DC, Disc, MC, V.*

Renovation was just what the doctor ordered for the jazz den below restaurateur Danny Meyer's Blue Smoke barbecue joint (*see p184* **Smokin' hot**). Now the room's marvelous sound matches its already splendid sight lines. In keeping with the rib-sticking chow, the jazz is of the groovy, hard-swinging variety, with such musicians as organist Dr. Lonnie Smith, Larry Goldings and Cedar Walton.

Knitting Factory

See p311 for listing.

Lenox Lounge

See p208 for listing.

A street hustler named Malcolm worked here before he got religion and added *X* to his name. The hardbop outfits that jam at this classy Harlem institution proudly carry on an old tradition.

Merkin Concert Hall

See p322 for listing.

Just across the street from Lincoln Center, Merkin's polished digs provide an intimate setting for jazz and experimental acts too offbeat for Avery Fisher Hall. Thomas Buckner's Interpretations series has presented many eclectic composer-performers over the years; other recent bookings include provocative jazz pianists Andrew Hill, Jason Moran and Matthew Shipp.

Smoke

2751 Broadway between 105th and 106th Sts (212-864-6662; www.smokejazz.com). Subway: 1, 9 to 103rd St. **Open** *Sun–Thu 5pm–4am; Fri, Sat 8pm–4am.* **Cover** *Sun–Thu free, $10 drink minimum; Fri, Sat $15–$25.* **Credit** *Disc, MC, V.*

Smoke is a classy little room that's figured out how to lure patrons from both uptown and downtown. Early in the week, evenings are themed: On Sunday, it's Latin jazz; Tuesday, organ jazz; and Wednesday, funk. On weekends, internationally renowned jazz locals (George Coleman, Eddie Henderson, Cedar Walton) hit the stage, relishing the opportunity to play informal gigs in their own backyard.

Stanley H. Kaplan Penthouse at Lincoln Center

70 Lincoln Center Plaza between Broadway and Amsterdam Ave, Rose Building, tenth floor (212-875-5050; www.jazzatlincolncenter.org). Subway: B, D, E to Seventh Ave; 1, 9 to 66th St–Lincoln Ctr. **Box office** *At Alice Tully Hall (see p323).* **Tickets** *$25–$75.* **Credit** *AmEx, DC, Disc, MC, V.*

Sax appeal The Laurent Coq Quartet blows its own horn at the **Jazz Gallery**. *See p316.*

A 100-seat room with a terrace that offers a scenic view of the Hudson River, the Penthouse is the place for the Lincoln Center jazz program's duets and solo recitals. It's almost like having Andy Bey or Bill Charlap tickle the ivories in your living room.

St. Nick's Pub

773 St. Nicholas Ave at 149th St (212-283-9728). Subway: A, C, B, D to 145th St. **Cover** *$3, two-drink minimum; shows start around 9pm.* **Credit** *Cash only.*

St. Nick's may be the closest thing to an old-fashioned juke joint you're likely to find in the city. Located in Harlem's Sugar Hill section, it has live music six nights a week, a charmingly makeshift decor, a soul-food menu and mature Heineken-sipping patrons nurturing their hedonistic impulses. The music runs from bebop and vocal-driven jazz to pumping funk.

Sweet Rhythm

88 Seventh Ave South between Bleecker and Grove Sts (212-255-3626; www.sweetrhythmny.com). Subway: 1, 9 to Christopher St–Sheridan Sq. **Open** *Sun–Thu 7pm–12:30am; Fri, Sat 7pm–2am.* **Cover** *$10–$25, $10 minimum per person per set.* **Credit** *AmEx, DC, MC, V.*

This West Village space was once the jazz club Sweet Basil, so the best kind of ghosts haunt Sweet Rhythm. The proprietors stir funk and world-music acts into the club's lineup, though fine jazz from such veterans as Sonny Fortune and Gary Bartz remains on the bill.

Swing 46

349 W 46th St between Eighth and Ninth Aves (212-262-9554; www.swing46.com). Subway: A, C, E to 42nd St–Port Authority. **Cover** *$5–$10; shows start Sun–Thu 8:30pm; Fri, Sat 9:30pm.* **Credit** *MC, V.*

You don't have to throw on a zoot suit to make the scene at this midtown bastion of retro, but it could help you fit in. Bands that jump, jive and wail await you, so be sure to wear your dancin' shoes.

Tonic

See p315 for listing.

Village Vanguard

178 Seventh Ave South at Perry St (212-255-4037; www.villagevanguard.com). Subway: A, C, E, 1, 2, 3, 9 to 14th St; L to Eighth Ave. **Tickets** *$25–$30, $10 drink minimum; reservations strongly recommended.* **Credit** *Cash only.*

After 68 years, this basement club's stage—a small but mighty step-up—still hosts the crème de la crème of mainstream jazz talent (Gary Bartz, Mark Turner, Roy Hargrove). Plenty of history has been made here: John Coltrane, Miles Davis and Bill Evans have all grooved in this hallowed hall. The 16-piece Vanguard Jazz Orchestra has been the Monday-night regular for more than 30 years. Doors open at 8pm.

Blues, country & folk

B.B. King Blues Club & Grill

See p309 for listing.

Paddy Reilly's Music Bar

519 Second Ave at 29th St (212-686-1210; www.paddyreillys.com). Subway: 6 to 28th St. **Cover** *$5–$7.* **Credit** *AmEx, MC, V.*

The premier local bar for Irish rock hosts nightly music from groups such as the Prodigals, with *seisiúns* (open jams) thrown in as well. Live music begins around 9:30pm on weeknights and 10 to 11pm on weekends (Sunday's first show is at 4pm).

Rodeo Bar & Grill

375 Third Ave at 27th St (212-683-6500). Subway: 6 to 28th St. **Cover** *free; shows start at 10pm.* **Credit** *AmEx, DC, Disc, MC, V.*

This laid-back roadhouse-in-the-city (there's even sawdust on the floor) books local roots outfits and visiting country, blues and rockabilly stars like Sleepy LaBeef and Bill Kirchen.

Latin, reggae & world

Babalu

327 W 44th St between Eighth and Ninth Aves (212-262-1111; www.babaluny.com). Subway: A, C, E to 42nd St–Port Authority; N, Q, R, W, 42nd St S, 1, 2, 3, 9, 7 to 42nd St–Times Sq. **Open** *Tue, Wed 5:30–11pm; music Thu–Sat 5:30pm–2am.* **Cover** *$5–$10.* **Credit** *AmEx, Disc, MC, V.*

This 21st-century version of the Tropicana supper club featured in *I Love Lucy* heats it up with live salsa, merengue and Latin pop.

Copacabana

560 W 34th St between Tenth and Eleventh Aves (212-239-2672; www.copacabanany.com). Subway: A, C, E to 34th St–Penn Station. **Cover** *$10–$40, $30 at tables; doors open Tue 6pm; Fri, Sat 10pm.* **Credit** *AmEx, Disc, MC, V.*

Copacabana, long the city's most iconic destination for Latin music, has now become a full-fledged party palace. It's still a prime stop for salsa, *cumbia* and merengue, but in addition to booking world-renowned stars (Ruben Blades, El Gran Combo, and Tito Nieves with Conjunto Clasico), the Copa now has an alternative nook called the House Room, where dancers can spin to disco, house and Latin freestyle.

Satalla

37 W 26th St between Broadway and Sixth Ave (212-576-1155; www.satalla.com). Subway: R, W to 28th St. **Cover** *$10–$25; shows start at either 8 or 10pm.* **Credit** *AmEx, Disc, MC, V.*

Every evening at Satalla transports you to another part of the world. It's a lounge dedicated to the globalist flavor of New York, which means that you might happen upon a Celtic band tonight, and then come back tomorrow to find African drummers or a Greek singing troupe. The decor is a tad psychedelic, but the couches are so comfy that it's easy to settle into the trip.

S.O.B.'s

See p315 for listing.

Zinc Bar

90 Houston St between La Guardia Pl and Thompson St (212-477-8337; www.zincbar.com). Subway: A, C, E, B, D, F, V to W 4th St. **Open** *6pm–3:30am daily.* **Cover** *$5.* **Credit** *AmEx, DC, Disc, MC, V.*

Located where Noho meets Soho, Zinc Bar is the place to hoot and holler with die-hard night owls. The after-hours atmosphere is enhanced by the cool mix of African, flamenco, jazz, Latin and samba bands.

Flirty dancing Salsa, merengue and more get dancers grooving at **Copacabana**. *See p318.*

Summer venues

Castle Clinton

Battery Park, Battery Pl at State St (212-835-2789). Subway: E to World Trade Ctr; R, W to Rector St; 2, 3 to Park Pl; 4, 5 to Bowling Green.

Space is limited but sight lines are swell at this historic fort in the heart of Battery Park. At the summer Thursday-night concert series, music hounds are within spitting distance of performers such as Neko Case and Rosanne Cash.

Central Park SummerStage

See p255 for listing.

On a humid summer weekend, SummerStage is one of New York's great treasures. The booking policy is delightfully ecumenical, from world music (Orchestra Baobab, Bembeya Jazz) and hip-hop (Common) to country (Lyle Lovett) and dance (Basement Jaxx). Bring sunscreen and show up early, as SummerStage is no secret.

Giants Stadium

For listing, *see p329* **New York Giants**.

At Giants Stadium, you can catch biggies like U2 and 'N Sync, while airplanes zoom overhead from nearby Newark Airport. Band members look like ants, and you'll wait a long, long time for beer, but the hot dogs aren't that bad. And because it's outdoors, it's the only remaining venue in the Meadowlands complex where you can smoke.

Lincoln Center Plaza

See p322 for listing.

The home of Lincoln Center's Midsummer Night Swing (*see p254*) and Out of Doors festivals, the Plaza becomes an alfresco musical paradise in the summertime. In one week, you might hear the world's hottest Latin and African bands, followed by such acts as tenor-saxophone god Sonny Rollins or pianists McCoy Tyner and Cyrus Chestnut.

Prospect Park Bandshell

For listing, *see p254* **Celebrate Brooklyn!**

Prospect Park Bandshell is to Brooklynites what Central Park SummerStage is to Manhattan residents: the place to hear great music in the great outdoors. The programming for the summer festival Celebrate Brooklyn! mirrors the borough's diversity: The music runs from salsa (the Spanish Harlem Orchestra) and Afropop (Oliver Mtukudzi) to reggae (Capleton) and hip-hop (Talib Kweli). Prospect Park also books indie-pop touring bands and excellent modern-dance troupes.

Tommy Hilfiger at Jones Beach Theatre

Jones Beach, Long Island (516-221-1000; www.tommyhilfigerjonesbeach.com). Travel: LIRR from Penn Station, Seventh Ave at 32nd St, to Freeport, then Jones Beach bus. **Tickets** *$18–$65.* **Credit** *AmEx, MC, V.*

Even though it's far away for the carless and the sound isn't that great, you can't beat the open-air setting at this beachside amphitheater. From July to September, most of the big tours make a pit stop. Expect bookings like Aerosmith, Coldplay, Toby Keith, Alicia Keys, OutKast, Weezer and the Who.

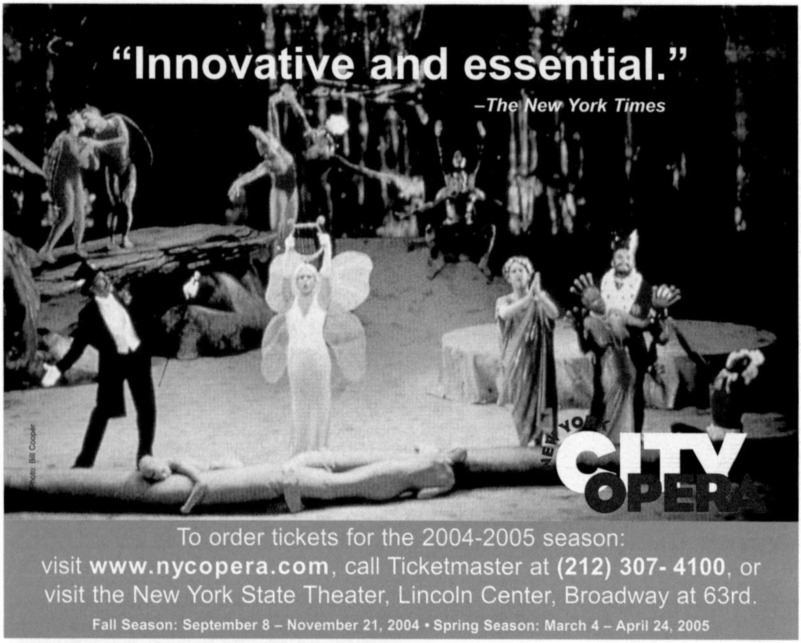
"Innovative and essential."
–The New York Times
Photo: Bill Cooper
NEW YORK CITY OPERA
To order tickets for the 2004-2005 season:
visit www.nycopera.com, call Ticketmaster at (212) 307- 4100, or
visit the New York State Theater, Lincoln Center, Broadway at 63rd.
Fall Season: September 8 – November 21, 2004 • Spring Season: March 4 – April 24, 2005

The ultimate guide to the city's nonstop nightlife
Time Out New York
Bars & Clubs
Get $100 worth of FREE DRINKS! COUPONS INSIDE
ON SALE NOW!
More than 1,000 bars, clubs, lounges, and music and comedy venues
More than 250 pages with color photos and maps
Available at newsstands, bookstores and at www.timeoutny.com/tonystore

Classical Music

If there's a single word one could use to describe the state of the local classical-music community in recent years, that word might well be *fusion*. At **Lincoln Center**, a great deal of attention has been devoted to better integrating the more traditional winter-season offerings—which have made the complex world-famous—with the more adventurous summer-season programs that have broadened its appeal enormously. The organization has also reached out from its tony campus to engage in coproductions with the funky, innovative **Brooklyn Academy of Music**. Likewise, **Carnegie Hall** teamed up with the **Miller Theatre** for a handful of recent collaborations, then made an even bigger splash with the opening of its new subterranean jewel box, **Zankel Hall**, which expands Carnegie's traditional purview to include jazz, pop and world-music artists.

Tickets

You can buy tickets directly from most venues, either in person at the box office or online. For some sites, you can also purchase tickets over the phone. However, a surcharge is generally added to tickets bought online and by phone. For more ticket information, *see p378.*

CarnegieCharge

212-247-7800; www.carnegiehall.org. **Box office** *By phone 8am–8pm daily.* **Fees** *$4.50 surcharge per ticket purchased online; $5 surcharge per ticket purchased by phone.* **Credit** *AmEx, DC, Disc, MC, V.*

Centercharge

212-721-6500. **Box office** *By phone Mon–Sat 10am–8pm; Sun noon–8pm.* **Fees** *$5.50 surcharge per ticket.* **Credit** *AmEx, Disc, MC, V.*
Centercharge sells tickets for events at Alice Tully Hall and Avery Fisher Hall, and for the Lincoln Center Festival (*see p255*).

Metropolitan Opera

212-362-6000; www.metopera.org. **Box office** *By phone Mon–Sat 10am–8pm; Sun 10am–6pm.* **Fees** *$5.50 surcharge per ticket.* **Credit** *AmEx, MC, V.*
The Met sells tickets for its own events and for those of American Ballet Theatre.

Backstage passes

It's possible to go behind the scenes at several of the city's major concert venues. **Backstage at the Met** *(212-769-7020)* shows you around the famous house during opera season, which runs from September to May; **Lincoln Center Tours** *(212-875-5350)* escorts you inside Avery Fisher and Alice Tully halls, as well as the New York State Theater; **Carnegie Hall** *(212-247-7800)* ushers you through what is perhaps the world's most famous concert hall. For a small fee, you may also sit in on rehearsals of the **New York Philharmonic** *(212-875-5656)*, usually held on the Thursday before a concert.

Concert halls

Brooklyn Academy of Music

30 Lafayette Ave between Ashland Pl and St. Felix St, Fort Greene, Brooklyn (718-636-4100; www.bam.org). Subway: B, Q, 2, 3, 4, 5 to Atlantic Ave; D, M, N, R to Pacific St; G to Fulton St. **Box office** *Mon–Sat noon–6pm; Sun noon–3:30pm (performance days only).* **Admission** *varies.* **Credit** *AmEx, MC, V.*
America's oldest academy for the performing arts has struggled with budgetary constraints (like everyone else lately), but it still manages to offer some of the freshest and most adventurous programming in the city. Every fall and winter, the Next Wave Festival provides an overview of avant-garde music, dance and theater, while the spring BAM Opera season brings lauded European productions to downtown Brooklyn. The recently renovated BAM Harvey Theater, located nearby, offers a smaller, more atmospheric setting for innovative works by such composers as Meredith Monk and Tan Dun. Meanwhile, the resident Brooklyn Philharmonic Orchestra has reached new heights of creative excellence under the direction of rising star conductor Robert Spano.

Carnegie Hall

154 W 57th St at Seventh Ave (212-247-7800; www.carnegiehall.org). Subway: B, D, E to Seventh Ave; F, N, Q, R, W to 57th St. **Box office** *Mon–Sat 11am–6pm; Sun noon–6pm.* **Admission** *varies.* **Credit** *AmEx, DC, Disc, MC, V.*
Carnegie Hall has been the talk of the town since the opening of Zankel Hall, a state-of-the-art theater located beneath venerable Isaac Stern Hall. While the biggest stars (soloists and orchestras) continue to appear upstairs, Zankel offers an eclectic mix of classical, contemporary, jazz, pop and world music. The smaller Weill Recital Hall plays host to intimate recitals and chamber-music programs.

Florence Gould Hall

French Institute–Alliance Française, 55 E 59th St between Madison and Park Aves (212-355-6160; www.fiaf.org). Subway: N, R, W to Fifth

► For information on concerts, times and locations, see ***Time Out New York***'s Classical & Opera listings.
► The **Theatre Development Fund** (*see p337*) provides information on all music events via its NYC/Onstage service.

Wunderbar The Vienna Symphony Orchestra performs at **Avery Fisher Hall**. *See p323.*

Ave–59th St. **Box office** *Tue–Fri 11am–7pm; Sat 11am–3pm.* **Admission** *$10–$35.* **Credit** *AmEx, MC, V.*
Programming in this small, comfortable hall has a decidedly French tone, in both artists and repertoire.

Merkin Concert Hall

Kaufman Center, 129 W 67th St between Broadway and Amsterdam Ave (212-501-3330; www.kaufman-center.org). Subway: 1, 9 to 66th St–Lincoln Ctr. **Box office** *Sun–Thu noon–7pm; Fri noon–4pm.* **Admission** *$10–$25.* **Credit** *AmEx, MC, V (for advance purchases only).*
Don't make the mistake of overlooking this gem, tucked away on a side street in the shadow of Lincoln Center. In addition to a robust mix of early music and avant-garde programming, Merkin has begun to offer still more disparate fare, including forward-thinking jazz artists and the always eclectic New York Festival of Song (which took up residency in fall 2003). Regular programs sponsored by WNYC-FM afford opportunities to interact with composers and performers in an appealing setting.

New Jersey Performing Arts Center

See p314 for listing.
You may think that Newark's sumptuous performing-arts complex is too far away to consider, but you'd be mistaken: It takes only 15 to 20 minutes to reach NJPAC from midtown, and the rewards are worth the trip. Big-name acts that may be sold out at Manhattan venues can often be found in the center's two halls, and some performers offer programs different from those they'll be playing in concurrent Gotham gigs.

92nd Street Y

See p271 for listing.
The Y emphasizes traditional orchestral, solo and chamber masterworks. But it also fosters the careers of young musicians, and has recently begun to seriously investigate European and Jewish-American music traditions in innovative, far-reaching ways.

Lincoln Center

Built in the 1960s, this massive complex is the nexus of Manhattan's performing-arts scene. Lincoln Center hosts lectures and symposia in the Rose Building, in addition to events in the main halls: **Alice Tully**, **Avery Fisher**, **Metropolitan Opera House**, **New York State Theater**, and the Vivian Beaumont and Mitzi E. Newhouse theaters (*see p323*). Also on the premises are the **Juilliard School** (*see p326*) and Fiorello La Guardia High School of the Performing Arts, which frequently hosts professional performances. Big stars like Anne-Sophie Mutter, Murray Perahia and Emanuel Ax are Lincoln Center's meat-and-potatoes. However, recent efforts by management have focused on narrowing the great divide between such old-school stalwarts as the flagship **Great Performers** season, and newer crowd-pleasers like the relatively audacious multidisciplinary **Lincoln Center Festival** in July (*see also p255*).

Lincoln Center

65th St at Columbus Ave (212-546-2656; www.lincolncenter.org). Subway: 1, 9 to 66th St–Lincoln Ctr.

This is the main entry point for Lincoln Center, but the venues that follow are spread out around the square of blocks from 62nd to 66th Streets, between Amsterdam and Columbus Avenues.

Alice Tully Hall

212-875-5050. **Box office** *Mon–Sat 11am–6pm; Sun noon–6pm; also open for 30 minutes after the start of a performance.* **Admission** *free–$75.* **Credit** *AmEx, Disc, MC, V.*

Built to house the Chamber Music Society of Lincoln Center *(212-875-5788; www.chambermusicsociety.org)*, Alice Tully Hall somehow makes its 1,096 seats feel cozy. It has no center aisle, and the rows have extra legroom. Its Art of the Song recital series is one of the most extensive in town.

Avery Fisher Hall

212-875-5030. **Box office** *Mon–Sat 10am–6pm; Sun noon–6pm.* **Admission** *$20–$114.* **Credit** *AmEx, Disc, MC, V.*

This handsome, comfortable 2,700-seat hall is the headquarters of the New York Philharmonic *(212-875-5656; www.nyphilharmonic.org)*, the country's oldest orchestra (founded in 1842) and one of its finest. It holds less expensive, early-evening concerts and open rehearsals on a regular basis. The hall presents top international soloists and ensembles in its Great Performers series, and every summer, fans flock to the renowned Mostly Mozart Festival (*see p255*).

Metropolitan Opera House

212-362-6000; www.metopera.org. **Box office** *Mon–Sat 10am–8pm; Sun noon–6pm.* **Admission** *$12–$295.* **Credit** *AmEx, Disc, MC, V.*

The Met is the grandest of the Lincoln Center buildings, and a spectacular place to see and hear opera. It's home to the Metropolitan Opera from September to May, and also to major visiting companies, such as a recent monthlong residency by the Kirov Opera of St. Petersburg, Russia. Opera's biggest stars (think Domingo, Fleming and Gheorghiu) appear here regularly, and artistic director James Levine has made the orchestra into a true symphonic force. Audiences are knowledgeable and fiercely partisan, with subscriptions remaining in families for generations. Still, the Met has tried to be more inclusive in recent years; digital English-language subtitles appear on screens affixed to railings in front of each seat, convenient for the novice and unobtrusive to his more seasoned neighbor. Tickets are expensive, and unless you can afford good seats, the view won't be great; standing-room-only tickets start at $12, and you'll have to wait in line on Saturday mornings to buy them. Innovative productions take the stage from time to time, but eye-popping, gasp-inducing sets by directors like Zeffirelli remain the gold standard here.

New York State Theater

212-870-5570. **Box office** *Mon 10am–7:15pm; Tue–Sat 10am–8:15pm; Sun 11:30am–7:15pm.* **Admission** *$25–$100 (Mon–Fri), $30–$110 (Sat, Sun).* **Credit** *AmEx, DC, Disc, MC, V.*

NYST houses the New York City Ballet *(www.nycballet.com)* as well as the New York City Opera *(www.nycopera.com)*—the latter of which has tried to overcome its second-best reputation by being both ambitious and defiantly populist. CityOp is the first place to catch rising young American singers (many of whom eventually make the trek across the plaza to the Met), and its casts and productions are often far younger and sexier than those of its more patrician counterpart. CityOp has an admirable commitment to the American repertoire, from offbeat fare by John Phillip Sousa to new works by Mark Adamo and Jake Heggie, as well as musical-theater gems by Stephen Sondheim. The company is also known for its stellar productions of Handel operas. Ultimately, CityOp is much cooler than its stodgier neighbor—and tickets are about half the price.

Walter Reade Theater

212-875-5600. **Box office** *2–6pm.* **Admission** *$12–$15.*

The Walter Reade Theater's acoustics are less than fabulous; still, the Chamber Music Society uses the space regularly, and the Great Performers series offers Sunday-morning events fueled by pastries and hot beverages sold in the lobby.

Opera

The Metropolitan Opera and New York City Opera may be the leading lights in the local firmament, but they're hardly the only game in town. Feisty upstarts, in addition to longstanding grassroots companies, assure that Manhattan's operaphiles are among the best served in the world. Call the organizations or visit their websites for ticket prices, schedules and venue details. The music schools (*see p326*) have opera programs, too.

Amato Opera Theatre

319 Bowery at 2nd St (212-228-8200; www.amato.org). Subway: B, D, F, V to Broadway–Lafayette St; 6 to Bleecker St. **Admission** *$30, seniors and children $25.* **Credit** *AmEx, Disc, MC, V.*

New York's beloved mom-and-pop opera shop offers charming, fully staged productions in a theater only 20 feet wide—it's almost like watching opera in your living room. Casting can be inconsistent, but many well-known singers have performed here.

American Opera Projects

South Oxford Space, 138 South Oxford St between Atlantic Ave and Hanson Pl, Fort Greene, Brooklyn (718-398-4024). Subway: B, Q, 2, 3, 4, 5 to Atlantic Ave; C to Lafayette St; D, M, N, R to Pacific St. **Admission** *varies.* **Credit** *Cash only.*

Renée Fleming in *La Traviata* at the **Metropolitan Opera House**. *See p323.*

AOP is not so much an opera company as a living, breathing workshop that allows you the opportunity to follow a new work from gestation to completion.

Dicapo Opera Theater

184 E 76th St between Lexington and Third Aves (212-288-9438; www.dicapo.com). Subway: 6 to 77th St. **Admission** *$47.50.* **Credit** *MC, V.*
This top-notch chamber-opera troupe benefits from City Opera–quality singers performing on intelligently designed, small-scale sets in the basement of St. Jean Baptiste Church.

New York Gilbert & Sullivan Players

For listing, see p325 **Symphony Space**.
Is Victorian camp your vice? This troupe presents a rotating schedule of the Big Three (*H.M.S. Pinafore*, *The Mikado* and *The Pirates of Penzance*), plus lesser-known G&S works.

Other venues

Bargemusic

Fulton Ferry Landing, next to the Brooklyn Bridge, Brooklyn Heights, Brooklyn (718-624-4061; www.bargemusic.org). Subway: A, C to High St; F to York St. **Admission** *$20–$40.* **Credit** *Cash only.*
This former coffee barge presents four chamber concerts a week—and a great view of the Manhattan skyline. It's a magical experience, but bundle up in winter. When the weather warms, you can enjoy a drink on the upper deck during intermission.

Frick Collection

See p148 for listing.
Concerts in this museum's elegantly appointed concert hall are a rare treat, featuring lesser-known but world-class performers in an intimate setting. Tickets are free, but acquiring them can be a chore: Written requests must be submitted in advance, and tickets are often gone weeks or months before the actual performance. A line for returned tickets forms one hour before each event.

The Kaye Playhouse

Hunter College, 68th St between Park and Lexington Aves (212-772-4448; www.kayeplayhouse.com). Subway: 6 to 68th St–Hunter College. **Box office** *Mon–Sat noon–6pm.* **Admission** *$10–$70.* **Credit** *AmEx, MC, V.*
Named for its benefactors—comedian Danny Kaye and his wife, Sylvia—this refurbished theater offers an eclectic program of professional music and dance.

The Kitchen

See p345 for listing.
Occupying a 19th-century icehouse, the Kitchen has been a meeting place for the avant-garde in music, dance and theater for more than 30 years. Show prices range from free to $25.

Kosciuszko Foundation

15 E 65th St at Fifth Ave (212-734-2130; www.kosciuszkofoundation.org). Subway: F to Lexington Ave–63rd St; 6 to 68th St–Hunter College. **Admission** *$15–$30.* **Credit** *MC, V.*
This East Side townhouse hosts a chamber-music series with a mission: Each program must feature at least one work by a Polish composer. You're less likely to choke on Chopin than to hear something novel by Bacewicz, Paderewski or Szymanowski.

Metropolitan Museum of Art

See p149 for listing.
To mark its 50th year of presenting live music, the Metropolitan Museum has pulled out all the stops with this season's programming: Respected veterans like the Beaux Arts Trio and the Guarneri Quartet have been rewarded with extensive series of their own, and the museum has also established a youthful resident ensemble, Metropolitan Museum Artists in Concert.

Miller Theatre at Columbia University

Broadway at 116th St (212-854-7799; www.millertheatre.com). Subway: 1, 9 to 116th St–Columbia Univ. **Box office** *Mon–Fri noon–6pm.* **Admission** *$20, students $12.* **Credit** *AmEx, MC, V.*
Columbia's Miller Theatre, which celebrates its 15th year this season, has singlehandedly made contemporary classical music sexy in New York City. The credit belongs to executive director George Steel, who proved that presenting challenging fare by such composers as Ligeti, Birtwistle and Zorn in a casual, unaffected setting could attract a young audience—and hang on to it.

New York Public Library for the Performing Arts

See p162 for listing. **Admission** *free.*

The library's Bruno Walter Auditorium regularly hosts recitals, solo performances and lectures.

Symphony Space

2537 Broadway at 95th St (212-864-5400; www.symphonyspace.org). Subway: 1, 2, 3, 9 to 96th St. **Box office** *Tue–Sun noon–7pm.* **Admission** *varies.* **Credit** *AmEx, MC, V ($5 per-order surcharge for tickets purchased by phone).*

The programming at Symphony Space is eclectic; best bets are the annual Wall to Wall marathons: a full day of music featuring a composer or theme, from Johann Sebastian Bach to Joni Mitchell. The marathons are free, so lines may go around the block.

Tishman Auditorium

The New School, 66 W 12th St at Sixth Ave (212-243-9937). Subway: F, V to 14th St; L to Sixth Ave. **Admission** *free–$14.* **Credit** *Cash only.*

The New School's modestly priced Schneider Concerts chamber-music series features up-and-coming young musicians, as well as established artists, who play here for a fraction of the prices charged elsewhere.

Churches

From sacred to secular, a thrilling variety of music is performed in New York's churches. Many resident choirs are out of this world, while superb acoustics and serene surroundings make churches particularly attractive venues. Bonus: Some concerts are free or very cheap.

Cathedral of St. John the Divine

See p116 for listing. **Box office** *10am–6pm.* **Admission** *varies.* **Credit** *AmEx, MC, V.*

The stunning neo-Gothic, 3,000-seat sanctuary provides a heavenly atmosphere for the church's own choir and visiting ensembles, though the acoustics are reliably murky.

Christ and St. Stephen's Church

120 W 69th St between Columbus Ave and Broadway (212-787-2755; www.csschurch.org). Subway: 1, 2, 3, 9 to 72nd St. **Admission** *varies.* **Credit** *Cash only.*

This West Side church offers one of the most diverse concert rosters in the city.

Church of the Ascension

12 W 11th St between Fifth and Sixth Aves (212-254-8553; www.voicesofascension.org). Subway: R, W to 8th St–NYU. **Admission** *$10–$50.* **Credit** *MC, V (for advance purchases only).*

There's a first-rate professional choir, the Voices of Ascension, at this little Village church. You can catch the choir at Lincoln Center on occasion, but home turf is the best place to hear it.

Church of St. Ignatius Loyola

980 Park Ave at 84th St (212-288-2520; www.saintignatiusloyola.org). Subway: 4, 5, 6 to 86th St. **Admission** *$10–$40.* **Credit** *MC, V.*

The Sacred Music in a Sacred Space series is a high point of Upper East Side music culture. Lincoln Center has also begun to take advantage of the church's fine acoustics and prime location.

Corpus Christi Church

529 W 121st St between Amsterdam Ave and Broadway (212-666-9266; www.mb1800.org). Subway: 1, 9 to 116th St–Columbia Univ. **Admission** *varies.* **Credit** *MC, V.*

Early-music fans can get their fix from Music Before 1800, a series that regularly imports the world's leading antiquarian artists and ensembles.

St. Bartholomew's Church

109 E 50th St between Park and Lexington Aves (212-378-0248; www.stbarts.org). Subway: E, V to Lexington Ave–53rd St; 6 to 51st St. **Admission** *varies.* **Credit** *AmEx, MC, V.*

This magnificent church hosts one of the city's most ambitious choral-music series every Sunday in summer, and fills the rest of the year with outstanding performances by resident ensembles and guests.

St. Thomas Church Fifth Avenue

1 W 53rd St at Fifth Ave (212-757-7013; www.saintthomaschurch.org). Subway: E, V to Fifth Ave–53rd St. **Admission** *$15–$60.* **Credit** *AmEx, MC, V.*

The choir of **St. Ignatius Loyola.**

Arts & Entertainment

String theory Former students perform in one of the chamber-music recitals at **Juilliard**.

The country's only fully accredited choir school for boys keeps the great Anglican choral tradition alive and well in New York. St. Thomas's annual performance of Handel's *Messiah* is a must-see.

Trinity Church/ St. Paul's Chapel

Broadway at Wall St (212-602-0747; www.trinitywallstreet.org). Subway: R, W to Rector St; 4, 5 to Wall St. **Admission** *Noonday Concerts series $2 donation.* **Credit** *Cash only.*

Historic Trinity, in the heart of the Financial District, plays host to the inexpensive Noonday Concerts series. Performances are held at 1pm on Mondays at St. Paul's Chapel *(Broadway at Fulton St)*, and on Thursdays at Trinity Church.

Schools

Juilliard and the **Manhattan School of Music** are renowned for their students, faculty and artists-in-residence, all of whom regularly perform for free or at low cost. Lately, **Mannes** has made great strides to rise to the same level. Noteworthy music and innovative programming can also be found at several other colleges and schools in the city.

Brooklyn Center for the Performing Arts at Brooklyn College

Campus Rd at Hillel Pl, one block west of the junction of Flatbush and Nostrand Aves, Flatbush, Brooklyn (718-951-4543; www.brooklyncenter.com). Subway: 2, 5 to Flatbush Ave–Brooklyn College. **Box office** *Tue–Sat 1–6pm.* **Admission** *$20–$50.* **Credit** *AmEx, MC, V.*

While its bread-and-butter is in booking pop stars on tour, this hall is also a destination for traveling opera troupes and performers of international acclaim.

The Juilliard School

60 Lincoln Center Plaza, Broadway at 65th St (212-769-7406; www.juilliard.edu). Subway: 1, 9 to 66th St–Lincoln Ctr. **Admission** *usually free.*

New York's premier conservatory stages weekly concerts by student soloists, orchestras and chamber ensembles, as well as elaborate opera productions that rival many professional presentations.

Manhattan School of Music

120 Claremont Ave at 122nd St (212-749-2802, ext 4428; www.msmnyc.edu). Subway: 1, 9 to 125th St. **Admission** *usually free.*

MSM offers master classes, recitals and off-site concerts by its students and faculty, and by visiting pros. The American String Quartet, in residence since 1984, gives concerts regularly, and the Augustine Guitar Series offers recitals by top soloists.

Mannes College of Music

150 W 85th St between Columbus and Amsterdam Aves (212-580-0210; www.mannes.edu). Subway: B, C, 1, 9 to 86th St. **Admission** *usually free.*

In addition to offering student concerts and faculty recitals, Mannes regularly mounts ambitious, historically themed concert series. The theme for 2004's festival is The Flowering of Romanticism: From Schumann to Brahms.

Sports & Fitness

So you like to watch? Fine with us. Prefer to play? Even better.

This city is a sports fan's dream. The metro area is home to three pro hockey teams, three basketball teams, two football teams, as well as two major-league and two minor-league baseball teams. You can find Irish hurling in the Bronx, an amateur cricket league supported by Brooklyn's West Indian community, and local facsimiles of World Cup soccer rivalries, in parks all over the city. Gyms (*see p333*) have long lists of traditional and offbeat exercise classes, in addition to every type of fitness equipment; massive sports complexes like Chelsea Piers have brought suburban-style recreational space to the city. You can kayak in the Hudson, go ice-skating at Rockefeller Center or ride a bike along well-maintained park trails in all five boroughs—and even over the George Washington Bridge to New Jersey. While you're checking out the city you'll be burning off last night's four-star meal.

Spectator sports

Baseball

In this town, from April through October, you're either a Yankees fan or a Mets fan. Please decide *now.* The American League's **Yankees** are the classic favorites, the team of Rudy Giuliani and Billy Crystal. This is the team with historical clout—Babe Ruth and the infamous "Murderer's Row" in the '20s, Mantle and Maris in the '60s—as well as current clout: The Bronx Bombers have appeared in the playoffs every year since 1996. The National League's **Mets** are the relatively new kids on the block. They represent a history forged by the old Brooklyn Dodgers, and their lovable underdog personality keeps many baseball fans pulling for them year after year. Minor-league excitement returned to the city in 2001, when the **Staten Island Yankees** and **Brooklyn Cyclones** (the Mets' minor-league team) opened new ballparks, both of which offer wonderful cityscape settings.

Brooklyn Cyclones

KeySpan Park, 1904 Surf Ave between West 17th and West 19th Sts, Coney Island, Brooklyn (718-449-8497; www.brooklyncyclones.com). Subway: D to Coney Island–Stillwell Ave. **Box office** *Mon–Fri 10am–4pm; Sat 10am–3pm.* **Tickets** *$5–$11.* **Credit** *AmEx, MC, V.*

New York Mets

Shea Stadium, 123-01 Roosevelt Ave at 126th St, Flushing, Queens (718-507-8499; www.mets.com). Subway: 7 to Willets Point–Shea Stadium. **Box office** *Mon–Fri 9am–6pm; Sat, Sun 9am–5pm.* **Tickets** *$8–$53.* **Credit** *AmEx, Disc, MC, V.*

New York Yankees

Yankee Stadium, River Ave at 161st St, Bronx (718-293-6000; www.yankees.com). Subway: B, D, 4 to 161st St–Yankee Stadium. **Box office** *Mon–Fri 9am–5pm; Sat 10am–3pm and during games.* **Tickets** *$8–$65.* **Credit** *AmEx, Disc, MC, V.*

Staten Island Yankees

For listing, *see p142* **Richmond County Ballpark**.

Basketball

Two National Basketball Association teams, the **New York Knicks** and the **New Jersey Nets**, dominate the local roundball scene from October through April. And while the Knicks had a long run in most New Yorkers' hearts, the Nets are coming off two consecutive NBA Finals appearances. The Knicks play at Madison Square Garden, the "world's most famous arena," and the seats are generally filled with true basketball diehards (like Spike Lee), while Nets games (at the Continental Airlines Arena in New Jersey) are more family-friendly. The ladies of the WNBA's **New York Liberty** hold court at MSG in summer.

New Jersey Nets

Continental Airlines Arena, East Rutherford, NJ (box office 201-935-3900, Nets tickets 800-7NJ-NETS; www.nba.com/nets). Travel: NJ Transit Meadowlands Sports Complex bus from Port Authority Bus Terminal (212-564-8484), Eighth Ave at 42nd St; $3.25 each way. **Tickets** *$10–$95.* **Credit** *AmEx, DC, Disc, MC, V.*

► ***Time Out New York*** lists upcoming games played by area teams.
► For details on major sporting events, contact **NYC & Company** *(212-484-1222; www.nycvisit.com).*
► Visit **www.nyc.gov/sports** for the latest news on all professional sports in the city.

Bronx cheer One of the best reasons for visiting the borough is **Yankee Stadium**. *See p327.*

New York Knicks

Madison Square Garden, Seventh Ave between 31st and 33rd Sts (box office 212-465-6741; www.nba.com/knicks). Subway: A, C, E, 1, 2, 3, 9 to 34th St–Penn Station. **Box office** *Mon–Sat noon–6pm.* **Tickets** *$27–$100.* **Credit** *AmEx, DC, Disc, MC, V.*

New York Liberty

Madison Square Garden, Seventh Ave between 31st and 33rd Sts (box office 212-465-6741; www.wnba.com/liberty). Subway: A, C, E, 1, 2, 3, 9 to 34th St–Penn Station. **Box office** *Mon–Sat noon–6pm.* **Tickets** *$10–$65.* **Credit** *AmEx, DC, Disc, MC, V.*

Boxing

Church Street Boxing Gym

25 Park Pl between Broadway and Church St (212-571-1333; www.nyboxinggym.com). Subway: 2, 3 to Park Pl; 4, 5, 6 to Brooklyn Bridge–City Hall. **Open** *Call or visit website for schedule.* **Tickets** *$20–$30.* **Credit** *Cash only.*

Church Street is a workout gym and amateur-boxing venue, housed in an atmospheric cellar. Evander Holyfield, Mike Tyson and other heavy hitters have trained here before Garden matches. About ten times a year, on Fridays, the gym hosts white-collar bouts that draw a young, single, energetic crowd.

Gleason's Gym

83 Front St between Main and Washington Sts, Dumbo, Brooklyn (718-797-2872; www.gleasonsgym.net). Subway: F to York St. **Open** *Call or visit website for schedule.* **Tickets** *$15.* **Credit** *Disc, MC, V.*

Occupying a nondescript second-floor space in an industrial Brooklyn neighborhood, Gleason's is *the* professional boxer's address in New York. The "sweet scientists" who have trained at the city's most storied gym include Muhammad Ali and Jake "Raging Bull" La Motta; these days, you'll run into lots of new-immigrant contenders. Monthly white-collar fights draw doctors, lawyers and stockbrokers—in and out of the ring.

Madison Square Garden

Seventh Ave between 31st and 33rd Sts (box office 212-465-6741; www.thegarden.com). Subway: A, C, E, 1, 2, 3, 9 to 34th St–Penn Station. **Box office** *Mon–Sat noon–6pm. All advance tickets must be purchased through Ticketmaster (212-307-7171; www.ticketmaster.com).* **Tickets** *$30–$305.* **Credit** *AmEx, DC, Disc, MC, V.*

Once the country's premier venue for boxing, the arena still hosts occasional pro fights. It also remains the site of the city's Golden Gloves amateur championships.

Dog show

Westminster Kennel Club Dog Show

Madison Square Garden, Seventh Ave between 31st and 33rd Sts (box office 212-465-6741; www.westminsterkennelclub.org). Subway: A, C, E, 1, 2, 3, 9 to 34th St–Penn Station. **Box office** *Mon–Sat noon–6pm.* **Tickets** *$41–$97.* **Credit** *AmEx, DC, Disc, MC, V.*

Each February, America's most prestigious dog show prances into Madison Square Garden for the oldest sporting event in the country. This is your chance to check out some of the most beautiful, well-trained pooches on the planet—and to be reminded more than once of Christopher Guest's hilarious *Best in Show*.

Football

From September through December—and often into the playoffs in January—New York fans live and breathe football. Officially, every **Giants** and **Jets** home game is sold out, but the teams sometimes release a few seats (those that weren't claimed by the visiting team) on the day of the game. Call for availability on the Friday before kickoff. You can also try your luck on eBay or (if you're discreet) with scalpers. Fans of the fast-paced, high-scoring arena-football league can truck out to Nassau Coliseum to see the **New York Dragons**, who play from February to May.

New York Dragons

Nassau Veterans Memorial Coliseum, 1255 Hempstead Tpke, Uniondale, Long Island (516-794-4100, tickets 866-AFL-TIXX; www.newyorkdragons.com). Travel: From Penn Station, Seventh Ave at 32nd St, take LIRR (www.lirr.org) to Hempstead, then N70, N71 or N72 bus to the coliseum. **Tickets** *$15–$65.* **Credit** *AmEx, Disc, MC, V.*

New York Giants

Giants Stadium, East Rutherford, NJ (box office 201-935-8222; www.giants.com). Travel: NJ Transit Meadowlands Sports Complex bus from Port Authority Bus Terminal (212-564-8484), Eighth Ave at 42nd St; $3.25 each way. **Tickets** *$60–$80.* **Credit** *Cash only.*

New York Jets

Giants Stadium, East Rutherford, NJ (box office 516-560-8200; www.newyorkjets.com). Travel: NJ Transit Meadowlands Sports Complex bus from Port Authority Bus Terminal (212-564-8484), Eighth Ave at 42nd St; $3.25 each way. **Tickets** *$60–$75.* **Credit** *Cash only.*

Hockey

The 2003 Stanley Cup champion **New Jersey Devils** are the team to beat; the two other local teams—the **New York Rangers** and **Islanders**—continue to struggle. Still, for many old-school hockey fans, the only games worth seeing are when the Rangers play the Garden. Tickets for all three teams are on sale throughout the season, which runs from October through April.

New Jersey Devils

Continental Airlines Arena, East Rutherford, NJ (201-935-6050, box office 201-935-3900; www.newjerseydevils.com). Travel: NJ Transit Meadowlands Sports Complex bus from Port Authority Bus Terminal (212-564-8484), Eighth Ave at 42nd St; $3.25 each way. **Tickets** *$20–$90.* **Credit** *AmEx, MC, V.*

New York Islanders

Nassau Veterans Memorial Coliseum, 1255 Hempstead Tpke, Uniondale, Long Island (800-882-4753; www.newyorkislanders.com). Travel: From Penn Station, Seventh Ave at 32nd St, take LIRR (www.lirr.org) to Hempstead, then N70, N71 or N72 bus to the coliseum. **Box office** *9:30am–4:45pm.* **Tickets** *$25–$140.* **Credit** *AmEx, MC, V.*

New York Rangers

Madison Square Garden, Seventh Ave between 31st and 33rd Sts (box office 212-465-6741; www.newyorkrangers.com). Subway: A, C, E, 1, 2, 3, 9 to 34th St–Penn Station. **Box office** *Mon–Sat noon–6pm.* **Tickets** *$30–$155.* **Credit** *AmEx, DC, Disc, MC, V.*

Horse racing

There are three major racetracks near Manhattan: Thoroughbreds run at **Aqueduct**, **Belmont** and the **Meadowlands**. If you don't want to trek to Queens or New Jersey, head to an Off-Track Betting (OTB) outpost to catch the action and (reliably seedy) atmosphere.

Top dog A **Westminster** winner. *See p328.*

Aqueduct Racetrack

110th St at Rockaway Blvd, Ozone Park, Queens (718-641-4700; www.aqueduct-racetrack.com). Subway: A to Aqueduct–North Conduit. **Races** *Thoroughbred Oct–May Wed–Sun.* **Admission** *clubhouse $2, grandstand $1.* **Credit** *Cash only.*
The Wood Memorial, held each April (April 10 in 2004), is a test run for promising three-year-olds headed for the Kentucky Derby.

Belmont Park

2150 Hempstead Tpke, Elmont, Long Island (718-641-4700; www.nyra.com/belmont). Travel: From Penn Station, Seventh Ave at 32nd St, take LIRR (www.lirr.org) to Belmont Park. **Races** *Thoroughbred May–Jul, Sept, Oct Wed–Sun.* **Admission** *clubhouse $4, grandstand $2.* **Credit** *Cash only.*
For review, *see below* **Belmont: A horse, a course**.

Meadowlands Racetrack

East Rutherford, NJ (201-935-8500; www.thebigm.com). Travel: NJ Transit Meadowlands Sports Complex bus from Port Authority Bus Terminal (212-564-8484), Eighth Ave at 42nd St; $3.25 each way. **Races** *Harness Jan–Aug; Thoroughbred Sept–Dec; check website for days.* **Admission** *clubhouse $3, grandstand $1.* **Credit** *Cash only.*

Belmont: A horse, a course

Fresh air, a scenic setting and nine chances a day to hit it big—no wonder thousands of would-be winners make the trip to **Belmont Park** racetrack (*see above*) every day during the spring and fall racing seasons. Belmont's claim to fame is, of course, the Belmont Stakes, run every June by the year's top three-year-olds. This renowned race is the last, longest leg of the Triple Crown, the annual three-race series that begins with the Kentucky Derby. Since 1875, only 11 horses (including the legendary Secretariat) have won all three. However, nearly every weekend features some notable stakes race. And you don't have to know a thing about racing to have a great day here.

Set amid towering oak trees on the Queens/Nassau border, the vintage (1905) track is as green as Central Park, complete with a lake in the infield. Picnic tables line the saddling ring and home stretch; bars and snack counters dot the grounds, grandstand and clubhouse. Plenty of first-time visitors show up just to enjoy a sunny day out of the city, or to see the horses—breathtaking aristocrats, every one—going through their paces in the paddock area before each race. Still, few trackgoers can resist the lure of the pari-mutuel betting windows; by the end of the day, the park is carpeted with scads of discarded tickets.

Into the turn at **Belmont**.

Spread over 430 acres, this charming course is also a thriving world unto itself. Belmont teems with homegrown lingo, lore and characters that sound like they just stepped off the set of *Guys and Dolls*. Nearly everyone—from Jesse the shuttle-bus driver to Yuri the barber ($15 for a shave and a haircut)—has a pick of the day that he *swears* can't lose. Belmont's unofficial mascot is red-jacketed, wisecracking Sam the Bugler, a conservatory-trained trumpeter who toots the "Call to the Post" before each race. "I got the job when the last bugler hit the Pick Six for a hundred and thirty grand," he says.

A lot of Belmont regulars consider picking winners their "real" job, but 31-year-old Kelly Gecewicz—the track's official handicapper—actually gets paid for it. Her big hit: A 70-to-1 colt named Skullbuster who paid $142 on a $2 bet. Kelly's daily picks can be found in the track's *Post Parade* program.

Over the loudspeakers, you'll hear the mellifluous baritone of race-caller nonpareil Tom Durkin, the voice of Belmont (as well as of Aqueduct, Saratoga, the Kentucky Derby and the Breeders' Cup Championship). Durkin is celebrated for his fast-tongued fluency with horse names like Shining City Shoes and his spine-tingling cry of "too close to call!"

Breezy Bicyclists and joggers can cruise six miles of pathway on the **Hudson River greenway**.

The Meadowlands runs both "trots" and "flats" (Thoroughbreds). Top harness racers compete for more than $1 million in the prestigious Hambletonian, held the first Saturday in August.

Soccer

Futbol may not yet rival the popularity of football in America, but soccer has plenty of fans around town. You'll find pickup games in many city parks, and for pro action, check out the **MetroStars**, who play across the river in New Jersey, at Giants Stadium.

MetroStars

Giants Stadium, East Rutherford, NJ (888-4-METRO-TIX; www.metrostars.com). Travel: NJ Transit Meadowlands Sports Complex bus from Port Authority Bus Terminal (212-564-8484), Eighth Ave at 42nd St; $3.25 each way. **Box office** *Mon–Fri 8:30am–6:30pm.* **Tickets** *$18–$75.* **Credit** *AmEx, Disc, MC, V.*

Tennis

U.S. Open

USTA National Tennis Center, Flushing Meadows–Corona Park, Queens (718-760-6200, tickets 866-673-6849; www.usopen.org). Subway: 7 to Willets Point–Shea Stadium. **Tickets** *$22–$115.* **Credit** *AmEx, MC, V.*

Tickets go on sale in May for this grand-slam thriller, which features the game's biggest names. Check website for match schedule.

Active sports

Visit New York Sports Online *(www.nysol.com)* for a comprehensive roundup of recreational sports options in the city. And always call ahead, in case there are last-minute changes.

Bicycling

Hundreds of miles of paths make it easy for the recreational biker to get pretty much anywhere in New York. The city continues construction on the paths that run alongside the East and Hudson rivers, and one day soon, it will be possible for riders to completely circumnavigate the island of Manhattan. Visitors can take a DIY trip using rental bikes and path maps, or go on organized rides. A word of caution: Cycling in the city is serious business. Riders must stay alert and abide by traffic laws, especially because drivers and pedestrians often don't. If you keep your ears and eyes open—and wear a helmet—you'll enjoy an adrenaline-pumping ride.

Bike-path maps

Department of City Planning Bookstore
22 Reade St between Broadway and Centre St (212-720-3667). Subway: J, M, Z to Chambers St; R, W to City Hall; 4, 5, 6 to Brooklyn Bridge–City Hall. **Open** *Mon–Fri 10am–4pm.* The Department of City Planning oversees the bike-path system. *The Bicycle Master Plan* outlines nearly 1,000 miles of cycling lanes.

Rink cycle Prometheus watches over skaters at **Rockefeller Center**. *See p333.*

Transportation Alternatives *115 W 30th St between Sixth and Seventh Aves, suite 1207 (212-629-8080; www.transalt.org). Subway: B, D, F, V, N, Q, R, W to 34th St–Herald Sq; 1, 2, 3, 9 to 34th St–Penn Station.* **Open** *Mon–Fri 10am–5pm.* This nonprofit citizens' group lobbies for more bike-friendly streets. You can pop into the office to get free maps, or download them from the website.

Bike rentals

Gotham Bike Shop *112 West Broadway between Duane and Reade Sts (212-732-2453; www.gothambikes.com). Subway: A, C, 1, 2, 3, 9 to Chambers St.* **Open** *Mon–Sat 10am–6:30pm; Sun 10:30am–5pm.* **Fees** *$30 for 24hrs, plus $5 helmet rental.* **Credit** *AmEx, MC, V.* Rent a sturdy set of wheels from this shop and ride the short distance to the Hudson River esplanade.

Loeb Boathouse *Central Park, entrance on Fifth Ave at 72nd St (212-517-2233; www.centralparknyc.org). Subway: 6 to 68th St–Hunter College.* **Open** *Apr–Nov 10am–5pm (weather permitting).* **Fees** *$9–$25 per hour (includes helmet).* **Credit** *Cash only.* If you want to cruise through Central Park, this is the place; it has more than 100 bikes available. Large groups should make reservations.

Organized bike rides

See also p70.

Fast and Fabulous *212-567-7160; www.fastnfab.org.* This "queer and queer-friendly" riding group leads tours throughout the year, usually meeting in Central Park and heading out of the city. Visit the website for a comprehensive calendar.

Time's Up! *212-802-8222; www.times-up.org.* An alternative-transportation advocacy group, Time's Up! sponsors rides year-round, including Critical Mass, in which hundreds of cyclists and skaters meet at Union Square Park (7pm on the last Friday of every month), and go tearing through the city, often ending up in Greenwich Village.

Bowling

AMF Chelsea Piers Lanes

23rd St at West Side Hwy, between Piers 59 and 60 (212-835-2695; www.chelseapiers.com). Subway: C, E to 23rd St. **Open** *Sun–Thu 9am–1am; Fri, Sat 9am–2am.* **Fees** *$5.50 per person per game weekdays, $7.50 weekends, $8.25 disco bowling; $3.50 shoe rental weekdays before 5pm, $4.50 weekdays after 5pm and weekends.* **Credit** *AmEx, MC, V.*
Enjoy 40 lanes, a huge bar and arcade, and glow-in-the-dark "disco" bowling on weekends.

Bowlmor Lanes

110 University Pl between 12th and 13th Sts (212-255-8188; www.bowlmor.com). Subway: L, N, Q, R, W, 4, 5, 6 to 14th St–Union Sq. **Open** *Mon 11am–3am; Tue, Wed, Sun 11am–1am; Thu 11am–2am; Fri, Sat 11am–4am.* **Fees** *$6.45 per person per game weekdays before 5pm, $7.95 weekdays after 5pm, $8.45 weekends and holidays; $5 shoe rental. Under 21 not admitted after 6pm.* **Credit** *AmEx, MC, V.*
Renovation turned a seedy but historic Greenwich Village alley (Richard Nixon bowled here!) into a hip downtown nightclub. Monday evening's Night

Strike features glow-in-the-dark pins and a techno-spinning DJ, in addition to unlimited bowling from 10pm to 3am ($20 per scenester).

Golf

Golf Club at Chelsea Piers

Pier 59, 23rd St at West Side Hwy (212-336-6400; www.chelseapiers.com). Subway: C, E to 23rd St. **Open** *Apr–Sept 6am–midnight; Oct–Mar 6:30am–11pm.* **Fees** *ball cards $20–$100; club rental $4–$12.* **Credit** *AmEx, Disc, MC, V.*

The four-story Golf Club has 52 heated and weather-protected driving stalls, an automatic ball-teeing system, two golf simulators and a 200-yard artificial fairway extending along the pier. The Golf Academy *(212-336-6444)* offers lessons with certified instructors. Rates vary.

Gyms

For travelers who can't bear to miss a workout, many gyms offer single-day memberships. If you can schedule a workout at nonrush hours (instead of just before or after the workday), you'll be better off. Call for class details.

Crunch

623 Broadway between Bleecker and Houston Sts (212-420-0507, 888-227-8624; www.crunch.com). Subway: B, D, F, V to Broadway–Lafayette St; 6 to Bleecker St. **Open** *Mon–Fri 6am–11pm; Sat 8am–8pm; Sun 9am–8pm.* **Fee** *day pass $24.* **Credit** *AmEx, Disc, MC, V.*

For a downtown feel without the attitude, Crunch wins hands-down. Most of the ten New York locations feature NetPulse cardio equipment, which lets you surf the Web or watch a personal TV while you exercise. Visit the website for other locations.

New York Sports Club

151 E 86th St between Lexington and Third Aves (800-301-1231; www.nysc.com). Subway: 4, 5, 6 to 86th St. **Open** *Mon–Thu 5:30am–11pm; Fri 5:30am–10pm; Sat, Sun 8am–9pm.* **Fee** *day pass $25.* **Credit** *AmEx, MC, V.*

A day membership at New York Sports Club includes aerobics classes, access to the weight room, cardio machines, steam room and sauna. The 62nd Street branch features squash courts. Visit the website for other gym locations.

The Printing House Fitness and Racquet Club

421 Hudson St between Clarkson and Leroy Sts (212-243-7600). Subway: 1, 9 to Houston St. **Open** *Mon–Fri 6am–11pm; Sat, Sun 8am–8pm.* **Fee** *day pass $25.* **Credit** *AmEx, MC, V.*

Not only can you sample the latest cardio machines or take a yoga or boxing class, but this penthouse gym also offers breathtaking views of midtown.

Horseback riding

Claremont Riding Academy

175 W 89th St between Columbus and Amsterdam Aves (212-724-5100). Subway: 1, 9 to 86th St. **Open** *Mon–Fri 6:30am–10pm; Sat, Sun 8am–5pm.* **Fees** *rental $50 per hour; lessons $60 per 30 minutes or 3 lessons for $165.* **Credit** *MC, V.*

The academy, originally built as a public livery stable, teaches English-style riding. Beginners use an indoor arena; experienced riders can take a leisurely canter along six miles of trails in Central Park. Be prepared to prove your mounted mettle: Claremont interviews all riders to determine their level of experience.

Kensington Stables

51 Caton Pl at East 8th St, Kensington, Brooklyn (718-972-4588; www.kensingtonstables.com). Subway: F to Fort Hamilton Pkwy. **Open** *10am–sunset.* **Fees** *guided trail ride $25 per hour; lessons $45 per hour.* **Credit** *AmEx, Disc, MC, V.*

The paddock is small, but there are miles of lovely trails in Prospect Park (*see p126* **Prospect Park**), particularly in the Ravine, which was designed to be seen from horseback.

Ice skating

Lasker Rink

Central Park, mid-park between 106th and 108th Sts (212-534-7639; www.centralparknyc.org). Subway: B, C to 110th St. **Open** *Nov–Mar Mon, Wed 10am–3:45pm; Tue, Thu, Fri 10am–10pm; Sat 12:30–10pm; Sun 12:30–4:30pm.* **Fees** *$4.50, children $2.25; skate rental $4.75.* **Credit** *MC, V.*

This low-profile alternative to Wollman Rink has two skate areas—one for high-school hockey teams and one for the average joe.

Rockefeller Center Ice Rink

1 Rockefeller Plaza, located between Fifth and Sixth Aves, from 49th to 50th St (recorded information 212-332-7654; www.therinkatrockcenter.com). Subway: B, D, F, V to 47–50th Sts–Rockefeller Ctr. **Open** *Oct–Apr; call or visit website for hours.* **Fees** *Mon–Thu $13, children under 12 $9; Fri–Sun $15, children under 12 $10; skate rental $7.* **Credit** *AmEx, Disc, MC, V.*

Rockefeller Center's famous outdoor rink, under the giant statue of Prometheus, is perfect for atmosphere—but bad for elbow room. The rink generally opens with an energetic ice show in mid-October, but attracts most of its visitors when the towering Christmas tree is lit.

Sky Rink at Chelsea Piers

Pier 61, 23rd St at West Side Hwy (212-336-6100; www.chelseapiers.com). Subway: C, E to 23rd St. **Open** *Call or visit website for hours.* **Fees** *$13, seniors and children $9.50; skate rental $6, helmet rental $3.* **Credit** *AmEx, Disc, MC, V.*

This is Manhattan's only year-round indoor ice-skating rink. There are several general-skating, figure-skating and ice-hockey sessions, as well as lessons and performances.

Wollman Rink

Central Park, mid-park at 62nd St (212-439-6900; www.wollmanskatingrink.com) Subway: N, R, W to Fifth Ave–59th St. **Open** *Late Oct–Mar Mon, Tue 10am–2:30pm; Wed, Thu 10am–10pm; Fri, Sat 10am–11pm; Sun 10am–9pm.* **Fees** *Mon–Thu $8.50, children $4.25; Fri–Sun $11, children $4.50; skate rental $4.75.* **Credit** *Cash only.*
Less crowded than Rock Center, the rink offers a lovely setting beneath the trees of Central Park.

In-line skating

In-line skaters, many of them tearing ass through traffic at 30mph, have made that *skish-skish* sound a familiar one on New York streets. Group skates—some mellow and social, others wild blitzkriegs on wheels—are a popular city pastime. Bring skates, a helmet and a sense of adventure. To give it a whirl, visit **Wollman Rink** April through mid-October (*see left*). If you don't want to be restricted to the rink, rent skates there for $15 a day (plus a $100 deposit) and take off on the park loop. The nearby gear shop **Blades, Board and Skate** *(120 W 72nd St between Columbus and Amsterdam Aves, 212-787-3911)* rents by the day.

Empire Skate Club of New York

P.O. Box 20070, London Terrace Station, New York, NY 10011 (212-774-1774; www.empireskate.org).
This club organizes in-line and roller-skating events throughout the city, including island-hopping tours and nighttime rides, such as the Thursday Evening Roll: Skaters meet May through October at Columbus Circle *(59th St at Broadway, southwest corner of Central Park)* at 6:45pm.

Pro picks: Run for it

Want to lope like a local? Gordon Bakoulis, of *New York Runner,* the official publication of the New York Road Runners club, offers her top five places to lace up.

Central Park Reservoir

Quite possibly the city's most popular running spot, the mile-and-a-half path ringing the lake offers uptown skyline views across the water, as well as a nice breeze.

The East River bridges

Brooklyn, Manhattan, Williamsburg and Queensboro. Zip between boroughs by taking the pedestrian paths that run across the bridges. They offer great views, too.

Hudson River Greenway

For long runs, the six-mile Greenway (which hugs the Hudson River shoreline from the Battery to Harlem) beats endless loops in Central Park.

Prospect Park, Brooklyn

The terrain is varied and, best of all, Brooklyn's monster green area is less crowded than Central Park.

Van Cortlandt Park, Bronx

This wooded park is as close as you'll get to *bucolic* in New York City. Runners can stick to the paths, or head off on a cross-country adventure.

Kayaking

Kayaking is a great way to explore New York Harbor and the Hudson River. But given the tricky currents, the tidal shifts and the hairy river traffic, it's best to go on an organized excursion.

Manhattan Kayak Company

Pier 63 Maritime, 23rd St at West Side Hwy (212-924-1788; www.manhattankayak.com). Subway: C, E to 23rd St. **Open** *Call or visit website for schedule and prices.* **Credit** *AmEx, Disc, MC, V.*
Run by veteran kayaker Eric Stiller, who once paddled halfway around Australia, Manhattan Kayak offers beginner to advanced classes and tours. Adventures include the Sushi Tour ($100 per person), in which the group paddles to Edgewater, New Jersey, to dine at a sushi restaurant.

Running

Join the joggers in Central and Riverside Parks or around Washington Square. Or just head anywhere you feel like exploring *(see also left* **Run for it**).

New York Road Runners

9 E 89th St between Fifth and Madison Aves (212-860-4455; www.nyrrc.org). Subway: 4, 5, 6 to 86th St. **Open** *Mon–Fri 10am–8pm; Sat 10am–5pm; Sun 10am–3pm.* **Fees** *Call or visit website.* **Credit** *AmEx, Disc, MC, V.*
Hardly a weekend passes without some sort of run or race sponsored by the NYRR, which is responsible for the New York City Marathon. Most races take place in Central Park and are open to the public. The club also offers classes and clinics, and can help you find a running partner.

Swimming

The Harlem, Vanderbilt and West Side YMCAs *(www.ymcanyc.org)* all have decent-size pools (accessible with a day pass), as do some private gyms. There are dozens of hotels with swimming pools, many of which provide day-pass access as well. The city of New York maintains several Olympic-size (and smaller) facilities. Its outdoor pools are free of charge and open from July to September: **Hamilton Fish** *(Pitt St between Houston and Stanton Sts, 212-387-7687);* **Asser Levy Pool** *(23rd St between First Ave and FDR Drive, 212-447-2020);* **Carmine Street Recreation Center** *(Clarkson St at Seventh Ave South, 212-242-5229);* **West 59th Street Pool** *(59th St between Tenth and Eleventh Aves, 212-397-3159).* For more information, call **New York Parks & Recreation** *(800-201-PARK; www.nyc.gov/parks).*

Tennis

From April through November, the city maintains excellent municipal courts throughout the five boroughs. Single-play (one-hour) tickets cost $5. The **Department of Parks** *(212-360-8131)* also issues permits that are valid for unlimited play during the season *($100, senior citizens $20, under 17 $10).* For a list of city courts, visit www.nycgovparks.org.

Trapeze

Trapeze School New York

Hudson River Park between Canal and Vestry Sts (917-797-1872; www.trapezeschool.com). **Open** *May–Nov, weather permitting.* **Fees** *two-hour class $35–$65.* **Credit** *AmEx, Disc, MC, V.*
If flying through the air with the greatest of ease (or at least with some facility) has ever been a dream of yours, this is the place for you. Set in a large cage-like construction on the bank of the Hudson River, the school offers classes for ages 6 and up. You can also watch while a loved one has a fling.

Yoga

Integral Yoga Institute

227 W 13th St between Seventh and Eighth Aves (212-929-0585; www.iyiny.org). Subway: A, C, E, 1, 2, 3, 9 to 14th St; L to Eighth Ave. **Open** *Mon–Fri 9:45am–8:30pm; Sat 8:15am–6pm; Sun 10am–2:30pm. Call or visit website for schedule.* **Fee** *$13 per class.* **Credit** *AmEx, MC, V.*
This studio offers a seemingly endless array of classes: hatha and vinyasa yoga, chanting, meditation and "yoga dance." Workshops on healthy living, nutrition and spirituality are also offered.
Other location *200 W 72nd St at Broadway, fourth floor (212-721-4000).*

Bend it like...yoga at **Jivamukti**.

Jivamukti

404 Lafayette St between Astor Pl and E 4th St, third floor (212-353-0214; www.jivamuktiyoga.com). Subway: 6 to Astor Pl or Bleecker St. **Open** *Call or visit website for schedule.* **Fees** *$17 per class; packages start at $90.* **Credit** *AmEx, Disc, MC, V.*
This intensely spiritual—and überpopular—yoga studio offers classes in Sanskrit and meditation alongside hatha and vinyasa classes. There's also great celeb-spotting here—look out for Sting or Christy Turlington.
Other location *853 Lexington Ave between 63rd and 64th Sts, second floor (212-396-4200).*

Om

826 Broadway at 12th St, sixth floor (212-254-9642; www.omyoga.com). Subway: L, N, Q, R, W, 4, 5, 6 to 14th St–Union Sq. **Open** *Mon–Fri 7am–9:45pm; Sat, Sun 9am–8:15pm. Call or visit website for schedule.* **Fees** *$16 per class; packages start at $25.* **Credit** *AmEx, Disc, MC, V.*
Owner Cyndi Lee weaves Buddhist meditation into her yoga teachings at this well-known studio.

► Check ***Time Out New York*** for current mind-and-body events and classes.

Theater & Dance

Places, everyone!

Theater

It's no secret that New York is synonymous with the hip-hooray and ballyhoo of **Broadway**—but did you know that, in the past couple of years, the Great White Way has grown more diverse than ever before? Just look at the current offerings. Sure, there are still Disney extravaganzas such as ***The Lion King*** and ***Beauty and the Beast***, and big musical revivals like ***Gypsy*** and ***42nd Street***. But now you can also see terrific examples of pop-driven musicals, such as Disney's ***Aida***, with its Elton John score, and ***Avenue Q***, an irreverent show best described as *Rent*–meets–*Sesame Street*. Increasingly, too, movie stars are lining up for a chance to step into Broadway's red-hot spotlight. Ashley Judd, Melanie Griffith, Antonio Banderas, John Lithgow and Mary Stuart Masterson have all starred in Broadway shows in the past few seasons.

From midtown's landmark palaces and slightly more intimate venues to downtown's offbeat **Off Broadway** and **Off-Off Broadway** spaces, there's a place—and a show—to suit every taste.

BUYING TICKETS

If you have a major credit card, buying Broadway tickets requires little more than picking up a phone. Nearly all Broadway and Off Broadway shows are served by one of the city's 24-hour booking agencies, which are listed in the show's print advertisements, or in the capsule reviews that run each week in *Time Out New York*. The venues' information lines can also refer you to ticket agents, sometimes merely by transferring your call (for additional ticketing info, *see p378*). Theater box offices usually charge a small additional fee for phone orders.

Some of the cheapest tickets on Broadway are rush tickets (purchased the day of a show at the theater's box office), which cost an average of $25—but not all theaters offer these, and some reserve them for students. Some theaters distribute rush tickets through a lottery, usually held two hours before the performance. If a show is sold out, it's worth waiting for standby tickets just before curtain time. Tickets are slightly cheaper for matinees and previews (typically on Wednesdays, Saturdays and Sundays), and for students or groups of 20 or more. For discount seats, your best bet is **TKTS** (*see p379*), where you can get tickets on the day of the performance for as much as 75 percent off the face value. Arrive early to beat—or at least get a jump on—the long lines. TKTS also sells matinee tickets the day before a show. (Beware of scam artists selling tickets to those waiting in line; the tickets are often fake.) If you're interested in seeing more than one Off-Off Broadway show or dance event, consider purchasing a book of vouchers from the **Theatre Development Fund**.

New York Shakespeare Festival at the Delacorte Theater

Park entrance on Central Park West at 81st St, then follow the signs (212-539-8750; www.publictheater.org). Subway: B, C to 81st St–Museum of Natural History.

The Delacorte Theater in Central Park is the fair-weather sister of the Public Theater (*see p345*). When not producing Shakespeare in the East Village, the Public offers the best of the Bard outdoors during the New York Shakespeare Festival *(Jun–Sept)*. Tickets are free (two per person), and are distributed at both theaters at 1pm on the day of the performance. Normally, 9am is a good time to begin waiting, though the line can start as early as 6am when big-name stars are on the bill.

Theatre Development Fund

1501 Broadway between 43rd and 44th Sts (212-221-0013; www.tdf.org). Subway: N, Q, R, W, 42nd St S, 1, 2, 3, 9, 7 to 42nd St–Times Sq. **Open** *Mon–Sat 3–8pm (for 8pm show); Wed, Sat 10am–2pm (for 2pm show); Sun 11am–7pm (for all shows).* **Credit** *Cash only.*

► To find out what's playing, see the listings and reviews in ***Time Out New York***.
► For plot synopses, show times and ticket info, call **NYC/Onstage** (*see p339*), a service of the Theatre Development Fund (*see above*). You'll learn about shows on Broadway, Off Broadway and Off-Off Broadway, as well as classical music, dance and opera.
► If you know what you want to see, call the **Broadway Line** *(212-302-4111, outside New York 888-276-2392; www.ilovenytheater.com) for tickets.*

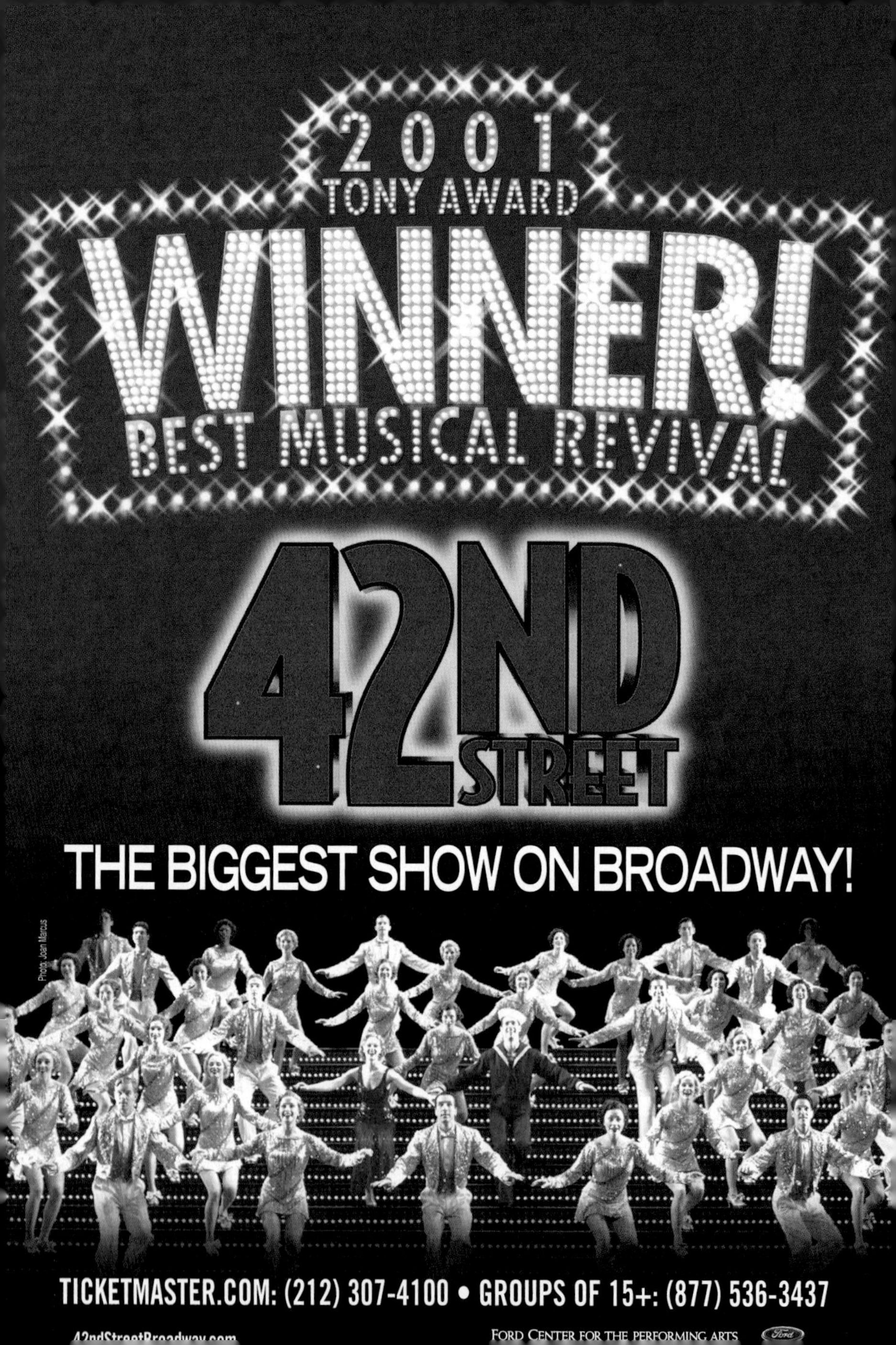
2001
TONY AWARD
WINNER!
BEST MUSICAL REVIVAL
42ND STREET
THE BIGGEST SHOW ON BROADWAY!
Photo: Joan Marcus
TICKETMASTER.COM: (212) 307-4100 • GROUPS OF 15+: (877) 536-3437
42ndStreetBroadway.com
FORD CENTER FOR THE PERFORMING ARTS
Ford

TDF offers a book of four vouchers for $28, which can be purchased only at its office by visitors who bring their passport or out-of-state driver's license, or by students and residents on the TDF mailing list. Each voucher is good for one admission to an Off-Off Broadway theater, dance or music event, at venues such as the Atlantic Theater Company, the Joyce, the Kitchen, P.S. 122 and many more. TDF's NYC/Onstage service *(212-768-1818)* provides information by phone on all theater, dance and music events in town.

Broadway

Technically speaking, "Broadway" is the Theater District that surrounds Times Square on either side of Broadway (the avenue), mainly between 41st and 53rd Streets. This is where you'll find the grand theaters, most of them built between 1900 and 1930. Officially, 38 are designated as being part of Broadway, for which full-price tickets can cost more than $100. The big shows are hard to ignore; high-profile revivals and new blockbusters announce themselves from giant billboards and drench the airwaves with radio advertisements. Still, there's more to Broadway than splashy musicals and flashy pop spectacles. In recent years, provocative dramas like *Take Me Out* and madcap comedies such as *Urinetown* have had remarkable success, as have British imports and American classics, including *Vincent in Brixton* and Eugene O'Neill's *Long Day's Journey into Night.*

The charming **Roundabout Theatre Company** *(American Airlines Theatre, 227 W 42nd St between Broadway and Eighth Ave, 212-719-1300)* is the critically acclaimed home of classics featuring all-star casts; it's also the force behind *Cabaret*'s latest

Around the dial

Cabaret-ready standards aren't the only sounds on Broadway these days. More musicals are going pop, a trend started in the '60s when breakthrough shows such as *Hair* and *Jesus Christ Superstar* wedded popular music to Broadway spectacle. These days, Elton John's ballads dramatize ***Aida***'s doomed love triangle, while synthesizer-saturated ABBA songs keep the plot moving in the crowd-pleasing ***Mamma Mia!*** You can still hum along to typical Broadway tunes at ***Thoroughly Modern Millie*** *and* ***The Producers,*** but pop fans now have plenty to choose from. (At press time, the lineup also included these shows.)

Bombay Dreams

Opening spring 2004. Based on an idea by composer/legend Andrew Lloyd Webber, this cross-cultural extravaganza features a lush musical score inspired by India's Bollywood films, and a straight-out-of-Hollywood boy-meets-girl plot.

The Boy from Oz

Imperial Theatre, 249 W 45th St between Broadway and Eighth Ave (212-239-6200). Subway: N, Q, R, W, 42nd St S, 1, 2, 3, 9, 7 to 42nd St–Times Sq. **Tickets** *$60–$100.*
For some people, "easy-listening music" isn't a bad thing. Starring Hugh Jackman (at press time), *Oz* tells the uplifting yet bittersweet story of flamboyant Australian singer-songwriter Peter Allen.

Movin' Out.

Movin' Out

Richard Rodgers Theatre, 226 W 46th St between Broadway and Eighth Ave (212-307-4100). Subway: N, Q, R, W, 42nd St S, 1, 2, 3, 9, 7 to 42nd St–Times Sq. **Tickets** *$80–$100.*
Combine the songs of Billy Joel ("Scenes from an Italian Restaurant" and "Big Shot," to name just a couple) with the sexy choreography of Twyla Tharp, and you have a unique show: part modern ballet, part music video.

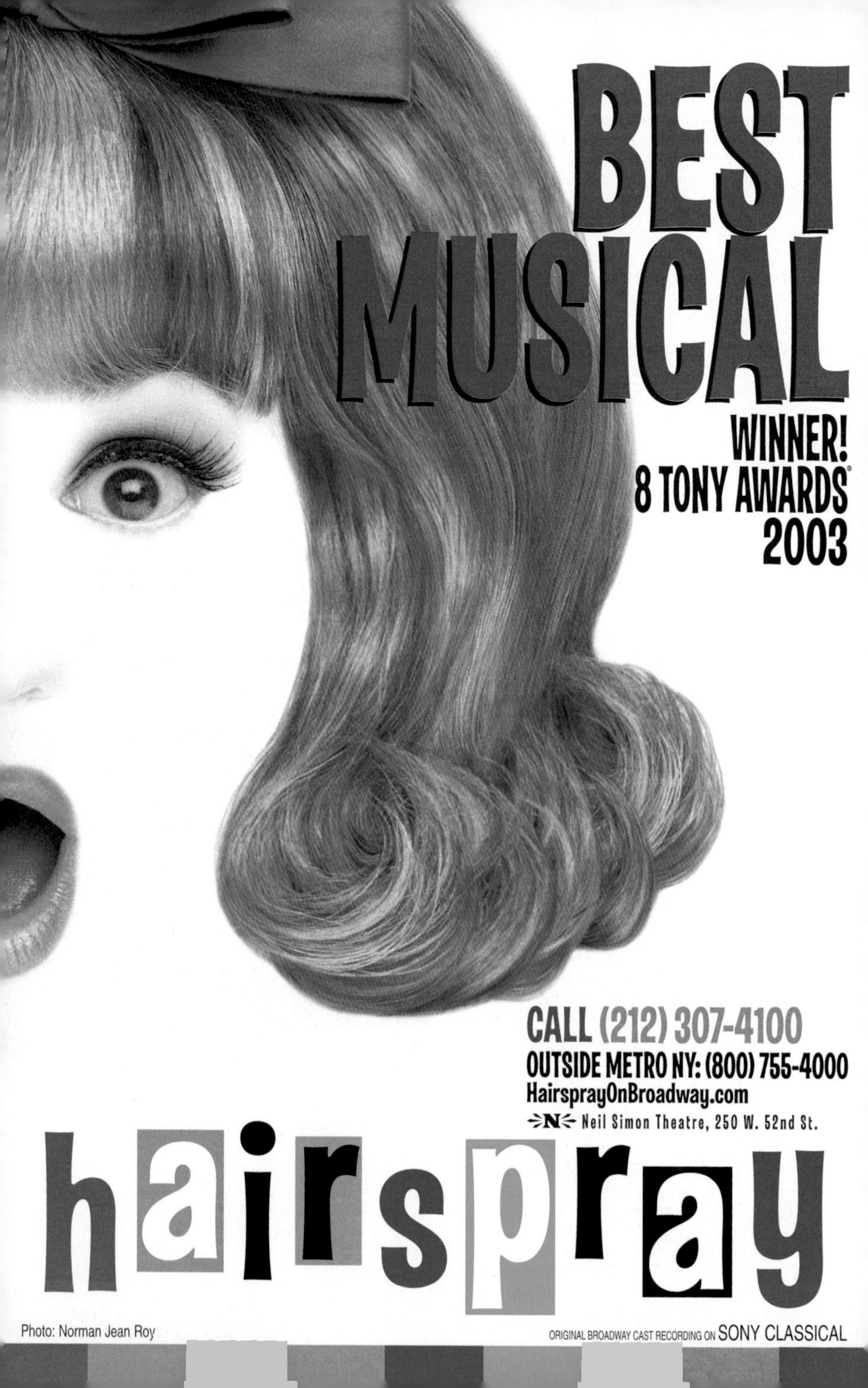
BEST
MUSICAL
WINNER!
8 TONY AWARDS®
2003
CALL (212) 307-4100
OUTSIDE METRO NY: (800) 755-4000
HairsprayOnBroadway.com
N Neil Simon Theatre, 250 W. 52nd St.
hairspray
Photo: Norman Jean Roy
ORIGINAL BROADWAY CAST RECORDING ON SONY CLASSICAL

incarnation. This deluxe Broadway space opened in 2000. You can subscribe to the Roundabout's full season or buy single tickets, if they're available.

Broadway (Theater District)

Subway: N, Q, R, W, 42nd St S, 2, 3, 7 to 42nd St–Times Sq; C, E, 1, 9 to 50th St.

Long-running shows

Straight (nonmusical) plays can provide some of Broadway's most stirring experiences, but they're less likely than musicals to enjoy long runs. If you aren't in search of a song, check *Time Out New York* for current listings and reviews of new or revived dramatic plays.

Avenue Q

Ambassador Theatre, 219 W 49th St between Broadway and Eighth Ave (212-239-6200; www.avenueq.com). Subway: C, E, 1, 9 to 50th St. **Tickets** *$45–$95.* **Credit** *AmEx, DC, Disc, MC, V.*
Mixing puppets and live actors with irreverent jokes and snappy songs, this clever, good-hearted musical comedy has been a surprise hit.

Hairspray

Neil Simon Theatre, 250 W 52nd St between Broadway and Eighth Ave (212-307-4100; www.hairsprayonbroadway.com). Subway: C, E, 1, 9 to 50th St. **Tickets** *$65–$100.* **Credit** *AmEx, DC, Disc, MC, V.*
John Waters's classic kitsch film has become an eye-popping song-and-dance extravaganza that's bigger, brighter, more satirical and much funnier.

The Producers

St. James Theatre, 246 W 44th St between Broadway and Eighth Ave (Telecharge 212-239-6200, Broadway Inner Circle 212-563-2929; www.producersonbroadway.com). Subway: N, Q, R, W, 42nd St S, 1, 2, 3, 9, 7 to 42nd St–Times Sq. **Tickets** *$31–$480.* **Credit** *AmEx, DC, Disc, MC, V.*
Mel Brooks's ode to tastelessness mixes Broadway razzmatazz with Borscht Belt humor. Original stars Nathan Lane and Matthew Broderick have left the cast (though they do return for periodic short-term runs), but the show still delivers plenty of laughs.

Off Broadway

As the cost of mounting a show on Broadway continues to soar, many serious playwrights are now opening their shows in the more adventurous (and less financially demanding) Off Broadway houses. Off Broadway theaters have between 200 and 500 seats, and tickets usually run from $20 to $70. Traditionally, the theaters were located in Greenwich Village, but these days, they're springing up all around the city, especially in Chelsea and the East Village. Below are some of our favorite long-running shows, followed by some of the best theaters and repertory companies.

Long-running shows

Blue Man Group: *Tubes*

Astor Place Theater, 434 Lafayette St between Astor Pl and E 4th St (212-254-4370; www.blueman.com). Subway: R, W to 8th St–NYU; 6 to Astor Pl. **Tickets** *$56–$70.* **Credit** *AmEx, MC, V.*
Three men with extraterrestrial imaginations (and head-to-toe blue body paint) carry this longtime favorite—a show that's as smart as it is ridiculous.

De La Guarda

Daryl Roth Theatre, 20 Union Sq East at 15th St (212-239-6200; www.delaguarda.com). Subway: L, N, Q, R, W, 4, 5, 6 to 14th St–Union Sq. **Tickets** *$55.* **Credit** *AmEx, DC, Disc, MC, V.*
A sexy mix of carnival, rave, concert and dance, with athletic performers flying through the air on bungee cords.

The Donkey Show

Club El Flamingo, 547 W 21st St between Tenth and Eleventh Aves (212-307-4100; www.thedonkeyshow.com). Subway: C, E to 23rd St. **Tickets** *$45–$85.* **Credit** *AmEx, DC, Disc, MC, V.*
Bring your dancing shoes to this *Midsummer Night's* disco, where Shakespearean comedy shakes it to '70s hits like *Car Wash* and *You Sexy Thing.*

Stomp

Orpheum Theater, 126 Second Ave between St. Marks Pl and E 7th St (212-477-2477). Subway: R, W to 8th St–NYU; 6 to Astor Pl. **Tickets** *$35–$60.* **Credit** *AmEx, MC, V.*
This show is billed as a "percussion sensation," because there's no other way to describe it. Using garbage-can lids, buckets, brooms, sticks and just about anything they can get their hands on, these aerobicized dancer-musicians make a lovely noise.

Repertory companies & venues

Atlantic Theater Company

336 W 20th St between Eighth and Ninth Aves (212-645-8015; www.atlantictheater.org). Subway: C, E to 23rd St. **Credit** *AmEx, DC, MC, V.*
Created in 1985 as an offshoot of acting workshops taught by playwright David Mamet and film star William H. Macy, this dynamic theater has presented nearly 100 plays, including Mamet's *American Buffalo* and the American premiere of Irish playwright Martin McDonagh's *The Beauty Queen of Leenane.*

Brooklyn Academy of Music

See p321 for listing.
Brooklyn's grand old opera house—along with the Harvey Theater, two blocks away on Fulton Street—stages the famous multidisciplinary Next

CHICAGO
THE MUSICAL
PHOTO: ULI WEBER
NOTORIOUS.
AMBASSADOR THEATRE
219 WEST 49TH STREET NYC
TELECHARGE.COM • 212-239-6200 • CHICAGOTHEMUSICAL.COM
GRAMMY® AWARD WINNING BROADWAY CAST RECORDING ON RCA VICTOR
Sprint

Wave Festival every October through December. The 2003 festival included downtown director Anne Bogart's fascinating homage to Robert Rauschenberg, *Bobrauschenbergamerica,* and the Improbable Theatre's existential comedy *The Hanging Man.*

Classic Stage Company

136 E 13th St between Third and Fourth Aves (212-677-4210; www.classicstage.org). Subway: L, N, Q, R, W, 4, 5, 6 to 14th St–Union Sq. **Credit** *AmEx, MC, V.*

From Greek tragedies to medieval mystery plays, the Classic Stage Company (now under the tutelage of artistic director Brian Kulick) makes the old new again. Productions scheduled for 2004 include Big Dance Theater's rendition of Mac Wellman's avant-garde musical *Antigone.*

Irish Repertory Theatre

132 W 22nd St between Sixth and Seventh Aves (212-727-2737; www.irishrepertorytheatre.com). Subway: F, V, 1, 9 to 23rd St. **Credit** *AmEx, MC, V.*

This Chelsea company puts on compelling shows by Irish playwrights. Past productions include Frank McCourt's *The Irish and How They Got That Way* and Enda Walsh's *Bedbound.*

Lincoln Center

See p323 for listing.

The majestic Lincoln Center complex includes two amphitheater-style drama venues: the 1,040-seat Vivian Beaumont Theater (the Broadway house) and the 290-seat Mitzi E. Newhouse Theater (Off Broadway). Expect polished, often star-studded productions of classic plays (*Henry IV* featuring Kevin Kline and Ethan Hawke) and new plays (the powerful South African drama *Nothing But the Truth*).

Manhattan Theatre Club

City Center, 131 W 55th St between Sixth and Seventh Aves (212-581-1212; www.mtc-nyc.org). Subway: B, D, E to Seventh Ave. **Credit** *AmEx, DC, Disc, MC, V.*

Manhattan Theatre Club has a reputation for sending young playwrights on to Broadway, as seen with such successes as David Auburn's *Proof.* The club's two theaters are located in the basement of City Center. The 299-seat Mainstage Theater features four plays a year by new and established playwrights; the Stage II Theater offers works-in-progress, workshops and staged readings. MTC also has a Broadway home in the newly renovated Biltmore Theatre (*261 W 47th St between Broadway and Eighth Ave; Telecharge 212-239-6200*).

The New Victory Theater

209 W 42nd St between Broadway and Eighth Ave (646-223-3020; www.newvictory.org). Subway: A, C, E to 42nd St–Port Authority; N, Q, R, W, 42nd St S, 1, 2, 3, 9, 7 to 42nd St–Times Sq. **Credit** *AmEx, DC, Disc, MC, V.*

The New Victory is a perfect symbol for the transformation of Times Square. Built in 1900 by Oscar Hammerstein II, Manhattan's oldest theater became a strip club and adult cinema in the '70s and '80s. Renovated by the city in 1995, the building now features a full season of family-friendly plays.

Breakthrough experiments

For those who prefer their theater way left of mainstream, there's plenty of avant-garde work thriving on the edge. Call ahead or check the website of the company or venue to find out what's playing and where.

Going up, up, up

Elevator Repair Service, founded in 1991, is still one of the freshest groups around. Mixing text and improvisation throughout a lengthy rehearsal process, ERS creates fascinating theatrical puzzles. A new work based on Tennessee Williams's plays, tentatively titled *Big Number,* is slated for the 2004 season *(212-529-7875; www.elevator.org).*

Hole lotta fun

Radiohole, a fab foursome based in Williamsburg, Brooklyn, turns out effervescent, anarchic work influenced by Soho's multimedia Wooster Group. Shows go up at the group's funky warehouse space, the Collapsable Hole *(718-388-2251; www.radiohole.com).*

The spice is right

Under the resourceful, witty direction of Emma Griffin, **Salt Theater** produces both canonical classics and brand-new works on a shoestring budget. Recent shows included lively productions of Chekhov's *The Cherry Orchard* and *Kaufman and Ferber's Stage Door.* In spring 2004, look for Charles Ludlam's campy sci-fi delight, *Conquest of the Universe (212-613-5740; www.salttheater.com).*

Your patriotic duty

Think absurdism is as dead as Samuel Beckett? Then you haven't seen the **National Theater of the United States of America**. Based in Brooklyn's artsy Dumbo neighborhood, the madcap collective of NTUSA develops its works through imaginative group improvisation. Its 2004 offering is called *What's That on My Head? (212-615-6607; www.ntusa.org).*

WINNER!
THE MOST TONY AWARDS® IN BROADWAY HISTORY!
THE PRODUCERS
the new
MEL BROOKS
musical
TELECHARGE.COM:(212) 239-5800 (800) 432-7250
GROUPS:(212)302-7000 (800)677-1164
ST. JAMES THEATRE, 246 W. 44th ST.
www.producersonbroadway.com
Original Broadway Cast Recording Available On Sony Classical
SONY CLASSICAL
Photo by:Paul Kolnik

New York Theatre Workshop

79 E 4th St between Bowery and Second Ave (212-460-5475; www.nytw.org). Subway: F, V to Lower East Side–Second Ave; 6 to Astor Pl. **Credit** *AmEx, DC, MC, V.*

Founded in 1979, the New York Theatre Workshop produces new plays with emerging directors who are eager to take on challenging pieces. Besides works by the likes of Caryl Churchill (*Far Away*) and Tony Kushner (the recent *Homebody/Kabul*), this Off Broadway company also premiered *Rent,* Jonathan Larson's Pulitzer Prize–winning musical, which still packs 'em in on Broadway.

Playwrights Horizons

416 W 42nd St between Ninth and Tenth Aves (Ticket Central 212-279-4200; www.playwrights horizons.org). Subway: A, C, E to 42nd St–Port Authority. **Credit** *AmEx, DC, Disc, MC, V.*

More than 300 important contemporary plays have premiered here, including dramas such as *Driving Miss Daisy* and *The Heidi Chronicles.* Recent seasons have included the works of Kenneth Lonergan (*Lobby Hero*), Doug Wright (*I Am My Own Wife*) and the brilliant Theresa Rebeck (*Bad Dates*).

Public Theater

425 Lafayette St between Astor Pl and E 4th St (212-539-8500; www.publictheater.org). Subway: R, W to 8th St–NYU; 6 to Astor Pl. **Credit** *AmEx, MC, V.*

Founded by the late Joseph Papp and dedicated to the work of new American playwrights and performers, this Astor Place landmark also presents new explorations of Shakespeare and other classics (*see p337* **New York Shakespeare Festival**). The building houses five stages, a coffee bar and the cabaret space Joe's Pub (*see p311*). The theater is under the direction of George C. Wolfe, who staged Suzan-Lori Parks's *Topdog/Underdog* on Broadway and the New York premiere of Tony Kushner's *Angels in America*.

Second Stage Theatre

307 W 43rd St at Eighth Ave (212-246-4422; www.secondstagetheatre.com). Subway: A, C, E to 42nd St–Port Authority; N, Q, R, W, 42nd St S, 1, 2, 3, 9, 7 to 42nd St–Times Sq. **Credit** *AmEx, MC, V.*

Second Stage produces the works of new American playwrights, including New York premieres of Mary Zimmerman's *Metamorphoses* and Ricky Jay's magic show *On the Stem.* Since 1999, the company has occupied a beautiful Rem Koolhaas–designed space near Times Square.

Signature Theatre Company

555 W 42nd St between Tenth and Eleventh Aves (212-244-7529; www.signaturetheatre.org). Subway: A, C, E to 42nd St–Port Authority. **Credit** *AmEx, MC, V.*

This award-winning company focuses on the work of a single playwright each season. This spring, it's world-renowned clown and New Vaudeville star Bill Irwin; come summer, he'll be followed by Pulitzer Prize–winner Paula Vogel.

The Vineyard Theatre

108 E 15th St at Union Sq East (212-353-3366; www.vineyardtheatre.org). Subway: L, N, Q, R, W, 4, 5, 6 to 14th St–Union Sq. **Credit** *AmEx, MC, V.*

This theater near Union Square produces excellent new plays and musicals. It also gives a second chance to lesser-known works.

Off-Off Broadway

The technical definition of Off-Off Broadway is a show presented at a theater with fewer than 100 seats, and one that's created by artists who aren't necessarily card-carrying union pros. It's where some of the most daring writers and performers create their edgiest work. The **New York International Fringe Festival** *(212-279-4488; www.fringenyc.org)* takes place every August, and it's a great way to catch the wacky side of theater. The cheekily titled group The **National Theater of the United States of America** (*see p343* **Breakthrough experiments**) performs its highly original work in Brooklyn. But Off-Off Broadway—where tickets run $10 to $25—is not restricted to experimental or solo shows. You can also see classical works and more traditional plays staged by companies such as the **Mint Theater** *(311 W 43rd St between Eighth and Ninth Aves, fifth floor, 212-315-0231; www.minttheater.org)* and at venues like **HERE** and **P.S. 122**.

Repertory companies & venues

HERE

145 Sixth Ave at Broome St (212-647-0202; www.here.org). Subway: C, E to Spring St; R, W to Prince St. **Credit** *Cash only.*

Containing three intimate performance spaces, an art gallery and a chic cafe, this lovely Tribeca arts complex has hosted a number of exciting companies, and was the launching pad for such well-known shows as Eve Ensler's *The Vagina Monologues.*

The Kitchen

512 W 19th St between Tenth and Eleventh Aves (212-255-5793). Subway A, C, E to 14th St; L to Eighth Ave. **Credit** *AmEx, MC, V.*

Founded in Soho in 1971, this cutting-edge performance space still cooks up thought-provoking avant-garde work.

Performance Space 122

150 First Ave at 9th St (212-477-5288; www.ps122.org). Subway: L to First Ave; 6 to Astor Pl. **Credit** *AmEx, MC, V.*

One of New York's most exciting venues, this non-profit arts center presents experimental dance, performance art, music, film and video. Eric Bogosian, Whoopi Goldberg, John Leguizamo and others have developed projects here.

Dance

Both classical and contemporary dance thrive in New York City. Despite a lack of substantial government funding, the city has a vibrant and wildly diverse community in which all kinds of dancers and choreographers sweat, stomp and spin. There are two major dance seasons—March to June, and October to December. The spring season is particularly busy: Not only does Paul Taylor present his marvelous troupe each March, but the resident American Ballet Theatre and the New York City Ballet are also in full force. And the offerings don't stop there; both the open-air **Central Park SummerStage** (*see p255*) and the **Lincoln Center Festival** (*see p323*) schedule performances throughout July. If watching those beautiful bodies inspires you, there are dozens of dance schools that offer classes (some are affiliated with established companies). Workshops are also listed in *Time Out New York*. You can call ahead for schedules, but walk-ins are welcome at most spaces. The **Mark Morris Dance Center** *(3 Lafayette Ave between Ashland and Flatbush Aves, Fort Greene, Brooklyn; 718-624-8400; www.markmorrisdancegroup.org)* is one of New York's most well-rounded options, offering ballet, modern and African techniques. When Morris is in town, he often teaches a class himself.

Venues

Brooklyn Academy of Music

See p321 for listing.

BAM, which showcases superb local and out-of-town companies, is one of New York's prominent cultural institutions. The Howard Gilman Opera House, with its Federal-style columns and carved marble, is one of the city's most beautiful dance venues. (The Mark Morris Dance Group generally performs there each spring.) The 1904 Harvey Theater *(651 Fulton St between Ashland and Rockwell Pls)*, formerly called the Majestic, has hosted such modern troupes as Susan Marshall & Company and the John Jasperse Company. Each fall, BAM's Next Wave Festival highlights established and experimental dance groups; in the spring, there's an assortment of ballet, hip-hop and modern dance.

City Center Theater

131 W 55th St between Sixth and Seventh Aves (212-581-7907; www.citycenter.org). Subway: B, D, E to Seventh Ave; N, Q, R, W to 57th St. **Tickets** *$25–$75.* **Credit** *AmEx, MC, V ($4.75 per-ticket surcharge).*

Before the creation of Lincoln Center changed the cultural geography of New York, this was the home of American Ballet Theatre, the Joffrey Ballet and the New York City Ballet (originally known as the Ballet Society). City Center's lavish decor is golden—as are the companies that pass through.

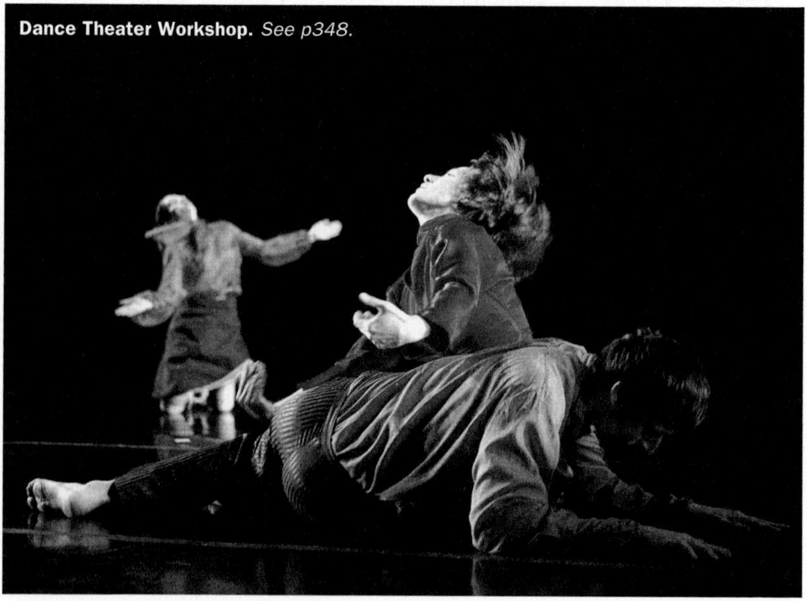

Dance Theater Workshop. *See p348.*

You can count on superb performances all year long, including those by ABT in the fall, the Alvin Ailey American Dance Theater in December, and the Paul Taylor Dance Company in the spring.

Joyce Theater

175 Eighth Ave at 19th St (212-242-0800; www.joyce.org). Subway: A, C, E to 14th St; 1, 9 to 18th St. **Tickets** *$25–$40.* **Credit** *AmEx, DC, Disc, MC, V.*

The intimate space, once a cinema, is one of the finest theaters in town. Of the 472 seats at the Joyce, there's not a single bad one. Companies and choreographers who present work here, including Ballet Hispanico, David Parsons and Doug Varone, tend to be more traditional than experimental. The Joyce also hosts out-of-town crowd-pleasers like Pilobolus Dance Theatre *(June),* and the annual Altogether Different Festival *(January),* which offers audiences the opportunity to check out less established choreographers. During the summer, when many theaters are dark, the Joyce continues its programming. At the Joyce Soho, emerging companies present work nearly every weekend.

Other location *Joyce Soho, 155 Mercer St between Houston and Prince Sts (212-431-9233).*

Metropolitan Opera House

See p[illegible] for listing.

The Met hosts a range of international companies, from the Paris Opéra Ballet to the Kirov Ballet. In spring, this majestic theater is home to American Ballet Theatre, which presents full-length classic story ballets as well as works by contemporary choreographers like Mark Morris and Twyla Tharp. The acoustics are wonderful, but the theater is immense, so sit as close to the stage as you can afford.

New York State Theater

Lincoln Center, 64th St at Columbus Ave (212-870-5570; www.nycballet.com). Subway: 1, 9 to 66th St–Lincoln Ctr. **Tickets** *$20–$93.* **Credit** *AmEx, DC, Disc, MC, V.*

The neoclassical New York City Ballet headlines at this opulent theater, which Philip Johnson designed to resemble a jewel box. NYCB has two seasons: Winter begins just before Thanksgiving and features more than a month of performances of George Balanchine's magical *The Nutcracker;* the season continues through February with repertory performances. The nine-week spring season usually begins in April. The best seats are in the first ring, where the music comes through loud and clear and—even better—one can enjoy the dazzling patterns of the dancers. Choreography is by Balanchine (the 89-by-58-foot stage was made to his specifications); Jerome Robbins; Peter Martins, the company's ballet master in chief; and Christopher Wheeldon, the resident choreographer, whose innovative work has injected the troupe with new life. In 2004, NYCB continues Balanchine 100: The Centennial Celebration, through June. Casting is usually announced the week of performance.

Merce Cunningham Studio. *See p348.*

Alternative venues

Aaron Davis Hall

City College, 135th St at Convent Ave (212-650-7100; www.aarondavishall.org). Subway: 1, 9 to 137th St–City College. **Tickets** *$15–$35.* **Credit** *AmEx, MC, V.*

Troupes here celebrate African-American life and culture. Companies that have performed in the modern, spacious theater include the Bill T. Jones/Arnie Zane Dance Company and the Alvin Ailey Repertory Ensemble.

Brooklyn Arts Exchange

421 Fifth Ave at 8th St, Park Slope, Brooklyn (718-832-0018; www.bax.org). Subway: F to Fourth Ave–9th St. **Tickets** *$6–$12.* **Credit** *Cash only.*

Brooklyn Arts Exchange presents a variety of dance concerts by emerging choreographers. There are also performances just for children.

Central Park SummerStage

See p255 for listing.

This outdoor dance series runs during the heat of summer. Temperatures can get steamy, but at least you're outside. Count on seeing relatively traditional dance; arrive early to secure a spot close to the stage.

Dance Theater Workshop

Bessie Schönberg Theater, 219 W 19th St between Seventh and Eighth Aves (212-691-6500, tickets 212-924-0077; www.dtw.org). Subway: A, C, E to 14th St; L to Eighth Ave; 1, 9 to 18th St. **Tickets** *$20–$25.* **Credit** *AmEx, MC, V.*

DTW, which hosts work by contemporary choreographers—both local and foreign—features a 192-seat theater, two dance studios and an artists' media lab. Choreographers on tap this spring are Donna Uchizono, Ron K. Brown and John Jasperse.

Danspace Project

St. Mark's Church in-the-Bowery, 131 E 10th St at Second Ave (212-674-8112, tickets 212-674-8194; www.danspaceproject.org). Subway: L to Third Ave; 6 to Astor Pl. **Tickets** *$12–$20.* **Credit** *Cash only.*

Choreographers are selected by the director, Laurie Uprichard, whose preference leans toward pure movement rather than technological experimentation. This spring, Neil Greenberg and Sally Silvers present new work. The gorgeous, high-ceilinged sanctuary for downtown dance is even more heavenly when the music is live.

Galapagos Art and Performance Space

See p311 for listing.

This casual Brooklyn club, which plays host to all sorts of creative types, also squeezes in up to four dance performances a week, including burlesque on Mondays.

The Kitchen

See p345 for listing.

Best known as an avant-garde theater space, the Kitchen also offers experimental dance by artists who are inventive and often provocative. Choreographers Yasmeen Godder and Sarah Michelson have both created work here.

Merce Cunningham Studio

55 Bethune St between Washington and West Sts, 11th floor (212-691-9751; www.merce.org). Subway: A, C, E to 14th St; L to Eighth Ave. **Tickets** *$10–$30.* **Credit** *Cash only.*

Located in the Westbeth complex on the edge of the West Village, the Cunningham Studio is rented by independent choreographers. As a result, performance quality can be mixed, but some shows are wonderful.

Man of the century

George Balanchine, one of the most extraordinary choreographers of the 20th century, revolutionized ballet. In stripping the art form of its earlier melodramatic artifice, he made his dancers embody pure movement, bringing the music to life in ways few choreographers had ever achieved.

Born in St. Petersburg, Russia, on January 22, 1904, Balanchine will be honored throughout the world in a grand centennial celebration this year. And there's no better city in which to honor him than New York, his longtime adopted home, where he and Lincoln Kirstein transformed the cultural landscape by founding, in 1948, what was to become the New York City Ballet.

Balanchine 100, conceived by Peter Martins, NYCB's ballet master in chief, celebrates the choreographer's genius. During the company's spring season *(Apr 27–Jun 27)*, 64 ballets will be performed, including a four-week **European Music Festival**, a two-week **American Festival** and a three-week **Russian Music Festival**. Additionally, during the final week of the season, NYCB will be joined by Tbilisi's Georgian State Dance Company, one of Balanchine's favorite troupes.

Of course, the celebration isn't limited to events at NYCB. Other centennial festivities include a Works & Process program at the **Guggenheim Museum of Art** ("Balanchine's Late Works" on April 18 and 19); film presentations at Lincoln Center's **Walter Reade Theater** in September; and two free performances at **Central Park SummerStage** in July. For SummerStage, dancers will be culled from NYCB, American Ballet Theatre and the Dance Theater of Harlem. In the fall of 2004, the **Manhattan School of Music** (*see p326*) presents a three-part symposium focusing on the choreographer's contributions to the music world.

According to Lourdes Lopez, the former NYCB principal who is now the executive director of the George Balanchine Foundation, coordinating such an extensive homage was less of a nightmare than she originally anticipated. "At the beginning of the spring, there was tremendous work, and everybody would say, 'What do we do?' " she recalls. "But I would always tell myself that it will work itself out. He did it for us. We have nothing to do but present his work. It's not like we have to make him into a genius or create buzz around him. This celebration is funny because it's very much like him. He would always say, 'Dear, they're *just* steps.' He was always so calm and reassuring, so patient and spiritual—in that sense, the celebration is exactly what he was like."

The stage and seating area are in Cunningham's large studio; be prepared to take off your shoes. Arrive early too, or you'll have to sit on the floor.

Movement Research at Judson Church

55 Washington Sq South at Thompson St (212-598-0551; www.movementresearch.org). Subway: A, C, E, B, D, F, V to W 4th St.

Director Carla Peterson carries on the tradition of free Monday-night performances at the Judson Church. At least two choreographers' works are shown each night, and the series runs from September to June. MR also offers several classes which are held at various venues, such as the Danspace Project (*see p348*).

New Jersey Performing Arts Center

See p314 for listing.

The New Jersey Performing Arts Center is the home base for the New Jersey Symphony Orchestra. It has also hosted the Alvin Ailey American Dance Theater, the Miami City Ballet and Suzanne Farrell Ballet. Large, open theaters make NJPAC a choice venue for dance. And it's not *that* far away.

The New Victory Theater

See p343 for listing.

Since opening in 1995, this intimate venue has offered exceptional dance programming. Much of it is geared toward children.

Performance Space 122

See p345 for listing.

An appealing range of up-and-coming choreographers like DD Dorvillier, Yasuko Yokoshi and Sarah Michelson present new, unconventional works.

Symphony Space

See p325 for listing.

The World Music Institute presents many international dance troupes here, but there are also seasons with contemporary choreographers like Wally Cardona and Sean Curran.

Williamsburg Art neXus

205 North 7th St between Driggs and Roebling Aves, Williamsburg, Brooklyn (718-599-7997; www.wax205.com). Subway: L to Bedford Ave.
Tickets *$10–$20.* **Credit** *Cash only.*

This Brooklyn venue features dance by local choreographers in an intimate environment. It's small, but the sight lines are great, and the mix of artists is usually intriguing.

There is a fresh generation of dancers performing Balanchine's works today, but NYCB's most burnished stars continue to dance, including the exquisite veteran Kyra Nichols, who has been a member of the company for 30 years. "I didn't expect myself to last this long," she admits, laughing. "The time has flown by because it's been such an incredible dream come true. So the centennial really reminds me of how much I love dancing and watching Balanchine. Of course, my favorite place is onstage, but it's also fun to be the viewer—to see the patterns and music in the choreography. I think it's a real treat for everybody to see so much Balanchine."

As Suzanne Farrell, the choreographer's greatest muse, sees it, the centennial is a chance to keep the vision of Balanchine flowing through the minds and bodies of audiences and dancers alike. "I don't feel I need a landmark number of years to celebrate him, because I *always* celebrate him," says Farrell, who was a member of the New York City Ballet for 28 years and now runs her own company, Suzanne Farrell Ballet. "But there are new lives being lived and new people coming to the ballet—I want to introduce [Balanchine] to young people and new audiences."

NYLB's Kyra Nichols.

Arts & Entertainment

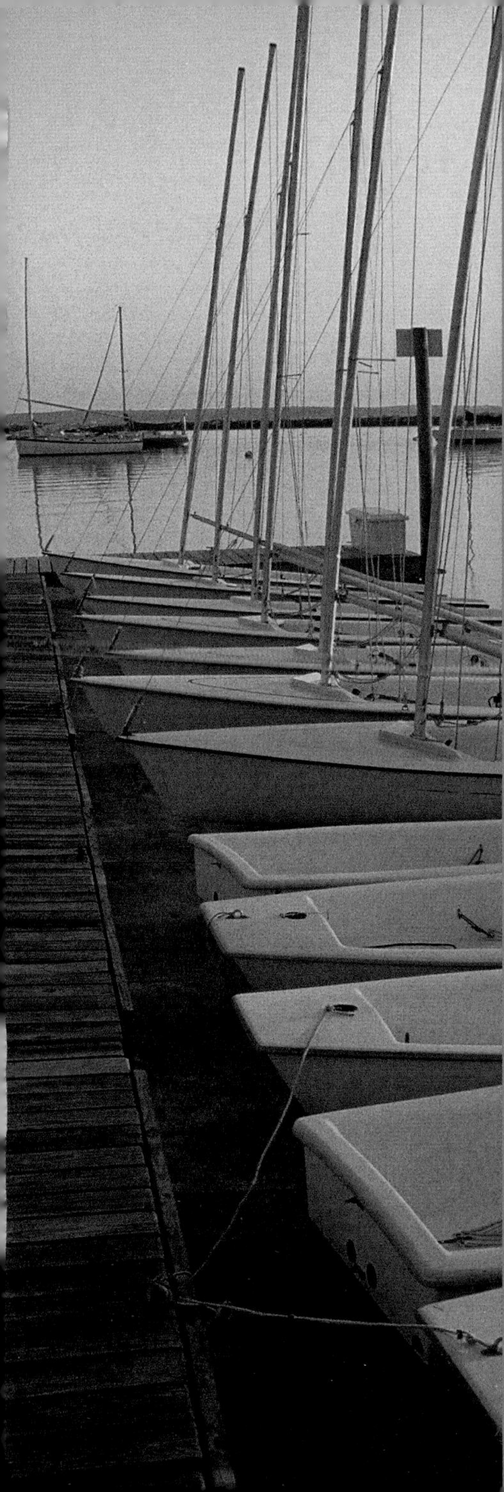

Trips Out of Town

Features

Trips Out of Town

Find an adventure beyond the city limits—and within a few hours' travel time.

Summer shares, winter shares, weekend shares—New Yorkers often claim to be dying to leave their favorite city, even if they rarely do. But as devoted as natives are to their work, they also need chill-out time. You might too: You may choose to socialize in a Hamptons beach town, hole up in a Hudson Valley retreat or go gamboling (or gambling) in the great outdoors. Whatever your destination, count on this: Traffic is hell on Fridays (leaving town) and Sundays (returning), so consider planning your trip for midweek—and think about taking public transportation.

GENERAL INFORMATION

NYC & Company, the New York visitors and convention bureau (*see p379*), has many brochures on upstate excursions. Look for special packages if you're planning to spend a few days away. *The New York Times* publishes a travel section every Sunday that carries advertised deals for transportation and lodging. *Time Out New York*'s annual Summer Getaways issue will also point you in the right direction.

TRANSPORTATION

We've included information on how to reach all listed destinations from New York City. **Metro-North** and the **Long Island Rail Road**, or LIRR (*see p362*), are the two main commuter rail systems. Both offer theme tours in the summer. Call the **Port Authority Bus Terminal** (*see p361*) for information on all bus transportation from the city. For a more scenic route, travel by water: **NY Waterway** (*see p70*) offers service to areas outside Manhattan. If you want to drive, be forewarned that New York's car-rental rates are exorbitant. For more information on airports, buses, car rentals and trains, *see pp360–362.*

Beaches

Manhattan may be an island, but its bedrock foundation makes for a deepwater shoreline that is better suited to boating than to bathing. However, you needn't travel far to find a proper beach. Coney Island and Brighton Beach make for picturesque day trips, as do the Rockaways, but most urban dwellers prefer the comparatively clean and serene beaches of Long Island. From Memorial Day (late May) to Labor Day weekend (early September), New Yorkers flock to summer rentals or day-trip destinations on Fire Island and in the Hamptons.

Nearby

When the city heats up, shore relief is only 45 minutes from Manhattan. Visitors head to **Jones Beach** *(516-785-1600; www.jonesbeach.org)* for picnicking and sunbathing. It's also the site of big-name headliner summer music concerts (*see p319*). Closer still is **Long Beach** *(516-431-1000; www.longbeachny.org),* which is easily accessible by the LIRR. At the tip of the Rockaways peninsula is **Jacob Riis Park** *(718-318-4300).* Riis is family-friendly at one end and a gay, nude beach at the eastern end, which almost touches Fire Island.

Getting there

Jacob Riis Park

NY Waterway offers round-trip ferry service from East 34th Street or from Pier 17 at South Street Seaport for $26 ($1 extra to bring a surfboard or bicycle).

Jones Beach

From late May through Labor Day, the **LIRR** offers a $14 package from Penn Station that covers train-and-bus fare, plus entry to the beach. Take the Babylon line of the LIRR to Freeport (change at Jamaica Station), then board a bus to the beach. Check the LIRR website for an updated schedule.

Long Beach

As with Jones Beach, the **LIRR** has a $15 deal from Penn Station that includes train fare and entry to the beach. Take the Long Beach line of the LIRR to its terminus; the beach is two blocks south of the station. Check the LIRR website for an updated schedule.

Fire Island

There are no automobiles allowed on most of Fire Island, making it quieter and prettier than many beach destinations. At its widest point, the island is only a quarter mile across; at its narrowest, only a few hundred feet. Yet this tiny isle is home to at least 15 different communities, each with a distinct personality.

Land's end The 1790 **Montauk lighthouse**, at Long Island's easternmost tip. *See p355.*

Cherry Grove and **Fire Island Pines** (commonly known as "The Pines"), at the eastern end of the island, together constitute Fire Island's gay outpost. Farther west are **Ocean Bay Park**, **Seaview** and **Ocean Beach**, the chosen playgrounds of college kids, young postgrads and many families. Ocean Beach in particular is well known for its thriving pickup scene, pricey restaurants and draconian laws governing public behavior: no drinking—not even water—on sidewalks and beaches; and no dogs or ball-playing on the beach. **Robert Moses State Park** *(631-669-0449),* located on the western tip, is a popular destination for day-trippers. A long stretch of white sand fronts grassy dunes. Head east along the shore toward the lighthouse and let it all hang out at the friendly nude beach. No matter which community you end up in, it's safe to say that *all* of Fire Island feels the way a beach resort should.

Where to stay, eat & drink

Most restaurants in resort areas are overpriced, but there are a few bargains. The **Out Restaurant** *(Bay Walk, Kismet; 631-583-7400; www.theoutrestaurant.com)* offers a standard seafood menu. It operates only five months out of the year, so check the website for details. **Flynn's** *(1 Cayuga St at Bay Ave, Ocean Bay Park; 631-583-5000)* is a partygoer's dream: cheap margaritas, DJs, live bands, a young boisterous crowd—and oh, yeah, decent seafood. Anyone with a taste for buttercream-frosted cakes and gooey brownies should stop by **Rachel's Bakery** *(325 Bay Walk between Bungalow Walk and Ocean Rd, Fire Island; 631-583-9340; www.rachelsfireisland.com).* If you don't know anyone with a summer rental, book a room at **Clegg's Hotel** *(478 Bayberry Walk, Ocean Beach, NY 11770; 631-583-5399)* or **Jerry's Accommodations** *(168 Cottage Walk, Ocean Beach, NY 11770; 631-583-8870).* In the Pines, guest rooms are available at **Botel** *(Harbor Walk, Fire Island Pines, NY 11782; 631-597-6500)* or **Pines Place** *(PO Box 5309, Fire Island Pines, NY 11782; 631-597-6162; www.pinesplace.com).*

Getting there

Ocean Beach

By train Take the Montauk line of the **LIRR** *($21)* to Bay Shore, then walk or cab it to the ferry station. *By van* **Tommy's Taxi** *(631-665-4800)* runs regular van service from various Manhattan locations *(Mon–Sat $17 per person, Sundays and holidays $20);* reservations are required. *By ferry* From Bay Shore, take the **Fire Island Ferry** *(99 Maple Ave near Aldrich Ct, Bay Shore; 631-665-3600; www.fireislandferries.com; round-trip $12.50, children $6).*

The Pines

By train Take the Montauk line of the **LIRR** *($15)* to Sayville, then walk or take a taxi to the ferry dock. *By bus* From May to October, **Islanders Horizon Coach & Buses** *(212-228-7100, 631-*

654-2622; www.islanderstravel.com; one-way $20) runs between Manhattan and the Sayville ferry station. *By ferry* From Sayville, take the **Sayville Ferry** *(41 River Rd at Willow St, 631-589-0810; www.sayvilleferry.com; round-trip $11, children under 12 $5).*

Robert Moses State Park

By train From late May through Labor Day, the **LIRR** offers a $15 train-and-bus package from Penn Station. Take the Babylon line to Babylon and board a bus to the park. Buses run approximately every half hour on weekend days and hourly on weekdays.

The Hamptons

The Hamptons, a string of small towns along the South Fork of Long Island, are known for attracting the rich and famous. Throughout the summer, socialites, artists and wannabes drift between beautiful sun-drenched beaches and sweat-drenched nightclubs, while locals grin and bear the vainglorious invasion. For an up-to-date social calendar, pick up the free local rags *Dan's Paper* or *Hamptons Country Magazine,* available at area stores. The glossy *Hamptons Magazine* displays plenty of red-carpet pics from parties past. The *East Hampton Star* carries local news. Check www.ihamptons.com for real-estate sales, rental listings, services (cleaning, etc.) and a live cam on the main street of every Hamptons community.

After Memorial Day, celebrities head to the Hamptons for rest and relaxation. **Two Mile Hollow Beach** *(Two Mile Hollow Rd, East Hampton)* and **Sagg Beach** *(Sagg Main St,*

The hills are alive!

The Catskills are among the oldest mountain ranges in all of North America, as their rolling, soft-shouldered shapes reveal. And for New Yorkers, they have served as a prime summer retreat for well over a century. The area of the Catskills that's really hopping these days is the northern part of Ulster County, especially around the town of Woodstock (not to be confused with the site of the legendary outdoor concerts, which were actually held in another Catskills county). Once a haven of urban-flight hippiedom, the area is now host to chic B&Bs; summer homes are being snapped up; and a new generation of artists, musicians and writers are making this upstate precinct a fashionable alternative to summering in the Hamptons.

THE CALL OF THE WILD

Outdoor recreation is a year-round source of entertainment in these parts. If it's winter, skiing and snowshoeing are the main events; the rest of the year, it's hiking and biking. For more information on hiking and biking trails, visit www.dec.state.ny.us/website/dlf/publands/cats. **Overlook Mountain Bikes** *(93 Tinker St off Old Forge Rd, Woodstock; 845-679-2122)* has the wheels to suit your needs. Ask about the trail that takes you past the ruins of a once massive Catskills hotel, and up to a summit with panoramic views. In winter, you can rent snowshoes and cross-country skis. **Hunter Mountain** *(888-HunterM; www.huntermtn.com)* and **Windham Mountain** *(800-754-9463; www.skiwindham.com)* are the ski resorts closest to the city and are quite popular. Hunter appeals to teens and boarders, while Windham is more family-friendly. During warmer months, the trails and runs are open to hikers and mountain bikers.

FESTIVALS AND SHOWS

One of the top draws to the area is the **Woodstock Film Festival** *(www.woodstockfilmfestival.com; Oct 13–17).* Events in Woodstock, Saugerties, Rhinebeck and Hunter include celebrity panels, concerts, parties and, of course, screenings. Previous participants have included Parker Posey and Marcia Gay Harden. Make sure to reserve early, as events sell out. Launched in 2001, the **Woodstock Poetry Festival** *(www.woodstockpoetryfestival.com)* takes place over several days at the end of August and features readings and open mikes. Pulitzer prize winner Paul Muldoon and poet laureate Billy Collins have participated in past years. Chamber-music lovers will want to check out the **Maverick Concerts** *(845-679-8217; www.maverickconcerts.org; Jun 27–Sept 5).* This summer series has been held every year since 1916, and it draws audiences from the city.

THE ART SCENE

The art community is still developing, but the **Woodstock Guild** *(845-679-2079; www.woodstockguild.org)* is a good starting point to find out what's happening locally. The guild operates the Kleinert/James Art Center,

Sagaponack) are good places to go star-spotting. Expect A-listers to show their faces after the Fourth of July at **Resort** *(44 Three Mile Harbor Rd between Boat Yard Dr and Fanyon Way, East Hampton; 631-329-6000).* The club exterior looks like a funeral parlor, but it's plenty sexy on the inside: a slick tunnel of a main room with turquoise floors, gold-leafed ceilings and white-leather bottle-service booths, plus an outdoor patio lined with private bottle-service cabanas.

To prepare for (or recover from) the nightlife, a visit to the spa is essential. **Style Bar** *(1 Bay St at Marine Park Dr, Sag Harbor; 631-725-6730; www.stylebarspa.com)* offers Endermologie, a mechanical massage technique that supposedly reduces cellulite. Also available are microdermabrasion for the hands, airbrush body tanning, the Tutti-Frutti pedicure and more. Those looking for more mind-body calm should visit **Samadhi House Yoga Studio and Spa** *(83 South Edison Ave at South Elmwood Ave, second floor, Montauk; 631-668-5555; www.samadhihouse.com).* You can get your pranayama on before or after your mani/pedi; other indulgences include custom herbal facials and Thai massage.

Montauk, a seaside village that's technically part of East Hampton, has little in common with its neighbors; the locals like to keep their ruffian reputation intact. **Montauk Point Lighthouse** *(Montauk Pt at end of Rte 27, Montauk; 888-MTK-POINT; www.montauklighthouse.com)* is the oldest in New York State (built in 1796), and historic memorabilia are displayed inside.

a gallery for visual and performing artists; the Fleur de Lis Gallery for local artisans; and the 1,500-acre Byrdcliffe Arts Colony, host to theater performances, walking tours and exhibits. Byrdcliffe, which was born out of the Arts and Crafts movement in the late 1800s, celebrated its centennial in 2003. **Opus 40** *(845-246-3400; www.opus40.org)* is a stirring piece of land art. Built by Harvey Fite over the course of 37 years, the sculpture covers more than six acres, with spirals and steps made of finely carved bluestone. As you walk across the piece, you'll come upon little ponds and sudden dead-ends.

Hunter Mountain.

WHERE TO STAY, EAT & DRINK

You can grab breakfast, lunch, or coffee and a cupcake at **Heaven Café** *(17 Tinker St off Old Forge Rd, Woodstock; 845-679-0011).* **Bread Alone Café and Bakery** *(22 Mill Hill Rd between Maple and Mower Lns, Woodstock; 845-679-2108)* offers hearty lunch fare like chili and sandwiches made with organic bread. A short drive from the center of Woodstock, you'll find the popular **Bear Café** *(295A Tinker St off Old Forge Rd, Bearsville; 845-679-5555),* which has a creative American menu and a lovely outdoor patio. The place fills up on weekends, so be sure to make a reservation. In nearby Saugerties, enjoy live music and Asian-Caribbean flavors at **New World Home Cooking Co.** *(1411 Rte 212 between Fish Creek Rd and Old Rte 212, Saugerties; 845-246-0900).* At **Sweet Sue's** *(Main St, Phoenicia; 845-688-7852),* you'll think you died and went to pancake heaven (choose from more than 22 different kinds!).

The **Woodstock Country Inn** *(845-679-9380; www.woodstockcountryinn.com)* is surrounded by rolling meadows and is located within easy hiking distance of the serene Cooper Lake. The staff at the inn will pick you up and drop you off at the Trailways bus stop in town. The young owners of the **Villa at Saugerties** *(845-246-0682; www.thevillaat saugerties.com)* bring a chic, modern aesthetic to their tiny B&B's lush country setting—and there's a pool.

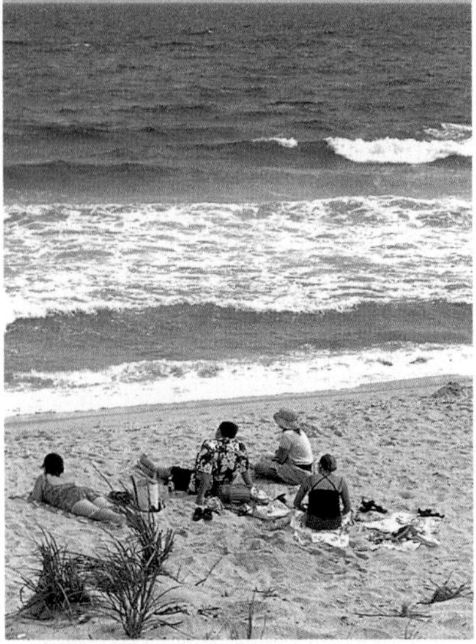

Chilling on a **Hamptons** beach.

Where to eat & drink

Dining trends in the Hamptons change frequently. **New Paradise Café** *(126 Main St at Madison St, Sag Harbor; 631-725-6080)* puts a spin on standard dishes. Fried calamari comes in salad form—the extraspicy rings are tossed with a mountain of lightly dressed frisée. Time your visit around sunset and get a seat on the back patio. The sunlight peering through the trees casts a glow that makes everyone look like a soap-opera star. For a break from the usual fare, try the Cajun eats at **Belles East** *(256 Elm St between Powell Ave and Pulaski St, Southampton; 631-204-0300)*. The jambalaya is bursting with piquant andouille sausage, and the sassily named Slap My Ass & Call Me Belle barbecued ribs live up to their name, if that's possible. Finally, if you need to detox, drag yourself to **Bogo's Food Spa** *(27 Race Ln between Gingerbread Ln and Railroad Ave, East Hampton; 631-329-1004)*. The market-style stand sells everything you need to cleanse and rehydrate, like fresh juices and smoothies, organic produce, and nutritional supplements. After excessive eating, drinking and sunbathing, it's the least you can do for your body.

► ***Time Out New York*** publishes an annual summer-getaway issue with info on places to go near the city. Find past years' articles at **www.timeoutny.com/archives**.

Getting there

By train Take the Montauk line of the **LIRR** *($10.25–$15.25)* to Southampton, East Hampton or Montauk. *By bus* The **Hampton Jitney** *(212-936-0440, 800-936-0440; www.hamptonjitney.com; one-way $23–$27)* runs regular bus service between three locations in Manhattan, and it stops in every town in the Hamptons.

Mountains

Carved by glaciers, the mountainous region just north of Manhattan has long been a seasonal playground for city dwellers. Gorgeous valley views, quaint towns and plenty of trees draw visitors year-round. While a trip there and back can be made in a day, plan on at least two days to enjoy all that the area affords.

The Catskill Mountains

Established in 1904, Catskill Park comprises both forest preserve and private land (more than 700,000 acres in all), and encompasses several counties of New York state. The artsy town of Woodstock, in Ulster County, is a natural base for a trip. For highlights of local events and activities, *see p354* **The hills are alive!**

Getting there

A two-and-a-half hour bus ride lands you in the center of Woodstock. Check **Trailways** *(800-858-8555; round trip $44.10)* from Port Authority for information and reservations. To really explore the area, rent a car. The drive from the city is a little more than two hours long. Take the New York State Thruway (I-87) to Exit 19, then Rte 375 to Woodstock. To get to Saugerties, take Exit 20. From there, you can take Rte 32 north into town, or continue up and take the lovely winding Rte 23A to Hunter Mountain.

The Hudson Valley

Magnificent historic homes (and their sprawling estates) dot the hills overlooking the Hudson River. The **Historic Hudson Valley** *(914-631-8200; www.hudsonvalley.org)* maintains most of these sites, which are open to the public throughout much of the year.

Kykuit

Pocantico Hills, Tarrytown, NY 10591 (914-631-9491; www.hudsonvalley.org). **Open** *Late Apr–early Nov Mon, Wed–Sun 9am–3pm.* **Admission** *$20, seniors $19, children 10–17 $17 (not recommended for children under 10).* **Credit** *AmEx, MC, V.*

John D. Rockefeller Jr.'s Kykuit, pronounced "KYE-kut," is located on the banks above the Hudson. In addition to the house and gardens, there are carefully maintained antique carriages and automobiles in the coach barn. Tickets are sold on a first-come basis at the Philipsburg Manor visitors' center (see website for directions), so arrive early.

Lyndhurst Castle

635 South Broadway, Tarrytown, NY 10591 (914-631-4481; www.lyndhurst.org). **Open** *Mid-Apr–Oct Tue–Sun, Monday holidays 10am–4:15pm. Nov–mid-Apr Sat, Sun, Monday holidays 10am–3:30pm.* **Admission** *$10, seniors $9, students 12–17 $4, children under 12 free; grounds fee $4.* **Credit** *AmEx, MC, V.*

Several notable figures have called this Gothic Revival mansion home, including former New York City mayor William Paulding and robber baron Jay Gould. The interior is sumptuously decorated and excellently maintained. From Grand Central, the estate is a scenic 40-minute trip by Metro-North (Hudson Line to Tarrytown), and a five-minute taxi ride from the train station.

Olana

Rte 9G, Hudson, NY 12534 (518-828-0135; www.olana.org). **Open** *Early Apr–Memorial Day, Jun 1–Oct 1 Wed–Sun 10am–5pm. Oct 2–31 Wed–Sun 10am–4pm. Nov Wed–Sun 10am–3pm. Dec–Mar by reservation only.* **Admission** *$7, seniors $5, children 5–12 $2, children under 5 free.* **Credit** *MC, V.*

Hudson River School artist Frederic Church built his home here after seeing the views from this site. The richly colored design incorporates many Moorish touches. Reservations are strongly recommended.

Springwood

4097 Albany Post Rd off Rte 9, Hyde Park, NY 12538 (800-967-2283; www.nps.gov/hofr). **Open** *Buildings 9am–5pm; grounds 7am–dusk; closed major holidays.* **Admission** *buildings $14, children under 16 free; grounds free.* **Credit** *AmEx, Disc, MC, V.*

Springwood, Franklin D. Roosevelt's boyhood home, is filled with family photos and the former president's artifacts. In the nearby library and museum, you can examine items such as presidential documents and FDR's pony cart. Reservations are required, since the home, library and museum are accessible only by guided tour. You can call or make reservations online at http://reservations.nps.gov.

Sunnyside

West Sunnyside Lane, off Rte 9, Tarrytown, NY 10591 (914-591-8763, 914-631-8200; www.hudsonvalley.org). **Open** *Mar Sat, Sun 10am–3pm. Apr–Oct Sun, Mon, Wed–Sat 10am–4pm. Nov, Dec Sun, Mon, Wed–Sat 10am–3pm.* **Admission** *$9, seniors $8, children 5–17 $5, children under 5 free.* **Credit** *AmEx, Disc, MC, V.*

Author Washington Irving renovated and expanded this 18th-century Dutch Colonial cottage in Tarrytown, adding a stepped gable entrance and a Spanish-style tower. To visit the cemetery of Sleepy Hollow, the village Irving immortalized in print, call for a taxi.

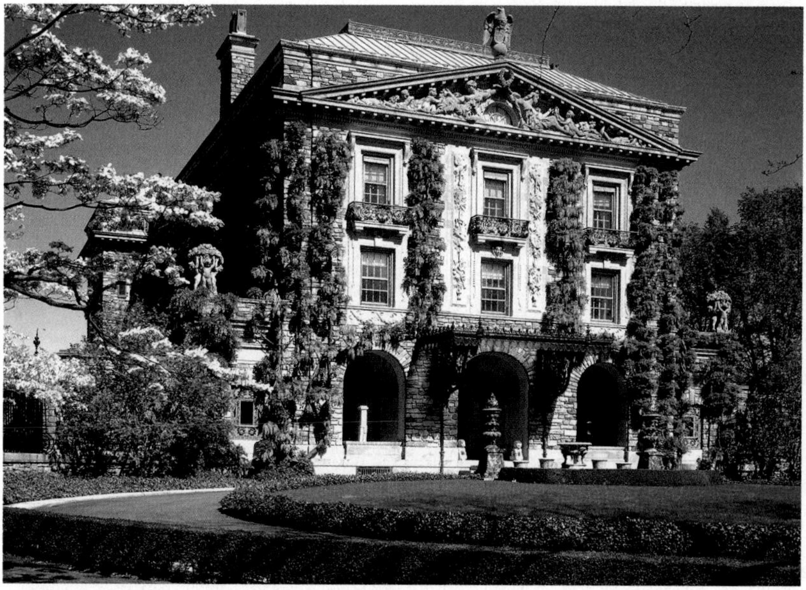

Home sweet home Four generations of the Rockefellers have lived at **Kykuit**. *See p356.*

Slotty behavior at the **Mohegan Sun** casino.

Vanderbilt

519 Albany Post Rd, Hyde Park, NY 12538 (845-229-9115; www.nps.gov/vama). **Open** *9am–5pm.* **Admission** *$8, children under 17 free.* **Credit** *AmEx, Disc, MC, V.*
Compared with the opulent homes of his siblings, Frederick Vanderbilt's estate is modest. Built on a bluff above the river, the Greek Revival structure and its grounds offer sweeping views.

Where to stay, eat & drink

The **Culinary Institute of America** *(1946 Campus Dr, Hyde Park; 845-471-6608; www.ciachef.edu)* boasts such illustrious alumni as celebrity chef Larry Forgione. Chefs-in-training prepare French, Italian, American contemporary and American regional cuisine in four different dining rooms. The CIA's **Apple Pie Bakery Café** is stocked with treats made by pastry majors. Rhinebeck's **Beekman Arms Inn** *(6387 Mill St, Rhinebeck, NY 12572; 845-876-7077, 800-361-6517; www.beekmandelamaterinn.com)* is the nation's oldest continuously operating hotel (more than 300 years), but the kitchen is au courant: Forgione is in charge of the Inn's **Traphagen Restaurant** *(845-876-1766)*. Show up in New Paltz with an appetite: The **Bakery** *(13A N Front St off Rte 32, 845-255-8840; www.ilovethebakery.com)* offers baked goods, sandwiches and salads, all made in-house. There's also an excellent selection of teas and coffees.

In Putnam County, the 1832 **Hudson House** *(2 Main St, Cold Spring, NY 10516; 845-265-9355; www.hudsonhouseinn.com)* is a peaceful, convenient inn with a notable contemporary American restaurant. A good place to rest in Hyde Park is **Fala Bed and Breakfast** *(East Market St, Hyde Park, NY 12538; 845-229-5937)*, a private one-bedroom guest house that was named after FDR's Scottish terrier (it features a pool). Call ahead for reservations.

Getting there

By train Ask about special package rates from **NY Waterway** (*see p70*). **Metro-North** runs trains daily along the Hudson Valley; the Hudson line ends at Poughkeepsie, a 20-minute taxi ride from Rhinebeck. Alternatively, you can take **Amtrak** (*see p362*), but it's more expensive. *By bus* **Short Line Buses** *(212-736-4700, 800-631-8405; www.shortlinebus.com; round-trip $28.35)* runs regular bus service to Hyde Park and Rhinebeck. Connecting service is available for some destinations. Check websites for more info.

Casinos

Side trips to nearby gambling resorts are a hot new trend. These options—only a short bus ride away—are your best, um, bets.

Atlantic City, NJ

Convention and Visitors Bureau (888-AC-VISIT, 800-BOARDWALK; www. atlanticcitynj.com). Travel: Greyhound from Port Authority Bus Terminal (round-trip $27). Call 800-231-2222 for schedule.
Markedly less fabulous than Las Vegas, this seaside resort still tries hard, with ten casinos, headline entertainment, boxing matches, the famed boardwalk and—let's not forget—the Miss America pageant.

Foxwoods

39 Norwich Westerly Rd, Mashantucket, CT 06338 (800-FOXWOODS; www.foxwoods.com). Travel: Greyhound from Port Authority Bus Terminal (round-trip $26; includes $10 match-play coupon and $5 keno coupon). Call 800-231-2222 for schedule.
Opened in 1986 as a high-stakes bingo hall (purportedly the world's largest), the casino now boasts 6,400 slots and 350 tables.

Mohegan Sun

1 Mohegan Sun Blvd, Uncasville, CT 06382 (888-226-7711; www.mohegansun.com). Travel: Academy Bus Tours from Port Authority Bus Terminal (round-trip $26; includes $10 food coupon and free match-play coupon). Call 800-442-7272 for schedule.
Coming off a $1 billion expansion, this massive (5.6-million-square-foot) enterprise has something for everyone: shopping, dining, cabaret, comedy and more than 6,000 slot machines.

Directory

Features

Directory

Getting to and from NYC

By air

Three major airports service the New York City area (there's also a smaller one in Long Island); for details, *see below* **Airports**. Here are some sources for purchasing airline tickets.

Websites

Sites to investigate for low fares: **www.airfare.com**, **www.cheaptickets.com**, **www.expedia.com**, **www.orbitz.com**, **www.priceline.com**, **www.travelocity.com**.

Newspapers

If the travel section of your local paper is no help, get a Sunday ***New York Times***. It has plenty of advertisements for discounted fares.

Satellite Airlines Terminal

125 Park Ave between 41st and 42nd Sts (212-986-0888). Subway: 42nd St S, 4, 5, 6, 7 to 42nd St–Grand Central. Mon–Fri 8am–7pm; Sat 9am–5pm.
This one-stop shop has ticket counters for major international airlines. You can exchange frequent-flier mileage; process passports, birth certificates and driver's licenses; and arrange for transportation and city tours. Call the information line above or individual carriers.
Other location *1 E 59th St at Fifth Ave.*

Travel agents

Agents are specialized, so find one who suits your needs. Do you want luxury? Around the world? Student? (*See p376* **Students**) Find an agent through word of mouth, newspapers, the Yellow Pages phone directory or the Internet. Knowledgeable travel agents can help with far more than air tickets, and a good relationship with an agent can be invaluable, especially if you travel often and prefer not to deal with travel details.

To and from the airport

For a list of transportation services between New York City and its major airports, call **800-AIR-RIDE** *(800-247-7433)*. Public transportation is the cheapest method, but it can be frustrating and time-consuming. Private bus or van services are usually the best bargain. Medallion (city-licensed) yellow cabs, which can be flagged on the street or at designated locations around the airports, are more expensive but offer convenient curb-to-door service. You may also reserve a car service in advance to pick you up or drop you off (*see p364* **Taxis & car services**). Although it is illegal, many car-service drivers and nonlicensed "gypsy cabs" solicit riders around the baggage-claim areas. Avoid them.

Airports

John F. Kennedy International Airport

718-244-4444; www.panynj.gov.
At $2, the subway-bus link from JFK is dirt-cheap, but it can take up to two hours to get to Manhattan. At the airport, look for the yellow shuttle bus to the Howard Beach station, then take the A train to Manhattan. In late 2003, JFK's Air Train began offering service between all eight terminals and the A, J, M and Z subway lines as well as the Long Island Railroad for $5. Visit www.airtrainjfk.com for more information. Private bus and van services are a good compromise between value and convenience (*see p361* **Bus services**). A medallion yellow cab from JFK to Manhattan will charge a flat $35 fare, plus toll (varies by route, but usually $4) and tip (if service is fair, give at least $5). There is no set fare to JFK from Manhattan; depending on traffic, it can be as high as $45. Or try a car service for around $40.

La Guardia Airport

718-244-4444; www.panynj.gov.
Seasoned New Yorkers take the M60 bus ($2), which runs between the airport and 106th Street at Broadway. The ride takes 40 minutes to an hour (depending on traffic) and runs from 5am to 1am. The route crosses Manhattan on 125th Street in Harlem. Get off at Lexington Avenue for the 4, 5 and 6 trains; at Malcolm X Boulevard (Lenox Avenue) for the 2 and 3; or at St. Nicholas Avenue for the A, C, B and D trains. You can also disembark on Broadway at the 116th St–Columbia Univ or 110th St–Cathedral Pkwy subway stations for the 1 and 9 trains. Less time-consuming options: Private bus services cost around $14 (*see p361* **Bus services**); taxis and car services charge about $25 plus toll and tip.

Newark Liberty International Airport

973-961-6000; www.newark airport.com
Although it's in next-door New Jersey, Newark has good public-transit access. The best bet is a 40-minute $11.55 trip by train and monorail to or from Penn Station. The airport's monorail, AirTrain Newark *(www.airtrainnewark.com)*, is now linked to the New Jersey Transit and Amtrak train systems. For inexpensive buses, *see p361* **Bus services**. A car service will run about $40 and a taxi around $45, plus toll and tip.

MacArthur Airport

631-467-3210; www.macarthur airport.com.
Some flights into this airport in Islip, Long Island, may be cheaper than flights into those above. Getting to Manhattan, of course, will take longer and be more expensive. Colonial Transportation *(631-589-3500)* will take up to four people to Manhattan for $143, including tolls and tip. Visit the airport's website for other alternatives.

Bus services

New York Airport Service

212-875-8200; www.nyairportservice.com. Call or visit website for schedule.
Buses operate frequently to and from JFK ($13 one-way, $23 round-trip) and La Guardia ($10 one-way, $17 round-trip) from early morning to late at night, with stops near Grand Central *(Park Ave between 41st and 42nd Sts),* near Penn Station *(33rd St at Seventh Ave),* inside the Port Authority terminal (*see below* **By bus**) and outside a number of midtown hotels (for an extra charge).

Olympia Trails

212-964-6233, 877-894-9155; www.olympiabus.com. Call or visit website for schedule.
Olympia operates between Newark Airport and Manhattan, stopping outside Penn Station *(34th St at Eighth Ave)* or Grand Central *(41st St between Park and Lexington Aves),* and inside Port Authority (*see below* **By bus**). The fare is $12 one-way ($19 round-trip); buses leave every 15 to 20 minutes, all day and night.

SuperShuttle

212-209-7000; www.supershuttle.com. 24hr.
Blue SuperShuttle vans offer door-to-door service between NYC and the three major airports. Allow extra time when catching a flight, as vans will be picking up other passengers. The fare varies from $13 to $22, depending on pickup location and destination. Always call to confirm.

By bus

Buses are an inexpensive means of getting to and from New York City, though the ride is longer and sometimes uncomfortable. They are particularly useful if you want to leave in a hurry; many don't require reservations. Most out-of-town buses come and go from the **Port Authority Bus Terminal**.

Bus stations

George Washington Bridge Bus Station

178th St between Broadway and Fort Washington Ave (800-221-9903; www.panynj.gov). Subway: A to 175th St; 1, 9 to 181st St. 5am–1am daily.
A few bus lines that serve New Jersey and Rockland County, New York, use this station.

Port Authority Bus Terminal

625 Eighth Ave between 40th and 42nd Sts (212-564-8484; www.panynj.gov). Subway: A, C, E to 42nd St–Port Authority.
This is the hub for many transportation companies serving New York City's commuter and long-distance bus travelers. Call for additional information.

Long-distance lines

Greyhound Trailways

800-229-9424; www.greyhound.com. 24hr. AmEx, Disc, MC, V.
Greyhound offers long-distance bus travel to destinations across North America.

New Jersey Transit

973-762-5100; www.njtransit.com. Call or visit website for schedules. AmEx, MC, V.
NJT provides bus service to nearly everywhere in the Garden State, and some destinations in New York State; most buses run around the clock.

Peter Pan

800-343-9999; www.peterpanbus.com. 24hr. AmEx, MC, V.
Peter Pan runs extensive service to cities across the Northeast; its tickets are also valid on Greyhound.

By car

If you drive to the city, you may encounter delays at bridge and tunnel crossings (check **www.nyc.gov** and **www.panynj.gov** before driving in). Tune your car radio to **WINS** (1010 on the AM dial) for up-to-the-minute traffic reports. Expect delays of 15 minutes to 2 hours—plenty of time to get your money out for the toll ($5 is average). Note that street parking in the city is very restricted, especially in the summer, so be prepared to shell out for a space in a parking garage (*see p362* **Parking**).

Car rental

If you're interested in heading out of town by car, rentals are much cheaper on the city's outskirts and in New Jersey and Connecticut; reserve ahead for weekends.
New York State honors valid foreign-issued driver's licenses. All car-rental companies listed below add sales tax (8.625 percent). Companies located outside of New York State offer a "loss damage waiver" (LDW). This is expensive, but without it, you are responsible for the cost of repairing even the slightest scratch. If you pay with an AmEx card or a gold Visa or MasterCard, the LDW *may* be covered by your credit-card company; it might also be covered by a reciprocal agreement with an automotive organization, such as AAA. Personal liability insurance is optional—and recommended (but see if your travel insurance or home policy already covers it). Rental companies in New York are required by law to insure their own cars, so the LDW is not a factor. Instead, the renter pays for the first $100 in damage to the vehicle, and the company is responsible for anything beyond that. You will need a credit card (or a large cash deposit) to rent a car, and you usually have to be at least 25 years old. If you know you want to rent a car before you travel, ask your travel agent or airline to check for special deals and discounts.

Avis

800-230-4898; www.avis.com. 24hr most locations. Rates from $60 a day, unlimited mileage. AmEx, DC, Disc, MC, V.

Budget Rent-a-Car

800-527-0700; www.budget.com. In the city, call for hours; airport counters 5am–2am. Rates from $35 per weekday, $70 per day on weekends; unlimited mileage. AmEx, DC, Disc, MC, V.

Enterprise

800-325-8007; www.enterprise.com. Mon–Fri 7:30am–6pm; Sat 9am–noon. Rates from $30 a day outside New York City; around $50 a day in New York City; unlimited

mileage restricted to New York, New Jersey and Connecticut. AmEx, DC, Disc, MC, V.
This inexpensive, reliable company has branches easily accessible from Manhattan. Try the Greenwich, Connecticut location (take Metro-North from Grand Central). Agents will pick you up at the station. Call or visit website for locations within the five boroughs.

Parking

If you drive to NYC, find a garage, park your car and leave it there. Parking on the street is subject to byzantine rules (for information on restrictions, call 311), ticketing is rampant (if you can't decipher the parking signs, find another spot), and car theft is common. Garages are plentiful but expensive. If you want to park for less than $15 a day, try a garage outside Manhattan and take public transportation. Listed below are Manhattan's better deals. For other options—there are many—try the Yellow Pages. (*See also p363* **Driving**.)

Central Kinney System

212-321-7500, press 5. 24hr most locations. AmEx, Disc, MC, V.
One of the city's largest parking companies, Kinney is accessible and reliable, though not the cheapest in town. Rates vary, so call for prices.

GMC Park Plaza

212-888-7400. 24hr most locations. AmEx, MC, V.
GMC has more than 70 locations in the city. At $22 overnight, including tax, the location at 407 E 61st St between First and York Aves *(212-838-4158)* is the least expensive.

Icon Parking

877-727-5464; www.iconparking.com. 24hr most locations. AmEx, MC, V.
Choose from more than 160 locations via the website to guarantee a spot and price ahead of time.

Mayor Parking

Pier 40, West St at West Houston St. (800-494-7007). 24hr. $14 for 12 hours. AmEx, MC, V.
Mayor Parking, another of the city's large chains, offers indoor and outdoor parking. Call for information and other locations.

By train

Thanks to Americans' love affair with the automobile, passenger trains are not as common here as in other parts of the world. American rails are used primarily for cargo, and passenger trains from New York are used mostly by commuters. For longer hauls, call **Amtrak** (*see also pp351–358* **Trips Out of Town**).

Train service

Amtrak

800 USA RAIL; www.amtrak.com.
Amtrak provides all long-distance train service in North America. Traveling by Amtrak is more comfortable than by bus, but it's also less flexible and more expensive (a sleeper will likely cost more than flying). All trains depart from Penn Station.

Long Island Rail Road

718-217-5477; www.lirr.org.
LIRR provides rail service to Long Island from Penn Station, Brooklyn and Queens.

Metro-North

212-532-4900, 800-638-7646; www.mnr.org.
Commuter trains leave from Grand Central Terminal and service towns north of Manhattan.

New Jersey Transit

973-762-5100; www.njtransit.com.
Service from Penn Station reaches most of New Jersey, some points in New York, and Philadelphia.

PATH Trains

800-234-7284; www.pathrail.com.
PATH (Port Authority Trans Hudson) trains run from five stations in Manhattan to various places across the Hudson River in New Jersey, including Hoboken, Jersey City and Newark. The system is fully automated and costs $1.50 per trip. You need change or crisp bills for the ticket machines, and trains run 24 hours a day. Manhattan PATH stations are marked on the subway map (*see p410*).

Train stations

Grand Central Terminal

From 42nd to 44th Sts, between Vanderbilt and Lexington Aves. Subway: 42nd St S, 4, 5, 6, 7 to 42nd St–Grand Central.
Home to Metro-North, which runs trains to more than 100 stations throughout New York State and Connecticut. Printed schedules are available at the terminal.

Penn Station

From 31st to 33rd Sts, between Seventh and Eighth Aves. Subway: A, C, E, 1, 2, 3, 9 to 34th St–Penn Station.
Amtrak, Long Island Rail Road and New Jersey Transit trains depart from this terminal, which has printed schedules available.

Holidays

Most banks and government offices close on these major U.S. holidays (except Election Day), but stores, restaurants and some museums are usually open. If you will be in New York during or around a holiday, call ahead to the venues you want to visit, to check for special hours.

New Year's Day
January 1

Martin Luther King Jr. Day
third Monday in January

Presidents' Day
third Monday in February

Memorial Day
last Monday in May

Independence Day
July 4

Labor Day
first Monday in September

Columbus Day
second Monday in October

Election Day
first Tuesday after first Monday in November

Veterans' Day
November 11

Thanksgiving Day
fourth Thursday in November

Christmas Day
December 25

Getting Around

Under normal circumstances, New York City is easy to navigate. However, subway and bus changes can occur at the last minute, so pay attention to the posters on station walls and listen carefully to any announcements you may hear in trains and on subway platforms.

Metropolitan Transportation Authority (MTA)

Travel info 718-330-1234, hourly updates 718-243-7777; www.mta.info.
The MTA runs the subways and buses, as well as a number of the commuter services to points outside Manhattan. You can get news of service interruptions and download the most current maps from the website.

City buses

MTA buses are fine, but only if you aren't in a hurry. They are white and blue, and display a route number (in Manhattan, look for the ones that begin with an *M*), and a digital destination sign on the front. If your feet hurt from walking around, a bus is a good way to continue your sightseeing. The $2 fare is payable with a **MetroCard** (*see right* **Subways**), or in exact change (silver coins only). Express buses usually head to the outer boroughs; these cost $4.

MetroCards allow automatic transfers from bus to bus, and between buses and subways. If you use coins, and you're traveling uptown or downtown and want to catch a crosstown bus (or vice versa), ask the driver for a transfer when you get on—you'll be given a ticket for use on the second leg of your journey. You can rely on other passengers for advice, but maps are posted on most buses and at all subway stations; they're also available from **NYC & Company** (*see p382* **Websites**). The Manhattan Bus Map is reprinted in this guide (*see p409*). Buses generally make only designated stops, but between 10pm and 5am, you can ask the driver to stop anywhere along the route. All buses are equipped with wheelchair lifts. Contact the MTA for further information.

Driving

Manhattan drivers—especially cabbies—are fearless; taking to the streets is not for the faint of heart. Try to restrict your driving to evening hours, when traffic is lighter and there's more street parking available. Even then, keep your eyes on the road and stay alert. New York will honor all valid foreign driver's licenses.

Street parking

Make sure you read the parking signs and never park within 15 feet (5 meters) of a fire hydrant (to avoid getting a $115 ticket). Parking is off-limits on most streets for at least a few hours each day. Even where meters exist, daytime parking can be restricted. The **Department of Transportation** *(dial 311)* provides information on daily changes to parking regulations. If precautions fail, call 718-935-0096 for NYC towing and impoundment information (*see also p362* **Parking**).

Emergency towing

Citywide Towing

514 W 39th St between Tenth and Eleventh Aves (212-244-4420). 24hr; repairs 9am–6pm. AmEx, MC, V.
All types of repairs are made on domestic and foreign autos.

24-hour gas stations

Exxon

24 Second Ave at 1st St (212-979-7000). AmEx, Disc, DC, MC, V.
Repairs.

Hess

502 W 45th St at Tenth Ave (212-245-6594). AmEx, Disc, MC, V.
No repairs.

Subways

Subways are the fastest way to get around town during the day, and they're cleaner and safer than they've been in 20 years. The city's system is one of the world's largest and cheapest—$2 will get you from the depths of Brooklyn to the northernmost reaches of the Bronx, and anywhere in between. Trains run around the clock, but with sparse service and fewer riders at night, it's advisable (and usually quicker) to take a cab after 10pm.

Ongoing improvements have resulted in several changes. This guide has the most current subway map at press time (*see pp410–411*), but you can also ask MTA workers in service booths for a free map.

To ensure safety, don't stand near the edge of the platform. During nonrush hours, board the train from the off-peak waiting area, near the middle of the platform (this area is safer than the ends of the platforms or the outermost cars, which are often less populated at night). Standard urban advisory: Hold your bag with the opening facing you or keep your wallet in a front pocket, and don't wear flashy jewelry. Remember, petty crime rises during the holidays.

MetroCards

To enter the subway system, you need a MetroCard (it also works on buses), which you can buy from a booth inside the station entrance, or from brightly colored MetroCard vending machines that accept cash, debit cards and credit cards *(AmEx, Disc, MC, V).*

If you're planning to use the subway or buses often, it's worth buying a multiple-ride MetroCard, which is also sold at some stores and hotels. Free transfers between subways and buses are available only with the MetroCard. There are two types: **pay-per-use cards** and **unlimited-ride cards**. Any number of passengers can use a pay-per-use card, which can be bought in denominations from $4 for two trips, up to $80. A $20 card offers 12 trips for the price of 10. The unlimited-ride MetroCard (an incredible value for frequent users) is offered in three amounts: a 1-day **Fun Pass** ($7, available at station vending machines but not at booths), a **7-day pass** ($21) and a **30-day pass** ($70). These are good for unlimited rides on subways and buses, but can be used only once every 18 minutes (so just one person can use the card per trip).

Subway lines

Trains are known by letters or numbers and are color-coded according to the line on which they run. Stations are named after the street at which they're located. Entrances are marked with a green globe or a red globe (the latter signifies that the entrance is not always open). Many stations (and most of the local stops) have separate entrances to the uptown and downtown platforms—look before you pay (for an explanation of the city's streets, *see p365* **Walking**). Local trains stop at every station; express trains run between major stations only. Check a subway map (posted in all stations and available at service booths; *see also pp410–411*) before you board. Be sure to look for posted notices indicating temporary changes along a particular line.

Taxis & car services

Taxicabs

Yellow cabs are hardly ever in short supply—except at rush hour. Use only yellow medallion (licensed) cabs; avoid unregulated "gypsy" cabs. If the center light on top of the taxi is lit, it means the cab is available and should stop if you flag it down. Jump in and *then* tell the driver where you're going (New Yorkers generally give cross streets, rather than building numbers).

Taxis carry up to four people for the same price: $2 plus 30¢ per fifth of a mile, with an extra 50¢ charge from 8pm to 6am. The average fare for a three-mile (4.5km) ride is $7 to $9, depending on time of day and on traffic (20¢ per minute while the car is idling). Cabbies rarely allow more than four passengers in a cab (it's illegal), though it may be worth asking.

Not all cabbies know their way around the city, so it helps if you know where you're going—and speak up. By law, taxis cannot refuse to take you anywhere inside the city limits (the five boroughs) or to New York airports, so don't be duped by a reluctant cabbie. They may still refuse; to avoid an argument, get out and try another cab. In general, tip as you would at a restaurant; 15 percent on average and 20 percent if the service is great. If you have a problem, take down the medallion number and driver's number that are posted on the partition. Or ask for a receipt—there's a meter number on it. To complain or trace lost property, call the **Taxi & Limousine Commission** *(212-692-8294; Mon–Fri 9am–5pm).*

Late at night, cabs stick to fast-flowing routes. Try the avenues and key streets (Canal, Houston, 14th, 23rd, 34th, 42nd, 57th, 72nd and 86th). Bridge and tunnel exits are also good for a steady flow returning from the airports, and passengerless cabbies will usually head for nightclubs and big hotels. Otherwise, try the following:

Chinatown

Chatham Square, where Mott Street meets the Bowery, is an unofficial taxi stand. You can also try hailing a cab exiting the Manhattan Bridge at the Bowery and Canal Street.

Lincoln Center

The crowd heads toward Columbus Circle for a cab; those in the know go west to Amsterdam Avenue.

Lower East Side

Katz's Deli *(Houston St at Ludlow St)* is a cabbies' hangout; also try Delancey Street, where cabs come in over the Williamsburg Bridge.

Midtown

Penn Station, Grand Central Terminal and the Port Authority Bus Terminal attract cabs all night.

Soho

If you're on the west side, try Sixth Avenue; east side, the intersection of Houston Street and Broadway.

Times Square

This busy area has 30 taxi stands—look for the yellow globes atop nine-foot poles.

Tribeca

Cabs head up Hudson Street. The Tribeca Grand *(2 Sixth Ave between Church and White Sts)* is also a good bet.

Car services

Car services are also regulated by the Taxi & Limousine Commission (*see p364*). What makes them different from cabs is that the cars aren't yellow and drivers can make only prearranged pickups. (If you see a black Lincoln Town Car, it most likely belongs to a car service; to be certain, look for a license plate that begins with the letter T.) Don't try to hail one, and be wary of those that offer you a ride; they may not be licensed or insured, and you might get ripped off.

The following companies will pick you up anywhere in the city, at any time of day or night, for a prearranged fare.

Carmel
212-666-6666

Tel Aviv
212-777-7777

Tri-State Limousine
212-777-7171, 212-410-7600

Walking

One of the best ways to take in NYC is on foot. Most of the streets are laid out in a grid pattern and are relatively easy to navigate. Our maps (*see pp398–408*) make it even easier. Manhattan is divided into three major sections: **downtown**, which includes all neighborhoods south of 14th Street; **midtown**, roughly the area from 14th to 59th Street; and **uptown**, the rest of the island north of 59th Street.

Generally, avenues run along the length of Manhattan from south to north. They are parallel to one another and are logically numbered—with a few exceptions, such as Broadway, Columbus and Lexington Avenues. Manhattan's center is Fifth Avenue, so all buildings located east of it will have "East" addresses, with numbers going higher toward the East River, and those west of it will have "West" numbers that go higher toward the Hudson River. Streets also run parallel to one another but they run east to west, or **crosstown**, and are numbered, beginning with 1st Street (a block north of East Houston Street), up to 220th Street. Almost all even-numbered streets run east and odd streets run west (the major crosstown streets, such as 42nd Street, are two-way).

The neighborhoods of lower Manhattan—the **Financial District**, **Tribeca**, **Chinatown** and **Greenwich Village**—were settled prior to urban planning and can be confusing to walk through. Their charming lack of logic makes the use of a map essential. (*See pp398–399.*)

Resources A to Z

Age restrictions

In most cases, you must be at least 25 years old to rent a car in the U.S. In NYC, you must be 18 to buy tobacco products and 21 to buy or be served alcohol. Some bars and clubs will admit patrons who are between 18 and 21, but you will be removed from the establishment if you are caught drinking alcohol (carry a picture ID at all times). The age of sexual consent in New York is 17. You must be 18 to purchase pornography and other adult material, or to play the lottery or gamble (where the law allows).

Baby-sitting

Avalon Nurse Registry & Child Service
212-245-0250; www.avalonhealthcare.com. Bookings: Mon–Fri 9am–5pm. AmEx, Disc, MC, V.
Avalon provides baby nurses and sitters (four-hour minimum) for between $15 and $20 per hour, plus travel expenses.

Babysitters' Guild
212-682-0227; www.babysittersguild.com. Bookings: 9am–9pm. Cash only.
Long- or short-term multilingual babysitters cost $17 and up per hour (four-hour minimum) plus cab fare ($5 to $7). Sitters are available round the clock.

Pinch Sitters
212-260-6005. Bookings: Mon–Fri 8am–5pm. Cash only.
Charges are $16 per hour (four-hour minimum) plus cab fare after 9pm (up to $10 max).

City Information

Citizen Service Center
311. 24hr.
The city's nonemergency help line. Calls can be handled in 171 different languages.

Computers

There are hundreds of computer dealers in Manhattan. You might want to buy out of state to avoid the New York sales tax (8.625 percent). Many out-of-state dealers advertise in New York papers and magazines (*see also p237* **Cameras & electronics**). Here are reliable places if you want to rent, or need repairs:

Computer Solutions Provider
45 W 21st St between Fifth and Sixth Aves, second floor (212-463-9744; www.cspny.com). Subway: F, V, R, W to 23rd St. Mon–Fri 9am–6pm. AmEx, MC, V.
Specialists in Macs, IBMs and related peripherals, CSP staffers can recover lost data and help you through other computer disasters, even on-site.

Fitch Graphics
25 W 45th St between Fifth and Sixth Aves (212-840-3091; www.fitchgroup.com). Subway: B, D, F, V to 42nd St–Bryant Park; 7 to Fifth Ave. Mon–Fri 7:30am–2am. AmEx, MC, V.
Fitch is a full-service desktop-publishing outfit, with color laser output and prepress facilities. Fitch works on Mac and Windows platforms and has a bulletin board so customers can reach the shop online.

Kinko's

240 Central Park South at Broadway (212-258-3750, 800-254-6567; www.kinkos.com). Subway: A, C, B, D, 1, 9 to 59th St–Columbus Circle. 24hr. AmEx, Disc, MC, V.
This is a very efficient, friendly place to use computers and copiers. Most branches have Windows and Macintosh workstations and design stations, plus all the major software. Color output is available, as are laptop hookups and Internet connections ($18 per hour, 50¢ per printed page). Check the phone book for other locations.

USRental.com

800-USRENTAL; www.usrental.com. Mon–Fri 8:30am–5pm. AmEx, MC, V.
Rent by the day, week, month or year. Rush delivery service (within three hours) is also available.

Consulates

Check the phone book for a complete list of consulates and embassies. *See also p379* **Travel advice**.

Australia

212-351-6500

Canada

212-596-1628

Great Britain

212-745-0200

Ireland

212-319-2555

New Zealand

212-832-4038

Consumer information

Better Business Bureau

212-533-6200; www.newyork.bbb.org.
The BBB offers advice on consumer-related complaints (shopping, services, etc.). Each phone inquiry costs $5 (plus New York City tax) and must be charged to a credit card; the online version is free.

New York City Department of Consumer Affairs

42 Broadway between Beaver St and Exchange Pl (311, 212-639-9675). Subway: 4, 5 to Bowling Green. Mon–Fri 9am–5pm.
You can file complaints on consumer-related matters here.

Customs & immigration

When planning your trip, check with a U.S. embassy or consulate to see if you need a visa to enter the country (*see p380* **Visas**). Standard immigration regulations apply to all visitors arriving from outside the United States, which means you may have to wait at least an hour in customs upon arrival. Owing to tightened security at all American airports, you can expect even slower moving lines. During your flight, you will be handed an immigration form and a customs-declaration form to be presented to an official when you land.

You may be expected to explain your visit, so be polite and prepared. You will usually be granted an entry permit to cover the length of your stay. Work permits are hard to get, and you are not allowed to work without one (*see p376* **Students**).

U.S. Customs allows foreigners to bring in $100 worth of gifts (the limit is $800 for Americans) before paying duty. One carton of 200 cigarettes (or 50 cigars) and one liter of liquor (spirits) are allowed. Plants, meat or fresh produce cannot be brought into the country. If you carry more than $10,000 in currency, you may have to fill out a form.

If you must bring prescription drugs into the U.S., make sure the container is clearly marked and that you bring your doctor's statement or a prescription. Marijuana, cocaine and most opiate derivatives, along with a number of other drugs and chemicals are not permitted. Possession of them is punishable by stiff fines and/or imprisonment. Check with the U.S. Customs Service *(www.customs.gov)* before you arrive if you have any questions about what you can bring. If you lose or need to renew your passport once inside the U.S., contact your country's embassy (*see left* **Consulates**).

Student immigration

Upon entering the U.S. as a student, you will need to show a passport, a special visa and proof of your plans to leave (such as a return airline ticket). You may be asked to show means of support during your stay (*see below*).

Before applying for a visa, nonnationals who want to study in the U.S. must obtain an I-20 Certificate of Eligibility from the school or university they plan to attend. If you are enrolling in an authorized visitor-exchange program, including a summer course, wait until you have been accepted before worrying about immigration. You will be guided through the process by the school.

You are admitted as a student for the length of your course. Requests for any extension or change must be submitted 30 days before your completion date. Approval is granted jointly between your school and the U.S. Citizenship and Immigrations Services. You may be allowed to stay in the country for an additional 12 months after completing your course work to pursue practical training. At the completion of your studies or training, you will be given 60 days to prepare to leave the country, unless you are granted a change to, or an extension of, your immigration status. The rules are strict, and you risk deportation if you break them.

Information on these and all other immigration matters is available from the **U.S. Citizenship and Immigration Services** (USCIS). The agency's 24-hour hot line *(800-375-5283)*

Weather or not

New York is fairly predictable: Winters are windy and frigid (with a sun that sits low in the southern sky, so you might want to plan your walks northward, from downtown to uptown, to avoid the glare), while summers are hot and humid, with occasional brief showers; spring is typically blustery and changeable, and fall is generally dry and cool. Below is a snapshot of the city's weather averages. Just remember that whatever it's like outside, there's always something to do indoors.

	Temperature		**Rain/Snow**	**Sun**
	Hi °F/°C	Low °F/°C	Days	Days
Jan	38/3	25/-4	11	8
Feb	40/5	27/-3	10	8
Mar	50/10	35/2	11	9
Apr	61/16	44/7	11	8
May	72/22	54/12	11	8
Jun	80/27	63/17	10	8
Jul	85/30	68/20	11	8
Aug	84/29	67/20	10	9
Sept	76/25	60/16	8	11
Oct	65/19	50/10	8	12
Nov	54/12	41/5	9	9
Dec	43/6	31/-1	10	9

Source: National Weather Service

has a vast menu of recorded information in English and Spanish; advisers are available from 8am to 6pm, Monday through Friday. You can visit the USCIS at its New York office, located in the Jacob Javits Federal Building *(26 Federal Plaza, Broadway between Duane and Worth Sts, third floor).* The office is open 7:30am to 3:30pm, Monday through Friday, and cannot be reached directly by telephone.

The **U.S. Embassy** also offers guidance on obtaining student visas *(in the U.S., 202-663-1225, www.travel.state.gov; in the U.K., 0-207-499-9000).* Or, in the U.K., you can write to the Visa Branch of the Embassy of the United States of America *(5 Upper Grosvenor Street, London W1A 2J).*

When you apply for your student visa, you'll be expected to prove your ability to support yourself financially (including the payment of school fees), without working, for at least the first full academic year of your studies. After those nine months, you may be eligible to work part-time, but you must have specific permission (again from both your school and the USCIS) to do so.

If you are a student from the U.K. who wants to spend a summer vacation working in the States, contact the **British Universities North America Club** (BUNAC) for help in arranging a temporary job and the requisite visa *(16 Bowling Green Lane, London EC1R 0QH; 0-20-7251-3472; www.bunac.org/uk).*

Disabled access

Under New York City law, all facilities constructed after 1987 must provide complete access for the disabled—rest rooms, entrances and exits included. In 1990, the Americans with Disabilities Act made the same requirement federal law. In the wake of this legislation, many owners of older buildings have voluntarily added disabled-access features. There has been widespread compliance with the law, so we have not specifically noted the availability of disabled facilities in our listings. However, it's always a good idea to call ahead and check.

Despite its best efforts, New York can be challenging for a disabled visitor. Support and guidance are readily available: One useful resource is *Access for All,* a guide to New York's cultural institutions published by **Hospital Audiences Inc.** *(212-575-7660; www.hospaud.org).* The online guide tells how accessible each place really is, and includes information on the height of telephones and water fountains; hearing and visual aids; and passenger-loading zones and alternative entrances. HAI also has a service for the visually impaired that provides descriptions of theater performances on audiocassettes.

All Broadway theaters are equipped with devices for the hearing impaired; call **Sound Associates** *(212-582-7678, 888-772-7686)* for more information. There are a number of other stage-related resources for the disabled. Call **Telecharge** *(212-239-6200)* to reserve tickets for wheelchair seating in Broadway and Off Broadway venues. **Theater Development Fund's Theater Access Project** (TAP) arranges sign-language interpretation and captioning in American Sign Language for Broadway and Off Broadway shows *(212-221-1103; www.tdf.org).* **Hands On** *(212-822-8550)* does the same.

Lighthouse International

111 E 59th St between Park and Lexington Aves (800-829-0500; www.lighthouse.org). Subway: N, R, W to Lexington Ave–59th St; 4, 5, 6 to 59th St. Mon–Fri 10am–6pm; Sat 10am–5pm.

In addition to running a store that sells handy items for sight-impaired people, this organization provides helpful information for blind residents of and visitors to New York City.

Mayor's Office for People with Disabilities

100 Gold St between Frankfort and Spruce Sts, second floor (212-788-2830). Subway: J, M, Z to Chambers St; 4, 5, 6 to Brooklyn Bridge–City Hall. Mon–Fri 9am–5pm.

This municipal office provides a broad range of services for disabled people.

New York Society for the Deaf

161 Williams St between Ann and Beekman Sts (212-777-3900; www.nysd.org). Subway: J, M, Z, 2, 3, 4, 5 to Fulton St. Mon–Thu 8:30am–6pm; Fri 8:30am–4pm.

The deaf and hearing-impaired come here for information and services.

The Society for Accessible Travel and Hospitality

347 Fifth Ave between 33rd and 34th Sts, suite 610 (212-447-7284; www.sath.org). Subway: B, D, F, V, N, Q, R, W to 34th St–Herald Sq.

This nonprofit group was founded in 1976 to educate people about travel facilities for the disabled, and to promote travel for the disabled worldwide. Membership is $45 a year ($30 for seniors and students) and includes access to an information service and a quarterly travel magazine. No drop-ins; membership by mail only.

Electricity

The U.S. uses 110–120V, 60-cycle alternating current, rather than the 220–240V, 50-cycle AC used in Europe and elsewhere. The transformers that power or recharge many newer electronic devices, such as laptop computers, are designed to handle either current and may need nothing more than an adapter for the wall outlet. However, most electrical appliances, including hair dryers, will require a power converter as well. Adapters and converters of various sorts are available at airport shops, at some pharmacies and department stores, and at Radio Shack branches around the city.

Emergencies

Ambulance

In an emergency only, dial **911** for an ambulance or call the operator (dial **0**). To complain about slow emergency service or poor treatment, call the **Fire Dept. Complaint Hot Line** *(718-999-2646).*

Fire

In an emergency only, dial **911**. For complaint line, *see above.*

Police

In an emergency only, dial **911**. For the location of the nearest police precinct, or for general information about police services, call 646-610-5000.

Health & medical facilities

The public health-care system is practically nonexistent in the United States, and the cost of private health care is exorbitant. If at all possible, make sure you have comprehensive medical insurance when you travel to New York.

Clinics

Walk-in clinics offer treatment for minor ailments. Most require immediate payment, though some will send their bill directly to your insurance company. You will have to file a claim to recover the cost of prescription medication.

D•O•C•S

55 E 34th St between Madison Ave and Park Ave South (212-252-6000). Subway: 6 to 33rd St. Walk-in Mon–Thu 8am–8pm; Fri 8am–7pm; Sat 9am–3pm; Sun 9am–2pm. Extended hours by appointment. Base fee $135–$300. AmEx, Disc, MC, V.

These excellent primary-care facilities, affiliated with Beth Israel Medical Center, offer by-appointment and walk-in services. If you need X rays or lab tests, go as early as possible—no later than 6pm, Monday through Friday.

Other locations *202 W 23rd St at Seventh Ave (212-352-2600); 1555 Third Ave at 88th St (212-828-2300).*

Dentists

NYU College of Dentistry

345 E 24th St between First and Second Aves (212-998-9872, off-hours emergency care 212-998-9828). Subway: 6 to 23rd St. Mon–Thu 8:30am–6pm; Fri 8:30am–3pm. Base fee $90. Disc, MC, V.

If you need your teeth fixed on a budget, the final-year students are slow but proficient, and an experienced dentist is always on hand to supervise. Go before 2pm to ensure a same-day visit.

Emergency rooms

You will be billed for emergency treatment. Call your travel-insurance company's emergency number before seeking treatment to find out which hospitals accept your insurance. Emergency rooms are always open at:

Bellevue Hospital

462 First Ave at 27th St (212-562-4141). Subway: 6 to 28th St.

Cabrini Medical Center

227 E 19th St between Second and Third Aves (212-995-6000). Subway: L, N, Q, R, W, 4, 5, 6 to 14th St–Union Sq.

Mount Sinai Hospital

Madison Ave at 100th St (212-241-7171). Subway: 6 to 103rd St.

St. Luke's–Roosevelt Hospital

1000 Tenth Ave at 59th St (212-523-6800). Subway: A, C, B, D, 1, 9 to 59th St–Columbus Circle.

St. Vincent's Hospital

153 W 11th St at Seventh Ave (212-604-7998). Subway: F, V, L to Sixth Ave; 1, 2, 3, 9 to 14th St.

Gay & lesbian health

See p297 **Centers & phone lines.**

House calls

NY Hotel Urgent Medical Services

952 Fifth Ave between 76th and 77th Sts, suite 1D (212-737-1212; www.travelmd.com). Subway: 6 to 77th St. Sun, Mon, Wed, Fri 10am–6pm; Tue, Thu 10am–10pm; Sat 9am–2pm. Weekday hotel-visit fee $250–$300; weekday office-visit fee $55–$165 (rates increase at night and on weekends). AmEx, MC, V.

Dr. Ronald Primas and his partners provide medical attention right in your Manhattan hotel room or private residence. Whether you need a simple prescription, urgent medical care or a thorough examination, this service can provide a specialist. In-office visits are available 24 hours.

Pharmacies

See also p232 **Pharmacists**. Be aware that pharmacies will not refill foreign prescriptions.

Duane Reade

224 W 57th St at Broadway (212-541-9708; www.duanereade.com). Subway: N, Q, R, W to 57th St. 24hr. AmEx, MC, V.

This chain operates all over the city, and some stores offer 24-hour service. Check the web site for additional locations.

Other 24-hour locations *24 E 14th St at University Pl (212-989-3632); 155 E 34th St at Third Ave (212-683-3042); 1279 Third Ave at 74th St (212-744-2668); 2465 Broadway at 91st St (212-799-3172).*

Rite Aid

303 W 50th St at Eighth Ave (212-247-8736; www.riteaid.com). Subway: C, E to 50th St. 24hr. AmEx, Disc, MC, V.

Select locations have 24-hour pharmacies. Call 800-748-3243 or check the web site for a complete listing of locations.

Other 24-hour locations *210 Amsterdam Ave between 69th and 70th Sts (212-873-7965); 144 E 86th St between Lexington and Third Aves (212-876-0600); 2833 Broadway at 110th St (212-663-8252).*

Women's health

Liberty Women's Health Care of Queens

37-01 Main St at 37th Ave, Flushing, Queens (718-888-0018). Subway: 7 to Flushing–Main St. By appointment only. AmEx, MC, V.

This facility provides both surgical and nonsurgical abortions until the 24th week of pregnancy. Unlike many other clinics, Liberty uses abdominal ultrasound before, during and after the abortion to ensure safety.

Parkmed Eastern Women's Center

44 E 30th St between Madison Ave and Park Ave South, fifth floor (212-686-6066). Subway: 6 to 28th St. By appointment only. AmEx, Disc, MC, V.

Urine pregnancy tests are free. Counseling, contraception services and nonsurgical abortions are also available.

Planned Parenthood of New York City

Margaret Sanger Center, 26 Bleecker St at Mott St (212-965-7000, 800-230-7526; www.ppnyc.org). Subway: B, D, F, V to Broadway–Lafayette St; 6 to Bleecker St. Mon, Tue 8am–4:30pm; Wed, Thu 8am–6:30pm; Sat 7am–4:30pm. AmEx, MC, V.

This is the best-known, most reasonably priced network of family-planning clinics in the U.S. Counseling and treatment are available for a full range of needs, including abortion, contraception, HIV testing and treatment of STDs. Call for more information on other services or to make an appointment at any of the centers. No walk-ins.

Other locations *44 Court St between Remsen and Joralemon Sts, Brooklyn Heights, Brooklyn; 349 E 149th St at Courtlandt Ave, Bronx.*

Help lines

Alcohol & drug abuse

Alcoholics Anonymous

212-647-1680. 9am–10pm.

Cocaine Anonymous

212-262-2463 (24-hour recorded info).

Drug Abuse Information Line

800-522-5353. 8am–10pm.

This hot line refers callers to recovery programs around the state as well as to similar programs in the rest of the U.S.

Pills Anonymous

212-874-0700 (24-hour recorded info).

You'll find information on drug-recovery programs for users of marijuana, cocaine, alcohol and other addictive substances, as well as referrals to Narcotics Anonymous meetings. You can also leave a message, and a counselor will call back to speak to you.

Child abuse

Childhelp USA's National Child Abuse Hotline

800-422-4453. 24hr.

Counselors provide general crisis consultation, and can help in an emergency. Callers include abused children, runaways and parents having problems with children.

Gay & Lesbian

See p297 **Centers & phone lines**.

Health

Visit the **Centers for Disease Control and Prevention** (CDC) website (www.cdc.gov) for up-to-date national health information, or call one of the toll-free hot lines below.

National STD & AIDS Hot Line

800-342-2437. 24hr.

Travelers' Health

877-394-8747 or visit CDC website. 24hr.

Provides alerts on disease outbreaks and other information via recording.

Psychological services

The Samaritans

212-673-3000. 24hr.

People thinking of committing suicide, or suffering from depression, grief, sexual anxiety or alcoholism, can call this organization for advice.

Rape & sex crimes

Safe Horizon Crisis Hotline

212-577-7777; www.safehorizon.org. 24hr.

SH offers telephone and in-person counseling for any victim of domestic violence, rape or other crime, as well as practical help with court procedures, compensation and legal aid.

Special Victims Liaison Unit of the New York Police Department

Rape hot line 212-267-7273. 24hr.
Reports of sex crimes are handled by a female detective from the Special Victims Liaison Unit. She will inform the appropriate precinct, send an ambulance if requested and provide counseling and medical referrals. Other issues handled: violence against gays and lesbians, child victimization, and referrals for the families and friends of crime victims.

St. Luke's–Roosevelt Hospital Crime Victims Treatment Center

212-523-4728. Mon–Fri 9am–5pm.
The Rape Crisis Center provides a trained volunteer who will accompany you through all aspects of reporting a rape and getting emergency treatment.

Holidays

See p362 **Holidays**.

Insurance

If you are not an American, it's advisable to take out comprehensive insurance before arriving here; insurance for foreigners is almost impossible to arrange in the U.S. Make sure you have adequate health coverage, since medical costs are high. For a list of New York urgent-care facilities, *see p368* **Emergency rooms**.

Internet & e-mail

Cyber Café

250 W 49th St between Broadway and Eighth Ave (212-333-4109). Subway: C, E to 50th St; N, R, W to 49th St. Mon–Fri 8am–11pm; Sat, Sun 11am–11pm. $6.40 per half hour; 50¢ per printed page. AmEx, MC, V.
This is a standard Internet-access café, but it serves great coffee.

Kinko's

See p366.

New York Public Library

See p162 **New York Public Library**

Toilet talk

Finding public rest rooms in the city requires a little savvy.

Visitors to New York are always on the go. But in between all that go, go, go, sometimes you've really got to...*go*. Contrary to what your nose may sometimes lead you to believe, the streets and alleys are no place to find relief. The real challenge lies in finding a legal public place to take care of your business. Although they don't exactly have an open-door policy, the numerous **McDonald's** restaurants, **Starbucks** coffeeshops and most of the **Barnes & Noble** bookstores contain (usually clean) rest rooms. If the door to the loo is locked, you may have to ask a cashier for the key. Don't announce that you're not a paying customer, and you should be all right. The same applies to most other fast-food joints (**Au Bon Pain**, **Wendy's**, etc.), major stores (**Barneys**, **Macy's**, **Toys "R" Us**; *see p211, p212 and p238*), and hotels and bars that don't have a host or maître d' at the door. Here are a few other options around town that can offer sweet relief (though you may have to hold your breath).

Downtown

Battery Park
Castle Clinton. Subway: 1, 9 to South Ferry; 4, 5 to Bowling Green.

Kmart
770 Broadway at Astor Pl. Subway: R, W to 8th St–NYU; 6 to Astor Pl.

Tompkins Square Park
Ave A at 9th St. Subway: L to First Ave; 6 to Astor Pl.

Washington Square Park
Thompson St at Washington Sq South. Subway: A, C, E, B, D, F, V to W 4th St.

Midtown

Bryant Park
42nd St between Fifth and Sixth Aves. Subway: B, D, F, V to 42nd St–Bryant Park; 7 to Fifth Ave.

Grand Central Terminal
42nd St at Park Ave, Lower Concourse. Subway: 42nd St S, 4, 5, 6, 7 to 42nd St–Grand Central.

Penn Station
Seventh Ave between 30th and 32nd Sts. Subway: A, C, E, 1, 2, 3, 9 to 34th St–Penn Station.

Uptown

Avery Fisher Hall at Lincoln Center
Broadway at 65th St. Subway: 1, 9 to 66th St–Lincoln Ctr.

Charles A. Dana Discovery Center
Central Park, north side of Harlem Meer, 110th St at Malcolm X Blvd (Lenox Ave). Subway: 2, 3 to 110th St–Central Park North.

Delacorte Theater
Central Park, mid-park at 81st St. Subway: B, C to 81st St–Museum of Natural History.

The branch libraries throughout the five boroughs are a great place to e-mail and surf the Web for free. However, the scarcity of computer stations may make for a long wait, and the user's time is limited. The Science, Industry and Business Library at Madison Ave and 34th St has more than 40 workstations that you can use for up to an hour per day.

NYC Wireless

www.nycwireless.net.
This group has established 178 nodes in the city for free wireless access. (For example, most parks below 59th Street are covered.) Visit the website for more information.

Starbucks

www.starbucks.com. AmEx, MC, V.
Many branches offer paid wireless access through T-Mobile (10¢ per minute).

Laundry

See also p380 **Wardrobe services.**

Dry cleaners

Madame Paulette Custom Couture Cleaners

1255 Second Ave between 65th and 66th Sts (212-838-6827). Subway: 6 to 68th St–Hunter College. Mon–Fri 7:30am–7pm; Sat 8am–5pm. AmEx, MC, V.
After more than 50 years in business, this luxury dry cleaner knows how to treat delicate garments. Take advantage of free pickup and delivery throughout Manhattan; there's also a worldwide shipping service.

Meurice Garment Care

31 University Pl between 8th and 9th Sts (212-475-2778). Subway: R, W to 8th St–NYU. Mon–Fri 8am–7pm; Sat 9am–6pm; Sun 9:30am–3pm. AmEx, MC, V.
Laundry is serious business here. Meurice's roster of high-profile clients includes Armani and Prada, and the company handles all kinds of tricky stain removal and repair jobs.
Other location *245 E 57th St between Second and Third Aves (212-759-9057).*

Midnight Express Cleaners

212-921-0111, 800-764-3648. Mon–Fri 7am–6:30pm. AmEx, MC, V.
Midnight Express will pick up your dry cleaning anywhere below 141st Street ($50 minimum may apply) at a mutually convenient time and return it to you the next day (that goes for bulk laundry too). It costs $6.95 for a man's suit to be cleaned, including pickup and delivery.

Self-service laundry

Most neighborhoods have self-service laundries with coin-operated machines, but in New York, it doesn't cost much more to drop off your wash and let someone else do the work. Check the Yellow Pages for specific establishments.

Ecowash

72 W 69th St between Central Park West and Columbus Ave (212-787-3890). Subway: B, C to 72nd St; 1, 9 to 66th St–Lincoln Ctr. 7:30am–9:30pm. Cash only.
For the green-minded, Ecowash uses only natural, nontoxic detergent. You can wash your own duds, starting at $1.75 per load, or drop off up to seven pounds for $6.50 (each additional pound is 75¢).

Legal assistance

If you're arrested for a minor violation (disorderly conduct, harassment, loitering, rowdy partying, etc.) and you're very polite to the officer during the arrest (and are carrying proper ID), you'll probably get fingerprinted and photographed at the station and be given a desk-appearance ticket with a date to show up at criminal court. Then you'll most likely get to go home.

Arguing with a police officer or engaging in more serious criminal activity (possession of a weapon, drunken driving, illegal gambling or prostitution, for example) might get you "processed," which means a 24- to 30-hour journey through the system.

If the courts are backed up (and they usually are), you'll be held temporarily at a precinct pen. You can make a phone call after you've been fingerprinted. When you get through central booking, you'll arrive at 100 Centre Street for arraignment. A judge will decide whether you should be released on bail and will set a court date. If you can't post bail, you'll be held at Rikers Island. The bottom line: Try not to get arrested, and if you are, don't act foolishly.

Legal Aid Society

212-577-3300; www.legalaidsociety.org. Mon–Fri 8am–5pm.
Legal Aid gives general information and referrals on legal matters.

Sandback, Birnbaum & Michelen Criminal Law

800-640-2000, 212-517-3200. 24hr.
You might want to carry these numbers with you, in case you find the cops reading you your rights in the middle of the night. If no one at this firm can help you, they'll direct you to lawyers who can.

Libraries

See p162 **New York Public Library.**

Locksmiths

The following emergency locksmiths are open 24 hours. Both require proof (license, registration, utility bill) of residency or car ownership plus ID.

Champion Locksmiths

19 locations in Manhattan (212-362-7000). $15 service charge, $25 after 8pm, plus $35 minimum to replace the lock they have to break. AmEx, Disc, MC, V.

Elite Locksmiths

470 Third Ave between 32nd and 33rd Sts (212-685-1472). Subway: 6 to 33rd St. $45 during the day; $75–$90 at night. Cash only.

Lost property

For property lost in the street, contact the police. For lost cards or traveler's checks, *see p372* **Money**.

Buses & subways

New York City Metropolitan Transit Authority, 34th St–Penn Station, near the A-train platform (212-712-4500). Mon–Wed, Fri 8am–noon; Thu 11am–6:30pm.
Call if you've left something on a subway train or bus.

Grand Central Terminal
212-340-2555. Mon–Fri 7am–6pm; Sat, Sun 9am–5pm.
Call if you've left something on a Metro-North train.

JFK Airport
718-244-4444, or contact your airline.

La Guardia Airport
718-533-3400, or contact your airline.

Newark Liberty International Airport
973-961-6230, or contact your airline.

Penn Station
212-630-7389. Mon–Fri 7:30am–4pm.
Call for items left on Amtrak, New Jersey Transit or the Long Island Rail Road.

Taxis
212-692-8294; www.nyc.gov/taxi.
Call for items left in a cab.

Messenger services

A to Z Couriers
106 Ridge St between Rivington and Stanton Sts (212-253-6500; www.atozcouriers.com). Subway: F to Delancey St; J, M, Z to Delancey–Essex Sts. Mon–Fri 8am–8pm. AmEx, MC, V.
These cheerful couriers will deliver to anywhere in the city (and Long Island too).

Breakaway
335 W 35th St between Eighth and Ninth Aves (212-947-4455; www.breakawaycourier.com). Subway: A, C, E to 34th St–Penn Station. Mon–Fri 7am–9pm; Sat 9am–5pm; Sun noon–5pm. AmEx, MC, V.
Breakaway is a highly recommended local delivery service that promises to pick up and deliver within 90 minutes. With 180 messengers, you can take its statement seriously.

Jefron Messenger Service
55 Walker St between Church St and West Broadway (212-431-6610; www.jefron.com). Subway: 1, 2, 3, 9 to Chambers St. Mon–Fri 8am–5pm. Cash only.
Jefron specializes in transporting import and export documents.

Money

Over the past few years, much of American currency has undergone a subtle face-lift—partly as a national celebration and partly to deter increasingly adept counterfeiters. However, the "old" money is still in circulation. One dollar ($) equals 100 cents (¢). Coins include copper pennies (1¢), silver-colored nickels (5¢), dimes (10¢), quarters (25¢) and half-dollars (50¢)—though the last of these, like the gold-colored dollar pieces used in vending machines, are less commonly seen.

Paper money is all the same size, so make sure you fork over the right bill. It comes in denominations of $1, $2, $5, $10, $20, $50 and $100 (and higher—but you'll never see those). All denominations, except for the $1 and $2 bills, have recently been updated by the U.S. Treasury, which chose a larger portrait (placed off-center) and extra security features; the new bills also have a large numeral on the back to help the visually impaired identify the denomination. The $2 bills are quite rare and make a smart souvenir. Small shops will seldom break a $50 or $100 bill (and cab drivers aren't required to change bills larger than $20), so it's best to carry smaller denominations.

ATMs

This City is full of automated teller machines (ATMs). Most accept American Express, MasterCard and Visa, along with most major bank cards, if they have been registered with a personal identification number (PIN). There is commonly a usage fee, though the convenience (and superior exchange rate) often make ATMs worth the extra charge.

Call the following for ATM locations: **Cirrus** *(800-424-7787);* **Plus Systems** *(800-843-7587);* or **Washington Mutual** *(800-788-7000),* which has no surcharge on transactions at their ATMs. Also, look for branch banks or delis, which often have mini ATMs by the front counter (which also charge fees). If you've lost your PIN number, or your card becomes demagnetized, most banks will give cash to cardholders with proper ID.

Banks & currency exchange

Banks are generally open from 9am to 3pm Monday through Friday, though some have longer hours. You need photo ID, such as a passport, to cash traveler's checks. Many banks will not exchange foreign currency, and the *bureaux de change,* limited to tourist-trap areas, close between 6 and 7pm.

It's best to arrive with a few dollars in cash but to pay mostly with credit cards or traveler's checks (accepted in most restaurants and larger stores—but ask first, and be prepared to show ID). In emergencies, most large hotels offer 24-hour exchange facilities; the catch is that they charge high commissions and don't give good rates.

People's Foreign Exchange
575 Fifth Ave at 47th St, third floor (212-883-0550). Subway: E, V to Fifth Ave–53rd St; 7 to Fifth Ave. Mon–Fri 9am–6pm; Sat, Sun 10am–3pm.
People's provides foreign exchange on banknotes and traveler's checks of any denomination for a $2 fee.

Travelex
29 Broadway at Morris St (212-363-6206). Subway: 4, 5 to Bowling Green. Mon–Fri 9am–5pm.
A complete range of foreign-exchange services is offered.
Other locations *317 Madison Ave at 42nd St (212-883-0401); 1590 Broadway at 48th St (212-265-6063); 1, 9 to 50th St; 511 Madison Ave at 53rd St (212-753-2595).*

Credit cards

Bring plastic if you have it, or be prepared for a logistical nightmare. Credit cards are essential for necessities like renting cars and booking hotels, and handy for buying tickets over the phone and the Internet. The five major cards accepted in the U.S. are American Express, Diners Club, Discover, MasterCard and Visa. If cards are lost or stolen, contact:

American Express
800-528-2122

Diners Club
800-234-6377

Discover
800-347-2683

MasterCard
800-826-2181

Visa
800-336-8472

Traveler's checks

Like credit cards, traveler's checks are also routinely accepted at banks, stores and restaurants throughout the city. Bring your driver's license or passport for identification. If checks are lost or stolen, contact:

American Express
800-221-7282

Thomas Cook
800-223-7373

Visa
800-336-8472

Wire services

If you find that you have run out of cash, don't expect anyone at your embassy or consulate to lend you money—they won't, though they may be persuaded to repatriate you. In case of an emergency, you can have money wired from your home.

MoneyGram
800-926-9400; www.moneygram.com

Western Union
800-225-5227; to find an agent 800-325-6000; www.westernunion.com

Newspapers & magazines

Daily newspapers

Daily News

The *News* has drifted politically from the Neanderthal right to a moderate but tough-minded stance under the ownership of real-estate mogul Mort Zuckerman. Labor-friendly pundit Juan Gonzalez has great street sense (and a Pulitzer).

New York Post

Founded in 1801 by Alexander Hamilton, the *Post* is the nation's oldest daily newspaper. After many decades as a standard-bearer for political liberalism, the *Post* has swerved sharply to the right under current owner Rupert Murdoch. The *Post* includes more column inches of gossip than any other local paper, and its headlines are often as sassy as they are sensational.

The New York Times

As Olympian as ever after almost 150 years, the *Times* remains the city's (and the nation's) paper of record. It has the broadest and deepest coverage of world and national events—as the masthead proclaims, it delivers "All the News That's Fit to Print." The mammoth *Sunday Times* can weigh a full five pounds and typically contains hundreds of pages of newsprint, including a magazine and book-review, arts, travel, finance, real-estate, sports and other sections.

Other dailies

The ***Amsterdam News***, one of the nation's oldest black newspapers, offers a trenchant African-American viewpoint. New York also supports two Spanish-language dailies, ***El Diario*** and ***Noticias del Mundo***. ***Newsday*** is the Long Island–based daily with a tabloid format but a sober tone (it has a city edition). ***USA Today*** keeps weary travelers abreast of national news. You may even find your own local paper at Universal News shops (check the phone book for locations).

Weekly papers

Downtown journalism is a battlefield, pitting the scabrous neocons of the ***New York Press*** against the unreconstructed hippies of ***The Village Voice***. The *Press* consists entirely of opinion columns; it's full of youthful energy and irreverence as well as cynicism and self-absorption. The *Voice* is sometimes passionate and ironic, but just as often strident and predictable. Both papers are free. In contrast, ***The New York Observer*** focuses on the doings of the upper echelons of business, finance, media and politics. ***Our Town*** and ***Manhattan Spirit*** are on the sidelines; these free sister publications feature neighborhood news and local political gossip, and can be found in street-corner bins around town. In a world of its own is the hilarious, satirical national weekly, ***The Onion***.

Weekly magazines

New York

This magazine is part newsweekly, part lifestyle report and part listings.

The New Yorker

Since the 1920s, *The New Yorker* has been known for its fine wit, elegant prose and sophisticated cartoons. In the postwar era, it established itself as a venue for serious long-form journalism. It usually makes for a lively, intelligent read.

Time Out New York

Of course, the best place to find out what's going on in town is *Time Out New York,* launched in 1995. Based on the tried-and-trusted format of its London parent, *TONY* is an indispensable guide to the life of the city (if we do say so ourselves).

Other magazines

Since its launch in 1996, the quarterly ***Black Book*** has covered New York high fashion and culture with intelligent bravado. ***Gotham***, a monthly from the publisher of the glossy gab-rags *Hamptons* and *Ocean Drive* (which focuses on Miami), unveiled its larger-than-life celeb-filled pages in 2001. And for two decades now, ***Paper*** has reported monthly on the city's trend-conscious set with plenty of insider buzz on bars, clubs, downtown boutiques—and the people you'll find in them.

Photocopying & printing

Dependable Printing

10 E 22nd St at Broadway (212-533-7560). Subway: R, W to 23rd St. Mon–Fri 8:30am–7pm; Sat 10am–4pm. AmEx, MC, V.
Dependable provides offset and color printing, large-size photocopies, color laser printing, binding, fax service and more.
Other location *71 W 23rd St between Fifth and Sixth Aves (212-689-2777).*

Fitch Graphics

See p365.

Kinko's

See p366.

Servco

56 W 45th St between Fifth and Sixth Aves (212-575-0991). Subway: B, D, F, V to 42nd St–Bryant Park; 7 to Fifth Ave. Mon–Fri 8:30am–8pm.
Photocopying, offset printing, blueprints and binding services are available.

Photo processing

Photo-developing services are offered by most drugstores (CVS and Rite Aid, for example) and megastores, such as Kmart, but the best results should be expected from labs that develop on the premises.

Duggal

3 W 20th St between Fifth and Sixth Aves (212-242-7000). Subway: F, V, R, W to 23rd St. Mon–Fri 7am–midnight; Sat, Sun 9am–6pm. AmEx, MC, V.
Duggal has amassed a dedicated following that includes artist David LaChapelle and companies like American Express and Armani. Started by Baldev Duggal more than 40 years ago, this shop is expert at developing any type of film, flawlessly. Prices reflect that mastery.

Postal services

Stamps are available at all U.S. post offices and from drugstore vending machines. It costs 37¢ to send a one-ounce (28g) letter within the U.S. Each additional ounce costs 23¢. Postcards mailed within the U.S. cost 23¢; for international postcards, it's 70¢. Airmailed letters to anywhere overseas cost 80¢ for the first ounce and 80¢ for each additional ounce.

For faster Express Mail service, you must use special envelopes and fill out a form, which can be done either at a post office or by arranging a pickup. Delivery within 24 hours, to major U.S. cities, is guaranteed. International delivery takes two to three days, with no guarantee. Call 800-275-8777 for more information on various deadlines.

General Post Office

421 Eighth Ave at 33rd St (800-275-8777 for 24-hour information; www.usps.com). Subway: A, C, E to 34th St–Penn Station. 24hr.
This is the city's main post office; call for the branch nearest you. Lines are long, but stamps are available from self-service vending machines. Branches are usually open Monday through Friday, 9am to 5pm; Saturday hours vary from office to office.

General Delivery

390 Ninth Ave at 30th St (212-330-3099). Subway: A, C, E to 34th St–Penn Station. Mon–Sat 10am–1pm.
U.S. visitors without local addresses can receive their mail here; it should be addressed to recipient's name, General Delivery, New York, NY 10001. You will need to show some form of identification—a passport or ID card—when picking up letters.

Poste Restante

421 Eighth Ave at 33rd St, window 29 (212-330-2912). Subway: A, C, E to 34th St–Penn Station. Mon–Sat 8am–6pm.
Foreign visitors without U.S. addresses can receive mail here; mail should be addressed to recipient's name, General Post Office, Poste Restante, 421 Eighth Avenue, attn: Window 29, New York, NY 10001. Be sure to bring some form of identification to claim your letters.

Couriers

DHL Worldwide Express

Various locations throughout the city; call and give your ZIP code to find the office nearest you, or arrange a pickup at your door (800-225-5345; www.dhl.com). AmEx, DC, Disc, MC, V.
DHL will send a courier to pick up packages at any address in New York City, or you can deliver packages to its offices and drop-off points in person. Cash is not accepted.

FedEx

Various locations throughout the city; call and give your ZIP code to find the office nearest you, or arrange a pickup at your door (800-247-4747; www.fedex.com). AmEx, DC, Disc, MC, V.
FedEx rates (like those of its main competitor, UPS) are based on the distance shipped, weight of the package and service chosen. A FedEx envelope to Los Angeles costs about $17; one to London, $30. Packages headed overseas should be dropped off by 6pm for International Priority delivery (depending on destination); by 9pm for packages to most destinations in the U.S. (some locations have a later cutoff time; call to check).

UPS

Various locations throughout the city; free pickup at your door (800-742-5877 for 24-hour service; www.ups.com). Hours vary by office; call for locations and times. AmEx, DC, MC, V.
Like DHL and FedEx, UPS will send a courier to pick up parcels at any address in New York City, or you can deliver packages to its offices and drop-off points in person. UPS offers domestic and international service.

Private mail services

Mail Boxes Etc. USA

1173A Second Ave between 61st and 62nd Sts (212-832-1390; www.mbe.com). Subway: F to Lexington Ave–63rd St. Mon–Fri 8:30am–7pm; Sat 10am–5pm. AmEx, MC, V.
Mailbox rental, mail forwarding, overnight delivery, packaging and shipping are available. Also on hand are a phone-message service, photocopying and faxing. There are more than 30 branches in Manhattan; check the phone book for locations.

Radio

There are nearly 100 stations in the New York area. On the AM dial, you can find intriguing talk radio and phone-in shows that attract everyone from priests to sports nuts. Flip to FM for everything from free jazz to the latest Rapture single. Radio highlights are printed weekly in *Time Out New York,* and daily in the *Daily News.*

Music

College radio

College radio is innovative and free of commercials. However, smaller transmitters mean that reception is often compromised by Manhattan's high-rise topography.

WNYU-FM 89.1 and **WKCR-FM 89.9** (*see also below* **Jazz**) are the stations of New York University and Columbia, and offer programming that ranges across the musical spectrum.

WFUV-FM 90.7, Fordham University's station, plays mostly folk and Irish music, but also airs a variety of shows, including "soul day" every Friday.

Dance & pop

American commercial radio is rigidly formatted, which makes most pop stations extremely tedious and repetitive during the day. Tune in on evenings and weekends for more interesting programming.

WWRL-AM 1600 features R&B, Caribbean music and oldies.

WPLJ-FM 95.5 and **WHTZ-FM 100.3** are Top 40 stations.

WQHT-FM 97.1, "Hot 97," is a commercial hip-hop station with rap and R&B throughout the day.

WRKS-FM 98.7, "Kiss FM," offers a "variety of old school and today's R&B," which translates to unremarkable pop.

WCBS-FM 101.1's playlist is strictly oldies.

WKTU-FM 103.5 is the city's premier dance-music station.

WWPR-FM 105.1, "Power 105," plays top hip-hop, with some old-school hits.

WLTW-FM 106.7, "Lite FM," plays the kind of music you hear in elevators.

WBLS-FM 107.5 plays classic and contemporary funk, soul and R&B. Highlights include Charles Mitchell's house and R&B mix on Saturday mornings, plus *Hal Jackson's Sunday Classics* (blues and soul).

Jazz

WCWP-FM 88.1, Long Island University's station, plays mostly jazz on weekdays, plus hip-hop, gospel and world music at night.

WBGO-FM 88.3 is strictly jazz. Dee Dee Bridgewater's weekly *JazzSet* program features many legendary artists, and there are also shows devoted to such categories as piano jazz.

WKCR-FM 89.9, the student-run radio station of Columbia University, is where you'll hear legendary jazz DJ Phil Schaap.

WQCD-FM 101.9 is a soft-jazz station.

Rock

WSOU-FM 89.5, the station of Seton Hall University, a Catholic college, focuses primarily on hard rock and heavy metal.

WFMU-FM 91.1 proves that the term *free-form radio* still has some meaning. This Jersey-based station airs an eclectic mix of music and other aural oddities.

WXRK-FM 92.3 and **WAXQ-FM 104.3** offer classic and alternative rock. WXRK attracts the city's largest group of morning listeners, thanks to Howard Stern's 6–10am weekday sleazefest.

WLIR-FM 92.7 plays alternative (indie and Goth) sounds with a British bias.

Other music

WEVD-AM 1050 carries wacky talk shows, sports games and music.

WQEW-AM 1560, "Radio Disney," has kids' programming.

WNYC-FM 93.9 and **WQXR-FM 96.3** serve up a range of classical music; WNYC is more progressive classical.

WXPK-FM 107.1 is the place for Spanish and Latin music.

News & talk

WABC-AM 770, **WCBS-AM 880**, **WINS-AM 1010** and **WBBR-AM 1130** offer news throughout the day, plus traffic and weather reports. WABC hosts a morning show featuring the street-accented demagoguery of Guardian Angels founder Curtis Sliwa along with radical attorney Ron Kuby (*weekdays 5–10am*). Right-winger Rush Limbaugh also airs his views here *(noon–3pm).*

WNYC-AM 820/FM 93.9 and **WBAI-FM 99.5** are commercial-free public radio stations providing news and commentary on current affairs. Highlights include WNYC's popular *All Things Considered (weekdays AM 4–6:30pm, 7–8pm; FM 4–6:30pm)* and guest-driven talk shows, notably WNYC's *The Leonard Lopate Show (AM 3–4am, noon–2pm; FM noon–2pm)* and WNYC-FM's *Fresh Air (weekdays 3–4pm).* WNYC also airs Garrison Keillor's *A Prairie Home Companion (AM Sat 6pm; Sun 11am; FM Sat 6pm)* and Ira Glass's *This American Life (AM Sat 11am, 6pm; FM Sun 6pm).* WBAI is a platform for left-wing politics with such shows as *Democracy Now! (weekdays 9–10am).*

WLIB-AM 1190 is the voice of black New York, airing news and talk from an Afrocentric perspective, interspersed with Caribbean music. Former mayor David Dinkins has a show on Wednesdays *(10–11am).*

WNEW-FM 102.7 is "music women love."

Sports

WFAN-AM 660 airs Giants, Knicks, Mets and Rangers games. In the mornings, talk-radio fixture Don Imus offers his opinion on whatever's going on in the world *(Mon–Fri 5:30–10am).*

WABC-AM 770 broadcasts Devils and Jets games.

WEVD-AM 1050 is devoted to news and sports talk and is the home of the Islanders.

WWRU-AM 1660, "Radio Unica," covers MetroStars soccer games in Spanish.

Religion

Here are just a few of the many places of worship in New York. Check the Yellow Pages for a more detailed listing.

Baptist

Abyssinian Baptist Church

See p119.

Buddhist

New York Buddhist Church

331-332 Riverside Dr between 105th and 106th Sts (212-678-0305). Subway: 1, 9 to 103rd St.

Catholic

St. Francis of Assisi

135 W 31st St between Sixth and Seventh Aves (212-736-8500; www.st.francis.org). Subway: B, D, F, V, N, Q, R, W to 34th St–Herald Sq; 1, 2, 3, 9 to 34th St–Penn Station.

St. Patrick's Cathedral

See p104.

Episcopal

Cathedral of St. John the Divine

See p116.

Jewish

UJA-Federation Resource Line

212-753-2288; www.youngleadership.org. Mon–Thu 9am–5pm; Fri 9am–4pm.

This hot line provides referrals to other organizations, groups, temples, philanthropic activities and synagogues, as well as advice on kosher food and restaurants in the city.

Methodist

Salem United Methodist Church

2190 Adam Clayton Powell Jr. Blvd (Seventh Ave) at 129th St (212-678-2700). Subway: A, C, B, D, 2, 3 to 125th St.

St. Paul and St. Andrew United Methodist Church

263 W 86th St between Broadway and West End Ave (212-362-3179; www.spsanyc.org). Subway: 1, 9 to 86th St.

Muslim

Islamic Cultural Center of New York

1711 Third Ave between 96th and 97th Sts (212-722-5234). Subway: 6 to 96th St.

Presbyterian

Madison Avenue Presbyterian Church

921 Madison Ave at 73rd St (212-288-8920; www.mapc.com). Subway: 6 to 72nd St.

Rest rooms

See p370 **Toilet talk**.

Safety

New York's crime rate, particularly for violent crime, has waned during the past decade. More than ever, most crime occurs late at night in low-income neighborhoods. Don't arrive thinking your safety is at risk wherever you go; it is unlikely that you will ever be bothered.

Still, a bit of common sense won't hurt. If you look comfortable rather than lost, you should deter troublemakers. Do not flaunt your money and valuables. Avoid desolate and poorly lit streets; if necessary, walk facing the traffic so no one can drive up alongside you undetected. On deserted sidewalks, walk close to the street—or even on it. Muggers prefer to hang back in doorways and shadows. If you do find yourself threatened, hand over your wallet or camera at once (your attacker will likely be as anxious to get it over with as you will be), then dial **911** as soon as you can (it's a free call).

Be extra alert to pickpockets and street hustlers—especially in crowded tourist areas like Times Square—and don't be seduced by any scam artists you may encounter. That shrink-wrapped camcorder you bought out of a car trunk for 50 bucks could turn out to be a couple of bricks when you open the box.

New York women are used to the brazenness with which they are stared at by men and usually develop a dismissive attitude toward it. If unwelcome admirers ever get verbal or start following you, ignoring them is better than responding. Walking into the nearest shop is the best way to get rid of persistent offenders. If you've been seriously victimized, *see p368* **Emergencies**, *or p369* **Rape & sex crimes** for assistance.

Smoking

New Yorkers live under some of the strictest antismoking laws on the planet. The 1995 NYC Smoke-Free Air Act makes it illegal to smoke in virtually all public places, including subways and movie theaters. Recent legislation went even further, banning smoking in nearly all restaurants *and* bars. Be sure to ask before you light up.

Students

Student life in NYC is unlike that anywhere else in the world. An endless extracurricular education exists right outside the dorm room—the city is both teacher and playground. For further guidance, check the ***Time Out New York Student Guide***, available free on campuses in August and for $2.95 at Hudson News outlets.

Student identification

Foreign students should get an **International Student Identity Card** (ISIC) as proof of student status and to secure discounts. These can be bought from your local student-travel agent (ask at your student union). If you buy the card in New York, you will also get basic accident insurance—a bargain. The New York branch of the **Council on International Educational Exchange** *(205 E 42nd St between Second and Third Aves, 212-822-2700)* can supply one on the spot. Note that a student identity card may not always be accepted as proof of age for drinking (you must be 21).

Student travel

Most agents offer discount fares for those under 26; specialists in student deals include:

STA Travel

205 E 42nd St between Second and Third Aves (212-822-2700; www.statravel.com; for other locations 800-777-0112). Subway: 42nd St S, 4, 5, 6, 7 to 42nd St–Grand Central. Mon–Fri 9am–7pm; Sat 10am–6pm.

Directory

Telephones

New York, like most of the world's busy cities, is overrun with telephones, cellular phones, pagers and faxes. (Check with your carrier to be sure that service will be available here.) This increasing dependence on a dial tone accounts for the city's abundance of area codes. As a rule, **you must dial 1** + area code before a number, even if the place you are calling is in the same area code. The area codes for Manhattan are 212 and 646; Brooklyn, Queens, Staten Island and the Bronx are 718 and 347; generally, 917 is reserved for cellular phones and pagers. The Long Island area codes are 516 and 631, and the codes for New Jersey are 201, 609, 732, 856, 908 and 973. Numbers preceded by 800, 877 and 888 are free of charge when dialed from anywhere in the United States. When numbers are listed as letters (e.g., 800-AIR-RIDE) for easy recall, dial the corresponding numbers on the telephone keypad.

Remember, if you carry a cellular phone, make sure you turn it off on trains and buses, and at restaurants, plays, movies, concerts and museums. New Yorkers are quick to show their annoyance at an ill-timed ring. Some establishments even post signs designating "cellular-free zones."

General information

The Yellow Pages and white pages directories have a wealth of useful information in the front, including theater-seating diagrams and maps; the blue pages in the center of the white pages directory list all government numbers and addresses. Hotels will have copies; otherwise, try libraries or Verizon (the local phone company) payment centers.

Collect calls & credit-card calls

Collect calls are also known as reverse-charge calls. Dial 0 followed by the area code and number, or dial AT&T's 800-CALL-ATT, MCI's 800-COLLECT or Sprint's 800-ONE-DIME.

Directory assistance

Dial 411 or 1 + area code + 555-1212. Doing so may be free, depending on the pay phone you're calling from; carrier fees may apply. Long-distance directory assistance may also incur long-distance charges.

Emergency

Dial **911**. All calls are free (including those from pay and cell phones).

International calls

Dial 011 + country code (Australia 61; New Zealand 64; U.K. 44), then the number.

Operator assistance

Dial 0.

Toll-free directory

Dial 1 + 800 + 555-1212 (no charge).

Pagers & cell phones

InTouch USA

212-391-8323, 800-872-7626. Mon–Fri 8am–5:30pm. AmEx, DC, Disc, MC, V.

InTouch, the city's largest cellular-phone rental company, leases equipment by the day, week or month.

Public pay phones & phone cards

Public pay phones are easy to find. Some of them even work. Verizon's phones are the most dependable (those from other phone companies tend to be poorly maintained). Phones take any combination of silver coins: Local calls usually cost 25¢ for three minutes; some require 50¢, but allow unlimited time on the call. If you're not used to American phones, know that the ringing tone is long; the "engaged" tone, or busy signal, is short and higher pitched.

If you want to call long-distance or make an international call from a pay phone, you need to go through one of the long-distance companies. Most pay phones in New York automatically use AT&T, but phones in and around transportation hubs usually contract other long-distance carriers, whose charges can be outrageous. Look in the Yellow Pages under Telephone Companies. MCI and Sprint are respected brand names (*see above* **Collect calls & credit-card calls**).

Make the call either by dialing 0 for an operator or by dialing direct (the latter is cheaper). To find out how much a call will cost, dial the number and a computerized voice will tell you how much money to deposit. You can pay for calls with your credit card.

The best way to make long-distance calls is with a **phone card**, available in various denominations from any post office branch or from chain stores like Duane Reade or Rite Aid (*see p369* **Pharmacies**). Delis and kiosks sell phone cards, including the New York Exclusive, which has favorable international rates. Dialing instructions are on the card.

Recorded information

For the exact time and temperature, plus lottery numbers and the weather forecast, call 212-976-2828—a free call 24 hours a day. At press time, this is the one number you can call without dialing a 1 first. You can also check www.time.gov.

Telephone answering service

Messages Plus Inc.

1317 Third Ave between 75th and 76th Sts (212-879-4144). Subway: 6 to 77th St. 24hr. AmEx, DC, Disc, MC, V.

Messages Plus provides telephone-answering service, with specialized (medical, bilingual, etc.) receptionists if required, and plenty of ways to deliver your messages. It also offers telemarketing, voice mail and interactive website services.

Television

A visit to New York often includes at least a small dose of TV time. American TV can cause culture shock, particularly for British and European visitors.

Time Out New York offers a rundown of weekly television highlights. For full TV schedules, save the Sunday *New York Times* TV section or buy a daily paper.

The networks

Six major networks broadcast nationwide. All offer ratings-driven variations on a theme.

CBS (Channel 2 in NYC) has the top investigative show, *60 Minutes*, on Sundays at 7pm, and the network's overall programming is geared to a middle-aged demographic (*Judging Amy; Without a Trace*). But check out *CSI* (Thursdays at 9pm) for fast-paced drama or *Everybody Loves Raymond* (Mondays at 9pm) and *The Late Show with David Letterman* (weeknights at 11:30pm) for solid humor.

NBC (4) is the home of the political-drama series *The West Wing*, the long-running sketch-comedy series *Saturday Night Live* (Saturdays at 11:30pm), and popular sitcoms such as *Will & Grace*.

Fox-WNYW (5) is popular with younger audiences for shows like *Malcolm in the Middle, The Simpsons* and *The O.C.*

ABC (7) is the king of daytime soaps and family-friendly sitcoms (*The Drew Carey Show; Life with Bonnie*).

UPN-WWOR (9) and **WB-WPIX** (11) don't attract huge audiences like other networks, but they feature some offbeat programming, including *Angel, Gilmore Girls* and *Smallville*.

WXTV (41) and **WNJU** (47) are Spanish-language channels that offer game shows and racy Mexican dramas. They're also your best noncable bet for soccer.

Public TV

Public TV is on channels 13, 21 and 25. Documentaries, arts shows and science series alternate with *Masterpiece Theatre* and reruns of British shows like *Inspector Morse*. Channel 21 broadcasts *BBC World News* daily at 6am and at 7 and 11pm.

Cable

All channel numbers listed are for Time Warner Cable in Manhattan. In other locations, or for other cable systems—such as Cablevision and RCN—check listings.

NY1 (1), **CNN** (10), **MSNBC** (43) and **Fox News** (46) offer news-heavy formats; NY1 has a local focus.

TNT (3), **TBS** (8) and **USA Network** (40) show notable reruns and feature films as well as sports action.

Nickelodeon (6) presents programming suitable for kids and nostalgic fans of shows like *The Brady Bunch, The Cosby Show* and *Happy Days*.

Lifetime (12) is "television for women."

A&E (16) airs the shallow but popular *Biography* documentary series.

The History Channel (17), **Sci-Fi Channel** (44) and **Weather Channel** (72) are self-explanatory. **Discovery Channel** (18) and **Learning Channel** (52) feature educational nature and science programs.

VH1 (19), MTV's more mature sibling, airs the popular *Behind the Music* series, which delves into the lives of artists like Vanilla Ice and the Partridge Family.

MTV (20) increasingly offers fewer music videos and more of its original programming (*Jackass, The Osbornes* and *The Real World*).

Court TV (23) scores big ratings when there's a hot trial going on.

E! (24) is "Entertainment Television," a mix of celebrity and movie news. This is where you'll find tabloidy segments like the unmissable *E! True Hollywood Story*, which profiles the likes of Mr. T and the Brat Pack.

Fox Sports (26), **MSG** (Madison Square Garden, 27), **ESPN** (28) and **ESPN2** (29) are all-sports stations.

Public Access TV is on channels 34, 56 and 57—surefire sources of bizarre camcorder-powered amusement.

Channel 35 carries the fun, risqué *Robin Byrd Show*.

Bravo (38) shows arts programming such as *Inside the Actors Studio*, art-house films and *Queer Eye for the Straight Guy*.

Comedy Central (45) is all comedy, airing the raunchy cartoon *South Park* (Wednesdays at 10pm), and *The Daily Show with Jon Stewart* (Monday through Thursday, at 7 and 11pm).

C-SPAN (64) is a forum for governmental-affairs programming.

Cinemax, Disney Channel, HBO, The Movie Channel and **Showtime** are premium channels often available for a fee in hotels. They show uninterrupted feature films, exclusive specials and acclaimed original series such as *The Sopranos* and *Six Feet Under*.

Tickets

It's always show time somewhere in New York. And depending on what you're after—music, sports, theater—scoring tickets can be a real hassle. Smaller venues often have their own box office that sells tickets. Large arenas like Madison Square Garden have ticket agencies—and many devoted spectators. You may have to try more than one tactic to get into a popular show.

Box-office tickets

Fandango

800-326-3264; www.fandango.com. 24hr. Surcharge $1.50 per ticket. AmEx, Disc, MC, V.

One of the newer services to offer advance credit-card purchase of movie tickets online or over the phone. Tickets can be picked up at an automated kiosk in the theater lobby (not available in all theaters).

Moviefone

212-777-FILM; www.moviefone.com. 24hr. Surcharge $1.50 ($1 if purchased online) per ticket. AmEx, Disc, MC, V.

Purchase advance movie tickets by credit card over the phone or online; pick them up at an automated kiosk in the theater lobby. Service is not available for every theater.

Telecharge

212-239-6200; www.telecharge.com. 24hr. Average $6 surcharge per Broadway and Off Broadway ticket. AmEx, DC, Disc, MC, V.

Broadway and Off Broadway shows are on offer here.

Ticket Central

416 W 42nd St between Ninth and Tenth Aves (212-279-4200; www.ticketcentral.org). Subway: N, Q, R, W, 42nd St S, 1, 2, 3, 9, 7 to 42nd St–Times Sq. Box office and phone orders 1–8pm. $1.50 surcharge ($1 charge if purchased online); $3 surcharge per phone or online order. AmEx, MC, V.

Off and Off-Off Broadway tickets are available at the office or by phone.

Ticketmaster

212-307-4100; www.ticketmaster.com. $3–$8 surcharge per ticket. AmEx, DC, Disc, MC, V.

This reliable service sells tickets to rock concerts, Broadway shows, sports events and more. You can buy tickets by phone, online or at outlets throughout the city—Tower Records, HMV, J&R Music World and Filene's Basement, to name a few.

TKTS

Duffy Square, 47th St at Broadway (212-221-0013; www.tdf.org). Subway: N, Q, R, W, 42nd St S, 1, 2, 3, 9, 7 to 42nd St–Times Sq. Mon–Sat 3–8pm; Sun 11am–7pm. Matinee tickets Wed, Sat 10am–2pm; Sun 11am–2pm. $3 surcharge per ticket. Cash only.
TKTS has become a New York tradition. Broadway and Off Broadway tickets are sold at discounts of 25 and 50 percent for same-day performances; tickets to other highbrow events are also offered. The line can be long, but it's often worth the wait.
Other location *199 Water St at the corner of Front and John Sts.*

Scalpers & standby tickets

Don't relinquish all hope when a show sells out: There's always the risky scalper option, though it is illegal and you might end up with a forged ticket. Before you part with any cash, make sure the ticket has the correct details, and be warned—the police have been cracking down on such trade.

Some venues also offer standby tickets right before show time, while others give reduced rates for tickets purchased on the same day as the performance.

Ticket brokers

Ticket brokers function like scalpers, though their activities are regulated. It's illegal in New York State to sell a ticket for more than its face value plus a service charge, so these companies operate by phone from other states. They can almost guarantee tickets, however costly, for sold-out events, and tend to deal only in better seats. Look under Ticket Sales in the Yellow Pages for brokers. Listed below are three of the more established outfits.

Apex Tours

800-248-9849; www.tixx.com. Mon–Fri 9am–5pm. AmEx, Disc, MC, V.

Prestige Entertainment

800-243-8849; www.prestigeentertainment.com. Mon–Fri 8am–6pm; Sat 8am–noon. AmEx, MC, V.

TicketCity

800-765-3688; www.ticketcity.com. Mon–Fri 8am–9pm; Sat 9am–7pm; Sun 11am–4pm. AmEx, Disc, MC, V.

Time & date

New York is on Eastern Standard Time, which extends from the Atlantic coast to the eastern shore of Lake Michigan and south to the Gulf of Mexico. This is five hours behind Greenwich Mean Time. Clocks are set forward one hour in early April and back one hour at the end of October. Going from east to west, Eastern Time is one hour ahead of Central Time, two hours ahead of Mountain Time and three hours ahead of Pacific Time. For the exact time of day, *see p377* **Recorded information**.

In the U.S., the date is written in this order: month, day, year; so February 5, 2004 is 2/5/04.

Toilets

See p370 **Toilet talk.**

Tourist information

Hotels are usually full of maps, brochures and free tourist magazines that include paid listings (so they cannot be viewed as objective). Plenty of local magazines, including *Time Out New York,* offer opinionated, yet reliable, info.

NYC & Company

810 Seventh Ave between 52nd and 53rd Sts (800-NYC-VISIT; www.nycvisit.com). Subway: B, D, E to Seventh Ave. Mon–Fri 8:30am–6pm; Sat, Sun 9am–5pm.
The city's official visitor and information center gives out leaflets, coupons, free maps and advice.
Other location *33–34 Carnaby St, London, UK, W1V 1CA (0-207-437-8300).*

Times Square Visitors Center

1560 Broadway between 46th and 47th Sts (212-869-1890). Subway: N, Q, R, W, 42nd St S, 1, 2, 3, 9, 7 to 42nd St–Times Sq. 8am–8pm
This center offers discount coupons for Broadway tickets, MetroCards, an Internet station and other useful goods and services.

Translation & language services

All Language Services

77 W 55th St between Fifth and Sixth Aves (212-986-1688; fax 212-582-5352). Subway: 42nd St S, 4, 5, 6, 7 to 42nd St–Grand Central. 24hr. AmEx, MC, V.

Travel advice

For current information on traveling to a specific country—including the latest news on health issues, safety and security, local laws and customs—contact your country's government department of foreign affairs. Most have websites with useful advice for would-be travelers.

Australia
www.dfat.gov.au/travel

Canada
www.voyage.gc.ca

Ireland
www.irlgov.ie/iveagh

New Zealand
www.mft.govt.nz/travel

United Kingdom
www.fco.gov.uk/travel

USA
www.state.gov/travel

ALS will type or translate documents in any of 59 languages and provide interpreters.

Visas

Some 27 countries participate in the Visa Waiver Program. Citizens of Andorra, Australia, Austria, Belgium, Brunei, Denmark, Finland, France, Germany, Iceland, Ireland, Italy, Japan, Liechtenstein, Luxembourg, Monaco, the Netherlands, New Zealand, Norway, Portugal, San Marino, Singapore, Slovenia, Spain, Sweden, Switzerland and the United Kingdom do not need a visa for stays shorter than 90 days (business or pleasure), as long as they have a machine-readable passport that is valid for the full 90-day period and a return ticket (the exemption includes children). An open standby ticket is acceptable. Anyone without a machine-readable passport will need a visa. If you are in any doubt as to whether your passport is machine-readable, check with the passport issuing authority of your country.

Canadians and Mexicans don't need visas but must have legal proof of residency. All other travelers must apply for visas. You can obtain information and application forms from your nearest U.S. embassy or consulate. In general, submit your application at least three weeks before you plan to travel. To apply for a visa on shorter notice, contact your travel agent.

For information on student visas, *see p366.*

U.S. Embassy Visa Information

In the U.S., 202-663-1225; in the U.K., 09068-200-2906, 60p/minute; travel.state.gov/visa_services.html.

Wardrobe services

See also p371 **Laundry**.

Clothing repair

Ramon's Tailor Shop

306 Mott St between Bleecker and Houston Sts (212-226-0747). Subway: F, V to Broadway–Lafayette St; 6 to Bleecker St. Mon–Fri 7:30am–8pm; Sat 8am–7:30pm; Sun 11am–4pm. Cash only.
Ramon's can alter or repair "anything that can be worn on the body." There's also an emergency service, and pickup and delivery is free in much of Manhattan.

Clothing rental

One Night Out/ Mom's Night Out

147 E 72nd St between Lexington and Third Aves (212-988-1122). Subway: 6 to 68th St–Hunter College. Mon–Wed 11am–6pm; Thu 11am–8pm; Fri 11am–6pm; Sat 11am–5pm. AmEx, MC, V.
One Night Out carries brand-new evening wear for uptown socialites—and for downtown girls having an uptown evening. Across the hall, Mom's Night Out provides its service to expectant mothers for $200 to $400.

Zeller Tuxedos

1010 Third Ave at 60th St (212-355-0707). Subway: N, R, W to Lexington Ave–59th St; 4, 5, 6 to 59th St. Mon–Fri 9am–6:30pm; Sat 10am–5:30pm; Sun 11am–4:30pm. AmEx, Disc, MC, V.
Calvin Klein and other tuxes are available. Check the phone book for other locations.

Jewelry & watch repair

Zig Zag Jewelers

1336A Third Ave between 76th and 77th Sts (212-794-3559). Subway: 6 to 77th St. Mon–Fri 11am–7pm; Sat 10am–6:30pm. AmEx, DC, Disc, MC, V.
These experts don't do costume jewelry, but they'll restring and reclasp your broken Bulgaris and Harry Winstons. Watch repairs are trustworthy, and estimates are free.
Other location *963 Madison Ave between 75th and 76th Sts (212-472-6373).*

Shoe repair

Andrade Shoe Repair

103 University Pl between 12th and 13th Sts (212-529-3541). Subway: L, N, Q, R, W, 4, 5, 6 to 14th St–Union Sq. Mon–Fri 7:30am–7pm; Sat 9am–6:30pm. Cash only.
Andrade is a basic but reliable shoe-repair chain around town. Check the phone book for other locations.

Weather

See p367 **Weather or not.**

Passport alert: Do you need a visa?

Passport regulations for visitors entering the US on the Visa Waiver Program are due to change on Oct 26, 2004, though details were unclear at press time. There may be no change for people with a passport issued before that date, but new passports must be machine-readable (most are) and, more problematically, they must contain a microchip of biometric data, such as fingerprints. Many countries, the U.K. included, don't yet have the technology to produce such information. Holders of foreign passports issued after October 26 without the microchip will need to get a visa, which can easily take two to three months. If you travel without the correct passport—and you don't have a visa—you risk being turned back when you try to enter the country. The best advice is to get your passport renewed before October 26, even if it won't expire for a couple of years. Well before you plan to travel, call the nearest U.S. Embassy or visit www.travel.state.gov/vwp.html. Children will need their own passports, and working journalists and business travelers who've been traveling without visas had better apply now.

Further Reference

In-depth guides

Edward Sibley Barnard: *New York City Trees.* Find the best places to hug a hickory.

Edward F. Bergman: *The Spiritual Traveler: New York City.* This is a guide to sacred and peaceful spaces.

Eleanor Berman: *Away for the Weekend: New York.* Trips within a 200-mile radius of New York City.

Eleanor Berman: *New York Neighborhoods.* Ethnic enclaves abound in this food lover's guide.

Laura Brown and Jill Fairchild: *Where to Wear.* A staple for shopaholics.

William Corbett: *New York Literary Lights.* An encyclopedic collection of info about NYC's literary past.

Dave Frattini: *The Underground Guide to New York City Subways.*

Suzanne Gerber: *Vegetarian New York City.* Includes restaurants, markets and lodging for veg-heads.

Alfred Gingold and Helen Rogan: *The Cool Parents Guide to All of New York.*

Hagstrom: *New York City 5 Borough Pocket Atlas.* You won't get lost with this thorough street map.

Colleen Kane (ed.): *Sexy New York City.* Discover erotica in the Naked City.

Chuck Katz: *Manhattan on Film 2.* A must for movie buffs who want to scope out the city on foot.

Landmarks Preservation Commission: *Guide to New York City Landmarks.*

Ruth Leon: *Applause: New York's Guide to the Performing Arts.* Detailed directory of performance venues.

Lyn Skreczko and Virginia Bell: *The Manhattan Health Pages.* Everything from aerobics to Zen.

Earl Steinbicker (ed.): *Daytrips New York.*

Linda Tarrant-Reid: *Discovering Black New York.* This guide presents important black museums and more.

Time Out New York Eating & Drinking: The annual comprehensive critics' guide to thousands of places to eat and drink in the five boroughs.

Zagat Survey: *New York City Restaurants.* The popular opinion survey.

Architecture

Richard Berenholtz: *New York New York.* Panoramic images of the city through the seasons.

Stanley Greenberg: *Invisible New York.* Photographic account of hidden architectural triumphs.

Karl Sabbagh: *Skyscraper.* How the tall ones are built.

Robert A.M. Stern et al.: *New York 1930.* A massive coffee-table slab with stunning pictures.

Norval White and Elliot Willensky (ed.): *AIA Guide to New York City.* A comprehensive directory of important buildings.

Gerard R. Wolfe: *New York: A Guide to the Metropolis.* Historical and architectural walking tours.

Culture & recollections

Candace Bushnell: *Sex and the City.* Smart women, superficial New York.

George Chauncey: *Gay New York.* The evolution of New York gay culture from 1890 to 1940.

William Cole (ed.): *Quotable New York.*

Martha Cooper and Henry Chalfant: *Subway Art.*

Josh Alan Friedman: *Tales of Times Square.* Sleaze, scum and degradation in the old Times Square.

Nelson George: *Hip-Hop America.* The history of hip-hop, from Grandmaster Flash to P. Diddy.

Pat Hackett (ed.): *The Andy Warhol Diaries.*

Robert Hendrickson: *New Yawk Tawk.* Dictionary of NYC slang.

A.J. Liebling: *Back Where I Came From.* Personal recollections from the famous *New Yorker* columnist.

Legs McNeil and Gillian McCain (ed.): *Please Kill Me.* Oral history of the city's 1970s punk scene.

Joseph Mitchell: *Up in the Old Hotel and Other Stories.* An anthology of the late journalist's most colorful reporting.

Frank O'Hara: *The Collected Poems of Frank O'Hara.* The great NYC poet found inspiration in his hometown.

Alice Leccese Powers et al.: *The Brooklyn Reader: 30 Writers Celebrate America's Favorite Borough.*

Andrés Torres: *Between Melting Pot and Mosaic.* African-American and Puerto Rican life in the city.

Heather Holland Wheaton: *Eight Million Stories in a New York Minute.*

E.B. White: *Here is New York.* A clear-eyed love letter to Gotham.

Fiction

Kurt Andersen: *Turn of the Century.* Millennial Manhattan seen through the eyes of media players.

Paul Auster: *The New York Trilogy: City of Glass, Ghosts, the Locked Room.* A search for the madness behind the method of Manhattan's grid.

Kevin Baker: *Dreamland.* A poetic novel about Coney Island's glory days.

James A. Baldwin: *Another Country.* Racism under the bohemian veneer of the 1960s.

Caleb Carr: *The Alienist.* Hunting a serial killer in New York's turn-of-the-19th-century demimonde.

Michael Chabon: *The Amazing Adventures of Kavalier and Clay.* Pulitzer Prize–winning account of Jewish comic-book artists in the 1940s.

Ralph Ellison: *Invisible Man.* Coming of age as a black man in 1950s New York dealing with intolerance.

Jack Finney: *Time and Again.* An illustrator travels back to 19th-century New York.

Larry Kramer: *Faggots.* Hilarious gay New York.

Jonathan Lethem: *The Fortress of Solitude.* Lethem's account of growing up in 1970s Brooklyn.

Phillip Lopate (ed.): *Writing New York.* An excellent anthology of short stories, essays and poems set in New York.

Toni Morrison: *Jazz.* The music, glamour and grit of 1920s Harlem.

Dawn Powell: *The Locusts Have No King.* A stinging satire of New York's intelligentsia.

David Schickler: *Kissing in Manhattan.* Explores the lives of quirky tenants in a Manhattan apartment building.

Hubert Selby Jr.: *Last Exit to Brooklyn.* Brooklyn dockland degradation, circa 1950s.

Time Out Book of New York Short Stories: Of course we like these original short stories by 23 American and British authors.

Edith Wharton: *Old New York.* Four novellas of 19th-century New York, by the author of *The Age of Innocence.*

Tom Wolfe: *The Bonfire of the Vanities.* Rich/poor, black/white. An unmatched slice of 1980s New York.

History

Irving Lewis Allen: *The City in Slang.* How New York living has spawned hundreds of new words and phrases.

Herbert Asbury: *The Gangs of New York: An Informal History of the Underworld.* Asbury's racy journalistic portrait of the city at the turn of the last century was reissued to coincide with the release of Martin Scorcese's film.

Patrick Bunyan: *All Around the Town.* A book about fun Manhattan facts and curiosities.

Robert A. Caro: *The Power Broker.* A biography of Robert Moses, the mid-20th-century master builder in New York, and his checkered legacy.

Federal Writers' Project: *The WPA Guide to New York City.* A wonderful snapshot of the 1930s by writers employed under FDR's New Deal.

Sanna Feirstein: *Naming New York.* An account of how Manhattan places got their names.

Mitchell Fink and Lois Mathias: *Never Forget: An Oral History of September 11, 2001.* A collection of first-person accounts.

Alice Rose George (ed.): *Here Is New York.* A collection of nearly 900 powerful amateur photos documents the aftermath of September 11, 2001.

Clifton Hood: *722 Miles: The Building of the Subways and How They Transformed New York.*

Kenneth T. Jackson (ed.): *The Encyclopedia of New York City.* An ambitious and useful reference guide.

Rem Koolhaas: *Delirious New York.* Urbanism, the culture of congestion and New York as a "terminal city."

David Levering Lewis: *When Harlem Was in Vogue.* A study of the 1920s Harlem Renaissance.

Shaun O'Connell: *Remarkable, Unspeakable New York.* The history of New York as literary inspiration.

Mitchell Pacelle: *Empire.* The story of the fight to build the Empire State Building.

Jacob A. Riis: *How the Other Half Lives.* A pioneering photojournalistic record of squalid tenement life.

Roy Rosenzweig and Elizabeth Blackmar: *The Park and the People.* A lengthy history of Central Park.

Marie Salerno and Arthur Gelb: *The New York Pop-Up Book.* Interactive historical account of NYC.

Luc Sante: *Low Life.* Opium dens, brothels and suicide salons in New York from the 1840s to the 1920s.

Mike Wallace and Edwin G. Burrows: *Gotham: A History of New York City to 1898.* The first volume in a planned mammoth history of NYC.

A few favorite films

Annie Hall (1977): Woody Allen costars with Diane Keaton in this appealingly neurotic valentine to living and loving in Manhattan.

Breakfast at Tiffany's (1961): Blake Edwards gave Audrey Hepburn her signature role as the lovable, cash-poor socialite Holly Golightly.

Dog Day Afternoon (1975): Al Pacino makes for a great antihero as a Brooklyn bank robber in Sidney Lumet's uproarious classic.

Do the Right Thing (1989): The hottest day of the summer leads to racial tensions in Bedford-Stuyvesant in Spike Lee's incisive drama.

The French Connection (1971): As detective Jimmy "Popeye" Doyle, Gene Hackman ignores all traffic lights as he chases down members of a drug ring in William Friedkin's thriller.

The Godfather (1972) and ***The Godfather: Part II*** (1974): Francis Ford Coppola's brilliant commentary about capitalism in America is told through the violent saga of Italian gangsters.

Mean Streets (1973): Robert De Niro and Harvey Keitel shine as small-time Little Italy hoods in Martin Scorsese's breakthrough film.

Midnight Cowboy (1969): Street creatures Ratso Rizzo and Joe Buck face an unforgiving Times Square in John Schlesinger's dark classic.

Spider-Man (2002): The comic-book web-slinger from Forest Hills comes to life in Sam Raimi's pitch-perfect crowd pleaser.

Taxi Driver (1976): Robert De Niro is a crazed cabbie who sees all of New York as a den of iniquity in Martin Scorsese's bold drama.

Websites

www.timeoutny.com
The *Time Out New York* website covers all the city has to offer. When you're planning your trip, check out the New York City Guide section for a variety of itineraries that you can use in conjunction with this guide.

eatdrink.timeoutny.com
Subscribe to TONY Eating & Drinking Online and instantly search thousands of reviews written by our critics.

www.nycvisit.com
The site of NYC & Company, the local convention and visitors bureau.

www.mta.info
Subway and bus service changes are always posted here. An interactive subway map points out sights near each stop.

www.nyc.gov
City Hall's "Official New York City Website" has lots of links.

www.ny1.com
NY1 News' site covers local events, news and weather.

www.nytimes.com
"All the News That's Fit to Print" online from *The New York Times.*

www.centralpark.org
Discover the nitty-gritty of the city's favorite park.

www.pagesix.com
Catch up on all the celeb canoodling going on around town, courtesy of the *New York Post*'s gossip site.

www.clubplanet.com
Follow the city's nocturnal scene and buy advance tickets to big events.

www.livebroadway.com
"The official website of Broadway" is the source for theaters, tickets and tours.

www.craigslist.org
A virtual community set up to find tickets, housing and even friendship.

www.hipguide.com
A short 'n' sweet site for those looking for what's considered hip.

www.forgotten-ny.com
Remember old New York here.

www.newyorkfirst.com
Gotham-inspired gifts, from T-shirts to cheesecake.

Index

Numbers in **bold** indicate key information on a topic; *italics* indicate photographs.

C

O

P

Q

R

T

Advertisers' Index

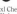

Maps

Street Index

MANHATTAN

BROOKLYN

QUEENS

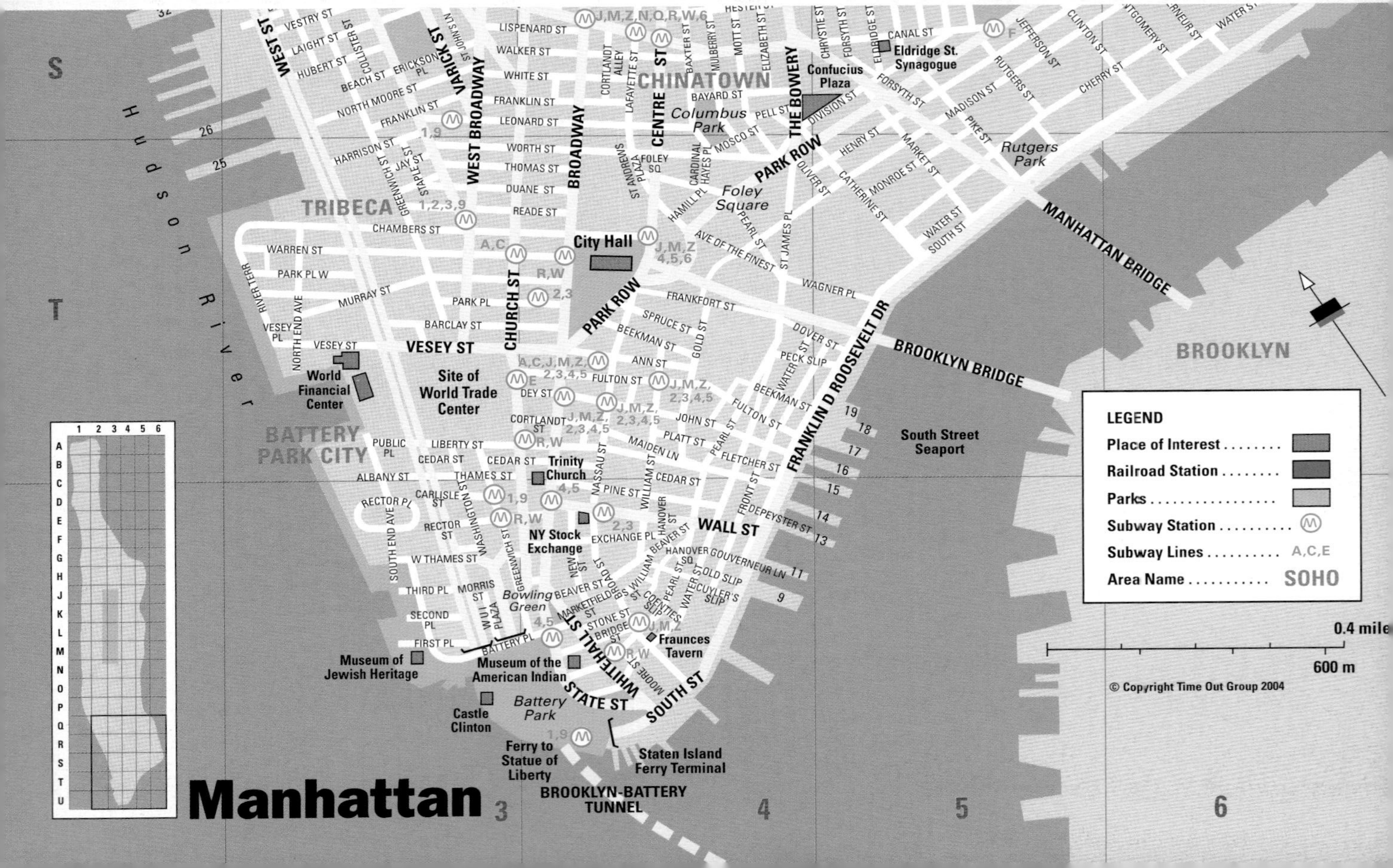

Manhattan
LEGEND
Place of Interest
Railroad Station
Parks
Subway Station
Subway Lines A,C,E
Area Name SOHO
0.4 mile
600 m
TRIBECA
BATTERY PARK CITY
CHINATOWN
BROOKLYN
Hudson River
City Hall
Site of World Trade Center
World Financial Center
Trinity Church
NY Stock Exchange
Museum of Jewish Heritage
Museum of the American Indian
Castle Clinton
Battery Park
Bowling Green
Ferry to Statue of Liberty
Staten Island Ferry Terminal
BROOKLYN-BATTERY TUNNEL
Fraunces Tavern
South Street Seaport
Foley Square
Columbus Park
Confucius Plaza
Eldridge St. Synagogue
Rutgers Park
BROOKLYN BRIDGE
MANHATTAN BRIDGE
FRANKLIN D ROOSEVELT DR
WEST ST
WEST BROADWAY
BROADWAY
CHURCH ST
VESEY ST
PARK ROW
CENTRE ST
THE BOWERY
VARICK ST
WALL ST
WHITEHALL ST
STATE ST
SOUTH ST

CHELSEA
FLATIRON
GRAMERCY PARK
GREENWICH VILLAGE
EAST VILLAGE
SOHO
LITTLE ITALY
LOWER EAST SIDE
Joyce Theater
Flatiron Building
Union Sq
Gramercy Park
Stuyvesant Square
Peter Cooper Village
Stuyvesant Town
Manhattan Marina
Grace Church
St. Mark's in the Bowery
Washington Square
New York University
Tompkins Square
East River Park
Seward Park
East River
W 23RD ST
E 23RD ST
W 14TH ST
E 14TH ST
BROADWAY
FOURTH AVE
THE BOWERY
SIXTH AVE
SEVENTH AVE S
HUDSON ST
WEST SIDE HWY (JOE DIMAGGIO HWY)
HOLLAND TUNNEL
CANAL ST
W HOUSTON ST
E HOUSTON ST
WEST BROADWAY
LAGUARDIA P
LAFAYETTE ST
CENTRE ST
VARICK ST
WILLIAMSBURG BRIDGE
GRAND ST
EAST BROADWAY
AVENUE A
AVENUE B
AVENUE C
AVENUE D

WEST SIDE HWY
TWELFTH AVE
Javits Center
ELEVENTH AVE
TENTH AVE
NINTH AVE
EIGHTH AVE
SEVENTH AVE
SIXTH AVE
FIFTH AVE
MADISON AVE
PARK AVE SOUTH
LEXINGTON AVE
THIRD AVE
SECOND AVE
FIRST AVE
FRANKLIN D ROOSEVELT DR
BROADWAY
FOURTH AVE
HUDSON ST
W 14TH ST
W 23RD ST
W 34TH ST
E 14TH ST
E 23RD ST
E 34TH ST
GARMENT DISTRICT
CHELSEA
FLATIRON
GREENWICH
GRAMERCY PARK
EAST VILLAGE
Chelsea Park
Dia Center for the Arts
General Post Office
Madison Square Garden
Penn Station
Macy's
Manhattan Mall
Empire State Building
Pierpont Morgan Library
Joyce Theater
Flatiron Building
Madison Square
Union Sq
Gramercy Park
Stuyvesant Square
Stuyvesant Town
Peter Cooper Village
Tompkins Square
Washington Square
New York University
Grace Church
St. Mark's in the Bowery
Manhattan Mari
DYER AVE
UNIVERSITY PL
IRVING PL
UNION SQ WEST
UNION SQ EAST
RUTHERFORD PL
NATHAN D PERLMAN PL
MT CARMEL PL
ASSER LEVY PL
STUYVESANT ST
ST MARKS PL
ASTOR PL
AVENUE A
AVENUE B
AVENUE C
WASH SQ WEST
WASH SQ EAST
WASHINGTON SQ NORTH
GREENE ST
WAVERLY PL
WASHINGTON PL
GROVE ST
WAVERLY PLACE
GREENWICH AVE
BLEECKER ST
W 4TH ST
GREENWICH ST
WASHINGTON ST
BANK ST
BETHUNE ST
PERRY ST
W 11TH ST
W 12TH ST
JANE ST
HORATIO ST
GANSEVOORT ST
LITTLE W 12TH ST
P
Q
R
1
2
3
4
5

WEST SIDE HWY
RIVERSIDE BLVD
FREEDOM PL
TWELFTH AVE
ELEVENTH AVE
WEST END AVE
TENTH AVE
AMSTERDAM AVE
NINTH AVE
COLUMBUS AVE
EIGHTH AVE
CENTRAL PARK WEST
SEVENTH AVE
SIXTH AVE
FIFTH AVE
MADISON AVE
PARK AVE
LEXINGTON AVE
THIRD AVE
SECOND AVE
FIRST AVE
YORK AVE
FRANKLIN D
BROADWAY
LINCOLN TUNNEL
QUEENS-MIDTOWN TUNNEL
QUEENSBORO BRIDGE (59TH ST)
TRAMWAY
Roosevelt Island
W 40TH ST
W 42ND ST
W 57TH ST
W 72ND ST
E 40TH ST
E 42ND ST
E 72ND ST
CENTRAL PARK SOUTH
CLINTON
THEATER DISTRICT
MIDTOWN
DeWitt Clinton Park
Times Square
Bryant Park
Lincoln Center
Columbus Circle
Port Authority Bus Terminal
NY Visitors Bureau
TKTS
Carnegie Hall
Rockefeller Center
Radio City Music Hall
ROCKEFELLER PLAZA
Museum of Modern Art
Grand Army Plaza
NY Public Library
Saks Fifth Ave
St. Patrick's Cathedral
Trump Tower
VANDERBILT AVE
Grand Central Terminal
Helmsley Building
Chrysler Building
Old Daily News Building
Bloomingdales
TUDOR CITY PL
UN PLAZA
United Nations Heaquarters
MITCHELL PL
BEEKMAN PL
SUTTON PL SOUTH
SUTTON PL
Heckscher Playground
Tavern on the Green
Strawberry Fields
Sheep Meadow
WEST DRIVE
EAST DRIVE
65TH ST TRANSVERSE RD
The Dairy
Wollman Memorial Rink
Naumburg Bandshell
Zoo
Frick Collection
Rockefeller University

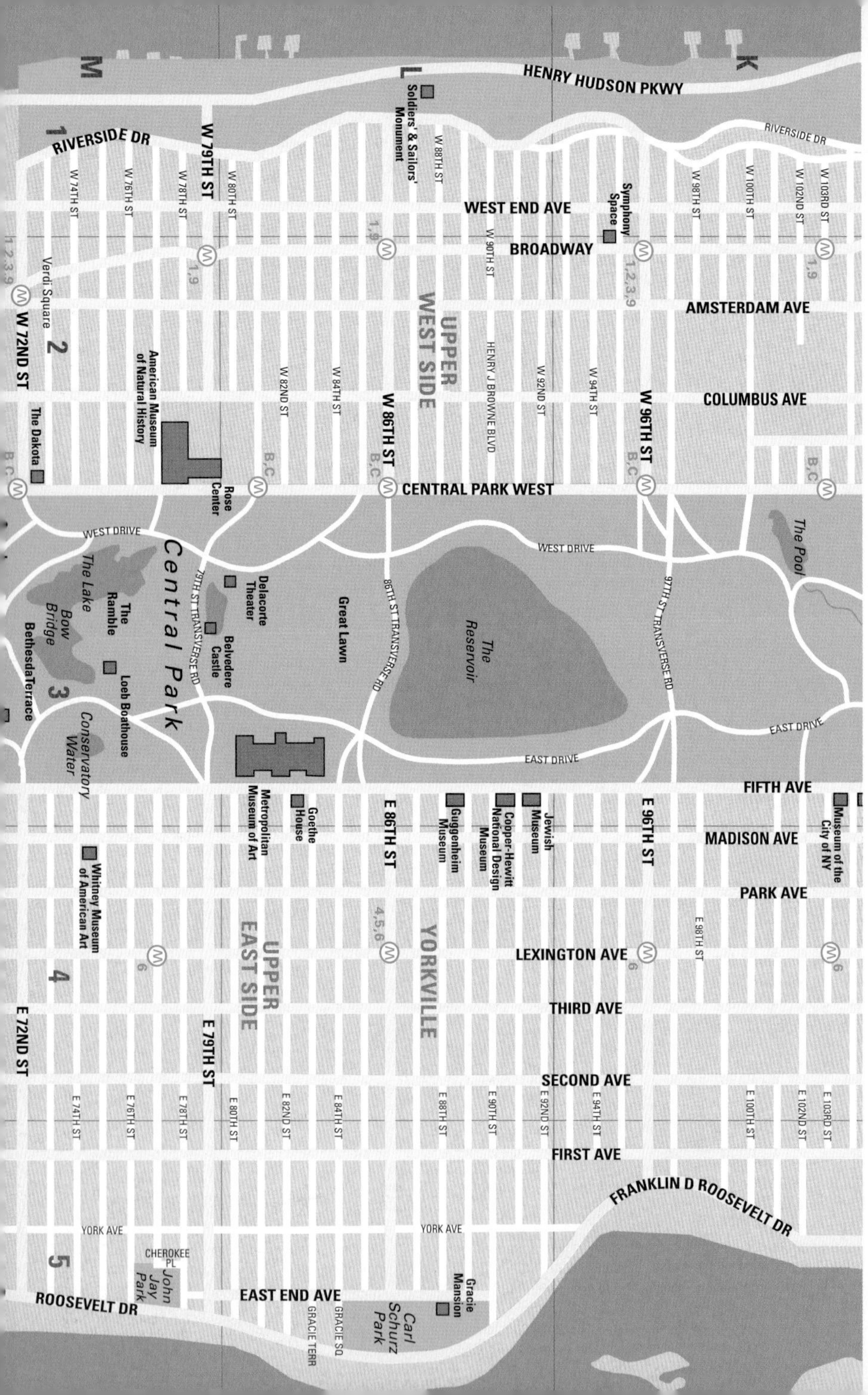

M
L
K
HENRY HUDSON PKWY
RIVERSIDE DR
Soldiers' & Sailors' Monument
W 79TH ST
W 74TH ST
W 76TH ST
W 78TH ST
W 80TH ST
W 88TH ST
W 98TH ST
W 100TH ST
W 102ND ST
W 103RD ST
Symphony Space
WEST END AVE
BROADWAY
W 90TH ST
Verdi Square
W 72ND ST
AMSTERDAM AVE
UPPER WEST SIDE
HENRY J BROWNE BLVD
W 82ND ST
W 84TH ST
W 86TH ST
W 92ND ST
W 94TH ST
W 96TH ST
COLUMBUS AVE
American Museum of Natural History
The Dakota
Rose Center
CENTRAL PARK WEST
WEST DRIVE
The Pool
Central Park
The Lake
Bow Bridge
The Ramble
Delacorte Theater
Belvedere Castle
79TH ST TRANSVERSE RD
Great Lawn
86TH ST TRANSVERSE RD
The Reservoir
97TH ST TRANSVERSE RD
Bethesda Terrace
Loeb Boathouse
Conservatory Water
EAST DRIVE
FIFTH AVE
Metropolitan Museum of Art
Goethe House
E 86TH ST
Guggenheim Museum
Cooper-Hewitt National Design Museum
Jewish Museum
E 96TH ST
Museum of the City of NY
MADISON AVE
Whitney Museum of American Art
PARK AVE
E 98TH ST
LEXINGTON AVE
UPPER EAST SIDE
YORKVILLE
THIRD AVE
E 72ND ST
E 79TH ST
SECOND AVE
E 74TH ST
E 76TH ST
E 78TH ST
E 80TH ST
E 82ND ST
E 84TH ST
E 88TH ST
E 90TH ST
E 92ND ST
E 94TH ST
E 100TH ST
E 102ND ST
E 103RD ST
FIRST AVE
FRANKLIN D ROOSEVELT DR
YORK AVE
CHEROKEE PL
John Jay Park
Gracie Mansion
ROOSEVELT DR
EAST END AVE
Carl Schurz Park
GRACIE TERR
GRACIE SQ
1
2
3
4
5

HENRY HUDSON PKWY
Riverside Park
RIVERSIDE DR WEST
RIVERSIDE DR EAST
TWELFTH AVE
W 135TH ST
Barnard College
Riverside Church
General Grant National Memorial
CLAREMONT AVE
BROADWAY
Columbia University
MARTIN LUTHER KING JR BLVD
OLD BROADWAY
City College of New York
AMSTERDAM AVE
Cathedral of St. John the Divine
Cathedral Close
MORNINGSIDE DRIVE
Morningside Park
CONVENT AVE
St Nicholas Park
MORNINGSIDE AVE
ST NICHOLAS TER
MANHATTAN AVE
FREDERICK DOUGLASS BLVD
(EIGHTH AVE)
Apollo Theater
ST NICHOLAS AVE
WEST DRIVE
ADAM CLAYTON POWELL JR. BLVD
(SEVENTH AVE)
W 125TH ST
HARLEM
Schomburg Center
Harlem Meer
Conservatory Gardens
MALCOLM X BLVD
(LENOX AVE)
MT MORRIS PARK WEST
Marcus Garvey Memorial Park
FIFTH AVE
El Museo del Barrio
MADISON AVE
E 135TH ST
SPANISH HARLEM
PARK AVE
E 125TH ST
LEXINGTON AVE
THIRD AVE BRIDGE
THIRD AVE
SECOND AVE
LUIS MUNOZ MARIN BLVD
TRIBOROUGH BRIDGE
FIRST AVE
Jefferson Park
PLEASANT AVE

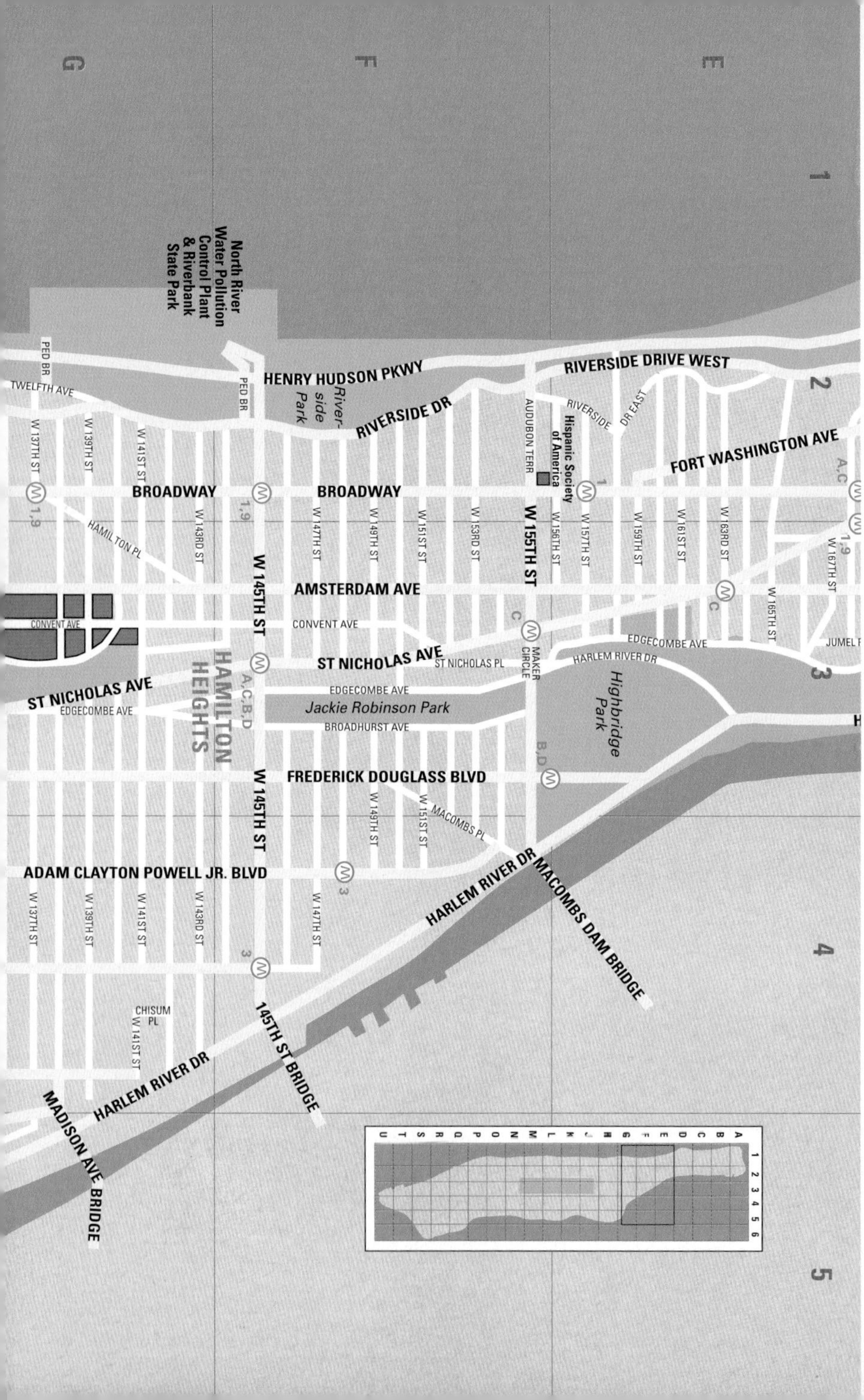
G
F
E
1
2
3
4
5
North River Water Pollution Control Plant & Riverbank State Park
HENRY HUDSON PKWY
RIVERSIDE DRIVE WEST
RIVERSIDE DR
RIVERSIDE DR EAST
River-side Park
FORT WASHINGTON AVE
Hispanic Society of America
AUDUBON TERR
PED BR
TWELFTH AVE
BROADWAY
HAMILTON PL
W 137TH ST
W 139TH ST
W 141ST ST
W 143RD ST
W 145TH ST
W 147TH ST
W 149TH ST
W 151ST ST
W 153RD ST
W 155TH ST
W 156TH ST
W 157TH ST
W 159TH ST
W 161ST ST
W 163RD ST
W 165TH ST
W 167TH ST
AMSTERDAM AVE
CONVENT AVE
ST NICHOLAS AVE
ST NICHOLAS PL
EDGECOMBE AVE
JUMEL PL
MAKER CIRCLE
HARLEM RIVER DR
Highbridge Park
HAMILTON HEIGHTS
Jackie Robinson Park
BROADHURST AVE
FREDERICK DOUGLASS BLVD
MACOMBS PL
ADAM CLAYTON POWELL JR. BLVD
MACOMBS DAM BRIDGE
145TH ST BRIDGE
CHISUM PL
MADISON AVE BRIDGE
1,9
A,C
A,C,B,D
B,D
C
3
A B C D E F G H J K L M N O P Q R S T U
1 2 3 4 5 6

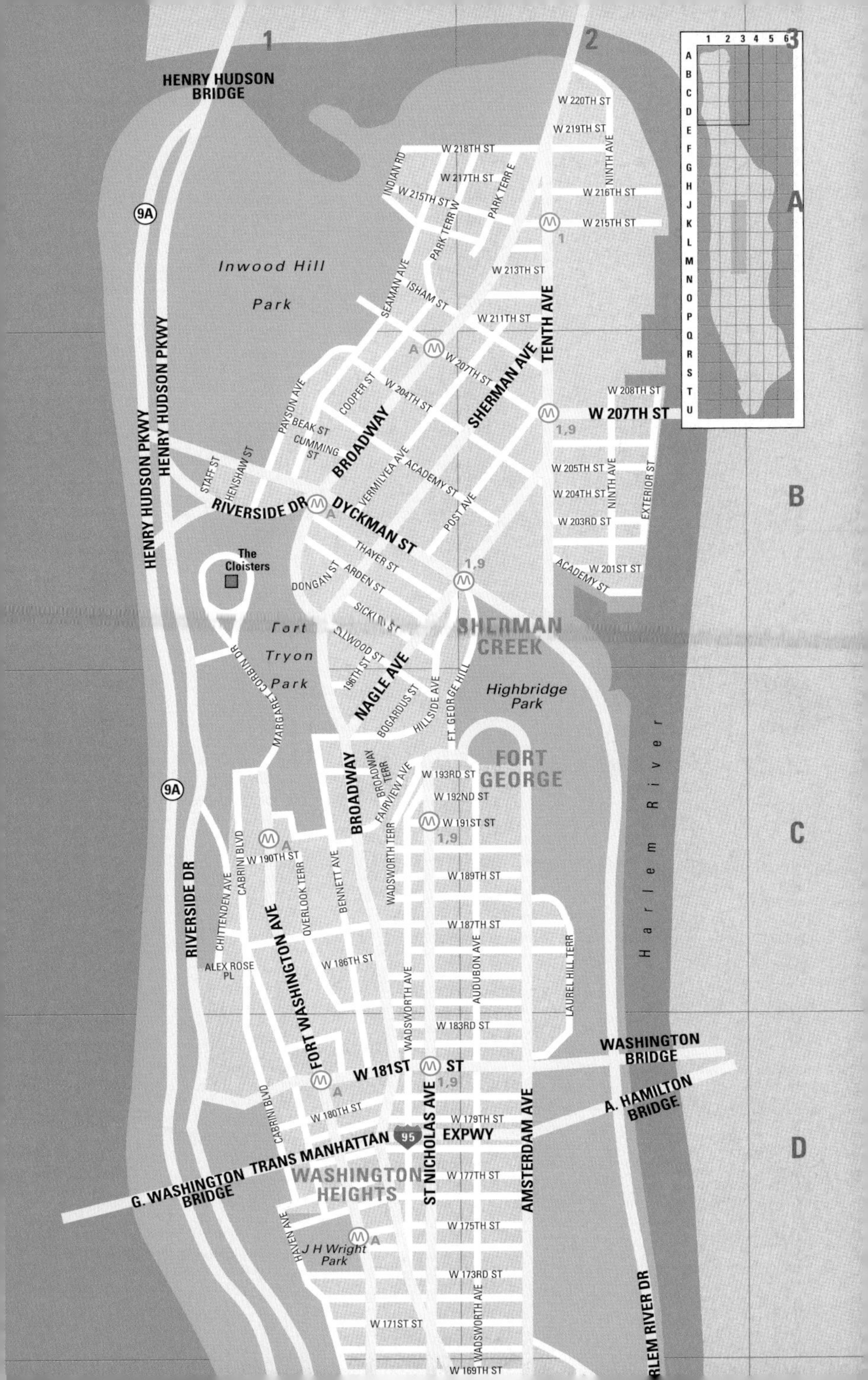

HENRY HUDSON BRIDGE
Inwood Hill Park
HENRY HUDSON PKWY
HENRY HUDSON PKWY
9A
W 220TH ST
W 219TH ST
W 218TH ST
W 217TH ST
W 216TH ST
W 215TH ST
W 213TH ST
W 211TH ST
W 208TH ST
W 207TH ST
W 205TH ST
W 204TH ST
W 203RD ST
W 201ST ST
INDIAN RD
W 215TH ST
PARK TERR W
PARK TERR E
NINTH AVE
TENTH AVE
SEAMAN AVE
ISHAM ST
W 207TH ST
SHERMAN AVE
COOPER ST
W 204TH ST
PAYSON AVE
BEAK ST
CUMMING ST
BROADWAY
VERMILYEA AVE
ACADEMY ST
POST AVE
EXTERIOR ST
STAFF ST
HENSHAW ST
RIVERSIDE DR
DYCKMAN ST
The Cloisters
THAYER ST
ARDEN ST
DONGAN ST
SICKLES ST
ELLWOOD ST
196TH ST
NAGLE AVE
Fort Tryon Park
SHERMAN CREEK
Highbridge Park
MARGARET CORBIN DR
BOGARDUS ST
HILLSIDE AVE
FT. GEORGE HILL
FORT GEORGE
BROADWAY TERR
FAIRVIEW AVE
W 193RD ST
W 192ND ST
W 191ST ST
W 190TH ST
W 189TH ST
W 187TH ST
W 186TH ST
W 183RD ST
W 181ST ST
W 180TH ST
W 179TH ST
W 177TH ST
W 175TH ST
W 173RD ST
W 171ST ST
W 169TH ST
RIVERSIDE DR
CHITTENDEN AVE
CABRINI BLVD
OVERLOOK TERR
BENNETT AVE
WADSWORTH TERR
FORT WASHINGTON AVE
ALEX ROSE PL
WADSWORTH AVE
AUDUBON AVE
LAUREL HILL TERR
Harlem River
WASHINGTON BRIDGE
A. HAMILTON BRIDGE
TRANS MANHATTAN EXPWY
95
G. WASHINGTON BRIDGE
WASHINGTON HEIGHTS
ST NICHOLAS AVE
AMSTERDAM AVE
HAVEN AVE
J H Wright Park
HARLEM RIVER DR
A
1
1,9
1
2
3
A
B
C
D

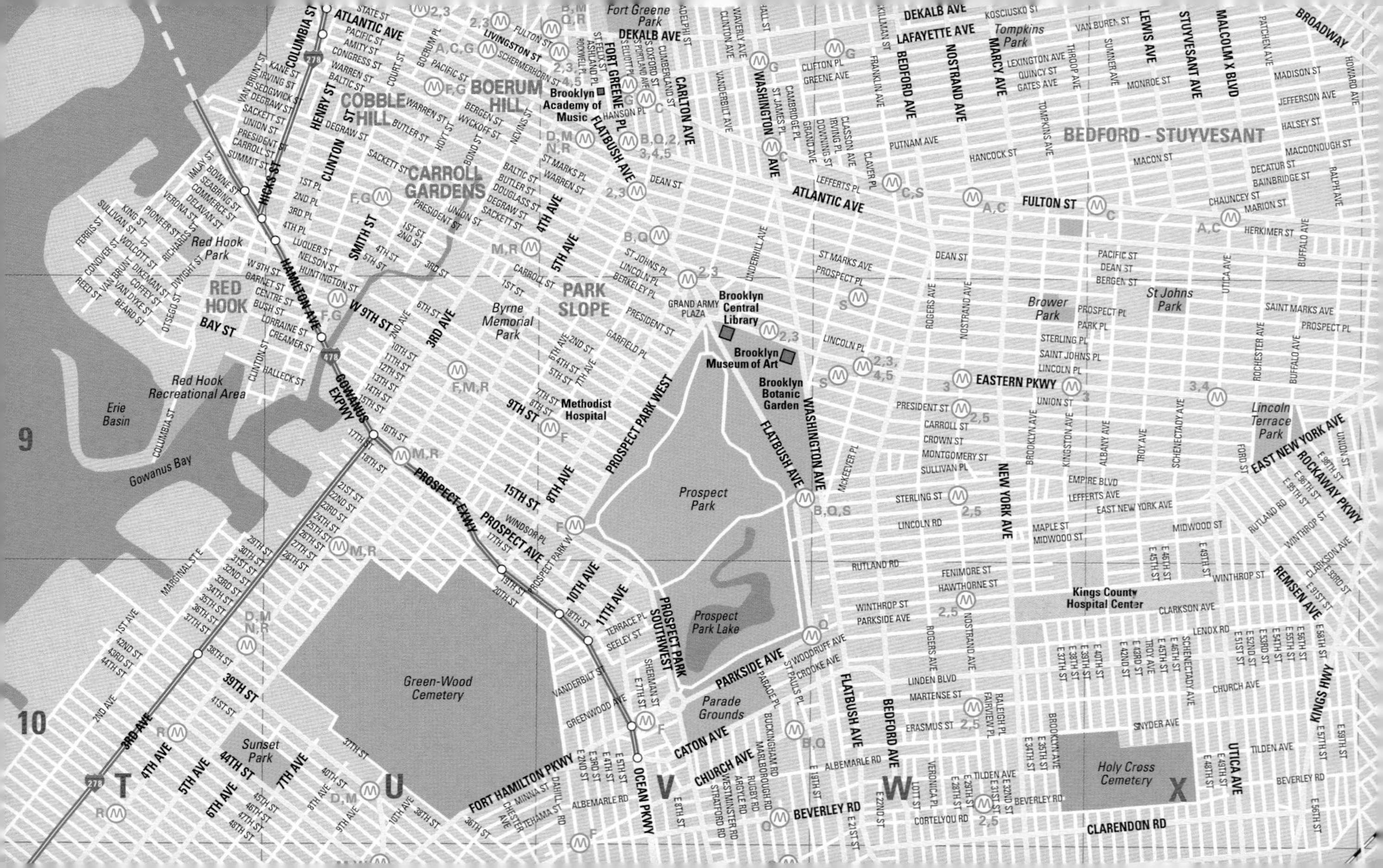

9
10
T
U
V
W
X
BEDFORD - STUYVESANT
BOERUM HILL
COBBLE HILL
CARROLL GARDENS
RED HOOK
PARK SLOPE
Fort Greene Park
Tompkins Park
Red Hook Park
Red Hook Recreational Area
Erie Basin
Gowanus Bay
Byrne Memorial Park
Methodist Hospital
Brooklyn Academy of Music
Brooklyn Central Library
Brooklyn Museum of Art
Brooklyn Botanic Garden
GRAND ARMY PLAZA
Prospect Park
Prospect Park Lake
Parade Grounds
Green-Wood Cemetery
Sunset Park
Brower Park
St Johns Park
Lincoln Terrace Park
Kings County Hospital Center
Holy Cross Cemetery
ATLANTIC AVE
COLUMBIA ST
HENRY ST
HICKS ST
CLINTON
SMITH ST
HAMILTON AVE
GOWANUS EXPWY
PROSPECT EXPWY
W 9TH ST
BAY ST
3RD AVE
4TH AVE
5TH AVE
6TH AVE
7TH AVE
8TH AVE
9TH ST
10TH AVE
11TH AVE
15TH ST
39TH ST
44TH ST
PROSPECT AVE
PROSPECT PARK WEST
PROSPECT PARK SOUTHWEST
FLATBUSH AVE
WASHINGTON AVE
DEKALB AVE
FORT GREENE PL
CARLTON AVE
LIVINGSTON ST
LAFAYETTE AVE
BEDFORD AVE
NOSTRAND AVE
MARCY AVE
LEWIS AVE
STUYVESANT AVE
MALCOLM X BLVD
BROADWAY
FULTON ST
EASTERN PKWY
NEW YORK AVE
EAST NEW YORK AVE
ROCKAWAY PKWY
REMSEN AVE
UTICA AVE
KINGS HWY
CLARENDON RD
BEVERLEY RD
CHURCH AVE
CATON AVE
PARKSIDE AVE
OCEAN PKWY
FORT HAMILTON PKWY

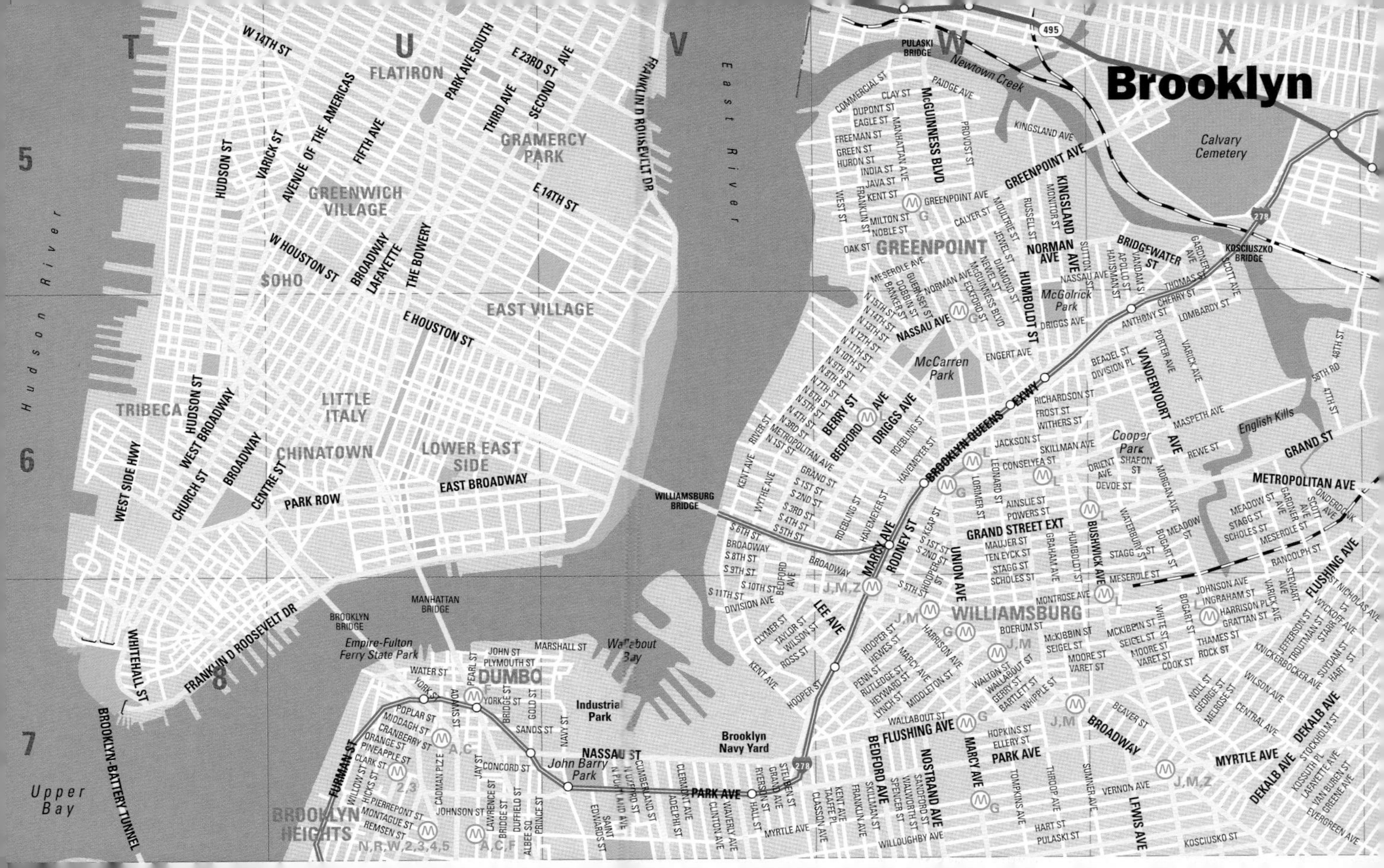

Brooklyn
T
U
V
W
X
5
6
7
8
Hudson River
East River
Upper Bay
W 14TH ST
FLATIRON
PARK AVE SOUTH
E 23RD ST
SECOND AVE
THIRD AVE
GRAMERCY PARK
FIFTH AVE
AVENUE OF THE AMERICAS
VARICK ST
HUDSON ST
GREENWICH VILLAGE
E 14TH ST
W HOUSTON ST
BROADWAY
LAFAYETTE
THE BOWERY
SOHO
EAST VILLAGE
E HOUSTON ST
FRANKLIN D ROOSEVELT DR
TRIBECA
LITTLE ITALY
CHINATOWN
LOWER EAST SIDE
EAST BROADWAY
WEST SIDE HWY
CHURCH ST
WEST BROADWAY
CENTRE ST
PARK ROW
WILLIAMSBURG BRIDGE
MANHATTAN BRIDGE
BROOKLYN BRIDGE
Empire-Fulton Ferry State Park
WHITEHALL ST
BROOKLYN-BATTERY TUNNEL
DUMBO
Industrial Park
Wallabout Bay
Brooklyn Navy Yard
John Barry Park
BROOKLYN HEIGHTS
FURMAN ST
NASSAU ST
PARK AVE
PULASKI BRIDGE
Newtown Creek
KOSCIUSZKO BRIDGE
Calvary Cemetery
GREENPOINT
McGUINNESS BLVD
GREENPOINT AVE
KINGSLAND AVE
NORMAN AVE
HUMBOLDT ST
BRIDGEWATER ST
McGolrick Park
McCarren Park
NASSAU AVE
BERRY ST
BEDFORD AVE
DRIGGS AVE
BROOKLYN QUEENS EXWY
VANDERVOORT AVE
Cooper Park
English Kills
GRAND ST
METROPOLITAN AVE
MARCY AVE
RODNEY ST
UNION AVE
GRAND STREET EXT
BUSHWICK AVE
WILLIAMSBURG
LEE AVE
FLUSHING AVE
NOSTRAND AVE
BROADWAY
MYRTLE AVE
DEKALB AVE
LEWIS AVE

Queens
W
X
Y
Z
1
2
3
4
5
6
7
Central Park
SPANISH HARLEM
FIFTH AVE
PARK AVE
LEXINGTON AVE
THIRD AVE
SECOND AVE
FIRST AVE
Jefferson Park
East River
Hell Gate
Con Edison
E 96TH ST
F D ROOSEVELT DR
YORKVILLE
E 86TH ST
UPPER EAST SIDE
EAST END AVE
Carl Schurz Park
E 79TH ST
John Jay Park
E 72ND ST
TRIBOROUGH BRIDGE
Astoria Park
Bowery Bay
La Guardia Airport
BIKERS ISLAND BRIDGE
MAIN AVE
ASTORIA BLVD
31ST ST
DITMARS BLVD
ASTORIA
Socrates Sculpture Park
Barnard College
Roosevelt Island
VERNON BLVD
21ST ST
34TH AVE
STEINWAY ST
St Michaels Cemetery
BROOKLYN QUEENS EXPY W
BROOKLYN QUEENS EXPY E
82ND ST
30TH AVE
31ST AVE
JACKSON HEIGHTS
QUEENSBORO BRIDGE
Queens Bridge Park
LONG ISLAND CITY
American Museum of the Moving Image
NORTHERN BLVD
81ST ST
Sunnyside Yard
39TH ST
SKILLMAN AVE
43RD AVE
48TH ST
Greenland Park
WOODSIDE
ROOSEVELT AVE
BROADWAY
BAXTER AVE
THOMSON AVE
QUEENS BLVD
P.S.1
MoMA QNS
SUNNYSIDE
VAN DAM ST
QUEENS-MIDTOWN TUNNEL
JACKSON AVE
49TH AVE
Dutch Kills
WOODSIDE AVE
45TH AVE
New Calvary Cemetery
58TH ST
61ST ST
PULASKI BRIDGE
11TH ST
Newtown Creek
BORDEN AVE
49TH AVE
MIDDLE VILLAGE
MCGUINNESS BLVD
Calvary Cemetery
BROOKLYN QUEENS EXPWY
Mount Zion Cemetery
MAURICE AVE
GREENPOINT AVE
NORMAN AVE
HUMBOLDT ST
MASPETH
GRAND AVE
69TH ST
MANHATTAN AVE
LOMBARDY ST
KINGSLAND AVE
VANDERVOORT AVE
MASPETH AVE
FRESH POND RD
Mt Olivet Cemetery
ELIOT AVE
Juniper Valley Park
McCarren Park
BERRY ST
BEDFORD AVE
DRIGGS AVE
English Kills
GRAND ST
FLUSHING AVE
METROPOLITAN AVE
Linden Hill Cemetery
MARCY AVE
RODNEY ST
UNION AVE
BUSHWICK AVE
Luttheran Cemetery
Glen Ridge Park
LEE AVE
BROADWAY
FLUSHING AVE
DEKALB AVE
CENTRAL AVE

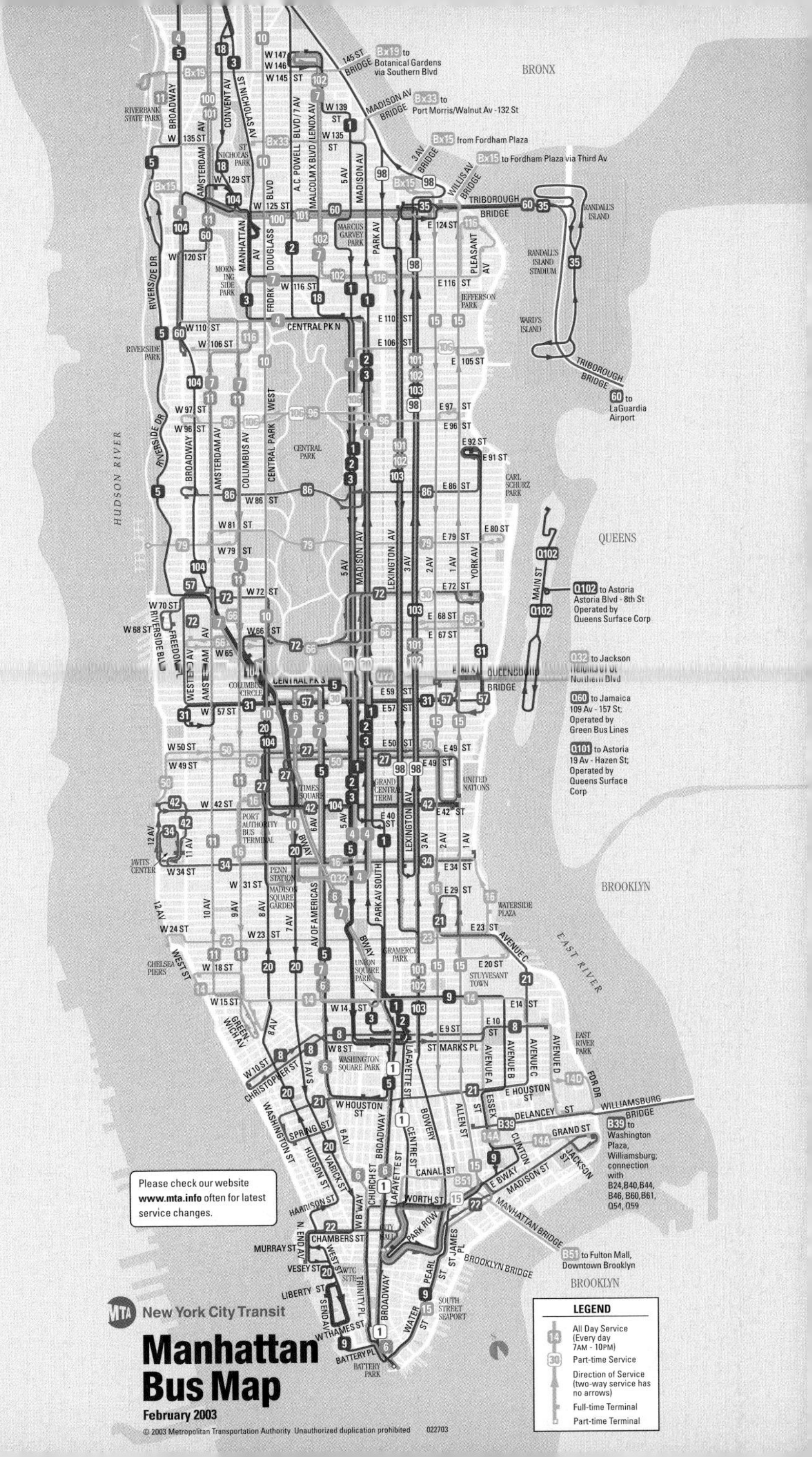
New York City Transit
Manhattan Bus Map
February 2003
© 2003 Metropolitan Transportation Authority Unauthorized duplication prohibited 022703
Please check our website www.mta.info often for latest service changes.
LEGEND
All Day Service (Every day 7AM - 10PM)
Part-time Service
Direction of Service (two-way service has no arrows)
Full-time Terminal
Part-time Terminal
Bx19 to Botanical Gardens via Southern Blvd
Bx33 to Port Morris/Walnut Av - 132 St
Bx15 from Fordham Plaza
Bx15 to Fordham Plaza via Third Av
60 to LaGuardia Airport
Q102 to Astoria Astoria Blvd - 8th St Operated by Queens Surface Corp
Q32 to Jackson Heights
Q60 to Jamaica 109 Av - 157 St; Operated by Green Bus Lines
Q101 to Astoria 19 Av - Hazen St; Operated by Queens Surface Corp
B39 to Washington Plaza, Williamsburg; connection with B24, B40, B44, B46, B60, B61, Q54, Q59
B51 to Fulton Mall, Downtown Brooklyn
BRONX
QUEENS
BROOKLYN
HUDSON RIVER
EAST RIVER
CENTRAL PARK
RANDALL'S ISLAND
WARD'S ISLAND
TRIBOROUGH BRIDGE
QUEENSBORO BRIDGE
WILLIAMSBURG BRIDGE
MANHATTAN BRIDGE
BROOKLYN BRIDGE

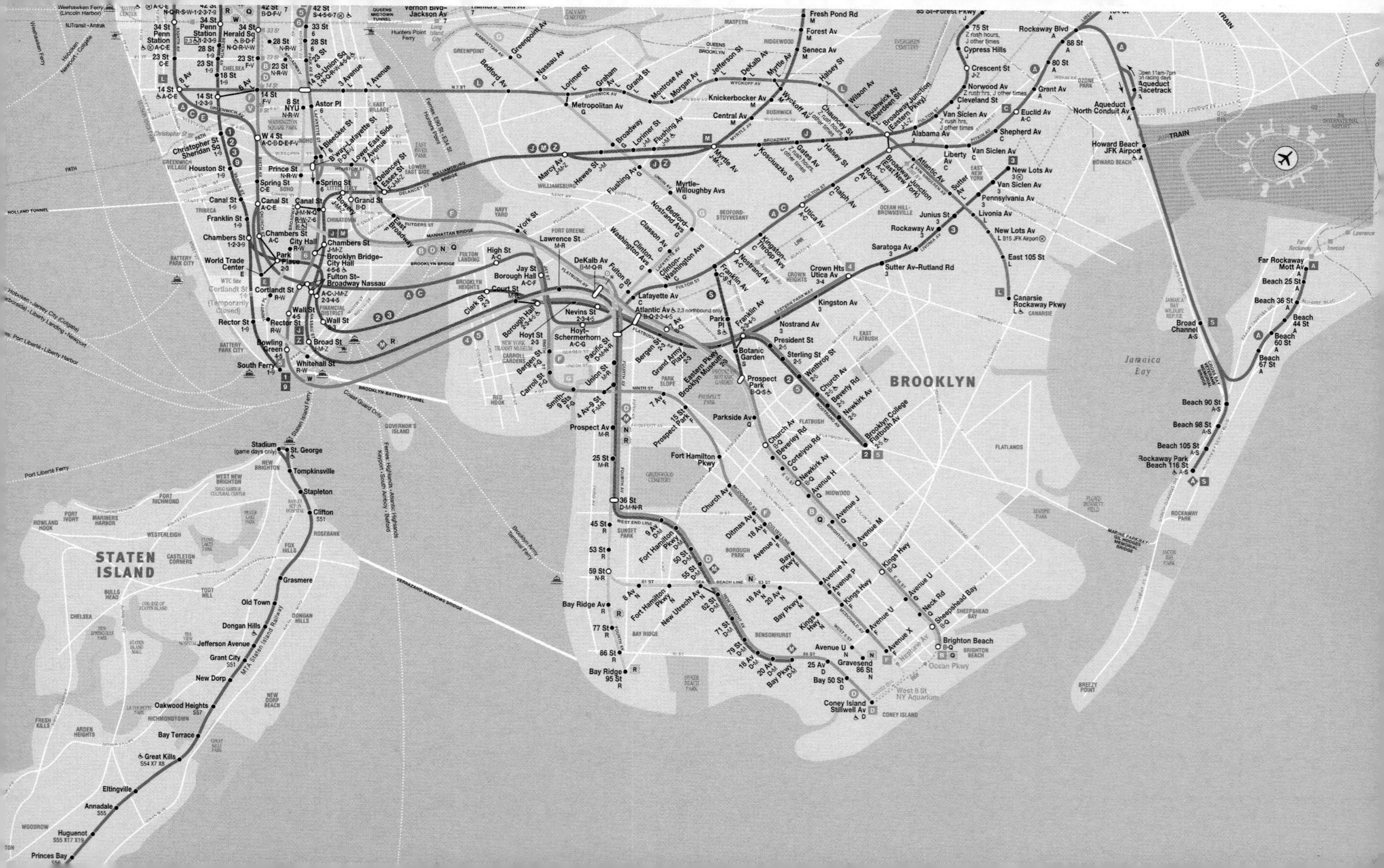

STATEN ISLAND
BROOKLYN
Jamaica Bay
MTA Staten Island Railway
Staten Island Ferry
Princes Bay
Huguenot
Annadale
Eltingville
Great Kills
Bay Terrace
Oakwood Heights
New Dorp
Grant City
Jefferson Avenue
Dongan Hills
Old Town
Grasmere
Clifton
Stapleton
Tompkinsville
St. George
Stadium
South Ferry
Bowling Green
Whitehall St
Rector St
Wall St
Broad St
Cortlandt St
World Trade Center
Chambers St
City Hall
Park Place
Brooklyn Bridge-City Hall
Fulton St-Broadway Nassau
Canal St
Franklin St
Spring St
Houston St
Christopher St Sheridan Sq
W 4 St
14 St
14 St-Union Sq
23 St
28 St
34 St Penn Station
34 St Herald Sq
42 St
Astor Pl
8 St NYU
Prince St
Bleecker St
B'way-Lafayette St
Lower East Side 2 Avenue
Delancey St Essex St
Grand St
Bowery
East Broadway
3 Avenue
1 Avenue
York St
High St
Clark St
Court St
Borough Hall
Jay St Borough Hall
Lawrence St
DeKalb Av
Nevins St
Hoyt St
Hoyt-Schermerhorn
Bergen St
Carroll St
Smith-9 Sts
4 Av-9 St
Union St
Pacific St
Atlantic Av
Lafayette Av
Fulton St
Clinton-Washington Avs
Washington Avs
Classon Av
Nostrand Av
Kingston-Throop Avs
Utica Av
Ralph Av
Rockaway Av
Broadway Junction
Atlantic Av
Liberty Av
Van Siclen Av
Shepherd Av
Euclid Av
Grant Av
80 St
88 St
Rockaway Blvd
Aqueduct North Conduit Av
Aqueduct Racetrack
Howard Beach JFK Airport
Broad Channel
Beach 90 St
Beach 98 St
Beach 105 St
Rockaway Park Beach 116 St
Beach 67 St
Beach 60 St
Beach 44 St
Beach 36 St
Beach 25 St
Far Rockaway Mott Av
Bedford Av
Lorimer St
Graham Av
Grand St
Montrose Av
Morgan Av
Jefferson St
DeKalb Av
Myrtle Av
Halsey St
Wilson Av
Bushwick Av Aberdeen St
Broadway Junction Eastern Pkwy
Alabama Av
Sutter Av
Livonia Av
New Lots Av
East 105 St
Canarsie Rockaway Pkwy
Greenpoint Av
Nassau Av
Metropolitan Av
Broadway
Flushing Av
Myrtle-Willoughby Avs
Bedford-Nostrand Avs
Marcy Av
Hewes St
Lorimer St
Flushing Av
Myrtle Av
Kosciuszko St
Gates Av
Halsey St
Chauncey St
Central Av
Knickerbocker Av
Wyckoff Av
Seneca Av
Forest Av
Fresh Pond Rd
Cypress Hills
75 St
Crescent St
Norwood Av
Cleveland St
Van Siclen Av
Franklin Av
Park Pl
Botanic Garden
Prospect Park
Eastern Pkwy Brooklyn Museum
Grand Army Plaza
7 Av
15 St Prospect Park
Fort Hamilton Pkwy
Church Av
Crown Hts Utica Av
Sutter Av-Rutland Rd
Saratoga Av
Rockaway Av
Junius St
Pennsylvania Av
Van Siclen Av
New Lots Av
Kingston Av
Nostrand Av
President St
Sterling St
Winthrop St
Church Av
Beverly Rd
Newkirk Av
Brooklyn College Flatbush Av
Parkside Av
Church Av
Beverley Rd
Cortelyou Rd
Newkirk Av
Avenue H
Avenue J
Avenue M
Kings Hwy
Avenue U
Neck Rd
Sheepshead Bay
Brighton Beach
Ocean Pkwy
West 8 St NY Aquarium
Coney Island Stillwell Av
Ditmas Av
18 Av
Avenue I
Bay Pkwy
Avenue N
Avenue P
Kings Hwy
Avenue U
Avenue X
Prospect Av
25 St
36 St
45 St
53 St
59 St
Bay Ridge Av
77 St
86 St
Bay Ridge 95 St
9 Av
Fort Hamilton Pkwy
50 St
55 St
62 St
71 St
79 St
18 Av
20 Av
Bay Pkwy
25 Av
Bay 50 St
8 Av
Fort Hamilton Pkwy
New Utrecht Av
18 Av
20 Av
Bay Pkwy
Kings Hwy
Avenue U
86 St
Gravesend
BROOKLYN-BATTERY TUNNEL
VERRAZANO-NARROWS BRIDGE
MANHATTAN BRIDGE
BROOKLYN BRIDGE
WILLIAMSBURG BRIDGE
HOLLAND TUNNEL
AIRTRAIN

Hudson River
Harlem River
East River
Long Island Sound
MANHATTAN
THE BRONX
QUEENS
Van Cortlandt Park 242 St
238 St
231 St
Marble Hill 225 St
215 St
207 St
Inwood 207 St
Dyckman St
191 St
190 St
181 St
175 St
168 St–Washington Hts
163 St Amsterdam Av
157 St
155 St
145 St
137 St City College
135 St
125 St
116 St Columbia University
116 St
Cathedral Pkwy (110 St)
Central Park North (110 St)
110 St
103 St
96 St
86 St
81 St–Museum of Natural History
79 St
77 St
72 St
68 St Hunter College
66 St Lincoln Center
59 St Columbus Circle
57 St
50 St
49 St
47–50 Sts/Rockefeller Ctr
5 Av/53 St
51 St
Lexington Av/53 St
Lexington Av/59 St
5 Av/59 St
Lexington Av/63 St
42 St Port Authority
Harlem 148 St
3 Av–149 St
149 St–Grand Concourse
138 St–Grand Concourse
3 Av 138 St
Brook Av
Cypress Av
E 143 St St Mary's St
E 149 St
Longwood Av
Hunts Point Av
Whitlock Av
Elder Av
Morrison–Sound View Avs
St Lawrence Av
Parkchester–E 177 St
Castle Hill Av
Zerega Av
Westchester Sq East Tremont Av
Middletown Rd
Buhre Av
Pelham Bay Park
Jackson Av
Prospect Av
Intervale Av
Simpson St
Freeman St
174 St
West Farms Sq E Tremont Av
E 180 St
Bronx Park East
Pelham Pkwy
Allerton Av
Burke Av
Gun Hill Rd
219 St
225 St
233 St
Nereid Av (238 St)
Wakefield 241 St
Morris Park
Baychester Av
Eastchester Dyre Av
161 St Yankee Stadium
167 St
170 St
Mt Eden Av
176 St
Burnside Av
183 St
Fordham Rd
Kingsbridge Rd
Bedford Pk Blvd Lehman College
Mosholu Pkwy
Woodlawn
174–175 Sts
Tremont Av
182–183 Sts
Bedford Pk Blvd
Norwood 205 St
Astoria Ditmars Blvd
Astoria Blvd
30 Av
Broadway
36 Av
39 Av
Queensboro Plaza
Queens Plaza
Court Sq
Long Island City
21 St Queensbridge
Roosevelt Island
23 St–Ely Av
45 Rd Court House Sq
21 St
Steinway St
46 St
Northern Blvd
65 St
74 St Broadway
82 St Jackson Hts
Jackson Hts Roosevelt Av
33 St
40 St
46 St
52 St
61 St Woodside
69 St
Elmhurst Av
90 St–Elmhurst Av
Junction Blvd
103 St–Corona Plaza
111 St
Willets Point–Shea Stadium
Flushing Main St
Grand Av Newtown
Woodhaven Blvd
63 Dr Rego Park
67 Av
Forest Hills 71 Av
75 Av
Kew Gardens Union Tpke
Briarwood/Van Wyck Blvd
Jamaica Van Wyck
Sutphin Blvd
Parsons Blvd
169 St
Jamaica 179 St
Sutphin Blvd Archer Av
Jamaica Center Parsons/Archer
121 St
111 St
104 St
Woodhaven Blvd
Ozone Park Lefferts Blvd
Middle Village Metropolitan Av
2
3
4
5
6
7
8
9
10
11
12

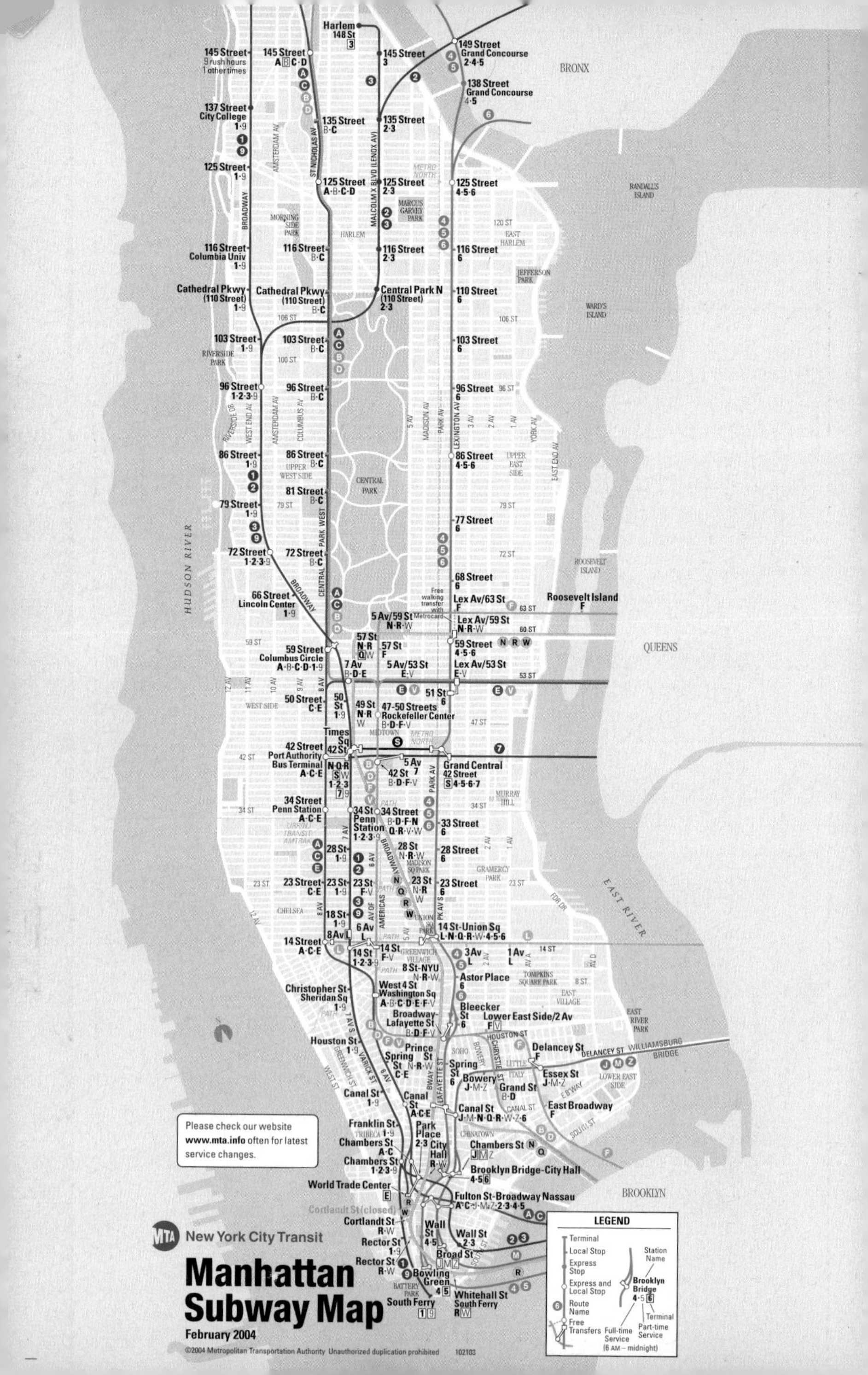
Harlem 148 St 3
145 Street 9 rush hours 1 other times
145 Street A B C D
145 Street 3
149 Street Grand Concourse 2·4·5
138 Street Grand Concourse 4·5
BRONX
137 Street City College 1·9
135 Street B·C
135 Street 2·3
125 Street 1·9
125 Street A·B·C·D
125 Street 2·3
125 Street 4·5·6
RANDALL'S ISLAND
MORNINGSIDE PARK
HARLEM
MARCUS GARVEY PARK
EAST HARLEM
116 Street Columbia Univ 1·9
116 Street B·C
116 Street 2·3
116 Street 6
JEFFERSON PARK
Cathedral Pkwy (110 Street) 1·9
Cathedral Pkwy (110 Street) B·C
Central Park N (110 Street) 2·3
110 Street 6
WARD'S ISLAND
103 Street 1·9
103 Street B·C
103 Street 6
RIVERSIDE PARK
96 Street 1·2·3·9
96 Street B·C
96 Street 6
86 Street 1·9
86 Street B·C
86 Street 4·5·6
UPPER WEST SIDE
CENTRAL PARK
UPPER EAST SIDE
81 Street B·C
79 Street 1·9
77 Street 6
HUDSON RIVER
72 Street 1·2·3·9
72 Street B·C
ROOSEVELT ISLAND
68 Street 6
66 Street Lincoln Center 1·9
Lex Av/63 St F
Roosevelt Island F
Free walking transfer with Metrocard
5 Av/59 St N·R·W
Lex Av/59 St N·R·W
57 St N·R Q W
57 St F
59 Street 4·5·6
59 Street Columbus Circle A·B·C·D·1·9
QUEENS
7 Av B·D·E
5 Av/53 St E·V
Lex Av/53 St E·V
51 St 6
50 Street C·E
50 St 1·9
49 St N·R W
47-50 Streets Rockefeller Center B·D·F·V
WEST SIDE
MIDTOWN
Times Sq 42 St
42 Street Port Authority Bus Terminal A·C·E
N·Q·R S W 1·2·3 7 9
5 Av 7
42 St B·D·F·V
Grand Central 42 Street S 4·5·6·7
MURRAY HILL
34 Street Penn Station A·C·E
34 St Penn Station 1·2·3·9
34 Street B·D·F·N Q·R·V·W
33 Street 6
28 St 1·9
28 St N·R·W
MADISON SQ PARK
28 Street 6
GRAMERCY PARK
23 Street C·E
23 St 1·9
23 St F·V
23 St N·R W
23 Street 6
CHELSEA
EAST RIVER
18 St 1·9
14 Street A·C·E
8 Av L
6 Av L
14 St 1·2·3·9
14 St F·V
14 St-Union Sq L·N·Q·R·W·4·5·6
UNION SQ PARK
3 Av L
1 Av L
GREENWICH VILLAGE
8 St-NYU N·R·W
Astor Place 6
TOMPKINS SQUARE PARK
Christopher St Sheridan Sq 1·9
West 4 St Washington Sq A·B·C·D·E·F·V
EAST VILLAGE
Bleecker St 6
Broadway-Lafayette St B·D·F·V
Lower East Side/2 Av F V
EAST RIVER PARK
Houston St 1·9
Prince St N·R·W
Spring St C·E
Spring St 6
SOHO
LITTLE ITALY
Delancey St F
WILLIAMSBURG BRIDGE
Essex St J·M·Z
LOWER EAST SIDE
Bowery J·M·Z
Grand St B·D
Canal St 1·9
Canal St A·C·E
Canal St J·M·N·Q·R·W·Z·6
East Broadway F
CHINATOWN
Franklin St 1·9
TRIBECA
Chambers St A·C
Park Place 2·3
City Hall R·W
Chambers St J M Z
Chambers St 1·2·3·9
Brooklyn Bridge-City Hall 4·5 6
World Trade Center E
Fulton St-Broadway Nassau A·C·J·M·Z·2·3·4·5
Cortlandt St (closed)
Cortlandt St R·W
BROOKLYN
Wall St 4·5
Wall St 2·3
Rector St R·W
Rector St 1·9
Broad St J M Z
Bowling Green 4 5
BATTERY PARK
South Ferry 1 9
Whitehall St South Ferry R W
Please check our website www.mta.info often for latest service changes.
LEGEND
Terminal
Local Stop
Express Stop
Express and Local Stop
Route Name
Free Transfers
Station Name
Brooklyn Bridge 4·5 6
Full-time Service (6 AM – midnight)
Part-time Service
Terminal
MTA New York City Transit
Manhattan Subway Map
February 2004
©2004 Metropolitan Transportation Authority Unauthorized duplication prohibited
102103